T0178669

Lecture Notes in Computer Science 14201

The series Lecture Notes in Computer Science (LNCS), including its subseries Lecture Notes in Artificial Intelligence (LNAI) and Lecture Notes in Bioinformatics (LNBI), has established itself as a medium for the publication of new developments in computer science and information technology research, teaching, and education.

LNCS enjoys close cooperation with the computer science R & D community, the series counts many renowned academics among its volume editors and paper authors, and collaborates with prestigious societies. Its mission is to serve this international community by providing an invaluable service, mainly focused on the publication of conference and workshop proceedings and postproceedings. LNCS commenced publication in 1973.

Claude Carlet · Kalikinkar Mandal ·
Vincent Rijmen
Editors

Selected Areas in Cryptography – SAC 2023

30th International Conference
Fredericton, Canada, August 14–18, 2023
Revised Selected Papers

Editors
Claude Carlet ⓘ
Université Paris 8
Saint-Denis Cedex, France

University of Bergen
Bergen, Norway

Vincent Rijmen ⓘ
KU Leuven
Heverlee, Belgium

University of Bergen
Bergen, Norway

Kalikinkar Mandal ⓘ
University of New Brunswick
Fredericton, NB, Canada

ISSN 0302-9743　　　　　　ISSN 1611-3349 (electronic)
Lecture Notes in Computer Science
ISBN 978-3-031-53367-9　　　ISBN 978-3-031-53368-6 (eBook)
https://doi.org/10.1007/978-3-031-53368-6

This Springer imprint is published by the registered company Springer Nature Switzerland AG
The registered company address is: Gewerbestrasse 11, 6330 Cham, Switzerland

Paper in this product is recyclable.

Preface

Selected Areas in Cryptography (SAC) is Canada's annual research conference on cryptography, held since 1994. The 30th edition of SAC took place at the University of New Brunswick in Fredericton, New Brunswick, Canada, during August 16–18, 2023.

There are four areas covered at each SAC conference. Three of the areas are permanent:

- Design and analysis of symmetric key primitives and cryptosystems, including block and stream ciphers, hash functions, MAC algorithms, cryptographic permutations, and authenticated encryption schemes.
- Efficient implementations of symmetric, public key, and post-quantum cryptography.
- Mathematical and algorithmic aspects of applied cryptology, including post-quantum cryptology.

The fourth area is selected as a special topic for each edition. The special topic for SAC 2023 was

- Counter-measures against side channel attacks in symmetric cryptography.

We received 48 submissions, among which 3 were withdrawn before reviewing. The remainng submissions were reviewed in a double-blind review process. Regular submissions received three reviews whereas submissions by Program Committee (PC) members were reviewed by five PC members. All in all, 139 reviews were written by our Program Committee, consisting of 39 members, and with the help of 30 subreviewers. Eventually, 21 papers were accepted for publication in these proceedings and presentation at the conference.

There were three invited talks at SAC 2023. The Stafford Tavares Invited Lecture, entitled "Robust and Non-malleable Threshold Schemes, AMD Codes and External Difference Families" was given by Doug Stinson. The first invited talk was given by Tim Güneysu on the topic of "Hardware Security—Directions and Challenges." The second invited talk was given by Tim Beyne on the topic of "A Geometric Approach to Symmetric-Key Cryptanalysis."

The program of SAC 2023 was completed by a preceding two-day summer school on August 14–15, 2023. During the summer school, there was one day of lectures about "Lattice-Based Cryptography" held by Adeline Roux-Langlois and "Post-quantum Cryptography" held by David Jao. The second day focused on "Linear and Differential Cryptanalysis" with lectures by Tim Beyne, and "Physical Attacks and Countermeasures" with lectures by Tim Güneysu.

We would like to thank all our colleagues who helped to make SAC 2023 a success. Especially, we would like to thank the Program Committee members and their subreviewers, for their hard work, and the invited speakers and the summer school lecturers who nicely enhanced the conference. We also thank all colleagues who submitted a paper and all speakers.

December 2023

Claude Carlet
Kalikinkar Mandal
Vincent Rijmen

Organization

Program Chairs

Claude Carlet — Université Paris 8, France and University of Bergen, Norway
Kalikinkar Mandal — University of New Brunswick, Canada
Vincent Rijmen — KU Leuven, Belgium and University of Bergen, Norway

Program Committee

Riham AlTawy — University of Victoria, Canada
Melissa Azouaoui — NXP Semiconductors, Germany
Paulo Barreto — University of Washington, Tacoma, USA
Jean-François Biasse — University of South Florida, USA
Olivier Blazy — Ecole Polytechnique, France
Wouter Castryck — KU Leuven, Belgium
Joan Daemen — Radboud University, The Netherlands
Maria Eichlseder — Graz University of Technology, Austria
Aurore Guillevic — Inria Nancy, France and Aarhus University, Denmark
Ryan Henry — University of Calgary, Canada
Takanori Isobe — University of Hyogo, Japan
Yunwen Liu — Cryptape Technology Co. Ltd, China
Subhamoy Maitra — Indian Statistical Institute, India
Barbara Masucci — University of Salerno, Italy
Cuauhtemoc Mancillas-López — CINVESTAV-IPN, Mexico
Bart Mennink — Radboud University, The Netherlands
Ruben Niederhagen — Academia Sinica, Taiwan and University of Southern Denmark, Denmark
Svetla Nikova — KU Leuven, Belgium and University of Bergen, Norway
Colin O'Flynn — NewAE Technology Inc., Canada
Stjepan Picek — Radboud University, The Netherlands
Elizabeth A. Quaglia — Royal Holloway, University of London, UK
Håvard Raddum — Simula UiB, Norway
Matthieu Rivain — CryptoExperts, France

Raghavendra Rohit	Technology Innovation Institute, UAE
Yann Rotella	Paris-Saclay University, Versailles, France
Yu Sasaki	NTT Social Informatics Laboratories, Japan
Palash Sarkar	Indian Statistical Institute, India
Nicolas Sendrier	Inria, France
Benjamin Smith	Inria and Ecole polytechnique, Institut Polytechnique de Paris, France
Sujoy Sinha Roy	Graz University of Technology, Austria
Douglas Stebila	University of Waterloo, Canada
Katsuyuki Takashima	Waseda University, Japan
Yosuke Todo	NTT Social Informatics Laboratories, Japan
Yuntao Wang	Osaka University, Japan
Wen Wang	Intel Labs, USA

Additional Reviewers

Ismail Afia	Lena Heimberger
Aikata Aikata	Akiko Inoue
Ravi Anand	Hilder Vitor Lima Pereira
Nicoleta-Norica Băcuieti	Loïc Masure
Mario Marhuenda Beltrán	Kohei Nakagawa
Olivier Bronchain	Shuhei Nakamura
Jan-Pieter D'Anvers	Angel L. Perez Del Pozo
Pratish Datta	Thomas Prest
Rafaël Del Pino	Mostafizar Rahman
Prastudy Fauzi	Shahram Rasoolzadeh
Paul Frixons	Azade Rezaeezade
Nick Frymann	Jacob Schuldt
Philippe Gaborit	Okan Seker
Clemente Galdi	Xiaoling Yu
John Gaspoz	Vincent Zucca

Invited Talks

Hardware Security—Directions and Challenges

Tim Güneysu

Abstract. The increasing integration of technology into our daily lives has also increased not only the significance of long-term secure cryptosystems but also its implementation and related aspects of hardware security. This talk explores some of the recent and multifaceted challenges that need to be tackled to ensure the integrity and confidentiality of modern security hardware. Often these vulnerabilities arise from physical attacks such as side-channel attacks (SCA) and fault injection attacks (FIA) that can easily target highly exposed devices of the embedded domain or the Internet of Things (IoT). This talk highlights the many misinterpretations and invalid assumptions of adversary models that are related to such physical attack vectors, revealing often simple vulnerabilities in the real-world that have been considered impossible under the initially assumed model. As technological advancements continue, understanding the achieved level of hardware security become essential – this includes to understand the features and capabilities of contemporary lab equipment, readily available, for example, in the domain of failure testing of integrated circuits, such as Laser Voltage Probing (LSP) or Laser Logic State Imaging (LLSI). This can be used to analyze internal states of modern integrated circuits, including the confidential information contained in the key storage of security devices. Further aspects of the talk highlight the important role of Electronic Design Automation (EDA) for the development of secure hardware devices such as the concept of dynamic reconfiguration of hardware circuits as a moving target defense countermeasure.

While the list of challenges in hardware security addressed by this invited talk is far from being complete, understanding and mitigating such aspects are crucial for preserving the confidentiality, integrity, and availability for the next generation of long-term secure hardware systems.

Robust and Non-malleable Threshold Schemes, AMD Codes and External Difference Families

Doug Stinson

Abstract. We began by reviewing the history of robust threshold schemes, which were introduced by Tampa and Woll in 1988. Various solutions over the years have used mathematical structures related to difference sets, including external difference families and algebraic manipulation detection codes. We presented several constructions for these structures and discussed their application to robust threshold schemes. Finally, we presented some recent (ongoing) work on non-malleable threshold schemes that employ a new variation of AMD codes, namely circular AMD codes.

A Geometric Approach to Symmetric-Key Cryptanalysis

Tim Beyne

Abstract. I presented recent results that show that linear, differential and integral cryptanalysis are different facets of a single theory. I introduced the basic principles of this point of view, and showed how the choice of base field (complex or p-adic) and basis (diagonalizing an action) correspond to existing techniques. A few applications of this point of view were given, starting with the analysis of invariants of cryptographic primitives and how they relate to (multiple) linear cryptanalysis. As a second application, I discussed how the geometric approach leads to quasidifferential trails and how these can be used to avoid statistical independence assumptions in differential cryptanalysis. Finally, I presented preliminary results on an extension of integral cryptanalysis called ultrametric integral cryptanalysis.

Contents

Differential Cryptanalysis

Cryptanalysis of Lightweight Ciphers

More Balanced Polynomials: Cube Attacks on 810- And 825-Round Trivium with Practical Complexities

Hao Lei[1,2], Jiahui He[1,2], Kai Hu[3], and Meiqin Wang[1,2,4(✉)]

[1] School of Cyber Science and Technology, Shandong University,
Qingdao, Shandong, China
{leihao,hejiahui2020}@mail.sdu.edu.cn, mqwang@sdu.edu.cn
[2] Key Laboratory of Cryptologic Technology and Information Security,
Ministry of Education, Shandong University, Jinan, China
[3] School of Physical and Mathematical Sciences, Nanyang Technological University,
Singapore, Singapore
kai.hu@ntu.edu.sg
[4] Quan Cheng Shandong Laboratory, Jinan, China

Abstract. The key step of the cube attack is to recover the special polynomial, the superpoly, of the target cipher. In particular, the balanced superpoly, in which there exists at least one secret variable as a single monomial and none of the other monomials contain this variable, can be exploited to reveal one-bit information about the key bits. However, as the number of rounds grows, it becomes increasingly difficult to find such balanced superpolies. Consequently, traditional methods of searching for balanced superpolies soon hit a bottleneck. Aiming at performing a cube attack on more rounds of Trivium with a practical complexity, in this paper, we present three techniques to obtain sufficient balanced polynomials.

1. Based on the structure of Trivium, we propose a variable substitution technique to simplify the superpoly.
2. Obtaining the additional balanced polynomial by combining two superpolies to cancel the two-degree terms.
3. We propose an experimental approach to construct high-quality large cubes which may contain more subcubes with balanced superpolies and a heuristic search strategy for their subcubes whose superpolies are balanced.

To illustrate the power of our techniques, we search for balanced polynomials for 810- and 825-round Trivium. As a result, we can mount cube attacks against 810- and 825-round Trivium with the time complexity of $2^{44.17}$ and $2^{53.17}$ round-reduced Trivium initializations, respectively, which can be verified in 48 min and 18 days on a PC with one A100 GPU. For the same level of time complexity, this improves the previous best results by 2 and 5 rounds, respectively.

Keywords: Trivium · cube attack · key-recovery attack · division property

Due to the page limit, the appendix of this paper is included in the full version [15].

C. Carlet et al. (Eds.): SAC 2023, LNCS 14201, pp. 3–21, 2024.
https://doi.org/10.1007/978-3-031-53368-6_1

1   Introduction

The cube attack, proposed by Dinur and Shamir at EUROCRYPT 2009 [7], is one of the most powerful cryptanalysis techniques for symmetric ciphers. It has been successfully used to attack various stream ciphers such as Kreyvium, Acorn and Trivium [2,4,5,18,23,26].

Trivium was designed by Cannière and Preneel, as a bit-oriented synchronous stream cipher which was selected as one of the eSTREAM hardware-oriented finalists, and the international standard under ISO/IEC 29192-3:2012 [4]. Trivium has attracted extensive attention because of its simple structure and high level of security. Since the cube attack was proposed, it has become one of the most effective cryptanalytic techniques to analyze the reduced-round variants of Trivium. Currently, the best cube attacks on Trivium are those enhanced by divsion-properties [23], which have reached 848 rounds [11] but with an impractical complexity that is very close to the exhaustive search.

At the same time, the cube attacks on reduced-round Trivium with practical complexities also attract much attention, for the practical attacks have the potential to reveal more internal structural properties of Trivium and inspire new techniques for cube attacks. In [7], the authors proposed the random walk method to attack 767-round Trivium with about 2^{45} initializations. Next, Fouque et al. found many cubes with linear superpolies by improving the time complexity of computing cubes, then the 784-round of Trivium could be attacked with about 2^{39} initializations [8]. Later, in [29], Ye et al. proposed an effective method to construct cubes for linear superpolies and they gave a practical attack against 805-round Trivium with about $2^{41.4}$ initializations. At FSE 2021, Sun proposed a new heuristic method to reject cubes without independent secret variables and they could perform practical attacks against 806- and 808-round Trivium with time complexity of $2^{39.88}$ and $2^{44.58}$ initializations, respectively [21]. Recently, Cheng et al. gave attacks on 815- and 820-round Trivium with $2^{47.32}$ and $2^{53.17}$ initializations, respectively [6]. These results are summarized in Table 1.

1.1   Our Contributions

This paper focuses on practical key-recovery attacks against reduced-round Trivium. In order to attack a higher number of rounds, we propose the following methods.

Simplify Superpolies by Variable Substitutions. At the cost of adding one extra variable, the variable substitution can greatly simplify the superpoly, so that some unbalanced superpolies can be transformed into balanced ones. Thanks to this technique, more simple and balanced superpolies are utilized, from which more information about secret variables can be extracted.

More Balanced Polynomials by Canceling the Quadratic Terms. Balanced superpolies are important for practical attacks on round-reduced Trivium. However, for Trivium with a higher number of rounds, it is hard to find cubes with balanced superpolies. We propose a method to obtain one additional balanced polynomial by canceling the quadratic terms in two superpolies. The new balanced polynomial is the sum of these two superpolies.

A Modified Algorithm to Construct a Better Mother Cube. Finding a large cube that contains many subcubes with balanced superpolies is important for the practical attack on round-reduced Trivium. In the following paper, this large cube is called a mother cube. By examining the relationship between the superpoly of a mother cube and the superpolies of its subcubes, we can more accurately judge whether a mother cube is suitable for a practical attack.

A Heuristic Strategy for Searching for Balanced Subcubes. It often takes a long time to recover the superpoly of a cube for high rounds of Trivium. Moreover, a high-dimensional mother cube has a large number of subcubes. To reduce the search space, we propose two strategies for dividing the search space by examining the relationship between the superpoly of a cube and the superpolies of its subcubes, which allows us to obtain sufficient balanced superpolies for a practical key-recovery attack with the reduced search space.

As an application, we apply our methods to 810-round Trivium and 825-round Trivium. The complexities of the cube attacks on 810 and 825 rounds of Trivium are respectively $2^{44.58}$ and $2^{53.09}$ round-reduced Trivium initializations. We list our attacks as well as the previous practical/theoretical cube attacks on Trivium for a better comparison in Table 1. We also implemented these two attacks on a PC with an A100 GPU. The experimental results showed that the whole keys can be recovered within 48 min and 18 days for 810 and 825 rounds of Trivium, respectively.

All source codes for our algorithms in this paper are provided at the git repository https://github.com/lhoop/ObtainMoreBS.

1.2 Outline

In Sect. 2, some related concepts and definitions are introduced. In Sect. 3, we propose three techniques to obtain a lot of balanced polynomials for round-reduced Trivium and a heuristic search strategy that reduces the cube search space of round-reduced Trivium. In Sect. 4, we mount cube attacks against 810- and 825-round Trivium by our techniques. Finally, we draw our conclusions in Sect. 5.

2 Preliminaries

2.1 Notation

We use bold italic lowercase letters to represent bit vectors, such as $x = (x_0, x_1, \ldots, x_{n-1})$ where x_i is the i-th element of x. For any n-bit vectors u and v, we define $u \succeq v$ if $u_i \geq v_i$ for all $0 \leq i < n$. Similarly, we define $u \preceq v$ if $u_i \leq v_i$ for all $0 \leq i < n$. Blackboard bold uppercase letters (e.g. $\mathbb{X}, \mathbb{K}, \mathbb{L}, \ldots$) are used to represent sets of bit vectors. And we use the composition operator ($\circ$) to compose two functions. For example, $g \circ f(x) = g(f(x))$.

Table 1. A summary of cube attacks on Trivium

Type	# of rounds	Cube size	# of key bits	Total time	Ref.
Practical	672	12	63	$2^{18.56}$	[7]
	709	22–23	79	$2^{29.14}$	[17]
	767	28–31	35	$2^{45.00}$	[7]
	784	30–33	42	$2^{39.00}$	[8]
	805	32–38	42	$2^{41.40}$	[29]
	806	33–37	45	$2^{39.88}$	[21]
	808	39–41	37	$2^{44.58}$	[21]
	810	**40–42**	**39**	$2^{44.17}$	**Section** 4.1
	815	44–46	35	$2^{47.32}$	[6]
	820	48–51	30	$2^{53.17}$	[6]
	825	**49–52**	**31**	$2^{53.09}$	**Section** 4.2
Theoretical	799	32–37	18	$2^{62.00}$	[8]
	802	34–37	8	$2^{72.00}$	[27]
	805	28	7	$2^{73.00}$	[16]
	806	34–37	16	$2^{64.00}$	[29]
	835	35	5	$2^{75.00}$	[16]
	832	72	1	$2^{79.01}$	[25]
	832	72	> 1	$< 2^{79.01}$	[28]
	840	78	1	$2^{79.58}$	[9]
	840	75	3	$2^{77.32}$	[14]
	841	78	1	$2^{79.58}$	[9]
	841	76	2	$2^{78.58}$	[14]
	842	78	1	$2^{79.58}$	[10]
	842	76	2	$2^{78.58}$	[14]
	843	54–57, 76	5	$2^{76.58}$	[13]
	843	78	1	$2^{79.58}$	[21]
	844	54–55	2	$2^{78.00}$	[13]
	845	54–55	2	$2^{78.00}$	[13]
	846	51–54	1	$2^{79.00}$	[11]
	847	52–53	1	$2^{79.00}$	[11]
	848	51–54	1	$2^{79.00}$	[11]

2.2   Boolean Functions and Algebraic Degree

Boolean Function. Let $f : \mathbb{F}_2^n \to \mathbb{F}_2$ be a Boolean function whose algebraic normal form (ANF) is

$$f(\boldsymbol{x}) = f(x_0, x_1, \ldots, x_{n-1}) = \bigoplus_{u \in \mathbb{F}_2^n} a_u \prod_{i=0}^{n-1} x_i^{u_i},$$

where $a_u \in \mathbb{F}_2$, and

$$x^u = \pi_u(x) = \prod_{i=0}^{n-1} x_i^{u_i} \text{ with } x_i^{u_i} = \begin{cases} x_i, & \text{if } u_i = 1, \\ 1, & \text{if } u_i = 0, \end{cases}$$

is called a **monomial**. We use the notation $x^u \to f$ to indicate that the coefficient a^u of x^u in f is 1, i.e., x^u appears in f. Otherwise, $x^u \nrightarrow f$. In this work, we will use x^u and $\pi_u(x)$ interchangeably to avoid the awkward notation $x^{(i)u^{(j)}}$ when both x and u have superscripts.

One important feature of a Boolean function is its algebraic degree which is denoted by $\deg(f)$ and defined as

$$\deg(f) = \max\{wt(u) \mid a_u \neq 0\},$$

where $wt(u)$ is the Hamming weight of u, i.e., $wt(u) = \sum_{i=0}^{n-1} u_i$.

Vectorial Boolean Function. Let $f : \mathbb{F}_2^n \to \mathbb{F}_2^m$ be a vectorial Boolean function with $y = (y_0, y_1, \ldots, y_{m-1}) = f(x) = (f_0(x), f_1(x), \ldots, f_{m-1}(x))$. For $v \in \mathbb{F}_2^m$, we use y^v to denote the product of some coordinates of y:

$$y^v = \prod_{i=0}^{m-1} y_i^{v_i} = \prod_{i=0}^{m-1} (f_i(x))^{v_i},$$

which is a Boolean function in x.

2.3 Pseudo-code of Trivium

Trivium is a bit oriented synchronous stream cipher, the main building block of Trivium is a 288-bit nonlinear feedback shift register which is divided into three small registers. For initialization, the 80 bit secret variables $k = (k_0, k_1, \ldots, k_{79})$ is loaded into the first register, and the 80-bit IV (i.e., public variables) $v = (v_0, v_1, \ldots, v_{79})$ is loaded into the second register. For the third register, all state bits are set to 0 except the last three bits. After 1152 state updates, Trivium starts to output keystream bits. The pseudo-code of Trivium is described in Algorithm 1.

2.4 Cube Attack

The cube attack was first proposed by Dinur and Shamir in EUROCRYPT 2009 [7]. It is a powerful cryptanalytic technique against stream ciphers. For a cipher with n public variables and m secret variables, each output bit of the cipher can be represented as a polynomial in these secret and public variables. Let z be an output bit, $x = (x_0, x_1, \ldots, x_{n-1})$ as the public variables and $k = (k_0, k_1, \ldots, k_{m-1})$ as the secret variables. z can be expressed as

$$z = f(k, x).$$

Algorithm 1: Pseudo-code of Trivium

1 $s_0, s_1, ..., s_{92} \leftarrow (k_0, ..., k_{79}, 0, ..., 0)$
2 $s_{93}, s_{94}, ..., s_{176} \leftarrow (v_0, ..., v_{79}, 0, ..., 0)$
3 $s_{177}, s_{178}, ..., s_{287} \leftarrow (0, ..., 0, 1, 1, 1)$
4 **for** i *from 1 to N (Number of initialization rounds)* **do**
5      $ta \leftarrow s_{65} \oplus s_{92} \oplus s_{90}s_{91} \oplus s_{170}$
6      $tb \leftarrow s_{161} \oplus s_{176} \oplus s_{174}s_{175} \oplus s_{263}$
7      $tc \leftarrow s_{242} \oplus s_{287} \oplus s_{285}s_{286} \oplus s_{68}$
8   **if** $i > 1152$ **then**
9        $\mid$ $z_{i-1152} \leftarrow s_{65} \oplus s_{92} \oplus s_{161} \oplus s_{176} \oplus s_{242} \oplus s_{287}$
10   **end**
11     $s_0, s_1, ..., s_{92} \leftarrow (tb, s_0, s_1, ..., s_{91})$
12     $s_{93}, s_{94}, ..., s_{176} \leftarrow (ta, s_{93}, s_{94}, ..., s_{175})$
13     $s_{177}, s_{178}, ..., s_{287} \leftarrow (tc, s_{177}, s_{178}, ..., s_{286})$
14 **end**

Let $I = \left\{x_{c_1}, x_{c_2}, ..., x_{c_d}\right\} \subset \{x_0, x_1, ..., x_{n-1}\}$ be a subset of public variables, assume $x^u = \prod_{x \in I} x$ is its corresponding term. Then, $f(x, k)$ can be uniquely expressed as

$$f(x, k) = p(x, k) \cdot x^u + q(x, k),$$

where $q(x, k)$ misses at least one variable in I. A **cube** determined by I is denoted as C_I and contains all 2^d possible combinations of the values of variables in I. C_I is a d-dimensional cube because the size of I is d. x^u is called a **cube term**. The public variables in I are called cube variables and the remaining public variables are called non-cube variables. $p(x, k)$ is called the **superpoly** of C_I which can be computed by

$$\bigoplus_{x \in C_I} f(x, k) = p(x, k).$$

Therefore, we can get the value of the superpoly $p(x, k)$ by $2^{|I|}$ calls to the initialization oracle.

For a superpoly P, if a variable k_i that appears only in a one-degree monomial, we say P is a **balanced superpoly** for the **balanced variable** k_i. Moreover, if all variables in P are balanced variables, we say P is a **linear superpoly**. For example, $P_1 = k_1 \oplus k_2 \oplus k_3k_4$ is a balanced superpoly for balanced variables k_1 and k_2, $P_2 = k_1 \oplus k_2$ is a linear superpoly. We say a cube is **balanced** if its superpoly is balanced for some balanced variables. For a balanced superpoly whose value is known, we can deduce its one balanced variable by enumerating the values of other variables.

2.5   The Bit-Based Division Property and Monomial Prediction

The division property is a generalization of integral property, which was proposed by Todo in [22, 24]. The conventional bit-based division property can be used to evaluate the algebraic degree of a cube and the three-subset division property without unknown subset can be used to recover superpoly. The definitions of the conventional bit-based division property and three-subset division property are provided in [15, Appendix A].

The monomial prediction, proposed by Hu et al. in [14], is another language of division property from a pure algebraic perspective. By counting the so-called monomial trails, the monomial prediction can determine if a monomial of IV appears in the polynomial of the output of the cipher.

Let $f : \mathbb{F}_2^{n_0} \to \mathbb{F}_2^{n_r}$ be a composite vectorial Boolean function of a sequence of r smaller function $f^{(i)} : \mathbb{F}_2^{n_i} \to \mathbb{F}_2^{n_{i+1}}, 0 \le i \le r - 1$ as

$$f = f^{(r-1)} \circ f^{(r-2)} \circ \cdots \circ f^{(0)}.$$

Let $x^{(i)} \in \mathbb{F}_2^{n_i}$ and $x^{(i+1)} \in \mathbb{F}_2^{n_{i+1}}$ be the input and output variables of $f^{(i)}$, respectively. Suppose $\pi_{u^{(0)}}(x^{(0)})$ is a monomial of $x^{(0)}$, it is easy to find all monomials of $x^{(1)}$ satisfying $\pi_{u^{(0)}}(x^{(0)}) \to \pi_{u^{(1)}}(x^{(1)})$. For every such $\pi_{u^{(1)}}(x^{(1)})$, we then find all the $\pi_{u^{(2)}}(x^{(2)})$ satisfying $\pi_{u^{(1)}}(x^{(1)}) \to \pi_{u^{(2)}}(x^{(2)})$. Finally, if we are interested in whether $\pi_{u^{(0)}}(x^{(0)}) \to \pi_{u^{(r)}}(x^{(r)})$, we collect some transitions from $\pi_{u^{(0)}}(x^{(0)})$ to $\pi_{u^{(r)}}(x^{(r)})$ as

$$\pi_{u^{(0)}}(x^{(0)}) \to \pi_{u^{(1)}}(x^{(1)}) \to \cdots \to \pi_{u^{(r)}}(x^{(r)}).$$

Every such transition is called a monomial trail from $\pi_{u^{(0)}}(x^{(0)}) \to \pi_{u^{(r)}}(x^{(r)})$, denoted by $\pi_{u^{(0)}}(x^{(0)}) \rightsquigarrow \pi_{u^{(r)}}(x^{(r)})$. All the trails from $\pi_{u^{(0)}}(x^{(0)})$ to $\pi_{u^{(r)}}(x^{(r)})$ are denoted by $\pi_{u^{(0)}}(x^{(0)}) \bowtie \pi_{u^{(r)}}(x^{(r)})$, which is the set of all trails. Then whether $\pi_{u^{(0)}}(x^{(0)}) \to \pi_{u^{(r)}}(x^{(r)})$ is determined by the size of $\pi_{u^{(0)}}(x^{(0)}) \bowtie \pi_{u^{(r)}}(x^{(r)})$, represented as $|\pi_{u^{(0)}}(x^{(0)}) \bowtie \pi_{u^{(r)}}(x^{(r)})|$. If there is no trail from $\pi_{u^{(0)}}(x^{(0)})$ to $\pi_{u^{(r)}}(x^{(r)})$, we say $\pi_{u^{(0)}}(x^{(0)}) \not\rightsquigarrow \pi_{u^{(r)}}(x^{(r)})$ and accordingly $|\pi_{u^{(0)}}(x^{(0)}) \bowtie \pi_{u^{(r)}}(x^{(r)})| = 0$.

Theorem 1 (Integrated from [9,10,12,14]). *Let* $f = f^{(r-1)} \circ f^{(r-2)} \circ \cdots \circ f^{(0)}$ *defined as above.* $\pi_{u^{(0)}}(x^{(0)}) \to \pi_{u^{(r)}}(x^{(r)})$ *if and only if*

$$|\pi_{u^{(0)}}(x^{(0)}) \bowtie \pi_{u^{(r)}}(x^{(r)})| \equiv 1 \pmod 2.$$

Propagation Rules of the Monomial Prediction. Any component of a symmetric cipher can be regarded as a vectorial Boolean function. To model the propagation of the monomial prediction for a vectorial Boolean function, a common method is to list all the possible (input, output) tuples according to the definition of the monomial prediction [14]. These tuples can be transformed into a set of linear inequalities and thus modeled with MILP [3,19,20]. Since any symmetric cipher can be decomposed into a sequence of the basic operations XOR, AND and COPY. Their concrete propagation rules for these basic functions and MILP models are provided in [15, Appendix B].

3   Obtain More Balanced Polynomials

To mount a practical key-recovery attack on high rounds of Trivium, we need a lot of small cubes whose superpolies are simple and balanced. However, small cubes for high rounds of Trivium tend to have complex and unbalanced superpolies.

In order to obtain more simple and balanced polynomials, we propose a method based on the variable substitution technique to simplify the superpolies and a method to obtain more balanced polynomials by canceling some quadratic terms between superpolies. We introduce these two methods in Sects. 3.1 and 3.2, respectively. Additionally, according to an observation, we modify the algorithm in [29, Section 3.1] to obtain a mother cube containing more subcubes whose superpolies are balanced and provide a heuristic search strategy to make a trade-off between the search space and the search quality. They are introduced in Sect. 3.3.

3.1   Variable Substitutions

The Principle of Variable Substitutions. Notice that after the state of Trivium was updated 24 times, the last 11 bits of the secret variables will only exist in the state in a specific form.

$$(s_0, s_1, \ldots, s_{92}) \leftarrow (k_0, k_1, \ldots, k_{79}, 0, \ldots, 0);$$

$$(s_{93}, s_{94}, \ldots, s_{176}) \leftarrow (v_0, v_1, \ldots, v_{79}, 0, \ldots, 0);$$

$$(s_{177}, s_{178}, \ldots, s_{287}) \leftarrow (0, \ldots, 0, 1, 1, 1).$$

After 24 rounds of updates,

$$(s'_0, s'_1, \ldots, s'_{92}) \leftarrow (tb_{23}, tb_{22}, \ldots, tb_0, k_0, \ldots, k_{68});$$

$$(s'_{93}, s'_{94}, \ldots, s'_{176}) \leftarrow (ta_{23}, ta_{22}, \ldots, ta_0, v_0, \ldots, v_{59});$$

$$(s'_{177}, s'_{178}, \ldots, s'_{287}) \leftarrow (tc_{23}, tc_{22}, \ldots, tc_0, 0, \ldots, 0),$$

where ta_i, tb_i, tc_i are three bits updated by the round function of the i-th round of Trivium.

From the expressions of $s'_0, s'_1, \ldots, s'_{287}$, we find that $k_{69}, k_{70}, \ldots, k_{79}$ are only involved in $s'_{94}, s'_{95}, \ldots, s'_{105}$.

$$s'_{94} = ta_{23} = k_{42} \oplus k_{69} \oplus k_{68}k_{67} \oplus v_{54},$$

$$s'_{95} = ta_{22} = k_{43} \oplus k_{70} \oplus k_{69}k_{68} \oplus v_{55},$$

$$\vdots$$

$$s'_{105} = ta_{12} = k_{53} \oplus 0 \oplus k_{79}k_{78} \oplus v_{65}.$$

We use new variables $p_{69}, \ldots, p_{80}$ to replace these polynomials of secret variables.

$$p_{69} = k_{42} \oplus k_{69} \oplus k_{68}k_{67},$$

$$p_{70} = k_{43} \oplus k_{70} \oplus k_{69}k_{68},$$

$$\vdots$$

$$p_{80} = k_{53} \oplus 0 \oplus k_{79}k_{78}.$$

For the sake of clarity, we also use $p_0, \ldots, p_{68}$ to replace the other secret variables $(p_0 = k_0, p_1 = k_1, \ldots, p_{68} = k_{68})$.

Then all state bits of round 24 are only related to the 81 new secret variables $\boldsymbol{p} = (p_0, p_1, \ldots, p_{80})$ and the 80 public variables $\boldsymbol{v} = (v_0, v_1, \ldots, v_{79})$. $(s'_0, \ldots, s'_{287})$ can be written as the output of a vectorial Boolean function of $\boldsymbol{p}$ and $\boldsymbol{v}$, namely,

$$\boldsymbol{y} = (s'_0, \ldots, s'_{287}) = \boldsymbol{g}(\boldsymbol{v}, \boldsymbol{p}) = (g_0(\boldsymbol{v}, \boldsymbol{p}), g_1(\boldsymbol{v}, \boldsymbol{p}), \ldots, g_{287}(\boldsymbol{v}, \boldsymbol{p})).$$

And the output bit after r rounds ($r > 24$) can be expressed as follows,

$$z^r = h(\boldsymbol{s}') \circ \boldsymbol{g}(\boldsymbol{v}, \boldsymbol{p}),$$

where $h(\boldsymbol{s}')$ is a Boolean function from $(s'_0, \ldots, s'_{287})$ to z^r.

This implies that we can represent the superpoly as a polynomial of only $\boldsymbol{p}$. Since polynomials of degree 2 in $\boldsymbol{k}$ (e.g., $k_{42} + k_{69} + k_{68}k_{67}$) are now replaced by single variables (e.g., p_{69}), the $\boldsymbol{p}$-representation of the superpoly is likely to have a lower algebraic degree and thus, is simpler.

Therefore, after representing superpolies as polynomials of $\boldsymbol{p}$, more simple and balanced superpolies may be obtained. We show this in Example 1.

Example 1. Let $A = k_{42} \oplus k_{69} \oplus k_{68}k_{67}$ and $B = k_{45} \oplus k_1(k_{45} \oplus k_{72} \oplus k_{71}k_{70})$ be a balanced superpoly and an unbalanced superpoly of $\boldsymbol{k}$, respectively. After variable substitutions, we have $A = p_{69}$, $B = p_{45} \oplus p_1 p_{72}$, which means A becomes a linear superpoly of $\boldsymbol{p}$ and B becomes a balanced superpoly of $\boldsymbol{p}$.

To illustrate the power of this technique, we search for balanced superpolies among the same set of cubes for 825-round Trivium before and after variable substitutions, respectively. We evaluate the simplicity of each superpoly by the number of variables it contains and record the number of occurrences of balanced superpolies at different levels of simplicity. See Table 2 for details.

Table 2. Distribution of balanced superpolies (B.S.) involving different numbers of variables.

# variables involved	#B.S. of k	#B.S. of p
≤ 5	34	42
≤ 10	42	67
≤ 20	90	122
≤ 40	187	235
≤ 60	275	318
≤ 80	322	354

Substituting Variables Back. The variable substitution technique simplifies superpolies at the cost of adding one extra variable, i.e., p_{80}. Notice that the values of $k_0, \ldots, k_{79}$ can be derived from the values of $p_0, \ldots, p_{79}$ as follows,

$$p_0, \ldots, p_{68} \Rightarrow k_0, \ldots, k_{68},$$
$$p_{69}, k_{42}, k_{67}, k_{68} \Rightarrow k_{69},$$
$$p_{70}, k_{43}, k_{68}, k_{69} \Rightarrow k_{70},$$
$$\vdots$$
$$p_{79}, k_{52}, k_{78}, k_{77} \Rightarrow k_{79}.$$

Therefore, p_{80} is actually redundant and can be expressed as a polynomial of $p_0, \ldots, p_{79}$. In other words, $f : (k_0, \ldots, k_{79}) \to (p_0, \ldots, p_{79})$ is actually a bijective function.

In this paper, we always consider the superpolies represented as polynomials of p. Once the values of all 81 new secret variables (i.e., $p_0, \ldots, p_{80}$) are obtained, we first derive the values of $k_0, \ldots, k_{79}$ from $p_0, \ldots, p_{79}$, then check whether the value of p_{80} is correct. The concrete process of substituting p back to obtain k is shown in Algorithm 2.

Algorithm 2: Recovering k from p

Input: $(p_0, p_1, \ldots, p_{80})$
Output: $(k_0, k_1 \ldots, k_{79})$ or $false$
1 **for** i *from 0 to 68* **do**
2 $\quad \lfloor \; k_i \leftarrow p_i \;$;
3 **for** i *from 69 to 79* **do**
4 $\quad \lfloor \; .k_i \leftarrow p_i \oplus k_{i-27} \oplus k_{i-1} k_{i-2} \;$;
5 $check \leftarrow k_{53} \oplus k_{78} k_{79} \;$;
6 **if** $p_{80} == check$ **then**
7 $\quad |\quad$ **return** $(k_0, k_1 \ldots, k_{79})$
8 **else**
9 $\quad \lfloor \;$ **return** $false$

3.2 More Balanced Polynomials by Canceling Quadratic Terms

After constructing a mother cube, we can obtain a large number of subcubes, but only a very small fraction of subcubes have balanced superpolies. More balanced polynomials are required when we perform the practical attack on high rounds of Trivium. In order to obtain more balanced polynomials, we provide an algorithm to obtain additional balanced polynomials by canceling the common quadratic terms between superpolies. First, we define two types of superpolies.

Definition 1 (Type-I Superpoly). *If there exists a single monomial p_i and a quadratic monomial $p_i p_j$, and none of the other monomials contain p_i, then we call this superpoly a type-I superpoly of a variable p_i.*

Definition 2 (Type-II Superpoly). *If there exists a variable p_i that appears in a quadratic monomial $p_i p_j$, and none of the other monomials contain this variable, then we call this superpoly a type-II superpoly of a variable p_i.*

For example, a superpoly $A = p_{73} \oplus p_{73} p_{25}$ is a type-I superpoly of a variable p_{73} and a superpoly $B = p_{73} p_{25}$ is a type-II superpoly of variables p_{73} and p_{25}.

Combining Rule. For a specific variable p_i, if we can find both a type-I superpoly of p_i and a type-II superpoly of p_i and the quadratic monomials containing p_i in these two superpolies are the same, then we can get a balanced polynomial by adding these two superpolies. For example, we can obtain a balanced polynomial C with p_{73} being a balanced variable by adding the type-I superpoly A and the type-II superpoly B,

$$C = A \oplus B = p_{73} \oplus p_{73} p_{25} \oplus p_{73} p_{25} = p_{73}.$$

In the superpolies recovery process, we use SageMath [1] to determine whether a superpoly is a type-I superpoly or a type-II superpoly.

For 825-round Trivium, we find 540 cubes with type-I superpolies or type-II superpolies. By the combining rule, we obtained 782 additional balanced polynomials. This increases our number of balanced polynomials from 451 to 1323.

3.3   Relationship Between a Cube and Its Subcubes

In our practical cube attacks on Trivium, we focus on balanced superpolies rather than superpolies of low degrees.

For example, consider two superpolies A and B.

$$A : p_1 p_2 \oplus p_2 p_3 = c_1,$$

$$B : p_1 \oplus p_3 p_{10} p_4 p_6 = c_2.$$

The degrees of A and B are 2 and 4, respectively. We prefer B to A because B is balanced so that we can use it to deduce p_1 by enumerating p_3, p_{10}, p_4, p_6.

Inspiration. In the search process, we obtain a set of cubes whose superpolies are estimated to have low degrees based on the division property, but the superpolies of these cubes are almost all unbalanced. While for another set of cubes, we find that a lot of their superpolies are balanced, although their superpolies are estimated to have high degrees. This inspires us to investigate how to locate the balanced superpolies more accurately. With experiments, we have the following observation.

Observation 1. *For a given x-dimensional cube I, if its superpoly is balanced, then the superpolies of its $(x-1)$-dimensional subcubes have a greater probability of being balanced.*

There are some data in [15, Appendix D] to support this observation. Based on this observation, we propose a method for constructing a better mother cube that may contain more subcubes with balanced superpolies and a heuristic search method to reduce the search space.

A Modified Algorithm to Construct a Mother Cube for Balanced Superpolies. We modify the algorithm for constructing the mother cube in [29, Section 3.1] to obtain a better mother cube that may have more subcubes with balanced superpolies.

First, at the stage of determining the starting cube, Ye et al. predicted a preference bit $s_\lambda^{(r)}$ for r-round Trivium. $s_\lambda^{(r)}$ can be written as

$$s_\lambda^{(r)} = s_{i_1^\lambda}^{(r-\lambda)} \cdot s_{i_2^\lambda}^{(r-\lambda)} \oplus s_{i_3^\lambda}^{(r-\lambda)} \oplus s_{i_4^\lambda}^{(r-\lambda)} \oplus s_{i_5^\lambda}^{(r-\lambda)},$$

it have five state bits from $(r - \lambda)$-round Trivium. Next, $s_{i_1^\lambda}^{(r-\lambda)}$ and $s_{i_2^\lambda}^{(r-\lambda)}$ are the dominant parts in determining whether $s_\lambda^{(r)}$ contributes to linear terms in the superpoly. Therefore, the starting cube should have a linear superpoly in $s_{i_1^\lambda}^{(r-\lambda)}$ or $s_{i_2^\lambda}^{(r-\lambda)}$. We are less strict about the starting cube because we focus on balanced superpolies, so our starting cube only need to have a simple balanced superpoly in $s_{i_1^\lambda}^{(r-\lambda)}$ or $s_{i_2^\lambda}^{(r-\lambda)}$.

Second, at the stage of extending the starting cube, we will obtain a lot of candidate mother cubes after the expansion. The criteria for selection from candidate mother cubes by Tian et al. is choosing the mother cube which has the most subcubes of degree less than 5 [6]. However, it may not be accurate enough to judge whether superpoly is more likely to be balanced by its degree. We propose a more accurate way to determine the best mother cube from the candidate mother cubes, i.e., the x-dimensional candidate mother cube that contains the most $(x - 1)$-dimensional subcubes with simple balanced superpolies is selected.

If an x-dimensional mother cube contains most $(x - 1)$-dimensional subcubes with simple balanced superpolies. Then by Observation 1, the superpolies of their $(x - 2)$-dimensional subcubes have a greater probability of being balanced and so do the superpolies of for $(x - 3)$- and $(x - 4)$-dimensional subcubes.

As an example, for 825-round Trivium, we select

$$I_2 = \{p_3, p_4, p_5, p_8, p_9, p_{10}, p_{16}, p_{17}, p_{20}, p_{22}, p_{25}, p_{26}, p_{28}, p_{29}, p_{32}, p_{34}, p_{37},$$
$$p_{39}, p_{40}, p_{43}, p_{44}, p_{45}, p_{46}, p_{47}, p_{48}, p_{49}, p_{51}, p_{52}, p_{53}, p_{54}, p_{55}, p_{56}, p_{57}, p_{58},$$
$$p_{59}, p_{60}, p_{61}, p_{62}, p_{64}, p_{66}, p_{67}, p_{69}, p_{70}, p_{71}, p_{72}, p_{74}, p_{76}, p_{78}, p_{79}, p_{80}\}$$

as our mother cube. The size of I_2 is 53 and it has 7 52-dimensional subcubes with simple balanced superpolies. Among the subcubes of these 7 52-dimensional subcubes, there are 44 51-dimensional subcubes with balanced superpolies. Further more, 87 50-dimensional subcubes with balanced superpolies can be discovered from these 44 51-dimensional subcubes.

A Heuristic Search Strategy for Searching Balanced Cubes. At ASI-ACRYPT 2022 [11], He et al. proposed an efficient method based on the core monomial prediction to recover the superpolies for up to 848 rounds of Trivium. We utilize this method as a tool to search for balanced subcubes (i.e., subcubes with balanced superpolies) among the subcubes of a mother cube by directly recovering the superpolies of subcubes.

According to our experiments, if the superpoly of a subcube is complex, it often takes a long time to recover it. Therefore, when recovering the superpoly for a specific subcube, we set a time limit. If the superpoly of a subcube is not recovered within the time limit, we consider the superpoly to be complex and discard this subcube. This simple trick speeds up the search for balanced subcubes of a mother cube. However, for a 53-dimensional mother cube, it has 53 52-dimensional subcubes, 1378 51-dimensional subcubes, and 23426 50-dimensional subcubes. Recovering the superpolies for these subcubes one by one is still impossible in a reasonable time, but reducing the search space for subcubes means some balanced superpolies may be missed.

To deal with this problem, we give two heuristic strategies based on Observation 1 to reject potentially useless subcubes in advance.

- **First strategy.** If an x-dimensional cube is determined to have an unbalanced and non-zero superpoly, all $(x - 1)$-dimensional subcubes of this cube are considered to have unbalanced superpolies and are rejected.
- **Second strategy.** If an x-dimensional cube is determined to have a balanced or zero superpoly, all $(x - 1)$-dimensional subcubes of this cube are considered to possibly have balanced superpolies and will be checked.

The difference between the first strategy and the second strategy is that when an $(x - 1)$-dimensional cube is simultaneously the subcube of several x-dimensional cubes and one of these x-dimensional cubes has an unbalanced and non-zero superpoly, then the $(x - 1)$-dimensional cube will be rejected according to the first strategy, but will be checked according to the second strategy. In other words, the first strategy is more aggressive in narrowing down the search space.

To further illustrate the effect of reducing the search space on the number of balanced superpolies, we give specific experimental data using the first strategy, the second strategy, and no strategy (i.e., the search over the whole $(x - 1)$-dimensional subcubes, called full search) in Table 3.

For an x-dimensional mother cube, we usually search over its $(x - 1)$- and $(x - 2)$-dimensional subcubes by the full search, then the second strategy is used to search over its $(x - 3)$-dimensional subcubes and $(x - 4)$-dimensional subcubes. Finally, we use the first strategy to search for $(x - 5)$-dimensional subcubes. These search strategies help us find a sufficient number of balanced superpolies with an acceptable computational effort.

4   Application

In this section, we apply our improved methods to 810- and 825-round Trivium. Due to the page limit, superpolies used in this section are provided at https://github.com/lhoop/ObtainMoreBS/tree/main/data.

Table 3. A comparison between search space and balanced cubes for 50-dimensional subcubes of a 53-dimensional mother cube A_0 for 825-round Trivium, where $A_0 = \{v_2, v_5, v_8, v_{10}, v_{12}, v_{15}, v_{17}, v_{19}, v_{23}, v_{29}, v_{31}, v_{41}, v_{44}, v_{46}, v_{51}, v_{55}, v_{63}, v_{66}, v_{72}, v_{78}, v_3, v_0, v_{69}, v_6, v_{26}, v_7, v_{50}, v_{68}, v_{25}, v_{48}, v_{33}, v_4, v_{21}, v_{76}, v_{36}, v_{16}, v_{14}, v_{37}, v_{38}, v_{39}, v_{59}, v_{61}, v_{18}, v_{53}, v_{34}, v_{74}, v_{40}, v_1, v_{57}, v_9, v_{13}, v_{22}, v_{35}\}$

Method	Search space	# of balanced cubes	Space rate[†]	Balanced cubes rate[‡]
first strategy	1365	63	5.83%	40.38%
second strategy	12201	156	52.1%	96.30%
no strategy	23426	162	100%	100%

†: Space rate = (search space)/(the whole search space).
‡: Balanced cubes rate = (balanced cubes)/(balanced cubes from the whole search space).

4.1   A Key-Recovery Attack on 810-Round Trivium with Practical Complexity

Determine a Mother Cube. Using the algorithm in [29], we predict $s_{66}^{(810)}$ as the preference bit for 810-round Trivium. We choose many cubes of size 19 and search for cubes whose superpolies in $s_{285}^{(744)}$ are balanced. Then, the cube

$$Sa_1 = \{v_2, v_6, v_8, v_{10}, v_{11}, v_{15}, v_{19}, v_{21}, v_{25}, v_{29}, v_{30}, v_{32}, v_{34}, v_{36}, v_{39}, v_{41}, v_{43},$$
$$v_{45}, v_{50}\}$$

is obtained. Its superpoly is p_{56}. Also, we search for cubes whose superpolies in $s_{286}^{(744)}$ are balanced. We get the cube

$$Sa_2 = \{v_0, v_2, v_4, v_8, v_{10}, v_{11}, v_{17}, v_{19}, v_{25}, v_{29}, v_{30}, v_{32}, v_{34}, v_{36}, v_{39}, v_{41}, v_{43},$$
$$v_{45}, v_{50}\}.$$

Its superpoly is p_{56}. We first choose Sa_1 as the starting cube to extend.

The public variables are added to Sa_1 iteratively to make the degree[1] of the superpoly decrease to a minimum value other than 0. Then Sa_3 is obtained.

$$Sa_3 = \{v_2, v_6, v_8, v_{10}, v_{11}, v_{15}, v_{19}, v_{21}, v_{25}, v_{29}, v_{30}, v_{32}, v_{34}, v_{36}, v_{39}, v_{41}, v_{43}, v_{45},$$
$$v_{50}, v_0, v_{75}, v_{12}, v_4, v_{14}, v_{20}, v_{22}, v_{16}, v_{27}, v_{23}, v_{72}, v_{52}, v_{55}, v_{60}, v_{37}, v_{79},$$
$$v_{62}, v_{64}, v_{47}, v_{54}, v_{70}\}.$$

The upper bound of the degree of its superpoly is 8 and its size is 40. We note that this set contains all elements in Sa_2 except v_{17}. So we replace v_{16} in Sa_3 with v_{17} to make it fully contain Sa_2.

$$Sa_3' = \{v_2, v_6, v_8, v_{10}, v_{11}, v_{15}, v_{19}, v_{21}, v_{25}, v_{29}, v_{30}, v_{32}, v_{34}, v_{36}, v_{39}, v_{41}, v_{43}, v_{45},$$
$$v_{50}, v_0, v_{75}, v_{12}, v_4, v_{14}, v_{20}, v_{22}, v_{17}, v_{27}, v_{23}, v_{72}, v_{52}, v_{55}, v_{60}, v_{37}, v_{79}, v_{62},$$
$$v_{64}, v_{47}, v_{54}, v_{70}\}.$$

---

[1] We evaluate the upper bound of the degree of the superpoly based on the division property modeled with MILP.

And after adding one element of set $A = \{v_{40}, v_{53}, v_{57}, v_{58}, v_{67}, v_{68}, v_{77}, v_{48}\}$, the degree of Sa'_3 is less than 5. Then, we select four elements from set A to add to Sa'_3 and get 70 44-dimensional candidate mother cubes. We examine the number of balanced superpolies in the 43-dimensional subcubes for each of the 70 candidate mother cubes, then the mother cube

$$Sa_4 = \{v_0, v_2, v_4, v_6, v_8, v_{10}, v_{11}, v_{12}, v_{14}, v_{15}, v_{17}, v_{19}, v_{20}, v_{21}, v_{22}, v_{23}, v_{25}, v_{27},$$
$$v_{29}, v_{30}, v_{32}, v_{34}, v_{36}, v_{37}, v_{39}, v_{41}, v_{43}, v_{45}, v_{47}, v_{50}, v_{52}, v_{54}, v_{55}, v_{60}, v_{62},$$
$$v_{64}, v_{70}, v_{72}, v_{75}, v_{79}, v_{68}, v_{57}, v_{53}, v_{48}\}$$

is selected. It has two simple 43-dimensional subcubes whose superpolies are linear.

Search for Balanced Subcubes. We add a time limit to the search time. A full search is performed over all 42- and 43-dimensional subcubes of Sa_4. The 40- and 41-dimensional subcubes are searched using the second strategy. The method used to recover superpolies is from [11], and we modify it to recover superpolies for new secret variables. Then several superpolies are obtained. After using Sage-Math to extract balanced or quadratic superpolies, 405 balanced superpolies and 526 quadratic superpolies are obtained. Then we obtain additional 275 balanced polynomials from 526 quadratic superpolies using the combining rule in Sect. 3.2.

Determine the Order of Derivation. We pick 39 polynomials from 680 balanced polynomials. The corresponding cubes and the independent bits contained by these polynomials are listed in [15, Appendix E]. 39 variables can be deduced from these polynomials. The specific polynomials are provided at https://github.com/lhoop/ObtainMoreBS/tree/main/data/810_superpoly.

A Practical Attack on a PC. The size of Sa_4 is 44, so it takes 2^{44} requests to obtain all the values of these 39 polynomials. Next, we need to enumerate the values of 42 variables: $\{p_0, p_2, p_3, p_4, p_6, p_7, p_9, p_{10}, p_{17}, p_{18}, p_{20}, p_{23}, p_{25}, p_{28}, p_{30}, p_{33}, p_{35}, p_{38}, p_{39}, p_{40}, p_{42}, p_{44}, p_{45}, p_{47}, p_{48}, p_{49}, p_{51}, p_{52}, p_{56}, p_{57}, p_{58}, p_{59}, p_{60}, p_{63}, p_{66}, p_{69}, p_{70}, p_{73}, p_{77}, p_{78}, p_{79}, p_{80}\}$.

For each enumeration, the values of the remaining 39 variables can be deduced iteratively in the order $(p_{76}, p_{61}, p_{64}, p_{74}, p_{62}, p_{41}, p_{46}, p_{11}, p_{37}, p_{34}, p_{21}, p_{22}, p_{54}, p_{24}, p_{50}, p_{12}, p_{36}, p_{19}, p_{65}, p_5, p_{29}, p_8, p_{16}, p_{53}, p_{26}, p_{14}, p_{43}, p_{68}, p_{55}, p_{67}, p_{71}, p_{27}, p_{75}, p_{31}, p_{15}, p_1, p_{32}, p_{13}, p_{72})$.

There are 2^{42} enumerations, for each enumeration, we use Algorithm 2 to substitute new secret variables back to original secret variables. Half of the enumerations will be excluded because the value of p_{80} does not match. This check only costs constant time. So actually, there are only 2^{41} enumerations of original secret variables. With 2^{41} round-reduced Trivium initializations, the correct key can be filtered out of these 2^{41} candidate keys. To sum up, the whole attack costs $2^{44} + 2^{41}$ round-reduced Trivium initializations. On a PC with an A100 GPU, we can perform the whole attack in 48 min.

4.2 A Key-Recovery Attack on 825-Round Trivium with Practical Complexity

Determine a Mother Cube. We predict $s_{66}^{(825)}$ as the preference bit for 825-round Trivium. Then we choose many cubes of sizes 20 and search for cubes whose superpolies in $s_{286}^{(759)}$ are balanced. Finally, the cube

$$Sb_1 = \{v_2, v_5, v_6, v_8, v_{10}, v_{12}, v_{15}, v_{19}, v_{23}, v_{29}, v_{34}, v_{41}, v_{44}, v_{46}, v_{53}, v_{55}, v_{63},$$
$$v_{66}, v_{72}, v_{78}\}$$

is selected. Its superpoly is $p_{66} \oplus p_{24} \oplus p_{22}p_{23} \oplus 1$. The public variables are added to Sb_1 iteratively to make the degree of the superpoly decrease to a minimum value other than 0. Then Sb_2 is obtained.

$$Sb_2 = \{v_2, v_5, v_8, v_{10}, v_{12}, v_{15}, v_{17}, v_{19}, v_{23}, v_{29}, v_{31}, v_{41}, v_{44}, v_{46}, v_{51}, v_{55}, v_{63}, v_{66},$$
$$v_{72}, v_{78}, v_3, v_0, v_{69}, v_6, v_{26}, v_7, v_{50}, v_{68}, v_{25}, v_{48}, v_{33}, v_4, v_{21}, v_{76}, v_{36}, v_{16},$$
$$v_{14}, v_{37}, v_{38}, v_{39}, v_{59}, v_{61}, v_{18}, v_{53}, v_{34}, v_{74}, v_{40}, v_1, v_{57}, v_9\}.$$

The upper bound of the degree of its superpoly is 6 and its size is 50. And after adding one variable of set $B = \{v_{40}, v_{53}, v_{57}, v_{58}, v_{67}, v_{68}, v_{77}, v_{48}\}$, the degree of Sb_2 is less than 5. Then we select three variables from set B to add to Sb_2 and obtain 280 53-dimensional candidate mother cubes. For each of the 280 candidate mother cubes, we examine the number of balanced superpolies that can be generated by its 52-dimensional subcubes, then the mother cube

$$Sb_3 = \{v_2, v_5, v_8, v_{10}, v_{12}, v_{15}, v_{17}, v_{19}, v_{23}, v_{29}, v_{31}, v_{41}, v_{44}, v_{46}, v_{51}, v_{55}, v_{63}, v_{66},$$
$$v_{72}, v_{78}, v_3, v_0, v_{69}, v_6, v_{26}, v_7, v_{50}, v_{68}, v_{25}, v_{48}, v_{33}, v_4, v_{21}, v_{76}, v_{36}, v_{16},$$
$$v_{14}, v_{37}, v_{38}, v_{39}, v_{59}, v_{61}, v_{18}, v_{53}, v_{34}, v_{74}, v_{40}, v_1, v_{57}, v_9, v_{13}, v_{22}, v_{35}\}$$

is selected. It has 7 52-dimensional subcubes whose superpolies are simple and balanced.

Search for Balanced Subcubes. A full search is performed over all 52- and 51-dimensional subcubes of Sb_3. The 50- and 49-dimensional subcubes are searched using the second strategy, respectively. Then several superpolies are obtained. We use SageMath to extract balanced or quadratic superpolies and obtain 354 balanced superpolies and 422 quadratic superpolies. Then we obtain an extra 872 balanced polynomials from 422 quadratic superpolies using the combining rule in Sect. 3.3.

Determine the Order of Derivation. We pick 31 polynomials from 1226 balanced polynomials. The corresponding cubes and the independent bits contained by these polynomials are listed in [15, Appendix E]. 31 variables can be deduced from these polynomials. The specific polynomials are provided at https://github.com/lhoop/ObtainMoreBS/tree/main/data/825_superpoly.

A Practical Attack on a PC. The size of Sb_3 is 53, so it takes 2^{53} requests to obtain all the values of these 31 polynomials. Next, we need to enumerate the values of 50 variables: $\{p_3, p_4, p_5, p_8, p_9, p_{10}, p_{16}, p_{17}, p_{20}, p_{22}, p_{25},$

$p_{26}, p_{28}, p_{29}, p_{32}, p_{34}, p_{37}, p_{39}, p_{40}, p_{43}, p_{44}, \quad p_{45}, p_{46}, p_{47}, p_{48}, p_{49}, p_{51}, \quad p_{52}, p_{53}, p_{54}, p_{55}, p_{56}, p_{57}, p_{58}, p_{59}, p_{60}, p_{61}, p_{62}, \quad p_{64}, p_{66}, p_{67}, p_{69}, p_{70}, p_{71}, p_{72}, p_{74}, p_{76}, p_{78}, p_{79}, p_{80}\}$.

For each enumeration, the values of the remaining 31 variables can be deduced iteratively in the order $(p_{73}, p_{75}, p_{77}, p_{63}, p_{14}, p_{31}, p_{11}, p_{35}, p_{27}, p_{33}, p_{12}, p_{41}, p_{30}, p_{65}, p_{38}, p_1, p_{13}, p_{15}, p_{50}, \quad p_{42}, p_6, p_7, p_{18}, p_{68}, p_{24}, p_{23}, p_2, p_0, p_{19}, p_{36}, p_{21})$.

There are 2^{50} enumerations, for each enumeration, we use Algorithm 2 to substitute new secret variables back to original secret variables. Half of the enumerations will be excluded because the value of p_{80} does not match. This check only costs a constant time. So actually, we only need 2^{49} enumerations of original secret variables. With 2^{49} round-reduced Trivium initializations, the correct key can be filtered out of these 2^{49} candidate keys. To sum up, the whole attack costs $2^{53} + 2^{49}$ round-reduced Trivium initializations. On a PC with an A100 GPU, we can perform the whole attack in 18 days.

5   Conclusion

In this paper, we focus on practical full key-recovery attacks on Trivium. We propose a variable substitution technique to simplify the superpoly and a new method to obtain a new balanced polynomial by combining two superpolies to cancel out the quadratic terms. Moreover, by an observation that the subcubes of a cube whose superpoly is balanced are more likely to have balanced superpolies, we modify the original algorithm to construct a better mother cube that contains more subcubes with balanced superpolies, and propose a heuristic strategy for searching for cubes with balanced superpolies. As a result, we use our new methods to perform full key-recovery attacks on 810- and 825-round Trivium, which can be done with time complexity $2^{44.17}$ and $2^{53.09}$ round-reduced Trivium initializations, respectively. It is experimentally verified that the two attacks could be completed in 48 min and 18 days on a PC with one A100 GPU (128×256 threads), respectively. We also time-test previous attacks on 808- and 820-round Trivium with the same number of threads [6,21]. For the attack on 808-round Trivium in [21], it could be completed in 12 h with our GPU. And for the attack on 820-round Trivium in [6], we estimate that the attack would be completed in 19 days with our GPU. These experiments confirm that we can improve the previous results for 2 and 5 rounds without increasing the time complexity.

Acknowledgment. The authors would like to thank Raghvendra Rohit as our shepherd and other anonymous reviewers that have helped us improve the quality of this paper. This research is supported by the National Key Research and Development Program of China (Grant No. 2018YFA0704702), the National Natural Science Foundation of China (Grant No. 62032014), the Major Basic Research Project of Natural Science Foundation of Shandong Province, China (Grant No. ZR202010220025).

References

1. Sagemath. https://www.sagemath.org
2. Aumasson, J.-P., Dinur, I., Meier, W., Shamir, A.: Cube testers and key recovery attacks on reduced-round MD6 and trivium. In: Dunkelman, O. (ed.) FSE 2009. LNCS, vol. 5665, pp. 1–22. Springer, Heidelberg (2009). https://doi.org/10.1007/978-3-642-03317-9_1
3. Boura, C., Coggia, D.: Efficient MILP modelings for Sboxes and linear layers of SPN ciphers. IACR Trans. Symmetric Cryptol. **2020**(3), 327–361 (2020). https://doi.org/10.13154/tosc.v2020.i3.327-361
4. De Cannière, C., Preneel, B.: Trivium. In: Robshaw, M., Billet, O. (eds.) New Stream Cipher Designs. LNCS, vol. 4986, pp. 244–266. Springer, Heidelberg (2008). https://doi.org/10.1007/978-3-540-68351-3_18
5. Canteaut, A., et al.: Stream ciphers: a practical solution for efficient homomorphic-ciphertext compression. J. Cryptol. **31**(3), 885–916 (2018). https://doi.org/10.1007/s00145-017-9273-9
6. Che, C., Tian, T.: An experimentally verified attack on 820-round trivium. In: Deng, Y., Yung, M. (eds.) Inscrypt 2022. LNCS, vol. 13837, pp. 357–369. Springer, Cham (2022). https://doi.org/10.1007/978-3-031-26553-2_19
7. Dinur, I., Shamir, A.: Cube attacks on tweakable black box polynomials. In: Joux, A. (ed.) EUROCRYPT 2009. LNCS, vol. 5479, pp. 278–299. Springer, Heidelberg (2009). https://doi.org/10.1007/978-3-642-01001-9_16
8. Fouque, P., Vannet, T.: Improving key recovery to 784 and 799 rounds of Trivium using optimized cube attacks. IACR Cryptol. ePrint Arch. 312 (2015). http://eprint.iacr.org/2015/312
9. Hao, Y., Leander, G., Meier, W., Todo, Y., Wang, Q.: Modeling for three-subset division property without unknown subset. In: Canteaut, A., Ishai, Y. (eds.) EUROCRYPT 2020. LNCS, vol. 12105, pp. 466–495. Springer, Cham (2020). https://doi.org/10.1007/978-3-030-45721-1_17
10. Hao, Y., Leander, G., Meier, W., Todo, Y., Wang, Q.: Modeling for three-subset division property without unknown subset. J. Cryptol. **34**(3), 22 (2021). https://doi.org/10.1007/s00145-021-09383-2
11. He, J., Hu, K., Preneel, B., Wang, M.: Stretching cube attacks: improved methods to recover massive superpolies. In: Agrawal, S., Lin, D. (eds.) ASIACRYPT 2022, Part IV. LNCS, vol. 13794, pp. 537–566. Springer, Cham (2022). https://doi.org/10.1007/978-3-031-22972-5_19
12. Hebborn, P., Lambin, B., Leander, G., Todo, Y.: Lower bounds on the degree of block ciphers. In: Moriai, S., Wang, H. (eds.) ASIACRYPT 2020, Part I. LNCS, vol. 12491, pp. 537–566. Springer, Cham (2020). https://doi.org/10.1007/978-3-030-64837-4_18
13. Hu, K., Sun, S., Todo, Y., Wang, M., Wang, Q.: Massive superpoly recovery with nested monomial predictions. In: Tibouchi, M., Wang, H. (eds.) ASIACRYPT 2021, Part I. LNCS, vol. 13090, pp. 392–421. Springer, Cham (2021). https://doi.org/10.1007/978-3-030-92062-3_14
14. Hu, K., Sun, S., Wang, M., Wang, Q.: An algebraic formulation of the division property: revisiting degree evaluations, cube attacks, and key-independent sums. In: Moriai, S., Wang, H. (eds.) ASIACRYPT 2020, Part I. LNCS, vol. 12491, pp. 446–476. Springer, Cham (2020). https://doi.org/10.1007/978-3-030-64837-4_15
15. Lei, H., He, J., Hu, K., Wang, M.: More balanced polynomials: cube attacks on 810- and 825-round Trivium with practical complexities. IACR Cryptol. ePrint Arch. 1237 (2023). https://eprint.iacr.org/2023/1237

16. Liu, M., Yang, J., Wang, W., Lin, D.: Correlation cube attacks: from weak-key distinguisher to key recovery. In: Nielsen, J.B., Rijmen, V. (eds.) EUROCRYPT 2018, Part II. LNCS, vol. 10821, pp. 715–744. Springer, Cham (2018). https://doi.org/10.1007/978-3-319-78375-8_23

17. Mroczkowski, P., Szmidt, J.: Corrigendum to: the cube attack on stream cipher Trivium and quadraticity tests. IACR Cryptol. ePrint Arch. 32 (2011). http://eprint.iacr.org/2011/032

18. Salam, M.I., Bartlett, H., Dawson, E., Pieprzyk, J., Simpson, L., Wong, K.K.-H.: Investigating cube attacks on the authenticated encryption stream cipher ACORN. In: Batten, L., Li, G. (eds.) ATIS 2016. CCIS, vol. 651, pp. 15–26. Springer, Singapore (2016). https://doi.org/10.1007/978-981-10-2741-3_2

19. Sasaki, Yu., Todo, Y.: New algorithm for modeling S-box in MILP based differential and division trail search. In: Farshim, P., Simion, E. (eds.) SecITC 2017. LNCS, vol. 10543, pp. 150–165. Springer, Cham (2017). https://doi.org/10.1007/978-3-319-69284-5_11

20. Sun, S., Hu, L., Wang, P., Qiao, K., Ma, X., Song, L.: Automatic security evaluation and (related-key) differential characteristic search: application to SIMON, PRESENT, LBlock, DES(L) and other bit-oriented block ciphers. In: Sarkar, P., Iwata, T. (eds.) ASIACRYPT 2014. LNCS, vol. 8873, pp. 158–178. Springer, Heidelberg (2014). https://doi.org/10.1007/978-3-662-45611-8_9

21. Sun, Y.: Automatic search of cubes for attacking stream ciphers. IACR Trans. Symmetric Cryptol. **2021**(4), 100–123 (2021). https://doi.org/10.46586/tosc.v2021.i4.100-123

22. Todo, Y.: Structural evaluation by generalized integral property. In: Oswald, E., Fischlin, M. (eds.) EUROCRYPT 2015. LNCS, vol. 9056, pp. 287–314. Springer, Heidelberg (2015). https://doi.org/10.1007/978-3-662-46800-5_12

23. Todo, Y., Isobe, T., Hao, Y., Meier, W.: Cube attacks on non-blackbox polynomials based on division property. In: Katz, J., Shacham, H. (eds.) CRYPTO 2017, Part III. LNCS, vol. 10403, pp. 250–279. Springer, Cham (2017). https://doi.org/10.1007/978-3-319-63697-9_9

24. Todo, Y., Morii, M.: Bit-based division property and application to SIMON family. In: Peyrin, T. (ed.) FSE 2016. LNCS, vol. 9783, pp. 357–377. Springer, Heidelberg (2016). https://doi.org/10.1007/978-3-662-52993-5_18

25. Wang, S., Hu, B., Guan, J., Zhang, K., Shi, T.: MILP-aided method of searching division property using three subsets and applications. In: Galbraith, S.D., Moriai, S. (eds.) ASIACRYPT 2019, Part III. LNCS, vol. 11923, pp. 398–427. Springer, Cham (2019). https://doi.org/10.1007/978-3-030-34618-8_14

26. Wu, H.: ACORN v3. Submission to CAESAR competition (2016)

27. Ye, C., Tian, T.: A new framework for finding nonlinear superpolies in cube attacks against trivium-like ciphers. In: Susilo, W., Yang, G. (eds.) ACISP 2018. LNCS, vol. 10946, pp. 172–187. Springer, Cham (2018). https://doi.org/10.1007/978-3-319-93638-3_11

28. Ye, C., Tian, T.: Algebraic method to recover superpolies in cube attacks. IET Inf. Secur. **14**(4), 430–441 (2020). https://doi.org/10.1049/iet-ifs.2019.0323

29. Ye, C.-D., Tian, T.: A practical key-recovery attack on 805-round trivium. In: Tibouchi, M., Wang, H. (eds.) ASIACRYPT 2021, Part I. LNCS, vol. 13090, pp. 187–213. Springer, Cham (2021). https://doi.org/10.1007/978-3-030-92062-3_7

A Closer Look at the S-Box: Deeper Analysis of Round-Reduced ASCON-HASH

Xiaorui Yu[1], Fukang Liu[2], Gaoli Wang[1(✉)], Siwei Sun[3], and Willi Meier[4]

[1] Shanghai Key Laboratory of Trustworthy Computing,
East China Normal University, Shanghai 200062, China
51215902051@stu.ecnu.edu.cn, glwang@sei.ecnu.edu.cn
[2] Tokyo Institute of Technology, Tokyo, Japan
[3] School of Cryptology, University of Chinese Academy of Sciences, Beijing, China
[4] FHNW, Windisch, Switzerland

Abstract. ASCON, a lightweight permutation-based primitive, has been selected as NIST's lightweight cryptography standard. ASCON-HASH is one of the hash functions provided by the cipher suite ASCON. At ToSC 2021, the collision attack on 2-round ASCON-HASH with time complexity 2^{103} was proposed. Due to its small rate, it is always required to utilize at least 2 message blocks to mount a collision attack because each message block is only of size 64 bits. This significantly increases the difficulty of the analysis because one almost needs to analyze equivalently at least 2ℓ rounds of ASCON in order to break ℓ rounds. In this paper, we make some critical observations on the round function of ASCON, especially a 2-round property. It is found that such properties can be exploited to reduce the time complexity of the 2-round collision attack to $2^{62.6}$. Although the number of attacked rounds is not improved, we believe our techniques shed more insight into the properties of the ASCON permutation and we expect they can be useful for the future research.

Keywords: ASCON · ASCON-HASH · Collision Attack · Algebraic Technique

1 Introduction

Lightweight cryptography algorithms are a class of ciphers designed for resource-constrained environments. They typically have low requirements in terms of computing power, storage space, and power consumption, and are suitable for resource-constrained application scenarios such as embedded systems, IoT devices, and sensors.

In 2013, NIST started the lightweight cryptography project. Later in 2016, NIST provided an overview of the project and decided to seek for some new algorithms as a lightweight cryptography standard. In 2019, NIST received 57

C. Carlet et al. (Eds.): SAC 2023, LNCS 14201, pp. 22–42, 2024.
https://doi.org/10.1007/978-3-031-53368-6_2

submissions and 56 of them became the first round candidates after the initial review. After the project proceeded into Round 2 [4], NIST selected 32 submissions as Round 2 candidates, including ASCON. After that, ASCON was selected to be one of the ten finalists of the lightweight cryptography standardization process. On February 7, 2023, NIST announced the selection of the ASCON family for the lightweight cryptography standardization.

ASCON [10] is a lightweight permutation-based primitive. It aims to provide efficient encryption and authentication functions while maintaining sufficiently high security.

Advantages. The main advantages of ASCON can be summarized as below:

- **Lightweight:** The design of ASCON is simple and suitable for hardware and software implementation. It is particularly suitable for resource constrained environments, such as IoT devices, embedded systems, and low-power devices.
- **High security:** ASCON provides high security and resists many different types of known attacks.
- **Adjustable:** ASCON supports different security levels and performance requirements. For example, ASCON-128 and ASCON-128a provide a 128-bit security level, suitable for high security requirements; ASCON-80pq provides an 128-bit security level, suitable for low-power and low-cost scenarios.
- **Authentication encryption:** ASCON can achieve both data encryption and integrity protection. It supports associated data and allows for verification of additional information during the encryption process, such as the identities of message senders and receivers.

History. ASCON was first published as a candidate in Round 1 [6] of the CAESAR competition [1]. This original design (version v1) specified the permutation as well as the mode for authenticated encryption with two recommended family members: The primary recommendation Ascon-128 as well as a variant Ascon-96 with 96-bit key. For the subsequent version V1.1 [7] and V1.2 [8], minor functional tweaks were applied, including a reordering of the round constants and the modification of the secondary recommendation to the current Ascon-128a. Then, V1.2 [8] and the status update file [9] were submitted to the NIST Lightweight Cryptography project. The submission to NIST includes not only the authenticated cipher family, but also introduces modes of operation for hashing: ASCON-HASH and ASCON-XOF, as well as a third parameterization for authenticated encryption: Ascon-80pq. For ASCON-HASH and ASCON-XOF, they support 256-bit and arbitrary-length hash values, respectively.

On the Collision Resistance of ASCON-HASH. Due to the used sponge structure, the generic time complexity to find a collision of ASCON-HASH is 2^{128} and the memory complexity is negligible with Floyd's cycle finding algorithm [11]. Due to its small rate, it is quite challenging to find collisions for a large number of rounds. In [21], the first 2-round collision attack on ASCON-HASH was presented with time complexity 2^{125}. However, it is shown that such an attack is invalid because the used 2-round differential characteristic is invalid according to [13]. Later, at ToSC 2021 [12], a new and valid 2-round differential characteristic with an optimal differential probability was found. Based on the same attack strategy as in [21], they gave a 2-round collision with time complexity of 2^{103} in [12]. Very recently, Qin et al. presented collision attacks on 3 and 4 rounds of ASCON-HASH by turning preimages for ASCON-XOF into collisions for ASCON-HASH [19]. However, it can be found that both the time complexity and memory complexity of the 3/4-round collision attacks are very high, i.e. larger than 2^{120}. From a practical view, it seems that these attacks may be slower than the generic attack. In any case, all the collision attacks are far from being practical, even for 2 rounds.

Table 1. Summary of collision attacks on ASCON-HASH

Attack Type	Rounds	Time complexity	Memory Complexity	Reference
collision attack	2	2^{125*}	negligible	[21]
	2	2^{103}	negligible	[12]
	2	$2^{62.6}$	negligible	Sect. 4
	3	$2^{121.85}$	2^{121}	[19]
	4	$2^{126.77}$	2^{126}	[19]

* The characteristic used is invalid.

Our Contributions. We aim to significantly improve the time complexity of the 2-round collision attack in [12] such that it can be much closer to a practical attack. Our contributions are summarized below:

1. We found that the 2-round collision attack in [12] is quite straightforward, i.e., the authors found a better characteristic but did not optimize the attack strategy. Hence, we are motivated to take a closer look at the used 2-round differential characteristic and aim to improve the attack by using some algebraic properties of the S-box as in the recent algebraic attack on LowMC [14,17], i.e., we are interested in the relations between the difference transitions and value transitions.
2. Based on our findings of the properties of the S-box, we propose to use a better attack framework and advanced algebraic techniques to improve the 2-round collision attack. As a result, the time complexity is reduced from 2^{103} to $2^{62.6}$, as shown in Table 1.

Organization of this paper. In Sect. 2, we define some notations that will be used throughout the paper and briefly describe ASCON-HASH. In Sect. 3, we describe the collision attack framework that will be used in the new attacks. In Sect. 4, we show how to optimize the existing 2-round collision attack with advanced algebraic techniques. Finally, the paper is concluded in Sect. 5.

2 Preliminaries

2.1 Notations

The notations used in this paper are summarized in Table 2.

Table 2. Notations

r	the length of the rate part for ASCON-HASH, $r = 64$
c	the length of the capacity part for ASCON-HASH, $c = 256$
S_j^i	the input state of round i when absorbing the message block M_j
$S^i[j]$	the j-th word (64-bit) of S_i
$S^i[j][k]$	the k-th bit of $S^i[j]$, $k = 0$ means the least significant bit and k is within modulo 64
x_i	the i-th bit of a 5-bit value x, x_0 represents the most significant bit
M	message
M_i	the i-th block of the padded message
$\ggg$	right rotation (circular right shift)
$a\%b$	$a \bmod b$
0^n	a string of n zeroes

2.2 Description of ASCON-HASH

The ASCON family offers 2 important hash functions: ASCON-HASH and ASCON-XOF. ASCON-HASH is a sponge-based hash function [2]. In its core, it is a 12-round permutation P^a over a state of 320 bits. The hashing mode is shown in Fig. 1.

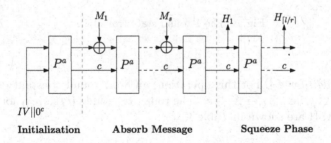

Initialization   Absorb Message   Squeeze Phase

Fig. 1. The mode of ASCON-HASH

For ASCON-HASH, the state denoted by X is divided into five 64-bit words, i.e., $X = X_0||X_1||X_2||X_3||X_4$. The first 64-bit word X_0 will be loaded in the rate part while the remaining 4 words (X_1, X_2, X_3, X_4) are loaded in the capacity part. The round function $f = f_L \circ f_S \circ f_C$ is composed of 3 operations: f_C is the constant addition, f_S is the substitution layer, and f_L is the linear diffusion layer. For simplicity, the ℓ-round ASCON permutation is simply denoted by f^ℓ.

On the Internal States. When absorbing the message block M_j, denote the 320-bit input state at round i ($0 \le i \le 11$) by S_j^i and the state transitions are described below.

$$S_j^i \xrightarrow{f_C} S_j^{i,a} \xrightarrow{f_S} S_j^{i,s} \xrightarrow{f_L} S_j^{i+1}.$$

Note that if we only consider one message block, we simply omit j as below:

$$S^i \xrightarrow{f_C} S^{i,a} \xrightarrow{f_S} S^{i,s} \xrightarrow{f_L} S^{i+1}.$$

The corresponding graphic explanations can be referred to Fig. 2 and Fig. 3, respectively.

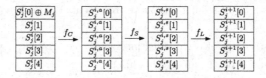

Fig. 2. The 1-round state transition when absorbing M_j

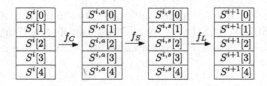

Fig. 3. The 1-round state transition

Constant Addition f_C. For this operation, an 8-bit round constant c_i is added to the word X_2, i.e., $X_2 \leftarrow X_2 \oplus c_i$. The round constants $(c_i)_{0 \le i \le 11}$ for 12-round ASCON-HASH are shown in Table 3.

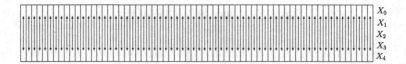

Fig. 4. The substitution layer

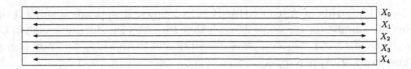

Fig. 5. The linear diffusion layer

Table 3. The round constants c_i

i	0	1	2	3	4	5	6	7	8	9	10	11
c_i	0xf0	0xe1	0xd2	0xc3	0xb5	0xa5	0x96	0x87	0x78	0x69	0x5a	0x4b

Substitution Layer f_S. At this operation, the state will be updated by 64 parallel applications of a 5-bit S-box. The S-box $(y_0, \ldots, y_4) = \mathrm{SB}(x_0, \ldots, x_4)$ is defined as follows:

$$
\begin{cases}
y_0 = x_4 x_1 \oplus x_3 \oplus x_2 x_1 \oplus x_2 \oplus x_1 x_0 \oplus x_1 \oplus x_0, \\
y_1 = x_4 \oplus x_3 x_2 \oplus x_3 x_1 \oplus x_3 \oplus x_2 x_1 \oplus x_2 \oplus x_1 \oplus x_0, \\
y_2 = x_4 x_3 \oplus x_4 \oplus x_2 \oplus x_1 \oplus 1, \\
y_3 = x_4 x_0 \oplus x_4 \oplus x_3 x_0 \oplus x_3 \oplus x_2 \oplus x_1 \oplus x_0, \\
y_4 = x_4 x_1 \oplus x_4 \oplus x_3 \oplus x_1 x_0 \oplus x_1.
\end{cases}
\tag{1}
$$

As shown in Fig. 4, the input $(x_0, \ldots, x_4)$ and output $(y_0, \ldots, y_4)$ correspond to one column of the state.

Linear Diffusion Layer f_L. This operation is used to diffuse each 64-bit word X_i, as shown in Fig. 5. Specifically, X_i is updated by the function $\sum_i$ where $0 \le i \le 4$, as specified below:

$$
\begin{cases}
X_0 \leftarrow \Sigma_0(X_0) = X_0 \oplus (X_0 \ggg 19) \oplus (X_0 \ggg 28), \\
X_1 \leftarrow \Sigma_1(X_1) = X_1 \oplus (X_1 \ggg 61) \oplus (X_1 \ggg 39), \\
X_2 \leftarrow \Sigma_2(X_2) = X_2 \oplus (X_2 \ggg 1) \oplus (X_2 \ggg 6), \\
X_3 \leftarrow \Sigma_3(X_3) = X_3 \oplus (X_3 \ggg 10) \oplus (X_3 \ggg 17), \\
X_4 \leftarrow \Sigma_4(X_4) = X_4 \oplus (X_4 \ggg 7) \oplus (X_4 \ggg 41).
\end{cases}
$$

On the Initial Value and State. The hash function initializes the 320-bit state using a constant $IV = 0x00400c0000000000$. Then, the 12-round ASCON permutation is applied and we obtain an initial state $S_1^0 = f^{12}(IV \| 0^{256})$, as specified below:

$$
S_1^0 \leftarrow
\begin{array}{l}
\text{0xee9398aadb67f03d} \\
\text{0x8bb21831c60f1002} \\
\text{0xb48a92db98d5da62} \\
\text{0x43189921b8f8e3e8} \\
\text{0x348fa5c9d525e140}
\end{array}
$$

The padding rule of ASCON-HASH is as follows: it appends a single 1 and the smallest number of zeroes to M such that the size of padded message in bits is a multiple of $r = 64$. The complete description of the hashing function is given in Algorithm 1 in Appendix A.

3   The Attack Frameworks

For differential-based collision attacks on a sponge-based hash function, one essential step is to find a collision-generating differential characteristic. The second step is to find conforming message pairs satisfying this differential characteristic.

With the development of automatic tools, there are many possible methods to search for a desired differential characteristic. However, when it comes to the second step, i.e., satisfying the conditions of the differential characteristic, it always involves dedicated efforts and sometimes requires nontrivial techniques. For example, the linearization techniques for the KECCAK round function have been widely used to speed up the differential-based collision attack on KECCAK, e.g., the 1/2/3-round connectors [5,18,20]. As can be seen from the current record of the Keccak crunchy crypto collision contest[1], it is quite challenging to analyze sponge-based hash functions with a small rate, which is exactly the case of ASCON. It is thus not surprising to see that the best differential-based collision attack on ASCON could only reach up to 2 rounds.

For a sponge-based hash function with a small rate, one main obstacle exists in the available degrees of freedom in each message block. For ASCON, each message block only provides at most 64 free bits. However, for a differential characteristic used for collision attacks, there may exist more than 128 bit conditions, which directly makes it mandatory to utilize at least 3 message blocks.

Let us consider a general case and suppose that we have an ℓ-round collision-generating differential characteristic. Furthermore, suppose we will use k message blocks $(M_1, \ldots, M_k)$ to fulfill the conditions, i.e., we aim to find $(M_1, \ldots, M_k)$ and $(M_1, \ldots, M_{k-1}, M'_k)$ such that

$$S^0_{j+1} = f^\ell\left(S^0_j \oplus (M_j \| 0^{256})\right) \text{ where } 1 \le j \le k-1,$$

$$\star \| 0^{256} = f^\ell\left(S^0_k \oplus (M_k \| 0^{256})\right) \oplus f^\ell\left(S^0_k \oplus \mathsf{SB}(M'_k \| 0^{256})\right),$$

where $M_k \ne M'_k$ and $\star$ is an arbitrary r-bit value.

From the differential characteristic, suppose that there are n_c bit conditions on the capacity part of S^0_k and the remaining conditions hold with probability 2^{-n_k}. Then, a straightforward method to find conforming message pairs is as follows:

Step 1: Find a solution of $(M_1, \ldots, M_{k-1})$ such that the n_c bit conditions on the capacity part of S^0_k can hold.

---

[1] https://keccak.team/crunchy_contest.html.

Step 2: Exhaust M_k and check whether remaining n_k bit conditions can hold. If there is a solution, a collision is found. Otherwise, return to Step 1.

For convenience, we call the above procedure *the general 2-step attack framework*. Note that this has been widely used and it is really not a new idea.

For a sponge with rate r, we need to perform Step 2 for about 2^{n_k-r} times and hence we need to perform Step 1 for 2^{n_k-r} times. Suppose the time complexity to find a solution of $(M_1, \ldots, M_{k-1})$ and M_k is T_{pre} and T_k, respectively. In this way, the total time complexity T_{total} is estimated as

$$T_{\text{total}} = (k-1) \cdot 2^{n_k-r} \cdot T_{\text{pre}} + 2^{n_k-r} \cdot T_k. \tag{2}$$

If T_k and T_{pre} are simply treated as 2^r and 2^{n_c}, respectively, i.e., only the naive exhaustive search is performed, then

$$T_{\text{total}} = (k-1) \cdot 2^{n_k+n_c-r} + 2^{n_k}.$$

In other words, the total time complexity is directly related to the probability of the differential characteristic, i.e., $2^{-n_c-n_k}$.

In many cases, the attackers can optimize T_k by using some advanced techniques to satisfy partial conditions implied in the differential characteristic, i.e., T_k can be smaller than 2^r. For example, the target difference algorithm proposed in [5] is one of such techniques. However, to optimize T_{pre}, one has to solve a problem similar to the ℓ-round preimage finding problem. In most cases, this is not optimized due to the increasing difficulty and it is simply treated as $T_{\text{pre}} = 2^{n_c}$.

3.1   The Literature and Our New Strategy

It is found that neither T_k nor T_{pre} has been optimized for the existing 2-round collision attacks on ASCON-HASH [12,21] and they exactly follow the above attack framework. In the collision attack on 6-round GIMLI-HASH [13], the attackers optimized both T_k and T_{pre} where $k = 2$.

As can be noted in our new attacks on ASCON-HASH, optimizing T_k is indeed quite straightforward after a little deeper analysis of the round function and its 5-bit S-box. However, optimizing T_{pre} looks infeasible at the first glance. Indeed even if T_k is optimized to 1, the improved factor is still quite small. Therefore, to achieve significant improvements, it is necessary to optimize T_{pre}.

Our idea to achieve this purpose is to further convert the n_c conditions on the capacity part of S_k^0 into some n_c^1 conditions on the capacity part of S_{k-1}^0, as Fig. 6 shows. In this way, our attack is stated as follows:

Step 1: Find a solution of $(M_1, \ldots, M_{k-2})$ such that the n_c^1 bit conditions on the capacity part of S_{k-1}^0 can hold.
Step 2: Enumerate all the solutions of M_{k-1} such that the conditions on the capacity part of S_k^0 can hold.
Step 3: Exhaust M_k and check whether remaining n_k bit conditions can hold. If there is a solution, a collision is found. Otherwise, return to Step 1.

To distinguish this from *the general 2-step attack framework*, we call the above procedure *the general 3-step attack framework*.

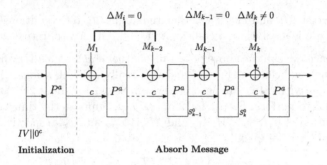

Fig. 6. The general 3-step attack framework

Analysis of the Time Complexity. For convenience, the time complexity of Step 1, 2 and 3 is denoted by T_{pre1}, $T_{\text{k-1}}$ and T_{k}, respectively. In this way, the total time complexity becomes

$$T_{\text{total}} = (k-2) \cdot 2^{n_k + n_c - 2r} \cdot T_{\text{pre1}} + 2^{n_k + n_c - 2r} \cdot T_{\text{k-1}} + 2^{n_k - r} \cdot T_{\text{k}}. \qquad (3)$$

Specifically, we need on average $2^{n_k - r}$ different valid solutions of $(M_1, \ldots, M_{k-1})$. In this sense, we need about $2^{n_k + n_c - 2r}$ different valid solutions of $(M_1, \ldots, M_{k-2})$ because for each valid $(M_1, \ldots, M_{k-2})$, we expect to have $2^{r - n_c}$ valid solutions of M_{k-1}.

Based on Eq. 3, if $n_c < r$ holds, we have

$$2^{n_k + n_c - 2r} < 2^{n_k - r}.$$

Compared with Eq. 2, this case has indicated the possibility to optimize the attack if $T_{\text{k-1}}$ can be significantly optimized and T_{pre1} is relatively small, i.e., we know $T_{\text{pre1}} \leq 2^{n'_c}$.

On the Purpose to Convert Conditions. As stated above, we have to optimize T_{pre1}. This is related to the original purpose to introduce conditions on the capacity part of S_{k-1}^0. Specifically, we expect that after adding these conditions, we can efficiently enumerate the solutions of M_{k-1} to satisfy the n_c conditions on the capacity part of S_k^0. In other words, without these conditions, we still can only perform the naive exhaustive search over M_{k-1} and no improvement can be obtained, i.e., the time complexity is

$$(k-2) \cdot 2^{n_k + n_c - 2r} + 2^{n_k + n_c - 2r} \cdot 2^r + 2^{n_k - r} \cdot T_{\text{k}}$$
$$= (k-2) \cdot 2^{n_k + n_c - 2r} + 2^{n_k + n_c - r} + 2^{n_k - r} \cdot T_{\text{k}}.$$

The Big Picture of Our New Attacks. In our attacks, we do not make more efforts to convert the n'_c conditions on S_{k-1}^0 into conditions on the previous input states due to the increasing difficulty. Hence, in our setting, we will make

$$T_{\text{pre1}} = 2^{n'_c}.$$

In this way, the total time complexity is estimated as

$$T_{\text{total}} = (k-2) \cdot 2^{n_k + n_c + n_c' - 2r} + 2^{n_k + n_c - 2r} \cdot T_{k-1} + 2^{n_k - r} \cdot T_k. \qquad (4)$$

In the following, we will describe how to significantly optimize T_{k-1} and T_k based on an existing 2-round differential characteristic of ASCON.

4   Collision Attacks on 2-Round ASCON-HASH

The collision attack in this paper is based on the 2-round differential characteristic proposed in [12], as shown in Table 4. Note that the first collision attack on 2-round ASCON-HASH was proposed in [21] but the differential characteristic is shown to be invalid in [13]. We have verified with the technique in [13] that the 2-round differential characteristic in [12] is correct.

Table 4. The 2-round differential characteristic in [12]

ΔS^0 (2^{-54})	ΔS^1 (2^{-102})	ΔS^2
0xbb450325d90b1581	0x2201080000011080	0xbaf571d85e1153d7
0x0	0x2adf0c201225338a	0x0
0x0	0x0	0x0
0x0	0x0000000100408000	0x0
0x0	0x2adf0c211265b38a	0x0

According to [12], there are 27 and 28 active S-boxes in the first and second round, respectively. Specifically, there are 54 bit conditions on the capacity part of the input S^0 and 102 bit conditions on the input state S^1 of the second round. With our notations, there are

$$n_c = 54, \quad n_k = 102.$$

With this differential characteristic, they used the technique in [21] to mount the collision attack with $k = 4$ message blocks and its time complexity is 2^{102}. It follows the general 2-step attack framework described above without optimization on T_{pre} and T_k, i.e.,

$$T_{\text{pre}} = 2^{54}, \quad T_k = 2^{64}.$$

In this way, the total time complexity can be computed based on Eq. 2, i.e.,

$$T_{\text{total}} = 2 \times 2^{102-64} \times 2^{54} + 2^{102-64} \times 2^{64} = 2^{93} + 2^{102} \approx 2^{102}. \qquad (5)$$

It should be noted that in [12], the authors simply checked whether M_3 and $M_3 \oplus \Delta S_3^0$ can follow the 2-round differential characteristic by exhausting M_3 and hence the time complexity in [12] is estimated as $2 \times 2^{102} = 2^{103}$. In other words, they do not take the specific conditions into account, while in the above, we only check whether the conditions on the S^1 hold for each M_3.

4.1   Optimizing T_k Using Simple Linear Algebra

Indeed, it is quite straightforward to optimize T_k. However, even if it is reduced to 1, the time complexity is still high, i.e., 2^{92} according to Eq. 5. Let us elaborate on how to significantly optimize T_k in this section. First, we need to study some properties of the S-box.

Studying the Active S-Boxes in the First Round. First, we describe why there are 54 bit conditions on the capacity part of S^0.

Property 1 [21]. *For an input difference $(\Delta_0, \ldots, \Delta_4)$ satisfying $\Delta x_1 = \Delta x_2 = \Delta x_3 = \Delta x_4 = 0$ and $\Delta x_0 = 1$, the following constraints hold:*

– *For the output difference:*

$$\begin{cases} \Delta y_0 \oplus \Delta y_4 = 1, \\ \Delta y_1 = \Delta x_0, \\ \Delta y_2 = 0. \end{cases} \tag{6}$$

– *For the input value:*

$$\begin{cases} x_1 = \Delta y_0 \oplus 1, \\ x_3 \oplus x_4 = \Delta y_3 \oplus 1. \end{cases} \tag{7}$$

Based on Property 1 and the 2-round differential characteristic in Table 4, we can derive $27 + 27 = 54$ bit conditions on the capacity part of S^0, i.e., 27 bit conditions on $S^0[1]$ and 27 bit conditions on $S^0[3] \oplus S^0[4]$. This also explains why $n_c = 54$.

Studying the Active S-Boxes in the Second Round. As the next step, we further study the 28 active S-boxes in the second round. We observe that from ΔS^1 to $\Delta S^{1,s}$, there are only 3 different possible difference transitions $(\Delta x_0, \ldots, \Delta x_4) \to (\Delta y_0, \ldots, \Delta y_4)$ through the S-box, as shown below:

$$(1, 1, 0, 0, 1) \to (1, 0, 0, 0, 0),$$
$$(0, 0, 0, 1, 1) \to (1, 0, 0, 0, 0),$$
$$(0, 1, 0, 0, 1) \to (1, 0, 0, 0, 0).$$

Similar to the algebraic attacks on LowMC [14,17], we study and exploit the properties of the $(x_0, \ldots, x_4)$ such that

$$\mathrm{SB}(x_0, \ldots, x_4) \oplus \mathrm{SB}(x_0 \oplus \Delta x_0, \ldots, x_4 \oplus \Delta x_4) = (\Delta y_0, \ldots, \Delta y_4) = (1, 0, 0, 0, 0)$$

where

$$(\Delta x_0, \ldots, \Delta x_4) \in \{(1, 1, 0, 0, 1), (0, 0, 0, 1, 1), (0, 1, 0, 0, 1)\}.$$

It is found that

- for $(\Delta x_0, \ldots, \Delta x_4) = (1,1,0,0,1)$, all possible $(x_0, \ldots, x_4)$ form an affine subspace of dimension 2, as shown below:

$$x_0 \oplus x_4 = 0, \quad x_1 = 1, \quad x_3 = 0; \tag{8}$$

- for $(\Delta x_0, \ldots, \Delta x_4) = (0,0,0,1,1)$, all possible $(x_0, \ldots, x_4)$ form an affine subspace of dimension 2, as shown below:

$$x_1 = 0, \quad x_2 = 0, \quad x_3 \oplus x_4 = 0; \tag{9}$$

- for $(\Delta x_0, \ldots, \Delta x_4) = (0,1,0,0,1)$, all possible $(x_0, \ldots, x_4)$ form an affine subspace of dimension 1, as shown below:

$$x_0 = 0, \quad x_1 \oplus x_4 = 1, \quad x_2 = 0, \quad x_3 = 0. \tag{10}$$

As a result, the difference transitions in the second round, i.e., the 28 active S-boxes, directly impose 102 *linear conditions* on S^1. Note that it is unclear whether the probability 2^{-102} is directly computed according to the differential distribution table (DDT) of the 5-bit S-box in [12]. At least, we do not see any such related claims in [12] that the probability 2^{-102} is caused by 102 linear conditions on S^1, i.e., the conditions may be *nonlinear* if we do not carefully study the relations between the difference transitions and values transitions. Indeed, we can simply generalize the above observations for any degree-2 S-box, as shown in Appendix B, i.e. all the conditions on the input bits must be linear for each valid difference transition of a degree-2 S-box.

More Nonlinear Conditions on the Capacity Part of S^0. As can be noted from Eq. 9 and Eq. 10, there will be conditions on $S^1[2]$, i.e., the conditions on x_2 in Eq. 9 and Eq. 10. However, according to the definition of the S-box, we know that

$$y_2 = x_4 x_3 \oplus x_4 \oplus x_2 \oplus x_1 \oplus 1.$$

Hence, after the capacity part of S_3^0 is fixed, $S^1[2]$ is irrelevant to $S^0[0]$. As a result, apart from the 54 linear conditions on the capacity part of S^0, there are also 21 nonlinear (quadratic) conditions on the capacity part of S^0. In other words, at the first glance, although there are 102 linear conditions on S^1, there are indeed only $102 - 21 = 81$ linear conditions on S^1 depending on $S^0[0]$ after the capacity part of S^0 is known. Hence, we can equivalently say that

$$n_c = 54 + 21 = 75, \quad n_k = 81.$$

With the general 2-step attack framework, the total time complexity is not affected as $n_c + n_k$ remains the same, i.e., it is still 2^{102}.

Optimizing T_k. After knowing that there are 81 linear conditions on S^1 depending on $S^0[0]$ after the capacity part of S^0 is known, optimizing T_k is quite straightforward. Recall the general 2-step attack framework described previously. Specifically, by using 3 message blocks (M_1, M_2, M_3), we first generate valid (M_1, M_2) such that the 75 bit conditions on the capacity part of S_3^0 can hold. Then, since

M_3 is only added to $S_3^0[0]$, S_3^1 directly becomes linear in M_3 and we know there are 81 linear conditions on S_3^1. Therefore, we can construct 81 linear equations in M_3, i.e., 64 variables. Similar to the idea in [15], solving this linear equation system is equivalent to exhausting all possible values of M_3 and hence T_k is reduced to the time complexity to solve 81 linear equations in 64 variables (Fig. 7) that requires $81 \times 81 \times 64 \approx 2^{19}$ bit operations. As explained before, only optimizing T_k is insufficient to significantly improve the attack and we need to further optimize T_{pre}.

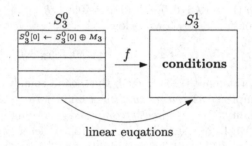

Fig. 7. Exhaust M_3 by solving linear equations

4.2   Finding Valid (M_1, M_2) with Advanced Techniques

To find valid (M_1, M_2), we are now only simply looping over (M_1, M_2) and checking whether the 75 bit conditions on the capacity part can hold. To improve the attack, we have to avoid such a naive loop. In what follows, we describe how to use the general 3-step attack framework stated above to overcome this obstacle.

The core idea is to utilize a 2-round property of ASCON. Let us explain it step by step.

Property 2. *For* $(y_0, \dots, y_4) = SB(x_0, \dots, x_4)$, *if* $x_3 \oplus x_4 = 1$, y_3 *will be independent to* x_0.

Proof. We can rewrite y_3 as follows:

$$y_3 = (x_4 \oplus x_3 \oplus 1)x_0 \oplus (x_4 \oplus x_3 \oplus x_2 \oplus x_1).$$

Hence, if $x_3 \oplus x_4 = 1$, y_3 is irrelevant to x_0.

Property 3. *Let*

$$(S^1[0], \dots, S^1[4]) = f(S^0[0], \dots, S^0[4]), \quad (S^2[0], \dots, S^2[4]) = f(S^1[0], \dots, S^1[4]),$$

where $(S^0[1], S^0[2], S^0[3], S^0[4])$ are constants and $S^0[0]$ is the only variable. Then, it is always possible to make u bits of $S^2[1]$ linear in $S^0[0]$ by adding at most $9u$ bit conditions on $S^0[3] \oplus S^0[4]$.

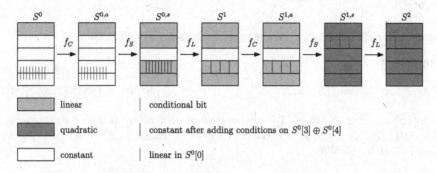

Fig. 8. Adding conditions on the capacity part to linearize $S^2[1]$

Proof. First, since $S^0[0]$ is the only variable, according to the definition of f, we know that $(S^1[0], S^1[1], S^1[3], S^1[4])$ are linear in $S^0[0]$ while $S^1[2]$ is still constant.

Each bit $S^2[1][i]$ can be expressed as

$$S^2[1][i] = S^{1,s}[1][i] \oplus S^{1,s}[1][i+61] \oplus S^{1,s}[1][i+39].$$

To make $S^2[1][i]$ linear in $S^0[0]$, we need to ensure

$$S^{1,s}[1][i] \oplus S^{1,s}[1][i+61] \oplus S^{1,s}[1][i+39]$$

is linear in $S^0[0]$. According to the definition of the S-box specified in Eq. 1, the expression of y_1 is

$$y_1 = x_4 \oplus x_1 x_3 \oplus x_3 \oplus x_2(x_3 \oplus x_1 \oplus 1) \oplus x_1 \oplus x_0.$$

Hence, if x_2 is constant, there is only one quadratic term $x_1 x_3$ in the expression of y_1.

According to the above analysis, $S^1[2]$ is always constant. Hence, we have

$$
\begin{aligned}
&S^{1,s}[1][i] \oplus S^{1,s}[1][i+61] \oplus S^{1,s}[1][i+39] \\
&= S^1[1][i]S^1[3][i] \oplus S^1[1][i+61]S^1[3][i+61] \oplus S^1[1][i+39]S^1[3][i+39] \\
&\oplus L_i(S^1[0], \ldots, S^1[4])
\end{aligned}
\tag{11}
$$

where L_i is a linear function.

Furthermore, according to Property 2, we can make $S^{0,s}[3][i]$ $(0 \le i \le 63)$ irrelevant to $S^0[0]$ by adding 1 bit condition on $S^0[3] \oplus S^0[4]$. In this way, we can add at most 9 bit conditions on $S^0[3] \oplus S^0[4]$ to make $(S^1[3][i], S^1[3][i + 61], S^1[3][i + 39])$ irrelevant to $S^0[0]$ since each bit of $S^1[3]$ is linear in 3 bits of $S^{0,s}[3]$. Once $(S^1[3][i], S^1[3][i+61], S^1[3][i+39])$ is irrelevant to $S^0[0]$, $S^{1,s}[1][i] \oplus S^{1,s}[1][i+61] \oplus S^{1,s}[1][i+39]$ becomes linear in $S^0[0]$ according to Eq. 11. Hence, to make u bits of $S^2[1]$ linear in $S^0[0]$, we need to add at most $9u$ bit conditions on $S^0[3] \oplus S^0[4]$.

A graphical explanation for Property 3 can be seen from Fig. 8.

Property 4. *Let*

$$(S^1[0], \ldots, S^1[4]) = f(S^0[0], \ldots, S^0[4]), \quad (S^2[0], \ldots, S^2[4]) = f(S^1[0], \ldots, S^1[4]),$$

where $(S^0[1], S^0[2], S^0[3], S^0[4])$ are constants and $S^0[0]$ is the only variable. Then, it is always possible to make u bits of $S^2[1]$ linear in $S^0[0]$ by guessing $3u$ linear equations in $S^0[0]$.

Proof. Similar to the proof of Property 3, we have

$$S^{1,s}[1][i] \oplus S^{1,s}[1][i + 61] \oplus S^{1,s}[1][i + 39]$$
$$= S^1[1][i]S^1[3][i] \oplus S^1[1][i + 61]S^1[3][i + 61] \oplus S^1[1][i + 39]S^1[3][i + 39]$$
$$\oplus L_i(S^1[0], \ldots, S^1[4])$$

where L_i is a linear function and $(S^1[0], S^1[1], S^1[2], S^1[3], S^1[4])$ are linear in $S^0[0]$. Hence, if we guess $(S^1[3][i], S^1[3][i + 61], S^1[3][i + 39])$, $S^2[1][i]$ will be linear in $S^0[0]$. In other words, by guessing 3 linear equations in $S^0[0]$, $S^2[1][i]$ can be linear in $S^0[0]$.

Improving the Attack. Based on the above discussions, it is now possible to further improve the 2-round collision attack. We utilize the general 3-step attack framework where $k = 3$, i.e., we use message blocks (M_1, M_2, M_3). From previous analysis, there are 54 linear conditions on the capacity part of S_3^0 and among them, 27 bit conditions are on $S_3^0[1]$ (or $S_2^2[1]$). Based on Property 3 and Property 4, it is possible to satisfy these 54 linear conditions more efficiently with advanced algebraic techniques, i.e., we can improve T_{k-1}. We emphasize that there are additional 21 quadratic conditions on the capacity part of S_3^0, but we will not consider them to speed up the exhaustive search over M_2 due to the increasing difficulty, i.e., it is required to solve degree-4 Boolean equations.

Specifically, based on Property 3, we can add $9u_1$ conditions on the capacity part of S_2^0 such that u_1 bits of $S_3^0[1]$ can be linear in M_2 after the capacity part of S_2^0 is known. Moreover, based on Property 4, after the capacity part of S_2^0 is known, we can guess $3u_2$ linear equations in M_2 such that u_2 bits of $S_3^0[1]$ can be linear in M_2. In total, we set up $u_1 + 4u_2$ linear equations in 64 variables to satisfy $u_1 + u_2$ out of 27 bit conditions. Then, we perform the Gaussian elimination on these $u_1 + 4u_2$ linear equations and obtain

$$u_3 = 64 - u_1 - 4u_2$$

free variables.

Note that the first round is always freely linearized and the remaining $54 - u_1 - u_2$ linear conditions on S_3^0 can be expressed as quadratic equations in these u_3 free variables. In a word, to efficiently exhaust M_2 such that the 54 conditions on S_3^0 can hold, we can perform the following procedure:

Step 1: Guess $3u_2 = 42$ bits of M_2 and construct $4u_2 + u_1$ linear equations.
Step 2: Apply the Gaussian elimination to the system and obtain $u_3 = 64 - u_1 - 4u_2$ free variables.
Step 3: Construct $54 - u_1 - u_2$ quadratic equations in these u_3 variables and solve the equations.
Step 4: Check whether the remaining 21 quadratic conditions on the capacity part of S_3^0 can hold for each obtained solution.

We use a similar method in [3,16] to estimate the time complexity to solve a quadratic equation system. After some calculations, the optimal choice of (u_1, u_2, u_3) is as follows:

$$u_1 = 3, \quad u_2 = 13 \quad u_3 = 9.$$

In other words, we need to perform the Gaussian elimination on 55 linear equations in 64 variables for $2^{3u_2} = 2^{39}$ times. Then, we need to solve 38 quadratic equations in 9 variables for 2^{39} times. The total time complexity is estimated as

$$2^{39} \times (55^2 \times 64 + 38^2 \times 45) \approx 2^{56.6}$$

bit operations. The cost of Step 4 is negligible since it is expected to perform such a check for about $2^{64-54} = 2^{10}$ times.

Time Complexity Evaluation. Based on the previous general 3-step attack framework using 3 message blocks (M_1, M_2, M_3), we have $9u_1 = 27$ conditions on S_2^0 and we need $2^{81+75-128} = 2^{28}$ different valid M_1. The cost of this step can be estimated as $2^{28+27} = 2^{55}$ calls to the 2-round ASCON permutation. Then, for each valid M_1, i.e., each valid S_2^0, we can exhaust M_1 with $2^{56.6}$ bit operations. At last, for each valid (M_1, M_2), we can exhaust M_3 with about 2^{19} bit operations. Assume that one round of the ASCON permutation takes about $15 \times 64 \approx 2^{10}$ bit operations, the total time complexity can be estimated as

$$T_{\text{total}} = 2^{28} \times 2^{27} + 2^{28} \times 2^{56.6-11} + 2^{17} \times 2^{19-11} \approx 2^{73.6}$$

calls to the 2-round ASCON permutation.

4.3   Further Optimizing the Guessing Strategy

In the above improved 2-round collision attack, we mainly exploit Property 3 and Property 4 to make some conditional bits of $S_2^2[1]$ linear in M_2. Specifically, the core problem is to make

$$(S_2^1[3][i], S_2^1[3][i+61], S_2^1[3][i+39])$$

constant by either guessing their values according to Property 4 or adding conditions on $S_2^0[3] \oplus S_2^0[4]$ according to Property 3. However, the two strategies are independently used for different bits of $S_2^2[1]$. It can be noted that for one specific conditional bit of $S_2^2[1]$, i.e., $S_2^2[1][i]$, we can guess g out of 3 bits of $(S_2^1[3][i], S_2^1[3][i+61], S_2^1[3][i+39])$ and add $3 \times (3-g)$ conditions on $S_2^0[3] \oplus S_2^0[4]$ to achieve the same goal. In other words, for the same conditional bit, we can use a hybrid guessing strategy.

As the next step, we aim to optimize the guessing strategy such that we can obtain a sufficient number of linear equations by guessing a smaller number of linear equations or adding a smaller number of extra conditions on $S_2^0[3] \oplus S_2^0[4]$. For example, for the above naive guess strategy, we need to add $9u_1 = 27$ bit conditions on $S_2^0[3] \oplus S_2^0[4]$ and we need to further guess $3u_2 = 39$ linear equations in order to get $u_1 + 4u_2 = 3 + 52 = 55$ linear equations in M_2. Can we guess fewer bits to achieve better results?

Note that there are 27 conditional bits in $S_2^2[1]$. For completeness, we denote the set of i such that $S_2^2[1][i]$ is conditional by $\mathcal{I}$ and we have

$$\mathcal{I} = \{0, 7, 8, 10, 12, 16, 17, 19, 24, 27, 28, 30, 31, 32, 34, 37,$$
$$40, 41, 48, 50, 54, 56, 57, 59, 60, 61, 63\}.$$

For each $i \in \mathcal{I}$, let

$$\mathcal{P}_i = \{i, (i+61)\%64, (i+39)\%64\}.$$

Further, let

$$\mathcal{P}_i = \mathcal{P}_{i,g} \cup \mathcal{P}_{i,a}, \quad \mathcal{P}_{i,g} \cap \mathcal{P}_{i,a} = \emptyset.$$

In other words, to linearize $S_2^2[1][i]$, we guess $S_2^1[3][j_0]$ where $j_0 \in \mathcal{P}_{i,g}$ and make $S_2^1[3][j_1]$ constant where $j_1 \in \mathcal{P}_{i,a}$ by adding 3 conditions on

$$S_2^0[3][j_1] \oplus S_2^0[4][j_1], \quad S_2^0[3][j_1+10] \oplus S_2^0[4][j_1+10], \quad S_2^0[3][j_1+17] \oplus S_2^0[4][j_1+17],$$

We can build a simple MILP model to determine the optimal choice of a subset $\mathcal{I}' \subseteq \mathcal{I}$ and the corresponding $\mathcal{P}_{i,g}$ and $\mathcal{P}_{i,a}$ where $i \in \mathcal{I}'$ such that the total time complexity of the attack is optimal. Specifically, assuming that after adding u_4 conditions on $S_2^0[3] \oplus S_2^0[4]$ and guessing u_5 bits of $S_2^1[3]$, we can set up u_6 linear equations for u_6 conditional bits of $S_2^2[1]$. In this way, we have in total $u_5 + u_6$ linear equations and after the Gaussian elimination, we can set up $54 - u_6$ quadratic equations in $u_7 = 64 - u_5 - u_6$ free variables. After some configurations, we propose to choose

$$u_4 = 31, \quad u_5 = 28, \quad u_6 = 27$$

as the optimal parameters. In other words, we can make all the 27 conditional bits of $S_2^2[1]$ linear in M_2 by guessing 28 linear equations in $S_2^1[3]$ and adding 31 bit conditions on $S_2^0[3] \oplus S_2^0[4]$. In this way, we need to perform the Gaussian elimination to $u_5 + u_6 = 55$ linear equations in 64 variables that requires about $2^{17.6}$ bit operations and then solve 27 quadratic equations in $u_7 = 64 - 55 = 9$

variables. Based on the method [3,16] to estimate the time complexity to solve such an overdefined quadratic equation system, it takes about $27^2 \times 45 + 2^3 \times 12^2 \times 6 \approx 2^{15.3}$ bit operations. Hence, the new total time complexity is

$$T_{\text{total}} = 2^{28} \times 2^{31} + 2^{28} \times 2^{28} \times (2^{17.6} + 2^{15.3}) \times 2^{-11} + 2^{17} \times 2^{19-11} \approx 2^{62.6}.$$

In conclusion, with the optimal guess strategy and advanced algebraic techniques, we can improve the best collision attack on 2-round ASCON-HASH by a factor of about $2^{40.4}$. For completeness, the required 28 guessed bits of $S_2^1[3]$ and the 31 condition bits of $S_2^0[3] \oplus S_2^0[4]$ are shown in Table 5.

Table 5. The optimal guessing strategy

$\bigcup_{i \in \mathcal{I}} \mathcal{P}_{i,g}$
$\{0, 3, 4, 7, 8, 10, 14, 15, 17, 21, 24, 25, 27, 28, 31, 32, 34, 35, 37, 38, 41, 45, 48, 51, 54, 55, 58, 61\}$
$\bigcup_{i \in \mathcal{I}} \mathcal{P}_{i,a}$
$\{2, 5, 6, 9, 12, 13, 16, 19, 23, 29, 30, 36, 39, 40, 46, 47, 49, 50, 53, 56, 57, 59, 60, 63\}$
$\{j, (j+10)\%64, (j+17)\%64 \mid j \in \bigcup_{i \in \mathcal{I}} \mathcal{P}_{i,a}\}$
$\{0, 2, 3, 5, 6, 9, 10, 12, 13, 15, 16, 19, 22, 23, 26, 29, 30, 33, 36, 39, 40, 46, 47, 49, 50, 53, 56, 57, 59, 60, 63\}$

5 Conclusion

By carefully studying the relations between the difference transitions and values transitions through the S-box, we show that the existing collision attacks on 2-round ASCON-HASH can be significantly improved with the aid of advanced algebraic techniques. We expect our close look at the algebraic properties of the S-box can inspire more efficient attacks on ASCON-HASH or ASCON-XOF.

Acknowledgements. This work is supported by the National Key Research and Development Program of China (No. 2022YFB2701900); the National Natural Science Foundation of China (Nos. 62072181, 62132005); the Shanghai Trusted Industry Internet Software Collaborative Innovation Center; and the "Digital Silk Roa" Shanghai International Joint Lab of Trustworthy Intelligent Software (No. 22510750100).

A The Algorithmic Description of ASCON-HASH

The Algorithmic Description of ASCON-HASH is shown in Algorithm 1.

Algorithm 1: ASCON-HASH

Input: $M \in \{0,1\}^*$
Output: hash $H \in \{0,1\}^{256}$
Initialization:
$S_1^0 \leftarrow f^{12}(IV \| 0^c)$;
Absorbing:
$M_1, \ldots, M_s \leftarrow M \| 1 \| 0^*$;
for $i = 1, \ldots, s$ **do**
$\quad \left| \quad S_{i+1}^0 \leftarrow f^{12}\left(S_i^0 \oplus (M_i \| 0^c) \right); \right.$
end
Squeezing:
$S^0 \leftarrow S_{s+1}^0$;
for $i = 1, \ldots, t = \lceil 256/r \rceil$ **do**
$\quad \left| \quad \begin{aligned} & H_i \leftarrow S^0[0]; \\ & S^0 \leftarrow f^{12}(S^0); \end{aligned} \right.$
end
return $\lfloor H_1 \| \ldots \| H_t \rfloor_{256}$;

B   On Degree-2 S-Box

For an n-bit S-box whose algebraic degree is 2, we can show that for any valid pair of input and output difference, the inputs satisfying this difference transition must form an affine subspace.

Let $(x_0, \ldots, x_{n-1}) \in \mathbb{F}_2^n$ and $(y_0, \ldots, y_{n-1}) \in \mathbb{F}_2^n$ be the input and output of the S-box. Further, let

$$y_i = f_i(x_0, \ldots, x_{n-1}), \ 0 \le i \le n-1,$$

where the algebraic degree of f_i is at most 2.

Given any valid input difference $(\Delta x_0, \ldots, \Delta x_{n-1})$ and output difference $(\Delta y_0, \ldots, \Delta y_{n-1})$, we aim to show that $(x_0, \ldots, x_{n-1})$ satisfying the following n equations must form an affine subspace:

$$f_0(x_0, \ldots, x_{n-1}) \oplus f_0(x_0 \oplus \Delta x_0, \ldots, x_{n-1} \oplus \Delta x_{n-1}) = \Delta y_0,$$

$$\ldots$$

$$f_{n-1}(x_0, \ldots, x_{n-1}) \oplus f_{n-1}(x_0 \oplus \Delta x_0, \ldots, x_{n-1} \oplus \Delta x_{n-1}) = \Delta y_{n-1}.$$

First, since $(\Delta x_0, \ldots, \Delta x_{n-1}) \to (\Delta y_0, \ldots, \Delta y_{n-1})$ is a valid difference transition, there must exist solutions to the above n equations. We only need to show that all the n equations are indeed linear in $(x_0, \ldots, x_{n-1})$ for each given $(\Delta x_0, \ldots, \Delta x_{n-1}, \Delta y_0, \ldots, \Delta y_{n-1})$ and then the proof is over. Note that the algebraic degree of f_i is at most 2. In this case,

$$f_i(x_0, \ldots, x_{n-1}) \oplus f_i(x_0 \oplus \Delta x_0, \ldots, x_{n-1} \oplus \Delta x_{n-1})$$

must be linear in $(x_0, \ldots, x_{n-1})$, thus completing the proof.

References

1. The CAESAR committee, CAESAR: competition for authenticated encryption: security, applicability, and robustness (2014). https://competitions.cr.yp.to/caesar-submissions.html
2. Bertoni, G., Daemen, J., Peeters, M., Van Assche, G.: Sponge functions. In: ECRYPT Hash Workshop, no. 9 (2007)
3. Bouillaguet, C., Delaplace, C., Trimoska, M.: A simple deterministic algorithm for systems of quadratic polynomials over F_2. In: Bringmann, K., Chan, T. (eds.) 5th Symposium on Simplicity in Algorithms, SOSA@SODA 2022, Virtual Conference, 10–11 January 2022, pp. 285–296. SIAM (2022). https://doi.org/10.1137/1.9781611977066.22
4. Bovy, E., Daemen, J., Mennink, B.: Comparison of the second round candidates of the NIST lightweight cryptography competition. Bachelor thesis, Radboud University (2020)
5. Dinur, I., Dunkelman, O., Shamir, A.: New attacks on Keccak-224 and Keccak-256. In: Canteaut, A. (ed.) FSE 2012. LNCS, vol. 7549, pp. 442–461. Springer, Heidelberg (2012). https://doi.org/10.1007/978-3-642-34047-5_25
6. Dobraunig, C., Eichlseder, M., Mendel, F., Schläffer, M.: ASCON v1. Submission to round 1 of the CAESAR competition (2014). https://competitions.cr.yp.to/round1/Asconv1.pdf
7. Dobraunig, C., Eichlseder, M., Mendel, F., Schläffer, M.: ASCON v1.1. Submission to round 2 of the CAESAR competition (2015). https://competitions.cr.yp.to/round2/Asconv11.pdf
8. Dobraunig, C., Eichlseder, M., Mendel, F., Schläffer, M.: Ascon v1.2. Submission to round 1 of the NIST lightweight cryptography project (2019). https://csrc.nist.gov/CSRC/media/Projects/Lightweight-Cryptography/documents/round-1/spec-doc/Ascon-spec.pdf
9. Dobraunig, C., Eichlseder, M., Mendel, F., Schläffer, M.: Status update on ASCON v1. 2 (2020)
10. Dobraunig, C., Eichlseder, M., Mendel, F., Schläffer, M.: ASCON v1.2: lightweight authenticated encryption and hashing. J. Cryptol. **34**(3), 33 (2021). https://doi.org/10.1007/s00145-021-09398-9
11. Floyd, R.W.: Nondeterministic algorithms. J. ACM **14**(4), 636–644 (1967). https://doi.org/10.1145/321420.321422
12. Gérault, D., Peyrin, T., Tan, Q.Q.: Exploring differential-based distinguishers and forgeries for ASCON. IACR Trans. Symmetric Cryptol. **2021**(3), 102–136 (2021). https://doi.org/10.46586/tosc.v2021.i3.102-136
13. Liu, F., Isobe, T., Meier, W.: Automatic verification of differential characteristics: application to reduced GIMLI. In: Micciancio, D., Ristenpart, T. (eds.) CRYPTO 2020, Part III. LNCS, vol. 12172, pp. 219–248. Springer, Cham (2020). https://doi.org/10.1007/978-3-030-56877-1_8
14. Liu, F., Isobe, T., Meier, W.: Cryptanalysis of full LowMC and LowMC-M with algebraic techniques. In: Malkin, T., Peikert, C. (eds.) CRYPTO 2021, Part III. LNCS, vol. 12827, pp. 368–401. Springer, Cham (2021). https://doi.org/10.1007/978-3-030-84252-9_13
15. Liu, F., Isobe, T., Meier, W., Yang, Z.: Algebraic attacks on round-reduced Keccak. In: Baek, J., Ruj, S. (eds.) ACISP 2021. LNCS, vol. 13083, pp. 91–110. Springer, Cham (2021). https://doi.org/10.1007/978-3-030-90567-5_5

16. Liu, F., Meier, W., Sarkar, S., Isobe, T.: New low-memory algebraic attacks on LowMC in the picnic setting. IACR Trans. Symmetric Cryptol. **2022**(3), 102–122 (2022). https://doi.org/10.46586/tosc.v2022.i3.102-122

17. Liu, F., Sarkar, S., Wang, G., Meier, W., Isobe, T.: Algebraic meet-in-the-middle attack on LowMC. In: Agrawal, S., Lin, D. (eds.) ASIACRYPT 2022, Part I. LNCS, vol. 13791, pp. 225–255. Springer, Cham (2022). https://doi.org/10.1007/978-3-031-22963-3_8

18. Qiao, K., Song, L., Liu, M., Guo, J.: New collision attacks on round-reduced Keccak. In: Coron, J.-S., Nielsen, J.B. (eds.) EUROCRYPT 2017, Part III. LNCS, vol. 10212, pp. 216–243. Springer, Cham (2017). https://doi.org/10.1007/978-3-319-56617-7_8

19. Qin, L., Zhao, B., Hua, J., Dong, X., Wang, X.: Weak-diffusion structure: meet-in-the-middle attacks on sponge-based hashing revisited. Cryptology ePrint Archive, Paper 2023/518 (2023). https://eprint.iacr.org/2023/518

20. Song, L., Liao, G., Guo, J.: Non-full Sbox linearization: applications to collision attacks on round-reduced Keccak. In: Katz, J., Shacham, H. (eds.) CRYPTO 2017, Part II. LNCS, vol. 10402, pp. 428–451. Springer, Cham (2017). https://doi.org/10.1007/978-3-319-63715-0_15

21. Zong, R., Dong, X., Wang, X.: Collision attacks on round-reduced GIMLI-HASH/ASCON-XOF/ASCON-HASH. Cryptology ePrint Archive, Paper 2019/1115 (2019). https://eprint.iacr.org/2019/1115

Improving the Rectangle Attack
on GIFT-64

Yincen Chen[1], Nana Zhang[2,3], Xuanyu Liang[1], Ling Song[1(✉)],
Qianqian Yang[2], and Zhuohui Feng[1]

[1] College of Cyber Security, Jinan University, Guangzhou 510632, China
cyincen@stu2021.jnu.edu.cn, songling@jnu.edu.cn
[2] Key Laboratory of Cyberspace Security Defense, Institute of Information
Engineering, Chinese Academy of Sciences, Beijing 100093, China
{zhangnana,yangqianqian}@iie.ac.cn
[3] School of Cyber Security, University of Chinese Academy of Sciences,
Beijing, China

Abstract. GIFT is a family of lightweight block ciphers based on SPN
structure and composed of two versions named GIFT-64 and GIFT-128.
In this paper, we reevaluate the security of GIFT-64 against the rectangle
attack under the related-key setting. Investigating the previous rectangle
key recovery attack on GIFT-64, we obtain the core idea of improving
the attack—trading off the time complexity of each attack phase. We
flexibly guess part of the involved subkey bits to balance the time cost of
each phase so that the overall time complexity of the attack is reduced.
Moreover, the reused subkey bits are identified according to the linear
key schedule of GIFT-64 and bring additional advantages for our attacks.
Furthermore, we incorporate the above ideas and propose a dedicated
MILP model for finding the best rectangle key recovery attack on GIFT-
64. As a result, we get the improved rectangle attacks on 26-round GIFT-
64, which are the best attacks on it in terms of time complexity so far.

Keywords: symmetric cryptography · GIFT-64 · rectangle attack ·
key recovery attack · related-key scenario · key guessing strategy

1 Introduction

Accompanied by the momentous expansion in emerging ubiquitous technologies, securing resource-limited devices has become increasingly important.
Lightweight block ciphers came into being in such a situation, which have more
advantages in terms of cost, speed, power, and execution time than traditional
block ciphers, but still provide a sufficiently high safety margin for resource-
limited devices.

Over the past three decades, researchers have committed to researching algorithms to efficiently and accurately evaluate the security of block ciphers. In 1990,
Biham and Shamir proposed differential cryptanalysis [5], which tracks the difference between a pair of inputs to outputs. One of the essential steps of differential

cryptanalysis is to find a high-probability differential trail over the target cipher. However, this goal is hard to achieve when the cipher contains many rounds. The boomerang attack [28] is an extension of differential cryptanalysis, which combines two short differential trails to get a long trail with a high probability. The rectangle attack [4] is a variant of the boomerang attack. The boomerang attack requires chosen plaintexts and chosen ciphertexts, while the rectangle attack only needs to choose plaintexts. Besides, the rectangle attack considers as many differences as possible in the middle to estimate the probability more accurately. The boomerang and rectangle attacks have been applied to many ciphers, and many good results have been obtained. For example, Biryukov *et al.* [6] put forward the rectangle attack on full AES-192 and AES-256, and Derbez *et al.* proposed the boomerang attack on full AES-192 in [12].

In recent years, many strategies emerged to mount key recovery attacks as efficiently as possible for the rectangle attack, such as [13,24,31]. Song *et al.* proposed the most efficient and generic rectangle key recovery algorithm at ASI-ACRYPT 2022 [24]. This algorithm supports flexible key guessing strategies and is compatible with all the previous rectangle key recovery algorithms. By trading off the overall complexity, Song *et al.* obtained the optimal results of rectangle key recovery attacks on a series of block ciphers.

GIFT is a family of SPN-based lightweight block ciphers proposed by Banik *et al.* at CHES'17 [3]. It is composed of two versions named GIFT-64 and GIFT-128, where the block sizes are 64 bits and 128 bits, and the numbers of rounds are 28 and 40, respectively. The key lengths of GIFT-64 and GIFT-128 are both 128 bits. As the inheritor of PRESENT [7], GIFT mends its weak points and achieves efficiency and security improvements. Because of the comprehensive treatment of the linear layer and the S-box, GIFT receives excellent performance in hardware and software implementations and has become one of the most energy-efficient ciphers. Benefiting from these advantages, GIFT plays the role of the underlying primitives of many lightweight authenticated encryption schemes, such as GIFT-COFB [2], HyENA [9], LOTUS-AEAD and LOCUS-AEAD [8], and SUNDAE-GIFT [1]. Notably, GIFT-COFB is one of the final round finalists of the NIST Lightweight Cryptography standardization project[1]. Thus, the security evaluation of GIFT is of great significance.

Previous Attacks on GIFT-64. GIFT has attracted the attention of many researchers since its publication and has been the subject of many cryptanalyses. The best result of the meet-in-the-middle attack is from [20], which attacks 15-round GIFT-64 under the single key scenario. Sun *et al.* proposed the best linear attack on GIFT-64 at present, which is a linear attack on 19-round GIFT-64 in [26]. The most efficient differential analysis for GIFT-64 under the related-key scenario is currently the 26-round differential attack of Sun *et al.* [25]. Dong *et al.* proposed the most efficient attack on GIFT-64 for the moment, which is a 26-round rectangle key recovery attack we are interested in [13]. We summarize the state-of-the-art attacks against GIFT-64 in Table 1, where RK and SK denote related-key and single-key settings, respectively, and enc. and m.a. represent time complexity in units of encryption and memory access.

---

[1] https://csrc.nist.gov/projects/lightweight-cryptography.

This paper focuses on the rectangle key recovery attack against GIFT-64. In 2019, Chen *et al.* executed the 23-round rectangle key recovery attack on GIFT-64 based on a 19-round related-key boomerang distinguisher [10]. Later, Zhao *et al.* [31] expanded this attack to 24 rounds with a more efficient key-guessing strategy. In 2020, Ji *et al.* [15] proposed the 20-round related-key boomerang distinguisher. Based on this distinguisher, they also proposed a 25-round related-key rectangle key recovery attack on GIFT-64 using Zhao *et al.*'s strategy in [15]. At EUROCRYPT 2022, Dong *et al.* [13] further improved the key guessing strategy and extended the attack of Ji *et al.* to 26 rounds, resulting in the most effective rectangle key recovery attack of GIFT-64 so far.

Table 1. Summary of relevant analysis results of GIFT-64

Method	Setting	Round	Time	Data	Memory	Source
Integral	**SK**	14	$2^{96.00}$ enc.	$2^{63.00}$	$2^{63.00}$	[3]
MITM	**SK**	15	$2^{112.00}$ enc.	$2^{64.00}$	$2^{16.00}$	[20]
Linear	**SK**	19	$2^{127.11}$ enc.	$2^{62.96}$	$2^{60.00}$	[26]
Boomerang	**RK**	23	$2^{126.60}$ enc.	$2^{63.30}$	–	[18]
Differential	**RK**	26	$2^{123.23}$ enc.	$2^{60.96}$	$2^{102.86}$	[25]
Rectangle	**RK**	23	$2^{107.00}$ m.a.	$2^{60.00}$	$2^{60.00}$	[10]
	RK	24	$2^{91.58}$ enc.	$2^{60.00}$	$2^{60.32}$	[31]
	RK	25	$2^{120.92}$ enc.	$2^{63.78}$	$2^{64.10}$	[15]
	RK	26	$2^{122.78}$ enc.	$2^{63.78}$	$2^{63.78}$	[13]
	RK	26	$2^{121.75}$ enc.	$2^{62.715}$	$2^{62.715}$	[17]
	RK	26	$2^{112.07}$ enc.	$2^{63.79}$	$2^{63.79}$	[30]
	RK	26	$2^{110.06}$ **enc. and** $2^{115.8}$**m.a.**	$2^{63.78}$	$2^{64.36}$	Sect. 3
	RK	26	$2^{111.51}$ **enc. and** $2^{115.78}$ **m.a.**	$2^{63.78}$	$2^{67.8}$	Sect. 3

Our Contributions. We investigate the previous rectangle attacks on GIFT-64 and find that the time complexities of different attack phases are not balanced. Inspired by the work of Song *et al.* [24], we study how to find a better strategy for the rectangle key recovery attack on GIFT-64 to trade off the complexity of each attack phase.

GIFT has a bit-wise linear layer and a bit-wise key schedule. We carefully study each component of GIFT and, for the first time, apply the generic rectangle key recovery algorithm [24] to such ciphers. For ciphers like GIFT, which mostly have bit-wise operations, finding the best key-guessing strategy is much more sophisticated than for cell-wise ciphers. In the attack on GIFT-64, we carefully analyzed the key schedule and identified all the reused key bits. To find the best attack for a given rectangle distinguisher, we build a MILP model in which all possible key guessing strategies are allowed and minimize the overall time complexity. As a result, we improve the rectangle attacks on 26-round GIFT-64 with new key-guessing strategies. Our attacks on GIFT-64 are better than the previous rectangle key recovery attacks and are the best attacks on GIFT-64 in terms of time complexity to date. The comparison of our attacks with previous works is shown in Table 1. Apart from this, we also study the rectangle key recovery attack on GIFT-128 and eventually reduce the complexity of the attack in [15] by a factor of 2^2. Limited by the piece space, the full version of this paper is available on eprint[2].

It's worth noting that Yu *et al.* [30] proposed remarkable cryptanalysis of GIFT-64 concurrently (available on-line on The Computer Journal on 14th July 2023). They constructed an automatic search model which treats the distinguisher and the key recovery phase as a whole for GIFT. Taking the linear key schedule into account, they also discovered a new boomerang distinguisher of GIFT-64. The complexity of their 26-round rectangle key recovery attack on GIFT-64 is $(T, D, M) = (2^{112.07} \text{ enc.}, 2^{63.79}, 2^{63.79})$.

Organization. The rest of the paper is organized as follows. In Sect. 2, we introduce the structure of GIFT-64 and review the rectangle attack and the key recovery algorithm. In Sect. 3, we propose the dedicated MILP model for finding the best rectangle key recovery attack on GIFT-64 and describe in detail the rectangle key recovery attack based on a new key guessing strategy. Sect. 4. concludes the paper.

2 Preliminary

2.1 Description of GIFT-64

GIFT is a block cipher with Substitution-Permutation-Network, which Banik *et al.* proposed at CHES' 2017 [3]. According to the 64-bit and 128-bit block sizes, GIFT has two versions, GIFT-64 and GIFT-128, with round numbers 28 and 40, respectively. Both versions of GIFT use a 128-bit master key. r in this subsection represents the number of rounds, where $r \in \{1, 2, ..., 28\}$.

Round Function. The round function of GIFT-64 consists of three operations. For convenience, we consider the 64-bit round state as 16 4-bit nibbles. The three operations of the round function are as follows:

1. **SubCells:** Nonlinear S-box substitutions are applied to each nibble, as is shown in Table 2. Denote X_r and Y_r as the inputs and outputs of the 16 S-boxes in the round r.
2. **PermBits:** For each bit of input, linear bit permutation $b_{P(i)} \leftarrow b_i, \forall i \in \{0, 1, ..., 63\}$ is applied. The permutation $P(i)$ is shown in Table 3. Denote the state which is transformed from Y_r by PermBits in round r as Z_r.
3. **AddRoundKey:** This step consists of adding the round key and round constants. At each round, a 32-bit round key is obtained from the master key. Denote round key as $RK_r = U || V = u_{15}, ..., u_0 || v_{15}, ..., v_0$. For each round, U and V are XORed with the cipher state, *i.e.* $b_{4i+1} \leftarrow b_{4i+1} \oplus u_i, b_{4i} \leftarrow$

---

2 https://eprint.iacr.org/2023/1419.

Table 2. The S-box of GIFT

x	0	1	2	3	4	5	6	7	8	9	a	b	c	d	e	f
$GS(x)$	1	a	4	c	6	f	3	9	2	d	b	7	5	0	8	e

Table 3. Specifications of GIFT-64 Bit Permutation

i	0	1	2	3	4	5	6	7	8	9	10	11	12	13	14	15
$P(i)$	0	17	34	51	48	1	18	35	32	49	2	19	16	33	50	3
i	16	17	18	19	20	21	22	23	24	25	26	27	28	29	30	31
$P(i)$	4	21	38	55	52	5	22	39	36	53	6	23	20	37	54	7
i	32	33	34	35	36	37	38	39	40	41	42	43	44	45	46	47
$P(i)$	8	25	42	59	56	9	26	43	40	57	10	27	24	41	58	11
i	48	49	50	51	52	53	54	55	56	57	58	59	60	61	62	63
$P(i)$	12	29	46	63	60	13	30	47	44	61	14	31	28	45	62	15

$b_{4i} \oplus v_i, \forall i \in \{0, ..., 15\}$. A single bit"1" and a 6-bit constant $C = c_5c_4c_3c_2c_1c_0$ are added to each state at bit position $63, 23, 19, 15, 11, 7, 3$ respectively, $i.e.$ $b_{63} \leftarrow b_{63} \oplus 1, b_{23} \leftarrow b_{23} \oplus c_5, b_{19} \leftarrow b_{19} \oplus c_4, b_{15} \leftarrow b_{15} \oplus c_3, b_{11} \leftarrow b_{11} \oplus c_2, b_7 \leftarrow b_7 \oplus c_1, b_3 \leftarrow b_3 \oplus c_0$. RK_r is added to the state Z_r in each round.

Key Schedule. Split the master key K into 8 16-bit subkeys $k_7||k_6||...||k_1||k_0 \leftarrow K$. For each round, the round key consists of the last two significant subkeys, and then, the key state is updated following $k_7||k_6||...||k_1||k_0 \leftarrow k_1 \ggg 2||k_0 \ggg 12||...||k_3||k_2$, where $\ggg i$ is an i-bit right rotation within a 16-bit word.

2.2 The Rectangle Attack

In this subsection, we review the rectangle attack and the generic rectangle key recovery algorithm [24] and explain the notations used in this paper.

Before introducing the rectangle attack, we must first review the boomerang attack. The boomerang attack was proposed by Wanger [28] in 1999, which is an adaptive chosen plaintext/ciphertext attack. As is illustrated in Fig. 1, it regards the target cipher as a composition of two sub-ciphers E_0 and E_1, $i.e.$ $E = E_0 \circ E_1$. The differential trail $\alpha \rightarrow \beta$ travels in E_0 with probability p, and the differential trail $\gamma \rightarrow \delta$ travels in E_1 with probability q, which composes the boomerang distinguisher with the probability p^2q^2. In [16], Kelsey et $al.$ developed a chosen-plaintext variant and formed the amplified boomerang attack with probability $p^2q^22^{-n}$, where n is the size of each block. The rectangle attack [4] improves the amplified boomerang attack, which estimates the probability more accurately by considering as many differences as possible in the middle. The probability of a rectangle distinguisher is $2^{-n}\hat{p}^2\hat{q}^2$, where $\hat{p} = \sqrt{\Sigma_i \mathrm{Pr}^2(\alpha \rightarrow \beta_i)}$,

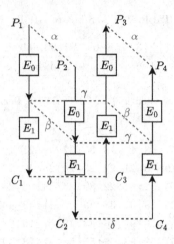

Fig. 1. Boomerang distinguisher

$\hat{q} = \sqrt{\Sigma_j \mathrm{Pr}^2(\gamma_j \to \delta)}$. Later, researchers discovered many methods to compute the probability more accurately and proposed an innovative tool named boomerang connectivity table (BCT) [11,23].

The Generic Key Recovery Algorithm. Another line of research on the rectangle attack is to mount key recovery attacks as efficiently as possible. The rectangle key recovery algorithm includes four steps: (1) data collection, (2) pair construction, (3) quartet generation and processing, and (4) exhaustive search. In the past few years, efforts have been made to find more effective key guessing strategies to improve the efficiency of key recovery attacks, like [13,31]. In the generic algorithm of Song *et al.* [24], which we are inspired by, one can select part of partial key bits involved in extended rounds to guess. Using the generic algorithm, the adversary can balance the complexities of each attack step by guessing the involved key reasonably. The outline of the key recovery algorithm can be profiled in Fig. 2.

The notations involved in the upcoming work will be described for a better understanding. As shown in Fig. 2, α' is the differential obtained by the propagation of α through E_b^{-1}, and δ' is the differential obtained by the propagation of δ through E_f. Note that not all quartets which satisfy the difference α' and δ' are useful to suggest and extract the right key. However, quartets that do not satisfy such conditions are necessarily useless. r_b and r_f are the number of unknown bits of input differential and output differential. k_b and k_f denote the subkey bits for verifying the differential propagation in E_b and E_f, respectively, where $m_b = |k_b|$ and $m_f = |k_f|$ are the size of k_b and k_f. In our attack, we guess part of k_b and k_f, so we denote k_b' and k_f' as the bits in k_b and k_f which have been guessed. Similarly, $m_b' = |k_b'|$, $m_f' = |k_f'|$, and r_b', r_f' are the number of inactive state bits which can be deduced by guessing key bits. Besides, in order

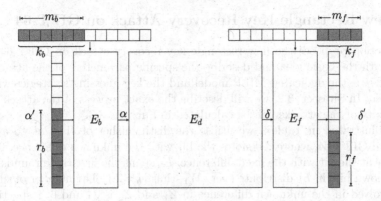

Fig. 2. Outline of rectangle key recovery attack [24]

to clearly describe the new attack, we define $r_b^* = r_b - r_b'$ and $m_b^* = m_b - m_b'$ (resp. r_f^* and m_f^*).

Related-Key Rectangle Attack. Under the related-key scenario, the rectangle attack and the rectangle key recovery attack differ slightly from those under the single-key setting. Let ΔK and ∇K be the key differences for E_0 and E_1. In the phase of data collection, the adversary needs to access four related-key oracles with K_1, $K_2 = K_1 \oplus \Delta K$, $K_3 = K_1 \oplus \nabla K$ and $K_4 = K_1 \oplus \Delta K \oplus \nabla K$ to obtain four plaintext-ciphertexts of (P_1, C_1), (P_2, C_2), (P_3, C_3) and (P_4, C_4) respectively. The remaining steps should be performed under the related-key oracles as well.

The Success Probability. From the method of [22], the success probability of the rectangle key recovery attack is calculated according to the Eq. 1, where $S_N = \hat{p}^2\hat{q}^2/2^{-n}$ is the signal/noise ratio, with an h-bit or higher advantage. s is the expected number of right quartets.

$$P_s = \Phi\left(\frac{\sqrt{sS_N} - \Phi^{-1}\left(1 - 2^{-h}\right)}{\sqrt{S_N + 1}}\right) \tag{1}$$

2.3 The Rectangle Distinguisher of GIFT-64

Our attack is based on the 20-round related-key boomerang distinguisher of Ji *et al.* [15]: $\alpha = 00\ 00\ 00\ 00\ 00\ 00\ a0\ 00$, $\delta = 04\ 00\ 00\ 00\ 01\ 20\ 10\ 00$, with $\Delta K = 0004\ 0000\ 0000\ 0800\ 0000\ 0000\ 0000\ 0010$ and $\nabla K = 2000\ 0000\ 0000\ 0000\ 0800\ 0000\ 0200\ 0800$.

The probability of the distinguisher above is $P_d = 2^{-58.557}$. Li *et al.* [17] have increased this probability to $2^{-57.43}$ by improving the BCT of the distinguisher (but otherwise using the same parameters as Ji *et al.*). Note that this paper does not discuss the calculation of the distinguisher probability but focuses on the key guessing strategy in the key recovery phase.

3   New Rectangle Key Recovery Attack on GIFT-64

This section proposes the new rectangle key recovery attack on GIFT-64. We begin with the basic idea and describe the specific parameters of the attack. In Subsect. 3.1, the dedicated MILP model and the key guessing strategies will be presented. In Subsect. 3.2, we will describe the exact process of the attack. The complexity of the attacks will be calculated in Subsect. 3.3.

As illustrated in Table 4, we utilise the distinguisher of Ji et $al.$ to attack 26-round GIFT-64, where ? denotes the bit with the unknown difference, 0 and 1 represent the bit with the fixed difference. E_b spans the first three rounds, and 44 unknown bits in E_b distribute over ΔY_1, thus $r_b = \textbf{44}$. The number of subkey bits involved in the unknown difference in Z_1 and Z_2 is 24 and 6, respectively, so $m_b = \textbf{30}$. E_f spans the last three rounds, and there are 64 unknown bits in E_f distributing over Z_{26}, thus $r_f = \textbf{64}$. The involved 32 bits, 24 bits, and 8 bits subkeys are added to state Z_{26}, Z_{25}, and Z_{24} respectively, so $m_f = \textbf{64}$. Hence, the number of subkey bits involved in k_b and k_f is $m_b + m_f = \textbf{94}$ bits.

Table 4. The 26-round related-key rectangle attack on GIFT-64. For round r, ΔX_r and ΔY_r are the input and output differences of the S-boxes, and ΔZ_r is the output difference of the linear layer. $r \in \{1, 2, ..., 26\}$

input	????	????	????	????	????	????	????	????	????	????	????	????	????	????	????	????
ΔY_1	??0?	1??0	01??	?0??	1?0?	?1?0	0???	?0??	??0?	???0	0???	?0??	??0?	???0	0???	?0??
ΔZ_1	????	????	????	????	0000	0000	0000	0000	11??	????	????	????	????	11??	????	????
ΔX_2	????	????	????	????	0000	0000	0000	0000	11??	????	????	????	????	11??	????	????
ΔY_2	0?01	00?0	000?	?000	0000	0000	0000	0000	0100	00?0	000?	?000	?000	0100	00?0	000?
ΔZ_2	????	0000	?1??	0000	0000	0000	0000	0000	0001	0000	0000	0000	0000	0000	0000	?1??
ΔX_3	????	0000	?1??	0000	0000	0000	0000	0000	0001	0000	0000	0000	0000	0000	0000	?1??
ΔY_3	1000	0000	0010	0000	0000	0000	0000	0000	0000	0000	0000	0000	0000	0000	0000	0010
ΔZ_3	0000	0000	0000	0000	0000	0000	0000	0000	0000	0000	0000	0010	1010	0000	0000	0000
$\Delta X_4(\alpha)$	0000	0000	0000	0000	0000	0000	0000	0000	0000	0000	0000	0000	1010	0000	0000	0000
$\vdots$							$\cdots$	$\cdots$								
$\Delta X_{24}(\delta)$	0000	0100	0000	0000	0000	0000	0000	0000	0000	0001	0010	0000	0001	0000	0000	0000
ΔY_{24}	0000	???1	0000	0000	0000	0000	0000	0000	0000	????	????	0000	????	0000	0000	0000
ΔZ_{24}	00?0	0000	00??	0?00	0001	0000	?00?	00?0	?000	0000	??00	000?	0?00	0000	0??0	?000
ΔX_{25}	00?0	0000	00??	0?00	0001	0000	?00?	00?0	?010	0000	??00	000?	0?00	0000	0??0	?000
ΔY_{25}	????	0000	????	????	????	0000	????	????	????	0000	????	????	????	0000	????	????
ΔZ_{25}	??0?	??0?	??0?	??0?	??0?	??0?	??0?	??0?	0???	0???	0???	0???	?0??	?0??	?0??	?0??
ΔX_{26}	??0?	??0?	??0?	??0?	??0?	??0?	??0?	??0?	0???	0???	0???	0???	?0??	?0??	?0??	?0??
ΔY_{26}	????	????	????	????	????	????	????	????	????	????	????	????	????	????	????	????
ΔZ_{26}	????	????	????	????	????	????	????	????	????	????	????	????	????	????	????	????
output	????	????	????	????	????	????	????	????	????	????	????	????	????	????	????	????

Thanks to the bit-wise linear key schedule of GIFT-64, the subkey bits are reused in certain rounds. For example, if we guess RK_1, we can obtain RK_{25} and vice versa. This relationship between subkey bits is also present in RK_2 and RK_{26}. As shown in Table 5, we mark the subkey bits involved in k_b and

k_f as bold, the subkey bits shared by RK_1 and RK_{25} as green, and the subkey bits shared in RK_2 and RK_{26} as cyan. Note that only the bolded-and-colored subkey bits are reusable. The number of reusable subkey bits is **26** (20 bits between RK_1 and RK_{25}, say $k_1|k_0$ in Table 5. 6 bits between RK_2 and RK_{26}, say $k_3|k_2$ in Table 5). Therefore, the number of subkey bits involved in the attack is $94 - 26 = \boldsymbol{68}$.

Table 5. The relation of the involved subkey bits in the key recovery phase

ΔZ_1	????	????	????	????	0000	0000	0000	0000	11??	????	????	????	????	11??	????	????
$k_1|k_0$	15|15	14|14	13|13	12|12	11|11	10|10	9|9	8|8	7|7	6|6	5|5	4|4	3|3	2|2	1|1	0|0
ΔZ_2	????	0000	?1??	0000	0000	0000	0000	0000	0001	0000	0000	0000	0000	0000	0000	?1??
$k_3|k_2$	15|15	14|14	13|13	12|12	11|11	10|10	9|9	8|8	7|7	6|6	5|5	4|4	3|3	2|2	1|1	0|0
...										... ...						
ΔZ_{25}	??0?	??0?	??0?	??0?	???0	???0	???0	???0	0???	0???	0???	0???	?0??	?0??	?0??	?0??
$k_1|k_0$	11|7	10|6	9|5	8|4	7|3	6|2	5|1	4|0	3|15	2|14	1|13	0|12	15|11	14|10	13|9	12|8
ΔZ_{26}	????	????	????	????	????	????	????	????	????	????	????	????	????	????	????	????
$k_3|k_2$	11|7	10|6	9|5	8|4	7|3	6|2	5|1	4|0	3|15	2|14	1|13	0|12	15|11	14|10	13|9	12|8

Based on the observation of the previous rectangle key recovery attack instance and the analysis of the GIFT-64 key schedule, we summarize the attack strategies into the following two observations:

- The phases of pair construction and quartet generation and processing dominate the time cost of our attacks. In general, there is a certain extent inverse relationship between the time consumption of pair construction and quartet generation and processing. Both of these parts are related to the number of guessed subkey bits and the number of filtering bits produced. Balancing the time complexity of these two parts with appropriate guessing subkey bits will be the core idea of our improvement.
- Our key guessing strategies are based on the idea of finding a method that requires less guessing time complexity but can obtain more conditional bits, i.e. $m'_b + m'_f \leq 2(r'_b + r'_f)$. The reused subkey bits can provide additional filtering bits for some guesses. However, excessive guessing of these subkey bits will make the complexity of pair construction and quartet generation and processing unbalanced. Under the consideration of trading off the time complexity, guessing as many reused subkey bits as possible will maximize the advantage of our attack.

3.1 The Dedicated Model and New Key Guessing Strategy

As a block cipher with the bit-wise key schedule and bit-wise linear layer, the structure of GIFT-64 allows us to directly reap the benefits of guessing each bit. These advantages provide greater flexibility for our attack. Our attack is under the related-key setting, so the filtering process corresponds to the guessed subkeys and their complement.

Since mouha *et al.*'s seminal paper [19], Mixed Integer Linear Programming (MILP) has been widely used in automated cryptanalysis and has yielded promising results in numerous cryptographic key recovery attacks [14,21,27,29]. In this paper, we present a dedicated model for automated key recovery attack for GIFT-64 based on our new subkey guessing strategy. We start our modeling with a selection of plaintexts and ciphertexts that satisfy the difference of Z_1 and Z_{26}, respectively. We use binary variables to indicate whether each bit is known and mark all the output bits of an S-box as known if and only if both its input bits and the 2 bits subkey involved are guessed. Guessing the subkey bits allows the propagation of the knownness to obtain the filtering bits. Note that the differential propagation in E_b is the exact opposite of the differential propagation in E_f. We then count the filtering bits of the S-box for which both the input and output differences are known and calculate the time complexity of each attack step. Naturally, we set our objective function to balance the time complexity of each attack step optimally. The parameters we used are listed in Table 6, and the dedicated model is described in Model 1.

Attack I: The guessing of the keys involved in the forward and backward extend rounds, shown in Fig. 3, and described as follows. Note that we have marked in red (resp. blue) the keys guessed in the E_b (resp. E_f) and the filters that can be used. Next, the guessed key bits and filters involved in E_b and E_f are explained.

○ **Involved in E_b:**
Choose the plaintexts that satisfy ΔZ_1. If $k_0[0]$ and $k_1[0]$ are guessed, we can obtain the value of $X_2[3:0]$ and filter out the pairs of plaintexts that do not satisfy the difference 000? by using the filter $GS(X_2[3:0]) \oplus GS(X_2[3:0] \oplus \Delta X_2[3:0]) = \Delta Y_2[3:0]$. As shown in Fig. 3, there are none bit in $\Delta X_2[3:0]$ with fixed difference and 3 bits in $\Delta Y_2[3:0]$ with fixed difference. When $k_1[0]$ and $k_0[0]$ are guessed, there exist 3 filtering bits (???? → 000?) via the corresponding S-box. We guess 24 bits $k_0[15,14,13,12,7,6,5,4,3,2,1,0]$ and $k_1[15,14,13,12,7,6,5,4,3,2,1,0]$ to obtain 34 filtering bits in round 2. We guess 6 bits $k_2[15,13,0]$ and $k_3[15,13,0]$ to obtain 10 filtering bits in round 3. Therefore, we guess **30 subkey bits** and obtain **44 filtering bits** in E_b, i.e. $m'_b = 30$ can verify $r'_b = 44$, and $r^*_b = r_b - r'_b = 0$.

○ **Involved in E_f:**
The filtering bits are obtained in the same way as described in E_b. We guess 16 bits $k_2[8,7,6,5,4,3,2,1]$ and $k_3[14,12,11,10,9,8,7,5]$, combined with the guessed subkey bits $k_2[15,13,0]$ and $k_3[15,13,0]$ which can be reused, this guess provides 11 filtering bits in round 26. We guess 2 bits $k_0[10,9]$, combined with $k_0[14,13,6,5]$ and $k_1[14,13,6,5,2,1]$ that can be reused. This guess provides 17 filtering bits in round 25. Therefore, we guess **18 subkey bits** and obtain **28 filtering bits** in E_f, i.e. $m'_f = 18$ can verify $r'_f = 28$, and $r^*_f = r_f - r'_f = 36$.

Table 6. Parameters of dedicated model

Parameter	Implication
$R_0 = \{1, 2, 3\}$	Extension rounds in E_b
$R_1 = \{24, 25, 26\}$	Extension rounds in E_f
$r \in \{R_0 \| R_1\}$	Round number in extension rounds
$m \in \{0, ..., 16\}$	S-box position in each round
$n \in \{0, ..., 4\}$	Bit position in the input (resp. output) of S-box
$s \in \{0, ..., 4\}$	Number of attack step
Binary $KX_{r,m,n}, KY_{r,m,n}$	Bit difference is known or not
Binary $FX_{r,m,n}, FY_{r,m,n}$	Bit difference is fixed or not
Binary $GK_{r,m}$	Subkey bits is guessed or not
Integer $A_{r,m}$	Number of filtering bits of each filter
General T_s	Time complexity of each attack step
General T	Upper bound of T_s

Algorithm 1. Optimal key guessing strategy searching

Require: R_0 rounds in E_b and R_1 rounds in E_f, the system of inequalities for linear layer and its inverse, the number of S-box in each round m, the size of each S-box n, multi binary variables $KX_{r,m,n}, KY_{r,m,n}, FX_{r,m,n}, FY_{r,m,n}, GK_{r,m}$, multi integer variables $A_{r,m}$, multi general variables T_s and T

Ensure: system of inequalities

   /* Initialization */

   Constraints: all $KX_0 = KY_{26} = 1$

   Constraints: $FX_{r,m,n}$ and $FY_{r,m,n}$ follow the differential in E_b and E_f

   /* Counting the number of filtering bits */

1: **for** r in R_0 **do**

2:    **for** $i = 0$ to m **do**

3:       Constraints: all $KY_{r,i,*} = 1$ if and only if all $KX_{r,i,*} = GK_{r,i} = GK_{r,i'} = 1$, otherwise all $KY_{r,i,*} = 0$

4:       Constraints: $A_{r,i} = KY_{r,i,*} \times (sum(FY_{r,i}) - sum(FX_{r,i}))$

5:    **end for**

6:    Constraints: Linear permutation from $KY_{r,*,*}$ to $KX_{r+1,*,*}$

7: **end for**

8: **for** r in R_1 **do**

9:    **for** $i = 0$ to m **do**

10:      Constraints: all $KX_{r,i,*} = 1$ if and only if all $KY_{r,i,*} = GK_{r,i} = GK_{r,i'} = 1$, otherwise all $KX_{r,i,*} = 0$

11:      Constraints: $A_{r,i} = KX_{r,i,*} \times (sum(FX_{r,i}) - sum(FY_{r,i}))$

12:    **end for**

13:    Constraints: Reversed linear permutation from $KX_{r,*,*}$ to $KY_{r-1,*,*}$

14: **end for**

   /* Computing time complexity */

15: **for** s in the number of attack steps **do**

16:    Constraints: T_s follow Eq. 6

17:    Constraints: $T >= T_s$

18: **end for**

   /* Objective function */

19: **MINIMIZE** T

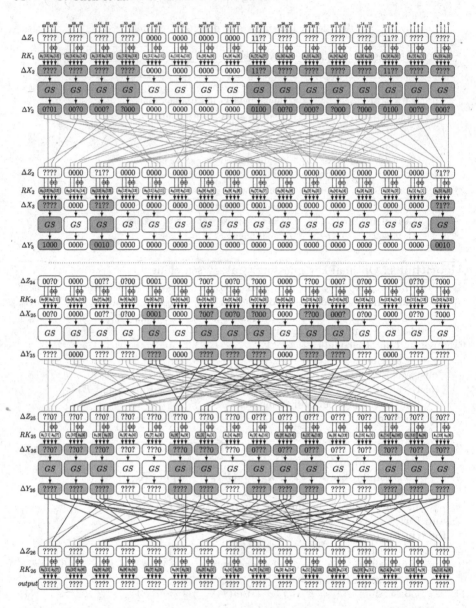

Fig. 3. Guessed key bits and the corresponding propagation relations for Attack I

3.2　New Rectangle Attack on GIFT-64

In this subsection, we conducted the rectangle key recovery attack against GIFT-64 using different key guessing strategies. For both attacks, we choose $y = \sqrt{s} \cdot 2^{\frac{n}{2}-r_b}/\sqrt{P_d}$ to be the number of structures that should be pre-constructed, where s is the number of quartets expected to be correct.

The key guessing strategy is detailed in Subsect. 3.1. The complexities will be calculated in Subsect. 3.3. The attack process is as follows:

1. Collect and store y structures of 2^{r_b} plaintexts each. Encrypt these structures under four related keys K_1, K_2, K_3, and K_4. We obtain four datasets containing the plaintext-ciphertexts under four related keys, denote as L_1, L_2, L_3, and L_4. Let $D = y \cdot 2^{r_b}$ for convenience, so the time, data, and memory complexity of this step is $T_0 = M_0 = D_{total} = 4 \cdot D = y \cdot 2^{r_b+2}$.
2. Guess $(m'_b + m'_f)$-bit key, and for each guess:
   (a) Initialize a list of key counters for the unguessed subkey bits of k_b and k_f, the memory complexity of key counters is $M_c = 2^{m_b^* + m_f^*}$.
   (b) For each plaintext-ciphertext collected in step 1, partially encrypt P_i and partially decrypt C_i under the key bits we guessed, i.e. $P_i^* = Enc_{k'_b}(P_i)$, $C_i^* = Dec_{k'_f}(C_i)$, where $i \in \{1, 2, 3, 4\}$. The time complexity of this step is $4 \cdot D = y \cdot 2^{r_b+2}$ partial encryptions.
   (c) Choose to construct pairs in the input of E_b. The reason is that constructing pairs in the input of E_b can get more filters for the phase of constructing pairs and balance the time complexity
      i. Insert L_1 into a hash table indexed by the r'_b inactive bits of P_1^*, so there are 2^{r_b} items, each of which comprises $2^{r_b^*}$ pairs (P_1^*, C_1^*). For L_2, find matches in the hash table according to the r'_b inactive bits of P_2^*. Each match corresponds to a pair $\{(P_1^*, C_1^*), (P_2^*, C_2^*)\}$. There are $y \cdot 2^{r_b}$ items in total, and there will be $2 \cdot \binom{2^{r_b^*}}{2}$ different combinations for each item. Perform the same operation to L_3 and L_4, so we can get two sets $S_1 = \{(P_1^*, C_1^*), (P_2^*, C_2^*)\}$ and $S_2 = \{(P_3^*, C_3^*), (P_4^*, C_4^*)\}$. The size of each is:

$$y \cdot 2^{r_b'} \cdot 2 \cdot \binom{2^{r_b^*}}{2} = D \cdot 2^{r_b^*}. \tag{2}$$

The memory complexity of this step is $M_1 = 2 \cdot D \cdot 2^{r_b^*}$ for storing sets S_1 and S_2. We need $D \cdot 2^{r_b^*}$ look-up tables to construct each set. The time complexity of this step is $2 \cdot D \cdot 2^{r_b^*}$ memory accesses.

      ii. Insert S_1 into a hash table indexed by the $2r'_f$ inactive bits of both C_1^* and C_2^*. Since each set contains $D \cdot 2^{r_b^*}$ pairs, there are $2^{2r'_f}$ items, each of which comprises $D \cdot 2^{r_b^* - 2r'_f}$ pairs $\{(P_1^*, C_1^*), (P_2^*, C_2^*)\}$. For S_2, find matches in the hash table according to the $2r'_f$ inactive bits of both C_3^* and C_4^*. Each matching provides a quartet $\{(P_1^*, C_1^*), (P_2^*, C_2^*), (P_3^*, C_3^*), (P_4^*, C_4^*)\}$ for us. For each item, similar to step 2(c)i, there are $2 \cdot \binom{D \cdot 2^{r_b^* - 2r'_f}}{2}$ different combinations. So the number of quartets we generate is

$$2^{2r'_f} \cdot 2 \cdot \binom{D \cdot 2^{r_b^* - 2r'_f}}{2} = D^2 \cdot 2^{2r_b^* + 2r_f^* - 2r_f}. \tag{3}$$

The time complexity of this step is $D^2 \cdot 2^{2r_b^* + 2r_f^* - 2r_f}$ memory accesses.

(d) Utilize the quartets we obtain above to determine the key candidates involved in E_b and E_f and increase the corresponding key counters. Denote the time cost of processing each quartet as ϵ. The time complexity of this step is $D^2 \cdot 2^{2r_b^* + 2r_f^* - 2n} \cdot \epsilon$. We will discuss the estimation of ϵ in detail in Subsect. 3.3.

(e) Select the top $2^{m_b^* + m_f^* - h}$ hits in the counters to be the key candidates, which delivers a h-bit or higher advantage, where $0 < h \leq m_b^* + m_f^*$.

(f) Guess the remaining $k - m_b - m_f$ bits key according to the key schedule and exhaustively search over them to recover the correct key, where k is the key size of GIFT-64. The time complexity of this step is $2^{k - m_b' - m_f' - h}$ encryptions.

3.3   Complexity Analysis

We will introduce two different methods to process quartets and extract key information, $i.e.$ calculation of ϵ, which will bring different time complexity to our attacks. We apply ϵ computed using the method of the pre-constructed hash table into the MILP model and compute the time complexity of Attack I accordingly. We also bring ϵ computed using the method of the guess and filter to the MILP model and compute the time complexity of Attack II accordingly. We mount this approach to our two attacks and take Attack I as an example to introduce it in detail. The complexity analysis of Attack II is calculated in detail in the eprint version.

Guess and Filter: Suppose we obtain N_q quartets after step 2d in the first attack. Guessing $k_2[14, 12]$ and $k_3[6, 4]$, we can use filters $GS(Y_{26}[15 : 12]) \oplus GS(Y_{26}[15 : 12] \oplus \Delta Y_{26}[15 : 12]) = ?0??$ and $GS(Y_{26}[47 : 44]) \oplus GS(Y_{26}[47 : 44] \oplus \Delta Y_{26}[47 : 44]) = ?0??$. Furthermore, combined with the subkey bits $k_0[15, 7, 3, 1]$ and $k_1[15, 7, 3]$, which have been guessed before, we can use filters $GS(Y_{25}[63 : 60]) \oplus GS(Y_{25}[63 : 60] \oplus \Delta Y_{25}[63 : 60] = 00?0$ and $GS(Y_{25}[55 : 48]) \oplus GS(Y_{25}[55 : 48] \oplus \Delta Y_{25}[63 : 48] = 00??, 0?00$. There are 10 filtering bits for pairs, so 20 filtering bits for quartets. Therefore, there are $2^4 \cdot N_q \cdot 2^{-20} = N_q \cdot 2^{-16}$ quartets remain, and the time cost is $2^4 \cdot N_q$ S-box accesses. Note that after this step, the number of quartets remaining is much lower than before. The time consumption of the remaining steps will be far less than $N_q \cdot 2^4$ S-box accesses. Therefore, $\epsilon \approx 2^4 / 26 \approx 2^{-0.7}$ encryption.

Pre-construct Hash Tables: As shown in Table 7, the time complexity of step 2d can be reduced by accessing the hash table instead of traversing subkeys. We can obtain the bits deduced according to the inputs of the filters, $i.e.$ starting bits and subkey bits. Utilize these bits to match pairs in the quartets. Each match can provide the corresponding subkey information. The time and memory cost of each subtable is determined by the underlined bits, and the filtering effect indicates the number of candidate subkeys obtained for each subtable access. Note that these hash tables in our paper are all built for quartets but can also be built for pairs in memory-limited cases.

Table 7. Precomputation tables for the 26-round attack on GIFT-64

No	Starting bits	Subkey bits	Bits deduced	Filter condition	T & M	Filter effect
1	$Y_{26}[47:44]$ $Y_{26}[15:12]$ $X_{26}[63:60]$ $X_{26}[31:28]$	$k_2[14,12]$ $k_3[6,4]$	$Y'_{26}[47:44]$ $Y'_{26}[15:12]$ $X_{26}[47:44]$ $X'_{26}[47:44]$ $X_{26}[15:12]$ $X'_{26}[15:12]$ $X_{25}[63:60]$ $X'_{25}[63:60]$ $X_{25}[55:48]$ $X'_{25}[55:48]$	$X_{26}[14] \oplus X'_{26}[14] = 0$ $X_{26}[44] \oplus X'_{26}[44] = 0$ $X_{25}[63:60] \oplus X'_{25}[63:60]$ $= 00?0$ $X_{25}[55:48] \oplus X'_{25}[55:48]$ $= 00??,0?00$	2^{48}	2^{-16}
	$Y^i_{26}[47:44], Y^i_{26}[15:12], X_{26}[63:60], X_{26}[31:28], i = 1,2,3,4$: $k_2[14,12], k_3[6,4]$					
2	$Y_{26}[51:48]$ $Y_{26}[35:32]$ $Y_{26}[19:16]$ $X_{26}[3:0]$	$k_0[8]$ $k_1[8]$ $k_2[14,10,9]$ $k_3[6,2,1]$	$Y'_{26}[51:48]$ $Y'_{26}[35:32]$ $Y'_{26}[19:16]$ $X_{26}[51:48]$ $X'_{26}[51:48]$ $X_{26}[35:32]$ $X'_{26}[35:32]$ $X_{26}[19:16]$ $X'_{26}[19:16]$ $X_{25}[15:12]$ $X'_{25}[15:12]$ $X_{25}[7:0]$ $X'_{25}[7:0]$	$X_{26}[49] \oplus X'_{26}[49] = 0$ $X_{26}[32] \oplus X'_{26}[32] = 0$ $X_{26}[19] \oplus X'_{26}[19] = 0$ $X_{25}[15:12] \oplus X'_{25}[15:12]$ $= 0?00$ $X_{25}[7:0] \oplus X'_{25}[7:0]$ $= 0??0, ?000$	2^{50}	2^{-14}
	$Y^i_{26}[51:48], Y_{26}[35:32], Y_{26}[19:16], X_{26}[3:1], i = 1,2,3,4$: $k_0[8], k_1[8], k_2[14,10,9], k_3[6,2,1]$					

As shown in Fig. 3, these uncoloured cells of ΔRK_i denote the subkey bits not used in previous steps, where $i = 24, 25, 26$. We should access subtable No.1 in Table 7 first. Combining state $Y_{26}[47:44], Y_{26}[15:12], X_{26}[63:60], X_{26}[31:28]$ with subkey bits $k_2[14,12], k_3[6,4]$, we can deduce the corresponding $Y'_{26}[47:44]$, $Y'_{26}[15:12]$, $X_{26}[47:44]$, $X'_{26}[47:44]$, $X_{26}[15:12]$, $X'_{26}[15:12]$, $X_{25}[63:60]$, $X'_{25}[63:60]$, $X_{25}[55:48]$, $X'_{25}[55:48]$. We can obtain filtering bits from $X_{26}[14] \oplus X'_{26}[14] = 0$, $X_{26}[44] \oplus X'_{26}[44] = 0$, $X_{25}[63:60] \oplus X'_{25}[63:60] = 00?0$, $X_{25}[55:48] \oplus X'_{25}[55:48] = 00??, 0?00$. Specifically, for a pair of plaintext, there are 10 filtering bits from $\Delta Y_{26}[47:44] =???? \to \Delta X_{26}[47:44] =???0, \Delta Y_{26}[15:12] =???? \to \Delta X_{26}[15:12] =?0??, \Delta Y_{25}[63:60] =???? \to \Delta X_{25}[63:60] = 00?0, \Delta Y_{25}[31:28] =????,???? \to \Delta X_{25}[31:28] = 00??, 0?00$. Therefore, we can get 20 filtering bits for a quartet using these filters. According to these filters, we can extract information of $k_2[14,12], k_3[6,4]$ and discard quartets that suggest nothing. We need to store subkey bits $k_2[14,12], k_3[6,4]$ into a hash table indexed by 64-bit $Y^i_{26}[47:44], Y^i_{26}[15:12], X^i_{26}[63:60], X^i_{26}[31:28]$ in total, where $i = 1,2,3,4$. The filter effect is 2^{-16}, which means 2^{16} quartets will be filtered out, so the time and memory cost to construct such a subtable is $2^{64-16} = 2^{48}$. For now, the number of quartets is much lower than before. To process the rest of the quartets and increase key counters, we need to access the remaining subtable No.2. The time cost of the following steps will be far less than that of accessing subtable No.1. Finally, we get $\epsilon \approx 1$ memory access.

The Complexity of Attack I: Considering the total complexity and success rate, we choose $s = 2$ and $h = 20$, so we need construct $y = \sqrt{s} \cdot 2^{\frac{n}{2} - r_b} / \sqrt{P_d} = 2^{17.78}$ structures in step 1 and $D = y \cdot 2^{r_b} = 2^{61.78}$.

- *Data complexity*: The plaintexts in step 1 are the total data we need to collect in this attack.

$$D_{total} = 4 \cdot D = 2^{63.78} \tag{4}$$

- *Memory complexity*: We need store data collected in step 1, key counters described in step 2a, and datasets S_1 and S_2 generated in step 2(c)i.

$$\begin{aligned}
M_{total} &= M_0 + M_1 + M_c \\
&= 4 \cdot D + 2 \cdot D \cdot 2^{r_b^*} + 2^{m_b^* + m_f^*} \\
&= 2^{63.78} + 2^{62.78} + 2^{36} \\
&\approx 2^{64.36}
\end{aligned} \tag{5}$$

- *Time complexity*: The time complexity consists of five parts: (1) data collection in step 1 denote as T_0, (2) partial encryption and partial decryption in step 2b denote as T_1, (3) pairs generation in step 2(c)i denote as T_2, (4) quartets generation and processing in step 2d denote as T_3 and (5) the exhaustive search of the remaining key in step 2f denote as T_4. Recall that our key guessing strategy provides the following parameters: $m_b' = 30, r_b' = r_b = 44, r_b^* = 0$ and $m_f' = 18, r_f' = 28, r_f^* = r_f - r_f' = 36$. For the last four parts, we need to consider all guessing of $(m_b' + m_f') = 48$ subkey bits.

$$\begin{aligned}
T_0 &= 4 \cdot D = 2^{63.78} \\
T_1 &= 2^{m_b' + m_f'} \cdot 4 \cdot D = 2^{111.78} \\
T_2 &= 2^{m_b' + m_f'} \cdot 2 \cdot D \cdot 2^{r_b^*} = 2^{110.78} \\
T_3 &= 2^{m_b' + m_f'} \cdot D^2 \cdot 2^{2r_b^* + 2r_f^* - 2n} \cdot \epsilon = 2^{115.56} \cdot \epsilon \\
T_4 &= 2^{m_b' + m_f' + k - m_b' - m_f' - h} = 2^{k-h} = 2^{108}
\end{aligned} \tag{6}$$

We obtain $\epsilon \approx 2^{-0.7}$ encryption with the method of the guess and filter. The time complexity of Attack I is $T_1 + T_3 + T_4 = \frac{6}{26} \cdot 2^{111.78} + 2^{115.56-0.7} + 2^{108} \approx \mathbf{2^{114.86}}$ encryption and $T_2 = \mathbf{2^{110.78}}$ memory access.

We obtain $\epsilon \approx 1$ memory access with the method of the pre-constructed hash table. The time complexity of Attack I is $T_1 + T_4 = \frac{6}{26} \cdot 2^{111.78} + 2^{108} \approx 2^{111.78-2.11} + 2^{108} \approx \mathbf{2^{110.06}}$ 26-round encryptions and $T_2 + T_3 = 2^{110.78} + 2^{115.56} \approx \mathbf{2^{115.80}}$ memory accesses.

Attack II: The key guessing strategy of this attack is $m_b' = \mathbf{26}, r_b' = \mathbf{39}, r_b^* = r_b - r_b' = \mathbf{5}$ and $m_f' = \mathbf{22}, r_f' = \mathbf{34}, r_f^* = r_f - r_f' = \mathbf{30}$. We choose $s = 2$ and $h = 20$, so $D = 2^{61.78}$. The data complexity is $D_{total} = 2^{63.78}$, memory complexity is $M_{total}' = 2^{67.8}$. We obtain that $\epsilon \approx 2^{-2.7}$ encryptions with the method of the guess and filter, so time complexity is $\mathbf{2^{111.51}}$ 26-round encryptions and $\mathbf{2^{115.78}}$ memory accesses. We obtain that $\epsilon \approx 1$ memory access with the method of the pre-construct hash table. Thence, the time complexity is $\mathbf{2^{110.06}}$ 26-round encryptions and $\mathbf{2^{116.06}}$ memory accesses. The detail of Attack II can be found in the eprint version.

In summary, we obtained that the best current rectangle key recovery attack on GIFT-64 is Attack I, which pre-constructs hash tables to process quartets. The attack complexity is: data complexity is $D_{total} = 2^{63.78}$, memory complexity is $M_{total} = 2^{64.36}$, time complexity is $T_{total} = 2^{110.06}$ 26-round encryption and $2^{115.80}$ memory accesses. Further, calculating using the probability which improved in [17], the overall complexity of the attack is: $D^*_{total} = 2^{63.22}$, $M^*_{total} = 2^{63.8}$, $T^*_{total} = 2^{109.5}$ 26-round encryption and $2^{115.24}$ memory accesses.

According to Eq. 1, the success rate of Attack I, II are both around 75%.

Reevaluate the Security of GIFT-128. We also re-evaluate the ability of GIFT-128 to resist rectangle key recovery attack. In [15], Ji *et al.* proposed the rectangle key recovery attack on 23-round GIFT-128. They guessed all the subkey bits involved in E_b, non-guessed any subkey bits in E_f. For improvement, we guess 2 fewer subkey bits in E_b than [15] and roughly reduce its total time complexity by a factor of 2^2, *i.e.* $2^{123.1}$ encryptions, and $T_2 = 2^{126.31}$ memory accesses. The data and memory complexity is the same as [15]. The details are given in eprint version.

4   Discussion and Conclusion

We propose new key guessing strategies to improve the attack of 26-round GIFT-64. The MILP model of the best key guessing strategy for GIFT-64 rectangle key recovery attack is constructed, and thus the optimal key guessing strategy for our attack scenario is obtained by searching and comparing. Our attacks against GIFT-64 are the best in terms of time complexity so far. For GIFT-64, its bit-wise linear permutation gives us great flexibility, and the reused subkey bits derived by the bit-wise key schedule provide additional filter bits for each guessing. Our attack starts from the bit-wise operations of GIFT-64 and considers the more accurate selection of the subkey bits involved in the attack so as to guess the key more effectively. This idea also provides a new possibility for better attacks on block ciphers structured by bit-wise operations.

We have observed that the designer of GIFT had not claimed the related-key security. For the community of symmetric cryptography, however, we believe that cryptographic security analysis under related-key settings is indispensable.

Acknowledgements. We would like to thank the anonymous reviewers for their helpful comments and suggestions. This paper is supported by the National Key Research and Development Program (No. 2018YFA0704704, No.2022YFB2701900, No.2022YFB2703003) and the National Natural Science Foundation of China (Grants 62022036, 62132008, 62202460, 62172410, 62372213).

References

1. Banik, S., et al.: SUNDAE-GIFT. In: Submission to the NIST Lightweight Cryptography Project (2019)
2. Banik, S., et al.: GIFT-COFB. In: Cryptology ePrint Archive (2020)

3. Banik, S., Pandey, S.K., Peyrin, T., Sasaki, Yu., Sim, S.M., Todo, Y.: GIFT: a small present - towards reaching the limit of lightweight encryption. In: Fischer, W., Homma, N. (eds.) CHES 2017. LNCS, vol. 10529, pp. 321–345. Springer, Cham (2017). https://doi.org/10.1007/978-3-319-66787-4_16

4. Biham, E., Dunkelman, O., Keller, N.: The rectangle attack—rectangling the serpent. In: Pfitzmann, B. (ed.) EUROCRYPT 2001. LNCS, vol. 2045, pp. 340–357. Springer, Heidelberg (2001). https://doi.org/10.1007/3-540-44987-6_21

5. Biham, E., Shamir, A.: Differential cryptanalysis of DES-like cryptosystems. J. Cryptol. **4**(1), 3–72 (1991). https://doi.org/10.1007/BF00630563

6. Biryukov, A., Khovratovich, D.: Related-key cryptanalysis of the full AES-192 and AES-256. In: Matsui, M. (ed.) ASIACRYPT 2009. LNCS, vol. 5912, pp. 1–18. Springer, Heidelberg (2009). https://doi.org/10.1007/978-3-642-10366-7_1

7. Bogdanov, A., et al.: PRESENT: an ultra-lightweight block cipher. In: Paillier, P., Verbauwhede, I. (eds.) CHES 2007. LNCS, vol. 4727, pp. 450–466. Springer, Heidelberg (2007). https://doi.org/10.1007/978-3-540-74735-2_31

8. Chakraborti, A., Datta, N., Jha, A., Lopez, C.M., Nandi, M., Sasaki, Y.: LOTUS-AEAD and LOCUS-AEAD. In: Submission to the NIST Lightweight Cryptography project (2019)

9. Chakraborti, A., Datta, N., Jha, A., Nandi, M.: HYENA. In: Submission to the NIST Lightweight Cryptography project (2019)

10. Chen, L., Wang, G., Zhang, G.: MILP-based related-key rectangle attack and its application to GIFT, Khudra, MIBS. Comput. J. **62**(12), 1805–1821 (2019). https://doi.org/10.1093/comjnl/bxz076

11. Cid, C., Huang, T., Peyrin, T., Sasaki, Yu., Song, L.: Boomerang connectivity table: a new cryptanalysis tool. In: Nielsen, J.B., Rijmen, V. (eds.) EUROCRYPT 2018, Part II. LNCS, vol. 10821, pp. 683–714. Springer, Cham (2018). https://doi.org/10.1007/978-3-319-78375-8_22

12. Derbez, P., Euler, M., Fouque, P., Nguyen, P.H.: Revisiting related-key boomerang attacks on AES using computer-aided tool. In: Agrawal, S., Lin, D. (eds.) ASIACRYPT 2022, Part III. LNCS, vol. 13793, pp. 68–88. Springer, Cham (2022). https://doi.org/10.1007/978-3-031-22969-5_3

13. Dong, X., Qin, L., Sun, S., Wang, X.: Key guessing strategies for linear key-schedule algorithms in rectangle attacks. In: Dunkelman, O., Dziembowski, S. (eds.) EUROCRYPT 2022, Part III. LNCS, vol. 13277, pp. 3–33. Springer, Cham (2022). https://doi.org/10.1007/978-3-031-07082-2_1

14. Fu, K., Wang, M., Guo, Y., Sun, S., Hu, L.: MILP-based automatic search algorithms for differential and linear trails for speck. In: Peyrin, T. (ed.) FSE 2016. LNCS, vol. 9783, pp. 268–288. Springer, Heidelberg (2016). https://doi.org/10.1007/978-3-662-52993-5_14

15. Ji, F., Zhang, W., Zhou, C., Ding, T.: Improved (related-key) differential cryptanalysis on GIFT. In: Dunkelman, O., Jacobson Jr., M.J., O'Flynn, C. (eds.) SAC 2020. LNCS, vol. 12804, pp. 198–228. Springer, Cham (2021). https://doi.org/10.1007/978-3-030-81652-0_8

16. Kelsey, J., Kohno, T., Schneier, B.: Amplified boomerang attacks against reduced-round MARS and serpent. In: Goos, G., Hartmanis, J., van Leeuwen, J., Schneier, B. (eds.) FSE 2000. LNCS, vol. 1978, pp. 75–93. Springer, Heidelberg (2001). https://doi.org/10.1007/3-540-44706-7_6

17. Li, C., Wu, B., Lin, D.: Generalized boomerang connectivity table and improved cryptanalysis of gift. In: Deng, Y., Yung, M. (eds.) Inscrypt 2022. LNCS, vol. 13837, pp. 213–233. Springer, Cham (2023). https://doi.org/10.1007/978-3-031-26553-2_11

18. Liu, Y., Sasaki, Y.: Related-key boomerang attacks on GIFT with automated trail search including BCT effect. In: Jang-Jaccard, J., Guo, F. (eds.) ACISP 2019. LNCS, vol. 11547, pp. 555–572. Springer, Cham (2019). https://doi.org/10.1007/978-3-030-21548-4_30

19. Mouha, N., Wang, Q., Gu, D., Preneel, B.: Differential and linear cryptanalysis using mixed-integer linear programming. In: Wu, C.-K., Yung, M., Lin, D. (eds.) Inscrypt 2011. LNCS, vol. 7537, pp. 57–76. Springer, Heidelberg (2012). https://doi.org/10.1007/978-3-642-34704-7_5

20. Sasaki, Yu.: Integer linear programming for three-subset meet-in-the-middle attacks: application to GIFT. In: Inomata, A., Yasuda, K. (eds.) IWSEC 2018. LNCS, vol. 11049, pp. 227–243. Springer, Cham (2018). https://doi.org/10.1007/978-3-319-97916-8_15

21. Sasaki, Yu., Todo, Y.: New impossible differential search tool from design and cryptanalysis aspects. In: Coron, J.-S., Nielsen, J.B. (eds.) EUROCRYPT 2017, Part III. LNCS, vol. 10212, pp. 185–215. Springer, Cham (2017). https://doi.org/10.1007/978-3-319-56617-7_7

22. Selçuk, A.A.: On probability of success in linear and differential cryptanalysis. J. Cryptol. 21(1), 131–147 (2008). https://doi.org/10.1007/s00145-007-9013-7

23. Song, L., Qin, X., Hu, L.: Boomerang connectivity table revisited. Application to SKINNY and AES. IACR Trans. Symmetric Cryptol. 2019(1), 118–141 (2019). https://doi.org/10.13154/tosc.v2019.i1.118-141

24. Song, L., et al.: Optimizing rectangle attacks: a unified and generic framework for key recovery. In: ASIACRYPT 2022, Part I. LNCS, vol. 13791, pp. 410–440. Springer, Cham (2023). https://doi.org/10.1007/978-3-031-22963-3_14

25. Sun, L., Wang, W., Wang, M.: Accelerating the search of differential and linear characteristics with the SAT method. IACR Trans. Symmetric Cryptol. 2021(1), 269–315 (2021). https://doi.org/10.46586/tosc.v2021.i1.269-315

26. Sun, L., Wang, W., Wang, M.: Improved attacks on GIFT-64. In: AlTawy, R., Hülsing, A. (eds.) SAC 2021. LNCS, vol. 13203, pp. 246–265. Springer, Cham (2022). https://doi.org/10.1007/978-3-030-99277-4_12

27. Sun, S., Hu, L., Wang, P., Qiao, K., Ma, X., Song, L.: Automatic security evaluation and (related-key) differential characteristic search: application to SIMON, PRESENT, LBlock, DES(L) and other bit-oriented block ciphers. In: Sarkar, P., Iwata, T. (eds.) ASIACRYPT 2014, Part I. LNCS, vol. 8873, pp. 158–178. Springer, Heidelberg (2014). https://doi.org/10.1007/978-3-662-45611-8_9

28. Wagner, D.: The boomerang attack. In: Knudsen, L. (ed.) FSE 1999. LNCS, vol. 1636, pp. 156–170. Springer, Heidelberg (1999). https://doi.org/10.1007/3-540-48519-8_12

29. Xiang, Z., Zhang, W., Bao, Z., Lin, D.: Applying MILP method to searching integral distinguishers based on division property for 6 lightweight block ciphers. In: Cheon, J.H., Takagi, T. (eds.) ASIACRYPT 2016. LNCS, vol. 10031, pp. 648–678. Springer, Heidelberg (2016). https://doi.org/10.1007/978-3-662-53887-6_24

30. Yu, Q., Qin, L., Dong, X., Jia, K.: Improved related-key rectangle attacks On GIFT. Comput. J. bxad071 (2023). https://doi.org/10.1093/comjnl/bxad071

31. Zhao, B., Dong, X., Meier, W., Jia, K., Wang, G.: Generalized related-key rectangle attacks on block ciphers with linear key schedule: applications to SKINNY and GIFT. Des. Codes Cryptogr. 88(6), 1103–1126 (2020). https://doi.org/10.1007/s10623-020-00730-1

Side-Channel Attacks
and Countermeasures

Mask Compression: High-Order Masking on Memory-Constrained Devices

Markku-Juhani O. Saarinen[1]([✉]) and Mélissa Rossi[2]

[1] PQShield Ltd., Oxford, UK
mjos@pqshield.com
[2] ANSSI, Paris, France
melissa.rossi@ssi.gouv.fr

Abstract. Masking is a well-studied method for achieving provable security against side-channel attacks. In masking, each sensitive variable is split into d randomized shares, and computations are performed with those shares. In addition to the computational overhead of masked arithmetic, masking also has a storage cost, increasing the requirements for working memory and secret key storage proportionally with d.

In this work, we introduce mask compression. This conceptually simple technique is based on standard, non-masked symmetric cryptography. Mask compression allows an implementation to dynamically replace individual shares of large arithmetic objects (such as polynomial rings) with κ-bit cryptographic seeds (or temporary keys) when they are not in computational use. Since κ does not need to be larger than the security parameter (e.g., $\kappa = 256$ bits) and each polynomial share may be several kilobytes in size, this radically reduces the memory requirement of high-order masking. Overall provable security properties can be maintained using appropriate gadgets to manage the compressed shares. We describe gadgets with Non-Interference (NI) and composable Strong-Non Interference (SNI) security arguments.

Mask compression can be applied in various settings, including symmetric cryptography, code-based cryptography, and lattice-based cryptography. It is especially useful for cryptographic primitives that allow quasilinear-complexity masking and are practically capable of very high masking orders. We illustrate this with a $d = 32$ (Order-31) implementation of the recently introduced lattice-based signature scheme Raccoon on an FPGA platform with limited memory resources.

Keywords: Side-Channel Security · Mask Compression · Raccoon Signature Scheme · Post-Quantum Cryptography

1 Introduction

Physical side-channel attacks exploit sensitive information leaked by a cryptography system via externally observable characteristics such as Timing [20], Power consumption (SPA/DPA) [21,22], and Electromagnetic emissions [30].

© The Author(s), under exclusive license to Springer Nature Switzerland AG 2024
C. Carlet et al. (Eds.): SAC 2023, LNCS 14201, pp. 65–81, 2024.
https://doi.org/10.1007/978-3-031-53368-6_4

Currently, NIST and the cryptographic community are engaged in a wide-reaching transition effort to use Post-Quantum Cryptography (PQC) algorithms such as Kyber [2] (a lattice-based key establishment scheme) and Dilithium [4] (a lattice-based signature scheme) to replace older quantum-vulnerable RSA and Elliptic Curve based cryptography [1,26]. In many prominent use cases, this transition requires physical side-channel security from PQC implementations: Authentication tokens, Mobile/IoT device platform security (secure boot, firmware update, attestation), smart cards, and other secure elements.

Masking. Masking is a general technique to attain side-channel security by splitting sensitive variables into d randomized shares, where $t = d - 1$ is the *masking order*. Each share individually appears uniformly random, and all d shares are required to determine their sum, which is the actual masked quantity. We write $[\![x]\!]$ to denote a masked representation of x. The relationship may be either an exclusive-or operation ("Boolean masking") or modular ("Arithmetic masking"):

$$\text{Boolean masking: } [\![x]\!] = x_0 \oplus x_1 \oplus \ldots \oplus x_t \qquad (1)$$
$$\text{Arithmetic masking: } [\![x]\!] = x_0 + x_1 + \ldots + x_{d-1} \pmod{q}. \qquad (2)$$

PQC algorithm side-channel countermeasures are primarily based on masking. For example, see [6,14] for details about masking Kyber, and [3,24] for Dilithium. High-order computation on the shares is relatively complex in the case of these two algorithms, requiring both Boolean and Arithmetic masking.

Complexity of Attack and Defence. In addition to practicality, one main advantage of masking over more ad-hoc approaches is that it allows one to prove side-channel security properties of implementations. In pioneering work, Chari et al. [7] showed that in the presence of Gaussian noise, the number of side-channel observations required to determine x from individual bits grows exponentially with the number of shares d. The understanding of this exponential relationship has since been made more precise both theoretically and in practice [13,18,23].

In [15], Ishai et al. introduced the probing model: the notion of t-probing security states that the joint distribution of any set of at most t internal intermediate values should be independent of any of the secrets. Thus, a circuit is t-probing secure iff it is secure against observations of $t = d-1$ wires. Reductions from the probing model to the noisy leakage model [12,29] exist and allow to link t-probing security with realistic leakage models.

In addition, [15] showed that any circuit can be transformed into a t-probing secure circuit of size $O(nt^2)$. It has since been demonstrated that quasilinear $O(t \log t)$ masking complexity can be achieved for some primitives, including the Lattice-based signature scheme Raccoon [27,28].

Structure of this Paper and Our Contributions. The mask compression technique is introduced in Sect. 2, which also discusses how it can be applied in practice. Further security discussion is given in Sect. 3, including requirements for composability (strong non-interference). Section 4 gives a practical example of a very high-order PQC scheme (Raccoon [28] with $d = 32$ shares) implemented with Mask Compression on FPGA with 128kB of physical SRAM, instead of several megabytes that would be required without it.

2   Mask Compression

Mask compression in a group G (Eqs. 1 or 2) requires a symmetric cryptography primitive $\mathsf{Sample}_G(z)$ that maps short binary keys z to elements in G. The function is used to manipulate sensitive variables, but thanks to the way it is used, $\mathsf{Sample}_G(z)$ itself does *not* need to be masked. Its input and output variables are generally ephemeral (single-use) individual shares.

Definition 1. *(Informal). The function $x \leftarrow \mathsf{Sample}_G(z)$ uses the input seed $z \in \{0,1\}^\kappa$ to sample a pseudorandom element $x \in G$ deterministically. We assume that Sample_G is cryptographically secure under a suitable definition.*

For a technical discussion of pseudorandomness, see [19, Section 3] (the definitions offered for binary strings can be easily extended to other uniform distributions.) Intuitively, we assume that the task of distinguishing x from a uniformly random element in set G is computationally hard. Typically key size κ is selected to match the overall security level of the system. In this case, distinguishing x should not be substantially easier than an exhaustive search for z.

Practical Instantiation. We can implement $\mathsf{Sample}_G(z)$ with an extendable output function (XOF) such as SHAKE [25][1] The function can also be instantiated with a stream cipher or a block cipher (in counter mode). If a mapping from XOF output to non-binary uniform distributions is required, one may use rejection sampling since each $\mathsf{XOF}(z)$ defines an arbitrarily long bit sequence.

Examples of sampled $|G| \gg 2^\kappa$ include large-degree polynomials that are ring elements $\mathbb{Z}_q[x]/(x^n + 1)$ in Kyber [2] and Dilithium [4]. Note that implementations Kyber and Dilithium already have subroutines that generate uniform polynomial coefficients in $\mathbb{Z}/q\mathbb{Z}$ from XOF output via rejection sampling. In common lattice algorithms, an efficient (unmasked) method for this task is required to create polynomials for $\mathbf{A}$ generator matrix on the fly. This is the reason why a PQC hardware implementation (such as the one discussed in Sect. 4) will often have an efficient instance of $\mathsf{Sample}_G(z)$ available.

Definition 2 (Compressed Mask Set). *A compressed mask set consists of a tuple $[\![x]\!]^z = (x_0, z_1, \cdots, z_t)$ satisfying $x \equiv x_0 + \sum_{i=1}^t \mathsf{Sample}_G(z_i)$ with $x_0 \in G$ and $z_i \in \{0,1\}^\kappa$ for $i \in [1,t]$.*

Theorem 1. *It is computationally infeasible to determine information about x from any subset of $t = d - 1$ elements in compressed masking d-tuple $[\![x]\!]^z$.*

---

[1] FIPS 202 presents a SHAKE specifically as an extensible output function (XOF), which is defined as a hash function with arbitrary-length input and output.

Proof. If x_0 is not known, x can be any value. If one of z_i is unavailable, the indistinguishability property of $\mathsf{Sample}_G(z_i)$ makes x similarly indistinguishable (Fig. 1).

Compress (x_0, x_1) as (x_0', z_1').   **Extract (x_0, x_1), refresh (x_0', z_1').**

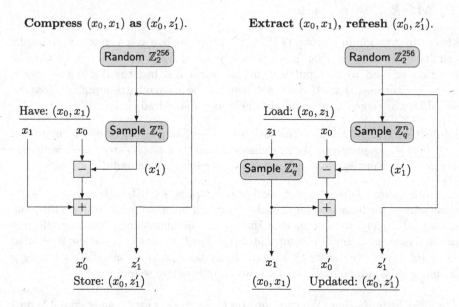

Fig. 1. Illustrating first-order ($t = 1$, $d = 2$) mask compression. Let $[\![x]\!] = (x_0, x_1)$ consist of a pair of degree-n polynomials ($n = 256$ for Kyber, Dilithium) with integer coefficients $\in \mathbb{Z}_q$. Function $\mathsf{Sample}_{\mathbb{Z}_q^n}(z)$ takes a 256-bit key z and uniformly samples a polynomial from it (similarly to $\mathsf{ExpandA}(z)$ in Dilithium and $\mathsf{Parse}(\mathsf{XOF}(z))$ in Kyber.) On the left-hand side, a "compression" algorithm (analogous to Algorithm 1) creates a 256-bit random z_1' and samples a random polynomial x_1' using it. It then subtracts x_1' from x_0 and then adds x_1 to the result, producing x_0'. This construction is exactly like a trivial first-order refresh algorithm, except that instead of (x_0', x_1'), we store (x_0', z_1'), which has a significantly smaller since z_1' is only 256 bits. While $x_1' \leftarrow \mathsf{Sample}_{\mathbb{Z}_q^n}(z_1')$ would suffice for decompression (once), on the right-hand side, we present a simultaneous refresh mechanism (analogous to Algorithm 2) that allows repeated extractions.

Encoding Size. From Theorem 1, we observe that the compressed masking inherits the basic security properties of regular masked encoding. However, the size of the representation is only $\log_2 |G| + d\kappa$ bits, while a regular representation requires $(d + 1) \log_2 |G|$ bits. In the case of Kyber, polynomials are typically packed in $12 * 256 = 3072$ bits, while Dilithium ring elements require $23 * 256 = 5888$ bits. In compressed masking, this is the size of the x_0^z element only, while z_i variables are $\kappa = 256$ bits.

Algorithm 1: $[\![x]\!]^z = \mathsf{MaskCompress}([\![x]\!])$ *(Proved t-NI in Th. 2)*

Input: Masking $[\![x]\!] = (x_0, x_1, \cdots, x_t)$.
Output: Compressed masking $[\![x]\!]^z$ with $x_0^z + \sum_{i=1}^{t} \mathsf{Sample}_G(z_i) = \sum_{i=0}^{t} x_i$.
1: $x_0^z = x_0$
2: **for** $i = 1, 2, \cdots, t$ **do**
3:    $z_i \leftarrow \mathsf{Random}(\kappa)$ ▷ Random Bit Generator, κ bits.
4:    $x_0^z \leftarrow x_0^z - \mathsf{Sample}_G(z_i)$
5:    $x_0^z \leftarrow x_0^z + x_i$
6: **return** $[\![x]\!]^z = (x_0^z, z_1, z_2, \cdots, z_t)$

Conversions. We obtain a trivial mapping from compressed encoding $[\![x]\!]^z$ to the general masked encoding $[\![x]\!]$ by setting $x_0 = x_0^z$ and $x_i = \mathsf{Sample}_G(z_i)$ for $i \in [1, d]$. Security follows from the observation that this conversion is "linear" in the sense that there is no interaction between shares.

Mapping from regular to compressed format requires interaction between the shares since Sample_G is not invertible. Algorithm 1 $\mathsf{MaskCompress}$ presents one way of performing this conversion. We note its resemblance to the $\mathsf{RefreshMasks}$ algorithm of Rivain and Prouff ([31, Algorithm 4]); its NI security follows similarly (see Sect. 3 for more details). While it is secure if used appropriately, combining it with other algorithms may expose leakage, as demonstrated in [9]. Depending on requirements, it can be combined with additional refresh steps to build an SNI [5] algorithm (also see Sect. 3 for more details).

Algorithm 2: $x_i = \mathsf{LoadShare}([\![x]\!]^z, i)$

Input: Compressed masking $[\![x]\!]^z$ satisfying $x = x_0^z + \sum_{i=1}^{t} \mathsf{Sample}_G(z_i)$
Input: Index i for the share to be accessed.
Output: If read in order, $i = 0, 1, \cdots t$, the returned $\{x_i\}$ is a fresh masking $[\![x]\!]$.
1: **if** $i = 0$ **then**
2:    $x_i^{\mathrm{out}} \leftarrow x_0^z$ ▷ Should be accessed first, the rest $i > 0$ only once.
3: **else**
4:    $x_i^{\mathrm{out}} \leftarrow \mathsf{Sample}_G(z_i)$ ▷ Expand the current z_i.
5:    $z_i \leftarrow \mathsf{Random}(\kappa)$ ▷ Update z_i with a Random Bit Generator.
6:    $x_0^z \leftarrow x_0^z - \mathsf{Sample}_G(z_i)$
7:    $x_0^z \leftarrow x_0^z + x_i^{\mathrm{out}}$ ▷ Update x_0^z accordingly.
8: **return** x_i^{out}

Algorithm 3: $[\![x]\!] = \mathsf{FullLoadShare}([\![x]\!]^z)$ *(Proved t-NI Th. 3)*

Input: Compressed masking $[\![x]\!]^z$ satisfying $x = x_0^z + \sum_{i=1}^{t} \mathsf{Sample}_G(z_i)$
Input: Index i for the share to be accessed.
Output: If read in order, $i = 0, 1, \cdots t$, the returned $\{x_i\}$ is a fresh masking $[\![x]\!]$.
  1: **for** $i = 0, 1, \cdots, t$ **do**
  2:    $x_i \leftarrow \mathsf{LoadShare}([\![x]\!]^z, i)$
  3: **return** $(x_0, x_1, \cdots, x_t)$

Computing with Compressed Masking. A key observation for memory conservation is that one does not need to uncompress all shares to perform computations with the compressed masked representation. One can decompress a single share, perform a transformation on that share, compress it, and proceed to the next one. Masked lattice cryptography implementations generally operate sequentially on each share, performing complex linear operations such as Number Theoretic Transforms (NTT) on individual shares without interaction with others. Furthermore, they require individual masked secret key shares only once (or a limited number of times) during a private key operation.

Algorithm 2, $\mathsf{LoadShare}([\![x]\!]^z, i)$ decodes a share $x_i \in G$ from a compressed masking $[\![x]\!]^z$. If the shares are accessed in the sequence $i = 0, 1, 2, \cdots, t$, like presented in Algorithm 3, it is easy to show that their sum will satisfy $x = \sum_{i=0}^{t} x_i$. The compressed masking is refreshed simultaneously (albeit not necessarily in an SNI-composable manner). Subsequent accesses to the same indices will return a different encoding $[\![x]\!]'$.

3 Security Arguments

Let us introduce some standard, intermediate security properties used in security proofs [5,9,31].

Definition 3 (t-Non Interference [5]). *An algorithm is said to be t-non-interfering (written t-NI for short) iff any set of at most t observed internal intermediate variables can be perfectly simulated from at most t shares of each input.*

One can see that t-non interference implies t-probing security. Such a precise definition allows simulation proofs for sequential compositions of non-interferent parts. Note that stronger security notions have been introduced in [5] like the t-strong non-interference to handle more than sequential compositions.

Definition 4 (t-Strong Non Interference[5]). *An algorithm is said t-strongly-non-interfering (written t-SNI for short) if and only if any set of at most $t = t_{\mathrm{int}} + t_{\mathrm{out}}$ observed variables where t_{int} are made on internal data and t_{out} are made on the outputs can be perfectly simulated from at most t_{int} shares of each input.*

We observe that t-strong non-interference implies t-non interference. Any non-interferent algorithm can achieve strong non-interference with an extra mask refreshing of its output [5].

Considering MaskCompress (Algorithm 1), we propose the following Theorem and prove it below.

Theorem 2. *Algorithm 1 is d-Non Interferent under the Pseudorandom Function hypothesis on the* Sample$_G$ *function (Definition 1). Hence, it is also t-probing secure.*

Let us first assume that there exists an index $i^* \in \{1, ..., d\}$ such that both the seed z_{i^*} and the input x_{i^*} are left unobserved by the probing attacker. With a hybrid argument, under the pseudorandomness hypothesis on the Sample$_G(z_{i^*})$ function, Sample$_G(z_{i^*})$ may be replaced by a uniform random value in G, denoted y^*. Hence, all the intermediate values that intervene in the i^*-th iteration can be simulated with uniform random. Therefore, the distribution of the observations can be simulated with at most t shares of the input (x_i for $i \neq i^*$) under the computational assumption.

Now assume that it is not possible to find such an index $i^* \in \{1, ..., d\}$. In that case, all the t observations are made on a combination of x_i for $i \in \{1, t\}$ and z_i for $i \in \{1, t\}$. Let us note that in that case, the input x_0 is always left unobserved. The distribution of x_0^z over all iterations is then statistically indistinguishable from uniform random in G. Hence, the distribution of the observations can be simulated with at most t shares of the input (x_i for $i \in \{1, t\}$).

Algorithm 4: $[\![x]\!]^z = $ SNIMaskCompress($[\![x]\!]$) *(Proved t-SNI in Th. 4)*

Input: Masking $[\![x]\!] = (x_0, x_1, \cdots, x_t)$.
Output: Compressed masking $[\![x]\!]^z$ with $x_0^z + \sum_{i=1}^{t} $ Sample$_G(z_i) = \sum_{i=0}^{t} x_i$.
1: $x_0^z = x_0$
2: **for** $i = 1, 2, \cdots, t$ **do**
3:    $z_i \leftarrow$ Random(κ)
4:    $x_0^z \leftarrow x_0^z - $ Sample$_G(z_i)$
5:    $x_0^z \leftarrow x_0^z + x_i$ ▷ Compared to Alg. 6, x_i is directly accessed
6: **for** $j = 1, 2, \cdots, t$ **do**
7:    **for** $i = 1, 2, \cdots, t$ **do**
8:       $x_i \leftarrow$ Sample$_G(z_i)$
9:       $z_i \leftarrow$ Random(κ)
10:       $x_0^z \leftarrow x_0^z - $ Sample$_G(z_i)$
11:       $x_0^z \leftarrow x_0^z + x_i$
12: **return** $[\![x]\!]^z = (x_0^z, z_1, z_2, \cdots, z_t)$

Let us now consider the LoadShare algorithm. As noted above, the full version of Algorithm 2, presented in Algorithm 3, is very similar to the Non-Interferent RefreshMasks algorithm introduced in [31]. Hence, we introduce the following Theorem.

Theorem 3. *Algorithm 3 is d-Non Interferent and thus t-probing secure under the pseudorandomness hypothesis on the* Sample$_G$ *function (Definition 1).*

Since there are $t+1$ iterations and at most t observations, there exists an index $i^* \in \{0, ..., t\}$ designating an iteration that is left unobserved by the probing attacker. Hence both the input seed z_{i^*} and the value x_0^z (of the i^*-th iteration) are left unobserved. In that case, all the subsequent updates of x_0^z can be replaced with uniform random under the same pseudorandomness hypothesis of Sample$_G$. Finally, all the attacker's observations may be simulated with $(x_0, (z_i)_{i \neq i^*})$ if $i^* \neq 0$ and all the (z_i) otherwise. There are no more than t shares of the input, which concludes the proof.

Algorithm 5: $x_i =$ SNILoadShare($[\![x]\!]^z, i$)

Input: Compressed masking $[\![x]\!]^z$ satisfying $x = x_0^z + \sum_{i=1}^{t}$ Sample$_G(z_i)$
Input: Index i for the share to be accessed.
Output: If read in order, $i = 0, 1, \cdots t$, the returned $\{x_i\}$ is a fresh masking $[\![x]\!]$.
  1: **if** $i = 0$ **then**
  2:    $x_i^{\text{out}} \leftarrow x_0^z$ $\triangleright$ Should be accessed first, the rest $i > 0$ only once.
  3: **else**
  4:    $x_i^{\text{out}} \leftarrow$ Sample$_G(z_i)$ $\triangleright$ Expand the current z_i.
  5: **for** $j = 1, 2, \cdots, t$ **do**
  6:    $x_j \leftarrow$ Sample$_G(z_j)$
  7:    $z_j \leftarrow$ Random(κ) $\triangleright$ Update z_i with a Random Bit Generator.
  8:    $x_0^z \leftarrow x_0^z -$ Sample$_G(z_j)$
  9:    $x_0^z \leftarrow x_0^z + x_j$ $\triangleright$ Update x_0^z accordingly.
10: **return** x_i^{out}

Strong Non Interference. Our mask compression design does not immediately reach the strong non-interference security notion; thus, it cannot be directly composed in complex designs. As outlined above, for safe composition properties, applying a Strong Non-Interferent mask refreshing like introduced in [8] is important. We present in Algorithm 6 an SNI refresh procedure on compressed masks. Applying Algorithm 6 at the beginning of FullLoadShare and at the end MaskCompress allows one to easily reach the strong Non-Interference property.

However, it is also possible to slightly save some randomness and directly transform both our algorithms such that they reach the SNI property. We introduce them in Algorithm 4, 5 and 7.

Please note that these three SNI gadgets will not be used in Sect. 4 for Raccoon, but they are provided here for potential other applications.

Algorithm 6: $[\![x]\!]^z = \mathsf{SNIRefresh}([\![x]\!])$ *(Proved t-SNI in Th. 4)*

Input: Compressed masking $[\![x]\!]^z$
Output: Compressed masking $[\![x]\!]^z$ with fresh shares.
1: **for** $j = 0, 1, \cdots, t$ **do**
2:    **for** $i = 1, 2, \cdots, t$ **do**
3:        $x_i \leftarrow \mathsf{Sample}_G(z_i)$
4:        $z_i \leftarrow \mathsf{Random}(\kappa)$
5:        $x_0^z \leftarrow x_0^z - \mathsf{Sample}_G(z_i)$
6:        $x_0^z \leftarrow x_0^z + x_i$
7: **return** $[\![x]\!]^z = (x_0^z, z_1, z_2, \cdots, z_t)$

Algorithm 7: $[\![x]\!] = \mathsf{FullLoadShare}([\![x]\!]^z)$ *(Proved t-SNI Th. 4)*

Input: Compressed masking $[\![x]\!]^z$ satisfying $x = x_0^z + \sum_{i=1}^t \mathsf{Sample}_G(z_i)$
Input: Index i for the share to be accessed.
Output: If read in order, $i = 0, 1, \cdots t$, the returned $\{x_i\}$ is a fresh masking $[\![x]\!]$.
1: **for** $i = 0 \cdots, t$ **do**
2:    $x_i \leftarrow \mathsf{SNILoadShare}([\![x]\!]^z, i)$
3: **return** $(x_0, x_1, \cdots, x_t)$

Theorem 4. *Algorithm 4, 6, and 7 are d-Strongly Non-Interferent under the Pseudorandomness hypothesis of* Sample_G *function (Definition Algorithm 1). They may be safely composed in complex designs.*

In Algorithm 4 and 6, since there are $t + 1 = d$ iterations (with one outside of the loop with index j for Algorithm 4) and t observations, at least one iteration is left unobserved. All the observations (including the observations on the output) performed after the unobserved iteration can be simulated with uniform random (under the same pseudorandomness hypothesis). All the observations performed before the unobserved iteration can be simulated with at most t shares of the input (inherited from the NI property of Algorithm 1). For Algorithm 7, one can switch the loops for i and j and apply the same reasoning.

4   Experiment: Order-31 Lattice Signatures

We illustrate Mask Compressions with Raccoon[2] at very high masking order 31 (number of shares $d = t + 1 = 32$) [28]. The unit performs all of the masked arithmetic in KeyGen(), and Sign(), and also implements Verif(). We will focus on the masked signing process, reproduced in Algorithm 8.

Overview of the Hardware. The FPGA implementation contains an RV32C controller, a 24-cycle Keccak accelerator, and a lattice unit with direct memory access via a 64-bit interface. The lattice unit has hard-coded support for Raccoon's mod q arithmetic. It can perform arbitrary-length vector arithmetic operations such as polynomial addition, coefficient multiplication, NTT butterfly operations, and shifts on 64-bit words. The FPGA implementation has a 5-cycle modular multiplier with a 64-to-49 bit fixed-modulus reduction circuit. All variants of Raccoon utilize the same modulus q, allowing "hard-coded" reduction circuitry to be used to implement them all.

Since the implementation is designed for masking, the circuitry also has a fast "random fill" function that generates non-deterministic masking randomness rapidly. In a production implementation, this function would require special attention to guarantee that the randomness used in each share is genuinely independent, but trivial entropy sources with simple ASCON [11] -based mixing function was used in the prototype.

4.1   Sample$_G(z)$ in Hardware

Crucially, the hardware can directly perform mod q rejection sampling from streaming SHAKE output to memory. Since a full Keccak round is implemented in hardware, it produces output at a very high rate, theoretically an entire block (136 bytes for SHAKE-256) every 24 cycles. This function works in parallel with other operations. We found that bus access and arithmetic steps tend to be the performance bottlenecks rather than the rejection sampling component.

In addition to implementing Sample$_G(z)$, the rejection sampler eliminates perhaps the most significant performance bottleneck in microcontroller lattice-based PQC implementations: It was initially intended to generate the $k \times \ell$ polynomial matrix **A** on the fly (Lines 2 and 12 in Algorithm 8, similar requirement in key generation and verification functions.) Such on-the-fly generation of **A** is also required in Kyber and Dilithium implementations. Hence, a rejection sampler of this type can be expected to be available in dedicated PQC hardware.

---

[2] The discussion applies to the version of Raccoon published at IEEE S&P 2023 [28]. There are differences to the Raccoon version submitted to the NIST PQC Call [27].

Share Access Gadgets. For this implementation, we used gadgets based on Algorithm 1 and 2, implemented as a library call with an "API" for loading and storing mask sets consistently (so that leakage characteristics would be uniform). Note that while the introduced SNI gadgets are not used in Raccoon – this would violate the quasilinear complexity requirement – the NI gadgets in Algorithm 1 and 2 suffice to ensure the probing security of Raccoon. One polynomial (x_0 in Definition 2) was held as full 64-bit integers to facilitate fast hardware arithmetic, while the rest ($t = 31$ shares) were stored as $\kappa = 256$ bit seeds. Note that each arithmetic step utilized the shares one at a time (thanks to the requirements of the quasilinear lattice cryptography) $i = 0, 1, \cdots, t$. When a share i was required for arithmetic, an implementation of Algorithm 2 gadget was called. For storing $i = 0, 1, \cdots, t$, the share $i = 0$ was stored in full, while the rest utilized Lines 3–6 of Algorithm 1 to update it. The implementation of Decode function does not require simultaneous refresh, so it is sufficient to compute $x_0 + \sum_{i=1}^{t} \mathsf{Sample}_G(z_i)$.

Memory Footprint. Algorithm 8 has been annotated with the share-access gadgets used in each stage, which allow the implementation to use mask compression on each sensitive variable. All of these are vectors of polynomial rings $\mathcal{R}_q$, with dimension depending on the security level $\lambda_{\mathsf{target}} \in \{128, 192, 256\}$ [28, Table 3]. Focusing on the "Category 1" Raccoon-128 parameter sets the vector length is either $\ell = 3$ (for $[\![r]\!]$, $[\![s]\!]$, and $[\![z]\!]$) or $k = 8$ (for $[\![u]\!]$ and $[\![w]\!]$.) For the masked variables, only the secret key $[\![s]\!]$ needs to be retained for repeated use. Not all internal variables are used concurrently, and hence e.g., $[\![u]\!]$ and $[\![w]\!]$ can occupy the same memory as $[\![r]\!]$ and $[\![z]\!]$. Hence this Raccoon implementation requires $\ell = 3$ masked polynomials for persistent storage (secret key), and additional $\ell + k = 11$ for working memory.

To estimate the minimum memory requirement at $t = 31$ without mask compression, we assume that each polynomial coefficient is bit-packed into $\lceil \log_2 q \rceil = 49$ bits; hence a masked polynomial requires $d \times n \times 49 = 802,816$ bits. For both secret key and working memory, this comes to roughly 1.4 megabytes (close to 2 MB if coefficients are stored in an access-friendly manner as 64-bit integers.)

With mask compression, the size of each masked polynomial drops to $n \times 49 + t \times \kappa = 33,024$ bits, or 4.1% of the uncompressed mask size. This is only a 31.6% increase over completely unmasked implementation, even for the very high masking order of 31; one can well say that the storage cost of masking becomes negligible with mask compression.

The physical FPGA implementation operated well with 128 kB of SRAM, while at least 2000 kB would have been required without compression. The secret key $[\![s]\!]$ size also shrunk from 294 kB to 12.1 kB, which is important as non-volatile storage can be more scarce than working memory.

Algorithm 8: Sign($[\![\mathsf{sk}]\!]$, vk, msg): "IEEE SP '23" Raccoon signing [28, Algorithm 7] with applicable mask compression gadgets annotated in the comments. (Note: There are differences to the "NIST" version [27].)

Input: A masked signing key $[\![\mathsf{sk}]\!]$, a message msg
Output: A signature sig of msg under sk

1: $[\![\mathbf{r}]\!] \leftarrow (\mathcal{R}_q^\ell)^d$ $\triangleright$ In the implementation: A random mask set!
2: $[\![\mathbf{u}]\!] := \mathbf{A} \cdot [\![\mathbf{r}]\!]$ $\triangleright$ Access: NI Alg. 1, 2 or SNI Alg. 4, 5.
3: $[\![\mathbf{u}]\!] \leftarrow \mathsf{Refresh}([\![\mathbf{u}]\!])$ $\triangleright$ Implicit with NI or SNI with Alg. 6.
4: $[\![\mathbf{w}]\!] := \mathsf{ApproxShift}_{q \to q_w}([\![\mathbf{u}]\!])$ $\triangleright$ Access: NI Alg. 1, 2 or SNI Alg. 4, 5.
5: $\mathbf{w} := \mathsf{Decode}([\![\mathbf{w}]\!])$ $\triangleright$ Commitment. NI: Alg. 3 or SNI Alg. 7.
6: $c_{\mathsf{hash}} := H(\mathbf{w}, \mathsf{msg})$ $\triangleright$ Challenge hash. (Not masked.)
7: $c_{\mathsf{poly}} := \mathsf{ChalPoly}(c_{\mathsf{hash}})$ $\triangleright$ Challenge polynomial. (Not masked.)
8: $[\![\mathbf{s}]\!] \leftarrow \mathsf{Refresh}([\![\mathbf{s}]\!])$ $\triangleright$ Implicit with NI or SNI with Alg. 6.
9: $[\![\mathbf{r}]\!] \leftarrow \mathsf{Refresh}([\![\mathbf{r}]\!])$ $\triangleright$ Implicit with NI or SNI with Alg. 6.
10: $[\![\mathbf{z}]\!] := c_{\mathsf{poly}} \cdot [\![\mathbf{s}]\!] + [\![\mathbf{r}]\!]$ $\triangleright$ Access: NI Alg. 1, 2 or SNI Alg. 4, 5.
11: $\mathbf{z} := \mathsf{Decode}([\![\mathbf{z}]\!])$ $\triangleright$ Response. NI: Alg. 3 or SNI Alg. 7.
12: $\mathbf{y} := \mathbf{A} \cdot \mathbf{z} - p_t \cdot c_{\mathsf{poly}} \cdot \mathbf{t}$ $\triangleright$ (The rest is not masked.)
13: $\mathbf{y}^{\mathsf{top}} := \lfloor \mathbf{y} \rfloor_{q \to q_w}$
14: $\mathbf{h} := \mathbf{w} - \mathbf{y}^{\mathsf{top}}$ $\triangleright$ Hint.
15: **if** $(\|\mathbf{h}\|_2 > B_2)$ **or** $(\|\mathbf{h}\|_\infty > B_\infty)$ **then**
16:     **goto** Line 1 $\triangleright$ Check the hint's norms.
17: **return** sig $:= (c_{\mathsf{hash}}, \mathbf{z}, \mathbf{h})$

4.2 Implementation Details and Basic Leakage Assessment

On an XC7A100T (Xilinx Artix 7) FPGA target, this size-optimized design (including a control Core, Keccak unit, lattice coprocessor, masking random number generator, and communication peripherals) was 10,638 Slice LUTs (16.78%), 4,140 Slice registers/Flip Flops, (3.26%) and only 3 DSPs (as logic was used for multipliers – the design is ASIC-oriented). The design was rated for 78.3 MHz. Table 1 summarizes its performance at various masking levels.

Table 1. FPGA cycle counts at various side-channel security levels.

Algorithm	Shares	Keygen()	Sign()	Verif()
Raccoon-128	$d = 2$	1,366,000	2,402,000	1,438,000
Raccoon-128	$d = 4$	2,945,000	3,714,230	1,433,034
Raccoon-128	$d = 8$	6,100,000	6,345,000	1,389,000
Raccoon-128	$d = 16$	12,413,000	11,605,000	1,389,000
Raccoon-128	$d = 32$	25,073,000	22,160,000	1,393,000

Leakage Assessments. We ran a TVLA/17825:2022(E) [17] type leakage assessment on all orders from $d = 2$ up to $d = 32$, with $N = 200,000$ traces at $d = 2$ showing no leakage. Such detection mechanisms are generally limited to first-order leakage, so testing a high-order implementation can be seen as unnecessary. However, in this particular case, there is a risk that the mask compression gadgets have unforeseen leaks.

Fixed vs. Random Test. A non-specific t-test [32] was conducted on the signing function to assess leakage of secret key $[\![s]\!]$. The fixed set of traces consisted of signing operations using synthetic keypairs where the secret $[\![s]\!]$ component was fixed (but refreshed for every operation), and the public $\mathbf{A}$ was randomized. For the signing operation, a synthetic $\mathbf{t}$ is derived with the fixed $[\![s]\!]$ and randomized $\mathbf{A}$. The second random set of traces used completely random keypairs. The message to be signed was constant in both tests.

Critical Value. At order $d = 32$, the leakage assessment was carried out with $N = 20,000$ full traces and passed well under a threshold value matching $\alpha = 10^{-5}$. As noted by several authors, for example, Ding et al. [10] and Oswald et al. [33], the common "TVLA" threshold value 4.5 needs to be adjusted for long traces (the overall false positive rate with millions of points would be close to 1.) The threshold value corresponding to significance level $\alpha = 10^{-5}$ with $l = 2.59 \times 10^6$ time points is $C = 6.94$, using the methodology of [10].

Signal Acquisition and Post-processing. Power signal was acquired from the FPGA chip on the CW305 board [16, Sect. C.3] with a PicoScope 2208B oscilloscope. The test was run with a 24ns (41.7 MHz) clock cycle. Power samples were gathered at the same rate. Each trace of the signature operation contained more than 22 million samples at $d = 32$. The DUT generated a cycle-precise trigger. Random delays and other non-masking countermeasures were disabled.

We applied post-processing steps to improve detection. The waveforms were computationally normalized so that each 1 ms sliding window had $\mu = 0$ and $\sigma^2 = 1$ (effectively, a 1 kHz high-pass filter and dynamic amplitude control). This allowed the traces to match more closely on the vertical axis. The traces were also aligned horizontally using the start and end triggers.

Results. At N=20,000 traces, the maximum t-value was 5.55 (Fig. 2), well under the threshold and corresponding to P-value 0.47. At N=10,000 traces, the test result was $t = 5.43$. We also verified that leakage detection is functional by disabling countermeasures in various ways; spikes rapidly appear in those cases.

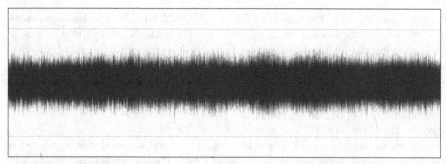

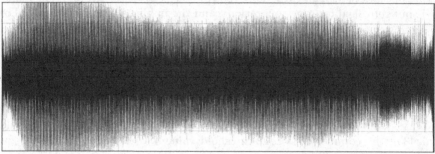

Fig. 2. On top, t-trace of Raccoon-128 ($d = 32$) signature function from $N = 20,000$ waveforms, each with 22.16×10^6 measurements (time on the horizontal axis). No leakage spikes were detected; the t-statistic values are within the critical value boundaries (thin red lines). This test only detects first-order leakage, so it is merely offered as additional evidence related to the implementation of the mask compression gadgets. The bottom figure has $N = 500$ traces of the same implementation with mask randomization disabled; this demonstrates that leakage detection was operational. (Color figure online)

5   Conclusions and Open Problems

We have introduced *Mask Compression*, a method to reduce the memory cost of high-order masking side-channel countermeasures using non-masked symmetric cryptography. This simple technique allows a set of t-order mask shares to have a storage requirement equivalent to a single share and t symmetric keys. The technique nearly halves the memory requirement for first-order Kyber and Dilithium, but its benefits are most significant in higher-order masking. We present security arguments in the well-known NI and SNI frameworks.

To illustrate the technique's utility, we describe an Order-31 implementation of the Raccoon signature scheme [28] where the size of the secret keys is reduced from 294kB to 12kB. The overall memory requirement is reduced from two megabytes to 128 kB, allowing the scheme to be implemented on a resource-constrained FPGA target while maintaining a quasilinear masking complexity and a high level of non-invasive side-channel security. However, this experiment was with NI gadgets only. As an open problem, we are working on closing SNI composability gaps for some of the components and providing SNI gadgets with quasilinear complexity.

References

1. Alagic, G., et al.: Status report on the third round of the NIST post-quantum cryptography standardization process. Interagency or Internal Report NISTIR 8413-upd1, National Institute of Standards and Technology (2022). https://doi. org/10.6028/NIST.IR.8413-upd1. https://csrc.nist.gov/publications/detail/nistir/8413/final

2. Avanzi, R., et al.: CRYSTALS-Kyber: Algorithm specifications and supporting documentation (version 3.02). NIST PQC Project, 3rd Round Submission Update (2021). https://pq-crystals.org/kyber/data/kyber-specification-round3-20210804. pdf

3. Azouaoui, M., et al.: Leveling Dilithium against leakage: revisited sensitivity analysis and improved implementations. IACR ePrint 2022/1406 (2022). https://eprint. iacr.org/2022/1406, fourth PQC Standardization Conference, NIST (Virtual) 29 Nov–1 Dec 2022

4. Bai, S., et al.: CRYSTALS-Dilithium: algorithm specifications and supporting documentation (version 3.1). NIST PQC Project, 3rd Round Submission Update (2021). https://pq-crystals.org/dilithium/data/dilithium-specification-round3-20210208.pdf

5. Barthe, G., et al.: Strong non-interference and type-directed higher-order masking. In: Weippl, E.R., Katzenbeisser, S., Kruegel, C., Myers, A.C., Halevi, S. (eds.) CCS 2016: Proceedings of the 2016 ACM SIGSAC Conference on Computer and Communications Security, Vienna, Austria, 24–28 October 2016, pp. 116–129. ACM (2016). https://doi.org/10.1145/2976749.2978427. http://dl.acm. org/citation.cfm?id=2976749

6. Bos, J.W., Gourjon, M., Renes, J., Schneider, T., van Vredendaal, C.: Masking kyber: first- and higher-order implementations. IACR Trans. Cryptogr. Hardw. Embed. Syst. **2021**(4), 173–214 (2021). https://doi.org/10.46586/tches.v2021.i4. 173-214

7. Chari, S., Jutla, C.S., Rao, J.R., Rohatgi, P.: Towards sound approaches to counteract power-analysis attacks. In: Wiener [34], pp. 398–412. https://doi.org/10. 1007/3-540-48405-1_26

8. Coron, J.-S.: Higher order masking of look-up tables. In: Nguyen, P.Q., Oswald, E. (eds.) EUROCRYPT 2014. LNCS, vol. 8441, pp. 441–458. Springer, Heidelberg (2014). https://doi.org/10.1007/978-3-642-55220-5_25

9. Coron, J.-S., Prouff, E., Rivain, M., Roche, T.: Higher-order side channel security and mask refreshing. In: Moriai, S. (ed.) FSE 2013. LNCS, vol. 8424, pp. 410–424. Springer, Heidelberg (2014). https://doi.org/10.1007/978-3-662-43933-3_21

10. Ding, A.A., Zhang, L., Durvaux, F., Standaert, F.-X., Fei, Y.: Towards sound and optimal leakage detection procedure. In: Eisenbarth, T., Teglia, Y. (eds.) CARDIS 2017. LNCS, vol. 10728, pp. 105–122. Springer, Cham (2018). https://doi.org/10. 1007/978-3-319-75208-2_7

11. Dobraunig, C., Eichlseder, M., Mendel, F., Schläffer, M.: Ascon v1.2. Submission to NIST (Lightweight Cryptography Project) (2021). https://csrc.nist.gov/CSRC/ media/Projects/lightweight-cryptography/documents/finalist-round/updated-spec-doc/ascon-spec-final.pdf

12. Duc, A., Dziembowski, S., Faust, S.: Unifying leakage models: from probing attacks to noisy leakage. J. Cryptol. **32**(1), 151–177 (2019). https://doi.org/10.1007/s00145-018-9284-1

13. Duc, A., Faust, S., Standaert, F.-X.: Making masking security proofs concrete. In: Oswald, E., Fischlin, M. (eds.) EUROCRYPT 2015. LNCS, vol. 9056, pp. 401–429. Springer, Heidelberg (2015). https://doi.org/10.1007/978-3-662-46800-5_16. https://eprint.iacr.org/2015/119, extended version is available as IACR ePrint Report 2015/015

14. Heinz, D., Kannwischer, M.J., Land, G., Pöppelmann, T., Schwabe, P., Sprenkels, D.: First-order masked Kyber on ARM Cortex-M4. IACR ePrint 2022/058 (2022). https://eprint.iacr.org/2022/058

15. Ishai, Y., Sahai, A., Wagner, D.: Private circuits: securing hardware against probing attacks. In: Boneh, D. (ed.) CRYPTO 2003. LNCS, vol. 2729, pp. 463–481. Springer, Heidelberg (2003). https://doi.org/10.1007/978-3-540-45146-4_27

16. ISO: IT security techniques - test tool requirements and test tool calibration methods for use in testing non-invasive attack mitigation techniques in cryptographic modules - part 2: Test calibration methods and apparatus. Standard ISO/IEC 20085-2:2020(E), International Organization for Standardization (2020). https://www.iso.org/standard/70082.html

17. ISO: Information technology - security techniques - testing methods for the mitigation of non-invasive attack classes against cryptographic modules. Draft International Standard ISO/IEC DIS 17825:2022(E), International Organization for Standardization (2023)

18. Ito, A., Ueno, R., Homma, N.: On the success rate of side-channel attacks on masked implementations: information-theoretical bounds and their practical usage. In: Yin, H., Stavrou, A., Cremers, C., Shi, E. (eds.) Proceedings of the 2022 ACM SIGSAC Conference on Computer and Communications Security, CCS 2022, Los Angeles, CA, USA, 7–11 November 2022, pp. 1521–1535. ACM (2022). https://doi.org/10.1145/3548606.3560579. https://eprint.iacr.org/2022/576

19. Katz, J., Lindell, Y.: Introduction to Modern Cryptography, 3rd edn. CRC Press, Boca Raton (2021). https://doi.org/10.1201/9781351133036

20. Kocher, P.C.: Timing attacks on implementations of Diffie-Hellman, RSA, DSS, and other systems. In: Koblitz, N. (ed.) CRYPTO 1996. LNCS, vol. 1109, pp. 104–113. Springer, Heidelberg (1996). https://doi.org/10.1007/3-540-68697-5_9

21. Kocher, P.C., Jaffe, J., Jun, B.: Differential power analysis. In: Wiener [34], pp. 388–397. https://doi.org/10.1007/3-540-48405-1_25

22. Kocher, P.C., Jaffe, J., Jun, B., Rohatgi, P.: Introduction to differential power analysis. J. Cryptogr. Eng. **1**(1), 5–27 (2011). https://doi.org/10.1007/s13389-011-0006-y

23. Masure, L., Rioul, O., Standaert, F.X.: A nearly tight proof of Duc et al.'s conjectured security bound for masked implementations. In: Buhan, I., Schneider, T. (eds.) CARDIS 2022. LNCS, vol. 13820, pp. 69–81. Springer, Cham (2023). https://doi.org/10.1007/978-3-031-25319-5_4. https://eprint.iacr.org/2022/600

24. Migliore, V., Gérard, B., Tibouchi, M., Fouque, P.-A.: Masking Dilithium - efficient implementation and side-channel evaluation. In: Deng, R.H., Gauthier-Umaña, V., Ochoa, M., Yung, M. (eds.) ACNS 2019. LNCS, vol. 11464, pp. 344–362. Springer, Cham (2019). https://doi.org/10.1007/978-3-030-21568-2_17

25. NIST: SHA-3 standard: Permutation-based hash and extendable-output functions. Federal Information Processing Standards Publication FIPS 202 (2015). https://doi.org/10.6028/NIST.FIPS.202

26. NSA: Announcing the commercial national security algorithm suite 2.0. National Security Agency, Cybersecurity Advisory (2022). https://media.defense.gov/2022/Sep/07/2003071834/-1/-1/0/CSA_CNSA_2.0_ALGORITHMS_.PDF

27. del Pino, R., et al.: Raccoon: a side-channel secure signature scheme. Submission to NIST Standardization Call for Additional PQC Signature Schemes (2023). https://github.com/masksign/raccoon/blob/main/doc/raccoon.pdf

28. del Pino, R., Prest, T., Rossi, M., Saarinen, M.J.O.: High-order masking of lattice signatures in quasilinear time. In: 44th IEEE Symposium on Security and Privacy, SP 2023, San Francisco, CA, USA, 22–25 May 2023, pp. 1168–1185. IEEE (2023). https://doi.org/10.1109/SP46215.2023.00160

29. Prouff, E., Rivain, M.: Masking against side-channel attacks: a formal security proof. In: Johansson, T., Nguyen, P.Q. (eds.) EUROCRYPT 2013. LNCS, vol. 7881, pp. 142–159. Springer, Heidelberg (2013). https://doi.org/10.1007/978-3-642-38348-9_9

30. Quisquater, J.-J., Samyde, D.: ElectroMagnetic analysis (EMA): measures and counter-measures for smart cards. In: Attali, I., Jensen, T. (eds.) E-smart 2001. LNCS, vol. 2140, pp. 200–210. Springer, Heidelberg (2001). https://doi.org/10.1007/3-540-45418-7_17

31. Rivain, M., Prouff, E.: Provably secure higher-order masking of AES. In: Mangard, S., Standaert, F.-X. (eds.) CHES 2010. LNCS, vol. 6225, pp. 413–427. Springer, Heidelberg (2010). https://doi.org/10.1007/978-3-642-15031-9_28

32. Schneider, T., Moradi, A.: Leakage assessment methodology. In: Güneysu, T., Handschuh, H. (eds.) CHES 2015. LNCS, vol. 9293, pp. 495–513. Springer, Heidelberg (2015). https://doi.org/10.1007/978-3-662-48324-4_25

33. Whitnall, C., Oswald, E.: A critical analysis of ISO 17825 ('testing methods for the mitigation of non-invasive attack classes against cryptographic modules'). In: Galbraith, S.D., Moriai, S. (eds.) ASIACRYPT 2019. LNCS, vol. 11923, pp. 256–284. Springer, Cham (2019). https://doi.org/10.1007/978-3-030-34618-8_9

34. Wiener, M. (ed.): CRYPTO 1999. LNCS, vol. 1666. Springer, Heidelberg (1999). https://doi.org/10.1007/3-540-48405-1

Not so Difficult in the End: Breaking the Lookup Table-Based Affine Masking Scheme

Lichao Wu[1], Guilherme Perin[2], and Stjepan Picek[1(✉)]

[1] Radboud University, Nijmegen, The Netherlands
lichao.wu9@gmail.com
[2] Leiden University, Leiden, The Netherlands

Abstract. The lookup table-based masking countermeasure is prevalent in real-world applications due to its potent resistance against side-channel attacks and low computational cost. The ASCADv2 dataset, for instance, ranks among the most secure publicly available datasets today due to two layers of countermeasures: lookup table-based affine masking and shuffling. Current attack approaches rely on strong assumptions. In addition to requiring access to the source code, an adversary would also need prior knowledge of random shares.

This paper forgoes reliance on such knowledge and proposes two attack approaches based on the vulnerabilities of the lookup table-based affine masking implementation. As a result, the first attack can retrieve all secret keys' reliance in less than a minute without knowing mask shares. Although the second attack is not entirely successful in recovering all keys, we believe more traces would help make such an attack fully functional.

Keywords: Side-channel analysis · Side-channel collision attack · Correlation

1 Introduction

Side-channel analysis (SCA) on symmetric-key cryptography implementations is typically divided into non-profiling [20,31] and profiling attacks [10,37], depending on the availability of a replica of the device under attack (profiling device). Non-profiling attacks operate without this assumption, and an adversary collects measurements that encode secret information and subsequently perform a statistical analysis to form a guess about the secrets. In contrast, profiling attacks assume that the adversary has unrestricted control over a duplicate of the targeted device. Using this duplicate, the adversary identifies and understands the device's side-channel behavior, subsequently leveraging this knowledge to extract secret information from the device under attack. Recent advancements, especially deep learning-based side-channel analysis, have significantly improved profiling attacks. Today, researchers can compromise various protected targets using a single measurement, underscoring the impressive progress in this field [24]. Such results were achieved on datasets only a few years ago considered difficult to

C. Carlet et al. (Eds.): SAC 2023, LNCS 14201, pp. 82–96, 2024.
https://doi.org/10.1007/978-3-031-53368-6_5

break: ASCAD with fixed key and ASCAD with random keys, both protected with the first-order Boolean masking.

However, one dataset is yet to be broken without prior knowledge about the random shares: ASCADv2 [2]. Indeed, this secure AES-128 implementation published by the Agence Nationale de la Sécurité des Systèmes d'Information (ANSSI) has been protected with multiple layers of hiding (shuffling) and masking countermeasures. Specifically, a lookup table-based masking scheme [9,13,28] is adopted, wherein a masked Sbox is pre-computed with random shares before the cryptographic operation. Consequently, any intermediate data leakages relating to the non-linear operation of the cipher are effectively eliminated. Although the weaknesses of lookup table-based masking schemes have been discussed in [32], to our knowledge, a direct key-recovery attack without any prior knowledge of mask shares never succeeded. One of the most significant challenges in overcoming this implementation is the masking schemes that incorporate both multiplicative mask computation with finite field multiplication over $GF(2^8)$ and additive (Boolean) masks. Traditional attacks on the Boolean masked implementation depend on the ability of the profiling model to combine mask shares and masked data to retrieve the sensitive data. For ASCADv2, even though the multiplicative masks significantly leak [23], the additive masked Galois field multiplication is complex for a profiling model to comprehend, even when leveraging deep learning [8]. Therefore, all existing attacks on this dataset are performed in a white-box setting with prior knowledge of the random shares, at least in the profiling phase or in both profiling and attack phases [22,23]. We argue that such assumptions could not be practical even in secure evaluation labs that perform white-box evaluations. Although cryptographic algorithms are evaluated with all implementation details (e.g., source code of the cryptographic library and hardware design details), the random shares would rarely be accessible to an evaluator. The reason is straightforward: the registers that store the random values for the system protection would never be accessible from the outside world unless severe implementation flaws exist. Although it is possible to predict the output of some weak pseudo-random number generators (PRNG) with modeling techniques [1], we consider it difficult considering the unknown random seeds and complexity (e.g., high-order polynomials) of PRNG. Other ways of bypassing such protections are monitoring the random number leakages on data bus with probes or forcing the PRNG stuck at some fixed value with fault injection. However, it highly depends on the implementation, and it is out of the scope of this paper that focus solely on SCA.

This paper presents two vulnerabilities in ASCADv2's affine masking implementation that could lead to successful key recovery without knowledge of the mask shares. With the knowledge of plaintexts, the implementation could be broken down in less than a minute with a CPU only. Note that we disable the shuffling countermeasure and concentrate solely on masking schemes. Although turning on this countermeasure would cause the proposed attack to fail with the number of traces we have, we expect it could be circumvented with, for instance, more leakage measurements [39]. For instance, without further means to overcome the shuffling, one would need approximately 120 times more traces to overcome a true random permutation. Our main contributions are:

1. We conduct an in-depth investigation into two vulnerabilities inherent in implementing the lookup table-based affine masking scheme, substantiating our findings with theoretical analysis.
2. We propose several strategies to execute second-order attacks that leverage the identified vulnerabilities.
3. We demonstrate two attack methodologies that lead to efficient key recovery without the knowledge of the mask shares.
4. We discuss several protection methods that would be resilient to our attack.

The rest of this paper is organized as follows. In Sect. 2, we provide the necessary background information. Section 3 discusses related works. Section 4 details the identified vulnerabilities. In Sect. 5, we provide experimental results. Section 6 discusses the identified vulnerability from a higher level, then offer possible protection methods to defend against proposed attacks. Finally, in Sect. 7, we conclude the paper and discuss potential future research directions.

2 Preliminaries

This section introduces the notation we follow. Afterward, the relevant information about the side-channel analysis, collision attack, and the targeted ASCADv2 dataset is discussed.

2.1 Notation

We utilize calligraphic letters such as $\mathcal{X}$ to represent sets, while the corresponding uppercase letters X denote random variables and random vectors $\mathbf{X}$ defined over $\mathcal{X}$. Realizations of X and $\mathbf{X}$ are denoted by lowercase letters x and $\mathbf{x}$, respectively. Functions, such as f, are presented in a sans-serif font.

The symbol k represents a candidate key byte in a key space $\mathcal{K}$. The notation k^* refers to the correct key byte or the key byte assumed to be correct by the adversary[1].

A dataset $\mathbf{T}$ comprises traces $\mathbf{t}_i$, which are associated with plaintext/ciphertext pairs $\mathbf{d}_i$ in plaintext/ciphertext space $\mathcal{D}$ and keys $\mathbf{k}_i$, or $k_{i,j}$ and $d_{i,j}$ when considering partial key recovery on byte j. Throughout this work, we focus on a fixed key scenario where $\mathbf{k}_i$ remains constant for each trace $\mathbf{t}_i$, resulting in the utilization of byte vector notation exclusively in equations.

2.2 Side-Channel Analysis

As briefly mentioned in the introduction section, side-channel analysis (SCA) can be broadly classified into two types, profiling SCA and non-profiling SCA, based on the availability of a fully-controlled cloned device. Non-profiling side-channel analysis exploits the correlation between key-related intermediate values

---

[1] It is important to note that subkey candidates can involve guessing any number of bits. Although we assume the AES cipher here, the concept remains algorithm-independent.

and leakage measurements. An adversary collects a series of traces generated during the encryption of different plaintexts. The adversary can guess a key portion by examining the correlation between the key-related intermediate values and the leakage measurements. The attack strategy typically involves a "divide-and-conquer" approach. First, an adversary divides the traces into groups based on the predicted intermediate value corresponding to the current key guess. If the groups exhibit noticeable differences (the definition of "difference" depends on the attack method), it suggests that the current key guess is likely correct. The non-profiling attacks assume relatively weaker adversaries who do not have access to a cloned device. Consequently, these attacks may require many measurements (potentially millions) to extract confidential information. Examples of non-profiling attacks include simple power analysis (SPA), differential power analysis (DPA) [20]/correlation power analysis (CPA) [7], and some machine learning-based attacks [16,31,38]. Note that side-channel collision attack [5,29] and its deep learning version [30] are also considered a non-profiling SCA but follows a slightly different strategy, discussed in the next section.

Profiling side-channel attacks aim to map a set of inputs (e.g., side-channel traces) to outputs (e.g., a probability vector of key hypotheses). Profiling attacks involve two phases. In the profiling phase, the adversary constructs a profiling model f_θ^M, parameterized by a leakage model M and a set of learning parameters θ. This model maps the inputs (side-channel measurements) to the outputs (classes obtained by evaluating the leakage model during a sensitive operation) using a set of N profiling traces. The notations f_θ^M and f_θ are used interchangeably. Then, in the attack phase, the trained model processes each attack trace t_i and produces a vector of probabilities p_j, representing the likelihood of the associated leakage value or label j. The adversary determines the best key candidate based on this vector of probabilities. If the adversary constructs an effective profiling model, only a few measurements from the target device may be sufficient to break its security. Examples of profiling attacks include the template attack [10], stochastic models [27], and supervised machine learning-based attacks [19,21,25].

2.3 Side-Channel Collision Attack

Side-channel Collision Attack (SCCA) represents a class of non-profiling attacks that leverage information dependence leaked during cryptographic processes. Traditional collision attacks capitalize on situations where two distinct inputs into a cryptographic algorithm yield an identical output, a circumstance known as a "collision". Since collisions are generally infrequent in robustly designed cryptographic systems, SCCA explicitly targets the internal state, which is more likely to be identical.

In SCCA, an adversary observes the side-channel information as the system processes different inputs. The adversary then scans for patterns or similarities in the side-channel data that indicate a collision has occurred. Upon identifying a collision, the adversary can utilize this knowledge to deduce information about the inter-dependencies of different key portions or the algorithm's internal state, thereby significantly reducing the remaining key space.

As an illustration, let us consider the SubBytes operation of the Advanced Encryption Standard (AES) [15]. The same intermediate data (Sbox input or output) could be processed if two different Sbox operations result in an identical side-channel pattern. Since the Sbox operation is bijective (i.e., a one-to-one correspondence between two sets), we have the following equations:

$$
\begin{aligned}
\mathsf{Sbox}(k_i \oplus p_i) &= \mathsf{Sbox}(k_j \oplus p_j) \\
\implies k_i \oplus p_i &= k_j \oplus p_j \\
\implies k_i \oplus k_j &= p_i \oplus p_j.
\end{aligned}
\tag{1}
$$

Note that a collision of Sbox input would also satisfy $k_i \oplus k_j = p_i \oplus p_j$. Indeed, in contrast to other SCA methods concentrating on key recovery, SCCA aims to uncover the linear difference between various keys. By making guesses on a single subkey, an adversary can leverage this linear difference to compute the remainder of the key. This essentially reduces the remaining key space to the equivalent of a single byte, 2^8.

2.4   The ANSSI's AES Implementation: ASCADv2

ANSSI has published a library implementing a secure AES-128 on an ARM Cortex-M4 architecture [2] together with 800 000 power measurements focusing on the full AES encryption. This implementation is equipped with several layers of countermeasures, such as affine secret-sharing [17] and random shuffling of independent operations [36]. We briefly discuss their implementations in this section. More implementation details can be found on the corresponding GitHub page [2] and paper [8,23].

An overview of generating a mask state C_i with an AES state X_i is shown in Eq. 2.

$$
C_i = (X_i \otimes \alpha) \oplus \beta,
\tag{2}
$$

where i stands for byte indices. Two random shares realize the affine masking scheme: the multiplicative share α and additive share β. Finite field multiplication over $\mathsf{GF}(2^8)$ and xor are denoted by $\otimes$ and $\oplus$, respectively. Note that β may denote Sbox's input mask r_{in}, Sbox's output mask r_{out}, or r_l, the mask used in the linear operation of AES[2]. To ensure there is no direct leakage on the AES state, a masked Sbox, denoted as Sbox_m, is pre-computed for all bytes based on r_{in}, r_{out} and α, enabling the processing of the masked data in the non-linear part of AES, illustrated in Eq. 3. Note that r_l is removed after r_{in} is applied and added before r_{out} is canceled. Therefore, sensitive states are masked during the entire AES process.

$$
(X_i \otimes \alpha) \oplus r_{in} \xrightarrow{\ \mathsf{Sbox}_m\ } (\mathsf{Sbox}(X_i) \otimes \alpha) \oplus r_{out}.
\tag{3}
$$

The random shares α, r_{in}, and r_{out} remain the same during the computations of each byte and are refreshed in the next AES operation.

---

[2] The proposed attack target the intermediate data when $\beta = r_{in}$ and $\beta = r_{out}$.

Random permutations are applied to ShiftRows, MixColumns, and Sbox executions; the permutations indices for each byte are generated based on random seeds.

3 Related Works

Side-channel analysis has been widely researched and applied to different cryptographic algorithms during past decades. Multiple attack methods have been developed, such as direct (non-profiled) attacks like Simple Power Analysis (SPA), Differential Power Analysis (DPA) [20], and two-stage (profiling) attacks like the template attack [10]. Machine learning-based attacks have been actively researched in recent years and could be used in both profiling [19,24,25,37,41] and non-profiling settings [16,31,38].

ASCAD [3], a first-order masked AES-128 implementation running on an 8-bit AVR microcontroller, is one of the most studied datasets by the side-channel community. While there are two versions of this ASCAD dataset (one with a fixed key and the other one with random keys), there is little difference in attacking those two datasets, see, e.g., [24], which is also discussed in more generic terms of portability difficulty in [4]. During only a few years of active research, the secret key of this dataset managed to be retrieved from around a thousand attack traces [3] to one trace [24]. For an overview of novel attack methodologies based on the publicly available implementations and the corresponding leakage measurements, as well as for the details on those datasets, we refer readers to [26]. Considering that almost all of the available datasets can be "easily" broken, there is a strong demand from the SCA community to have more robust open-source implementations and leakage measurements. Indeed, knowing the complexity of modern devices, we see a large disbalance between the realistic implementations and those studied in academia. The release of new cryptographic implementations implemented with different hardware, software, and protections fills the gap between academics and the real world.

Lookup table-based masking is a common countermeasure against SCA. This strategy, particularly when applied to mask the Sbox, stands out for its computational efficiency. The pre-computed Sbox notably reduces the computational load during operations. The initial provably secure first-order lookup table-based masking scheme was proposed by Chari et al. [9]. A randomized Sbox lookup table undergoes a shift and receives protection with an output mask. Following this seminal work, enhancements have been made in terms of enhancing its secure order [11,12,28] and decreasing its memory requirement [33,34]. In 2019, ANSSI publicly released a hardened AES-128 implementation. This secure variant employs a lookup table-based affine masking scheme in line with [17], incorporating both multiplicative and additive masking. This combination poses a significant challenge to the profiling attack on first-order leakages. Initial security analysis of this implementation was undertaken by Bronchain et al., who proposed several attack strategies given knowledge of the source code, the secret key, and the random shares processed during the profiling phase [8]. Following this, Cristiani et al. [14] uses non-profiled SCA with Joint Moments Regression to break the ASCADv2 dataset with 100M traces. Masure et al. conducted partial attacks on various shares and permutation indices [23]. The knowledge they garnered from these attacks was subsequently used to orchestrate a global attack on the protected data. Marquet et al. further contributed to the field by highlighting the superiority of multi-task learning over single-task learning when the analysis is focused exclusively on secret data [22]. Recently, Vasselle et al. published an AES implementation that included both masking and artificially implemented shuffling as countermeasures [35]. They successfully breached the target using a spatial dependency analysis. Their research has helped to further our understanding of the strengths and weaknesses of these countermeasures and offers new avenues for exploration in securing AES implementations.

4   Vulnerability Analysis

This section first discusses the constant affine mask shares used in ASCADv2. Afterward, we discuss the zero input to the affine masking scheme.

4.1   Constant Affine Mask Shares for an Encryption

As mentioned, the ASCADv2 implementation is protected by an affine masking scheme consisting of independent additive and multiplicative mask shares (see Eq. 2). This implementation increases the security level of the implementation [8,23]. Nonetheless, upon analyzing the code, we observe that the same pre-computation table is used for all state bytes, meaning that additive and multiplicative masks remain constant throughout a single AES encryption. Random values are pre-loaded into mask registers before encryption and are retrieved during mask calculations. Such an implementation presents the opportunity to bypass these masking schemes altogether. Formally, assuming $C_i = C_j$ during an AES processing, we have:

$$(X_i \otimes \alpha) \oplus \beta = (X_j \otimes \alpha) \oplus \beta$$
$$\implies X_i = X_j, \ \alpha \neq 0. \tag{4}$$

Lemma 1. *Given* $X_i \otimes \alpha \oplus \beta = X_j \otimes \alpha \oplus \beta$, *we xor both sides of the equation with* β *to cancel it out*

$$X_i \otimes \alpha = X_j \otimes \alpha. \tag{5}$$

Since we work with finite field multiplication (in $GF(2^8)$*), each element has a unique inverse (except the element 0). Since* α *is non-zero (otherwise, both sides of the original equation would equal* β*, which would not provide any information), we can multiply both sides of the equation by the multiplicative inverse of* α*, denoted as* α^{-1}*:*

$$X_i \otimes \alpha \otimes \alpha^{-1} = X_j \otimes \alpha \otimes \alpha^{-1}, \ \alpha \neq 0. \tag{6}$$

Applying the associative property of finite field multiplication over $GF(2^8)$, *we have:*

$$X_i \otimes (\alpha \otimes \alpha^{-1}) = X_j \otimes (\alpha \otimes \alpha^{-1})$$
$$\implies X_i \otimes 1 = X_j \otimes 1 \tag{7}$$
$$\implies X_i = X_j.$$

Therefore, a collision between X_i *and* X_j *is created without the knowledge of* α *and* β.

Equation 4 illustrates the vulnerability of this AES implementation. Indeed, a fixed mask can be easily canceled by comparing intermediate data protected by the same mask shares. Note that X_i and X_j could be key-related intermediate data, represented by $\mathsf{Sbox}(k_j \oplus p_j)$. In this case, Eq. 1 is satisfied if X_i equals X_j. Since the plaintext is known, we adopt a side-channel collision attack to retrieve $k_i \oplus k_j$ for all keys, detailed in Sect. 5.1.

4.2 Zero Input of Affine Masking Scheme

As discussed in Eq. 7, the multiplicative mask α is non-zero, so each element has a unique inverse. However, it is also possible that X_i is zero (e.g., $\mathsf{Sbox}(\cdot) = 0$). Formally speaking, when $X_i = 0$, Eq. 2 can be rewritten as:

$$C_i = (X_i \otimes \alpha) \oplus \beta$$
$$= 0 \oplus \beta \tag{8}$$
$$= \beta.$$

The masked state C_i only relies on β, and the multiplicative mask α is disabled in this scenario, links to the zero-value 2nd-order leakage mentioned in [17]. To exploit this attack path, an adversary would try all possible keys to calculate X_i and select the traces that satisfy $X_i = 0$. Then, the chosen traces are correlated with β. The traces set with the highest correlation would indicate the correct key.

There are two ways to perform such an attack. The first attack path requires the knowledge of β, indicating that an adversary should, for instance, access the output of a PRNG that provides the mask value. In this case, one could conduct the attack in the profiling SCA setting similar to other researches [8,22,23], namely learning β on the cloned and fully controlled device and predict β on a victim device, finally performing correlation analysis using the predicted values and leakage measurements. Since this attack path relies on the knowledge of the mask shares, it is less interesting considering the scope of this paper that aims at breaking ASCADv2 with no assumption on prior knowledge about the mask shares.

The second attack path is similar to a side-channel collision attack in which an adversary compares two trace segments. Instead of correlating with the β value, an adversary could correlate with the leakage segments that process β.

According to the source code, since β is handled in plaintext (which makes sense as there is no need to protect a random value from side-channel leakages), we expect significant leakages of the β processing. The relevant features would correlate well with the trace segments that process SubBytes with zero Sbox inputs. The attack results are shown in Subsect. 5.2.

5 Attack Results

This section provides experimental results, first the collision attack on canceling mask shares, followed by correlation attack on GF(0). Instead of regenerating leakage traces [8,23], the original traces provided by ANSSI are used for attacks[3].

5.1 Side-Channel Collision Attack on Canceling Mask Shares

The collision attacks require the trace segments of each intermediate data processing. Therefore, the leakage analysis is crucial for the success of such an attack. Figure 1a presents an averaged trace representing the first round of the AES. Y-axis stands for the leakage amplitude. The sixteen SubBytes operations are highlighted in red. Repeated patterns can be observed when zooming in on each SubBytes operation, as shown in Fig. 1b. The trace segments for each operation ($T^0, T^1, \cdots T^{15}$) are selected based on the lowest value of each repetitive pattern (e.g., the end of T^0, T^1, and T^2 interval in Fig. 1b). Note that the selection of the trace segment is neither restricted to the highlighted ranges nor requires any additional knowledge regarding the data being processed or random shares. For instance, one could include intervals between T^0, T^1, and T^2 (according to the source code, these intervals could represent operations such as register writing). Based on our preliminary experiments, such a setting would also break the target.

Algorithm 1. Side-channel collision attack on ASCADv2

Input: trace segments $\mathbf{T}^i$ and $\mathbf{T}^j$, plaintext bytes $\mathbf{d}_i$ and $\mathbf{d}_j$
Output: most-likely key difference δ^*
1: **for** δ in $\mathcal{K}$ **do**
2:     indices = arg where($\mathbf{d}_i \oplus \delta == \mathbf{d}_j$)
3:     $diff_\delta = \mathsf{E}(\|\mathbf{T}^i_{\text{indices}} - \mathbf{T}^j_{\text{indices}}\|)$
4: **end for**
5: $\delta^* = \arg\min_\delta diff$

Following Algorithm 1, we perform a side-channel collision attack with the selected trace segments. Given trace segments $\mathbf{T}^i$ and $\mathbf{T}^j$ and plaintext bytes $\mathbf{d}_i$ and $\mathbf{d}_j$, we first find the trace indices that satisfies $k_i \oplus k_j = p_i \oplus p_j$ (Eq. 1) with the current $k_i \oplus k_j$ guess in an AES encryption, denoted as δ. Then, the similarity

---

[3] https://github.com/ANSSI-FR/ASCAD/tree/master/STM32_AES_v2.

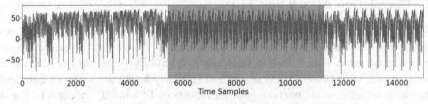

(a) Leakage trace and **SubBytes** operations.

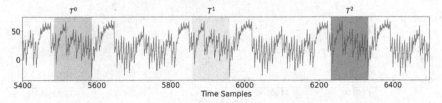

(b) Zoom-in view of the leakage trace and selected time intervals.

Fig. 1. An overview of the leakage trace and the target time interval.

of the two trace segments is measured with squared Euclidean distance [6] and averaged (represented by E in Algorithm 1) over indices. After looping through all possible δ candidates, the δ guess that leads to the lowest averaging difference would be the most likely candidate δ^*.

The experimental result is shown in Fig. 2. When attacking with 30 000 traces, only $k_1 \oplus k_2$ and $k_{13} \oplus k_{14}$ cannot be successfully recovered (δ rank are 3 and 12, respectively). In this case, one could adopt error correction methods [18,40] to recover the true key differences. With around 70 000 attack traces, all δ^* that represents the correct subkey difference can be recovered. Given this information, the entropy of the key is reduced to 256 and can be easily brute-forced.

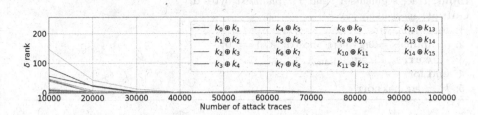

Fig. 2. Side-channel collision attack on all bytes.

5.2   Correlation Attack on GF(0)

The same trace segments used in the previous section, namely $\mathbf{T}^0$ to $\mathbf{T}^{15}$, are adopted for the attack presented in this section. Based on the source code, Sbox's output mask r_{out} is loaded right after the SubBytes operation is finished. Therefore, the time interval of β is selected similarly to the selection of SubBytes operations with the same pattern gap, for instance, $\mathbf{T}^{14}$ and $\mathbf{T}^{15}$ shown in Fig. 3.

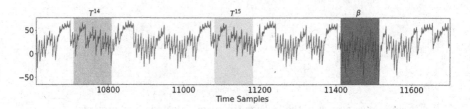

Fig. 3. The selected time intervals including the additive mask (β).

The attack method is presented in Algorithm 2. Since the goal is to correlate the β leakages with the trace segments of SubBytes, the pairwise correlation corr is performed column-wise. Note that each column in trace segments $\mathbf{T}^i$ represents a leakage feature at a specific time location; the pairwise correlation ensures the dissimilarity of traces segments, due to different operation steps and data handling methods, less influence the correlation results. After averaging the output correlation matrix with E, the k guess that leads to the highest correlation value would be the most likely candidate k^*.

Algorithm 2. Correlation attack on ASCADv2

Input: trace segments $\mathbf{T}^i$ and $\mathbf{T}^\beta$, plaintext bytes $\mathbf{d}_i$
Output: most-likely key k^*
1: **for** k in $\mathcal{K}$ **do**
2:      indices = arg where($\mathsf{Sbox}(\mathbf{d}_i \oplus k) == 0$)
3:      $\mathrm{corr}_k = \mathsf{E}(\mathrm{corr}(\mathbf{T}^i_{\text{indices}}, \mathbf{T}^\beta_{\text{indices}}))$
4: **end for**
5: $k^* = \arg\max \mathrm{corr}$

The experimental result is shown in Fig. 4. Although most of the correct key does not reach a key rank of zero (the most-likely key), we see a clear convergence of the key rank with increased attack traces. Table 1 shows the detailed key rank of each subkey with 500 000 attack traces. Two subkeys are successfully recovered, and the rest (except k_5 and k_6) reach low values of the key rank. As a rough estimation, eight times more traces would lead to successful δ recovery of all subkeys.

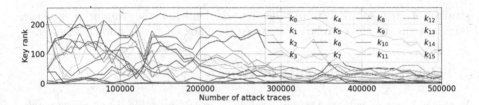

Fig. 4. Correlation attack results on all bytes.

Table 1. The rank of each subkey with 500 000 attack traces.

	k_0	k_1	k_2	k_3	k_4	k_5	k_6	k_7	k_8	k_9	k_{10}	k_{11}	k_{12}	k_{13}	k_{14}	k_{15}
Key rank	1	22	0	3	1	112	113	0	37	1	21	23	12	24	24	8

6 Discussion and Protection Methods

The implementation of AES by ANSSI provides an excellent example of a secure AES execution. It employs masking schemes that protect the entire AES process while shuffling serves to minimize potential leakages further. From the viewpoint of a first-order attack focusing on the leakage of a single intermediate data, this implementation exhibits robust security, only breakable under strong attack assumptions. However, this masking scheme could be easily compromised with straightforward techniques when examining second-order leakages. A solitary shuffling countermeasure could be defeated by employing more traces.

Analyzing its design reveals that the reliance on a single Sbox_m facilitates the attacks discussed in this paper. Despite all AES states being masked and unknown to an adversary, the deterministic association between the Sbox input and output leaves the computation of each byte susceptible to second-order attacks. One might propose the generation of sixteen distinct Sbox_m to facilitate byte substitution. However, in the specific case of the affine masking scheme outlined in [17], it's crucial that the multiplicative share *must* remain consistent across every byte in the state. Deviating from this principle would result in linear operations, such as AddRoundKey and MixColumns, losing their homomorphic property with the affine encoding. This, in turn, implies that each operation would necessitate 16 pre-computed lookup tables, each with a size of 256^2, which makes the cryptographic implementation prohibitively resource-intensive. Alternatively, implementing hiding countermeasures may be a simple and effective strategy against the proposed attacks. The proposed attacks require the comparison of trace segments. The original implementation's random shuffling significantly increases the required attack traces. Adding to this, countermeasures introducing temporal randomnesses, such as clock jitters and random branch insertion, could further complicate the process of identifying and comparing the target operations, enhancing the security of the implementation.

Addressing the second vulnerability would involve carefully redesigning the implementation, ensuring that $\mathsf{GF}(0)$ results in a random output. A more straightforward solution would involve randomizing the timing β process, thereby reducing the correlation between the Sbox operation and β leakages.

7   Conclusions and Future Work

In this paper, we evaluate two vulnerabilities in lookup table-based affine masking implementation, then leverage them to perform efficient second-order attacks on the ASCADv2 dataset. Specifically, we notice that some mask shares remain constant during an AES encryption, which leads to an easy cancellation of masks with a side-channel collision attack. Another vulnerability relies on implementing the Galois field multiplication, which always outputs zero when one input is zero. In this case, an adversary could choose specific traces that generate zero input. In this case, the affine masking scheme is significantly weakened, as only additive mask shares remain as the output.

Multiple aspects would be interesting to consider in future research. First, the proposed attacks rely on the single masked SBox used during encryption. It will be interesting to investigate the applicability of the proposed attack when two or more masked $SBox_m$ are used in a cryptographic operation. Next, the proposed attacks are grounded on the squared Euclidean distance and Pearson correlation coefficient for similarity assessment. It would be interesting to explore deep learning in initiating attacks under more noisy circumstances, such as those involving desynchronization. Further, it would be compelling to study and augment the attack performance hinging on our second identified vulnerability: the zero output of the finite field multiplication. Finally, an optimal objective would be to devise innovative techniques to overcome the complexity inherent in finite field multiplication, enabling direct attacks on this dataset's intermediate data.

References

1. Amigo, G., Dong, L., Ii, R.J.M.: Forecasting pseudo random numbers using deep learning. In: 2021 15th International Conference on Signal Processing and Communication Systems (ICSPCS), pp. 1–7. IEEE (2021)
2. Benadjila, R., Khati, L., Prouff, E., Thillard, A.: Hardened library for AES-128 encryption/decryption on ARM Cortex M4 architecture (2019). https://github.com/ANSSI-FR/SecAESSTM32
3. Benadjila, R., Prouff, E., Strullu, R., Cagli, E., Dumas, C.: Deep learning for side-channel analysis and introduction to ASCAD database. J. Cryptogr. Eng. 10(2), 163–188 (2020)
4. Bhasin, S., Chattopadhyay, A., Heuser, A., Jap, D., Picek, S., Ranjan, R.: Mind the portability: a warriors guide through realistic profiled side-channel analysis. In: Network and Distributed System Security Symposium, NDSS 2020, pp. 1–14 (2020)
5. Bogdanov, A.: Improved side-channel collision attacks on AES. In: Adams, C., Miri, A., Wiener, M. (eds.) SAC 2007. LNCS, vol. 4876, pp. 84–95. Springer, Heidelberg (2007). https://doi.org/10.1007/978-3-540-77360-3_6

6. Bogdanov, A., Kizhvatov, I.: Beyond the limits of DPA: combined side-channel collision attacks. IEEE Trans. Comput. **61**(8), 1153–1164 (2011)
7. Brier, E., Clavier, C., Olivier, F.: Correlation power analysis with a leakage model. In: Joye, M., Quisquater, J.-J. (eds.) CHES 2004. LNCS, vol. 3156, pp. 16–29. Springer, Heidelberg (2004). https://doi.org/10.1007/978-3-540-28632-5_2
8. Bronchain, O., Standaert, F.X.: Side-channel countermeasures' dissection and the limits of closed source security evaluations. IACR Trans. Cryptographic Hardware Embed. Syst. 1–25 (2020)
9. Chari, S., Jutla, C.S., Rao, J.R., Rohatgi, P.: Towards sound approaches to counteract power-analysis attacks. In: Wiener, M. (ed.) CRYPTO 1999. LNCS, vol. 1666, pp. 398–412. Springer, Heidelberg (1999). https://doi.org/10.1007/3-540-48405-1_26
10. Chari, S., Rao, J.R., Rohatgi, P.: Template attacks. In: Kaliski, B.S., Koç, K., Paar, C. (eds.) CHES 2002. LNCS, vol. 2523, pp. 13–28. Springer, Heidelberg (2003). https://doi.org/10.1007/3-540-36400-5_3
11. Coron, J.-S.: Higher order masking of look-up tables. In: Nguyen, P.Q., Oswald, E. (eds.) EUROCRYPT 2014. LNCS, vol. 8441, pp. 441–458. Springer, Heidelberg (2014). https://doi.org/10.1007/978-3-642-55220-5_25
12. Coron, J.S., Rondepierre, F., Zeitoun, R.: High order masking of look-up tables with common shares. Cryptology ePrint Archive (2017)
13. Coron, J.S., Rondepierre, F., Zeitoun, R.: High order masking of look-up tables with common shares. IACR Trans. Cryptographic Hardware Embed. Syst. 40–72 (2018)
14. Cristiani, V., Lecomte, M., Hiscock, T., Maurine, P.: Fit the joint moments: how to attack any masking scheme. IEEE Access **10**, 127412–127427 (2022)
15. Daemen, J., Rijmen, V.: AES proposal: Rijndael (1999)
16. Dol, N.T., Le, P.C., Hoang, V.P., Doan, V.S., Nguyen, H.G., Pham, C.K.: MODLSCA: deep learning based non-profiled side channel analysis using multi-output neural networks. In: 2022 International Conference on Advanced Technologies for Communications (ATC), pp. 245–250. IEEE (2022)
17. Fumaroli, G., Martinelli, A., Prouff, E., Rivain, M.: Affine masking against higher-order side channel analysis. In: Biryukov, A., Gong, G., Stinson, D.R. (eds.) SAC 2010. LNCS, vol. 6544, pp. 262–280. Springer, Heidelberg (2011). https://doi.org/10.1007/978-3-642-19574-7_18
18. Gérard, B., Standaert, F.-X.: Unified and optimized linear collision attacks and their application in a non-profiled setting. In: Prouff, E., Schaumont, P. (eds.) CHES 2012. LNCS, vol. 7428, pp. 175–192. Springer, Heidelberg (2012). https://doi.org/10.1007/978-3-642-33027-8_11
19. Hospodar, G., Gierlichs, B., De Mulder, E., Verbauwhede, I., Vandewalle, J.: Machine learning in side-channel analysis: a first study. J. Cryptogr. Eng. **1**(4), 293–302 (2011)
20. Kocher, P., Jaffe, J., Jun, B.: Differential power analysis. In: Wiener, M. (ed.) CRYPTO 1999. LNCS, vol. 1666, pp. 388–397. Springer, Heidelberg (1999). https://doi.org/10.1007/3-540-48405-1_25
21. Maghrebi, H., Portigliatti, T., Prouff, E.: Breaking cryptographic implementations using deep learning techniques. In: Carlet, C., Hasan, M.A., Saraswat, V. (eds.) SPACE 2016. LNCS, vol. 10076, pp. 3–26. Springer, Cham (2016). https://doi.org/10.1007/978-3-319-49445-6_1
22. Marquet, T., Oswald, E.: A comparison of multi-task learning and single-task learning approaches. Cryptology ePrint Archive (2023)

23. Masure, L., Strullu, R.: Side-channel analysis against ANSSI's protected AES implementation on ARM: end-to-end attacks with multi-task learning. J. Cryptographic Eng. 1–19 (2023)
24. Perin, G., Wu, L., Picek, S.: Exploring feature selection scenarios for deep learning-based side-channel analysis. IACR Trans. Cryptographic Hardware Embed. Syst. 828–861 (2022)
25. Picek, S., et al.: Side-channel analysis and machine learning: a practical perspective. In: 2017 International Joint Conference on Neural Networks, IJCNN 2017, Anchorage, AK, USA, 14–19 May 2017, pp. 4095–4102 (2017)
26. Picek, S., Perin, G., Mariot, L., Wu, L., Batina, L.: SoK: deep learning-based physical side-channel analysis. ACM Comput. Surv. **55**(11), 1–35 (2023)
27. Schindler, W., Lemke, K., Paar, C.: A stochastic model for differential side channel cryptanalysis. In: Rao, J.R., Sunar, B. (eds.) CHES 2005. LNCS, vol. 3659, pp. 30–46. Springer, Heidelberg (2005). https://doi.org/10.1007/11545262_3
28. Schramm, K., Paar, C.: Higher order masking of the AES. In: Pointcheval, D. (ed.) CT-RSA 2006. LNCS, vol. 3860, pp. 208–225. Springer, Heidelberg (2006). https://doi.org/10.1007/11605805_14
29. Schramm, K., Wollinger, T., Paar, C.: A new class of collision attacks and its application to DES. In: Johansson, T. (ed.) FSE 2003. LNCS, vol. 2887, pp. 206–222. Springer, Heidelberg (2003). https://doi.org/10.1007/978-3-540-39887-5_16
30. Staib, M., Moradi, A.: Deep learning side-channel collision attack. IACR Trans. Cryptographic Hardware Embed. Syst. 422–444 (2023)
31. Timon, B.: Non-profiled deep learning-based side-channel attacks with sensitivity analysis. IACR Trans. Cryptographic Hardware Embed. Syst. 107–131 (2019)
32. Tunstall, M., Whitnall, C., Oswald, E.: Masking tables—an underestimated security risk. In: Moriai, S. (ed.) FSE 2013. LNCS, vol. 8424, pp. 425–444. Springer, Heidelberg (2014). https://doi.org/10.1007/978-3-662-43933-3_22
33. Vadnala, P.K.: Time-memory trade-offs for side-channel resistant implementations of block ciphers. In: Handschuh, H. (ed.) CT-RSA 2017. LNCS, vol. 10159, pp. 115–130. Springer, Cham (2017). https://doi.org/10.1007/978-3-319-52153-4_7
34. Valiveti, A., Vivek, S.: Second-order masked lookup table compression scheme. IACR Trans. Cryptographic Hardware Embed. Syst. 129–153 (2020)
35. Vasselle, A., Thiebeauld, H., Maurine, P.: Spatial dependency analysis to extract information from side-channel mixtures: extended version. J. Cryptographic Eng. 1–17 (2023)
36. Veyrat-Charvillon, N., Medwed, M., Kerckhof, S., Standaert, F.-X.: Shuffling against side-channel attacks: a comprehensive study with cautionary note. In: Wang, X., Sako, K. (eds.) ASIACRYPT 2012. LNCS, vol. 7658, pp. 740–757. Springer, Heidelberg (2012). https://doi.org/10.1007/978-3-642-34961-4_44
37. Wu, L., Perin, G., Picek, S.: The best of two worlds: Deep learning-assisted template attack. IACR Trans. Cryptographic Hardware Embed. Syst. 413–437 (2022)
38. Wu, L., Perin, G., Picek, S.: Hiding in plain sight: non-profiling deep learning-based side-channel analysis with plaintext/ciphertext. Cryptology ePrint Archive (2023)
39. Wu, L., Picek, S.: Remove some noise: on pre-processing of side-channel measurements with autoencoders. IACR Trans. Cryptographic Hardware Embed. Syst. 389–415 (2020)
40. Wu, L., Tiran, S., Perin, G., Picek, S.: An end-to-end plaintext-based side-channel collision attack without trace segmentation. Cryptology ePrint Archive (2023)
41. Zaid, G., Bossuet, L., Habrard, A., Venelli, A.: Methodology for efficient CNN architectures in profiling attacks. IACR Trans. Cryptographic Hardware Embed. Syst. 1–36 (2020)

Threshold Implementations with Non-uniform Inputs

Siemen Dhooghe$^{(\boxtimes)}$ and Artemii Ovchinnikov

COSIC, KU Leuven, Leuven, Belgium
{siemen.dhooghe,artemii.ovchinnikov}@esat.kuleuven.be

Abstract. Modern block ciphers designed for hardware and masked with Threshold Implementations (TIs) provide provable security against first-order attacks. However, the application of TIs leaves designers to deal with a trade-off between its security and its cost, for example, the process to generate its required random bits. This generation cost comes with an increased overhead in terms of area and latency. Decreasing the number of random bits for the masking allows to reduce the aforementioned overhead.

We propose to reduce the randomness to mask the secrets, like the plaintext. For that purpose, we suggest *relaxing the requirement for the uniformity* of the input shares and *reuse randomness* for their masking in first-order TIs. We apply our countermeasures to first-order TIs of the Prince and Midori64 ciphers with three shares. Since the designs with non-uniform masks are no longer perfect first-order probing secure, we provide further analysis by calculating bounds on the advantage of a noisy threshold-probing adversary. We then make use of the PROLEAD tool, which implements statistical tests verifying the robust probing security to compare its output with our estimates. Finally, we evaluate the designs on FPGA to highlight the practical security of our solution. We observe that their security holds while requiring four times less randomness over uniform TIs.

Keywords: FPGA · Masking · Probing Security · Threshold Implementations · Uniformity

1 Introduction

For the past two decades after Kocher *et al.* [16] presented differential power analysis in 1999, one example of a side-channel attack, the development of protected cryptographic hardware devices has turned into an important goal for researchers and designers. To that end, masking has become a reliable countermeasure. In masking, a secret is split into several parts to confound the correlation between its value and some physical characteristics, like its power consumption. However, to eliminate the mentioned statistical dependence, the shares of the masking have to be uniform random such that they are independent

C. Carlet et al. (Eds.): SAC 2023, LNCS 14201, pp. 97–123, 2024.
https://doi.org/10.1007/978-3-031-53368-6_6

of the secret. Threshold Implementations (TIs), introduced in 2006 by Nikova et al. [21], allow to preserve this uniformity of the masks and provide for first-order security. As a result, one only needs some fixed number of random bits to be generated at the initial stage and no fresh random bits are needed for further re-masking. The process of randomness generation needed for this uniformity lacks attention in terms of cost and security from the research community. As a result, to be on the safe side, researchers recommend heavy-duty random number generators based on standardised cryptographic primitives. However, in practice, lighter non-cryptographic generators are used whose security remains unknown. Instead of deducting which lightweight random number generator can be used, designers of masking schemes focus on reducing the total number of random bits required for the masking to be secure. The security of this question can more easily be verified by using the probing model by Ishai et al. [15] which has become the standard model for masking countermeasures.

The research on reducing the randomness cost for maskings has significantly progressed. The work by Shahmirzadi and Moradi [22] reduces the fresh randomness needed for first-order designs using only two shares while their follow-up work [23] does the same for second-order designs. The work by Beyne et al. [7] in 2020 introduces the bounded-query probing model which allows to obtain a concrete bound on the adversary's advantage by means of a security framework based on linear cryptanalysis. In 2021, Beyne et al. [6] applied their scheme to make a low-randomness masked AES. This work was followed up in 2022 [5] to include the noise on probes to improve the bounds on the adversary and to improve the efficiency of their designs. For all three previous works, the security framework was always applied to second-order masked designs but never to the first-order designs. Its application to first-order designs provides an opportunity of using non-uniform randomness to generate secret shares. Via careful analysis, it can provide a way to reduce the cost of the initial randomness for TIs.

Contributions. In this paper, we investigate TIs of lightweight ciphers and their security when given non-uniform inputs. We provide a framework, based on the works by Beyne et al. [5,7], to show when the implementations are secure and when they are not, and provide practical evidence to support it.

For the analysis, we work with the Prince [10] and Midori64 [1] ciphers and take previously established TIs of them, namely the one by Bozilov et al. [11] for Prince and by Moradi et al. [18] for Midori64. The goal of the analysis is to reduce the initial randomness needed to mask the plaintext for both ciphers. To that end, we investigate cases where we can re-use randomness for the initial masking and provide, for each cipher, insecure and secure cases using the same number of total random bits. This shows that it is not the total entropy of the masked input which counts, but instead, its relation to the properties of the masking of the cipher. We demonstrate that using the security framework via a trail based approach where we obtain bounds on a probing adversary's advantage.

In order to complete the research, we provide practical experiments on top of the previous mentioned theoretical analysis. We test the designs with non-uniform masked inputs using two different approaches. First, we use the PRO-

LEAD tool by Müller and Moradi [19] which allows for a noiseless statistical leakage evaluation based on the glitch-extended probing model. Second, we provide the results of a practical evaluation of our designs on FPGA. For the observed power consumption, we apply first-order statistical fixed vs. random t-tests [2]. The results of those tests are closer to practice as the noise is included in the sampled traces. As an end result, we show that the TIs by Bozilov et al. and by Moradi et al. can be used with a non-uniform masked input reducing the total needed randomness four times over while still providing practical security of up to 50M traces.[1]

2 Preliminaries

In this section, we introduce the probing security model together with the basics of masking and threshold implementations. We also introduce the cryptanalysis-based evaluation we use to determine which non-uniform inputs of threshold implementations are secure.

2.1 Glitch-Extended Bounded-Query Probing Security

We first introduce the bounded-query probing model [7] with a noisy probing variant [5]. The security model is depicted in Fig. 1.

In this model, the security of a circuit C with input k against a t-threshold-probing adversary is quantified as follows. The challenger picks a random bit b and provides an oracle $\mathcal{O}^b$ (the masked circuit with b hardwired), to which adversary $\mathcal{A}$ is given query access. The adversary queries the oracle by choosing up to t wires of the masked circuit to probe, we denote this set by $\mathcal{P}$, and sends it to the oracle along with the inputs (for a cipher, both key and plaintext) k_0 and k_1. The oracle responds by giving back a noisy leakage function $\mathbf{f}$ (following the definition given in [5]) of the glitch-extended probed wire values of the masked circuit with input k_b. After a total of q queries, the adversary responds to the challenger with a guess for b. For $b \in \{0,1\}$, denote the result of the adversary after interacting with the oracle $\mathcal{O}^b$ using q queries by $\mathcal{A}^{\mathcal{O}^b}$. For left-or-right security, the advantage of the adversary $\mathcal{A}$ is then defined as

$$\mathrm{Adv}_{t\text{-thr}}(\mathcal{A}) = |\Pr[\mathcal{A}^{\mathcal{O}^0} = 1] - \Pr[\mathcal{A}^{\mathcal{O}^1} = 1]|.$$

Since we are working on hardware, we make use of the glitch-extended probing model by Faust et al. [13]. Whereas one of the adversary's probes normally results in the value of a single wire, a glitch-extended probe allows obtaining the values of all wires in a bundle, with the limit that glitches do not propagate through memory gates.

---

[1] The HDL representations of the constructed ciphers will be made publicly available on https://github.com/KULeuven-COSIC/TIs_with_Non-Uniform_Inputs.

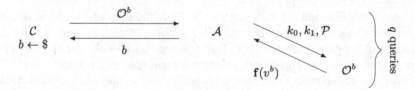

Fig. 1. [5] The privacy model for the glitch-extended t-threshold-probing security consisting of a challenger $\mathcal{C}$, an adversary $\mathcal{A}$, a left-right oracle $\mathcal{O}^b$, two inputs k_0, k_1, a set of probes $\mathcal{P}$, and a noisy leakage function $\mathbf{f}(v^b)$ of the probed wire values v^b in the circuit $C(k_b)$.

2.2   Boolean Masking and Threshold Implementations

Boolean masking is a technique based on splitting each secret variable $x \in \mathbb{F}_2$ in the circuit into shares $\bar{x} = (x^0, x^1, \ldots, x^{s_x-1})$ such that $x = \sum_{i=0}^{s_x-1} x^i$ over $\mathbb{F}_2$. A random Boolean masking of a fixed secret is uniform if all maskings of that secret are equally likely. There are several approaches to masking a circuit. In this work, we make use of threshold implementations proposed by Nikova et al. [21].

Let $\bar{F}$ be a masked function in the threshold implementation corresponding to the unmasked function $F : \mathbb{F}_2^n \to \mathbb{F}_2^m$. Then $\bar{F}$ can have the following properties.

Definition 1 (Threshold implementations [21]). *Let $F : \mathbb{F}_2^n \to \mathbb{F}_2^m$ be a function and $\bar{F} : \mathbb{F}_2^{ns_x} \to \mathbb{F}_2^{ms_y}$ be a masking of F. The masking $\bar{F}$ is said to be*

1. *correct if $\forall x^0, \ldots, x^{s_x-1} \in \mathbb{F}_2^n$, $\sum_{i=0}^{s_y-1} F^i(x^0, \ldots, x^{s_x-1}) = F(\sum_{i=0}^{s_x-1} x_i)$,*
2. *non-complete if any function share F^i depends on at most $s_x - 1$ input shares,*
3. *uniform if $\bar{F}$ maps a uniform random masking of any $x \in \mathbb{F}_2^n$ to a uniform random masking of $F(x) \in \mathbb{F}_2^m$.*

2.3   Linear Cryptanalysis of Maskings

To prove the first-order probing security of a circuit, it is sufficient to show that the probed values consist only of uniform randomness and public values. To that end, we make use of the theory by Beyne et al. [7] which bounds the distribution of probed values (in a bounded query model) by their Fourier distribution. We also make use of the later work [5], where this framework was expanded to include the noise on the traces. We recall the main results of these works.

Bound on the Advantage. We first discuss the bound on a bounded-query probing adversary which uses λ-noisy probes. We refer to [5] on the specific definition of the used noisy leakage function. In the rest of this description, the noise parameter λ characterises the level of the noise. In principle, the noise parameters could be computed empirically from estimates of the probability distributions of the leakage (i.e. trace points) under all possible secrets.

We assume that any probed wire value can be labelled as 'good' or 'bad'. The values labelled 'good' jointly reveal nothing about the secret. The 'bad' values may reveal secret information, but the leakage can be bounded in terms of λ and ε. The parameter λ is determined by physical aspects such as the leakage model and noise level. The parameter ε is instead determined by the mathematical properties of the masking. Specifically, it will be shown later how these parameters can be determined using linear cryptanalysis. Below is the definition of the bound on a first-order noisy probing adversary given a bound on ε and λ.

Theorem 1 ([5]). *Let $\mathcal{A}$ be a noisy threshold-probing adversary for a circuit C. Take $\lambda \geq 1$, and $\varepsilon \leq 1$ as non-negative real numbers. Assume that for every query made by $\mathcal{A}$ on the oracle $\mathcal{O}^b$ with result $\mathbf{z}$, there exists a partitioning (depending only on the probe positions) of the probed wire values into two random variables $\mathbf{x}$ ('good') and $\mathbf{y}$ ('bad') such that*

1. *The noisy leakage function $\mathbf{f}$ such that $\mathbf{z} = \mathbf{f}(\mathbf{x}, \mathbf{y})$ is λ-noisy.*
2. *The conditional probability distribution $p_{\mathbf{y}|\mathbf{x}}$ satisfies $\mathbb{E}_{\mathbf{x}}\|\widehat{p}_{\mathbf{y}|\mathbf{x}}\|_2^2 \leq \varepsilon$.*
3. *Any t-threshold-probing adversary for the same circuit C and making the same oracle queries as $\mathcal{A}$, but which only receives the 'good' wire values (i.e. corresponding to $\mathbf{x}$) for each query, has advantage zero.*

The advantage of $\mathcal{A}$ can be upper bounded as

$$\mathrm{Adv}_{\mathsf{noisy}}(\mathcal{A}) \leq \sqrt{2q\,\varepsilon/\lambda},$$

where q is the number of queries to the oracle $\mathcal{O}^b$.

The security bound obtained in Theorem 1 depends on the parameter ε. This value will be determined by performing linear cryptanalysis of the masked cipher. Essentially, this follows regular linear cryptanalysis, except that masking schemes naturally incorporate linear relations (namely that the sum of the shares form the secret). As a result, the basic definitions of linear cryptanalysis need to be adapted to work over a quotient space where, in short, the last share is removed to avoid the previously mentioned linear relation. Viewing linear cryptanalysis over this quotient space is justified by the non-completeness property of threshold implementations, namely that a probe does not view all shares of a secret at once, and as a result, we only investigate relations over non-complete sets of shares.

Correlation of Maskings. For any linear masking scheme, there exists a vector space $\mathbb{V} \subset \mathbb{F}_2^\ell$ of valid maskings of zero. More specifically, an $\mathbb{F}_2$-linear secret sharing scheme is an algorithm that maps a secret $x \in \mathbb{F}_2^n$ to a random element of a corresponding coset of the vector space $\mathbb{V}$. Let $\rho : \mathbb{F}_2^n \to \mathbb{F}_2^\ell$ be a map that sends secrets to their corresponding coset representative. For convenience, we denote $\mathbb{V}_a = a + \mathbb{V}$.

We use the following definition of correlation matrices of a masking.

Definition 2 (Correlation matrix). *For a subspace $\mathbb{V} \subseteq \mathbb{F}_2^\ell$, let $F : \mathbb{V} \to \mathbb{V}$ be a function. The correlation matrix C^F of F is a real $|\mathbb{V}| \times |\mathbb{V}|$ matrix with coordinates indexed by elements $u, v \in \mathbb{F}_2^n/\mathbb{V}^\perp$ and equal to*

$$C_{v,u}^F = \frac{1}{|\mathbb{V}|} \sum_{x \in \mathbb{V}} (-1)^{u^\top x + v^\top F'(x)}.$$

for a function $F' : \mathbb{V}_a \to \mathbb{V}_b$ with $F'(x) = F(x + a) + b$.

The link between ε from Theorem 1 and linear cryptanalysis is completed by the theorem below. It shows that the coordinates of $\widehat{p}_{\mathbf{z}}$ are entries of the correlation matrix of the state-transformation between the specified probe locations. In Theorem 2, the restriction of $x \in \mathbb{V}_a$ to an index set $I = \{i_1, \ldots, i_m\}$ is denoted by $x_I = (x_{i_1}, \ldots, x_{i_m}) \in \mathbb{F}_2^{|I|}$. This definition depends on the specific choice of the representative a, but the result of the theorem does not.

Theorem 2 ([7], §5.2). *Let $F : \mathbb{V}_a \to \mathbb{V}_b$ be a function with $\mathbb{V} \subset \mathbb{F}_2^\ell$ and $I, J \subset \{1, \ldots, \ell\}$. For $\mathbf{x}$ uniform random on $\mathbb{V}_a$ and $\mathbf{y} = F(\mathbf{x})$, let $\mathbf{z} = (\mathbf{x}_I, \mathbf{y}_J)$. The Fourier transformation of the probability mass function of $\mathbf{z}$ then satisfies $|\widehat{p}_{\mathbf{z}}(u, v)| = |C_{\widetilde{v}, \widetilde{u}}^F|$, where $\widetilde{u}, \widetilde{v} \in \mathbb{F}_2^\ell/\mathbb{V}^\perp$ are such that $\widetilde{u}_I = u$, $\widetilde{u}_{[\ell] \setminus I} = 0$, $\widetilde{v}_J = v$ and $\widetilde{v}_{[\ell] \setminus J} = 0$.*

The above theorem relates the linear approximations of F to $\widehat{p}_{\mathbf{z}}(u, v)$ and hence provides a method to upper bound ε based on linear cryptanalysis.

Applying the Bound with Non-uniform Inputs. The analysis by Beyne *et al.* originally applied to threshold implementations working on a uniform input or consisting of uniform functions. In this work, we extend this framework by analysing threshold implementations with a non-uniform input, namely an input which is shared via a non-uniform function. More specifically, we use a limited number of random bits to mask the input of the threshold implementation and analyse the impact on its first-order security. While previous works focus on reducing the online randomness of a masking, we instead propose to use the cryptanalysis technique to reduce the randomness requirement at the start of the masking.

We model this limited-random input by considering a non-uniform input encoder *Enc* (shown in Fig. 2) which takes in the circuit's input k (e.g. plaintext and key) and random bits $\mathbf{r}$ (modelled as shares of zero and as 'bad' values), and provides a shared input for the masked circuit. In particular, where this shared input is larger in size than the randomness that was given as input.

Due to *Enc* being a non-uniform function, the correlation matrix's entries $C_{\widetilde{v},0}^{Enc}$ for $\widetilde{v} \in \mathbb{F}_2^\ell/\mathbb{V}^\perp$ are non-zero. As a result, when $|\widehat{p}_{\mathbf{y}_J}(v)| = |C_{\widetilde{v},0}^H| \neq 0$ for $H = F \circ Enc$ (some non-uniform function which maps the limited randomness $\mathbf{r}$ to the probed values), $\widetilde{v}_J = v$ and $\widetilde{v}_{[\ell] \setminus J} = 0$ where a single probe is placed on $\mathbf{y}_J$, it is possible that this probe reveals a secret. The specific value $\varepsilon = |\widehat{p}_{\mathbf{y}_J}(v)|$ determines the advantage of the first-order probing adversary via Theorem 1. In other words, due to the threshold implementation using a non-uniform input,

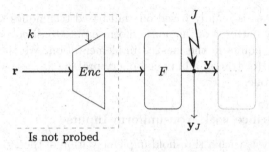

Fig. 2. Depiction of the non-uniform encoder *Enc* masking the input (e.g., plaintext and key) k using a few uniform random bits r.

a first-order probing attack is possible. However, we show the probability of success is limited in function of ε.

In the rest of the work, we will look at trails over F (which is a uniform function) where we can pick non-zero input linear masks with certain conditions depending on how the input of the cipher was masked. We thus analyse the trails of the masked cipher ending in a single probe position with conditions on the input mask related to how it is masked.

Cautionary Note. In this work, we use the piling-up principle [17,25] to obtain estimates of ε using a trail-based approach (which is often used in the field of cryptanalysis). However, since *Enc* is a non-uniform (read non-balanced) function, a zero input mask will correlate to several output masks. As a result, and due to the first S-box layer, many input masks of F from Fig. 2 are related to an output mask. As a result, the actual correlations may differ from the trail-based estimates. More specifically, we make the assumption that the correlation of the probed values is determined by a trail with an outstanding value. In case a trail with high correlation is found, we can assume that there is an attack. However, we emphasise that the absence of such trails does not trivially imply that no attack is possible. For that reason, we use this piling-up principle as a heuristic to find and verify promising non-uniform inputs for the threshold implementations. We then base ourselves on a practical verification to analyse the promising candidates via tools like PROLEAD [19] for a noiseless verification and via FPGA experiments for more realistic and noisy verification.

3   Analysis of TIs with Non-uniform Inputs

We analyse threshold implementations of the Midori64 and Prince ciphers which are given non-uniform masked inputs. The threshold implementations consist of uniform functions which do not need fresh randomness for their computation. The security calculations of the non-uniform inputs are done via the cryptanalytic technique explained in Sect. 2.3. In essence, this analysis allows to bound the deviation of a masking from uniform. When this deviation is low, the masking is "almost uniform" and we can expect the masking to still be first-order secure. The analysis is mainly based on trail-based techniques where we investigate the activity patterns of the non-uniform inputs to discover whether there are weak probing points in the masked implementation. We then estimate the number of queries (or traces) a bounded-query probing adversary needs in order to get advantage one.

3.1   Masked Prince with Non-uniform Inputs

We start the analysis with a threshold implementation of the Prince cipher with a non-uniform input. We provide the details of the cipher and its masking as well as a secure and an insecure example of a non-uniform masked input. We provide the theoretical analysis of both cases. The experimental analysis is found in Sect. 4.

Prince Cipher. Prince [10] is an AES-like cipher which consists of a 64-bit state divided in 4×4 rosters of nibbles and a 128-bit key. The S-box is a 4-bit cubic function and the linear layer consists of a MixColumns operation with a quasi-MDS matrix and a ShiftRows operation. The key schedule is simple where the first and last whitening keys contain the first 64-bits of the master key and the other round keys form the last 64-bits of the master key. The cipher consists of 12 nonlinear layers, where the first half applies the S-box and the second half applies the inverse S-box. The S-box and its inverse are affine equivalent.

Masking Details. Consider the threshold implementation of the Prince cipher, we choose the design presented in work by Bozilov $et\ al.$ [11], where the S-box is decomposed using three identical quadratic functions

$$S = A_4 \circ Q_{294} \circ A_3 \circ Q_{294} \circ A_2 \circ Q_{294} \circ A_1$$

with A_1, A_2, A_3, A_4 affine layers and Q_{294} a quadratic representative of a particular affine equivalence class as described by Bilgin $et\ al.$ [8,9]. Since the inverse S-box of Prince used in the second part of the algorithm is an affine equivalent of the regular S-box, only two additional affine layers are required to implement it. The masking of the above functions is achieved via direct sharing using three shares. Similarly, the masking of Prince's linear layer is done share-wise. Both are non-complete and uniform, and such that a register layer is placed after the only nonlinear layer, namely after Q_{294}. Since the cipher is implemented in parallel and calculates regular and inverse diffusion layers simultaneously, the chosen approach may significantly decrease the security with non-uniform inputs against noisy-probing adversary. To reduce the probability of leakage, we add two more registers in the design. One register is added before inverse diffusion to disable it, as it is unnecessary until the end of fifth round. The other register is added after ShiftRows operation. The details on the S-box and its inverse decomposition and maskings of its quadratic substitutions are given in Appendix A.

The architecture of the masking follows a round-based design. In total, the original version needs 36 cycles and does not require fresh randomness for its computation. Our modified version needs 48 clock cycles, due to the presence of new registers. The schematic of the design can be found in Figure 5 in [11]. The data path is 64×3 bits width indicating a masked state. Round constants and the key are XORed with the first share of the state.

The threshold implementation of the S-box has interesting cryptanalytic properties which we can use when evaluating the security of the cipher with non-uniform inputs. Namely, the masked S-box has a nontrivial upper bound on the maximum absolute correlation.

Lemma 1 (Correlation of the Masked Prince S-box). *Let $\bar{S} : \mathbb{V}_a \to \mathbb{V}_b$ be any restriction of the sharing of the masked Prince S-box S. Denote its absolute correlation matrix by $|C^{\bar{S}}|$. For any $u, v \in \mathbb{F}_2^\ell / \mathbb{V}^\perp$ such that $u \neq 0$, it holds that $|C_{u,v}^{\bar{S}}| \leq 2^{-1.41}$.*

The above result will be used in the analysis of non-uniform inputs.

For simplicity of the analysis, we keep the key as a constant (as a result, we do not need to consider trails including the key schedule). Meaning that for the theoretical and experimental analysis, we do not consider the influence of the key and instead only consider a non-uniform masking of the plaintext. We note that with this analysis, the security of the masked cipher including the key (given that the key is uniformly masked) is also included (with the possible effect that the masked key improves the security due to the increased entropy).

An Insecure Non-uniform Input. We first detail the non-uniform masking of the plaintext which shows negative experimental results in PROLEAD and on FPGA as featured in Sect. 4. For the masking of the plaintext we use 32 random bits (versus 128 bits for a uniform three-sharing), and we re-use this randomness row-by-row. We depict this as follows

$$\begin{pmatrix} r_1 \ r_2 \ r_3 \ r_4 \\ r_1 \ r_2 \ r_3 \ r_4 \\ r_1 \ r_2 \ r_3 \ r_4 \\ r_1 \ r_2 \ r_3 \ r_4 \end{pmatrix}, \tag{1}$$

with r_i eight bits of (ideal) randomness. Namely, each cell in a column of the state is masked using the same randomness.

We analyse the effect of this non-uniform input masking using the linear cryptanalytic techniques detailed in Sect. 2.3. To recap, we use a trail based approach. To that end, we study the activity patterns through the masked Prince given the non-uniform input (or given the uniform input with the non-uniform encoder *Enc* from Fig. 2). When we call some parts of the state *active*, we mean the non-zero linear approximations are applied to those parts. We consider (masked) cells of the cipher's state as main indicators of the activity propagation. Using the resulting trails, we find the dependency between the probed values and the initially masked input secret. Due to the way the plaintext is shared, when activating a cell masked with r_i, we have to activate at least one other cell masked with the same randomness r_i. This results in the constraint that each row either has no cells activated or at least two cells activated. We then analyse the resulting activity patterns. We stop the activity pattern when a single probe can cover the output activity. Namely, in Prince, this is when only one input of a single MixColumns function is active or when only one S-box is active.

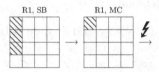

Fig. 3. The trail for the threshold implementation of Prince with the non-uniform input from Eq. (1) activating at most 3 masked S-boxes in the first round. SB stands for SubCell, MC for MixColumn. The lighting indicates a single-bit probe in the active cell before it and will be omitted on the following pictures.

Considering the described approach, we can see in Fig. 3 that the input of the first MixColumns function is already non-uniform. As a result, at most three masked S-boxes are in the trail (the branch number of Prince's Mix-Columns minus one), each with a maximum absolute correlation of $2^{-1.41}$ following Lemma 1. When probing the S-box, a glitch-extended probe can view up to 16 bits due to the parallel architecture. A probe placed after MixColumns reveals 9 bits, because due to affine layers, each glitch-extended probe can view several bits of cells in the first round. Considering the bound from Theorem 1, we find that $\varepsilon \approx 1$. As a result, the non-uniformity is so high that no relevant bound can be found. Thus, this method should be insecure and, in practice, it should leak. In Sects. 4.1 and 4.2, we have implemented this case study in PROLEAD and on FPGA and observed this leakage.

A Secure Non-uniform Input. The previous example already shows that badly chosen non-uniform inputs can lead to insecurities. We now detail a non-uniform masking (with the same entropy as the insecure example) of the plaintext which shows positive experimental results in PROLEAD and on FPGA as detailed in Sects. 4.1 and 4.2.

For this example, we again need 32 random bits which are re-used now in a different, row-wise, manner. We mask the plaintext as follows

$$\begin{pmatrix} r_1 & r_1 & r_1 & r_1 \\ r_2 & r_2 & r_2 & r_2 \\ r_3 & r_3 & r_3 & r_3 \\ r_4 & r_4 & r_4 & r_4 \end{pmatrix}, \tag{2}$$

with r_i eight bits of (ideal) randomness.

Applying the same strategy as for the insecure case, we find that the trail activating the least number of masked S-boxes ends in an S-box operation of the round three and activates 12 masked S-boxes. The trail is depicted in Fig. 4.

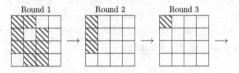

Fig. 4. The best trail for the threshold implementation of Prince with the non-uniform input from Eq. (2) activating 12 masked S-boxes.

Considering the above trail, we calculate the advantage of a bounded-query noisy-probing adversary. A probe in a masked S-box views at most 16 bits, namely when propagating through the affine layers and branching, the probe returns two shares of two clock cycles. Moreover, the best trail activates 12 masked S-boxes each with a maximum absolute correlation of $2^{-1.41}$ following Lemma 1. As a result,

$$\varepsilon := \|\widehat{p}_{\mathbf{z}} - \delta_0\|_2^2 \leq |\text{supp}\,\widehat{p}_{\mathbf{z}}|\,\|\widehat{p}_{\mathbf{z}} - \delta_0\|_\infty^2 \leq 2^{16}\,2^{-33.84} = 2^{-17.84}.$$

The above calculation gives the following bound on the advantage of a noisy-probing adversary.

$$\text{Adv}_{\text{2-thr}}(\mathcal{A}) \leq \sqrt{\frac{q}{\lambda 2^{16.84}}},$$

where λ is the addition of noise that would be observed during practical experiments. It was mentioned in the paper of Beyne *et al.* that the noise that was observed during evaluation on an FPGA was bounded by $\lambda < 2^9$. Given that we take around 50M $\approx 2^{25}$ traces, the above bound looks to be a promising candidate to be tested. In Sect. 4, we provide PROLEAD and FPGA experimental results.

Given that Prince's MixColumns works on four cells at a time and since we require the input of this operation to be (close-to) uniform, using less than 32-bits of randomness to mask the input would likely lead to insecure designs. Nevertheless, a carefully chosen masking of the S-box and the input might allow for a further reduction in cost. Such an optimisation would be non-trivial and we leave it as an open problem.

3.2   Masked Midori64 with Non-uniform Inputs

We apply the analysis on a second case study. Namely, we investigate non-uniform inputs to a threshold implementation of the Midori64 cipher. Like in the Prince example, we use no less than 32 bits to mask the plaintext because we aim to preserve the uniformity of the first MixColumns operation.

Midori64 Cipher. Midori [1] is a block cipher optimised for low-energy usage. The S-box is also used in other block ciphers including CRAFT [4] and MAN-TIS [3]. In this work, we specifically look at the Midori64 variant which has a 128-bit key and a 64-bit state that is split into 4-bit cells. An involutive binary quasi-MDS matrix together with a permutation of the 4-bit cells form the diffusion layer and it uses a 4-bit cubic S-box as the non-linear layer. Midori64 has a simple key schedule where each round either the left or right half of the master key is XORed to the state of the cipher.

Masking Details. To create the first-order secure masking of Midori64 we adopt the approach described in the work by Moradi *et al.* [18] with a change of the decomposition choice where we switch the quadratic class Q_{12} for the classes Q_{294} and Q_{299}. The architecture comprises only the encryption of the Midori64 and follows a pipelined structure as depicted in Fig. 5.

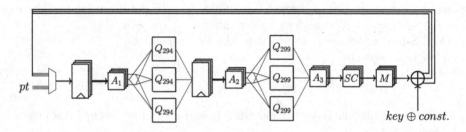

Fig. 5. Midori64 encryption round-based architecture.

Midori64 S-box is affine equivalent to the cubic class C_{266} and can be decomposed into two quadratic bijections. The decomposition we choose for our experiments is

$$S = A_3 \circ Q_{299} \circ A_2 \circ Q_{294} \circ A_1$$

with the affine functions A_1, A_2, A_3 and the quadratic classes Q_{299}, Q_{294}. More details on the decomposition and its masking are given in Appendix B. The pipelined architecture implies two register stages: one placed before the S-box and another one inside of it to split the nonlinear layers. It increases the latency of the implementation; nevertheless allowing to encrypt two plaintexts at the same time. The chosen design needs 32 clock cycles to perform one encryption and does not require fresh randomness for its computation. Similar to the design of the threshold implementation of Prince, the key is considered a constant. As a result, the secure example of a non-uniform input below would also be secure in case the key is (uniformly) masked.

The threshold implementation of the S-box has the following cryptanalytic property.

Lemma 2 (Correlation of the Masked Midori64 S-box). *Let $\bar{S} : \mathbb{V}_a \to \mathbb{V}_b$ be any restriction of the masking of S defined above. Denote its absolute* *correlation matrix by* $|C^{\bar{S}}|$. *For any* $u, v \in \mathbb{F}_2^{\ell}/\mathbb{V}^{\perp}$ *such that* $u \neq 0$, *it holds that* $|C_{u,v}^{\bar{S}}| \leq 2^{-2}$.

An Insecure Non-uniform Input. An insecure example is designed following the same principle as for the corresponding case in Sect. 3.1 for Prince. We initialise the state with 32-bits of randomness placing them as follows

$$\begin{pmatrix} r_1 & r_2 & r_3 & r_4 \\ r_2 & r_1 & r_4 & r_3 \\ r_3 & r_4 & r_1 & r_2 \\ r_4 & r_3 & r_2 & r_1 \end{pmatrix}. \tag{3}$$

With the above masking of the plaintext, an input to an S-box on the second round is non-uniform. The trail to such an S-box activates three cells with the same randomness because of the diffusion layer.

To verify whether the advantage of the noisy probing adversary is high, we use the analysis from Sect. 2.3. Recall from Lemma 2 that a masked S-box has a maximum absolute correlation of 2^{-2} and that we activate only three of them. A probe placed in the S-box after the first round will reveal at most 8 bits of information because of the Q_{299} quadratic layer. If the probe is placed after the MixColumn operation, it views at most $8 \cdot 3 = 24$ bits due to the quasi-MDS matrix and the absence of a register between Q_{299} and the MixColumns layer. Thus, we find that $\varepsilon \approx 1$. As a result, we expect to quickly observe leakage in this case. In Sects. 4.1 and 4.2, we have implemented this case study in PROLEAD and on FPGA and observed this leakage.

A Secure Non-uniform Input. For the secure non-uniform masking of the plaintext, we need again a total of 32 random bits and reuse the randomness over the rows the same way as it was done in Sect. 3.1 for the secure non-uniform input example. We represent the masking of the plaintext as a matrix

$$\begin{pmatrix} r_1 & r_1 & r_1 & r_1 \\ r_2 & r_2 & r_2 & r_2 \\ r_3 & r_3 & r_3 & r_3 \\ r_4 & r_4 & r_4 & r_4 \end{pmatrix}, \tag{4}$$

with r_i eight bits of randomness.

We analyse activity patterns for Midori64 which end in a single S-box or a single active column and which start with the constraint that a row either has no activations or at least two active cells. The best trail with these constraints activates at least 12 masked S-boxes and is depicted in Fig. 6.

As we already mentioned for the insecure case, a probe placed after MixColumn can observe up to 24 wires and the masked S-box has a maximum absolute correlation of 2^{-2}. From the above, we find that

$$\varepsilon := \|\widehat{p_{\mathbf{z}}} - \delta_0\|_2^2 \leq |\mathrm{supp}\, \widehat{p_{\mathbf{z}}}| \, \|\widehat{p_{\mathbf{z}}} - \delta_0\|_{\infty}^2 \leq 2^{24}\, 2^{-48} = 2^{-24},$$

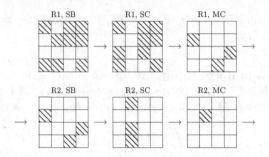

Fig. 6. An example of the best trail for the masked Midori64 with a non-uniform input activating 12 masked S-boxes in 2 rounds (denoted R1 and R2). SB stands for SubCell, SC for ShuffleCell, and MC for MixColumn.

which provides the following advantage for a non-uniform input masking

$$\mathrm{Adv}_{2\text{-thr}}(\mathcal{A}) \leq \sqrt{\frac{q}{\lambda 2^{23}}}.$$

Similar to Prince's secure case, the above advantage shows the masking is a promising candidate for practical verification. Its results are found in Sect. 4.

We also tested another way to re-use the same amount of initial random bits (32-bits), namely a column-wise masking similar to the masking in Eq. (1) of Prince (which was an insecure example). The case of a column-wise masking for Midori64 provides the same security bound as for the row-wise masking which is detailed above. This case was also tested in PROLEAD and lead to a secure result. We provide these test results in Appendix C.4.

4 Practical Evaluation and Efficiency

In this section, we provide experimental analyses of the proposed security claims for both the Prince cipher from Sect. 3.1 and the Midori64 cipher from Sect. 3.2. The section is divided into three parts: a noiseless verification is done using the PROLEAD tool from Müller *et al.* [19] in Sect. 4.1, a more realistic noisy result is obtained from FPGA experiments in Sect. 4.2, and an efficiency analysis is done in Sect. 4.3.

4.1 PROLEAD Experiments

PROLEAD is a recently developed automated tool which allows to analyse the statistical independence of simulated intermediates probed by a robust-probing adversary following the definition by Faust *et al.* [12]. Among its benefits are the abilities to handle full masked cipher implementations and to detect flaws related to the occurrence of glitches. The tool does not require any power model as it processes only gate-level netlists.

We use PROLEAD to check the correctness of our assumptions about the threshold-probing adversary advantage claimed in Sects. 3.1 and 3.2 following the analysis detailed in Sect. 2.3. Since the tool does not consider noise during statistical evaluation, we omit the noise parameter λ used in the Theorem 1 (we set $\lambda = 1$). To evaluate any leakage, PROLEAD uses a likelihood ratio G-test of independence [24] as a statistical hypothesis test based on multinomial distributions. It tests the goodness of fit of observed frequencies to their expected frequencies. The method is applied to contingency tables containing the distributions for all glitch-extended probing sets generated for the design. The sizes of those probing sets depend on the glitch-extended probing model which can reveal many bits under a single probe making the tables significantly large. For example, the maximum number of probes per largest set is 32 and 39[2] for the Midori64 and Prince designs, respectively.

PROLEAD operates in two modes, namely a normal mode and a compact mode. The difference lies in the contingency table calculation. In normal mode, the columns of the distribution tables are calculated using the concatenated values of all probed bits from the particular set that are called *labels*. Each label represents an entry of a contingency table where the frequency of the label's appearance per group is stored. Thus, it is possible to acquire the tables with up to 2^{n_p} columns, where n_p equals the number of wires within one probe in the glitch-extended probing set. In compact mode, the labels for the distribution tables are provided based on the Hamming weight of a probing set which allows for a more computation friendly verification at the cost of accuracy. To summarise, the normal mode provides more accurate information on the observed leakage, whereas it is possible to conduct more experiments for larger inputs in the compact mode.

We begin the evaluation process with checking our implementations in a compact mode to verify their security against first-order glitch-extended probing adversaries when uniform randomness is used. We perform up to 100M simulations. The results for those and the following experiments are shown in Table 1. We find that the implementations with uniform inputs do not leak during the simulations as would be expected. Excerpts with the results from the PROLEAD reports can be found in Appendix C.

Then, we use PROLEAD to evaluate leakage for the same designs with non-uniform inputs. Since the tool is only designed to create uniform maskings of the input, we add an intermediate module to our design, that is excluded from the probing list, to reuse generated randomness in composition of the non-uniform shares. For the cases with "insecure" inputs, the tool shows immediate[3] leakage significantly exceeding the threshold for the statistical tests in both modes which

---

[2] The size of the largest set may include control logic wires of the algorithm (like counter, start, and select). These bits do not contribute to the advantage of the noisy threshold-probing adversary.

[3] Simulations in PROLEAD are split into several iterations with a chosen step. Here, we set a step of 1M and 128k traces for the compact and normal modes, respectively.

is in line with the theoretical analyses in Sect. 3. Moreover, the leakage is observed only in some particular rounds of the ciphers (see Table 1).

Finally, we test the "secure" non-uniform designs. Again, we observe growing leakage during the simulations. However, this time the threshold is achieved only after significantly more experiments, and the leakage is detected during the later rounds in accordance with our trails from Sect. 3. We pay closer attention to the tests in normal mode, since those are more related to a threshold-probing adversary model, and see the leakage again. This time the number of traces needed to conclude the insecurity of a design is closely related to the bounds we proposed considering the absence of noise ($\lambda = 1$).

Table 1. Results of PROLEAD experiments of the Prince masking detailed in Sect. 3.1 and of the Midori64 cipher from Sect. 3.2. We detail after how many experiments PRO-LEAD finds leakage and in which clock cycles the leakage occurs (including two cycles to initialise the cipher) and in which round of the cipher the leakage occurs.

Cipher	Case	Mode	Passed	#Traces	#Cycle	#Round
Prince	Uniform	compact	✓	100M	NA	NA
	"Insecure" Non-Uniform	compact	✗	1M	4, ..., 10	1, 2, 3
		normal	✗	128k	4, ..., 10	1, 2, 3
	"Secure" Non-Uniform	compact	✗	48M	10	3
		normal	✗	3.8M	10	3
Midori64	Uniform	compact	✓	100M	NA	NA
	"Insecure" Non-Uniform	compact	✗	1M	5,6,7	2,3
		normal	✗	128k	5,6,7	2,3
	"Secure" Non-Uniform	compact	✗	2M	7	3
		normal	✗	6.4M	8	3

4.2   FPGA Experiments

For the practical experiments, we used a Xilinx Spartan-6 FPGA on a SAKURA-G evaluation board [14] and supplied the device with a stable 6.144 MHz clock. For the randomness generation, we focus on providing comprehensive results whether randomness can be re-used when masking the input of the cipher. As a result, we use a heavy cryptographic random number generator, namely one based on AES-128, to ensure the limited randomness given to the threshold implementation is of good quality such that it does not bias our results.

We collect power consumption traces by monitoring the voltage drop over a 1Ω shunt resistor placed on the VDD path of the target FPGA and using a digital oscilloscope at a sampling rate of 500 MS/s. For the measurement's analysis, we follow TVLA requirements [2] to conduct first-order fixed vs. random plaintext t-tests. The encryption is performed up to 50M times receiving either masked fixed or masked random plaintexts. This technique allows to detect the first-order side-channel leakage without implementing an actual key-recovery attack.

We perform an analysis for each example introduced in Sect. 3. To do the first-order t-test, we collect 4000 and 3000 sample points (the number of points that comprise a complete waveform record, determined by the amount of data that can be captured by an oscilloscope.) for the Prince and Midori64 implementations, respectively. The corresponding results are shown in Figs. 7 and 8 including the absolute t-value changes through the number of traces sampled.

From Fig. 7, we observe that the threshold implementation of Prince with a uniform input is secure (as expected). As a sanity check, we also evaluated the implementation with the random number generator turned off to find that the implementation leaks (again, as expected). The "insecure" non-uniform input leaks almost immediately and we see a spike of leakage each cycle of the implementation. However, the "secure" non-uniform input does not leak even at 50M traces. Together with the theoretical analysis and the PROLEAD analysis, we can conclude that it is viable to use the threshold implementation of Prince with such a non-uniform input.

From Fig. 8, we observe similar results for the threshold implementation of the Midori64 cipher. It is interesting to note that the "insecure" non-uniform input only leaks in the second round of the cipher, but then becomes secure. This can be explained from the strong cryptanalytic properties of its diffusion layer and its masked S-box. As the computation of the cipher continues, the non-uniform randomness is processed more-and-more via a good cryptographic function making it less-and-less distinguishable from uniform random. We note that Prince's behaviour with the "insecure" non-uniform input should be the same, but that due to the multiplexers in the architecture the same leakage from the first round is repeated each cycle. Again, the "secure" non-uniform input shows no leakage in the t-test showing that it is possible to work with the threshold implementation without giving a full entropy input.

4.3   Efficiency Comparison

We quickly provide the efficiency measures of the threshold implementations of the Prince and Midori64 ciphers from Sects. 3.1 and 3.2 though we note that we worked with tried-and-tested threshold implementations and that their efficiency was not the goal of the work. Table 2 provides the cost in terms of area, latency, and total random bits all designs use. We note that while we report on the randomness cost in bits, we have not investigated the related cost of the RNG which generates this randomness.

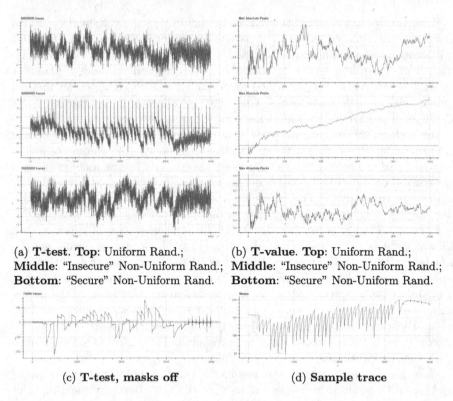

(a) **T-test. Top**: Uniform Rand.;   (b) **T-value. Top**: Uniform Rand.;
Middle: "Insecure" Non-Uniform Rand.;   **Middle**: "Insecure" Non-Uniform Rand.;
Bottom: "Secure" Non-Uniform Rand.   **Bottom**: "Secure" Non-Uniform Rand.

(c) **T-test, masks off**   (d) **Sample trace**

Fig. 7. Masked Prince implementation with 50M traces where we test the implementation with uniform randomness and the non-uniform case studies from Sect. 3.1. We show sample traces with masks off and masks on and we show the final t-test together with the maximum absolute t-test value evolution over the number of traces.

For the Midori64 case, we find that the non-uniform input allows a four times reduction of the total randomness cost without requiring a trade-off in area or latency. However, the Prince masking requires an extra register layer in order to have a sufficient theoretical bound. We have performed leakage tests with a non-uniform input without this extra layer and have seen secure results. Thus, we believe the cheaper Prince masking with the non-uniform input can still be used in practice and that the discrepancy comes from the theoretical framework's overestimation on glitches, similar to the observations from [6] on glitches in a masked AES S-box.

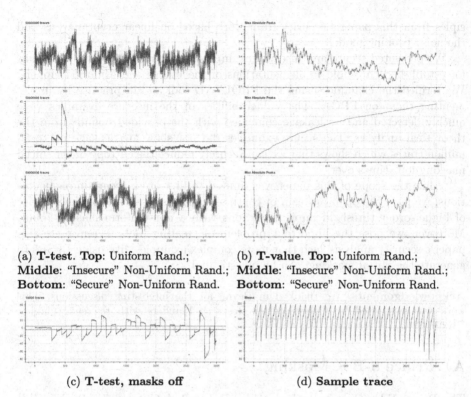

(a) **T-test**. **Top**: Uniform Rand.;
Middle: "Insecure" Non-Uniform Rand.;
Bottom: "Secure" Non-Uniform Rand.

(b) **T-value**. **Top**: Uniform Rand.;
Middle: "Insecure" Non-Uniform Rand.;
Bottom: "Secure" Non-Uniform Rand.

(c) **T-test, masks off**

(d) **Sample trace**

Fig. 8. Masked Midori64 implementation with 50M traces where we test the implementation with uniform randomness and the case studies from Sect. 3.2. We show sample traces with masks off and masks on and we show the final t-test together with the maximum absolute t-test value evolution over the number of traces.

Table 2. The efficiency measures in area, latency, and total randomness cost of both the Prince and Midori64 threshold implementations using uniform or non-uniform randomness with the NANGATE 45nm Open Cell Library [20].

Cipher	#Shares	Area (GE)	Latency (Cycles)	Rand. (Bits)
Prince	3	8353	36	128
		11050	48	32
Midori64	3	7324	32	128
		7324	32	32

5 Conclusion

In this paper, we have shown that using a non-uniform masked input for a threshold implementation can remain first-order secure in face of a practical evaluation. We have also shown that the non-uniform masking itself should be chosen carefully and differently for each symmetric primitive following the principles from this paper's security framework based on linear cryptanalysis and the noisy probing model.

We presented secure and insecure examples of non-uniform initial maskings for established threshold implementations of the Prince and Midori64 ciphers. We verified the examples using the PROLEAD tool and in practice by implementing them on FPGA. The vulnerabilities of the insecure examples were quickly detected and its leakage coincided with the provided bounds from the theoretical analyses. The secure examples did not show any leakage up to 50 million traces which shows that we can securely reduce the entropy of the initial masking four times over.

While the scope of this paper was limited to first-order secure implementations, we pose the open problem of continuing the investigation of the security of higher-order threshold implementations with a non-uniform masked input. Moreover, we pose the important problem of creating tools to automate this paper's security analysis such that more complex examples, like using LFSRs to generate the initial masking, can be investigated.

Acknowledgements. We thank Tim Beyne for the interesting discussions. This work was supported by CyberSecurity Research Flanders with reference number VR20192203.

A   Prince S-Box Masking

The Prince S-box has its lookup table $[B, F, 3, 2, A, C, 9, 1, 6, 7, 8, 0, E, 5, D, 4]$ and is decomposed as follows

$$S = A_1 \circ Q_{294} \circ A_2 \circ Q_{294} \circ A_3 \circ Q_{294} \circ A_4.$$

The inverse S-box has its lookup table $[B, 7, 3, 2, F, D, 8, 9, A, 6, 4, 0, 5, E, C, 1]$ and is decomposed as

$$S^{-1} = A_5 \circ Q_{294} \circ A_2 \circ Q_{294} \circ A_3 \circ Q_{294} \circ A_6.$$

The inputs of the following 4-bit functions are designated with a nibble (x, y, z, w), where x is the most significant bit and w s the least significant bit.

$$A_1 = [1 + x + z; 1 + y; z + w; z]$$
$$A_2 = [x + z + w; 1 + x + z; 1 + y + z + w; x + y + z + w]$$
$$A_3 = [w; z; y; x]$$
$$A_4 = [1 + x + y + z + w; x; 1 + x + z + w; w]$$
$$A_5 = [1 + y; x + z; 1 + y + w; 1 + z + w]$$
$$A_6 = [1 + x + w; y; w; 1 + z],$$

with

$$A_1 = [C, E, 7, 5, 8, A, 3, 1, 4, 6, F, D, 0, 2, B, 9]$$
$$A_2 = [6, D, 9, 2, 5, E, A, 1, B, 0, 4, F, 8, 3, 7, C]$$
$$A_3 = [0, 8, 4, C, 2, A, 6, E, 1, 9, 5, D, 3, B, 7, F]$$
$$A_4 = [A, 1, 0, B, 2, 9, 8, 3, 4, F, E, 5, C, 7, 6, D]$$
$$A_5 = [B, 8, E, D, 1, 2, 4, 7, F, C, A, 9, 5, 6, 0, 3]$$
$$A_6 = [9, 3, 8, 2, D, 7, C, 6, 1, B, 0, A, 5, F, 4, E].$$

The above affine functions are masked share-by-share. The quadratic layer $Q_{294} = [a, b, c, d] = [x, y, z + xy, w + xz]$ is masked as follows

$$a^i = x^i$$
$$b^i = y^i$$
$$c^i = z^i + x^i y^i + x^i y^{i+1} + x^{i+1} y^i$$
$$d^i = w^i + x^i z^i + x^i z^{i+1} + x^{i+1} z^i,$$

for the shares $i \in \{0, 1, 2\}$, where the convention is used that superscripts wrap around at two. The above masking is uniform and non-complete.

B Midori64 S-Box Masking

The Midori64 S-box has its lookup table $[C, A, D, 3, E, B, F, 7, 8, 9, 1, 5, 0, 2, 4, 6]$ and is decomposed as

$$S = A_1 \circ Q_{299} \circ A_2 \circ Q_{294} \circ A_3.$$

The inputs of the following 4-bit functions are designated with a nibble (x, y, z, w), where x is the most significant bit and w s the least significant bit.

$$A_1 = [1 + x + y + z; 1 + x + y + w; 1 + x + y + z + w; y + w]$$
$$A_2 = [w; x; y; z]$$
$$A_3 = [1 + y + w; 1 + y + z + w; w; x + z + w],$$

with

$$A_1 = [E, 9, 4, 3, 1, 6, B, C, 0, 7, A, D, F, 8, 5, 2]$$
$$A_2 = [0, 8, 1, 9, 2, A, 3, B, 4, C, 5, D, 6, E, 7, F]$$
$$A_3 = [C, 3, 9, 6, 0, F, 5, A, D, 2, 8, 7, 1, E, 4, B].$$

The above affine functions are masked share-by-share. The quadratic layer $Q_{294} = [a, b, c, d] = [x, y, z + xy, w + xz]$ is masked as follows

$$a^{i-1} = x^i$$
$$b^{i-1} = y^i$$
$$c^{i-1} = z^i + x^i y^i + x^i y^{i+1} + x^{i+1} y^i$$
$$d^{i-1} = w^i + x^i z^i + x^i z^{i+1} + x^{i+1} z^i,$$

and the quadratic layer $Q_{299} = [a, b, c, d] = [x, y + xy + xz, z + xy + xz + xw, w + xy + xw]$ is masked as

$$a^{i-1} = x^i$$
$$b^{i-1} = y^i + (x^i y^i + x^i y^{i+1} + x^{i+1} y^i) + (x^i z^i + x^i z^{i+1} + x^{i+1} z^i)$$
$$c^{i-1} = z^i + (x^i y^i + x^i y^{i+1} + x^{i+1} y^i) + (x^i z^i + x^i z^{i+1} + x^{i+1} z^i)$$
$$\qquad + (x^i w^i + x^i w^{i+1} + x^{i+1} w^i)$$
$$d^{i-1} = w^i + (x^i y^i + x^i y^{i+1} + x^{i+1} y^i) + (x^i w^i + x^i w^{i+1} + x^{i+1} w^i).$$

for the shares $i \in \{0, 1, 2\}$, where the convention is used that superscripts wrap around at two. The above maskings are uniform and non-complete.

C   PROLEAD Experiments

The PROLEAD tool outputs data in two formats: tables with an overview of the current status of the evaluation process and reports for each simulation step. We further provide shortened versions of the tables for our experiments and add them with the overview of some probing sets from the reports. In the following tables, we will write probe sets (such as _00480_[35] (7)). Such sets include several register values from the implementation together with the cycle of the computation (in this example seven).

C.1   Designs with Uniform Randomness

(See Tables 3, 4 and 5).

Table 3. Evaluation info: Uniform randomness.

Cipher	#Standard Probes	#Extended Probes	Security Order	#Probing Sets	Maximum #Probes per Set
Prince	17600	20880	1	9080	101
Midori64	50880	29120	1	14480	32

Table 4. Evaluation results: Prince, uniform case.

Elapsed Time (s)	Required RAM (GB)	Processed Simulations	Probe Set with Highest Information Leakage	−log10(p)	Status
101	26.23	1000000	_03951_[61] (18)	4.887129	OKAY
202	26.23	2000000	_04211_[21] (22)	7.141349	LEAKAGE
304	26.23	3000000	_04081_[32] (6)	5.383576	LEAKAGE
406	26.23	4000000	_04211_[39] (27)	3.671223	OKAY
9655	26.23	99000000	_03951_[53] (40)	4.154447	OKAY
9751	26.23	100000000	_04081_[19] (1)	4.118873	OKAY

Table 5. Evaluation results: Midori64, uniform case.

Elapsed Time (s)	Required RAM (GB)	Processed Simulations	Probe Set with Highest Information Leakage	−log10(p)	Status
89	33.32	1000000	Sbox[15].register.in[5] (20)	4.004151	OKAY
179	33.32	2000000	ciphertext_1[63] (9)	2.891629	OKAY
269	33.32	3000000	Sbox[7].register.in[1] (4)	3.397437	OKAY
8560	33.32	99000000	_00226_[19] (1)	4.151201	OKAY
8646	33.32	100000000	_00226_[19] (1)	4.091332	OKAY

C.2   Midori64, Non-uniform Randomness

(See Tables 6, 7 and 8).

Table 6. Evaluation info: Midori64, non-uniform cases.

Case	Mode	#Stand. Probes	#Extend. Probes	#Probe Sets	Maximum #Probes per Set
"Insecure"	compact	43200	29100	14480	32
	normal	10800	7280	3620	
"Secure"	compact	43200	29120	14480	
	normal	10800	7280	3620	

Table 7. Evaluation results: Midori64, "insecure", normal mode.

Elapsed Time (s)	Required RAM (GB)	Processed Simulations	Probe Set with Highest Information Leakage	−log10(p)	Status
34	8.24	128000/ 438057	_00208_[63] (5)	inf	LEAKAGE
457	45.70	1280000/ 1346575	_00208_[63] (5)	inf	LEAKAGE

Table 8. Evaluation results: Midori64, "secure", normal mode.

Elapsed Time (s)	Required RAM (GB)	Processed Simulations	Probe Set with Highest Information Leakage	−log10(p)	Status
33	9.21	128000/ 438083	Sbox[7].register.in[5] (6)	3.912678	OKAY
73	13.74	256000/ 615365	Sbox[14].register.in[5] (10)	3.354810	OKAY
4318	273.38	6272000/ 2767077	Sbox[9].register.in[4] (8)	4.880834	OKAY
4473	282.42	6400000/ 2790153	Sbox[9].register.in[4] (8)	5.094253	LEAKAGE

C.3   Prince, Non-uniform Randomness

(See Tables 9, 10 and 11)

Table 9. Evaluation info: Prince, non-uniform cases.

Case	Mode	#Stand. Probes	#Extend. Probes	#Probe Sets	Maximum #Probes per Set
"Insecure"	compact	16500	14300	8380	39
	normal	7425	6435	3771	
"Secure"	compact	16500	14300	8380	
	normal	7425	6435	3771	

Table 10. Evaluation results: Prince, "insecure", normal mode.

Elapsed Time (s)	Required RAM (GB)	Processed Simulations	Probe Set with Highest Information Leakage	−log10(p)	Status
46	10.26	128000/ 293647	beta_reg_3.in[22](4)	inf	LEAKAGE
276	45.70	768000/ 316035	beta_reg_3.in[22](4)	inf	LEAKAGE

Table 11. Evaluation results: Prince, "secure", normal mode.

Elapsed Time (s)	Required RAM (GB)	Processed Simulations	Probe Set with Highest Information Leakage	−log10(p)	Status
48	11.05	128000/ 293811	_05111_ (4)	3.485201	OKAY
95	11.79	256000/ 313129	beta_reg_2.in[53] (6)	3.070294	OKAY
1385	11.99	3968000/ 316035	_04193_[16] (10)	5.983958	LEAKAGE
1431	11.99	4096000/ 316035	_04193_[17] (10)	5.668399	LEAKAGE

C.4   Midori64, "Secure" Non-uniform Case, Column-Wise

(See Tables 12, 13 and 14)

Table 12. Evaluation info: Midori64, column-wise.

Case	Mode	#Stand. Probes	#Extend. Probes	#Probe Sets	Maximum #Probes per Set
Column-wise	compact	43200	29120	14480	32
	normal	6480	4368	2172	

Table 13. Evaluation results: Midori64, column-wise, compact mode.

Elapsed Time (s)	Required RAM (GB)	Processed Simulations	Probe Set with Highest Information Leakage	−log10(p)	Status
94	33.34	1000000	ciphertext_1[35] (27)	4.696523	OKAY
187	33.34	2000000	Sbox[3].register.in[1] (20)	3.945218	OKAY
9222	33.34	101000000	Sbox[7].register.in[9] (8)	4.789482	OKAY
9312	33.34	102000000	Sbox[7].register.in[9] (8)	5.164452	LEAKAGE
13539	33.34	150000000	_00480_[35] (7)	8.223624	LEAKAGE

Table 14. Evaluation results: Midori64, column-wise, normal mode.

Elapsed Time (s)	Required RAM (GB)	Processed Simulations	Probe Set with Highest Information Leakage	−log10(p)	Status
21	7.71	128000/ 438075	Sbox[9].register.in[1]·(8)	2.371509	OKAY
46	10.60	256000/ 615407	_00480_[14] (3)	2.493538	OKAY
6551	238.73	9984000/ 3316723	_00220_[61] (3)	3.992771	OKAY
6712	239.51	10112000/ 3332201	_00220_[61] (3)	3.959946	OKAY

References

1. Banik, S., et al.: Midori: a block cipher for low energy. In: Iwata, T., Cheon, J.H. (eds.) ASIACRYPT 2015. LNCS, vol. 9453, pp. 411–436. Springer, Heidelberg (2015). https://doi.org/10.1007/978-3-662-48800-3_17
2. Becker, G.T., et al.: Test vector leakage assessment (TVLA) methodology in practice (2013)
3. Beierle, C., et al.: The SKINNY family of block ciphers and its low-latency variant MANTIS. In: Robshaw, M., Katz, J. (eds.) CRYPTO 2016. LNCS, vol. 9815, pp. 123–153. Springer, Heidelberg (2016). https://doi.org/10.1007/978-3-662-53008-5_5
4. Beierle, C., Leander, G., Moradi, A., Rasoolzadeh, S.: CRAFT: lightweight tweakable block cipher with efficient protection against DFA attacks. IACR Trans. Symmetric Cryptol. **2019**(1), 5–45 (2019)
5. Beyne, T., Dhooghe, S., Moradi, A., Shahmirzadi, A.R.: Cryptanalysis of efficient masked ciphers: applications to low latency. IACR Trans. Cryptogr. Hardw. Embed. Syst. **2022**(1), 679–721 (2022)
6. Beyne, T., Dhooghe, S., Ranea, A., Šijačić, D.: A low-randomness second-order masked AES. In: AlTawy, R., Hülsing, A. (eds.) SAC 2021. LNCS, vol. 13203, pp. 87–110. Springer, Cham (2022). https://doi.org/10.1007/978-3-030-99277-4_5
7. Beyne, T., Dhooghe, S., Zhang, Z.: Cryptanalysis of masked ciphers: a not so random idea. In: Moriai, S., Wang, H. (eds.) ASIACRYPT 2020. LNCS, vol. 12491, pp. 817–850. Springer, Cham (2020). https://doi.org/10.1007/978-3-030-64837-4_27
8. Bilgin, B., Nikova, S., Nikov, V., Rijmen, V., Stütz, G.: Threshold implementations of all 3 × 3 and 4 × 4 S-boxes. In: Prouff, E., Schaumont, P. (eds.) CHES 2012. LNCS, vol. 7428, pp. 76–91. Springer, Heidelberg (2012). https://doi.org/10.1007/978-3-642-33027-8_5
9. Bilgin, B., Nikova, S., Nikov, V., Rijmen, V., Stütz, G.: Threshold implementations of all 3 × 3 and 4 × 4 s-boxes. IACR Cryptology ePrint Archive, p. 300 (2012). https://eprint.iacr.org/2012/300
10. Borghoff, J., et al.: PRINCE – a low-latency block cipher for pervasive computing applications. In: Wang, X., Sako, K. (eds.) ASIACRYPT 2012. LNCS, vol. 7658, pp. 208–225. Springer, Heidelberg (2012). https://doi.org/10.1007/978-3-642-34961-4_14

11. Bozilov, D., Knezevic, M., Nikov, V.: Optimized threshold implementations: securing cryptographic accelerators for low-energy and low-latency applications. J. Cryptogr. Eng. **12**(1), 15–51 (2022). https://doi.org/10.1007/s13389-021-00276-5

12. Faust, S., Grosso, V., Pozo, S.M.D., Paglialonga, C., Standaert, F.: Composable masking schemes in the presence of physical defaults and the robust probing model. IACR Cryptology ePrint Archive, p. 711 (2017). https://eprint.iacr.org/2017/711

13. Faust, S., Grosso, V., Pozo, S.M.D., Paglialonga, C., Standaert, F.: Composable masking schemes in the presence of physical defaults & the robust probing model. IACR Trans. Cryptogr. Hardw. Embed. Syst. **2018**(3), 89–120 (2018)

14. Guntur, H., Ishii, J., Satoh, A.: Side-channel attack user reference architecture board SAKURA-G. In: IEEE 3rd Global Conference on Consumer Electronics, GCCE 2014, Tokyo, Japan, 7–10 October 2014, pp. 271–274. IEEE (2014). https://doi.org/10.1109/GCCE.2014.7031104

15. Ishai, Y., Sahai, A., Wagner, D.: Private circuits: securing hardware against probing attacks. In: Boneh, D. (ed.) CRYPTO 2003. LNCS, vol. 2729, pp. 463–481. Springer, Heidelberg (2003). https://doi.org/10.1007/978-3-540-45146-4_27

16. Kocher, P., Jaffe, J., Jun, B.: Differential power analysis. In: Wiener, M. (ed.) CRYPTO 1999. LNCS, vol. 1666, pp. 388–397. Springer, Heidelberg (1999). https://doi.org/10.1007/3-540-48405-1_25

17. Matsui, M.: Linear cryptanalysis method for DES cipher. In: Helleseth, T. (ed.) EUROCRYPT 1993. LNCS, vol. 765, pp. 386–397. Springer, Heidelberg (1994). https://doi.org/10.1007/3-540-48285-7_33

18. Moradi, A., Schneider, T.: Side-channel analysis protection and low-latency in action. In: Cheon, J.H., Takagi, T. (eds.) ASIACRYPT 2016. LNCS, vol. 10031, pp. 517–547. Springer, Heidelberg (2016). https://doi.org/10.1007/978-3-662-53887-6_19

19. Müller, N., Moradi, A.: PROLEAD: a probing-based hardware leakage detection tool. IACR Trans. Cryptogr. Hardw. Embed. Syst. **2022**(4), 311–348 (2022). https://doi.org/10.46586/tches.v2022.i4.311-348

20. NANGATE: The NanGate 45 nm Open Cell Library, version: PDKv1.3_v2010-12.Apache.CCL. https://github.com/The-OpenROAD-Project/OpenROAD-flow-scripts/tree/master/flow/platforms/nangate45

21. Nikova, S., Rechberger, C., Rijmen, V.: Threshold implementations against side-channel attacks and glitches. In: Ning, P., Qing, S., Li, N. (eds.) ICICS 2006. LNCS, vol. 4307, pp. 529–545. Springer, Heidelberg (2006). https://doi.org/10.1007/11935308_38

22. Shahmirzadi, A.R., Moradi, A.: Re-consolidating first-order masking schemes nullifying fresh randomness. IACR Trans. Cryptogr. Hardw. Embed. Syst. **2021**(1), 305–342 (2021). https://doi.org/10.46586/tches.v2021.i1.305-342

23. Shahmirzadi, A.R., Moradi, A.: Second-order SCA security with almost no fresh randomness. IACR Trans. Cryptogr. Hardw. Embed. Syst. **2021**(3), 708–755 (2021). https://doi.org/10.46586/tches.v2021.i3.708-755

24. Sokal, R., Rohlf, F.: Biometry: The Principles and Practice of Statistics in Biological Research. W. H. Freeman (1981). https://books.google.be/books?id=C-OTQgAACAAJ

25. Tardy-Corfdir, A., Gilbert, H.: A known plaintext attack of FEAL-4 and FEAL-6. In: Feigenbaum, J. (ed.) CRYPTO 1991. LNCS, vol. 576, pp. 172–182. Springer, Heidelberg (1992). https://doi.org/10.1007/3-540-46766-1_12

Post-Quantum Constructions

SMAUG: Pushing Lattice-Based Key Encapsulation Mechanisms to the Limits

Jung Hee Cheon[1,2] ⓘ, Hyeongmin Choe[1](✉) ⓘ, Dongyeon Hong[2],
and MinJune Yi[1]

[1] Seoul National University, Seoul, South Korea
{jhcheon,sixtail528,yiminjune}@snu.ac.kr
[2] CryptoLab Inc., Seoul, South Korea

Abstract. Recently, NIST has announced Kyber, a lattice-based key encapsulation mechanism (KEM), as a post-quantum standard. However, it is not the most efficient scheme among the NIST's KEM finalists. Saber enjoys more compact sizes and faster performance, and Mera et al. (TCHES '21) further pushed its efficiency, proposing a shorter KEM, Sable. As KEM are frequently used on the Internet, such as in TLS protocols, it is essential to achieve high efficiency while maintaining sufficient security.

In this paper, we further push the efficiency limit of lattice-based KEMs by proposing SMAUG, a new post-quantum KEM scheme whose IND-CCA2 security is based on the combination of MLWE and MLWR problems. We adopt several recent developments in lattice-based cryptography, targeting the *smallest* and the *fastest* KEM while maintaining high enough security against various attacks, with a full-fledged use of sparse secrets. Our design choices allow SMAUG to balance the decryption failure probability and ciphertext sizes without utilizing error correction codes, whose side-channel resistance remains open.

With a constant-time C reference implementation, SMAUG achieves ciphertext sizes up to 12% and 9% smaller than Kyber and Saber, with much faster running time, up to 103% and 58%, respectively. Compared to Sable, SMAUG has the same ciphertext sizes but a larger public key, which gives a trade-off between the public key size versus performance; SMAUG has 39%–55% faster encapsulation and decapsulation speed in the parameter sets having comparable security.

Keywords: Key Encapsulation Mechanism · Public Key Encryption · Post Quantum Cryptography · Module Learning With Errors · Module Learning With Roundings

1 Introduction

Recent advances in quantum computers raise the demand for quantum-resistant cryptographic protocols, i.e., the Post-Quantum Cryptographic (PQC) schemes.

© The Author(s), under exclusive license to Springer Nature Switzerland AG 2024
C. Carlet et al. (Eds.): SAC 2023, LNCS 14201, pp. 127–146, 2024.
https://doi.org/10.1007/978-3-031-53368-6_7

As a consequence, the American National Institute of Standards and Technology (NIST) has established a standardization process focusing on Public Key Encryption (PKE), digital signature, and Key Encapsulation Mechanism (KEM). In particular, KEM is one of the most widely used algorithms over the Internet, such as in Transport Layer Security (TLS) protocols; however, the KEM currently used in the protocol is considered vulnerable to quantum attacks.

Various lattice-based KEMs [4,10,14,15,19,24,43,50] have been proposed and submitted to NIST PQC standardization to secure the Internet in the quantum world. During the standardization process, diverse techniques improving efficiency or security were introduced. In 2020, NIST selected Kyber [14], Saber [50], and NTRU [19] as the lattice-based KEM finalists, having enough efficiency and quantum security based on the Module Learning With Errors (MLWE), Module Learning With Roundings (MLWR), and NTRU problems, respectively. Recently Kyber was selected as a future standard among the candidates.

As of independent interest to NIST's standardization, the KEM's efficiency is crucial since it is executed and transmitted frequently on the Internet. In particular, the TLS protocols are also necessary for embedded devices, so the efficiency requirement has become even more pressing with the proliferation of the Internet of Things (IoT). To this end, some variants of Saber focusing on efficiency, Scabbard [46], have been recently proposed by Mera et al. Scabbard consists of three schemes based on the Ring Learning With Roundings (RLWR) or MLWR problems, Floreta, Espada, and Sable, each targeting HW/SW-efficient, parallelizable, and shorter KEM than Saber. In particular, Sable achieves the smallest public key and ciphertext sizes among the KEM schemes targetting the NIST's security level 1 and low enough Decryption Failure Probability (DFP).

1.1   Our Results

In this work, we ask:

Can we further push the efficiency of the lattice-based KEMs to the limits?

Specifically, we propose a new lattice-based KEM, SMAUG, constructed based on both MLWE and MLWR problems. By bringing the MLWE-based public key generation and the sparse secret to Sable, SMAUG can enhance efficiency further. We aimed to achieve *the shortest* ciphertext among the LWE/LWR-based KEM schemes while maintaining the security level with *even better* performance.

The SMAUG. The design rationale of SMAUG aims to achieve small ciphertext and public key with low computational cost while maintaining security against various attacks. In more detail, we target the following practicality and security requirements considering real applications:

Practicality

- Both the public key and ciphertext must be short to minimize communication costs. We especially focus on the ciphertext size as it is more frequently transmitted.

- The key exchange protocol is frequently required on various personal devices, so a KEM algorithm with low computational costs is desirable.
- A compact secret key is beneficial in restricted settings such as embedded or IoT devices. Maintaining a secure zone is imperative to thwart physical attacks on the storage storing secret keys.

Security

- The shared key should have a large enough entropy, at least ≥ 256 bits, to prevent Grover's search [35].
- Security should be concretely guaranteed concerning the attacks on the underlying assumptions.
- The low enough DFP is essential to avoid the attacks boosting the failure and exploiting the decryption failures [26,40].
- As KEMs are widely used in various devices and systems, countermeasures against implementation-specific attacks should also be considered. Especially combined with DFP, using Error Correction Codes (ECC) on the message to reduce decryption failures should be avoided since masking ECC against side-channel attacks remains a challenging problem (Table 1).

Table 1. Parameter sets of SMAUG for NIST's security levels 1, 3, and 5. Security (Sec.) is given in classical core-SVP hardness. One core of Intel Core i7-10700k is used for cycle counts.

Scheme	Sizes (bytes)			Security			Cycle		
	sk	pk	ct	Lvl.	Sec.	DFP	KeyGen	Encap	Decap
SMAUG-128	176	672	672	1	120	2^{-120}	77k	77k	92k
SMAUG-192	236	1088	1024	3	181	2^{-136}	153k	136k	163k
SMAUG-256	218	1792	1472	5	264	2^{-167}	266k	270k	305k

To achieve this goal, we exploit the possible combination of the known techniques in lattice-based cryptography, such as underlying lattice assumptions, ciphertext compression, Fujisaki-Okamoto (FO) transforms, and the secret and error distribution.

Among the possibilities on the choice of lattice assumptions, we conclude to use LWE-based key generation and LWR-based encapsulation with sparse secrets in module lattices. This choice allows SMAUG to enjoy the conservative secret key security from the hardness of the un-rounded MLWE problem and explore efficiency on encapsulation and decapsulation from the MLWR-based approach.

Sparse secret allows SMAUG to enjoy fast polynomial multiplications and small secret keys. The sparse secret is widely used in homomorphic encryption (HE) schemes to speed up the expensive homomorphic operations and to reduce the noise [22,36], whose ability is attractive for efficient KEMs. By using the SampleInBall algorithm of Dilithium [29], we can efficiently sample the sparse ternary secrets. Regarding security, the hardness reductions for sparse LWE and LWR problems [23,24] from LWE problem exists; however, the concrete security should be treated carefully[1].

The MLWE-based public key of SMAUG uses the discrete Gaussian noise, which is scaled and approximated. While this approximation may result in a security loss compared to the ideal case, we can efficiently upper-bound with a small scaling factor due to Rényi divergence. By utilizing the logic minimization technique SMAUG uses a boolean discrete Gaussian sampler.

We take the recent approaches in FO transform for key exchange in the Quantum Random Oracle Model (QROM) [39] and apply it to our IND-CPA PKE, SMAUG.PKE. We use the FO transform with implicit rejection and no ciphertext contributions ($FO_m^{\not\perp}$).

We delicately choose three parameter sets for SMAUG regarding NIST's security levels 1, 3, and 5 (classical core-SVP hardness of 120, 180, and 260, respectively) and having DFP at least smaller than Saber.

Comparison to Other KEMs. We compare SMAUG with Kyber, Saber, and its variant Sable in Table 2.

Table 2. Comparison of recent KEM schemes. Security is given in the classical core-SVP hardness with DFP. The cycle counts are given relative to that of SMAUG's. The C implementations without AVX optimizations are used.

Schemes	Sizes (bytes)			Security		Cycle (ratio)		
	sk	pk	ct	Classic.	DFP	KeyGen	Encap	Decap
NIST's security level 1 (120)								
Kyber512 [14]	1632	800	768	118	2^{-139}	1.70	2.10	2.03
LightSaber [50]	832	672	736	118	2^{-120}	1.21	1.58	1.44
LightSable [46]	800	608	672	114	2^{-139}	1.10	1.48	1.39
SMAUG-128	176	672	672	120	2^{-120}	1	1	1
NIST's security level 3 (180)								
Kyber768 [14]	2400	1184	1088	183	2^{-164}	1.38	1.84	1.75
Saber [50]	1248	992	1088	189	2^{-136}	1.21	1.64	1.47
Sable [46]	1152	896	1024	185	2^{-143}	1.10	1.48	1.39
SMAUG-192	236	1088	1024	181	2^{-136}	1	1	1
NIST's security level 5 (260)								
Kyber1024 [14]	3168	1568	1568	256	2^{-174}	1.25	1.38	1.36
FireSaber [50]	1664	1312	1472	260	2^{-165}	1.21	1.58	1.44
FireSable [46]	1632	1312	1376	223	2^{-208}	1.03	1.25	1.22
SMAUG-256	218	1792	1472	264	2^{-167}	1	1	1

---

[1] We used the lattice-estimator [2], from https://github.com/malb/lattice-estimator (commit 9687562), while additionally considering other attacks targeting the sparsity.

Compared to Kyber-512 [14], the NIST-selected standard having security level 1, SMAUG-128 has 16% and 12% smaller public key and ciphertext, respectively. The secret key size of SMAUG is tiny and ready to use, which enable efficient management of secure zone in restricted IoT devices. With high enough security and low enough DFP, SMAUG further achieves 110% and 103% speed up in encapsulation and decapsulation.

Compared to LightSaber [50], one of the round 3 finalists with the security level 1, SMAUG-128, has 9% smaller ciphertext and the same public key size. Again, the secret key is significantly smaller than LightSaber, with a 58% and 44% speed up in encapsulation and decapsulation, respectively.

When compared to LightSable [46], SMAUG-128 has the same ciphertext size but a larger public key size. It can be seen as a trade-off as SMAUG achieves 48% and 39% faster encapsulation and decapsulation.

In NIST's security levels 3 and 5, SMAUG similarly outperforms Kyber and provides a trade-off with Saber and Sable. We refer to Sect. 6.2 for detailed comparisons.

Paper Organization. The rest of the paper is organized as follows. Section 2 defines the notations and summarizes the formal definitions of key encapsulation mechanisms with the relevant works. In Sect. 3, we introduce the design choices of SMAUG. In Sect. 4, we introduce SMAUG and its security proofs. We provide concrete security analysis and the recommended parameter sets in Sect. 5. Lastly, we give the performance result with comparisons to recent KEM schemes and the implementation details in Sect. 6.

2 Preliminaries

2.1 Notation

We denote matrices with bold and upper case letters (e.g., $\mathbf{A}$) and vectors with bold type and lower case letters (e.g., $\mathbf{b}$). Unless otherwise stated, the vector is a column vector.

We define a polynomial ring $\mathcal{R} = \mathbb{Z}[x]/(x^n + 1)$ where n is a power of 2 integers and denote a quotient ring by $\mathcal{R}_q = \mathbb{Z}[x]/(q, x^n + 1) = \mathbb{Z}_q[x]/(x^n + 1)$ for a positive integer q. For an integer η, we denote the set of polynomials of degree less than n with coefficients in $[-\eta, \eta] \cap \mathbb{Z}$ as S_η. Let $\tilde{S}_\eta$ be a set of polynomials of degree less than n with coefficients in $[-\eta, \eta) \cap \mathbb{Z}$. We denote a discrete Gaussian distribution with standard deviation σ as $\mathcal{D}_{\mathbb{Z},\sigma}$.

2.2 Public Key Encryption and Key Encapsulation Mechanism

We refer to [21] for the formalism of Public Key Encryption (PKE) and Key Encapsulation Mechanism (KEM). Note that we only focus on the adaptive IND-CCA attacks, i.e., IND-CCA2 attacks.

2.3   Fujisaki-Okamoto Transform

Fujiskai and Okamoto proposed a novel generic transform [33,34] that turns a weakly secure PKE scheme into a strongly secure PKE scheme in the Random Oracle Model (ROM), and various variants have been proposed to deal with tightness, non-correct PKEs, and in the quantum setting, i.e., QROM. Here, we recall the FO transformation for KEM as introduced by Dent [28] and revisited by Hofheinz et al. [38], Bindel et al. [12], and Hövelmanns et al. [39].

We recap the QROM proof of Bindel et al. [12] allowing the KEMs constructed over non-perfect PKEs to have IND-CCA security.

Theorem 1 ([12], Theorem 1 & 2). *Let G and H be quantum-accessible random oracles, and the deterministic PKE is ϵ-injective. Then the advantage of* IND-CCA *attacker $\mathcal{A}$ with at most Q_{Dec} decryption queries and Q_G and Q_H hash queries at depth at most d_G and d_H, respectively, is*

$$\mathsf{Adv}_{\mathsf{KEM}}^{\mathsf{IND\text{-}CCA}}(\mathcal{A}) \leq 2\sqrt{(d_G+2)\left(\mathsf{Adv}_{\mathsf{PKE}}^{\mathsf{IND\text{-}CPA}}(\mathcal{B}_1) + 8(Q_G+1)/|\mathcal{M}|\right)}$$
$$+\mathsf{Adv}_{\mathsf{PKE}}^{DF}(\mathcal{B}_2) + 4\sqrt{d_H Q_H/|\mathcal{M}|} + \epsilon,$$

where $\mathcal{B}_1$ is an IND-CPA *adversary on PKE and $\mathcal{B}_2$ is an adversary against finding a decryption failing ciphertext, returning at most Q_{Dec} ciphertexts.*

3   Design Choices

In this section, we explain the design choices for SMAUG.

3.1   MLWE Public Key and MLWR Ciphertext

One of the core designs of SMAUG uses the MLWE hardness for its secret key security and MLWR hardness for its message security. This choice is adapted from Lizard and RLizard, which use LWE/LWR and RLWE/RLWR, respectively. Using both LWE and LWR variant problems makes the conceptual security distinction between the secret key and the ephemeral sharing key: a more conservative secret key with more efficient en/decapsulations. Combined with the sparse secret, bringing the LWE-based key generation to the LWR-based scheme enables balancing the speed and the DFP.

Public Key. Public key of SMAUG consists of a vector $\mathbf{b}$ over a polynomial ring $\mathcal{R}_q$ and a matrix $\mathbf{A}$, which can be viewed as an MLWE sample,

$$(\mathbf{A}, \mathbf{b} = -\mathbf{A}^\top \mathbf{s} + \mathbf{e}) \in \mathcal{R}_q^{k \times k} \times \mathcal{R}_q^k,$$

where $\mathbf{s}$ is a ternary secret polynomial with hamming weight h_s, and $\mathbf{e}$ is an error sampled from discrete Gaussian distribution with standard deviation σ. The matrix $\mathbf{A}$ is sampled uniformly, using a seed and an eXtendable Output Function (XOF).

Ciphertext. The ciphertext of SMAUG is a tuple of a vector $\mathbf{c}_1 \in \mathcal{R}_p^k$ and a polynomial $c_2 \in \mathcal{R}_{p'}$. The ciphertext is generated by multiplying a random vector $\mathbf{r}$ to the public key with scaling and rounding:

$$\mathbf{c} = \begin{bmatrix} \mathbf{c}_1 \\ c_2 \end{bmatrix} = \left\lfloor \frac{p}{q} \cdot \begin{pmatrix} \mathbf{A} \\ \mathbf{b}^\top \end{pmatrix} \cdot \mathbf{r} \right\rceil + \frac{p}{t} \cdot \begin{bmatrix} 0 \\ \mu \end{bmatrix},$$

Along with the public key, it can be seen as an MLWR sample added by a scaled message, as $(\mathbf{A}', \lfloor p/q \cdot \mathbf{A}' \cdot \mathbf{r} \rceil) + (0, \mu')$, where $\mathbf{A}'$ is a concatenated matrix of $\mathbf{A}$ and $\mathbf{b}^\top$.

The public key and ciphertext can be further compressed by scaling but introduces a larger error. In SMAUG, we only compress the ciphertext which gives less significant errors.

3.2 Sparse Secret

The sparse secret is widely used in homomorphic encryption to reduce the noise propagation and running time during the homomorphic operations [22,36]. As the lattice-based KEM schemes have inherent decryption error from LWE or LWR noise, the sparse secret can also improve the lattice-based KEMs.

Concretely, the decryption error can be expressed as $\langle \mathbf{e}, \mathbf{r} \rangle + \langle \mathbf{e}_1, \mathbf{s} \rangle + e_2$, where $\mathbf{e} \leftarrow \chi_{pk}^k$ and $(\mathbf{e}_1, e_2) \leftarrow \chi_{ct}^{k+1}$ are noises added in the public key and a ciphertext. As the vectors $\mathbf{r}$ and $\mathbf{s}$ are binary (ternary, resp.), each coefficient of the decryption error is an addition (signed addition, resp.) of h_r variables from χ_{pk} and $h_s + 1$ variables from χ_{ct}. So, the magnitude of the decryption error depends greatly on the Hamming weights h_r and h_s; thus, we can take advantage of the sparse secrets.

Other major advantages of sparse secrets include reducing the secret key size and enabling fast polynomial multiplication. As the coefficients of the secret key are sparse with a fixed hamming weight, we can store only the information of the nonzero coefficients. We can further use this structure for the polynomial multiplications, which we will describe in Sect. 3.4.

As the sparse secret reduces the secret key entropy, the hardness of the lattice problem may be decreased. For the security of LWE problem using sparse secret, a series of works have been done, including [23] for asymptotic security, and [11,31,49] for concrete security. Independent of the secret distribution, the module variant (MLWE) is regarded as hard as LWE problem with appropriate parameters, including a smaller modulus. Also, a reduction from ordinary MLWE to MLWE using sparse secret or small errors is studied in [17]. The MLWR problem also has a simple reduction from MLWE independent of the secret distribution, and its concrete security is heuristically discussed in [27].

For the specific parameters of SMAUG, we exploit the lattice-estimator [2]. We also consider some attacks not in the estimator. Using a smaller modulus, SMAUG can maintain high security.

To sample such fixed Hamming weight secrets, we adapted the SampleInBall algorithm in Dilithium [29]. As a result, HWT$_h$ samples a ternary polynomial vector having a hamming weight of h in a secret-independent running time. A detailed algorithm is given in the full version of this paper [21].

3.3 Discrete Gaussian Noise

For the public key noise, we use an approximated discrete Gaussian distribution to a narrow range. As this approximated noise is used only once for each secret key, the security loss of using the approximated Gaussian can be efficiently bounded.

We construct dGaussian, a constant-time approximate discrete Gaussian noise sampler, upon a Cumulative Distribution Table (CDT) but is not used during sampling, as it is expressed with bit operations. We first scale the discrete Gaussian distribution and make a CDT approximating the discrete Gaussian distribution. We choose an appropriate scaling factor based on the analysis in [15, 42] using Rényi divergence. We then deploy the Quine-McCluskey method[2] and apply logic minimization technique on the CDT. As a result, even though our dGaussian is constructed upon CDT, it is expressed with bit operations and is constant-time. The algorithms are easily parallelizable and suitable for IoT devices as their memory requirement is low. The algorithms and the detailed analysis for the approximation can be found in the full version of this paper [21].

3.4 Polynomial Multiplication Using Sparsity

SMAUG uses the power-of-two moduli to ease the correct scaling and roundings. However, this makes the polynomial multiplications hard to benefit from Number Theoretic Transform (NTT). To address this issue, we propose a new polynomial multiplication that takes advantage of sparsity, which we adapt from [1, 43]. Our new multiplication, given in Fig. 1, is constant-time and is faster than the previous approaches.

3.5 FO Transform, $\mathsf{FO}_m^{\not\perp}$

We construct SMAUG upon the FO transform with implicit rejection and without ciphertext contribution to the sharing key generation, say $\mathsf{FO}_m^{\not\perp}$. This choice makes the encapsulation and decapsulation algorithm efficient since the sharing key can be directly generated from a message. The public key is additionally fed into the hash function with the message to avoid multi-target decryption failure attacks.

4   The SMAUG

4.1 Specification of SMAUG.PKE

We now describe the public key encryption scheme SMAUG.PKE in Fig. 2:

---

[2] We use the python package, from https://github.com/dreylago/logicmin.

```
poly_mult_add(a, b, neg_start):                                    ▷ a ∈ ℛ_q, b ∈ 𝒮_η
 1:  c = 0
 2:  for i from 0 to neg_start − 1 do
 3:      degree = b[i]
 4:      for j from 0 to n − 1 do
 5:          c[degree + j] = c[degree + j] + a[j];
 6:  for i from neg_start to len(b) − 1 do
 7:      degree = b[i]
 8:      for j from 0 to n − 1 do
 9:          c[degree + j] = c[degree + j] − a[j];
10:  for j from 0 to n − 1 do
11:      c[j] = c[j] − c[n + j];
12:  return c
```

Fig. 1. Polynomial multiplication using sparsity.

We now give the completeness of SMAUG.PKE. Please see the full version of this paper [21] for the detailed algorithm of the uniform random matrix sampler, expandA, which is adapted from the gen algorithm in Saber [50].

Theorem 2 (Completeness of SMAUG.PKE). *Let* $\mathbf{A}$, $\mathbf{b}$, $\mathbf{s}$, $\mathbf{e}$, *and* $\mathbf{r}$ *are defined as in Fig. 2. Let the moduli* t, p, p', *and* q *satisfy* $t \mid p \mid q$ *and* $t \mid p' \mid q$. *Let* $\mathbf{e}_1 \in \mathcal{R}_{\mathbb{Q}}^k$ *and* $e_2 \in \mathcal{R}_{\mathbb{Q}}$ *be the rounding errors introduced from the scalings and roundings of* $\mathbf{A} \cdot \mathbf{r}$ *and* $\mathbf{b}^T \cdot \mathbf{r}$. *That is,* $\mathbf{e}_1 = \frac{q}{p}(\lfloor \frac{p}{q} \cdot \mathbf{A} \cdot \mathbf{r} \rceil \mod p) - (\mathbf{A} \cdot \mathbf{r} \mod q)$ *and* $e_2 = \frac{q}{p'}(\lfloor \frac{p'}{q} \cdot \langle \mathbf{b}, \mathbf{r} \rangle \rceil \mod p') - (\langle \mathbf{b}, \mathbf{r} \rangle \mod q)$. *Let* $\delta = \Pr\left[\|\langle \mathbf{e}, \mathbf{r} \rangle + \langle \mathbf{e}_1, \mathbf{s} \rangle + e_2\|_\infty > \frac{q}{2t}\right]$, *where the probability is taken over the randomness of the encryption. Then* SMAUG.PKE *in Fig. 2 is* $(1 - \delta)$-*correct.*

4.2 Specification of SMAUGKEM

The key encapsulation mechanism SMAUG.KEM is given in Fig. 3. SMAUG.KEM is designed following the Fujisaki-Okamoto transform with implicit rejection using the non-perfectly correct public key encryption SMAUG.PKE.

The Fujisaki-Okamoto transform used in Fig. 3 defers from the $\mathrm{FO}_m^{\not\perp}$ transform in [39] in encapsulation and decapsulation. When generating the sharing key and randomness, SMAUG's Encap utilizes the hashed public key, which prevents certain multi-target attacks. As for Decap, if ct $\neq$ ct' holds, an alternative sharing key should be re-generated so as not to leak failure information against Side-Channel Attacks (SCA).

We also remark that the randomly chosen message μ should also be hashed in the environments using a non-cryptographic Random Number Generator (RNG) system. Using a True Random Number Generator (TRNG) is recommended to sample the message μ in such devices.

We now give the completeness of SMAUG.KEM based on the completeness of the underlying public key encryption scheme, SMAUG.PKE.

KeyGen(1^λ):

  1: seed $\leftarrow \{0,1\}^{256}$
  2: $(\text{seed}_A, \text{seed}_{sk}, \text{seed}_e) \leftarrow \text{XOF}(\text{seed})$
  3: $A \leftarrow \text{expandA}(\text{seed}_A) \in \mathcal{R}_q^{k \times k}$
  4: $s \leftarrow \text{HWT}_{h_s}(\text{seed}_{sk}) \in S_\eta^k$
  5: $e \leftarrow \text{dGaussian}_\sigma(\text{seed}_e) \in \mathcal{R}^k$
  6: $b = -A^\top \cdot s + e \in \mathcal{R}_q^k$
  7: **return** $pk = (\text{seed}_A, b)$, $sk = s$

Enc(pk, μ; seed$_r$):   ▷ $pk = (\text{seed}_A, b)$, $\mu \in \mathcal{R}_t$

  1: $A = \text{expandA}(\text{seed}_A)$
  2: **if** seed$_r$ is not given **then** seed$_r \leftarrow \{0,1\}^{256}$
  3: $r \leftarrow \text{HWT}_{h_r}(\text{seed}_r) \in S_\eta^k$
  4: $c_1 = \lfloor p/q \cdot A \cdot r \rceil \in \mathcal{R}_p^k$
  5: $c_2 = \lfloor p'/q \cdot \langle b, r \rangle + p'/t \cdot \mu \rceil \in \mathcal{R}_{p'}$
  6: **return** $ct = (c_1, c_2)$

Dec(sk, c):   ▷ $sk = s$, $c = (c_1, c_2)$

  1: $\mu' = \lfloor t/p \cdot \langle c_1, s \rangle + t/p' \cdot c_2 \rceil \in \mathcal{R}_t$
  2: **return** μ'

Fig. 2. Description of SMAUG.PKE

Theorem 3 (Completeness of SMAUG.KEM). *We borrow the notations and assumptions from Theorem 2 and Fig. 3. Then* SMAUG.KEM *in Fig. 3 is also* $(1 - \delta)$*-correct.*

4.3 Security Proof

When proving the security of the KEMs constructed using FO transform in the (Q)ROM, on typically relies on the generic reductions from one-wayness or IND-CPA security of the underlying PKE. In the ROM, SMAUG.KEM has a tight reduction from the IND-CPA security of the underlying PKE, SMAUG.PKE. However, like other lattice-based constructions, the underlying PKE has a chance of decryption failures, which makes the generic reduction unapplicable [47] or non-tight [12,38,39] in the QROM. Therefore, we prove the IND-CCA security of SMAUG.KEM based on the non-tight QROM reduction of [12] as explained in Sect. 2 by proving the IND-CPA security of SMAUG.PKE.

Theorem 4 (IND-CPA security of SMAUG.PKE). *Assuming pseudorandomness of the underlying sampling algorithms, the* IND-CPA *security of* SMAUG. PKE *can be tightly reduced to the decisional MLWE and MLWR problems. Specifically, for any* IND-CPA*-adversary* $\mathcal{A}$ *of* SMAUG.PKE*, there exist adversaries* $\mathcal{B}_0$, $\mathcal{B}_1$, $\mathcal{B}_2$, *and* $\mathcal{B}_3$ *attacking the pseudorandomness of* XOF*, and the pseudorandomness of sampling algorithms, the hardness of MLWE, and the hardness of MLWR,*

```
KeyGen(1^λ):
 1: (pk, sk') ← SMAUG.PKE.KeyGen(1^λ)
 2: d ← {0,1}^256
 3: return pk, sk = (sk', d)

Encap(pk):                                          ▷ pk = (seed_A, b)
 1: μ ← {0,1}^256
 2: (K, seed) ← G(μ, H(pk))
 3: ct ← SMAUG.PKE.Enc(pk, μ; seed)
 4: return ct, K

Decap(sk, ct):                                      ▷ sk = (sk', d)
 1: μ' = SMAUG.PKE.Dec(sk', ct)
 2: (K', seed') ← G(μ', H(pk))
 3: ct' = SMAUG.PKE.Enc(pk, μ'; seed')
 4: if ct ≠ ct' then
 5:     (K', ·) ← G(d, H(ct))
 6: return K'
```

Fig. 3. Description of SMAUG.KEM

respectively, such that,

$$\mathsf{Adv}_{\mathsf{SMAUG.PKE}}^{\mathsf{IND\text{-}CPA}}(\mathcal{A}) \leq \mathsf{Adv}_{\mathsf{XOF}}^{\mathsf{PR}}(\mathcal{B}_0) + \mathsf{Adv}_{\mathsf{expandA,HWT,dGaussian}}^{\mathsf{PR}}(\mathcal{B}_1)$$
$$+ \mathsf{Adv}_{n,q,k,k}^{\mathsf{MLWE}}(\mathcal{B}_2) + \mathsf{Adv}_{n,p,q,k+1,k}^{\mathsf{MLWR}}(\mathcal{B}_3).$$

The secret distribution terms omitted in the last two advantages (of $\mathcal{B}_1$ and $\mathcal{B}_2$) are uniform over ternary polynomials with Hamming weights h_s and h_r, respectively. The error distribution term omitted in the advantage of $\mathcal{B}_2$ is a pseudorandom distribution following the corresponding CDT.

In the classical random random oracle model, the classical IND-CCA security of SMAUG.KEM is obtained directly from FO transforms [38]. Theorem 1 implies the quantum IND-CCA security of SMAUG.KEM in the quantum random oracle model.

Due to space limitations, we omit the proofs. Please see the full version [21].

5   Parameter Selection and Concrete Security

In this section, we give concrete security analysis and recommended parameters.

5.1   Concrete Security Estimation

We exploit the best-known lattice attacks to estimate the concrete security of SMAUG.

Core-SVP Methodology. Most of the known attacks are essentially finding a nonzero short vector in Euclidean lattices, using the Block-Korkine-Zolotarev (BKZ) lattice reduction algorithm [20,37,48]. BKZ has been used in various lattice-based schemes [3,14,29,32,50]. The security of the schemes is generally estimated as the time complexity of BKZ in core-SVP hardness introduced in [4]. It depends on the block size β of BKZ reporting the best performance. According to Becker et al. [8] and Chailloux et al. [18], the β-BKZ algorithm takes approximately $2^{0.292\beta+o(\beta)}$ and $2^{0.257\beta+o(\beta)}$ time in the classical and quantum setting, respectively. We ignore the polynomial factors and $o(\beta)$ terms in the exponent to ease the analysis. We use the lattice estimator [2] to estimate the concrete security of SMAUG in core-SVP hardness.

Beyond Core-SVP Methodology. In addition to lattice reduction attacks, we also take into consideration the cost of other types of attacks, e.g., algebraic attacks like the Arora-Ge attack or Coded-BKW attacks and their variants. In general, these attacks have considerably higher costs and memory requirements compared to previously introduced attacks. We use the lattice estimator for estimating such attacks.

We also focus on the attacks targeting sparse secrets, such as the Meet-LWE [45] attack. This attack is inspired by Odlyzko's Meet-in-the-Middle approach and involves using representations of ternary secrets in additive shares. We use a Python script to estimate the cost of the Meet-LWE attack, following the original description in [45].

MLWE Hardness. We estimated the cost of the best-known attacks for MLWE, including *primal attack, dual attack,* and their hybrid variations, in the core-SVP hardness. We remark that any $\mathsf{MLWE}_{n,q,k,\ell,\eta}$ instance can be viewed as an $\mathsf{LWE}_{q,nk,n\ell,\eta}$ instance. Although the MLWE problem has an additional algebraic structure compared to the LWE problem, no attacks currently take advantage of this structure. Therefore, we assess the hardness of the MLWE problem based on the hardness of the corresponding LWE problem. We also consider the distributions of secret and noise when estimating the concrete security of SMAUG. We have also analyzed the costs of recent attacks that aim to target the MLWE problem with sparse secrets.

MLWR Hardness. To measure the hardness of the MLWR problem, we treat it as an MLWE problem since no known attack utilizes the deterministic error term in the MLWR structure. Banerjee et al. [7] provided the reduction from the MLWE problem to the MLWR problem, which was subsequently improved in [5,6,13]. Basically, for given an MLWR sample $(\mathbf{A}, \lfloor p/q \cdot \mathbf{A} \cdot \mathbf{s} \rceil \mod p)$ with uniformly chosen $\mathbf{A} \leftarrow \mathcal{R}_q^k$ and $\mathbf{s} \leftarrow \mathcal{R}_p^\ell$, it can be expressed as $(\mathbf{A}, p/q \cdot (\mathbf{A} \cdot \mathbf{s} \mod q) + \mathbf{e} \mod p)$. The MLWR sample can be converted to an MLWE sample over $\mathcal{R}_q$ by multiplying q/p as $(\mathbf{A}, \mathbf{b} = \mathbf{A} \cdot \mathbf{s} + q/p \cdot \mathbf{e} \mod q)$. Assuming that the error term in the resulting MLWE sample is a random variable, uniformly distributed within the interval $(-q/2p, q/2p]$, we can estimate the hardness of the MLWR problem as the hardness of the corresponding MLWE problem.

5.2 Parameter Sets

The SMAUG is parameterized by various integers such as n, k, q, p, p', t, h_s and h_r, as well as a standard deviation $\sigma > 0$ for the discrete Gaussian noise. Our main focus when selecting these parameters is to minimize the ciphertext size while maintaining security. We set SMAUG parameters to make SMAUG at least as safe as Saber.

We first set our ring dimension to $n = 256$ and plaintext modulus to $t = 2$ to have a 256-bit message space (or sharing key space). Then, we search for parameters with enough security to select the smallest ciphertext size. The compression factor p' can be set to a small integer if the DFP is low enough. Otherwise, we can keep $p' = 256$ as in the level-3 parameter and not compress the ciphertext.

Table 3 shows the three parameter sets of SMAUG, corresponding to NIST's security levels 1, 3, and 5. For security levels 3 and 5, we can not find the parameters for $q = 1024$, so we use $q = 2048$. Especially, the standard deviation $\sigma = 1.0625$ is too low for security level 3, so we move to $\sigma = 1.453713$. For the level-5 parameters set, we use $k = 5$ since $k = 4$ is too small for enough security.

Table 3. The NIST security level, selected parameters, classical and quantum core-SVP hardness and security beyond core-SVP (see Sect. 5.1), DFP (in $\log_2$), and sizes (in bytes) of SMAUG.

Parameters sets	SMAUG-128	SMAUG-192	SMAUG-256
Security level	1	3	5
n	256	256	256
k	2	3	5
(q, p, p', t)	$(1024, 256, 32, 2)$	$(2048, 256, 256, 2)$	$(2048, 256, 64, 2)$
(h_s, h_r)	$(140, 132)$	$(198, 151)$	$(176, 160)$
σ	1.0625	1.453713	1.0625
Classical core-SVP	120.0	181.7	264.5
Quantum core-SVP	105.6	160.9	245.2
Beyond core-SVP	144.7	202.0	274.6
DFP	−119.6	−136.1	−167.2
Secret key	176	236	218
Public key	672	1088	1792
Ciphertext	672	1024	1472

The core-SVP hardness is estimated[3] via the lattice estimator [2] using the cost model "ADPS16" introduced in [4] and "MATZOV" [44]. In the table, the smaller cost is reported. We assumed that the number of 1s is equal to the number of −1 s for simplicity, which conservatively underestimates security.

The security beyond core-SVP is estimated via the lattice estimator [2] and the Python script implementing the Meet-LWE attack cost estimation. It shows the lowest attack costs among coded-BKW, Arora-Ge, and Meet-LWE attack and their variants. We note that these attacks require a minimum memory size of 2^{130} to 2^{260}.

5.3 Decryption Failure Probability

As our primary goal is to push the efficiency of the lattice-based KEMs toward the limit while keeping roughly the same level of security, we follow the frameworks given in the NIST finalist Saber. In particular, we set the DFP to be similar to or lower than that of Saber's.

The impact of DFP on the security of KEM is still being investigated. However, we can justify our decision to follow Saber's choice and why it is sufficient for real-world scenarios. We can deduce that the number of observable decryption failures can be upper bounded by $2^{64+33+8+8} \cdot 2^{-20} = 2^{93}$ base on the following assumptions:

1. Each key pair has a limit of $Q_{\text{limit}} = 2^{64}$ decryption queries, as specified in NIST's proposal call.
2. There are approximately 2^{33} people worldwide, each with hundreds of devices. Each device has hundreds of *usable* public keys broadcasted for KEM.
3. We introduce an observable probability and assume it is far less than 2^{-20}. Even though the decryption failure occurs, it can only be used for an attack when it is observed. However, it is hard to observe all of the failures due to physical constraints.

The best-known (multi-target) attacks for Saber [25, Figure 6 (a), 7(a)] shows that the quantum cost for finding a single failing ciphertext of SMAUG security level 3 (Resp. 5) is much higher than 2^{160} (Resp. 2^{245}), as desired. Regardless of the attack cost estimated above, the scenario of checking the failures in more than 2^{40} different devices is already way too far from the real-world attack scenario.

6   Implementation

In this section, we give the implementation performance for each parameter set. We compare the sizes and the reported performance with prior works such as Kyber, Saber, and Sable. The constant-time reference implementation of SMAUG, along with the supporting scripts, can be found in our website: www.kpqc.cryptolab.co.kr/smaug.

---

[3] There are some suspicions on the unsubstantiated dual-sieve attacks assuming the flawed heuristic [30]. However, we hereby estimate the security of SMAUG following the methods in Kyber, Saber, and Sable for a fair comparison.

6.1   Performance

We instantiate the hash functions G, H and the extendable output function XOF with the following symmetric primitives: G is instantiated with SHAKE256, H is instantiated with SHA3-256, and XOF is instantiated with SHAKE128.

Table 4 presents the performance results of SMAUG. For a fair comparison, we also performed measurements on the same system with identical settings of the reference implementation of Kyber, Saber, and Sable[4].

Table 4. Median cycle counts of 1000 executions for Kyber, Saber, Sable, and SMAUG (and their ratios). Cycle counts are obtained on one core of an Intel Core i7-10700k, with TurboBoost and hyperthreading disabled, using the C implementations without AVX optimizations.

Schemes	Cycles			Cycles (ratio)		
	KeyGen	Encap	Decap	KeyGen	Encap	Decap
Kyber512	131560	162472	18930	1.7	2.1	2.03
LightSaber	93752	122176	133764	1.21	1.58	1.44
LightSable	85274	114822	128990	1.1	1.48	1.39
SMAUG-128	77220	77370	92916	1	1	1
Kyber768	214160	251308	285378	1.38	1.84	1.75
Saber	18722	224686	239590	1.21	1.64	1.47
Sable	170400	211290	23724	1.1	1.55	1.45
SMAUG-192	154862	136616	163354	1	1	1
Kyber1024	332470	371854	415498	1.25	1.38	1.36
FireSaber	289278	347900	382326	1.08	1.29	1.25
FireSable	275156	337322	371486	1.03	1.25	1.22
SMAUG-256	266704	270123	305452	1	1	1

6.2   Comparison to Prior/Related Work

In this section, we compare the sizes, security, and performance of SMAUG to the recent lattice-based KEM schemes.

Kyber and SMAUG . Tables 4 and 5 demonstrate that SMAUG outperforms Kyber in almost every aspect, except for the DFP and public key size in level 5. Compared to Kyber-512 [14], SMAUG-128 has a 16% and 12% smaller public key and ciphertext, respectively. Additionally, the secret key size of SMAUG is significantly smaller than that of Kyber. This makes it easy to manage secure zones in restricted IoT devices, as it is tiny and ready to use. Note that most of

---

[4] From https://github.com/pq-crystals/kyber (518de24), https://github.com/KULeuven-COSIC/SABER (f7f39e4), and https://github.com/josebmera/scabbard (4b2b5de), respectively.

Table 5. Comparison of Kyber, Saber, Sable, and SMAUG. Sizes are given in bytes, and the ratios are given relative to the sizes of SMAUG. Security is provided in the classical core-SVP hardness with DFP (in logarithm base two).

Schemes	Sizes (bytes)			Sizes (ratio)			Security	
	sk	pk	ct	sk	pk	ct	Classic.	DFP
Kyber512	1,632	800	768	9.4	1.2	1.1	118	−139
LightSaber	832	672	736	4.8	1	1.1	118	−120
LightSable	800	608	672	4.6	0.9	1	114	−139
SMAUG-128	176	672	672	1	1	1	120	−120
Kyber768	2,400	1,184	1,088	10.4	1.1	1.1	183	−164
Saber	1,248	992	1,088	5.4	0.9	1.1	189	−136
Sable	1,152	896	1,024	5	0.8	1	185	−143
SMAUG-192	236	1,088	1,024	1	1	1	181	−136
Kyber1024	3,168	1,568	1,568	15.2	0.9	1.1	256	−174
FireSaber	1,664	1,312	1,472	8	0.7	1	260	−165
FireSable	1,632	1,312	1,376	7.8	0.7	0.9	223	−208
SMAUG-256	218	1,792	1,472	1	1	1	264	−167

the KEMs can store a secret key as a seed, having 32 bytes, making them more vulnerable to side-channel attacks.

Furthermore, SMAUG-128 achieves a 110% and 103% speed-up in encapsulation and decapsulation, respectively, while maintaining high security and low DFP. Similar results are presented for security levels 3 and 5, except that the public key size of Kyber is shorter than SMAUG's in level 5. We note that the speed-ups decrease in higher security parameters.

Saber, Sable, and SMAUG. When compared to Saber, one of NIST's round 3 finalists, SMAUG-128 has a 9% smaller ciphertext and the same public key size as LightSaber. The secret key is significantly smaller, with a 58% and 44% speed up in encapsulation and decapsulation, respectively. Compared to Sable, an efficient variant of Saber, SMAUG-128, has the same ciphertext size but a larger public key size. This can be seen as a trade-off between smaller public keys versus faster running time. SMAUG-128 achieves 48% and 39% faster encapsulation and decapsulation, a smaller secret key, and a bit higher security at the cost of a larger public key.

This trade-off is also observed in security levels 3 and 5, between the public key size versus the secret key size and running time. In level 3, the encapsulation and decapsulation speed of SMAUG outperforms by 44% to 64% with a much smaller, ready-to-use secret key. In level 5, FireSable has a classical core-SVP hardness of 223, much lower than 260. It achieves a smaller public key and ciphertext than SMAUG-256 but still with slower speeds.

6.3   Security Against Physical Attacks

As the full masked implementation is not the target of this paper, we left it as a future work. However, how easy a masking is can also be one of the efficiency measures. Therefore, we justify how we can make SMAUG secure against physical attacks based on the profiled Differential Power Analysis (DPA). As Kyber and Saber share many design aspects with SMAUG, we can follow recent works on masking Kyber and Saber [9, 16] to add SCA countermeasures. Our new sampler, dGaussian, is expressed with bit operations, so adding SCA countermeasures like boolean masking is easy. While Krausz et al. [41] have recently proposed masking methods for the fixed hamming weight sampler, their efficiency is lacking, so we see it as future work. The new multiplication method may be vulnerable to memory access patterns, but we can efficiently mask it using coefficient-wise shuffling.

Acknowledgments. This work was submitted to the 'Korean Post-Quantum Cryptography Competition' (www.kpqc.or.kr). Part of this work was done while MinJune Yi was in CryptoLab Inc.

References

1. Akleylek, S., Alkım, E., Tok, Z.Y.: Sparse polynomial multiplication for lattice-based cryptography with small complexity. J. Supercomput. **72**, 438–450 (2016)
2. Albrecht, M.R., Player, R., Scott, S.: On the concrete hardness of learning with errors. J. Math. Cryptol. **9**(3), 169–203 (2015)
3. Alkim, E., Barreto, P.S.L.M., Bindel, N., Kramer, J., Longa, P., Ricardini, J.E.: The lattice-based digital signature scheme qtesla. Cryptology ePrint Archive, Paper 2019/085 (2019). https://eprint.iacr.org/2019/085
4. Alkim, E., Ducas, L., Pöppelmann, T., Schwabe, P.: Post-quantum key exchange - a new hope. In: Holz, T., Savage, S. (eds.) USENIX Security 2016, pp. 327–343. USENIX Association, August 2016
5. Alperin-Sheriff, J., Apon, D.: Dimension-preserving reductions from LWE to LWR. Cryptology ePrint Archive, Paper 2016/589 (2016). https://eprint.iacr.org/2016/589
6. Alwen, J., Krenn, S., Pietrzak, K., Wichs, D.: Learning with rounding, revisited. In: Canetti, R., Garay, J.A. (eds.) Advances in Cryptology - CRYPTO 2013. CRYPTO 2013. LNCS, vol. 8042, pp. 57–74. Springer, Berlin, Heidelberg (2013). https://doi.org/10.1007/978-3-642-40041-4_4
7. Banerjee, A., Peikert, C., Rosen, A.: Pseudorandom functions and lattices. In: Pointcheval, D., Johansson, T. (eds.) Advances in Cryptology - EUROCRYPT 2012. EUROCRYPT 2012. LNCS, vol. 7237, pp. 719–737. Springer, Berlin, Heidelberg (2012). https://doi.org/10.1007/978-3-642-29011-4_42
8. Becker, A., Ducas, L., Gama, N., Laarhoven, T.: New directions in nearest neighbor searching with applications to lattice sieving, pp. 10–24. Society for Industrial and Applied Mathematics (2016). https://doi.org/10.1137/1.9781611974331.ch2
9. Beirendonck, M.V., D'anvers, J.P., Karmakar, A., Balasch, J., Verbauwhede, I.: A side-channel-resistant implementation of saber. J. Emerg. Technol. Comput. Syst. **17**(2) (2021). https://doi.org/10.1145/3429983

10. Bernstein, D.J., Chuengsatiansup, C., Lange, T., Van Vredendaal, C.: Ntru prime. IACR Cryptol. ePrint Arch. **2016**, 461 (2016)

11. Bi, L., Lu, X., Luo, J., Wang, K.: Hybrid dual and meet-LWE attack. In: Nguyen, K., Yang, G., Guo, F., Susilo, W. (eds.) Information Security and Privacy. ACISP 2022. LNCS, vol. 13494, pp. 168–188. Springer, Heidelberg (2022). https://doi.org/10.1007/978-3-031-22301-3_9

12. Bindel, N., Hamburg, M., Hövelmanns, K., Hülsing, A., Persichetti, E.: Tighter proofs of CCA security in the quantum random oracle model. In: Hofheinz, D., Rosen, A. (eds.) Theory of Cryptography. TCC 2019, Part II. LNCS, vol. 11892, pp. 61–90. Springer, Heidelberg (2019). https://doi.org/10.1007/978-3-030-36033-7_3

13. Bogdanov, A., Guo, S., Masny, D., Richelson, S., Rosen, A.: On the hardness of learning with rounding over small modulus. In: Kushilevitz, E., Malkin, T. (eds.) Theory of Cryptography. TCC 2016. LNCS, vol. 9562, pp. 209–224. Springer, Berlin, Heidelberg (2016). https://doi.org/10.1007/978-3-662-49096-9_9

14. Bos, J., et al.: Crystals-kyber: a CCA-secure module-lattice-based KEM. In: 2018 IEEE European Symposium on Security and Privacy (EuroS&P), pp. 353–367. IEEE (2018)

15. Bos, J.W., et al.: Frodo: take off the ring! Practical, quantum-secure key exchange from LWE. In: Weippl, E.R., Katzenbeisser, S., Kruegel, C., Myers, A.C., Halevi, S. (eds.) ACM CCS 2016, pp. 1006–1018. ACM Press, October 2016. https://doi.org/10.1145/2976749.2978425

16. Bos, J.W., Gourjon, M., Renes, J., Schneider, T., van Vredendaal, C.: Masking kyber: first- and higher-order implementations. IACR TCHES **2021**(4), 173–214 (2021). https://doi.org/10.46586/tches.v2021.i4.173-214, https://tches.iacr.org/index.php/TCHES/article/view/9064

17. Boudgoust, K., Jeudy, C., Roux-Langlois, A., Wen, W.: On the hardness of module learning with errors with short distributions. J. Cryptol. **36**(1), 1 (2023). https://doi.org/10.1007/s00145-022-09441-3

18. Chailloux, A., Loyer, J.: Lattice sieving via quantum random walks. In: Tibouchi, M., Wang, H. (eds.) Advances in Cryptology - ASIACRYPT 2021. ASIACRYPT 2021. LNCS, vol. 13093, pp. 63–91. Springer, Cham (2021). https://doi.org/10.1007/978-3-030-92068-5_3

19. Chen, C., et al.: Ntru: algorithm specifications and supporting documentation (2020). nIST PQC Round 3 Submision

20. Chen, Y., Nguyen, P.Q.: BKZ 2.0: better lattice security estimates. In: Lee, D.H., Wang, X. (eds.) Advances in Cryptology – ASIACRYPT 2011. ASIACRYPT 2011. LNCS, vol. 7073, pp. 1–20. Springer, Berlin, Heidelberg (2011). https://doi.org/10.1007/978-3-642-25385-0_1

21. Cheon, J.H., Choe, H., Hong, D., Yi, M.: Smaug: pushing lattice-based key encapsulation mechanisms to the limits. Cryptology ePrint Archive, Paper 2023/739 (2023). https://eprint.iacr.org/2023/739

22. Cheon, J.H., Han, K., Kim, A., Kim, M., Song, Y.: Bootstrapping for approximate homomorphic encryption. In: Nielsen, J.B., Rijmen, V. (eds.) Advances in Cryptology - EUROCRYPT 2018. EUROCRYPT 2018, Part I. LNCS, vol. 10820, pp. 360–384. Springer, Cham (2018). https://doi.org/10.1007/978-3-319-78381-9_14

23. Cheon, J.H., Han, K., Kim, J., Lee, C., Son, Y.: A practical post-quantum public-key cryptosystem based on spLWE. In: Hong, S., Park, J.H. (eds.) Information Security and Cryptology - ICISC 2016. ICISC 2016. LNCS, vol. 10157, pp. 51–74. Springer, Cham (2017). https://doi.org/10.1007/978-3-319-53177-9_3

24. Cheon, J.H., Kim, D., Lee, J., Song, Y.: Lizard: cut off the tail! A practical post-quantum public-key encryption from LWE and LWR. In: Catalano, D., De Prisco, R. (eds.) Security and Cryptography for Networks. SCN 2018. LNCS, vol. 11035, pp. 160–177. Springer, Heidelberg (2018). https://doi.org/10.1007/978-3-319-98113-0_9

25. D'Anvers, J.P., Batsleer, S.: Multitarget decryption failure attacks and their application to saber and Kyber. In: Hanaoka, G., Shikata, J., Watanabe, Y. (eds.) Public-Key Cryptography - PKC 2022. PKC 2022, Part I. LNCS, vol. 13177, pp. 3–33. Springer, Cham (2022). https://doi.org/10.1007/978-3-030-97121-2_1

26. D'Anvers, J.P., Guo, Q., Johansson, T., Nilsson, A., Vercauteren, F., Verbauwhede, I.: Decryption failure attacks on IND-CCA secure lattice-based schemes. In: Lin, D., Sako, K. (eds.) Public-Key Cryptography – PKC 2019. PKC 2019, vol. 11443, pp. 565–598. Springer, Cham (2019). https://doi.org/10.1007/978-3-030-17259-6_19

27. D'Anvers, J.P., Karmakar, A., Roy, S.S., Vercauteren, F.: Saber: module-LWR based key exchange, CPA-secure encryption and CCA-secure KEM. In: Joux, A., Nitaj, A., Rachidi, T. (eds.) Progress in Cryptology – AFRICACRYPT 2018. AFRICACRYPT 2018. LNCS, vol. 10831, pp. 282–305. Springer, Heidelberg (2018). https://doi.org/10.1007/978-3-319-89339-6_16

28. Dent, A.W.: A designer's guide to KEMs. In: Paterson, K.G. (eds.) Cryptography and Coding. Cryptography and Coding 2003. LNCS, vol. 2898, pp. 133–151. Springer, Berlin, Heidelberg (2003). https://doi.org/10.1007/978-3-540-40974-8_12

29. Ducas, L., et al.: CRYSTALS-Dilithium: a lattice-based digital signature scheme. IACR TCHES 2018(1), 238–268 (2018). https://doi.org/10.13154/tches.v2018.i1.238-268, https://tches.iacr.org/index.php/TCHES/article/view/839

30. Ducas, L., Pulles, L.: Does the dual-sieve attack on learning with errors even work? Cryptology ePrint Archive, Paper 2023/302 (2023). https://eprint.iacr.org/2023/302

31. Espitau, T., Joux, A., Kharchenko, N.: On a dual/hybrid approach to small secret LWE - a dual/enumeration technique for learning with errors and application to security estimates of FHE schemes. In: Bhargavan, K., Oswald, E., Prabhakaran, M. (eds.) Progress in Cryptology - INDOCRYPT 2020. INDOCRYPT 2020. LNCS, vol. 12578, pp. 440–462. Springer, Cham (2020). https://doi.org/10.1007/978-3-030-65277-7_20

32. Fouque, P.A., et al.: Falcon: fast-fourier lattice-based compact signatures over NTRU. Submiss. NIST's Post-quantum Cryptogr. Stand. Process 36(5) (2018)

33. Fujisaki, E., Okamoto, T.: Secure integration of asymmetric and symmetric encryption schemes. In: Wiener, M.J. (ed.) Advances in Cryptology – CRYPTO'99. CRYPTO 1999. LNCS, vol. 1666, pp. 537–554. Springer, Berlin, Heidelberg (1999). https://doi.org/10.1007/3-540-48405-1_34

34. Fujisaki, E., Okamoto, T.: Secure integration of asymmetric and symmetric encryption schemes. J. Cryptol. 26(1), 80–101 (2013). https://doi.org/10.1007/s00145-011-9114-1

35. Grover, L.K.: A fast quantum mechanical algorithm for database search. In: Proceedings of the Twenty-Eighth Annual ACM Symposium on Theory of Computing, pp. 212–219 (1996)

36. Halevi, S., Shoup, V.: Bootstrapping for HElib. In: Oswald, E., Fischlin, M. (eds.) EUROCRYPT 2015, Part I. LNCS, vol. 9056, pp. 641–670. Springer, Heidelberg (2015). https://doi.org/10.1007/978-3-662-46800-5_25

37. Hanrot, G., Pujol, X., Stehlé, D.: Algorithms for the shortest and closest lattice vector problems. In: Chee, Y.M., et al. (eds.) Coding and Cryptology. IWCC 2011. LNCS, vol. 6639, pp. 159–190. Springer, Berlin, Heidelberg (2011). https://doi.org/10.1007/978-3-642-20901-7_10

38. Hofheinz, D., Hövelmanns, K., Kiltz, E.: A modular analysis of the Fujisaki-Okamoto transformation. In: Kalai, Y., Reyzin, L. (eds.) Theory of Cryptography. TCC 2017, Part I. LNCS, vol. 10677, pp. 341–371. Springer, Cham (2017). https://doi.org/10.1007/978-3-319-70500-2_12

39. Hövelmanns, K., Kiltz, E., Schäge, S., Unruh, D.: Generic authenticated key exchange in the quantum random oracle model. In: Kiayias, A., Kohlweiss, M., Wallden, P., Zikas, V. (eds.) Public-Key Cryptography - PKC 2020. PKC 2020, Part II. LNCS, vol. 12111, pp. 389–422. Springer, Heidelberg (2020). https://doi.org/10.1007/978-3-030-45388-6_14

40. Howgrave-Graham, N., et al.: The impact of decryption failures on the security of NTRU encryption. In: Boneh, D. (ed.) Advances in Cryptology – CRYPTO 2003. CRYPTO 2003. vol. 2729, pp. 226–246. Springer, Berlin, Heidelberg (2003). https://doi.org/10.1007/978-3-540-45146-4_14

41. Krausz, M., Land, G., Richter-Brockmann, J., Güneysu, T.: A holistic approach towards side-channel secure fixed-weight polynomial sampling. In: Boldyreva, A., Kolesnikov, V. (eds.) Public-Key Cryptography – PKC 2023. PKC 2023, Part II. LNCS, vol. 13941, pp. 94–124. Springer, Cham (2023). https://doi.org/10.1007/978-3-031-31371-4_4

42. Langlois, A., Stehlé, D., Steinfeld, R.: GGHLite: more efficient multilinear maps from ideal lattices. In: Nguyen, P.Q., Oswald, E. (eds.) Advances in Cryptology – EUROCRYPT 2014. LNCS, vol. 8441, pp. 239–256. Springer, Berlin, Heidelberg (2014). https://doi.org/10.1007/978-3-642-55220-5_14

43. Lee, J., Kim, D., Lee, H., Lee, Y., Cheon, J.H.: RLizard: post-quantum key encapsulation mechanism for IoT devices. IEEE Access **7**, 2080–2091 (2018)

44. MATZOV: Report on the Security of LWE: Improved Dual Lattice Attack, April 2022. https://doi.org/10.5281/zenodo.6493704

45. May, A.: How to meet ternary LWE keys. In: Malkin, T., Peikert, C. (eds.) Advances in Cryptology – CRYPTO 2021, Part II. LNCS, vol. 12826, pp. 701–731. Springer, Cham (2021). https://doi.org/10.1007/978-3-030-84245-1_24

46. Mera, J.M.B., Karmakar, A., Kundu, S., Verbauwhede, I.: Scabbard: a suite of efficient learning with rounding key-encapsulation mechanisms. IACR TCHES **2021**(4), 474–509 (2021). https://doi.org/10.46586/tches.v2021.i4.474-509, https://tches.iacr.org/index.php/TCHES/article/view/9073

47. Saito, T., Xagawa, K., Yamakawa, T.: Tightly-secure key-encapsulation mechanism in the quantum random oracle model. In: Nielsen, J.B., Rijmen, V. (eds.) Advances in Cryptology - EUROCRYPT 2018. EUROCRYPT 2018, Part III. LNCS, vol. 10822, pp. 520–551. Springer, Cham (2018). https://doi.org/10.1007/978-3-319-78372-7_17

48. Schnorr, C.P., Euchner, M.: Lattice basis reduction: improved practical algorithms and solving subset sum problems. Math. Program. **66**(1), 181–199 (1994)

49. Son, Y., Cheon, J.H.: Revisiting the hybrid attack on sparse secret LWE and application to he parameters. In: Proceedings of the 7th ACM Workshop on Encrypted Computing & Applied Homomorphic Cryptography, pp. 11–20. WAHC'19, Association for Computing Machinery, New York, NY, USA (2019). https://doi.org/10.1145/3338469.3358941

50. Vercauteren, I.F., Sinha Roy, S., D'Anvers, J.P., Karmakar, A.: Saber: mod-LWR based KEM, nIST PQC Round 3 Submision

A Post-Quantum Round-Optimal Oblivious PRF from Isogenies

Andrea Basso[1,2]([✉])([iD])

[1] University of Birmingham, Birmingham, UK
andrea.basso@bristol.ac.uk
[2] University of Bristol, Bristol, UK

Abstract. An oblivious pseudorandom function, or OPRF, is an important primitive that is used to build many advanced cryptographic protocols. Despite its relevance, very few post-quantum solutions exist.

In this work, we propose a novel OPRF protocol that is post-quantum, verifiable, round-optimal, and moderately compact.

Our protocol is based on a previous SIDH-based construction by Boneh, Kogan, and Woo, which was later shown to be insecure due to an attack on its one-more unpredictability. We first propose an efficient countermeasure against this attack by redefining the PRF function to use irrational isogenies. This prevents a malicious user from independently evaluating the PRF. The SIDH-based construction by Boneh, Kogan, and Woo is also vulnerable to the recent attacks on SIDH. We thus demonstrate how to efficiently incorporate the countermeasures against such attacks to obtain a secure OPRF protocol. To achieve this, we also propose the first proof of isogeny knowledge that is compatible with masked torsion points, which may be of independent interest. Lastly, we design a novel non-interactive proof of knowledge of parallel isogenies, which reduces the number of communication rounds of the OPRF to the theoretically-optimal two.

Putting everything together, we obtain the most compact post-quantum verifiable OPRF protocol.

Keywords: Oblivious Pseudorandom Functions · Isogenies · SIDH

1 Introduction

An oblivious pseudorandom function (OPRF) is a two-party protocol between a user and a server. The two parties obliviously evaluate a PRF on a user-controlled input with a secret key held by the server. After engaging in the protocol, the user learns only the output of the PRF on their chosen input, while the server does not learn anything, neither the user's input nor the output of the function. Oblivious PRFs can also satisfy a stronger property called *verifiability*: in a verifiable OPRF (vOPRF), the server initially commits to its secret key, and during the execution of the protocol it provides a proof that it has behaved honestly and it has used the previously committed secret key.

C. Carlet et al. (Eds.): SAC 2023, LNCS 14201, pp. 147–168, 2024.
https://doi.org/10.1007/978-3-031-53368-6_8

It is possible to build an OPRF using generic multi-party computation techniques, but such solutions can be inefficient, and they require more rounds of communication than what an ad-hoc construction can achieve. Indeed, highly-efficient and round-optimal (i.e., with two rounds) constructions exist based on Diffie-Hellman [15] or RSA blind signatures [9]. All such constructions are vulnerable to quantum attacks, and very few quantum-resistant OPRFs are reported in the literature. The first quantum-secure verifiable OPRF was proposed by Albrecht, Davidson, Deo and Smart [1]. The protocol is based on the learning-with-errors problem and the short-integer-solution problem in one dimension, and it only requires two rounds of communication. However, the construction can be characterized as a feasibility result, as a single OPRF execution requires communicating hundreds of gigabytes of data. The only other post-quantum solutions were proposed by Boneh, Kogan, and Woo [5]. The authors proposed two moderately-compact OPRFs based on isogenies, one relying on SIDH and one on CSIDH. The OPRF based on SIDH is verifiable, but requires an even higher number of communication rounds, since the verifiability proof is highly interactive. A later work by Basso, Kutas, Merz, Petit and Sanso [4] cryptanalyzed the SIDH-based OPRF by demonstrating two attacks against the one-more unpredictability of the protocol, i.e. it showed that a malicious user can recover sufficient information to independently evaluate the PRF on any input. The first attack is polynomial-time, but it can be easily prevented with a simple countermeasure; the second attack is subexponential but still practical, and the authors argue that there is no simple countermeasure against it. More recently, a series of works [7,19,22] developed an efficient attack on SIDH that also extends to the SIDH-based OPRF.

Contributions. In this work, we propose an OPRF protocol that is post-quantum secure, verifiable, round-optimal, and moderately compact ($\approx$9 MB per execution), with a security proof in the UC framework [6] in the random-oracle model. To do so, we follow the same high-level approach as the SIDH-based OPRF by Boneh, Kogan, Woo [5], but with the following changes:

- We propose an efficient countermeasure against the one-more unpredictability attack by Basso, Kutas, Merz, Petit, and Sanso [4]. We modify the PRF definition, and in particular we use irrational isogenies to map the user's input to an elliptic curve. In this way, the information that allowed an attacker to independently evaluate the PRF is no longer defined over a field of small extension. A malicious user may still attempt to carry out the attack from [4], but this would now require the attacker to work with points with exponentially many coordinates over the base field, which makes the attack infeasible. Besides preventing the attack, this change results in a smaller prime and a more compact protocol.
- We discuss how to integrate M-SIDH, a recently-proposed countermeasure [12] against the SIDH attacks that relies on masked torsion, into the OPRF protocol. This requires using longer isogenies and a larger prime, but a series of optimizations allow us to maintain a reasonable communication

cost. To integrate M-SIDH, we also propose the first zero-knowledge proof of knowledge that can guarantee the correctness of an M-SIDH public key, which may be of independent interest. The proof relies on splitting the masking value into three multiplicative shares: this enables the prover to build a commutative SIDH square and reveal a single edge, together with the torsion point images, without leaking any information about the witness. Repeating the process multiple times yields a proof with negligible soundness error.

- We propose a novel proof of knowledge that can guarantee that two isogenies are parallel, i.e. they are computed by applying the same secret key to two starting curves and torsion points. The protocol is obtained by evaluating two proofs of isogeny knowledge in parallel *with correlated randomness*. The proof can be proved zero-knowledge under a new yet mild assumption. Such a proof can be used by the server to show that it has used a previously committed secret key, which is the key ingredient to make the OPRF verifiable. Since the proof is a proof of knowledge, it can be made non-interactive through standard transformations; this makes the proposed OPRF the first isogeny-based OPRF to be round-optimal.

2 Preliminaries

The Existing OPRF Construction. Boneh, Kogan, and Woo [5] introduced a verifiable OPRF protocol based on SIDH (for further preliminaries on SIDH, we refer to the full version of this paper [2]), which uses a prime p of the form $p = N_M N_B N_K N_1 N_2 f - 1$, where the values N_i are coprime smooth integers and f is a small cofactor. Initially, the server commits to its key k by publishing the curve E_C obtained as the codomain of the N_K-isogeny starting from $\tilde{E}$ with kernel $\langle \tilde{P} + [k]\tilde{Q} \rangle$, where the values $\tilde{E}, \tilde{P}, \tilde{Q}$ are protocol parameters. The commitment also includes a zero-knowledge proof π_C of the correctness of the computation. Then, to evaluate the PRF on input $m \in \mathcal{M}$, where $\mathcal{M}$ defines the input space, the user computes an isogeny ϕ_m of degree N_M by hashing the input with a function H and computing $\phi_m : E_0 \rightarrow E_m := E_0/\langle P + [H(m)]Q \rangle$, where the curve E_0 and the points P, Q are also protocol parameters. Then, the user blinds the curve E_m by computing a second isogeny $\phi_b : E_m \rightarrow E_{mb}$ of degree N_B. The user sends the curve E_{mb} and the torsion images $R_K = \phi_b \circ \phi_m(P_K), S_K = \phi_b \circ \phi_m(Q_K)$ to the server, where the points P_K, Q_K are also protocol parameters of order N_K. The user also provides a non-interactive zero-knowledge proof that torsion information was honestly computed. The server validates the proof, computes the isogeny $\phi_k : E_{mb} \rightarrow E_{mbk} := E_{mb}/\langle R_K + [k]S_K \rangle$ based on its secret key k, and sends the curve E_{mrk}, the image $\phi_k(E_{mb}[N_B])$, and a non-interactive zero-knowledge proof of correctness to the user. Then, the server and the user engage in an interactive protocol where the server proves that the isogeny ϕ_k has used the same key k as the committed value. If the user is convinced, they use the provided torsion information to undo the blinding isogeny, i.e. to compute the translation of the dual of the blinding isogeny, to obtain the curve E_{mk}. The output of the OPRF is then the hash $H(m, j(E_{mk}), (E_C, \pi_C))$. The main exchange, without the commitments and the proofs, is represented in Fig. 1.

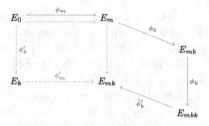

Fig. 1. The OPRF construction by Boneh, Kogan, and Woo. The protocol, without the relevant zero-knowledge proofs, is represented by the solid lines: the isogenies $\longrightarrow$ (ϕ_m, ϕ_b, $\hat{\phi}_b'$) are computed by the client, while the isogeny $\longrightarrow$ (ϕ_k) is computed by the server. The isogenies $\rightsquigarrow$ represent the PRF evaluation, and the isogenies $\dashrightarrow$ are relevant to the attack presented in [4]. The figure is based on Fig. 1 of [4].

The BKMPS Attacks. Basso, Kutas, Merz, Petit, and Sanso [4] proposed two attacks against the one-more unpredictability of the OPRF protocol by Boneh, Kogan, Woo [5] OPRF. In the first attack, an attacker who acts as a malicious user engages in the OPRF with a message isogeny ϕ_m with kernel generator a point M, of order ℓ^e. The attacker repeats the process with message isogenies with kernel generators $[\ell]M, [\ell^2]M, \ldots, [\ell^e]M$. The outputs of the PRF are the curves that lie on the isogeny path of $\phi_m' : E_k \rightarrow E_{mk}$ (see Fig. 1), which allows the attacker to compute a generator of the kernel of such isogeny. The recomputed generator is a scalar multiple $\phi_k'(M)$, where ϕ_k' is the isogeny parallel to the server's secret isogeny, i.e. its kernel is generated by $P_k + [k]Q_k$. By repeating this process three times with points M_1, M_2 and $M_3 := M_1 + M_2$ (where M_1 and M_2 are linearly independent), the attacker obtains the points $R := [\alpha]\phi_k'(M_0), S := [\beta]\phi_k'(M_1), T := [\gamma]\phi_k'(M_3) = [\gamma/\alpha]R + [\gamma/\beta]S$, for some unknown values α, β, γ. By expressing T in terms of R and S, the attacker obtains the values γ/α and γ/β and the points $R' := [\gamma/\alpha]R = [\gamma]\phi_k'(M_0)$ and $S' := [\gamma/\beta]S = [\gamma]\phi_k'(M_1)$. Finally, the attacker can evaluate the PRF on any input m by computing $E_K/\langle R' + [H(m)]S'\rangle$. The attack runs in polynomial time, but it crucially relies on using message isogenies ϕ_m of varying degree. The attack can be thwarted by server checking the order of the isogeny ϕ_m, which is possible because of the proof of knowledge provided by user.

The authors of [4] also propose a second attack that cannot be easily prevented. The attack proceeds in a similar way to the previous one, but the malicious user uses only isogenies of full degree. To obtain the curves on the path of ϕ_m, the attacker needs to find the middle curve between two PRF outputs. This introduces a trade-off between the complexity of the attack and the number of queries. Minimizing both yields a subexponential yet practical attack on the one-more unpredictability of the protocol.

3   Oblivious Pseudorandom Functions

The security properties of an OPRF can be hard to define. Oblivious pseudorandom functions were originally proposed by Naor and Reingold [21], who defined an OPRF via an ideal functionality. Subsequent work [13,18] defined OPRFs in terms of the two-party computation $(k, x) \mapsto (\bot, f(k, x))$, but such a definition has several drawbacks. On one side, it is hard to build protocols that satisfy such a definition, because the security proof would require extracting the user's input, while at the same the definition is not secure enough, because it does not guarantee any security under composability. Since OPRFs are mainly used as building blocks in larger protocols, such a security guarantee is highly needed. For these reasons, Jarecki et al. [15,17] proposed new definitions in the UC framework [6]. To avoid extracting the user's input, the ideal functionality introduces a ticketing system that increases a counter when the PRF is evaluated and decreases the counter when the user receives the PRF output. This captures the idea that a malicious user should learn only the PRF output for one input for each interaction. This results in the definition of Fig. 2, which is based on the definitions by Jarecki et al. [15–17].

Parameters: The PRF output ℓ, polynomial in the security parameter λ.

Convention: For every identifier S, the counter $\mathsf{tx}[S]$ is initially set to zero. For every value $\pi \in \{0, 1\}^*$ and $x \in \{0, 1\}^*$, the value $F(\pi, x)$ is initially undefined, and whenever such a value is referenced, the functionality assigns a random ℓ-bit string $F(\pi, x) \xleftarrow{\$} \{0, 1\}^\ell$.

Initialization

- On message INIT from party S, forward (INIT, S) to the adversary $\mathcal{A}$.
- On message (PARAM, S, π) from adversary $\mathcal{A}$, and if $\mathsf{param}[S]$ is undefined, then set $\mathsf{param}[S] = \pi$.

Evaluation

- On message (EVAL, S, x) from $P \in \{U, \mathcal{A}\}$, record $\langle P, x \rangle$ and forward the message (EVAL, P, S) to $\mathcal{A}$.
- On message SERVERCOMPLETE from server S, send (SERVERCOMPLETE, S) to $\mathcal{A}$ and increment $\mathsf{tx}[S]$.
- On message (USERCOMPLETE, P, π) from $\mathcal{A}$, retrieve the record $\langle P, x \rangle$, delete it from the list of records, and decrement $\mathsf{tx}[S]$ if there exists an honest server S such that $\mathsf{param}[S] = \pi$; abort if no such record exists or if $\mathsf{tx}[S] = 0$. Then, send (EVAL, $\pi, F(\pi, x)$) to P.

Fig. 2. The $\mathcal{F}_{\mathsf{vOPRF}}$ functionality.

3.1   Security Assumptions

To prove that the OPRF protocol we propose implements the functionality of Fig. 2, we will make use of the properties listed in this section. Since our protocol and security proof follows the same high-level structure as that of the OPRF protocol by Boneh, Kogan, and Woo [5], these properties are also based on those of the augmentable commitment framework proposed in [5]. Unlike [5], we avoid the abstraction of augmentable commitments due to its restrictiveness (the counteremasures of Sect. 4 would not be possible within that framework), and we prefer an explicit description throughout this work.

Correctness. Firstly, we require the OPRF to be correct, i.e. the output of the protocol is the output of function that deterministically depends only on the user's input and the server's secret key. In other words, we want that the blinding process that guarantees the obliviousness of the user's input does not affect the final output. In the context of our protocol, we want that the unblinding isogeny undoes the effect of the blinding isogeny. This is contained in the following lemma, whose proof follows from the correctness of the SIDH protocol [14].

Lemma 1 (Correctness). *Let p be a prime of the form $p = N_B N_K f - 1$, where N_B, N_K, f are smooth coprime integers. Let E_0 be a supersingular elliptic curve defined over $\mathbb{F}_{p^2}$ and let P_B, Q_B and P_K, Q_K be respectively a basis of $E_0[N_B]$ and $E_0[N_K]$. Let also b and k be two values in $\mathbb{Z}_{N_B}$ and $\mathbb{Z}_{N_K}$. Then, consider the isogenies*

$$\phi_B : E_0 \to E_B := E_0/\langle P_B + [b]Q_B \rangle,$$
$$\phi_K : E_0 \to E_K := E_0/\langle P_K + [k]Q_K \rangle,$$
$$\phi'_k : E_B \to E_{BK} := E_B/\langle \phi_B(P_K) + [k]\phi_B(Q_K) \rangle.$$

If R_B, S_B is a basis of $E_B[N_B]$ and the values b_0, b_1 satisfy $\ker \hat{\phi}_B = \langle [b_0]R_B + [b_1]S_B \rangle$, then we have

$$j\left(E_{BK}/\langle [b_0]\phi'_k(R_B) + [b_1]\phi'_k(S_B) \rangle\right) = j(E_K).$$

Input Hiding. To ensure that the OPRF is oblivious, we want that the server does not learn the user's input. That holds in the strongest sense, i.e. the server should not learn the user's input even when the input is randomly chosen between two inputs *chosen by the server*. In other words, the user must apply a blinding step that fully hides the chosen input. In the context of isogenies, we want the following problem to be hard.

Problem 2. Let p be a prime of the form $p = N_B N_K f - 1$, where $N_B N_K, f$ are smooth coprime integers. Let E_0 and E_1 be two supersingular elliptic curves defined over $\mathbb{F}_{p^2}$ and chosen by the adversary, and let P_0, Q_0 and P_1, Q_1 be a basis of $E_0[N_K]$ and $E_1[N_K]$, respectively, such that $e_{N_K}(P_0, Q_0) = e_{N_K}(P_1, Q_1)$. Let i be a random bit, i.e. $i \xleftarrow{\$} \{0,1\}$, and B a random point in $E_i[N_B]$, and write $\phi : E_i \to E' := E_i/\langle B \rangle$. Output i given E' and $f_{\mathsf{aux}}(\phi(P_i), \phi(Q_i))$, where the latter is some auxiliary torsion information.

The hardness of the problem clearly depends on the function f_{aux}; if the torsion images were directly revealed, Problem 2 would be easy due to the SIDH attacks. We thus delay describing the function f_{aux} until Sect. 5, where we discuss the SIDH countermeasures and choose f_{aux} to reveal the values $\phi(P_i), \phi(Q_i)$, both scaled by the same unknown value. In the section, we also state the variant of the Decisional Isogeny problem that Problem 2 reduces to.

One-More Unpredictability. A key property of an OPRF is that the user learns the output of the PRF only on its input of choice. That means that a malicious user should not learn the output on more inputs than the number of OPRF executions. The BKMPS attack [4] on the OPRF by Boneh, Kogan, and Woo [5] targets the one-more unpredictability, since it shows that a malicious user can extract enough information to independently evaluate the OPRF on any input of their choice. We propose an efficient countermeasure against the one-more unpredictability attack in the next section; we thus delay until then a formalization of the isogeny-related assumption (see Problem 5) we need to guarantee the one-more unpredictability of the OPRF protocol.

Commitment Binding. At the beginning of the OPRF protocol, the server commits to a secret key k, so that during each OPRF execution it can prove that the same key was used. To guarantee verifiability, we want a commitment scheme with an associated proof of input reuse. We propose to commit to a key k by fixing a special curve $\tilde{E}$ with a basis $\tilde{P}, \tilde{Q}$ of $\tilde{E}[N_{\mathsf{K}}]$ and revealing $j(\tilde{E}/\langle \tilde{P} + [k]\tilde{Q} \rangle)$. The proof of input reuse, which in the context of isogenies becomes a proof of parallel isogenies, is presented in Sect. 5.1. To guarantee that the commitment is binding, we want that the following problem to be hard.

Problem 3 (Collision finding problem). Let E_0 be a supersingular elliptic curve of unknown endomorphism ring. Find two distinct isogenies $\phi_0 : E_0 \to E$ and $\phi_1 : E_0 \to E'$ such that $j(E_0) = j(E_1)$.

Problem 3 has been studied in the context of the CGL hash function [8], and it has been shown to be heuristically equivalent to the following problem, which underpins every isogeny-based protocol [10].

Problem 4 (Endomorphism Ring problem). Let E be a supersingular elliptic curve. Find its endomorphism ring $\mathrm{End}(E)$.

4   Countermeasures Against the Unpredictability Attacks

The original protocol by Boneh, Kogan and Woo starts by mapping an input m to an isogeny ϕ_m. If we denote with N_{M} the torsion space dedicated to the message, the protocol fixes a basis P, Q of $E_0[N_M]$ and computes the isogeny ϕ_m given by

$$\phi_m : E_0 \to E_0/\langle P + [H(m)]Q \rangle =: E_m, \tag{1}$$

where $H(\cdot)$ maps the message m onto an element of $\mathbb{Z}_{N_M}$.

The subexponential attack [4] recovers the image P_k, Q_k of the torsion basis P, Q, up to scalar multiplication, under the secret isogeny $\phi'_k : E_0 \to E_k$. With such information, the attacker can evaluate the PRF on any input of their choice. The output curve of the PRF is the curve computed as $E_k/\langle P_k + [H(m)]_k \rangle$. The attack is subexponential, and it is possible to obtain λ bits of security if the isogeny ϕ_m has degree 2^{λ^2} (this can be reduced if we limit the number of queries the attacker can make). This would require using very long isogenies (the degree would be $2^{16,384}$ for $\lambda = 128$) and very large primes.

Instead, in this section we propose a novel and efficient countermeasure that sidesteps these issues. Our main idea is to accept that an attacker may recover the curve E_k and points P_k, Q_k on it, but to prevent those points from being sufficient to evaluate the desired isogeny. To do so, we require that the isogeny ϕ_m has an irrational kernel, i.e. its kernel is defined over a sufficiently-large extension field. Such an isogeny can be efficiently computed as a composition of rational isogenies. More formally, assume that $N_M = \ell^e$, and e is the highest power of ℓ that divides $p + 1$. Then, given an input $m \in \mathcal{M}$, we compute the isogeny ϕ_m in the following way:

1. We first map the message m to two elements in $\mathbb{Z}_{\ell^e}$ through two hash functions H_0, H_1 that are collision resistant. We thus have $m_0 = H_0(m)$ and $m_1 = H_1(m)$.
2. Given the starting curve E_0 and two points P_0, Q_0 spanning $E_0[\ell^e]$, we compute the isogeny $\phi_0 : E_0 \to E_1 := E_0/\langle P_0 + [m_0]Q_0 \rangle$.
3. We determine a canonical basis P_1, Q_1 of $E_1[\ell^e]$ and compute the isogeny $\phi_1 : E_1 \to E_m := E_1/\langle P_1 + [m_1]Q_1 \rangle$,
4. The isogeny $\phi_m : E_0 \to E_m$ is the composition $\phi_1 \circ \phi_0$.

An attacker may still try to apply the one-more unpredictability attack. In the original case, the attacker recovers three isogenies from E_k to E_{mk} and they combine their kernel generators to obtain the image points P_k, Q_k. In the proposed construction, the attacker can still recover three (or more) isogenies from E_k to E_{mk}. However, the kernel generators of these isogenies are points of order ℓ^{2e}, and thus they are defined only over the extension field $\mathbb{F}_{p^{2\ell^e}}$. This is an exponentially large field, and even just representing such a point—let alone doing any computation—would be exponential in the security parameter. To guarantee security, it is important that the degree of ϕ_m is a prime power. If the degree were a product of prime powers, it is possible to represent a large extension by working over several smaller extensions because of the Chinese Remainder Theorem. This can reduce the complexity of working over a large extension and thus reduce the security of the proposed countermeasures.

The attacker can work with the kernel generators of only the first half of the isogenies and obtain a basis P_k, Q_k of order ℓ^e (see Fig. 3). This allows them

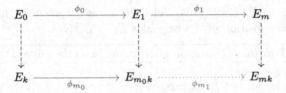

Fig. 3. Summary of the proposed countermeasure (this does not depict the blinding/unblinding phase). Isogenies in red are known or can be computed by the attacker, isogenies in black are unknown to the attacker, and the dotted isogeny represents the missing isogeny that the attacker needs to compute to succeed in the attack. (Color figure online)

to evaluate the first isogeny ϕ_{m_0} to obtain the curve $E_{m_0 k}$ for any message m. However, the attacker has no way of computing the remaining isogeny ϕ_{m_1}. To do so, the attacker would need to map the canonical basis on E_1 to $E_{m_0 k}$, which does not seem to be possible without knowing the server secret key. Alternatively, the attacker could map the points P, Q and P_k, Q_k under the isogenies ϕ_0 and ϕ'_k. At least one of the image points on each curve has full order, and the point of full order on $E_{m_0 k}$ is the image of the point of full order on E_1. This suggest such an approach could be used to find a basis, but the second point on each curve is always a scalar multiple of the first point.[1] Hence, guessing the remaining point has exponential complexity ℓ^e. Lastly, the attacker cannot use a similar strategy as the one-more unpredictability attack to recover a basis on $E_{m_0 k}$ because the curve $E_{m_0 k}$ depends on the message m. It thus changes at every interaction, and it is hard for an attacker to find two messages that have the same first curve E_1 and $E_{m_0 k}$ since we assume that the hash function H_0 is collision-resistant. Note that we require H_0 and H_1 to be collision-resistant, but we conjecture that only H_0 needs to be. Overall, the knowledge of $E_{m_0 k}$ does not help the attacker learn any information on the curve E_{mk}, which successfully prevents the one-more unpredictability attack.

Optimizations. We can extend this approach to obtain a more compact protocol. Rather than limiting ourselves to two isogenies, we can extend this to an arbitrary number I. We obtain the optimal case when I is maximal, i.e. when $\deg \phi_m = \ell^I$.

Let H_i be I distinct random oracles for every $i \in \{1, \ldots, I\}$. Then, given an input m and a starting curve E_0, the isogeny ϕ_m and the curve E_m by computing an isogeny ϕ_i determined by $H_i(m)$, generating a canonical basis on the codomain curve, and repeating the process I times (see Algorithm 1). We refer to this hashing as $\mathcal{H}_I(x)$, and in the rest of the paper, we write $(\phi_m, E_m) = \mathcal{H}_I(x)$ to refer to the function in Algorithm 1; we also write $[P_0, P_1, \ldots, P_{I-1}]_{E,N}$ to denote a list points of order N where the point P_0 belongs to E, and the point

---

[1] If $\ker \phi = \langle P + \alpha Q \rangle$, it follows that $\phi(P) = -\alpha \phi(Q)$.

P_i belongs to $E_i := E_{i_1}/\langle P_{i-1}\rangle$. We refer to this as a *sequence*, whose associated isogeny is the composition of the isogenies $E_i \twoheadrightarrow E_i/\langle P_i\rangle$.

Algorithm 1 Function $\mathcal{H}_I$ mapping the input m to the curve E_m

---

1: **for** $i \leftarrow 0$ to $I - 1$ **do**
2:     Set $m_i = H_i(m)$ and $P_i, Q_i = \mathcal{B}_M(E)$;
3:     Compute $\phi_i : E_i \to E_{i+1} := E_i/\langle P_i + [m_i]Q_i\rangle$;
4: Set $\phi_m = \phi_{I-1} \circ \ldots \circ \phi_0$ and $E_m = E_{I-1}$;
5: **return** ϕ_m, E_m;

This technique to compute message isogenies results in a more compact OPRF protocol because only the shorter isogenies ϕ_i need to be defined over $\mathbb{F}_{p^2}$; thus, using more isogenies can result in a smaller prime p while maintaining the same degree of the isogeny ϕ_m. However, this approach has also a security advantage: an attacker can use the BKMPS attack to recover the image of basis on E_k, which could potentially be used to recover the isogeny between E_0 and E_k using the SIDH attacks. While this could be avoided by picking a sufficiently long isogeny ϕ_k, choosing $I = e$, i.e. setting parameters such that only isogenies of degree ℓ have a kernel defined over $\mathbb{F}_{p^2}$, ensures that an attacker obtains only a basis of very small order, which prevents the attack altogether.

A New Assumption. We proposed a modified protocol that prevents the existing one-more unpredictability attacks. As in the original construction, the one-more unpredictability of the resulting protocol relies on the hardness of a novel problem, which is the following.

Problem 5 (One-more unpredictability). Let p be a prime of the form $p = N_M N_K f - 1$, where N_M and N_K are smooth coprime integers, and f a cofactor. Let $\mathcal{H}_I$ be a function as in Algorithm 1. Let E_0 be a supersingular curve defined over $\mathbb{F}_{p^2}$, and let K be a point on E_0 of order N_K. Write ϕ_K for the isogeny $\phi_K : E_0 \to E_K := E_0/\langle K\rangle$. Given the curves E_0, E_K and an oracle that responds to the following queries:

- challenge: returns a random sequence $[M_0, \ldots, M_{I-1}]_{E_0, N_M}$,
- solve($[V_0, \ldots, V_{I-1}]_{E_0, N_M}$): returns $j(E_V/\langle\phi_V(K)\rangle)$, where ϕ_V is the isogeny associated to the input sequence,
- decide(i, j): returns true if j is equal to the output of a solve query with input the response of the i-th challenge query, and false otherwise,

For any value n, produce n pairs (i, j) such that decide(i, j) = true with less than n solve queries.

The problem is based on Game 12 of [5], but compared to it, this game involves multiple points during the challenge and solve query to abstract the behavior described in the previous section. Moreover, the problem includes the countermeasures against the polynomial time attack of [4], i.e. the attacker can only query points of the correct order. This can be replicated in the OPRF setting by checking the order of the isogenies in the proof of isogeny knowledge.

We included these countermeasures to prevent possible attacks since they are inexpensive. However, we conjecture that the problem remains hard even if the adversary is allowed to submit solve queries with points of arbitrary order. Furthermore, the problem remains hard after the SIDH attacks since it does not involve exchanging any torsion points.

Countermeasure Costs. We briefly discuss the impact of the proposed countermeasures on the performance of the OPRF protocol. Firstly, we need to determine the parameters ℓ, e, and I. Keeping in mind the possible SIDH attacks based on the recovered torsion on E_k, we choose I to be maximal. We require that the degree of the message isogeny is about $\approx 2^{5/2\lambda}$ to prevent the attack proposed in [20]. Hence, we set $e = 1$ and $I = \log_\ell(2^{5/2\lambda})$.

The message component N_M can then be chosen to be ℓ, to ensure that isogenies of degree ℓ have kernel in $\mathbb{F}_{p^2}$, or one, if torsion points of order ℓ are defined over a small extension field. In the latter case, the prime p does not need to change to allow computations of the message isogeny. In both cases, not only do the proposed countermeasures protect against existing attacks, but also they reduce the prime size leading to a more compact and efficient protocol.

5   Countermeasures Against the SIDH Attacks

The recent series of attacks by Castryck and Decru [7], Maino, Martindale, Panny, Pope, and Wesolowski [19], and Robert [22] exploits torsion-point information to break SIDH. These attacks trivially translate to the OPRF, where any third party can recover both the user's hashed input (which breaks obliviousness) and the server's secret key. Thus, to guarantee the security of the SIDH-based OPRF we need to rely on the masked-torsion countermeasures, as in masked SIDH (M-SIDH) [12]. We can now formulate the following problem, on whose hardness the input hiding property of the OPRF is based.

Problem 6 (Decisional M-SIDH Isogeny problem). Let E_0 be a supersingular elliptic curve, with a basis P, Q be of $E_0[n]$. Distinguish between the following distributions:

- (E_1, R, S), where E_1 is the codomain of a d-isogeny $\phi : E_0 \to E_1$, where d is coprime with n, and the points R, S are the masked images of P, Q, i.e. $R = [\alpha]\phi(P)$ and $S = [\alpha]\phi(Q)$ for some $\alpha \xleftarrow{\$} \mathbb{Z}_n^*$;
- (E_1, R, S), where E_1 is a random supersingular elliptic curve and the points R, S are a random basis of $E_1[n]$ such that $e(R, S) = e(P, Q)^{\alpha^2 d}$, for some value α.

The hardness of the problem clearly depends on the choices of n and d; the problem (conjecturally) requires $O(2^\lambda)$ operations to solve when $n > f_{\text{M-SIDH}}(\lambda, d)$, i.e. the product of the λ largest prime powers dividing n is smaller than $\sqrt{d}$.

Concrete Cost. We have shown it is possible to protect the OPRF protocol from the SIDH attacks. Unfortunately, the proposed countermeasure do come at a significant cost. The degrees of the blinding isogeny and the server's isogeny are the same as in SIDH with the same countermeasures. At security level $\lambda = 128$, that corresponds to isogenies of degree $\approx 2^{2956}$. More generally, we see experimentally that the degree of the isogenies scales log-linearly in the security parameter with a constant of ≈ 6.7. We thus have that the degree of the blinding isogeny and the server's isogeny must be $\approx 2^{6.7\lambda \log \lambda}$ to guarantee the security of the protocol.

5.1 Adapting the Proof of Isogeny Knowledge

In this section, we propose a zero-knowledge proof, based on that in [5], of isogeny knowledge that can guarantee the correctness of torsion points up to a scalar, i.e. a proof for the following relation:

$$\mathcal{R}_{\text{iso}} = \left\{ ((E_0, P_0, Q_0, E_1, P_1, Q_1), (\phi, \alpha)) \; \middle| \; \begin{array}{c} \phi : E_0 \to E_1 \text{ is a cyclic } d\text{-isogeny,} \\ P_1 = [\alpha]\phi(P_0), \\ Q_1 = [\alpha]\phi(Q_0). \end{array} \right\}.$$

The main idea is that the masking constant α can be split into three shares $\alpha = \alpha_1 \alpha_2 \alpha_3$. The prover can mask the torsion points with α_i when computing the i-th side of the SIDH square, so that the composition of the three isogenies, together with their masking values, forms a commutative diagram with the isogeny ϕ with masking value α. The proof remains zero-knowledge because each single value α_i is independent of α.

More formally, let E_0 and E_1 be supersingular elliptic curves with points $P_0, Q_0 \in E_0[n]$ and $P_1, Q_1 \in E_1[n]$. The prover wants to prove knowledge of a d-isogeny $\phi : E_0 \to E_1$ and a value $\alpha \in \mathbb{Z}_n$ such that $P_1 = [\alpha]\phi(P_0)$ and $Q_1 = [\alpha]\phi(Q_0)$. Let us assume $n = f_{\text{M-SIDH}}(\lambda, d)$, so that the isogeny ϕ is hard to extract from public information. The prover generates a random isogeny $\psi : E_0 \to E_2$ of degree s, where $s \approx n$ is a smooth number coprime with both n and d, and generates the SIDH square (E_0, E_1, E_2, E_3) with edges $(\phi, \psi, \phi', \psi')$. To guarantee soundness, the prover needs to show that ψ and ψ' are parallel: the prover thus generates a s-basis R_2, S_2 on E_2, maps it to E_3 to obtain R_3, S_3, and expresses the kernels of $\hat{\psi}$ and $\hat{\psi}'$ in terms of R_2, S_2 and R_3, S_3 with the same linear coefficients. The prover also splits α in three shares $\alpha = \alpha_1 \alpha_2 \alpha_3$ and maps the points P_0, Q_0 through ψ and ϕ' with masking values α_1 and α_2 to obtain the points $P_2 = [\alpha_1]\psi(P_0), Q_2 = [\alpha_1]\psi(Q_0)$, and $P_3 = [\alpha_2]\phi'(P_2), Q_3 = [\alpha_2]\phi'(Q_2)$, which implies that P_3 and Q_3 also satisfy the relation $[\alpha_3]P_3 = \psi'(P_1), [\alpha_3]Q_3 = \psi'(Q_1)$. Hence, the SIDH square commutes with respect to the points P_i, Q_i, i.e. if we restrict ourselves to the n-torsion, we have $[\alpha][s]\phi = [\alpha_3]\hat{\psi}' \circ [\alpha_2]\phi' \circ [\alpha_1]\psi$.

Thus, the witness can be split into three components, and hence we obtain a proof with ternary challenges. The prover initially commits to the curves E_2, E_3 and the relevant points on them with a commitment scheme $\mathsf{C}(\cdot)$. Then, depending on the challenge, the prover responds with one edge of the SIDH square, the relevant curves and points, and the corresponding commitment openings. The proof is described in details in the full version [2]. Since each iteration has soundness error $2/3$, the proof must be repeated $-\lambda \log_{2/3}(2) \approx 1.71$ times to achieve a soundness error of $2^{-\lambda}$.

Remark 7. If the kernel of the isogeny ϕ is not defined over a small extension field, as in the case of the message isogeny, the proof can be computed by gluing together multiple SIDH squares, as shown in [3].

We now sketch the proofs of correctness, three-special soundness and zero-knowledge. Given the similarity of the zero-knowledge proof with those in [5], the proofs also follow a similar approach.

Correctness. A honest prover always generates proofs that are accepted by the verifier. The verifier recomputes the same operations as the prover and checks that the outputs match. The only difference is in the chall $= \pm 1$ cases, where the verifier computes the dual of ψ and ψ', which then introduces a factor s in the point equality check.

Three-special Soundness. The protocol is three-special sound because there exists an extractor that extracts the witness given three accepting transcripts with the same commitments and different challenges. The isogeny ϕ can be computed by mapping the kernel of ϕ' (from chall $= 0$) under the isogeny $\hat{\psi}$ (from chall $= -1$). Since the isogenies ψ and ψ' are parallel (from all the challenges combined), this guarantees that ϕ is a d-isogeny from E_0 to E_1. The masking value α can be recomputed as the product of α_1, α_2, and α_3.

Zero-knowledge. We sketch a simulator that given a statement $(E_0, P_0, Q_0, E_1, P_1, Q_1)$ and a challenge chall can simulate a valid transcript without knowledge of the witness. For the case chall $= -1$, the simulator behaves like an honest prover. For chall $= +1$, the situation is similar: the simulator can compute a d-isogeny ψ', pick a random basis R_3, S_3 of $E_3[d]$ and a random value $\alpha_3 \in \mathbb{Z}_n^*$, and compute the values a, b and points P_3, Q_3 that pass verification. Note that the points R_3, S_3 are uniformly random among the bases of $E_3[d]$, and the value α_3 is uniformly random and independent of α; the simulated values are thus distributed as the honestly-generated ones. The case of chall $= 0$ is more complicated: the simulator can sample a random curve E_2, generate a random basis P_2, Q_2 of $E_2[n]$ that satisfies $e(P_2, Q_2) = e(P_0, Q_0)^{x^2 s}$ for some random x, pick a random d-isogeny $\phi' : E_2 \to E_3$, and compute the image points on E_3. In this case, the indistinguishability of the simulator's output is only computational. It is thus based on the conjectured hardness of the following problem, which is a modified version of the Decisional Supersingular Product (DSSP) problem introduced in [14].

Problem 8 (DSSP with Torsion (DSSPwT) problem). Given an isogeny $\phi : E_0 \to E_1$ and points $P_0, Q_0 \in E_0[n]$, where $n = f_{\text{M-SIDH}}(\lambda, d)$, distinguish between the following distributions:

- $\mathcal{D}_0 = \{(E_2, P_2, Q_2, E_3, \phi')\}$, where E_2 is the codomain of an s-isogeny $\psi :$ $E_0 \to E_2$, the points P_2, Q_2 satisfy $P_2 = [\alpha]\psi(P_0)$, $Q_2 = [\alpha]\psi(Q_0)$ for some $\alpha \in \mathbb{Z}_n^*$, and $\phi' : E_2 \to E_3$ is a d-isogeny with kernel $\ker \phi' = \psi(\ker \phi)$.
- $\mathcal{D}_1 = \{(E_2, P_2, Q_2, E_3, \phi')\}$, where E_2 is a random supersingular curve with the same cardinality as E_0, P_2 and Q_2 are two random points of order n such that $e(P_2, Q_2) = e(P_0, Q_0)^s$, and the isogeny ϕ' is a d-isogeny between E_2 and E_3.

Note that [5] argues that a similar proof can only reveal one torsion point (either P_i or Q_i) at a time to prevent a distinguishing attack on the simulator. The attack they present relies on computing the Weil pairing between two points of coprime order, and thus their pairing is always one. The attack thus does not apply, and the simulated transcript remains indistinguishable under Weil pairing checks because the sampled points P_2, Q_2 are guaranteed to have the same pairing as the honestly-generated points. By revealing both points P_i and Q_i we obtain a significantly more efficient proof, since it has $1/3$ soundness rather than $1/6$. We discuss potential optimizations and the concrete cost of such a proof in the full version of this paper [2].

6   Verifiability

Oblivious PRFs can satisfy a stronger security property called *verifiability*. Informally, this guarantees that the server behaves honestly and always uses the same long-term static key. This is needed to guarantee the privacy of the user in those instances where the user may later reveal the output of the OPRF. A malicious server may behave "honestly" while also using different secret keys on different interactions. After learning the OPRF output of the user, the server can then test which secret key was used to produce that specific output and thus link the user to a specific user-server interaction.

The OPRF protocol by Boneh, Kogan, and Woo achieves verifiability by relying on many SIDH exchanges: not only is this broken by the attacks on SIDH [7,19,22], this requires five rounds of interaction.

We avoid such issues by introducing a novel public-coin proof protocol of parallel isogeny. Since the proof does not rely on private randomness, we obtain a proof *of knowledge* that can be made non-interactive via the Fiat-Shamir transform [11] or the Unruh transform [23]. In the OPRF setting, we will rely on the latter to achieve the online-extractability without rewinding needed to get a proof in the UC model. Our main approach relies on executing two proofs of isogeny knowledge in parallel *with correlated randomness*. Since part of the randomness used is shared, we can obtain a proof of parallelness without needing additional computations.

Firstly, we formalize the notion of parallelness. We say that two d-isogenies $\phi :$ $E_0 \to E_1$ and $\tilde{\phi} : \tilde{E}_0 \to \tilde{E}_1$ are parallel with respect to the bases $T_0, V_0 \in E_0[d]$ and $\tilde{T}_0, \tilde{V}_0 \in E_0'[d]$ if there exists coefficients $a, b \in \mathbb{Z}_d$ such that $\ker \phi = \langle [a]T_0 + [b]V_0 \rangle$ and $\ker \tilde{\phi} = \langle [a]\tilde{T}_0 + [b]\tilde{V}_0 \rangle$. This suggests that the parallelness relation that we are proving is the following:

$$\mathcal{R}_{\mathsf{par}} = \left\{ ((E_0, T_0, V_0, E_1, \tilde{E}_0, \tilde{T}_0, \tilde{V}_0, \tilde{E}_1), (k_0, k_1)) \;\middle|\; \begin{array}{l} E_0/\langle [k_0]T_0 + [k_1]V_0 \rangle \cong E_1, \\ \tilde{E}_0/\langle [k_0]\tilde{T}_0 + [k_1]\tilde{V}_0 \rangle \cong \tilde{E}_1 \end{array} \right\}$$

However, as discussed before, we are combining several proofs together to obtain a larger proof that simultaneously proves knowledge of two isogenies and guarantees the two isogenies are parallel. We thus obtain a proof for the following relation, where we consider the case of a secret key with two coefficients for completeness. For practical reasons, the OPRF will fix $k_0 = 1$ without any loss of security.

$$\mathcal{R}_{\mathsf{par}}^* = \left\{ \begin{array}{l} ((E_0, T_0, V_0, P_0, Q_0, E_1, P_1, Q_1, \\ \tilde{E}_0, \tilde{T}_0, \tilde{V}_0, \tilde{P}_0, \tilde{Q}_0, \tilde{E}_1, \tilde{P}_1, \tilde{Q}_1), \\ (k_0, k_1, \alpha, \alpha')) \end{array} \;\middle|\; \begin{array}{l} \ker \phi = \langle [k_0]T_0 + [k_1]V_0 \rangle, \\ \ker \phi' = \langle [k_0]\tilde{T}_0 + [k_1]\tilde{V}_0 \rangle, \\ (E_0, P_0, Q_0, E_1, P_1, Q_1), (\phi, \alpha) \in \mathcal{R}_{\mathsf{iso}}, \\ (\tilde{E}_0, \tilde{P}_0, \tilde{Q}_0, \tilde{E}_1, \tilde{P}_1, \tilde{Q}_1), (\phi', \alpha') \in \mathcal{R}_{\mathsf{iso}} \end{array} \right\}$$

Now, let the curve $\tilde{E}_0$ with a d-basis $\tilde{T}_0, \tilde{V}_0$ be fixed protocol parameters. Using the same notation as before, assume that server has committed to its key (k_0, k_1) by publishing the codomain of the d-isogeny $\tilde{\phi}$ that has kernel $\langle [k_0]\tilde{T}_0 + [k_1]\tilde{V}_0 \rangle$. The server may also reveal some torsion information in its commitment, but as we will discuss later, this is not strictly needed. During the OPRF execution, the server receives a curve E_0 with a d-basis T_0, V_0 on it, and it computes $\phi : E_0 \to E_1 := E_0/\langle [k_0]T_0 + [k_1]V_0 \rangle$. The server then wants to prove that it knows the isogenies ϕ and $\tilde{\phi}$ and that they are parallel.

If the server simply ran two instances of the PoIK $\mathcal{R}_{\mathsf{iso}}$ in parallel, there would be no way to convince the prover that the isogenies are indeed parallel. If the proofs share the same challenges, i.e. the verifier sends the same challenges to both proofs, the server would respond with both ϕ' and $\tilde{\phi}'$ when $\mathsf{chall} = 0$. However, the isogenies ϕ' and $\tilde{\phi}'$ are parallel with respect to the bases $\psi(T_0), \psi(V_0)$ and $\tilde{\psi}(\tilde{T}_0), \tilde{\psi}(\tilde{V}_0)$ (where ψ is the vertical isogeny used in the proof of knowledge), which are not revealed in the proof. If we were to reveal them, the proof would not be zero-knowledge, because when $\mathsf{chall} = 0$, the verifier could recompute the secret isogeny ψ and $\tilde{\psi}$ through the SIDH attacks. Instead, we want to modify the proof to reveal different bases $T_2, V_2 \in E_2[d]$ and $\tilde{T}_2, \tilde{V}_2 \in \tilde{E}_2[d]$ such that ϕ' and $\tilde{\phi}'$ are parallel with regards to them, but also such that they do not reveal much information about ψ and $\tilde{\psi}$. We thus propose that the prover generates four random coefficients $w, x, y, z \in \mathbb{Z}_d$ such that $wz - xy \neq 0 \bmod d$, and computes T_2 and V_2 as the solution of $\psi(T_0) = [w]T_2 + [x]S_2, \psi(V_0) = [y]T_2 + [z]V_2$, and similarly for $\tilde{T}_2$ and $\tilde{V}_2$. This is then secure, because the basis T_2, V_2 is uniformly random. Thus, for a single proof, this change only does not affect the security of the proof since no additional information is revealed. The rest of the proof needs to be modified to ensure that the process is followed correctly, i.e. we want the prover to reveal the values w, x, y, z together with ψ so that the verifier can verify the correctness of T_2 and V_2. The modified proof is denoted by $\mathcal{P}_{\mathsf{iso}}^*$, and it is represented explicitly in the full version of this paper [2].

Now, if the prover executes the modified proof of isogeny knowledge for ϕ and $\tilde{\phi}$ in parallel, with the same challenges, and with the same values x, w, y, z, the isogenies $\phi', \tilde{\phi}'$ revealed when chall $= 0$ are parallel when the isogenies $\phi, \tilde{\phi}$ are also parallel, as shown in the following lemma.

Lemma 9. *Let notation be as above. The isogenies $\phi, \tilde{\phi}$ are parallel if and only if the isogenies $\phi', \tilde{\phi}'$ are also parallel.*

Proof. Assume the isogeny ϕ has kernel $\langle [k_0]T_0 + [k_1]V_0 \rangle$ and the isogeny $\tilde{\phi}$ has kernel $\langle [\tilde{k}_0]\tilde{T}_0 + [\tilde{k}_1]\tilde{V}_0 \rangle$. The kernel of ϕ' is the image of the kernel of ϕ under ψ, i.e. $\ker \phi' = \psi(\ker \phi)$. Since $\ker \phi = \langle [k_0]T_0 + [k_1]V_0 \rangle$, it follows that

$$\ker \phi' = \langle [k_0]\psi(T_0) + [k_1]\psi(V_0) \rangle = \langle [wk_0 + yk_1]T_2 + [xk_0 + zk_1]V_2 \rangle.$$

Similarly, we obtain

$$\ker \tilde{\phi}' = \langle [w\tilde{k}_0 + y\tilde{k}_1]\tilde{T}_2 + [x\tilde{k}_0 + z\tilde{k}_1]\tilde{V}_2 \rangle.$$

Since the coefficients w, x, y, z were chosen such that the matrix $\begin{pmatrix} w & x \\ y & z \end{pmatrix}$ is invertible, we obtain that $k_0 = \tilde{k}_0$ and $k_1 = \tilde{k}_1$ holds if and only if $wk_0 + yk_1 = w\tilde{k}_0 + y\tilde{k}_1$) and $xk_0 + zk_1 = x\tilde{k}_0 + z\tilde{k}_1$ holds. □

We can now use the proof $\mathcal{P}^*_{\text{iso}}$ to construct our proof of parallel isogeny knowledge. The prover runs two such proofs in parallel, with the same randomness (w, x, y, z), and responds to the verifier's challenges with the responses of the individual proofs. The resulting proof is represented explicitly in the full version of this paper [2]. The security proofs follow closely those of the PoIK $\mathcal{P}_{\text{iso}}$ in Sect. 5.1: correctness of $\mathcal{P}_{\text{iso}}$ implies correctness of $\mathcal{P}_{\text{par}}$, while the soundness of $\mathcal{P}_{\text{par}}$ follows from the soundness of $\mathcal{P}_{\text{iso}}$ and Lemma 9. The argument for zero-knowledge is also similar, but it is based on the hardness of the following problem, which takes into consideration that the two parallel instance partially share the same randomness.

Problem 10 (Double DSSP with Torsion (DDSSPwT) problem). Let $\mathcal{D}_0$ and $\mathcal{D}_1$ be as in Problem 8. Given:

1. two d-isogenies $\phi : E_0 \to E_1$, $\tilde{\phi} : \tilde{E}_0 \to \tilde{E}_1$,
2. the points $T_0, V_0 \in E_0[d]$ and $\tilde{T}_0, \tilde{V}_0 \in \tilde{E}_0[d]$,
3. the points $P_0, Q_0 \in E_0[n]$ and $\tilde{P}_0, \tilde{Q}_0 \in \tilde{E}_0[n]$, where $n = f_{\text{M-SIDH}}(\lambda, d)$,

distinguish between the following distributions:

- $\mathcal{D}^*_0 = \left\{ \begin{array}{l} (E_2, T_2, V_2, P_2, Q_2, E_3, \phi'), \\ (\tilde{E}_2, \tilde{T}_2, \tilde{V}_2, \tilde{P}_2, \tilde{Q}_2, \tilde{E}_3, \tilde{\phi}'), \end{array} \right\}$, where the curves and the n-torsion points follow the $\mathcal{D}_0$-distribution, i.e. we have $(E_2, P_2, Q_2, E_3, \phi') \leftarrow \mathcal{D}_0$, and $(\tilde{E}_2, \tilde{P}_2, \tilde{Q}_2, \tilde{E}_3, \tilde{\phi}') \leftarrow \mathcal{D}_0$, and moreover

$$\begin{bmatrix} T_2 \\ V_2 \end{bmatrix} = B \begin{bmatrix} \psi(T_0) \\ \psi(V_0) \end{bmatrix}, \quad \text{and} \quad \begin{bmatrix} \tilde{T}_2 \\ \tilde{V}_2 \end{bmatrix} = B \begin{bmatrix} \tilde{\psi}(\tilde{T}_0) \\ \tilde{\psi}(\tilde{V}_0) \end{bmatrix},$$

for some $B \in \text{GL}_2(\mathbb{Z}_n)$, and ψ and $\tilde{\psi}$ being respectively the s-isogenies between E_0 and E_2 and $\tilde{E}_0$ and $\tilde{E}_2$ that are guaranteed to exist because of the $\mathcal{D}_0$ distribution;

- $\mathcal{D}_1^* = \left\{ \begin{array}{l} (E_2, T_2, V_2, P_2, Q_2, E_3, \phi'), \\ (\tilde{E}_2, \tilde{T}_2, \tilde{V}_2, \tilde{P}_2, \tilde{Q}_2, \tilde{E}_3, \tilde{\phi}'), \end{array} \right\}$, where the curves and the n-torsion
points follow the $\mathcal{D}_1$-distribution, i.e. we have $(E_2, P_2, Q_2, E_3, \phi') \leftarrow \mathcal{D}_1$, and $(\tilde{E}_2, \tilde{P}_2, \tilde{Q}_2, \tilde{E}_3, \tilde{\phi}') \leftarrow \mathcal{D}_1$, and moreover the points T_2, V_2 and $\tilde{T}_2, \tilde{V}_2$ form a random basis of $E_2[d]$ and $\tilde{E}_2[d]$, respectively.

The proof $\mathcal{P}_{par}$ is a proof of knowledge, and it can be made non-interactive with standards transformations, such as the Fiat-Shamir [11] or the Unruh [23] transform. This is the first non-interactive proof of parallelness. We discuss potential optimizations and the concrete cost of such a proof in the full version of this paper [2].

7   A New OPRF Protocol

In this section, we combine the countermeasures presented in Sect. 4, the SIDH countermeasures and the novel proof of isogeny knowledge discussed in Sect. 5, and the non-interactive proof of parallel isogeny introduced in Sect. 6 to obtain a verifiable OPRF protocol that is post-quantum secure, round-optimal, and moderately compact.

The OPRF protocol is a two-party protocol between a user U and a server S. Let N_M, N_B, N_K be coprime numbers representing the degrees of the message isogeny, the blinding isogeny, and the server's isogeny, respectively. Let p be a prime of the form $p = N_M N_B N_K f - 1$, for some cofactor f, and let $E_0, \tilde{E}$ be two supersingular elliptic curves defined over $\mathbb{F}_{p^2}$. Moreover, let P, Q be a fixed basis of $E_0[N_M]$ and let $\tilde{P}, \tilde{Q}$ be a fixed basis of $\tilde{E}[N_K]$. The first curve is used to compute the PRF, while the second is used within the server's commitment.

At a high-level, to evaluate the OPRF on an input x, the user maps the input to a curve E_m according to Algorithm 1 and computes a blinding isogeny $\phi_b : E_m \to E_{mb}$. The user then sends the codomain curve, together with torsion images and a proof of their correctness, to the server, which computes a second isogeny $\phi_k : E_{mb} \to E_{mbk}$. The torsion information is appropriately masked to avoid the SIDH attacks. The server then responds with the curve E_{mbk}, some torsion information, a proof of their correctness, and a proof that it has used the previously-committed secret key. The user then concludes by using the torsion information provided by the server to undo the blinding isogeny and compute the curve E_{mk}. Its j-invariant is then hashed together with the input and the server's public key to form the PRF output. The protocol is described in Fig. 4, and it realizes the OPRF ideal functionality of Fig. 2, which allows us to state the following theorem.

Theorem 11. *The protocol described in Fig. 4 realizes the ideal functionality $\mathcal{F}_{vOPRF}$ of Fig. 2 in the random oracle model.*

We sketch a proof in the full version of this paper [2].

Parameters. A prime p of the form $p = N_M N_B N_K f - 1$, where N_M, N_B, N_K are smooth coprime integers and f a smooth cofactor. E_0 and $\tilde{E}$ are supersingular elliptic curves defined over $\mathbb{F}_{p^2}$, where $\text{End}\,\tilde{E}$ is unknown, and $P, Q \in E_0[N_M]$ and $\tilde{P}, \tilde{Q} \in E[N_K]$ are fixed bases. The protocol also relies on the following functions:

- $H_i : \{0,1\}^* \to \mathbb{Z}_M$ for $i \in \{1,\dots,I\}$, where I is such that $N_M^I > 2^{4\lambda}$
- $\bar{H} : \{0,1\}^* \to \{0,1\}^\lambda$, to hash the final PRF output,

and two non-interactive proofs of knowledge: $\mathcal{P}_{\text{iso}}$, for the user to prove correctness of torsion images, and $\mathcal{P}_{\text{par}}$, for the server to prove it computed honestly with the committed key.

Initialization. On input INIT from the environment, the server S:

- sample $k \leftarrow \mathbb{Z}_K$ and stores it,
- computes the curve $\tilde{E}_C = \tilde{E}/\langle \tilde{P} + [k]\tilde{Q} \rangle$,
- stores $\mathsf{pk} = (j(E_C))$ and outputs (INIT, pk).

Evaluation. On input INIT from the environment, the server S:

- On input (EVAL, S, x), the user U proceeds as follows:
  1. Sample $\alpha \leftarrow \mathbb{Z}_N^*$ and $b \leftarrow \mathbb{Z}_B$,
  2. Compute $(\phi_m, E_m) = \mathcal{H}_I(x)$;
  3. Compute $\phi_b : E_m \to E_{mb} := E_m/\langle P_m + [b]Q_m \rangle$, where $P_m, Q_m = \mathcal{B}_B(E_m)$,
  4. Set $\phi_{mb} = \phi_b \circ \phi_1 \circ \phi_0$, $R = [\alpha]\phi_{mb}(P)$, $S = [\alpha]\phi_{mb}(Q)$,
  5. Compute $\pi_c \leftarrow \mathcal{P}_{\text{iso}}(E_0, P, Q, E_{mb}, R, S, \phi_{mb}, \alpha)$,
  6. Send message (E_{mb}, R, S, π_c) to the server and store ϕ_b.

- On input SERVERCOMPLETE from the environment and message (E_{mb}, R, S, π_c) from the user U, the server S proceeds as follows:
  1. Verify the proof π_c and sample $\alpha_k \leftarrow \mathbb{Z}_n^*$,
  2. Compute $\phi_k : E_{mb} \to E_{mbk} := E_{mb}/\langle R + [k]S \rangle$,
  3. Compute $R_k = [\alpha_k]\phi_k(P_b)$, $S_k = [\alpha_k]\phi_k(Q_b)$, where $P_b, Q_b = \mathcal{B}_B(E_{mb})$,
  4. Compute $\pi_k \leftarrow \mathcal{P}_{\text{par}}((E_{mb}, P_b, Q_b, E_{mbk}, R_k, S_k), (\tilde{E}, \tilde{P}, \tilde{Q}, \tilde{E}_C), k, \alpha_k)$,
  5. Send $(\mathsf{pk}, E_{mbk}, R_k, S_k, \pi_k)$ to the user U.

- On input $(\mathsf{pk} = j(E_c), E_{mbk}, R_k, S_k, \pi_k)$ from the server S, the user U proceeds as follows:
  1. Verify the proof π_k,
  2. Compute b_0, b_1 such that $\langle [b_0]P_b + [b_1]Q_b \rangle = \ker \hat{\phi}_b$, where $P_b, Q_b = \mathcal{B}_d(E_{mb})$,
  3. Compute $\phi_u : E_{mbk} \to E_{mk} := E_{mbk}/\langle [b_0]R_k + [b_1]S_k \rangle$,
  4. Compute $y = \bar{H}(x, \mathsf{pk}, j(E_mk))$ and output (EVAL, pk, y).

Fig. 4. The verifiable OPRF protocol.

Parameter Selection. Firstly, we discuss how to select the starting curves E_0 and $\tilde{E}$. As mentioned in Sect. 5, the cryptanalysis on masked-torsion SIDH with a starting curve with small endomorphism [12, Section 4.2] does not apply here, since the message isogeny removes this property from the starting curve of the blinding isogeny. Hence, the curve E_0 does not need to have unknown endomorphism ring. However, the situation is different for $\tilde{E}$: as observed in [4], knowledge of End $\tilde{E}$ allows to find collisions in the server's commitment. Thus, knowing End $\tilde{E}$ would allow the server to break verifiability, since it could prove parallelness to two distinct isogenies. It is thus necessary that the curve $\tilde{E}$ is generated by a trusted party or through a multiparty trusted setup ceremony, such as the one presented in [3].

The main parameter of the OPRF protocol is the prime p. Firstly, if the message isogeny is the composition of many isogenies whose kernel is defined over $\mathbb{F}_{p^4}$, the value $p + 1$ does not need have a dedicated factor. Then, for the main exchange, i.e. the blinding, server's isogeny, unblinding part, we need to smooth coprime integers N_B and N_K that are highly composite to prevent the SIDH attacks. Following the analysis of Sect. 5, we have $N_B \approx N_K \approx 2^{2956}$. Lastly, the proofs of knowledge $\mathcal{P}_{\text{iso}}$ and $\mathcal{P}_{\text{par}}$ require a third cofactor N_S that is coprime with both N_B and N_K. To guarantee the hardness of Problems 8 and 10, the integer N_S needs to be of the same length as N_B and N_K. However, since torsion points of order N_S do not need to be masked, the value N_S can be a prime power. Putting this together, we obtain that the prime p needs to be of the form $p = N_B N_S N_K f - 1$ and be at least 8868-bit long to guarantee $\lambda = 128$ bits of security. Note that the new computation of the message isogeny and the new proofs of knowledge has significantly reduced the size of the prime; compared to the OPRF protocol by Boneh, Kogan, and Woo, we use a prime that is 5.8× larger, while relying on an SIDH protocol with isogenies that are 9.2× longer.

Efficiency. We now estimate the communication cost of the OPRF protocol. The largest components are the non-interactive proofs of knowledge: given the analysis of the previous sections, they are less than $1.7\lambda(35 \log p + 51\lambda)$-bit long. Since $\log p \approx 10\lambda \log \lambda$, we obtain that one OPRF execution requires $1.7\lambda^2(350 \log \lambda + 51)$ bits of communication. For $\lambda = 128$, this corresponds to a transcript of 8.7 MB. We remark that the size of the proofs is particularly large due to the Unruh transform needed to prove security in the UC framework. If the proofs were made non-interactive via the Fiat-Shamir transform, a single execution of the verifiable OPRF with $\lambda = 128$ would require 1.9 MB of communication on average and 3.8 MB in the worst case. Such an OPRF may be used in instances where security in the UC framework is not necessary.

A direct comparison with the protocol by Boneh, Kogan, and Woo [5] is not simple since their bandwidth estimate does not appear to include the Unruh transform overhead. We estimate that one execution of the OPRF from [5] requires at least 10.9 MB. Our protocol is thus more compact than that in [5], despite being round-optimal and secure against both the one-more unpredictability attack and the SIDH attacks. This is made possible by the fact that the sigma protocols are highly optimized and have ternary challenges, which significantly reduces the overhead introduced in the Unruh transform. Indeed, if we compare a version of the two protocols with the Fiat-Shamir transform, our OPRF uses 31% more bandwidth than the one in [5]. We summarize the state of post-quantum OPRF protocols in Table 1.

Table 1. Post-quantum OPRF protocols secure against malicious clients.

Protocol	Rounds	Bandwidth (avg.)	Verifiable	Secure
[1] (LWE)	2	>128 GB	✓	✓
[5] (CSIDH)	3	424 kB	✗	✓
[5] (SIDH)^{FO}	6	1.4 MB	✓	✗
[5] (SIDH)^{Unruh}	6	>10.9 MB	✓	✗
[This work]^{FO}	2	1.9 MB	✓	✓
[This work]^{Unruh}	2	8.7 MB	✓	✓

8   Conclusion

In this work, we presented a post-quantum verifiable OPRF protocol that is moderately compact and round-optimal. The protocol is the first round-optimal OPRF based on isogenies, and it is several orders of magnitude more compact than the existing round-optimal protocol. To obtain this protocol, we started from an insecure protocol by Boneh, Kogan, and Woo, and we proposed an efficient countermeasure against the one-more unpredictability attack, integrated the existing SIDH countermeasures, developed a new zero-knowledge proof of isogeny that works with the SIDH countermeasures, and proposed a new non-interactive proof of parallel isogeny that reduced the number of rounds to two.

The protocol is an important stepping stone towards fully practical post-quantum OPRFs, but its performance is hindered by the inefficiency of the SIDH countermeasures. In future work, we aim at developing more efficient solutions: a moderate reduction in the degree of the isogenies would significantly improve the efficiency of the protocol. It is also interesting to improve the proof of parallel isogeny by avoiding validating the commitment isogeny at every interaction.

Acknowledgements. The author thanks Christophe Petit and Luca de Feo for various suggestions, and Tako Boris Fouotsa, Christophe Petit, Chloe Martindale, and the anonymous reviewers of Crypto and the PQCifris workshop for feedback on earlier versions of this work. The author would also like to thank Luca de Feo, Antonin Leroux, and Benjamin Wesolowski for fruitful discussions on isogeny-based zero-knowledge proofs at the Banff International Research Station workshop "Supersingular Isogeny Graphs in Cryptography".

This work has been supported in part by EPSRC via grant EP/R012288/1, under the RISE (http://www.ukrise.org) programme.

References

1. Albrecht, M.R., Davidson, A., Deo, A., Smart, N.P.: Round-optimal verifiable oblivious pseudorandom functions from ideal lattices. In: Garay, J. (ed.) PKC 2021, Part II. LNCS, vol. 12711, pp. 261–289. Springer, Heidelberg (2021). https://doi.org/10.1007/978-3-030-75248-4_10
2. Basso, A.: A post-quantum round-optimal oblivious PRF from isogenies. Cryptology ePrint Archive, Report 2023/225 (2023). https://eprint.iacr.org/2023/225
3. Basso, A., et al.: Supersingular curves you can trust. In: Hazay, C., Stam, M. (eds.) EUROCRYPT 2023, Part II. LNCS, vol. 14005, pp. 405–437. Springer, Heidelberg (2023). https://doi.org/10.1007/978-3-031-30617-4_14
4. Basso, A., Kutas, P., Merz, S.P., Petit, C., Sanso, A.: Cryptanalysis of an oblivious PRF from supersingular isogenies. In: Tibouchi, M., Wang, H. (eds.) ASIACRYPT 2021, Part I. LNCS, vol. 13090, pp. 160–184. Springer, Heidelberg (2021). https://doi.org/10.1007/978-3-030-92062-3_6
5. Boneh, D., Kogan, D., Woo, K.: Oblivious pseudorandom functions from isogenies. In: Moriai, S., Wang, H. (eds.) ASIACRYPT 2020, Part II. LNCS, vol. 12492, pp. 520–550. Springer, Heidelberg (2020). https://doi.org/10.1007/978-3-030-64834-3_18
6. Canetti, R.: Universally composable security: a new paradigm for cryptographic protocols. In: 42nd FOCS, pp. 136–145. IEEE Computer Society Press, October 2001. https://doi.org/10.1109/SFCS.2001.959888
7. Castryck, W., Decru, T.: An efficient key recovery attack on SIDH. In: Hazay, C., Stam, M. (eds.) Advances in Cryptology – EUROCRYPT 2023. EUROCRYPT 2023, Part V. LNCS, vol. 14008, pp. 423–447. Springer, Heidelberg (2023). https://doi.org/10.1007/978-3-031-30589-4_15
8. Charles, D.X., Lauter, K.E., Goren, E.Z.: Cryptographic hash functions from expander graphs. J. Cryptol. 22(1), 93–113 (2009). https://doi.org/10.1007/s00145-007-9002-x
9. Chaum, D.: Blind signatures for untraceable payments. In: Chaum, D., Rivest, R.L., Sherman, A.T. (eds.) CRYPTO'82, pp. 199–203. Plenum Press, New York, USA (1982)
10. Eisenträger, K., Hallgren, S., Lauter, K.E., Morrison, T., Petit, C.: Supersingular isogeny graphs and endomorphism rings: reductions and solutions. In: Nielsen, J.B., Rijmen, V. (eds.) EUROCRYPT 2018, Part III. LNCS, vol. 10822, pp. 329–368. Springer, Heidelberg (2018). https://doi.org/10.1007/978-3-319-78372-7_11
11. Fiat, A., Shamir, A.: How to prove yourself: Practical solutions to identification and signature problems. In: Odlyzko, A.M. (ed.) CRYPTO'86. LNCS, vol. 263, pp. 186–194. Springer, Heidelberg (1987). https://doi.org/10.1007/3-540-47721-7_12
12. Fouotsa, T.B., Moriya, T., Petit, C.: M-SIDH and MD-SIDH: countering SIDH attacks by masking information. In: Hazay, C., Stam, M. (eds.) EUROCRYPT 2023, Part V. LNCS, vol. 14008, pp. 282–309. Springer, Heidelberg (2023). https://doi.org/10.1007/978-3-031-30589-4_10
13. Freedman, M.J., Ishai, Y., Pinkas, B., Reingold, O.: Keyword search and oblivious pseudorandom functions. In: Kilian, J. (ed.) TCC 2005. LNCS, vol. 3378, pp. 303–324. Springer, Heidelberg (2005). https://doi.org/10.1007/978-3-540-30576-7_17
14. Jao, D., De Feo, L.: Towards quantum-resistant cryptosystems from supersingular elliptic curve isogenies. In: Yang, B.Y. (ed.) Post-Quantum Cryptography - 4th International Workshop, PQCrypto 2011, pp. 19–34. Springer, Heidelberg (2011). https://doi.org/10.1007/978-3-642-25405-5_2

15. Jarecki, S., Kiayias, A., Krawczyk, H.: Round-optimal password-protected secret sharing and T-PAKE in the password-only model. In: Sarkar, P., Iwata, T. (eds.) ASIACRYPT 2014, Part II. LNCS, vol. 8874, pp. 233–253. Springer, Heidelberg (2014). https://doi.org/10.1007/978-3-662-45608-8_13

16. Jarecki, S., Kiayias, A., Krawczyk, H., Xu, J.: TOPPSS: cost-minimal password-protected secret sharing based on threshold OPRF. In: Gollmann, D., Miyaji, A., Kikuchi, H. (eds.) ACNS 17. LNCS, vol. 10355, pp. 39–58. Springer, Heidelberg (2017). https://doi.org/10.1007/978-3-319-61204-1_3

17. Jarecki, S., Krawczyk, H., Xu, J.: OPAQUE: an asymmetric PAKE protocol secure against pre-computation attacks. In: Nielsen, J.B., Rijmen, V. (eds.) EUROCRYPT 2018, Part III. LNCS, vol. 10822, pp. 456–486. Springer, Heidelberg (2018). https://doi.org/10.1007/978-3-319-78372-7_15

18. Jarecki, S., Liu, X.: Efficient oblivious pseudorandom function with applications to adaptive OT and secure computation of set intersection. In: Reingold, O. (ed.) TCC 2009. LNCS, vol. 5444, pp. 577–594. Springer, Heidelberg (2009). https://doi.org/10.1007/978-3-642-00457-5_34

19. Maino, L., Martindale, C., Panny, L., Pope, G., Wesolowski, B.: A direct key recovery attack on SIDH. In: Hazay, C., Stam, M. (eds.) EUROCRYPT 2023, Part V. LNCS, vol. 14008, pp. 448–471. Springer, Heidelberg (2023). https://doi.org/10.1007/978-3-031-30589-4_16

20. Merz, S.P., Minko, R., Petit, C.: Another look at some isogeny hardness assumptions. In: Topics in Cryptology - CT-RSA 2020 - the Cryptographers' Track at the RSA Conference 2020, San Francisco, CA, USA, 24–28 February 2020, Proceedings, pp. 496–511 (2020)

21. Naor, M., Reingold, O.: Number-theoretic constructions of efficient pseudo-random functions. In: 38th FOCS, pp. 458–467. IEEE Computer Society Press, October 1997. https://doi.org/10.1109/SFCS.1997.646134

22. Robert, D.: Breaking SIDH in polynomial time. In: Hazay, C., Stam, M. (eds.) EUROCRYPT 2023, Part V. LNCS, vol. 14008, pp. 472–503. Springer, Heidelberg (2023). https://doi.org/10.1007/978-3-031-30589-4_17

23. Unruh, D.: Non-interactive zero-knowledge proofs in the quantum random oracle model. In: Oswald, E., Fischlin, M. (eds.) EUROCRYPT 2015, Part II. LNCS, vol. 9057, pp. 755–784. Springer, Heidelberg (2015). https://doi.org/10.1007/978-3-662-46803-6_25

Traceable Ring Signatures from Group Actions: Logarithmic, Flexible, and Quantum Resistant

Wei Wei[iD], Min Luo[✉][iD], Zijian Bao[iD], Cong Peng[iD], and Debiao He[✉][iD]

Key Laboratory of Aerospace Information Security and Trusted Computing,
Ministry of Education, School of Cyber Science and Engineering,
Wuhan University, Wuhan, China
{weiwei_only,mluo,cpeng}@whu.edu.cn, bao_zijian@163.com, hedebiao@163.com

Abstract. Traceable ring signature (TRS) is a variation of ring signature, allowing to expose the user's identity whenever he signs two different messages under the same tag. The accountable anonymity of TRS makes it widely used in many restrained anonymous applications, e.g., e-voting system, offline coupon service. Traditional TRS schemes are built on mathematical problems, which are believed to be easy to solve by quantum computers. While numerous post-quantum (traceable) ring signature schemes have been proposed so far, there has been no TRS scheme based on isogenies proposed. We construct two TRS schemes from group actions that can be instantiated with isogenies and lattices. The critical technique is to generate multiple tags for the message and design an OR sigma protocol to generate proofs for multiple tag sets, which provides traceability for the TRS scheme. The signature size can be expressed as $O(\log N)$, where N represents the ring size. Based on different instantiation parameters, our proposed scheme enables ring members to negotiate the signature size and signing time according to their specific requirements. Moreover, we prove the security of our scheme under the standard random oracle model.

Keywords: Traceable ring signature · Post-Quantum cryptography · Isogeny-based cryptography · Lattice-based cryptography · OR sigma protocol

1 Introduction

Ring Signature (RS) [30] allows the signer to sign a message on behalf of the group without revealing the signer's identity. Traceable ring signature (TRS) is a variation of the RS, if a signer produces two signatures for different messages under the same tag, then the identity of the signer can be extracted by the ring

This work was supported by the Key Research and Development of Shandong Province under Grant 2021CXG010107; in part by the National Natural Science Foundation of China under Grant U21A20466, Grant 62172307, Grant 61972294 and Grant 61932016.

C. Carlet et al. (Eds.): SAC 2023, LNCS 14201, pp. 169–188, 2024.
https://doi.org/10.1007/978-3-031-53368-6_9

members, if signatures are for the same message, everyone can know that the two signatures were generated by the same signer. TRS limits the indubitable anonymity of ring signature, the tag in TRS consists of a group of members and a topic, the topic string refers to a social issue or voting. In many anonymous information systems such as e-voting [9] and offline coupon services [21], users are not expected to sign messages twice under the same tag, e.g., double-spending, multiple voting. The TRS scheme mitigates this dishonest behavior, and further protects the privacy of members, therefore, it becomes a powerful cryptographic tool in such systems.

The concept of TRS was proposed by Fujisaki and Suzuki [22] in 2007. Since then, several variant schemes [2,21] have been proposed to improve security or performance. However, these proposals are built on number theory, which can be solved by a large-scale quantum computer running Shor's algorithm [33]. Consequently, a quantum-resistant ring signature and related variant schemes have drawn much attention over the past ten years. Lattice-based cryptography is one of the most promising candidates in post-quantum cryptography. In addition to resisting quantum attacks, it has the advantage of better performance. Isogeny-based cryptography was first proposed by [11,31], it is an extension and thorough study of classical elliptic curve cryptography. Compared with other post-quantum cryptography candidates, isogeny-based cryptography stands out for its comparatively shorter key sizes [24].

Recently, various schemes based on isogeny assumption have been proposed: signature schemes [5,19], ring signature scheme [4], revocable ring signature scheme [24] and accountable ring signature scheme [10]. Although these constructions and many post-quantum ring signature schemes (including variants) from lattices, code and symmetric cryptographic primitives have been proposed successively, an efficient isogeny-based TRS scheme has yet to be reported in the literature.

To fill this gap, we propose a general TRS scheme from group actions and instantiate the group action with isogenies and lattices. To the best of our knowledge, the isogeny-based instantiation is the first isogeny-based TRS scheme. It provides a smaller signature size than lattice-based instantiation. However, its significant overhead is signing time which is caused by the complex operation of isogeny. Under different instantiation parameters, users can flexibly customize the signature size and signing time according to their requirements with different instantiation parameters. Note that the isogeny-based instantiation in this paper is from CSIDH [8]. The latest attack on isogenies proposed by Castryck and Decru [7] leads to key leakage in SIDH. This method has no impact on the security of primitives such as CSIDH and SQISign [19]. The efficiency of our TRS scheme is discussed in detail in Sect. 5.1.

1.1   Related Work on Post Quantum Ring Signature

Lattice-based schemes. The first lattice-based ring signature was proposed by Libert et al. [26], which is non-linkable. Lu et al. [27] developed a general lattice-based (linkable) ring signature scheme from the short integer solution

(SIS) and NTRU assumptions. Esgin et al. [15] extended discrete logarithm proof techniques to the lattice setting in the one-out-of-many proofs, and designed a short ring signature scheme. They further optimized one out of many proofs, resulting in a smaller size ring signature scheme [14]. Then, they introduced a zero-knowledge proof and extractable commitment scheme from lattices, and designed an efficient RingCT protocol [16]. Feng et al. [17] constructed an efficient TRS scheme and instantiated the scheme with lattice-based building blocks: non-interactive zero-knowledge proof, collision-resistant hash function, and pseudorandom function. Nguyen et al. [28] proposed a unique ring signature (URS) scheme from lattices, which exploited a Merkle tree based accumulator as the building block.

Isogeny-Based Schemes. Beullens et al. [4] constructed an efficient (linkable) ring signature scheme and gave two concrete instances from isogenies and lattices. The signature size of their scheme scales with the number of ring members. Then, they constructed an accountable ring signature based on isogeny and lattice assumptions [3]. Through adding a valid ciphertext proof to their OR protocol and building an online extractable non-interactive zero-knowledge proof system, the signature size grows in $O(\log N)$. Chung et al. [10] proposed a group signature and accountable ring signature scheme based on the decisional CSIDH assumptions (D-CSIDH) and proved the security of scheme under the quantum random oracle model (QROM), the signature size grows in $O(N^2)$. Lai and Dobson [24] introduced the first revocable ring signature (RRS) scheme from isogenies, which is proved secure under the QROM, the signature size grows in $O(N \log(N))$.

Other Post-quantum Schemes. Branco and Mateus [6] built a post-quantum resistant TRS scheme based on the syndrome decoding problem. Their scheme was built on the Fiat-Shamir heuristic [20], they gave the security proof under the classic random oracle. Derler et al. [13] proposed the first sub-linear ring signature scheme from symmetric primitives. Scafuro and Zhang [32] introduced a one-time TRS scheme based on hash-function symmetric-key primitive.

Overall, the TRS schemes based on lattices, code and symmetric primitives have better performance, but the signature size of these schemes is large. Especially, the post-quantum TRS schemes that can be instantiated by isogenies and lattices are still in their infancy. This work proposes a general OR sigma protocol construction and constructs two TRS schemes from isogeny-based and lattice-based group action primitives. Both instantiations of the TRS schemes have a logarithmic communication complexity. Compared with other post-quantum schemes, the isogeny-based instantiation has the advantage of a smaller signature size, the lattice-based instantiation has a shorter signing time. Finally, we prove the security of our TRS scheme under the random oracle model.

1.2   Contribution

The major contribution of this work is the construction of a TRS from restricted group action in the random oracle model (ROM). As far as we know, this is the *first* TRS scheme that can be instantiated with isogenies.

- We propose a general TRS scheme based on restricted pair of group actions, OR sigma protocol and collision-resistant hash function. Furthermore, we instantiate the group action from *isogenies* and *lattices* to construct two TRS schemes.
- We design a special OR protocol for the TRS scheme. The core of our technique is to provide *traceability* by generating *tag sets* based on messages and user identities. Traceability will be possible by checking whether each tag/vector in the two tag/vector sets is equal. Further, we add OR proof for multiple tag sets to ensure validity.
- The scheme has *logarithmic communication complexity*. In order to reduce the signature size, we generate two Merkle trees and set the response as two paths in the tree in case challenge bit chall = 0, when challenge bit chall = 1, we send a seed as the response. Compared with other post-quantum TRS schemes, the signature size of our proposed TRS extends well with the ring size N, and our multiplicative factor on $\log N$ is much lower since the signatures mainly consist of two paths in a Merkle tree of depth $\log N$.
- The time and size of the signature can be *flexibly customized* from different instantiation parameters of the OR sigma protocol. The isogeny-based instantiation has a smaller signature size and lattice-based instantiation has better performance.

1.3   Overview of Results

In this paper, we will construct a general TRS scheme with generic security in terms of tag-linkability, anonymity and exculpability. With isogeny and lattice instantiation, it is resistant to attacks by quantum adversaries.

There is a (linkable) ring signature framework [4] that has been proposed, this general construction utilizes the "admissible group action" primitive and is built upon a OR sigma protocol. However, for the dishonest users who signs the same message or two different messages twice, it does not have the ability to track the identity of dishonest users. By adding multiple tags to the OR proof, we prove that the tag was generated by the signer while tracing the identity of the signer by comparing each tag in the tag set.

The security of TRS scheme from isogenies in Sect. 3 relies on the group action inverse problem and its equivalent hard problems [34], the security of lattice-based instantiation relies on the module short integer solution problem and module learning with errors problem [25], which are believed to be resistant to attacks by quantum adversaries. According to the experimental results, the smaller the value of Q is, the less time it takes for signature generation and verification. The minimum signature size is obtained when $K = 36$, where K and $Q - K$ are the number of 0 and the number of 1 in the challenge space.

Specifically, we have the 64/4096 bytes public key size under two different instantiations. The secret key of a user is 16 bytes. The signature size of our TRS scheme relies on the proof size of the OR protocol, which is logarithmic. It is approximately $2 \log N + 2.45/2 \log N + 55.37$ **KB** under the specific instantiation parameters and outperforms the post-quantum traceable signature size of [6,17,32].

Among the post-quantum signature schemes we investigated, these schemes support either linkability or traceability. In the case of supporting two properties, the signature size scales linearly with the ring size. Compared with lattice-based TRS schemes, our signature size under lattice-based instantiation is acceptable. Compared with isogeny-based linkable ring signature (without traceability), our scheme provides traceability with a smaller signature size. The details of the performance of TRS will be presented in Sect. 5.1.

2   Preliminaries

2.1   Traceable Ring Signature

In this section, we review the TRS scheme proposed by Fujisaki and Suzuki [22]. Assuming that N is the number of users in the ring, $\mathsf{PK} = (pk_1, \ldots, pk_N)$ is ring member's public keys set, *issue* is a string representing the specific event of the signature and $L = (issue, \mathsf{PK})$ is the tag of the signature. A TRS scheme consists of five algorithms $\mathsf{TRS} = (\mathsf{Setup}, \mathsf{KeyGen}, \mathsf{Sign}, \mathsf{Verify}, \mathsf{Trace})$ described as follows:

- $\mathsf{pp} \leftarrow \mathsf{Setup}(1^\lambda)$: The algorithm run by the trusted authority, which takes as input security parameter $\lambda \in \mathbb{N}$ and outputs public parameter pp.
- $(pk, sk) \leftarrow \mathsf{KeyGen}(\mathsf{pp})$: The algorithm run by the ring member, which takes as input public parameter pp and returns public key pk and secret key sk.
- $\sigma \leftarrow \mathsf{Sign}(sk_\pi, L, M)$: The algorithm run by the ring member, which takes as input the secret key sk_π, a tag L and a message $M \in \{0,1\}^*$, and returns a signature σ.
- $\{\mathsf{accept}, \mathsf{reject}\} \leftarrow \mathsf{Verify}(L, M, \sigma)$: The algorithm run by the signature receiver, which takes as input the tag L, message M and signature σ, and returns either accept or reject.
- $\{\mathsf{indep}, \mathsf{linked}, pk\} \leftarrow \mathsf{Trace}(L, M, \sigma, M', \sigma')$: The algorithm run by the ring member or trusted authority, which takes as input two traceable ring signatures σ on message M and σ' on message M' with the same tag L, and returns a string that is either $\mathsf{indep}, \mathsf{linked}$ or an element $pk \in \mathsf{PK}$. If $\sigma = \mathsf{Sign}(sk_\pi, L, M)$ and $\sigma' = \mathsf{Sign}(sk_{\pi'}, L, M')$, it holds that :

$$\mathsf{Trace}(L, M, \sigma, M', \sigma') = \begin{cases} \mathsf{indep} & \text{if } \pi \neq \pi', \\ \mathsf{linked} & \text{else if } M = M', \\ pk_i & \text{otherwise } (\pi = \pi' \wedge M \neq M'). \end{cases}$$

2.2   Security Model

A secure TRS scheme should satisfy the following properties: *correctness* and *security*. We use the security model in [21]. The security requirement for a TRS scheme has three: *tag-linkability, anonymity* and *exculpability*. The *unforgeability* can be derived from tag-linkability and exculpability [21].

Tag-linkability. Given N pairs of public and secret keys and N pairs of message-signature under tag L, the adversary can output $N + 1$ valid pairs of message-signature. If for all PPT adversaries $\mathcal{A}$, we have $Adv^{\text{tag}-\text{link}}_{\mathcal{A},\text{Game}}(\lambda) \leq \text{nelg}(\lambda)$, then we say that TRS scheme is tag-linkable.

Anonymity. It is infeasible for the adversary to know who signed the message. If for all PPT adversaries $\mathcal{A}$, we have $Adv^{\text{anon}}_{\mathcal{A},\text{Game}}(\lambda) \leq \text{nelg}(\lambda)$, then we say that TRS scheme is anonymous.

Exculpability. This ensures that the adversary cannot construct two valid pairs of message-signature under tag L without knowing the secret key of the user. Consider the exculpability game $\text{Game}^{\text{excu}}_{\mathcal{A}}$, if for all PPT adversaries $\mathcal{A}$, we have $Adv^{\text{excu}}_{\mathcal{A},\text{Game}}(\lambda) \leq \text{nelg}(\lambda)$, then we say that TRS scheme is exculpable.

2.3   Restricted Pair of Group Actions

The restricted effective group actions (REGA) can be endowed with the properties: *one-wayness* (OW), *weak unpredictability* (wU), and *weak pseudorandomness* (wPR) [1]. The special restricted pair of group actions used in this paper is called "admissible pair of group actions", which is proposed by Beullens et al. [4].

Definition 1. *Given a finite commutative group $\mathcal{G}$, $\mathcal{G}_1$ and $\mathcal{G}_2$ are two subsets of $\mathcal{G}$. Let $\mathcal{S}$ and $\mathcal{T}$ be two finite sets, $D_\mathcal{S}$ and $D_\mathcal{T}$ are distributions over two group actions $\star : \mathcal{G} \times \mathcal{S} \to \mathcal{S}, \mathcal{G} \times \mathcal{T} \to \mathcal{T}$. For $(S_0, T_0) \in \mathcal{S} \times \mathcal{T}$, we say that $\mathsf{ResPGA} = (\mathcal{G}, \mathcal{S}, \mathcal{T}, \mathcal{G}_1, \mathcal{G}_2, D_\mathcal{S}, D_\mathcal{T})$ is a ξ-restricted pair of group actions if the following holds:*

1. **Efficient Group Action:** *For any $g \in \mathcal{G}_1 \cup \mathcal{G}_2$ and $(S, T) \in \mathcal{S} \times \mathcal{T}$, it is efficient to compute $g \star S$ and $g \star T$, and uniquely represent the element of set $\mathcal{G}$, $\mathcal{S}$ and $\mathcal{T}$.*
2. **Efficient Rejection Sampling:** *For all $g \in \mathcal{G}_1$, the intersection of all sets $\mathcal{G}_2 + g$ is large enough. Let $\mathcal{G}_3 = \bigcap_{g \in \mathcal{G}_1} \mathcal{G}_2 + g$, then $|\mathcal{G}_3| = \xi |\mathcal{G}_2|$.*
3. **Efficient Membership Testing:** *It is efficient to verify that an element $z \in \mathcal{G}_1$, or $z \in \mathcal{G}_2$, or $z \in \mathcal{G}_3$.*
4. *Given $(g \star S_0, g \star T_0)$ for any element g sampled from $\mathcal{G}_1$ uniformly, it is indistinguishable from the elements (S, T) sampled from $\mathcal{S} \times \mathcal{T}$ uniformly.*
5. *It is difficult to find two elements $g, g' \in \mathcal{G}_2 + \mathcal{G}_3$, that satisfy $g \star S_0 = g' \star S_0$ and $g \star T_0 \neq g' \star T_0$.*
6. *For the element g sampled from set $\mathcal{G}_1$ uniformly, given $S = g \star S_0$ and $T = g \star T_0$, it is difficult to find $g' \in \mathcal{G}_2 + \mathcal{G}_3$ such that $T = g' \star T_0$.*

2.4 Collision-Resistant Hash Function

In this paper, the cryptographic primitives used in the TRS scheme, such as pseudo-random number generators (PRG) and commitment schemes, are instantiated by the hash function. Specifically, we define five collision-resistant hash functions: $\mathcal{H}_1$, $\mathcal{H}_2$, $\mathcal{H}_3$, $\mathcal{H}_4$ and $\mathcal{H}_5$, where:

$$\mathcal{H}_1 : \{0,1\}^* \to \mathcal{G}_1,$$
$$\mathcal{H}_2 : \{0,1\}^* \to \{0,1\}^{2\lambda},$$
$$\mathcal{H}_3 : \{0,1\}^* \to C_K^Q,$$
$$\mathcal{H}_4 : \{0,1\}^* \to \mathcal{G}_1^\dagger, \mathcal{H}_5 : \{0,1\}^* \to \mathcal{G}_1^{\dagger\dagger}.$$

For the Fiat-Shamir transform, we define a hash function $\mathcal{H}_3$ to produce an unbalanced challenge space C_K^Q, which is a set of string in $\{0,1\}^Q$, such that K bits are 0. The integers Q, K satisfying $\binom{Q}{K} \geq 2^{\lambda 1}$.

2.5 Sigma Protocol

A sigma protocol is a three-move public coin interactive protocol between the prover and verifier for the relation $R \subseteq X \times W$, where X is the space of statements and W is the space of witnesses. The sigma protocol under the random oracle includes the following three properties: *correctness, special honest-verifier zero-knowledge* and *special soundness* [12].

Definition 2. *A sigma protocol Π_Σ for the relation $R \subseteq X \times W$ consists of four PPT algorithms $(P = (P_1, P_2), V = (V_1, V_2))$, where V_2 is deterministic, P_1 and P_2 share the same information. Under the random oracle, the Π_Σ protocol has the three-move flow as follows:*

- $P_1(X, W) \to$ com. *The prover runs $P_1(X, W)$ on input $(X, W) \in R$ to generate a commitment* com, *and sends it to the verifier.*
- $V_1(\text{com}) \to$ chall. *The verifier runs $V_1(\text{com})$ on input* com *to generate a random challenge bit* chall, *and sends it to the prover.*
- $P_2(X, W, \text{chall}) \to$ rsp. *The prover, after receiving* chall, *runs $P_2(X, W, \text{chall})$ to obtain the response* rsp *and sends it to the verifier. In the case of P_2 termination, the prover sets* rsp *with symbol $\perp$ and sends it to the verifier.*
- $V_2(X, \text{com}, \text{chall}, \text{rsp}) \to \{\text{accept}, \text{reject}\}$. *The verifier runs $V_2(X, \text{com}, \text{chall}, \text{rsp})$ to check whether X is valid under the transcript* (com, chall, rsp), *and outputs* accept *or* reject.

---

[1] Under the and lattice-based instantiations, $\mathcal{G}_1^\dagger$ and $\mathcal{G}_1^{\dagger\dagger}$ are two different subsets of $\mathcal{G}$, the specific sets are shown is Sect. 5.

3   General Construction of Traceable Ring Signature

In this section, we will present a general construction of the TRS scheme from restricted pair of group actions. We first design a sigma protocol for the OR relation, then obtain a TRS scheme by applying the Fiat-Shamir transformation to the OR sigma protocol.

3.1   Our Special or Sigma Protocol for Traceable Ring Signature

Our construction is based on a special OR sigma protocol, a variant of OR sigma protocol presented in [4] by adding the tag set. The essential technique of the protocol is to generate proofs for multiple tags and multiple public-secret key pairs, and the proof size of our sigma protocol grows logarithmically in N.

Let the relation $R \subset \boldsymbol{S}^{N+1} \times \boldsymbol{T}^{N+1} \times (\boldsymbol{G_1}, \mathbb{Z}_N)$, where $R = \{(S_0, S_1, \ldots, S_N),$ $(T_0, T_1, \ldots, T_N), (g, \pi), | g \in \boldsymbol{G_1}, S_i \in \boldsymbol{S}, T_i \in \boldsymbol{T}, S_\pi = g \star S_0, T_\pi = g \star T_0\}$. We define a relation R' slightly wider than the relation R, and (R, R') satisfies $R \subseteq R'$, in addition to the relation R, R' contains two pairs of hash-preimage, and the extractor in special-soundness only extracts the witness of relation R'. Under the relation (R, R'), the OR sigma protocol is still useful as long as the relation (R, R') is sufficiently difficult.

$$R' = \left\{ (S_0, \ldots, S_N), (T_0, \ldots, T_N), w \left| \begin{array}{c} S_i \in \boldsymbol{S}, T_i \in \boldsymbol{T} \text{ and} \\ w = (g, \pi) : g \in \boldsymbol{G_2} + \boldsymbol{G_3}, S_\pi = g \star S_0, \\ T_\pi = g \star T_0 \text{ or} \\ w = (x, x') : x \neq x', \mathcal{H}_2(x) = \mathcal{H}_2(x') \end{array} \right. \right\}$$

The difficulty of applying the accumulator to our construction is that each instance in the relation (R, R') is a pair of elements (S_i, T_i) rather than a single element. We solve this problem by hashing the commitments after applying the accumulator scheme to get the final commitments.

Based on the relation (R, R'), the OR sigma protocol proves that: 1) the prover owns a secret g and there exists $i \in N$, such that $g \star S_0 = S_i, g \star T_0 = T_i$, without revealing the secret g and specific index i. Otherwise, 2) the prover owns a pair of collisions for $\mathcal{H}_2$.

Given $(S_0, S_1, \ldots, S_N)$, $(T_0, T_1, \ldots, T_N)$, we propose a sigma protocol $(P, V) = ((P_1, P_2), (V_1, V_2))$ under binary challenge space, for proving the ring member $\mathcal{P}_\pi$ possesses the secret key sk that satisfies relation (R, R'). A simple OR sigma protocol is shown in Fig. 1 and the specific OR sigma construction as Fig. 2.

Through repeating the basic OR sigma protocol under binary space, we construct a main OR sigma protocol under large challenge space and optimize it using three optimizations: unbalanced challenge space, Seed tree, and adding salt [4].

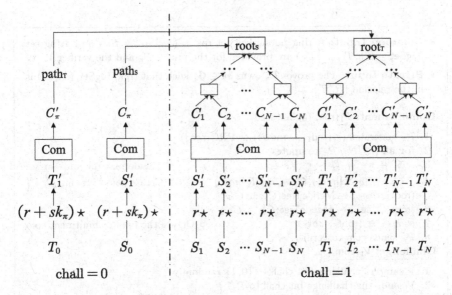

Fig. 1. The base OR sigma protocol, which proves that secret (sk_π, π) satisfies $sk_\pi \star S_0 = S_\pi$ and $sk_\pi \star T_0 = T_\pi$. If $\mathsf{chall} = 0$, then the commitments C_π and C'_π will be revealed, otherwise all commitments will be revealed.

3.2 Traceable Ring Signature from or Sigma Protocol

We now present two concrete TRS schemes based on isogenies and lattices. The instantiation of both schemes is built on the aforementioned main OR sigma protocol, mainly by combining the design principles of Fujisaki and Suzuki [22] with restricted pair of group actions. Given the security parameters λ, the main OR sigma protocol (P_{main}, V_{main}), and the collision-resistant hash function $\mathcal{H}_1$, $\mathcal{H}_2$, $\mathcal{H}_3$, $\mathcal{H}_4$ and $\mathcal{H}_5$, we construct two secure TRS schemes Π_{ISO} and Π_{LAT} by applying FS transform to main OR sigma protocol. Figure 3 illustrates two instantiations of the TRS scheme under lattice and isogeny. The general construction of the Setup and KeyGen in both schemes is as follows.

- Setup(1^λ): takes security parameter λ as input, selects $S_0 \leftarrow \mathcal{S}$, and outputs public parameter $\mathsf{rpp} = S_0, \mathsf{ResPGA} = (\mathcal{G}, \mathcal{S}, \mathcal{T}, \mathcal{G}_1, \mathcal{G}_2, \mathbf{D}_{\mathcal{S}}, \mathbf{D}_{\mathcal{T}})$.
- KeyGen(rpp): takes public parameter as input, selects $g \leftarrow \mathcal{G}_1, S = g \star S_0$, and outputs public key $pk_i = S$ and secret key $sk_i = g$.

To ensure that the secret key is embedded in the tag, and that the components in the signature do not disclose any information about the secret key and the identity of the member, we apply group action operations in the calculation of the tags and auxiliary parameters. Concretely, we set $T_0 = \mathcal{H}_1(L) \star S_0$ and the auxiliary parameter $T = (sk_\pi - \mathcal{H}_1(a, \pi)) \star T_0$ in the isogeny-based instantiation. The lattice-based instantiation is slightly different since the secret key is not sampled in the addition group, but in the polynomial ring, which supports

- **Common Input:** A ring public key set $\mathsf{rpk} = (S_0, S_1, \ldots, S_N)$ and a tag set $\mathsf{TagSet} = (T_0, T_1, \ldots, T_N)$ are provided for the prover $\mathcal{P}_\pi$ and the verifier $\mathcal{V}$.
- **Private Input:** The prover $\mathcal{P}_\pi$ owns $sk \in \mathcal{G}_1$ such that $(\mathsf{rpk}, \mathsf{TagSet}, (sk, \pi))$ is in the relation (R, R').

Commitment: $P_1(\mathsf{rpk}, \mathsf{TagSet}, \mathsf{seed})$

1. $\mathcal{P}_\pi$ generates $(r, (\mathsf{rnd}_1, \ldots, \mathsf{rnd}_N)) \leftarrow \mathsf{PRG}(\mathsf{seed})$
2. **for all** $i \in [N]$, $\mathcal{P}_\pi$ computes
3. $S_i' \leftarrow r \star S_i, T_i' \leftarrow r \star T_i$ ▷ Randomize rpk and TagSet
4. $C_i \leftarrow \mathcal{H}_2(S_i' \| \mathsf{rnd}_i), C_i' \leftarrow \mathcal{H}_2(T_i' \| \mathsf{rnd}_i)$ ▷ Create commitments C_i, C_i'
5. $(\mathsf{root}_S, \mathsf{tree}_S) \leftarrow \mathsf{MerkleTree}(C_1, \ldots, C_N)$
6. $(\mathsf{root}_T, \mathsf{tree}_T) \leftarrow \mathsf{MerkleTree}(C_1', \ldots, C_N')$
7. $\mathsf{com} \leftarrow \mathcal{H}_2(\mathsf{root}_S, \mathsf{root}_T)$ ▷ Create the final commitment com
8. $\mathcal{P}_\pi$ sends com to verifier $\mathcal{V}$.

Challenge: $V_1(\mathsf{com})$

1. $\mathcal{V}$ samples challenge bit $\mathsf{chall} \leftarrow \{0, 1\}$ randomly
2. $\mathcal{V}$ sends the challenge bit chall to $\mathcal{P}_\pi$.

Response: $P_2((sk_\pi, \pi), \mathsf{chall}, \mathsf{seed})$

1. **if** $\mathsf{chall} = 0$, $\mathcal{P}_\pi$ computes $z = r + sk_\pi$, if $z \notin \mathcal{G}_3$, abort, else $\mathcal{P}_\pi$ computes:
2. $\mathsf{path}_S \leftarrow \mathsf{getMerklePath}(\mathsf{tree}_S, \pi)$ ▷ Generate the path for rpk
3. $\mathsf{path}_T \leftarrow \mathsf{getMerklePath}(\mathsf{tree}_T, \pi)$ ▷ Generate the path for TagSet
4. $\mathsf{rsp} \leftarrow (z, \mathsf{path}_S, \mathsf{path}_T, \mathsf{rnd}_\pi)$
5. **else**
6. $\mathsf{rsp} \leftarrow \mathsf{seed}$
7. $\mathcal{P}_\pi$ sends rsp as response to $\mathcal{V}$.

Verification: $V_2(\mathsf{com}, \mathsf{chall}, \mathsf{rsp})$

1. **if** $\mathsf{chall} = 0$, $\mathcal{V}$ computes:
2. $(z, \mathsf{path}_S, \mathsf{path}_T, \mathsf{rnd}_\pi) \leftarrow \mathsf{rsp}$
3. $\hat{S} = z \star S_0, \hat{T} = z \star T_0$
4. $\hat{C} = \mathcal{H}_2(\hat{S} \| \mathsf{rnd}_\pi), \hat{C}' = \mathcal{H}_2(\hat{T} \| \mathsf{rnd}_\pi)$
5. $\widehat{\mathsf{root}_S} = \mathsf{ReconstructRoot}(\hat{C}, \mathsf{path}_S)$ ▷ Recovery root for rpk
6. $\widehat{\mathsf{root}_T} = \mathsf{ReconstructRoot}(\hat{C}', \mathsf{path}_T)$ ▷ Recovery root for TagSet
7.   **if** $z \in \mathcal{G}_3 \wedge \mathcal{H}_2(\widehat{\mathsf{root}_S}, \widehat{\mathsf{root}_T}) = \mathsf{com}$ ▷ Verify the final commitment
8. $\mathcal{V}$ outputs accept.
9.   **else** $\mathcal{V}$ outputs reject.
10. **else**
11. $\mathsf{seed} \leftarrow \mathsf{rsp}$
12. $\mathcal{V}$ computes $\mathsf{com} \leftarrow P_1(\mathsf{rpk}, \mathsf{TagSet}, \mathsf{seed})$
13.   **if** $\mathsf{com} = \mathcal{H}_2(\mathsf{root}_S, \mathsf{root}_T)$
14. $\mathcal{V}$ outputs accept.
15.   **else** $\mathcal{V}$ outputs reject.

Fig. 2. The details of binary challenge space OR sigma protocol $(P, V) = ((P_1, P_2), (V_1, V_2))$, under a restricted pair of group actions $\mathsf{ResPGA} = (\mathcal{G}, \mathcal{S}, \mathcal{T}, \mathcal{G}_1, \mathcal{G}_2, D_\mathcal{S}, D_\mathcal{T})$ and $(S_0, T_0) \in \mathcal{S} \times \mathcal{T}$, PRG and hash function $\mathcal{H}_2$ is an instantiation of random oracle.

RSign_ISO$((sk_\pi, \pi), L, M)$

1. $(issue, \mathsf{rpk}) \leftarrow L$
2. $T_0 = \mathcal{H}_1(L) \star S_0, a = \mathcal{H}_1(L, M)$
3. $T = (sk_\pi - \mathcal{H}_1(a, \pi)) \star T_0$
4. **for all** $i \in N$
5. $\quad k = \mathcal{H}_1(a, i)$
6. $\quad T_i = k \star T$
7. TagSet $\leftarrow (T_0, T_1, ... T_N)$
8. com $\leftarrow P^1_{main}(M, \mathsf{rpk}, \mathsf{TagSet})$
9. chall $\leftarrow \mathcal{H}_3(M, \mathsf{rpk}, \mathsf{TagSet}, \mathsf{com})$
10. rsp $\leftarrow P^2_{main}((sk_\pi, \pi), \mathsf{chall})$
11. **return** $\sigma = (T, \mathsf{com}, \mathsf{chall}, \mathsf{rsp})$.

RVer_ISO(L, M, σ)

1. $(issue, \mathsf{rpk}) \leftarrow L$
2. $(T, \mathsf{com}, \mathsf{chall}, \mathsf{rsp}) \leftarrow \sigma$
3. $T_0 = \mathcal{H}_1(L) \star S_0, a = \mathcal{H}_1(L, M)$
4. **for all** $i \in N$
5. $\quad k = \mathcal{H}_1(a, i)$
6. $\quad T_i = k \star T$
7. TagSet $\leftarrow (T_0, T_1, ... T_N)$
8. **if** $V^2_{main}(\mathsf{com}, \mathsf{chall}, \mathsf{rsp}) = \mathsf{accept}$
$\quad \land \mathcal{H}_3(M, \mathsf{rpk}, \mathsf{TagSet}, \mathsf{com}) = \mathsf{chall}$
9. $\quad$ **return** accept.
10. **else return** reject.

RTrace_ISO$(L, M, \sigma, M', \sigma')$

1. $(issue, \mathsf{rpk}) \leftarrow L$
2. $(T, \mathsf{com}, \mathsf{chall}, \mathsf{rsp}) \leftarrow \sigma$
3. $(T', \mathsf{com}', \mathsf{chall}', \mathsf{rsp}') \leftarrow \sigma'$
4. $a = \mathcal{H}_1(L, M), a' = \mathcal{H}_1(L, M')$
5. **for all** $i \in N$
6. $\quad k = \mathcal{H}_1(a, i), k' = \mathcal{H}_1(a', i)$
7. $\quad T_i = k \star T, T_i' = k' \star T'$
8. **if for all** $i \in [N], T_i = T_i'$
9. $\quad$ **return** linked.
10. **if only exist one** $i \in [N]$, such that $T_i = T_i'$
11. $\quad$ **return** pk_i.
12. **else return** indep.

RSign_LAT$((sk_\pi, \pi), L, M)$

1. $(issue, \mathsf{rpk}) \leftarrow L$
2. $T_0 = \mathcal{H}_4(L), a = \mathcal{H}_5(L, M)$
3. $T_\pi = sk_\pi \star T_0, \mathsf{aux} = \frac{(T_\pi - a)}{\pi}$
4. **for all** $i \in N, i \neq \pi$
5. $\quad k = a + \mathsf{aux} \cdot i$
6. $\quad T_i = k \star T_0$
7. TagSet $\leftarrow (T_0, T_1, ... T_N)$
8. com $\leftarrow P^1_{main}(M, \mathsf{rpk}, \mathsf{TagSet})$
9. chall $\leftarrow \mathcal{H}_3(M, \mathsf{rpk}, \mathsf{TagSet}, \mathsf{com})$
10. rsp $\leftarrow P^2_{main}((sk_\pi, \pi), \mathsf{chall})$
11. **return** $\sigma = (\mathsf{aux}, \mathsf{com}, \mathsf{chall}, \mathsf{rsp})$.

RVer_LAT(L, M, σ)

1. $(issue, \mathsf{rpk}) \leftarrow L$
2. $(\mathsf{aux}, \mathsf{com}, \mathsf{chall}, \mathsf{rsp}) \leftarrow \sigma$
3. $T_0 = \mathcal{H}_4(L) \star S_0, a = \mathcal{H}_5(L, M)$
4. **for all** $i \in N$
5. $\quad k = a + \mathsf{aux} \cdot i$
6. $\quad T_i = k \star T_0$
7. TagSet $\leftarrow (T_0, T_1, ... T_N)$
8. **if** $V^2_{main}(\mathsf{com}, \mathsf{chall}, \mathsf{rsp}) = \mathsf{accept}$
$\quad \land \mathcal{H}_3(M, \mathsf{rpk}, \mathsf{TagSet}, \mathsf{com}) = \mathsf{chall}$
9. $\quad$ **return** accept.
10. **else return** reject.

RTrace_LAT$(L, M, \sigma, M', \sigma')$

1. $(issue, \mathsf{rpk}) \leftarrow L$
2. $(\mathsf{aux}, \mathsf{com}, \mathsf{chall}, \mathsf{rsp}) \leftarrow \sigma$
3. $(\mathsf{aux}', \mathsf{com}', \mathsf{chall}', \mathsf{rsp}') \leftarrow \sigma'$
4. $a = \mathcal{H}_5(L, M), a' = \mathcal{H}_5(L, M')$
5. **for all** $i \in N$
6. $\quad k_i = a + \mathsf{aux} \cdot i$
7. $\quad k_i' = a' + \mathsf{aux}' \cdot i$
8. **if for all** $i \in [N], k_i = k_i'$
9. $\quad$ **return** linked.
10. **if only exist one** $i \in [N]$, such that $k_i = k_i'$
11. $\quad$ **return** pk_i.
12. **else return** indep.

Fig. 3. The isogeny-based TRS scheme (left column) and lattice-based TRS scheme (right column) from group actions.

multiplication and addition, we set $T_0 = \mathcal{H}_4(L), T_\pi = sk_\pi \star T_0$ and auxiliary parameter $\mathsf{aux} = \frac{(T_\pi - a)}{\pi}$.

As a result, the cost of the Trace algorithm differs between the two instantiations, with the isogeny-based instantiation requiring $2N$ group actions and the lattice-based instantiation requiring only $2N$ polynomial multiplications and additions.

Let $(S_0, S_1, \ldots, S_N)$ be the public parameter, each member $\mathcal{P}_i$ possesses a pair of public and secret keys: $sk_i = g, pk_i = g \star S_0$. Moreover, each member will generate N different tags $(T_0, T_1, \ldots, T_N)$ to link or trace signatures.

In order to generate the ring signature σ for the message $M \in \{0, 1\}^*$ under the tag $L = (issue, \mathsf{rpk})$, the ring member $\mathcal{P}_\pi$ invokes $\mathsf{RSign}_{\{ISO,LAT\}}(sk_\pi, L, M)$. The receivers verify signature σ on (L, M) by running $\mathsf{RVer}_{\{ISO,LAT\}}(L, M, \sigma)$. To trace the relation between two valid signatures σ on M and σ' on M' with the same tag L, the ring members invoke $\mathsf{RTrace}_{\{ISO,LAT\}}(L, M, \sigma, M', \sigma')$ which outputs linked, indep or pk_i.

4   Analysis of Our Traceable Ring Signature Scheme

In this section, we analyzed the correctness and security of TRS scheme under isogeny-based instantiation. A detailed proof of the lattice-based TRS scheme is presented in full version of paper.

4.1   Correctness

The correctness of our TRS scheme Π_{ISO} is composed of *completeness* and *traceability*. The completeness can be deduced from the correctness of the main OR sigma protocol. The detailed proof is presented in full version of paper.

4.2   Security

Theorem 1. *If the OR sigma protocol is soundness and zero-knowledge, the hash function $\mathcal{H}_1, \mathcal{H}_2$ are collision-resistant, the ResPGA is a restricted pair of group actions, then our TRS scheme Π_{ISO} satisfies tag-linkability, anonymity and exculpability.*

Proof. **Tag-Linkability.** Conversely, assuming there exists an adversary $\mathcal{A}$ that makes at most B random oracle queries, the probability of $\mathcal{A}$ winning the game is not negligible. Then we demonstrate how to construct an algorithm $\mathcal{B}$ using $\mathcal{A}$, $\mathcal{B}$ breaks the Item 5 of ResPGA and collision resistance of $\mathcal{H}_2$. The simulation of $\mathcal{B}$ under random oracle is as follows:

- $\mathsf{Sim}^1_\mathcal{B}$: The output of $\mathcal{A}$ in winning the tag-linkability game is the input of $\mathcal{B}$. Let $\{(L, (M_1, \sigma_1)), \ldots, (L, (M_{N+1}, \sigma_{N+1}))\}$ be the output of $\mathcal{A}$, $\sigma_i = (T^i, \mathsf{com}_i, \mathsf{chall}_i, \mathsf{rsp}_i)$, chall_i is the output of $\mathcal{H}_3$ on input $(M_i, \mathsf{rpk}_i, \mathsf{TagSet}_i, \mathsf{com}_i)$, $\mathcal{A}$ records these transcripts into list $\mathsf{List} = \{i, T^i, (\mathsf{com}_i, \mathsf{chall}_i, \mathsf{rsp}_i), M_i\}_{i \in [N+1]}$.

- $\mathsf{Sim}_\mathcal{B}^2$: $\mathcal{B}$ re-invokes $\mathcal{A}$ until $\mathcal{A}$ wins the tag-linkability game. Different from $\mathsf{Sim}_\mathcal{B}^1$, $\mathcal{B}$ controls the randomness used in the underlying main OR sigma protocol to generate signatures in each query. Specifically, for responding to the j-th signing query, the randomness used by the underlying main OR sigma protocol is the same as $\mathsf{Sim}_\mathcal{B}^1$ before q_i-th ($q_i \in [B]$) random oracle, after that, $\mathcal{B}$ uses fresh randomness to interact with $\mathcal{A}$. Assuming that the output form of $\mathcal{A}$ is $\sigma' = (T^{j'}, (\mathsf{com}_j', \mathsf{chall}_j', \mathsf{rsp}_j'), M_j', L)_{j \in [N+1]}$. If the signature σ_j' does not appear in the q_j-th random oracle query, the simulation of $\mathcal{B}$ starts again from $\mathsf{Sim}_\mathcal{B}^2$, otherwise, $\mathcal{B}$ updates list $\mathsf{List} = \mathsf{List} \cup \{j, T^{j'}, (\mathsf{com}_j', \mathsf{chall}_j', \mathsf{rsp}_j'), M_j'\}$, chall_j' is the result of the q_j-th random oracle query. Since we fix the randomness before q_j-th for both simulations, for all the entries in the list, we have $(M_j, T^j, \mathsf{com}_j) = (M_j', T^{j'}, \mathsf{com}_j')$.
- $\mathsf{Sim}_\mathcal{B}^3$: $\mathcal{B}$ extracts two entries from List that satisfy the above requirements, which one generated in $\mathsf{Sim}_\mathcal{B}^1$: $(T^j, (\mathsf{com}_j, \mathsf{chall}_j, \mathsf{rsp}_j), M_j)$ and the other generated in $\mathsf{Sim}_\mathcal{B}^2$: $(T^j, (\mathsf{com}_j, \mathsf{chall}_j', \mathsf{rsp}_j'), M_j)$. If $\mathsf{chall}_j = \mathsf{chall}_j'$, $\mathcal{B}$ aborts the simulation, otherwise, $\mathcal{B}$ invokes the underlying main OR sigma protocol extraction algorithm, on input the statement $(\mathsf{rpk}_j, \mathsf{TageSet}_j)$ and two accepted transcripts $(\mathsf{com}_j, \mathsf{chall}_j, \mathsf{rsp}_j), (\mathsf{com}_j, \mathsf{chall}_j', \mathsf{rsp}_j')$, where TagSet_j is generated by the public input T^j, M_j and L, it outputs a witness w_j.
- $\mathsf{Sim}_\mathcal{B}^4$: For $j, j' \in [N+1]$, if there exists $w_j = (sk_j, \pi), w_j' = (sk_j', \pi)$, then $\mathcal{B}$ outputs (sk_j, sk_j'), if w_j forms a collision of $\mathcal{H}_2$, $\mathcal{B}$ outputs w_j, otherwise, $\mathcal{B}$ aborts the simulation.

We can see that the witness $(w_j)_{j \in [N+1]}$ has the form: $w_j = (sk_j, \pi_j)$ such that $S_{\pi_j} = sk_j \star S_0, T_{\pi_j} = sk_j \star T_0$ or a collision of $\mathcal{H}_2$. If no collision occurs, then there must have two indexes $j', j \in [N+1]$ such that $w_j = (sk_j, \pi), w_j' = (sk_j', \pi)$, since the pigeonhole principle and the conditions for winning the tag-linkability game, which indicate that $sk_j \star S_0 = sk_j' \star S_0$ but $sk_j \star T_0 \neq sk_j' \star T_0$, this violates the Item 5 of the restricted pair of group actions. Otherwise w_j is a collision of $\mathcal{H}_2$. □

Anonymity. We demonstrated the anonymity of the scheme by building a sequence of games. The first game is the same as the original anonymity game, where $c = 0$. Similarly, the last game is exactly like the original anonymity game, where $c = 1$. We will prove that for any PPT adversary $\mathcal{A}$, the probability that he distinguishes between any two games is negligible. Let $Adv_{\mathcal{A}, \mathsf{Game}_i}^{\mathsf{anon}}$ denotes the advantage of adversary $\mathcal{A}$ in Game_i.

- Game_1: This is an actual anonymity game $\mathsf{Game}_\mathcal{A}^{\mathsf{anon}}$ where $c = 0$, the adversary $\mathcal{A}$ is allowed to query $\mathsf{RSign}(sk_0, \cdot), \mathsf{RSign}(sk_1, \cdot)$ and $\mathsf{RSign}(sk_c, \cdot)$. Challenger $\mathcal{C}$ invokes the actual signing algorithm with the secret key to generate the signature, and outputs it as the result of a signing query.
- Game_2: In the second game, challenger $\mathcal{C}$ invokes the underlying main OR sigma protocol zero-knowledge simulation protocol Sim to respond to the signing query of $\mathcal{A}$ instead of running the real main OR sigma protocol.

From the zero-knowledge property of the underlying main OR sigma protocol, the output distribution of Game_1 and Game_2 is indistinguishable, we have: $Adv^{anon}_{\mathcal{A},\mathsf{Game}_1}(\lambda) \approx Adv^{anon}_{\mathcal{A},\mathsf{Game}_2}(\lambda)$.

- Game_3: In the third game, the challenger $\mathcal{C}$ simulates N public-secret key pairs $\{(sk_i, pk_i)\}_{i \in [N]}$ instead of running the Setup algorithm, then $\mathcal{C}$ guesses that the pair of public keys $\{pk_j^*, pk_k^*\}$ sent by the adversary happens to be the j-th and k-th public keys, and generates two tag sets:

$$\mathsf{TagSet}_0 = \left(T_0, T_j = sk_j^* \star T_0, (T_i = (sk_j^* + \mathcal{H}_1(a,i) - \mathcal{H}_1(a,j)) \star T_0)_{i \in [N] \setminus j}\right)$$

$$\mathsf{TagSet}_1 = \left(T_0, T_k = sk_k^* \star T_0, (T_i = (sk_k^* + \mathcal{H}_1(a,i) - \mathcal{H}_1(a,k)) \star T_0)_{i \in [N] \setminus k}\right)$$

where $a = \mathcal{H}_1(L, M), T_0 = \mathcal{H}_1(L) \star S_0$. If the guess is incorrect, the challenger randomly samples a bit as the output of $\mathcal{A}$ and terminates the game. Otherwise, it responds to the signing queries using a pre-computed $\mathsf{TagSet}_0, \mathsf{TagSet}_1$ and $T^0 = (sk_j^* - \mathcal{H}_1(a,j)) \star T_0, T^1 = (sk_k^* - \mathcal{H}_1(a,k)) \star T_0$ at the beginning of Game_2. Since the probability of the challenger correctly guessing the two public keys is at most $1/N^2$, thus we have: $Adv^{anon}_{\mathcal{A},\mathsf{Game}_3}(\lambda) \approx \frac{1}{N^2} Adv^{anon}_{\mathcal{A},\mathsf{Game}_2}(\lambda)$.

- Game_4: Different from Game_3, the challenger $\mathcal{C}$ samples $\{i_0, i_1\} \leftarrow [N]$ and simulates $N - 2$ public-secret key pairs $\{(sk_i, pk_i)\}_{i \in [N] \setminus \{i_0, i_1\}}$, then samples (E_0, E_1) uniformly from $\mathcal{T}$ and computes:

$$T^0 = (-\mathcal{H}_1(a,i_0)) \star E_0, \mathsf{TagSet}_0 = \left(T_0, (T_i = \mathcal{H}_1(a,i) \star T^0)_{i \in [N]}\right)$$

$$T^1 = (-\mathcal{H}_1(a,i_1)) \star E_1, \mathsf{TagSet}_1 = \left(T_0, (T_i = \mathcal{H}_1(a,i) \star T^1)_{i \in [N]}\right)$$

where $T_0 = \mathcal{H}_1(L) \star S_0$, the rest is the same as Game_3. Using the *weak-pseudrandom* of the restricted pair of group actions, we have: $(sk \star T_0 : sk \leftarrow \mathcal{G}_1) \approx (E : E \leftarrow \mathcal{T})$. Thus Game_4 is computationally indistinguishable from Game_3: $Adv^{anon}_{\mathcal{A},\mathsf{Game}_1}(\lambda) \approx Adv^{anon}_{\mathcal{A},\mathsf{Game}_3}(\lambda)$. Now, the secret key is no longer used to generate the signature, i.e., the output of signing query does not reveal any information about the bit c in Game_4.

- Game_5: This is the same as an actual anonymous game, where $c = 1$.

It can be deduced from the above game sequence, there is no such adversary $\mathcal{A}$ that can distinguish any two games with a non-negligible probability, thus the probability of the adversary winning the real anonymity game is negligible. □

Exculpability. If there exists an adversary $\mathcal{A}$ wins $\mathsf{Game}^{excu}_{\mathcal{A}}$ with non-negligible probability, then we show how to construct an algorithm $\mathcal{B}$ from $\mathcal{A}$ that breaks the property Item 6 of restricted pair of group actions and collision resistance of $\mathcal{H}_1, \mathcal{H}_2$.

First, we simulate a game Game_1, it is indistinguishable from the real game $\mathsf{Game}^{excu}_{\mathcal{A}}$. In Game_1, the challenger invokes the OR sigma protocol zero-knowledge simulation protocol Sim to simulate the signature, and generates N public-secret key pairs $\{(sk_i, pk_i)\}_{i \in [N]}$, let $T^i = (sk_i - \mathcal{H}_1(a,i)) \star T_0$, then challenger computes N tag sets $\mathsf{TagSet}_i = \left(T_{0,i} = \mathcal{H}_1(L) \star S_0, (T_{j,i} = \mathcal{H}_1(a,j) \star T^i)_{j \in [N]}\right)_{i \in [N]}$

before the game starts. If the signing query made by the adversary contains index i, then the challenger uses N public-secret key pairs, precomputed N tag sets TagSet_i and N elements T^i to generate the response. From the zero-knowledge of OR sigma protocol, indistinguishable of tag sets and collision resistance of $\mathcal{H}_1$, we have $Adv_{\mathcal{A},\mathsf{Game}_1}^{\mathsf{excu}} \approx Adv_{\mathcal{A},\mathsf{Game}^{\mathsf{excu}}}^{\mathsf{excu}}$. We show that when $\mathcal{A}$ wins Game_1, the simulation of $\mathcal{B}$ on the input (S, T) as follows:

- $\mathsf{Sim}_{\mathcal{B}}^1$: $\mathcal{B}$ randomly samples index $j \leftarrow [N]$, sets $pk_j = S$, $T^j = (-\mathcal{H}_1(a,j)) \star T$, and computes $\mathsf{TagSet}_j = (T_0 = \mathcal{H}_1(L) \star S_0, (T_i = \mathcal{H}_1(a,i) \star T^j)_{i \in [N]})$, then generates the remaining $N-1$ public-secret key pairs $\{(pk_i, sk_i)\}_{i \in [N] \backslash j}$.
- $\mathsf{Sim}_{\mathcal{B}}^2$: $\mathcal{B}$ simulates the view of Game_1, since Game_1 does not contain any information of secret key. After interacting with $\mathcal{B}$, $\mathcal{A}$ outputs a forgery $(M, \mathsf{rpk}^*, \sigma^* = (T^*, \mathsf{com}^*, \mathsf{chall}^*, \mathsf{rsp}^*))$. To make sure the signature σ^* wins the Game_1, $\mathcal{B}$ must have responded to the signing query (i, M, rpk) with signature $\sigma = (T', \mathsf{com}', \mathsf{chall}', \mathsf{rsp}')$. If $i \neq j$, $\mathcal{B}$ terminates the simulation, otherwise, we have $T' = T$ and $T^* = T$, then $\mathcal{B}$ can extract witness w from the signature σ^* by rerunning $\mathcal{A}$. It is the same as what we have shown in the proof for tag-linkability.
- $\mathsf{Sim}_{\mathcal{B}}^3$: If w does not constitute a collision of $\mathcal{H}_2$, then we have $w = (sk, \pi)$ such that $sk \star T_0 = T_\pi$, $\mathcal{B}$ outputs $w = (sk, \pi)$, which violates the Item 6 of the underlying restricted pair of group actions, otherwise $\mathcal{B}$ outputs a pair of collisions of $\mathcal{H}_1$. □

5 Instantiations

Isogeny-based Instantiation. Theoretically, our TRS scheme can be instantiated with any CSIDH parameter set, e.g., CSIDH-512, CSIDH-1024 and CSIDH-1792 [4,18]. Nevertheless, taking into account that efficiency plays a vital role in the implementation, we implemented our TRS with the first group action parameter set proposed by Beullens et al. [5], which relies on the CSIDH group action proposed by [8], cSHAKE proposed by [23]. Let the ideal class group $\mathcal{Cl}(\mathcal{O})$ be a cyclic group, and the order of generator $\mathfrak{g}$ is N. Then the group action $\star := \mathcal{Cl}(\mathcal{O}) \times \mathcal{Ell}(\mathcal{O}, \pi) \to \mathcal{Ell}(\mathcal{O}, \pi)$ can be instantiated $(a, E) :\neq \mathfrak{g}^a \star E$. We set $\mathcal{G} = \mathcal{G}_1 = \mathcal{G}_2 = \mathcal{Cl}(\mathcal{O}) = \mathbb{Z}_N$, $\xi = 1$, $\mathcal{T} = \mathcal{Ell}(\mathcal{O}, \pi)$, $S = \mathcal{Ell}(\mathcal{O}, \pi)$, and $S_0 = E_0, T_0 = \mathcal{H}_1(L) \star E_0$, where E_0 is the elliptic curve $y^2 = x^3 + x$ over $\mathbb{F}_p$.

Lattice-Based Instantiation. Let $q = 5 \mod 4$, and let k, m be integers, n be a power of 2, B_1 and B_2 are integers such that $B_1 < B_2 < q$. Then the group action $\star := (\mathbf{s}, \mathbf{e}) \star \mathbf{t} \to \mathbf{As} + \mathbf{e} + \mathbf{t}$. We set $(\mathcal{G}, S, \mathcal{T}) = (R_q^{k \times m} \times R_q^k \times R_q^m, R_q^m, R_q^m)$, $\mathcal{G}_1 = \{(\mathbf{s}, \mathbf{e}_1) \in \mathcal{G} \mid \|\mathbf{s}\|_\infty, \|\mathbf{e}_1\|_\infty \leq B_1\}$, $\mathcal{G}_2 = \{(\mathbf{s}, \mathbf{e}_2) \in \mathcal{G} \mid \|\mathbf{s}\|_\infty, \|\mathbf{e}_2\|_\infty \leq B_2\}$, where $R_q = \mathbb{Z}[X]/(q, X^n + 1)$. For the collision-resistant hash function, let $\mathcal{H}_4 : \{0,1\}^* \to R_q^{k \times m}$, $\mathcal{H}_5 : \{0,1\}^* \to R_q^m$.

5.1 Implementation and Performance

Table 1 presents a detailed performance of our scheme, including signature size and time. Note that the addition of traceability necessitates additional group action computations, which impact the efficiency of our TRS scheme, especially for groups with large numbers of members. This explains why our scheme may be less efficient than the original linkable ring signature scheme proposed by Beullens et al. [4].

Table 1. Performance of proposed TRS scheme under different instantiations.

N			2^1	2^2	2^3	2^4	2^5	2^6
TRS_ISO	Time	KeyGen(ms)	39	39	39	39	39	39
		Sign(s)	3.37×10^1	6.63×10^1	1.31×10^2	2.64×10^2	5.23×10^2	1.07×10^3
		Verify(s)	3.20×10^1	6.02×10^1	1.16×10^2	2.31×10^2	4.64×10^2	9.22×10^2
	Size	Public Key(Byte)	64					
		Secret Key(Byte)	16					
		Signature(KB)	4.45	6.43	8.25	10.09	12.06	13.87
TRS_LAT	Time	KeyGen(ms)	0.2	0.2	0.2	0.2	0.2	0.2
		Sign(ms)	68.5	101.3	131.4	230.8	390.3	764.0
		Verify(ms)	27.4	34.9	50.3	81.1	144.0	265.4
(NIST 2)	Size	Public Key(Byte)	4096					
		Secret Key(Byte)	16					
		Signature(KB)	56.37	57.37	58.37	59.37	60.37	61.37

Table 2. Comparison of public key size, secret key size and signature size of our TRS scheme with post-quantum (traceable) ring signature schemes.

Schemes		Public key (KB)	Secret key (KB)	Signature size (KB)				Security Level
				2^1	2^3	2^6	2^{10}	
Calamari [4]		64 (Byte)	16 (Byte)	3.5	5.4	8.2	10	*
Beullens_ISO [3]		64 (Byte)	16 (Byte)	3.6	–	6.6	9.0	*
Raptor [27]		0.9	9.1	2.6	11	82	1331.2	100bits
Beullens_LAT [3]		5120 (Byte)	16 (Byte)	124	–	126	129	NIST 2
Falafl [4]		5120 (Byte)	16 (Byte)	49	50	52	55	NIST 2
Branco [6]		1577	0.5	–	1920	1536	245(MB)	NIST 5
Alessandra [32]		6	4	4	16	131	1024	NIST 5
Feng H [17]		–	–	135.1	136.3	138.2	140.7	NIST 5
Esign [15]		≤ 8.33	≤ 0.83	–	–	774	1021	NIST 5
this work	ISO	64 (Byte)	16 (Byte)	4.5	8.3	13.9	22.2	*
	LAT	4096 (Byte)	16 (Byte)	56.3	58.3	61.3	65.3	NIST 2
	LAT	6144 (Byte)	16 (Byte)	74.3	76.3	79.3	83.3	NIST 5

*: 128bits classical security and 60bits quantum security [29]

We compare our TRS with existing post-quantum (traceable) ring signature schemes. The results are shown in Table 2. The signature size of our lattice-based TRS scheme outperforms the size of [3,6,15,17]. When the ring members are small, the signature size of [32] and [27] is advantageous. However, once the ring members exceed 2^6, the signature size of [32] and [27] becomes significantly larger than in our lattice-based TRS scheme. Compared with the original scheme [4] and [3], Our isogeny-based instantiation has a larger signature size.

With isogeny-based instantiation, it can be concluded from Fig. 4 (right) that the smaller the value of Q is, the less time it takes for signature generation and verification. We conducted experiments with $N = 2$ to analyze the relationship between signature size and the value of K. The results are presented on the left side of Fig. 4. It can be seen that the minimum signature size is obtained when $K = 36$.

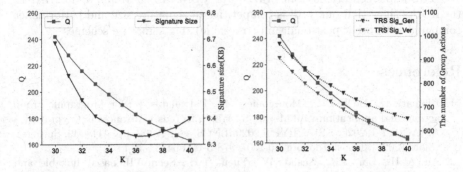

Fig. 4. The signature size of TRS (left) and number of group actions (right) under different (Q, K).

With the same security level, we set constant rounds for OR sigma protocol to observe the effect of different values of K on the signature size and signing time. The results are shown on the right in Fig. 5, the value of K increases, the time required for signature verification decreases while the signature size increases. Users can customize the value of K according to their specific requirements. In addition, we provide three optimal (Q, K) pairs under different ring sizes in Fig. 5 (left), which result in smaller signature sizes.

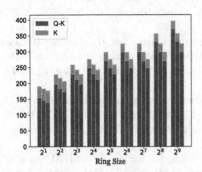
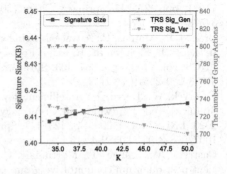

Fig. 5. Three superior (Q, K) pairs under different ring sizes (left) and the relationship among K, signature size and time spent on signature generation and verification (right) under the same Q.

6 Conclusion

This work presents a quantum-resistant TRS scheme from group action. First, we construct a special OR sigma protocol based on the restricted group action, which can be instantiated by isogenies and lattices. Then, using Fiat-Shamir transform to the OR sigma protocol, we derive two concrete TRS schemes. The core of our technique is to construct an OR proof for multiple tags and public key set. Under the random oracle model, we further prove the security of our TRS scheme in terms of tag-linkability, anonymity and exculpability. Finally, we give two TRS implementations from CSIDH-512/CSI-Fish, Dilithium and cSHAKE, the results show that our TRS is competitive in signature size and performance compared with other post-quantum (traceable) ring signature schemes.

References

1. Alamati, N., De Feo, L., Montgomery, H., Patranabis, S.: Cryptographic group actions and applications. In: Moriai, S., Wang, H. (eds.) Advances in Cryptology – ASIACRYPT 2020. ASIACRYPT 2020. LNCS, vol. 12492, pp. 411–439. Springer, Cham (2020). https://doi.org/10.1007/978-3-030-64834-3_14

2. Au, M.H., Liu, J.K., Susilo, W., Yuen, T.H.: Secure ID-based linkable and revocable-iff-linked ring signature with constant-size construction. Theor. Comput. Sci. **469**, 1–14 (2013). https://doi.org/10.1016/j.tcs.2012.10.031

3. Beullens, W., Dobson, S., Katsumata, S., Lai, Y.F., Pintore, F.: Group signatures and more from isogenies and lattices: generic, simple, and efficient. Des. Codes Cryptogr. **91**(6), 2141–2200 (2023). https://doi.org/10.1007/s10623-023-01192-x

4. Beullens, W., Katsumata, S., Pintore, F.: Calamari and Falafl: Logarithmic (linkable) ring signatures from isogenies and lattices. In: Moriai, S., Wang, H. (eds.) Advances in Cryptology –ASIACRYPT 2020. ASIACRYPT 2020. LNCS, vol. 12492, pp. 464–492. Springer, Cham (2020). https://doi.org/10.1007/978-3-030-64834-3_16

5. Beullens, W., Kleinjung, T., Vercauteren, F.: CSI-FiSh: Efficient isogeny based signatures through class group computations. In: Galbraith, S., Moriai, S. (eds.) Advances in Cryptology – ASIACRYPT 2019. ASIACRYPT 2019. LNCS, vol. 11921, pp. 227–247. Springer, Cham (2019). https://doi.org/10.1007/978-3-030-34578-5_9

6. Branco, P., Mateus, P.: A traceable ring signature scheme based on coding theory. In: Ding, J., Steinwandt, R. (eds.) Post-Quantum Cryptography. PQCrypto 2019. LNCS, vol. 11505, pp. 387–403. Springer, Cham (2019). https://doi.org/10.1007/978-3-030-25510-7_21

7. Castryck, W., Decru, T.: An efficient key recovery attack on SIDH. In: Hazay, C., Stam, M. (eds.) Advances in Cryptology – EUROCRYPT 2023. EUROCRYPT 2023. LNCS, vol. 14008, pp. 423–447. Springer, Cham (2023). https://doi.org/10.1007/978-3-031-30589-4_15

8. Castryck, W., Lange, T., Martindale, C., Panny, L., Renes, J.: CSIDH: an efficient post-quantum commutative group action. In: Peyrin, T., Galbraith, S. (eds) Advances in Cryptology – ASIACRYPT 2018. ASIACRYPT 2018. LNCS, vol. 11274, pp. 395–427. Springer, Cham (2018). https://doi.org/10.1007/978-3-030-03332-3_15

9. Chow, S.S., Liu, J.K., Wong, D.S.: Robust receipt-free election system with ballot secrecy and verifiability. In: NDSS, vol. 8, pp. 81–94 (2008)

10. Chung, K.M., Hsieh, Y.C., Huang, M.Y., Huang, Y.H., Lange, T., Yang, B.Y.: Group signatures and accountable ring signatures from isogeny-based assumptions. arXiv e-prints pp. arXiv-2110 (2021)

11. Couveignes, J.M.: Hard homogeneous spaces. Cryptology ePrint Archive, Paper 2006/291 (2006). https://eprint.iacr.org/2006/291

12. Cramer, R., Damgård, I., Schoenmakers, B.: Proofs of partial knowledge and simplified design of witness hiding protocols. In: Desmedt, Y.G. (eds.) Advances in Cryptology – CRYPTO '94. CRYPTO 1994. LNCS, vol. 839, pp. 174–187. Springer, Berlin, Heidelberg (1994). https://doi.org/10.1007/3-540-48658-5_19

13. Derler, D., Ramacher, S., Slamanig, D.: Post-quantum zero-knowledge proofs for accumulators with applications to ring signatures from symmetric-key primitives. In: Lange, T., Steinwandt, R. (eds.) Post-Quantum Cryptography. PQCrypto 2018. LNCS, vol. 10786, pp. 419–440. Springer, Cham (2018). https://doi.org/10.1007/978-3-319-79063-3_20

14. Esgin, M.F., Steinfeld, R., Liu, J.K., Liu, D.: Lattice-based zero-knowledge proofs: new techniques for shorter and faster constructions and applications. In: Boldyreva, A., Micciancio, D. (eds.) Advances in Cryptology – CRYPTO 2019. CRYPTO 2019. LNCS, vol. 11692, pp. 115–146. Springer, Cham (2019). https://doi.org/10.1007/978-3-030-26948-7_5

15. Esgin, M.F., Steinfeld, R., Sakzad, A., Liu, J.K., Liu, D.: Short lattice-based one-out-of-many proofs and applications to ring signatures. In: Deng, R., Gauthier-Umana, V., Ochoa, M., Yung, M. (eds.) Applied Cryptography and Network Security. ACNS 2019. LNCS, vol. 11464, pp. 67–88. Springer, Cham (2019). https://doi.org/10.1007/978-3-030-21568-2_4

16. Esgin, M.F., Zhao, R.K., Steinfeld, R., Liu, J.K., Liu, D.: MatRiCT. In: Proceedings of the 2019 ACM SIGSAC Conference on Computer and Communications Security. ACM, November 2019. https://doi.org/10.1145/3319535.3354200

17. Feng, H., Liu, J., Wu, Q., Li, Y.N.: Traceable ring signatures with post-quantum security. In: Jarecki, S. (eds.) Topics in Cryptology - CT-RSA 2020. CT-RSA 2020. LNCS, vol. 12006, pp. 442–468. Springer, Cham (2020). https://doi.org/10.1007/978-3-030-40186-3_19

18. Feo, L.D., Galbraith, S.D.: SeaSign: compact isogeny signatures from class group actions. In: Ishai, Y., Rijmen, V. (eds.) Advances in Cryptology–EUROCRYPT 2019. EUROCRYPT 2019. LNCS, vol. 11478, pp. 759–789. Springer, Cham (2019). https://doi.org/10.1007/978-3-030-17659-4_26

19. Feo, L.D., Kohel, D., Leroux, A., Petit, C., Wesolowski, B.: SQISign: compact post-quantum signatures from quaternions and isogenies. In: Moriai, S., Wang, H. (eds.) Advances in Cryptology – ASIACRYPT 2020. ASIACRYPT 2020. LNCS, vol. 12491, pp. 64–93. Springer, Cham (2020). https://doi.org/10.1007/978-3-030-64837-4_3

20. Fiat, A., Shamir, A.: How to prove yourself: practical solutions to identification and signature problems. In: Odlyzko, A.M. (eds.) Advances in Cryptology – CRYPTO' 86. CRYPTO 1986. LNCS, vol. 263, pp. 186–194. Springer, Berlin, Heidelberg (1987). https://doi.org/10.1007/3-540-47721-7_12

21. Fujisaki, E.: Sub-linear size traceable ring signatures without random oracles. In: Kiayias, A. (eds.) Topics in Cryptology - CT-RSA 2011. CT-RSA 2011. LNCS, vol. 6558, pp. 393–415. Springer, Berlin, Heidelberg (2011). https://doi.org/10.1007/978-3-642-19074-2_25

22. Fujisaki, E., Suzuki, K.: Traceable ring signature. In: Okamoto, T., Wang, X. (eds.) Public Key Cryptography - PKC 2007. PKC 2007. LNCS, vol. 4450, pp. 181–200. Springer, Berlin, Heidelberg (2007). https://doi.org/10.1007/978-3-540-71677-8_13   •

23. Kelsey, J., Jen Change, S., Perlner, R.: SHA-3 derived functions: cSHAKE, KMAC, TupleHash and ParallelHash. Technical report (2016). https://doi.org/10.6028/nist.sp.800-185

24. Lai, Y.F., Dobson, S.: Collusion resistant revocable ring signatures and group signatures from hard homogeneous spaces. Cryptology ePrint Archive, Paper 2021/1365 (2021). https://eprint.iacr.org/2021/1365

25. Langlois, A., Stehlé, D.: Worst-case to average-case reductions for module lattices. Des. Codes Cryptogr. **75**(3), 565–599 (2014). https://doi.org/10.1007/s10623-014-9938-4

26. Libert, B., Ling, S., Nguyen, K., Wang, H.: Zero-knowledge arguments for lattice-based accumulators: logarithmic-size ring signatures and group signatures without trapdoors. J. Cryptol. **36**(3) (2023). https://doi.org/10.1007/s00145-023-09470-6

27. Lu, X., Au, M.H., Zhang, Z.: Raptor: a practical lattice-based (linkable) ring signature. In: Deng, R., Gauthier-Umana, V., Ochoa, M., Yung, M. (eds.) Applied Cryptography and Network Security. ACNS 2019. LNCS, vol. 11464, pp. 110–130. Springer, Cham (2019). https://doi.org/10.1007/978-3-030-21568-2_6

28. Nguyen, T.N., et al.: Efficient unique ring signatures from lattices. In: Atluri, V., Di Pietro, R., Jensen, C.D., Meng, W. (eds.) Computer Security - ESORICS 2022. ESORICS 2022. LNCS, vol. 13555, pp. 447–466. Springer, Cham (2022). https://doi.org/10.1007/978-3-031-17146-8_22

29. Peikert, C.: He gives c-sieves on the CSIDH. In: Canteaut, A., Ishai, Y. (eds.) Advances in Cryptology – EUROCRYPT 2020. EUROCRYPT 2020. LNCS, vol. 12106, pp. 463–492. Springer, Cham (2020). https://doi.org/10.1007/978-3-030-45724-2_16

30. Rivest, R.L., Shamir, A., Tauman, Y.: How to leak a secret. In: Boyd, C. (eds.) Advances in Cryptology - ASIACRYPT 2001. ASIACRYPT 2001. LNCS, vol. 2248, pp. 552–565. Springer, Berlin, Heidelberg (2001). https://doi.org/10.1007/3-540-45682-1_32

31. Rostovtsev, A., Stolbunov, A.: Public-key cryptosystem based on isogenies. Cryptology ePrint Archive, Paper 2006/145 (2006). https://eprint.iacr.org/2006/145

32. Scafuro, A., Zhang, B.: One-time traceable ring signatures. In: Bertino, E., Shulman, H., Waidner, M. (eds.) Computer Security - ESORICS 2021. ESORICS 2021. LNCS, vol. 12973, pp. 481–500. Springer, Cham (2021). https://doi.org/10.1007/978-3-030-88428-4_24

33. Shor, P.W.: Polynomial-time algorithms for prime factorization and discrete logarithms on a quantum computer. SIAM Rev. **41**(2), 303–332 (1999). https://doi.org/10.1137/s0036144598347011

34. Stolbunov, A.: Cryptographic schemes based on isogenies (2012)

Symmetric Cryptography and Fault Attacks

The Random Fault Model

Siemen Dhooghe[✉][iD] and Svetla Nikova[iD]

COSIC, KU Leuven, Leuven, Belgium
{Siemen.Dhooghe,Svetla.Nikova}@esat.kuleuven.be

Abstract. In this work, we introduce the *random fault model* - a more advanced fault model inspired by the random probing model, where the adversary can fault all values in the algorithm but the probability for each fault to occur is limited. The new adversary model is used to evaluate the security of side-channel and fault countermeasures such as Boolean masking, error detection techniques, error correction techniques, multiplicative tags, and shuffling methods. The results of the security analysis reveal new insights both in the novel random fault model as well as in the established random probing model including: shuffling masked implementations does not significantly improve the random probing security over regular masking; error correction providing little security when faults target more bits (versus the significant improvement when using error detection); and the order in which masking and duplication are applied providing a trade-off between random probing and fault security. Moreover, the results also explain the experimental results from CHES 2022 and find weaknesses in the shuffling method from SAMOS 2021.

Keywords: Encoding · Masking · Physical Security · Random Probing · Shuffling

1 Introduction

The field of side-channel analysis, following Differential Power Analysis (DPA) by Kocher *et al.* [17], has made significant progress over the years. Currently, we are capable of practically protecting hardware applications against side-channel attacks using masking. However, such progress did not come without difficulty. Often masking schemes were proposed, broken, and patched. This trial-and-error approach caused the need for theoretical proofs to guarantee the security of new masking methods. The main adversary in the academic literature is considered in the *probing model* proposed by Ishai *et al.* [16]. While this probing model already captures basic attacks and allows for easy proofs, it does not cover more advanced attacks in practice. Instead, the model proposed by Chari *et al.* [6], called the *noisy leakage model*, is much closer to practice but requires a complicated security analysis for countermeasures making the model less used in papers. In 2014, Duc *et al.* [12] made a reduction between the probing and noisy leakage models. This reduction introduced a new intermediate model called the *random probing model* which allows to capture attacks such as horizontal attacks introduced by Clavier

C. Carlet et al. (Eds.): SAC 2023, LNCS 14201, pp. 191–212, 2024.
https://doi.org/10.1007/978-3-031-53368-6_10

et al. [8] and which has an easier security analysis compared to the noisy leakage model. A security analysis in the random probing model allows for better insight in the security provided by different countermeasures, such as Boolean masking or shuffling, versus those provided in the standard probing model.

Compared to side-channel analysis, the field of fault attacks, following differential fault analysis by Biham and Shamir [4], is less studied and has not seen the same progress as side-channel analysis. As a result, standard fault security models are not yet accepted. The current most used academic model is an active variant of the probing model where the adversary can inject faults in a circuit up to a threshold number of wires or gates. However, experimental works such as the results by Bartkewitz *et al.* [3] note that a threshold fault model does not properly capture the practice where a single laser fault typically affects multiple values. Other adversary models from this threshold model have not been used to investigate and compare countermeasures. As such, the question remains how effective certain countermeasures are in a more realistic security model. Some popular countermeasures include: Boolean masking introduced by Patarin [14] and Chari *et al.* [6]; error detection methods such as in ParTI [20] and Impeccable Circuits [1]; error correction methods such as in Impeccable Circuits II [21]; multiplicative tags such as in CAPA [19] and M&M [9]; and shuffling such as Rocky [18]. However, none of the above countermeasures have been properly analyzed or compared to one another in a similar adversary model.

Contributions. The work essentially provides contributions in two fields: on random probing security, and on random fault security.

Considering random probing security, we investigate the security of the following countermeasures: Boolean masking, duplication, masked duplication, and shuffling. From the analysis, we made the following interesting observations.

- There is a security difference between masking-then-duplicating a variable versus duplicating-then-masking it.
- Both shuffling and shuffling with masking provides little improvement in random probing security no matter how the shuffling is performed.

Considering fault security, inspired by the random probing model, we propose a new fault adversary, the *random fault model*, which is allowed to fault all values in an algorithm but where each fault has a limited probability to apply. We then use the random fault model to analyze countermeasures in two security models: *correctness*, where the adversary's goal is to have an incorrect output, and *privacy*, where the adversary's goal is to retrieve secret information from the abort state of the algorithm. We analyze Boolean masking, error detection methods, error correction methods, multiplicative tags, and shuffling. From the analysis, we made the following interesting observations.

- There is a security difference between masking-then-duplicating a variable versus duplicating-then-masking it.
- We give a theoretical foundation to the experiments of Bartkewitz *et al.* [3] on faulting encoded variables with a different number of parity bits.

- Triplication provides significantly less security than duplication methods when the fault targets many bits.
- We observe that the random fault model can explain the success rate of statistical ineffective faults targeting multiple values similar to the random probing model explaining horizontal attacks.
- Multiplicative tags provide an exponential security gain in the field size in the correctness model.
- Shuffling exhibits several weaknesses when used to secure against fault attacks. As a result, we show that the work by Miteloudi *et al.* [18] has vulnerabilities.

2   Background

2.1   Notation

We consider stochastic variables, denoted as capital letters, over a finite field $\mathbb{F}_2$. We denote the probability of a stochastic variable attaining a value x as $\Pr[X = x]$ and the probability of X conditioned on Y as $\Pr[X = x | Y = y]$.

   We define random functions as stochastic variables over a set of functions. For example, a function uniform randomly drawn from a set of functions.

2.2   Algorithmic Representation

We represent algorithms as a string of elements or elementary operations over a finite field $\mathbb{F}$. In this work, we consider only the field $\mathbb{F}_2$ for which the elementary operations are the field addition (XOR) and multiplication (AND). We assume that algorithms can sample uniform random field elements. Moreover, an algorithm is also able to abort the computation providing $\perp$ as the output. We give an example of a binary algorithm

$$(x, y, r \leftarrow \$, z \leftarrow x + y, w \leftarrow zy, v \leftarrow y + r).$$

   An algorithm can have an *encoding* phase, where its input is, for example, masked or encoded. Oppositely, an algorithm can have a *decoding* phase where, for example, masked variables can be revealed and encoded variables can be checked for errors. For clarity, an error check in a duplication countermeasure is not part of the decoding phase, only the verification of the final output is. These phases are important in the security models of Sect. 2.3 and Sect. 3 since the adversaries cannot target these parts of the algorithm.

2.3   Random Probing Model

In this section, we introduce the *random probing model* as originally introduced by Duc *et al.* [12]. More specifically, its adversary and its security model. Later in Sect. 3, we study the main contribution of the work, namely the random fault model, which can be seen as the fault counterpart of the random probing model.

Random Probing Adversary. Consider the set of two functions $\mathcal{N} = \{f_0, f_1\}$ with $f_0 : \mathbb{F}_2 \to \mathbb{F}_2 \cup \{\bot\} : x \mapsto x$ and $f_1 : \mathbb{F}_2 \to \mathbb{F}_2 \cup \{\bot\} : x \mapsto \bot$. Namely, the function which maps a bit to itself and the function which returns nothing ($\bot$). We consider a Bernoulli distribution over $\mathcal{N}$ with mean $0 \leq \varepsilon \leq 1$. Thus, from the set $\mathcal{N}$ we draw the function f_0 with probability ε and the function f_1 with probability $1 - \varepsilon$. In words, when drawing a random function and evaluating a variable, the adversary has an ε probability to view that variable.

We note for clarity that the adversary can **precisely target** the location of the probes, but the probability for each probe to provide a value is random.

In this paper, we only consider random probes over bits. The model is easily generalized to work over larger fields. However, we note that in practice, the adversary never views the leakage of a large field element but, rather, a function of the bit vector (such as its Hamming weight) which was processed. As a result, the link with practice is weaker when a direct generalization of the random probing model is made.

Security Model. Consider an algorithm and denote the set of all its variables (excluding the encoding and decoding phases) by $\mathcal{V}$, the set of ε-*random probes* on $\mathcal{V}$ is the set $\{F(v)|v \in V, F \overset{Bern(\varepsilon)}{\leftarrow} \mathcal{N}\}$ with V the values the variables $\mathcal{V}$ in the algorithm attained with its input and internal randomness, and where for each value an independent random probe is chosen.

The *random probing security model* is the bounded query, left-right security game represented in Fig. 1. The game consists of a challenger picking a random bit b, the challenger then creates an oracle $\mathcal{O}^b$ from the algorithm C and provides this to the adversary $\mathcal{A}$. This adversary is computationally unbounded, but it is bounded in the number of queries to the oracle. The adversary provides two secrets k_0, k_1 (for a cipher, a secret is the plaintext and the key) and the set of variables $\mathcal{V}$ which it wants to probe. The oracle then picks the secret k_b, generates its internal randomness, computes the values V on $\mathcal{V}$, and provides the random probing leakage to the adversary. After q queries (for ease, in this work $q = 1$), the adversary guesses the bit b which was chosen by the challenger.

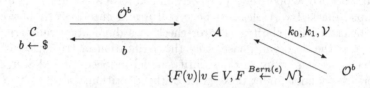

Fig. 1. The random probing leakage model.

The advantage of $\mathcal{A}$ is defined as

$$\text{Adv}(\mathcal{A}) = |\Pr[\mathcal{A}^{\mathcal{O}^0} = 1] - \Pr[\mathcal{A}^{\mathcal{O}^1} = 1]|.$$

3   Random Fault Model

We propose a novel adversary model inspired by the previous explained random probing model where the adversary can fault the entire state but there is a limited probability for each fault to occur (following the mechanisms of statistical fault analysis [13]). This random fault security model is novel and is meant to improve over the standard threshold fault model where an adversary can fault a fixed number of values.

3.1   Random Fault Adversary

Consider a function $g : \mathbb{F}_2 \to \mathbb{F}_2$ which is the fault the adversary wants to inject. Denote the set of functions $\mathcal{F}_g = \{g, id\}$, with $id : \mathbb{F}_2 \to \mathbb{F}_2 : x \mapsto x$, and consider a Bernoulli distribution $Bern(\kappa)$ on the set to take a random function F. For this random function F, we have that

$$F(x) = \begin{cases} g(x) \text{ with probability } \kappa, \\ x \text{ with probability } 1 - \kappa. \end{cases}$$

Considering the possible fault injections g an adversary can make over bits, there are three possibilities.

- *bitflip*: $\mathbb{F}_2 \to \mathbb{F}_2 : x \mapsto x + 1$.
- *set to zero*: $\mathbb{F}_2 \to \mathbb{F}_2 : x \mapsto 0$.
- *set to one*: $\mathbb{F}_2 \to \mathbb{F}_2 : x \mapsto 1$.

In Sect. 5 and Sect. 6, we use the above function names to indicate which fault is injected. We note for clarity that the adversary can **precisely target** the faults (over bits), but the probability for the fault to occur is random.

We only consider fault over bits and not over larger fields. Since our hardware and software works over bits and not over abstract algebraic structures, faults would hit separate gates or wires causing them to affect bit-by-bit. We leave the generalization of using realistic distributions of fault attacks in the random fault model over words (larger sets of bits) as an open problem.

3.2   Security Model: Correctness

The random fault model has two security models, namely a correctness and a privacy model (after the models by Ishai *et al.* [16]). The goal of the adversary in the correctness game is for the algorithm to output a wrong value (different than the value in case no faults were injected). In case the algorithm detected a fault and aborts, the adversary does not win the game. A fault attack covered by this model is for example differential fault analysis by Biham and Shamir [4]. However, the correctness model is more general as it does not look whether secret information can be gathered from an incorrect output.

Consider an algorithm and denote the set of the variables the adversary targets (excluding the encoding and decoding phases) by $\mathcal{V}$. Denote the set of κ-*random faults* by a set of functions $\mathcal{G} = \{g_i \mid i \in \mathcal{V}\}$.

The correctness game of the random fault model consists of an adversary querying the oracle implementing the algorithm providing it with the input secret k and the set of faults $\mathcal{G}$. The oracle then implements the algorithm with the secret k faulting its values with random functions $\mathcal{F}_\mathcal{G}$ following a $Bern(\kappa)$ distribution. The oracle outputs 1 if the output was correct or abort $\perp$, and 0 if the output was incorrect. This is depicted in Fig. 2. We require, for the algorithm to be useful, that it outputs a correct result in case no faults were present.

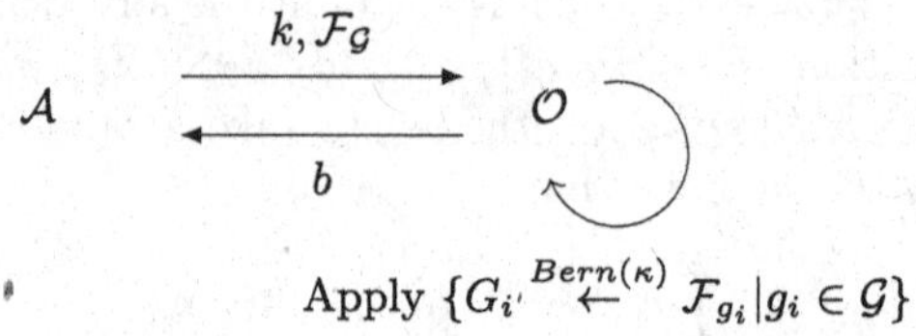

$$\mathcal{A} \quad \xrightarrow{\quad k, \mathcal{F}_\mathcal{G} \quad} \quad \mathcal{O}$$
$$\xleftarrow{\quad\quad}$$
$$b$$

Apply $\{G_{i'} \xleftarrow{Bern(\kappa)} \mathcal{F}_{g_i} | g_i \in \mathcal{G}\}$

Fig. 2. The correctness game of the random fault model.

The advantage is the probability the oracle outputs zero after a single query.

$$\mathrm{Adv}(\mathcal{A}) = \Pr[\mathcal{O}(k, \mathcal{F}_\mathcal{G}) = 0]$$

3.3   Security Model: Privacy

The goal of the adversary in the privacy game is to uncover internal information (the input) of the algorithm from the algorithm's abort state after faulting it. In case the algorithm does not have an abort signal (such as with masking or error correction), the countermeasure is automatically secure in the privacy model and its protection is solely determined by the correctness model. Examples of fault attacks in the privacy model include Clavier's ineffective faults [7] and statistical ineffective faults by Dobraunig et al. [11].

The privacy game of the *random fault model* is the bounded query, left-right security game represented in Fig. 3. The game consists of a challenger picking a random bit b, the challenger then creates an oracle $\mathcal{O}^b$ from the algorithm and provides this to the adversary $\mathcal{A}$. This adversary is computationally unbounded, but it is bounded in the number of queries to the oracle. The adversary provides two secrets k_0, k_1 together with a set of functions on the values (excluding encoding and decoding phases) $\mathcal{G} = \{g_i \mid i \in \mathcal{V}\}$. The oracle then picks the secret k_b, generates its internal randomness, computes the algorithm, and applies the random fault functions $\mathcal{F}_\mathcal{G}$ on the targeted variables $\mathcal{V}$ (following a $Bern(\kappa)$ distribution). The oracle returns the state of the abort signal of the algorithm. After q queries (for ease, in this work $q = 1$), the adversary returns the bit b which was chosen by the challenger.

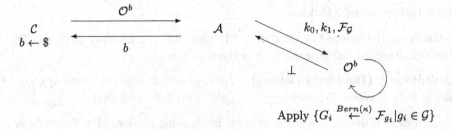

Fig. 3. The privacy game of the random fault model.

The advantage of $\mathcal{A}$ is defined as

$$\text{Adv}(\mathcal{A}) = |\Pr[\mathcal{A}^{\mathcal{O}^0} = 1] - \Pr[\mathcal{A}^{\mathcal{O}^1} = 1]|.$$

4   Case Studies: Random Probing Model

In order to showcase the random fault model, we apply it to several popular countermeasures with the goal to find general bounds over the parameters of the countermeasure. However, in order to properly provide the security of each countermeasure, we also evaluate them over the established random probing model (as introduced in Sect. 2.3). For example, to show that masking might not improve the bound over the random fault model, but that it does increase the security in the random probing model.

Although the random probing model has already been established for some time, some of the results in this section are novel. For example, as far as we are aware, no concrete random probing bounds have been given for duplicate-and-mask countermeasures. In addition, we show that shuffling methods do not significantly improve the security over the random probing model.

4.1   Influence of Duplication

We investigate what happens if you view the same variable m times (for example if the value is duplicated to defend against fault attacks) or when the variable is an element of $\mathbb{F}_{2^m}$.

Consider a uniform random variable $X \in \mathbb{F}_2$ ($\Pr[X = x] = 1/2$) and m independent random probes $F_0, ..., F_{m-1}$ taken from the set $\mathcal{N}$ following a $Bern(\varepsilon)$ distribution. Then, the probability that at least one probe views a value is $1 - (1 - \varepsilon)^m$. Thus, the advantage of a random probing adversary is

$$\text{Adv}(\mathcal{A}) = |\Pr[\mathcal{A}^{\mathcal{O}^0} = 1] - \Pr[\mathcal{A}^{\mathcal{O}^1} = 1]|$$
$$= 1 - (1 - \varepsilon)^m \le m\varepsilon,$$

where the last inequality is Bernoulli's inequality.

It is the above observed gain in advantage when viewing the same variable multiple times which causes horizontal attacks [8] to be effective.

4.2   Influence of Masking

Masking was introduced by Goubin and Patarin [14] and Chari *et al.* [6] in 1999. The definition for Boolean masking is given as follows.

Definition 1 (Boolean masking). *The n-shared Boolean masking of a variable $x \in \mathbb{F}_2$ consists of a vector $(x^0, \ldots, x^{n-1}) \in (\mathbb{F}_2)^n$ such that $x = \sum_{i=0}^{n-1} x^i$.*

In a countermeasure, a share vector is made using random bits. For example, to mask a secret x in two shares one can use a random bit r and create the vector $(x + r, r) = (x^0, x^1)$. That way, each share x^0 or x^1 is uniform random.

We start by showing that masking indeed improves the protection against a random probing adversary. Given a uniform value X^0 and X^1 such that $X^0 + X^1 = 0$ and two independent random probing functions F_0 and F_1 with probability ε to observe the value, then

$$\Pr[F_0 = f_{id}, F_1 = f_{id}] \Pr[X^0 \oplus X^1 = 0 | F_0(X^0), F_1(X^1)] = \varepsilon^2$$
$$\Pr[F_0 = f_{\perp}, F_1 = f_{id}] \Pr[X^0 \oplus X^1 = 0 | F_0(X^0), F_1(X^1)] = \varepsilon(1 - \varepsilon)/2$$
$$\Pr[F_0 = f_{\perp}, F_1 = f_{\perp}] \Pr[X^0 \oplus X^1 = 0 | F_0(X^0), F_1(X^1)] = (1 - \varepsilon)^2/2,$$

with $f_{id} : x \mapsto x$ and $f_{\perp} : x \mapsto \perp$. Similarly,

$$\Pr[F_0 = f_{id}, F_1 = f_{id}] \Pr[X^0 \oplus X^1 = 1 | F_0(X^0), F_1(X^1)] = 0$$
$$\Pr[F_0 = f_{\perp}, F_1 = f_{id}] \Pr[X^0 \oplus X^1 = 1 | F_0(X^0), F_1(X^1)] = \varepsilon(1 - \varepsilon)/2$$
$$\Pr[F_0 = f_{\perp}, F_1 = f_{\perp}] \Pr[X^0 \oplus X^1 = 1 | F_0(X^0), F_1(X^1)] = (1 - \varepsilon)^2/2,$$

As a result, the advantage of the adversary is ε^2 (the absolute subtraction of the three corresponding equations). Similarly, for n shares, the adversary only guesses correctly when all random probes return a value which happens with probability ε^n (which is then the advantage).

4.3   Influence of Masked Duplication

Consider the case where a variable is both masked and duplicated. In practice, this happens when we require both fault protection and side-channel security. We distinguish two cases.

- Mask-then-duplicate: A variable is first masked and then duplicated. For two shares and two duplicates, this means a bit $x \in \mathbb{F}_2$ is encoded to $(x_0^0, x_0^1), (x_1^0, x_1^1)$ where $x_0^0 + x_0^1 = x$ and $x_0^0 = x_1^0$, $x_0^1 = x_1^1$. Examples of countermeasures which use this technique include [10,15].
- Duplicate-then-mask: A variable is first duplicated and then masked. For two shares and two duplicates, this means a bit $x \in \mathbb{F}_2$ is encoded to $(x_0^0, x_1^1, x_2^0, x_3^1)$ where $x_0^0 + x_1^1 = x_2^0 + x_3^1 = x$. Examples of countermeasures which use this technique include [9,19,20].

Mask-then-Duplicate. For the first case with two shares ($n = 2$) and two duplicates ($k = 2$), we have that

$$\text{Adv}(\mathcal{A}) = |\Pr[\mathcal{A}^{\mathcal{O}^0} = 1] - \Pr[\mathcal{A}^{\mathcal{O}^1} = 1]| = (1 - (1 - \varepsilon)^2)^2.$$

Namely, the adversary only gets an advantage if it observes both shares, but since each share is duplicated, observing a single share happens with probability $1 - (1 - \varepsilon)^2$. By combining the advantages for duplication and for masking, for n shares and k duplicates, we have an advantage of

$$\text{Adv}(\mathcal{A}) = (1 - (1 - \varepsilon)^k)^n \leq (k\varepsilon)^n.$$

Duplicate-then-Mask. For the second case with $n, k = 2$, we have that

$$\text{Adv}(\mathcal{A}) = |\Pr[\mathcal{A}^{\mathcal{O}^0} = 1] - \Pr[\mathcal{A}^{\mathcal{O}^1} = 1]| = 1 - (1 - \varepsilon^2)^2.$$

Namely, the adversary has a ε^2 advantage to when observing a masking and the adversary has two chances to break it. For n shares and k duplicates, we have a random probing advantage of

$$\text{Adv}(\mathcal{A}) = 1 - (1 - \varepsilon^n)^k \leq k\varepsilon^n.$$

We observe that the duplicate-then-mask method protects better against a random probing adversary compared to the mask-then-duplicate method. We depict the differences between the advantages in Fig. 4.

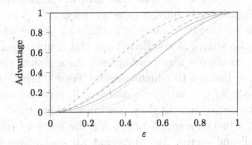

Fig. 4. The random probing advantage of the mask-then-duplicate method (in green) and the duplicate-then-mask method (in red). The full lines depict $(n, k) = (2, 2)$, the dashed lines depict $(n, k) = (2, 3)$, and the dotted lines depict $(n, k) = (3, 2)$. (Color figure online)

4.4 Influence of Shuffling

We take a look at shuffling as a countermeasure and assess its security in the random probing model. We then move to the shuffling of masked values.

Consider two values $x, y \in \mathbb{F}_2$. With shuffling, the encoding phase of the algorithm randomly shifts the two values from place. Consider the security model from Sect. 2.3. Since the adversary can choose the two secret inputs, we can take $x = y$ (meaning, $x = y = 0$ or $x = y = 1$ for the two cases of inputs). The advantage of the adversary using random probes (denoted F_0 and F_1 and calling the first operation O_0 and the second O_1) is

$$\text{Adv}(\mathcal{A}) = | \Pr[F_0(O_0) = 1 \vee F_1(O_1) = 1 | X = 1] |$$
$$= 1 - (1 - \varepsilon)^2 \leq 2\varepsilon .$$

The above adversary randomly guesses the secret when both random probes return $\perp$ and provides the answer to the probes when a value is returned. The above bound generalizes to $n\varepsilon$ for shuffling n bits.

We observe that the bound of the shuffling method is the same as the bound of an unshuffled n-bit state. As a result, shuffling provides no additional security when the adversary chooses weak inputs.

Shuffled Masking. We consider a state of k-bit n-shared values. For example, for $k = 3$ and $n = 2$, we have a state $(x_0, x_1), (y_0, y_1), (z_0, z_1)$ such that $x = x_0 + x_1$, $y = y_0 + y_1$, $z = z_0 + z_1$ for three bits $x, y, z \in \mathbb{F}_2$. Consider then that the total of nk bits are randomly permuted, meaning that a permutation is uniform randomly drawn for the set of all $\mathbb{F}_2^{nk} \rightarrow \mathbb{F}_2^{nk}$ permutations and is applied to the nk bits. We note that practical implementations of shuffling often consider a weaker case where the permutation is drawn from a smaller set, such as cyclical shifts of the shares. The security mentioned in related works such as [2, Sect. 2.4] is that shuffling these masked values at least improves the side-channel security by a factor k. We will show that in the random probing model, shuffling does not significantly improve the security.

We consider the advantage of random probing all the nk shares in the state. Since the order of the shares is shuffled (from the countermeasure), the values returned to the adversary are also randomized. As a result, the adversary does not know which value belongs to which variable. For example, the adversary can receive the transcript $(1, 0, 0)$ for $n = 2$ and $k = 3$, meaning that the adversary receives three values out of six but does not know which three it received.

We consider an adversary which takes, for the security model, the all-zero secret versus the all-one secret. Meaning that all k sharings are of either the secret zero (in the first case) or the secret all-one (in the second case). The adversary then considers all possible n-sums of the received values. In case the majority of the sums are zero, the adversary decides it is in the first case (with the secrets all equal to zero), otherwise it decides it is in the second case. We calculate the advantage of this adversary.

The probability that the adversary receives exactly i bits from the random probes is $\binom{nk}{i}\varepsilon^i(1-\varepsilon)^{nk-i}$. Given that the adversary has i values, it can calculate a total of $\binom{i}{n}$ n-sums out of the total of $\binom{nk}{n}$ n-sums. Finally, there are a total of k sums which sum to the secret (we call these "correct sums"). The advantage is thus given as follows.

$$\text{Adv}(\mathcal{A}) = \sum_{i=0}^{nk} \binom{nk}{i} \varepsilon^i (1 - \varepsilon)^{nk-i} \sum_{j=0}^{k} C(i,j) K(i,j),$$

with $C(i,j)$ the probability to have j correct sums over the total of $\binom{i}{n}$ sums, and $K(i,j)$ the probability to win the game minus the probability to lose the game given j correct sums over a total of $\binom{i}{n}$ sums.

In more detail,

$$C(i,j) = \frac{\binom{a}{j}\binom{b-a}{k-j}}{\binom{b}{k}},$$

with $a = \binom{i}{n}$ and $b = \binom{nk}{n}$ since $C(i,j)$ is the probability of j successes in the hypergeometric distribution. The value

$$K(i,j) = \sum_{\ell=\lceil \frac{a+1}{2} \rceil - j}^{a-j} \frac{1}{2^{a-j}} \binom{a-j}{\ell} - \sum_{\ell=0}^{\lfloor \frac{a}{2} \rfloor - j} \frac{1}{2^{a-j}} \binom{a-j}{\ell},$$

with $a = \binom{i}{n}$ is the probability that the majority of the n-sums are equal to the secret (given that j sums are correct) minus the probability that the majority of the sums equal zero.

It is clear that an upper bound for the above advantage is equal to the advantage of an k times n-sharing without shuffling, which is equal to $1 - (1 - \varepsilon^n)^k$. For $n, k = 2$, we also find that the above advantage is equal to $2\varepsilon^2 - 2\varepsilon^3 + \frac{3}{8}\varepsilon^4$, which is lower than the $2\varepsilon^2 - \varepsilon^4$ advantage without shuffling. This shows that shuffling indeed increases the security of an implementation. However, we see that both advantages have a leading coefficient $2\varepsilon^2$. Meaning that the advantage of shuffling equals the advantage without shuffling plus terms in ε^3 or higher. In words, shuffling only achieves a very insignificant (i.e. less than linear) increase in random probing security.

We prove this "less than linear" security gain more formally. First, since $C(i,j) = 0$ for $i < n$, we can write $\text{Adv}(\mathcal{A}) = c\varepsilon^n + \mathcal{O}(\varepsilon^{n+1})$. Second, we find that $c = k$ since $c = \binom{nk}{n}C(n,1)K(n,1)$ with $C(n,1) = \frac{k}{\binom{nk}{n}}$ and $K(n,1) = 1$. As a result, we find that $\text{Adv}(\mathcal{A}) = k\varepsilon^n + \mathcal{O}(\varepsilon^{n+1})$ which can be compared to the advantage of the state without shuffling $1 - (1 - \varepsilon^n)^k = k\varepsilon^n + \mathcal{O}(\varepsilon^{n+1})$. Thus, we have proven that shuffling can only improve the random probing security by a less-than-linear amount when the adversary chooses weak inputs.

We mention that similar results were found by Bogdanov et al. [5] on using higher-order differential computational analysis on white-box implementations using masking and shuffling.

5   Case Studies: Random Fault Correctness

We investigate the random fault security of several popular countermeasures including duplication, error correcting codes, masking, multiplicative tags, and shuffling. Recall from Sect. 3.2 that the random fault model has two security models, namely the correctness and the privacy model. In this section, we evaluate the countermeasures in the correctness model.

To better understand the bounds given in this section, we establish a baseline. Namely, we investigate the correctness security of storing a single bit. The advantage of a random fault adversary changing this single bit value is κ. In case there are m variables (or m queries), then the advantage is $1 - (1 - \kappa)^m \le m\kappa$.

5.1   Influence of Masking

Consider masking from Sect. 4.2 where a variable $x \in \mathbb{F}_2$ is split in two parts x^0, x^1 such that $x^0 + x^1 = x$. Then using a random bitflip fault F with probability κ only on x^0, the advantage of the adversary against an n-masking is still

$$\mathrm{Adv}(\mathcal{A}) = \Pr[F(X^0) + X^1 \neq X^0 + X^1] = \kappa.$$

However, the adversary can bitflip both shares (denoted F_0 and F_1) to attain the advantage $2\kappa(1 - \kappa)$. For n shares, this advantage becomes

$$\mathrm{Adv}(\mathcal{A}) = \sum_{i=0}^{\lfloor \frac{n}{2} \rfloor} \binom{n}{2i + 1} \kappa^{2i+1}(1 - \kappa)^{n-2i-1} = \frac{1}{2}(1 - (1 - 2\kappa)^n) \le n\kappa.$$

We observe that, if $\kappa \le 1/2$, masking increases the advantage of a faulting adversary in the correctness model over a non-masked alternative.

5.2   Influence of Duplication

We then investigate the effect of duplicating the variable and error checking the duplicates at the end of the computation.

Definition 2 (Duplication). *The n-duplication of a variable $x \in \mathbb{F}_2$ consists of a vector $(x_0, \ldots, x_{n-1}) \in (\mathbb{F}_2)^n$ such that $x_0 = \ldots = x_{n-1}$.*

The above is combined with an error check which verifies if $x_i = x_j$ with $i \neq j$ and aborts the computation if they are not equal.

We calculate the advantage of a random fault adversary injecting a *bitflip* (see Sect. 3) in both duplicates for a two-duplication using random faults (F_0, F_1) with probability κ to occur. We find the following advantage

$$\mathrm{Adv}(\mathcal{A}) = \Pr[F_0(X_0) = F_1(X_1), F_0(X_0) \neq X_0] = \kappa^2.$$

This is extended to k-duplication with an advantage of κ^k. As a result, duplication (or any linear code with nontrivial distance) exponentially decreases the advantage of the adversary in the correctness game.

For m-bit k-duplicated variables, the advantage of the adversary is still κ^k if the adversary attacks only one pair of duplicates. In case the adversary attacks all duplicates, the advantage becomes

$$\text{Adv}(\mathcal{A}) = \sum_{i=1}^{m} \binom{m}{i} \kappa^{ik}(1-\kappa)^{k(m-i)} = (\kappa^k + (1-\kappa)^k)^m - (1-\kappa)^{km},$$

where the equality comes from the binomial theorem. The above advantage is higher compared to attacking one pair of duplicates in case κ is small.

Specific Codes. We consider the advantage for encodings using different linear codes from the repetition (duplication) code. Consider a value $x \in \mathbb{F}_{2^m}$ encoded as a codeword $c \in \mathcal{C}$ with $\mathcal{C}$ and $[n, m, d]$ code. It is clear that if the adversary faults c to the nearest other codeword, the advantage is κ^d.

For a different attack, the adversary bitflips each bit of c where the advantage is the probability they form a codeword. In particular, if $\kappa = 0.5$, one gets a random m-bit fault for which the advantage is $\frac{2^m-1}{2^n}$. This result is, for example, given by Schneider et al. [20] where it is called the "fault coverage" of the code. For more accurate results when $\kappa \neq 0.5$, the specific advantage of the adversary depends on the actual code that is used. We provide some examples.

Consider the $[m + 1, m, 2]$ parity code (i.e. $(x[0], ..., x[m-1], c)$ with $c = \sum_{i=0}^{m-1} x[i]$). The advantage of a random fault adversary is

$$\text{Adv}(\mathcal{A}) = \sum_{i=1}^{\lfloor \frac{m+1}{2} \rfloor} \binom{m+1}{2i} \kappa^{2i}(1-\kappa)^{m-2i+1}$$

$$= \frac{1}{2}(1 + (1-2\kappa)^{m+1}) - (1-\kappa)^{m+1}.$$

For other examples, we need the weight distribution of the codes we are investigating.

- For the $[7, 4, 3]$ Hamming code, the weight distribution, ranging from zero to seven, of the codewords is $[1, 0, 0, 7, 7, 0, 0, 1]$. As a result, the advantage is $7\kappa^3(1-\kappa)^4 + 7\kappa^4(1-\kappa)^3 + \kappa^7$.
- Similarly, the weight distribution of the $[8, 4, 4]$ extended Hamming code, ranging from zero to eight, is $[1, 0, 0, 0, 14, 0, 0, 0, 1]$. Thus, the advantage is $14\kappa^4(1-\kappa)^4 + \kappa^8$.

The difference in advantages between the codes is shown in the first graph of Fig. 5. From this figure, we find that the number of parity bits have a significant effect on the advantage of a random fault adversary and that not only the minimal distance of the code matters. Note that the "kink" in the graphs is given by the difference of advantages of different attacks.

In the work by Bartkewitz et al. [3], experiments were performed by faulting only the message bits in an implementation (leaving the parity bits unaltered). Assuming that a κ-random fault in the message bits was injected (and that indeed the parity bits were unaffected), the result of the advantage for the different codes investigated by Bartkewitz et al. is given in the second graph of Fig. 5. The difference between the codes becomes more significant when faulting only the message bits versus faulting all bits in the codeword.

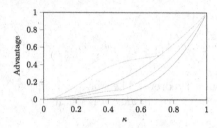 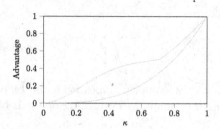

Fig. 5. The advantage of a random fault adversary against encoded values on the left and on the right when only the message bits are attacked. Blue depicts the $[5, 4, 2]$ code, green $[8, 4, 2]$, yellow $[7, 4, 3]$, and red $[8, 4, 4]$. For the right figure, the $[8, 4, 2]$ and $[8, 4, 4]$ codes have advantage zero. (Color figure online)

5.3   Influence of Triplication

Consider the duplication method from before, but with a minimum of three duplicates (x_0, x_1, x_2). Instead of using error detection where the algorithm can abort, we correct the errors using a majority voting.

We consider an adversary which bitflips two out of three duplicates of a single bit. This adversary has the following advantage

$$\mathrm{Adv}(\mathcal{A}) = \Pr[F_0(X_0) = F_1(X_1), F_0(X_0) \neq X_0] = \kappa^2 \,.$$

For k duplicates, the advantage would be $\kappa^{\lceil k/2 \rceil}$.

We extend the above analysis by considering m bits. When each variable is duplicated and an error detection method is used, the advantage of the adversary is $(\kappa^2 + (1-\kappa)^2)^m - (1-\kappa)^{2m}$ when attacking all variables, and κ^2 when attacking one pair of duplicates. However, with error correction, the advantage against an m-bit three-duplicate correction method becomes

$$\mathrm{Adv}(\mathcal{A}) = 1 - (1 - \kappa^2)^m \,,$$

as the adversary can re-try the attack with each variable and win when one of the m variables is error-corrected to the wrong output. The advantage is depicted in Fig. 6. We find that triplication performs significantly worse when faults can target a large state size compared to duplication. We note that the combination of Boolean masking with triplication would not improve the advantage.

5.4   Influence of Masked Duplication

Recall the two methods of both masking and duplicating variables from Sect. 4.3.

Mask-then-Duplicate. We consider the first case where each share is duplicated. If the adversary only bitflips one pair of duplicates, the advantage is κ^2

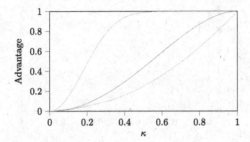

Fig. 6. The advantage against error correction (with three duplicates) is shown in red (for $m = 2$) and yellow ($m = 16$). The advantage against error detection (with two duplicates) is shown in green (for $m = 2$) and blue ($m = 16$). (Color figure online)

(or κ^k for k duplicates). In case the adversary bitflips all values (denoting the random faults F_0, F_1, F_2, F_3), the advantage for $n, k = 2$ is

$$\mathrm{Adv}(\mathcal{A}) = \Pr[F_0(X_0^0) = F_1(X_1^0), F_2(X_0^1) = F_3(X_1^1), F_0(X_0^0) + F_2(X_0^1) \neq X]$$
$$= 2\kappa^2(1 - \kappa)^2.$$

Given that the probability to break the correctness of a k-duplication is κ^k and the probability to leave each duplicate unchanged is $(1 - \kappa)^k$, the advantage with n shares and k duplicates becomes

$$\mathrm{Adv}(\mathcal{A}) = \sum_{i=0}^{\lfloor \frac{n-1}{2} \rfloor} \binom{n}{2i+1} \kappa^{k(2i+1)}(1 - \kappa)^{k(n-2i-1)}$$
$$= \frac{1}{2}((1 - \kappa)^k + \kappa^k)^n - ((1 - \kappa)^k - \kappa^k)^n.$$

Duplicate-then-Mask. Recall that for the second case, the variable is first duplicated and then each duplicate is shared separately. When attacking only one share per duplicate, the advantage is κ^k. When attacking all variables (denoting the random faults F_0, F_1, F_2, F_3), for $n, k = 2$, the advantage becomes

$$\mathrm{Adv}(\mathcal{A}) = \Pr[F_0(X_0^0) + F_1(X_0^1) = F_2(X_2^0) + F_3(X_3^1), F_0(X_0^0) + F_1(X_0^1) \neq X]$$
$$= 4\kappa^2(1 - \kappa)^2.$$

For n shares and k duplicates, the probability to change the correctness of an n-sharing is $\frac{1}{2}(1 - (1 - 2\kappa)^n)$, so we have

$$\mathrm{Adv}(\mathcal{A}) = 2^{-k}(1 - (1 - 2\kappa)^n)^k.$$

We observe that for small parameters κ, the mask-then-duplicate method provides more security as opposed to the duplicate-then-mask method. This is depicted for small variables n, k in Fig. 7.

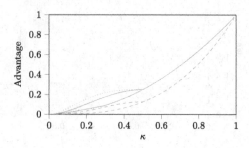

Fig. 7. The random fault advantage in the correctness model of the mask-then-duplicate method (in green) and the duplicate-then-mask method (in red). The full lines depict $(n, k) = (2, 2)$, the dashed lines depict $(n, k) = (2, 3)$, and the dotted lines depict $(n, k) = (3, 2)$. (Color figure online)

5.5   Influence of Multiplicative Tags

We can encode variables against fault attacks by multiplying the duplicate with a random value. We call this a multiplicative tag.

Definition 3 (Multiplicative Tag). *A multiplicative tag of $x \in \mathbb{F}_{2^m}$ is a value $\alpha x \in \mathbb{F}_{2^m}$ with $\alpha \in \mathbb{F}_{2^m}$ chosen uniformly random with each query.*

Consider the encoding of $x \in \mathbb{F}_{2^m}$ with a multiplicative tag $(x, \alpha x) \in (\mathbb{F}_{2^m})^2$ and $\alpha \in \mathbb{F}_{2^m}$ chosen randomly with every query. Error detection is performed by taking the message x, multiplying it with the tag α, and verifying it against the duplicate αx. We investigate the security of this method in the correctness game with a random fault adversary.

We consider a first adversary which changes a single bit of x assuming $\alpha = 0$. Consider F a random fault flipping the first bit of x. Then, the advantage is

$$\mathrm{Adv}(\mathcal{A}) = \Pr[F(X_0) \neq X_0, \alpha = 0] = 2^{-m}\kappa.$$

For a second adversary, we take $x = 1$ and fault both x and αx with set-to-zero faults. We number the bits of x by $(x[0], ..., x[m-1])$ and the bits of αx by $(\alpha x[0], ..., \alpha x[m-1])$. Then, the advantage of the adversary applying random faults $F_0, ..., F_m$ against an m-bit multiplicative tag is given as follows

$$\mathrm{Adv}(\mathcal{A}) = \Pr[F_0(X[0]) = 0, F_1(\alpha X[0]) = 0, ..., F_m(\alpha X[m-1]) = 0]$$
$$= \kappa \left(\frac{1+\kappa}{2}\right)^m.$$

While, in this work, we are not able to provide bounds for general adversaries, we observe that multiplicative tags provide a promising countermeasure against faults compared to using linear codes from Sect. 5.2.

5.6   Influence of Shuffling

Consider the shuffling countermeasure from Sect. 4.4. Without duplication, the adversary can bitflip each value for the same advantage as in the non-shuffled case. Since there is no detection step, as long as one fault hits, the adversary wins.

In case duplication is used on top of the shuffling, similar to the weak input attack in Sect. 4.4, there are weak inputs in the correctness model. Namely, for two two-duplicated bits $(x_0, y_0), (x_1, y_1)$, pick the secret $(0, 1)$. By applying a set-to-zero fault on all values, only one variable can change in its value providing the same advantage as in the non-shuffled case where the adversary only targets one pair of duplicates. Moreover, recall from Sect. 5.2 that when k is small, the best attack of the adversary is to fault all duplicates. Such an attack has the same probability to break correctness when shuffling the duplicates. As a result, for small κ, shuffling does not improve security in the random fault model (independent of how the shuffling is done). Together with the weak inputs when attacking only one pair of duplicates, we conclude that we cannot find a non-trivial upper bound on the security of shuffling in the correctness model.

6 Case Studies: Random Fault Privacy

In Sect. 5, we investigated the correctness security of several countermeasures. In this section, we investigate the privacy security (from Sect. 3.3). Recall that the privacy model is only relevant to countermeasures which can abort the computation. Therefore, we do not investigate countermeasures such as masking.

6.1 Influence of Duplication

Consider the duplication method from Sect. 5.2 (the advantage is similar when using multiplicative tags from Sect. 5.5). A privacy adversary (taking $x = 0$ and $x = 1$) faulting one variable to zero with probability κ has an advantage

$$\mathrm{Adv}(\mathcal{A}) = |\Pr[\mathcal{A}^{\mathcal{O}^0} = \bot] - \Pr[\mathcal{A}^{\mathcal{O}^1} = \bot]| = \kappa.$$

This is because, when $x = 0$, the countermeasure can never abort or, when $x = 1$, it aborts with probability κ. The bound for m-bit variables (or viewing the variable m times) is $1 - (1 - \kappa)^m \leq m\kappa$.

In case the adversary faults all k duplicates to zero, the advantage becomes

$$\mathrm{Adv}(\mathcal{A}) = \sum_{i=1}^{k-1} \binom{k}{i} \kappa^i (1 - \kappa)^{k-i} = 1 - \kappa^k - (1 - \kappa)^k.$$

6.2 Influence of Masked Duplication

Similar to Sect. 5.4, we consider a variable which is both masked and duplicated.

Mask-then-Duplicate. Consider a masked and encoded value $(x_0^0, x_0^1, x_1^0, x_1^1)$ where the shares are duplicated. When faulting both x_0^0 and x_0^1 to zero, we get

$$\mathrm{Adv}(\mathcal{A}) = |\Pr[\mathcal{A}^{\mathcal{O}^0} = \bot] - \Pr[\mathcal{A}^{\mathcal{O}^1} = \bot]| = \kappa - (1 - (1 - \kappa)^2)/2 = \kappa^2/2.$$

When considering n shares, the probability to change at least one share out of n (due to a set fault) when the sharing has secret zero κ_0 or secret one κ_1 is

$$\kappa_0 = \sum_{i=0}^{\lfloor \frac{n}{2} \rfloor} 2^{1-n} \binom{n}{2i} (1 - (1-\kappa)^{2i}), \quad \kappa_1 = \sum_{i=0}^{\lfloor \frac{n-1}{2} \rfloor} 2^{1-n} \binom{n}{2i+1} (1 - (1-\kappa)^{2i+1}).$$

The advantage of the above attack is $|\kappa_0 - \kappa_1| = 2^{1-n} \kappa^n$.

When faulting $(x_0^0, x_0^1, x_1^0, x_1^1)$ all to zero, the advantage becomes $2\kappa^2(1-\kappa)^2$. For small κ, the advantage is higher when faulting all duplicates and shares. For the bound when faulting all k duplicates and n shares is

$$\mathrm{Adv}(\mathcal{A}) = 2^{1-n}(1 - (1-\kappa)^k - \kappa^k)^n,$$

since the advantage when faulting a k-duplication is $1 - (1-\kappa)^k - \kappa^k$.

Duplicate-then-Mask. Consider the masking $(x_0^0, x_1^1, x_2^0, x_3^1)$ such that $x_2^0 + x_3^1 = x_0^0 + x_1^1$. When faulting x_0^0 and x_1^1 both to zero, we have an advantage

$$\mathrm{Adv}(\mathcal{A}) = |\Pr[\mathcal{A}^{\mathcal{O}^0} = \bot] - \Pr[\mathcal{A}^{\mathcal{O}^1} = \bot]| = \kappa^2.$$

For n shares, this attack generalizes to the advantage κ^n. When faulting all bits $(x_0^0, x_1^1, x_2^0, x_3^1)$ to zero, the advantage is $2\kappa^2(1-\kappa)^2$. When investigating the advantage for n shares and k duplicates, when faulting all shares to zero, the probability to change the value of the secret when it is equal to zero is

$$\kappa_0 = \sum_{i=1}^{\lfloor \frac{n}{2} \rfloor} 2^{1-n} \binom{n}{2i} \left(\sum_{j=0}^{i-1} \binom{2i}{2j+1} \kappa^{2j+1}(1-\kappa)^{2i-2j-1} \right)$$

$$= \sum_{i=1}^{\lfloor \frac{n}{2} \rfloor} 2^{-n} \binom{n}{2i} (1 - (1-2\kappa)^{2i}) = 1/2(1 - (1-\kappa)^n - \kappa^n),$$

where the equalities are derived from the binomial expansion theorem. Similarly, the probability to change the secret of a sharing of one is

$$\kappa_1 = \sum_{i=0}^{\lfloor \frac{n-1}{2} \rfloor} 2^{1-n} \binom{n}{2i+1} \left(\sum_{j=0}^{i} \binom{2i+1}{2j+1} \kappa^{2j+1}(1-\kappa)^{2i-2j} \right)$$

$$= 1/2(1 - (1-\kappa)^n + \kappa^n).$$

Then, when faulting all shares in the duplication, the probability to abort for secret zero is $1 - \kappa_0^k - (1 - \kappa_0)^k$. Similarly, for secret one the probability is $1 - \kappa_1^k - (1 - \kappa_1)^k$. Thus, the advantage against n shares and k duplicates is

$$\text{Adv}(\mathcal{A}) = |\kappa_0^k - \kappa_1^k + (1 - \kappa_0)^k - (1 - \kappa_1)^k|.$$

We observe that the mask-then-duplicate method scales better for higher parameters n and the duplicate-then-mask method scales better for higher parameters k (with the mask-then-duplicate method performing better for equal parameters n, k) as depicted in Fig. 8.

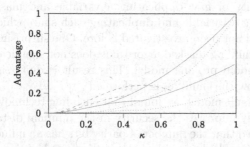

Fig. 8. The privacy advantage of the mask-then-duplicate method (in green) and the duplicate-then-mask method (in red). The full lines depict $(n, k) = (2, 2)$, the dashed lines depict $(n, k) = (2, 3)$, and the dotted lines depict $(n, k) = (3, 2)$. (Color figure online)

6.3   Influence of Shuffling

Consider the shuffling method from Sect. 4.4 but with duplicated values. Similar to Sect. 4.4 and Sect. 5.6, there are weak inputs in the privacy model. Namely, when shuffling $(x, y) \in \mathbb{F}_2^2$ and taking the two secrets $x = y$, shuffling becomes obsolete as the same values are shuffled. Moreover, the same attack described in Sect. 6.1 still applies. Namely, to attack all duplicates with a set-to-zero fault between the all-zero and all-one secrets. As a result, shuffling with duplication does not improve the random fault security in the privacy model. Moreover, when using a masking countermeasure, for small parameters κ the best attack is to fault all shares and duplicates with the same fault. The advantage of this attack would not change when shuffling the values.

Together with the weaknesses found in the correctness model in Sect. 5.6, we conclude that shuffling against fault attacks exhibits several weaknesses. The vulnerabilities found in this work directly apply to the Rocky countermeasure [18] which we show is weak in both the correctness and privacy models of the random fault model for certain parameters κ and for certain weak inputs. In addition with the weaknesses found for shuffling in the random probing model from Sect. 4.4, we do not believe shuffling can provide a significant improvement for security against either random probing or random fault adversaries.

7   Conclusion

In this work, we proposed a new fault adversary model called *the random fault model* which is a model inspired from the known random probing model. The goal of the work was to investigate and compare different countermeasures and observe which can promise good security against fault attacks. To make this comparison properly, we also investigated the countermeasures in the random probing model.

Most results in the random probing model are intuitive. Masking provides exponential protection in the number of shares and duplication linearly decreases security in the number of duplicates. However, we did observe a difference between the security of first duplicating a variable and masking each duplicate versus masking a variable and duplicating each share which, to the best of our knowledge, had not been investigated before. One surprising result was that both shuffling or shuffling masked algorithms does not significantly increase the security in the random probing model. This result is quite significant since it holds no matter how the shuffling is performed.

In the random fault model, we found that encoding techniques such as duplication exponentially improves the security in the minimal distance of the code. But we also observed that the number of parity bits has an influence to the countermeasure's security which provides a theoretical explanation for the practical results by Bartkewitz *et al.* [3]. Interestingly enough, we also find that triplication methods (error correction) are significantly less secure than duplication methods (error detection) when the adversary faults several bits. Since there is a lot of work on error correction methods, it remains a question whether these works can provide any good security in a formal security model and we are left with the open question of investigating their security in practice. Moving to masking, we showed that masking reduces the security of a countermeasure against fault attacks and, similar to results in the random probing model, that there is a trade-off in security between duplicate-then-masking a variable versus masking-then-duplicating one. Finally, similar to the results in the random probing model, we show that shuffling does not improve a countermeasure's security against fault attacks which implies that the countermeasure Rocky [18] does not currently provide a theoretical foundation for its security.

Acknowledgement. A special thanks to Vincent Rijmen for the helpful discussions. This work was supported by CyberSecurity Research Flanders with reference number VR20192203.

References

1. Aghaie, A., Moradi, A., Rasoolzadeh, S., Shahmirzadi, A.R., Schellenberg, F., Schneider, T.: Impeccable circuits. IEEE Trans. Comput. **69**(3), 361–376 (2020). https://doi.org/10.1109/TC.2019.2948617
2. Azouaoui, M., Bronchain, O., Grosso, V., Papagiannopoulos, K., Standaert, F.: Bitslice masking and improved shuffling: how and when to mix them in software? IACR Trans. Cryptogr. Hardw. Embed. Syst. **2022**(2), 140–165 (2022)

3. Bartkewitz, T., Bettendorf, S., Moos, T., Moradi, A., Schellenberg, F.: Beware of insufficient redundancy an experimental evaluation of code-based FI countermeasures. IACR Trans. Cryptogr. Hardw. Embed. Syst. **2022**(3), 438–462 (2022)
4. Biham, E., Shamir, A.: Differential fault analysis of secret key cryptosystems. In: Kaliski, B.S., Jr. (ed.) CRYPTO 1997. LNCS, vol. 1294, pp. 513–525. Springer, Heidelberg (1997). https://doi.org/10.1007/BFb0052259
5. Bogdanov, A., Rivain, M., Vejre, P.S., Wang, J.: Higher-order DCA against standard side-channel countermeasures. In: Polian, I., Stöttinger, M. (eds.) COSADE 2019. LNCS, vol. 11421, pp. 118–141. Springer, Cham (2019). https://doi.org/10.1007/978-3-030-16350-1_8
6. Chari, S., Jutla, C.S., Rao, J.R., Rohatgi, P.: Towards sound approaches to counteract power-analysis attacks. In: Wiener, M. (ed.) CRYPTO 1999. LNCS, vol. 1666, pp. 398–412. Springer, Heidelberg (1999). https://doi.org/10.1007/3-540-48405-1_26
7. Clavier, C.: Secret external encodings do not prevent transient fault analysis. In: Paillier, P., Verbauwhede, I. (eds.) CHES 2007. LNCS, vol. 4727, pp. 181–194. Springer, Heidelberg (2007). https://doi.org/10.1007/978-3-540-74735-2_13
8. Clavier, C., Feix, B., Gagnerot, G., Roussellet, M., Verneuil, V.: Horizontal correlation analysis on exponentiation. In: Soriano, M., Qing, S., López, J. (eds.) ICICS 2010. LNCS, vol. 6476, pp. 46–61. Springer, Heidelberg (2010). https://doi.org/10.1007/978-3-642-17650-0_5
9. De Meyer, L., Arribas, V., Nikova, S., Nikov, V., Rijmen, V.: M&M: masks and macs against physical attacks. IACR Trans. Cryptographic Hardw. Embed. Syst. **2019**(1), 25–50 (2018). https://doi.org/10.13154/tches.v2019.i1.25-50, https://tches.iacr.org/index.php/TCHES/article/view/7333
10. Dhooghe, S., Nikova, S.: My gadget just cares for me - how NINA can prove security against combined attacks. In: Jarecki, S. (ed.) CT-RSA 2020. LNCS, vol. 12006, pp. 35–55. Springer, Cham (2020). https://doi.org/10.1007/978-3-030-40186-3_3
11. Dobraunig, C., Eichlseder, M., Korak, T., Mangard, S., Mendel, F., Primas, R.: SIFA: exploiting ineffective fault inductions on symmetric cryptography. IACR Trans. Cryptographic Hardw. Embed. Syst. **2018**(3), 547–572 (2018). https://doi.org/10.13154/tches.v2018.i3.547-572, https://tches.iacr.org/index.php/TCHES/article/view/7286
12. Duc, A., Dziembowski, S., Faust, S.: Unifying leakage models: from probing attacks to noisy leakage. In: Nguyen, P.Q., Oswald, E. (eds.) EUROCRYPT 2014. LNCS, vol. 8441, pp. 423–440. Springer, Heidelberg (2014). https://doi.org/10.1007/978-3-642-55220-5_24
13. Fuhr, T., Jaulmes, É., Lomné, V., Thillard, A.: Fault attacks on AES with faulty ciphertexts only. In: Fischer, W., Schmidt, J. (eds.) 2013 Workshop on Fault Diagnosis and Tolerance in Cryptography, Los Alamitos, CA, USA, 20 August 2013, pp. 108–118. IEEE Computer Society (2013). https://doi.org/10.1109/FDTC.2013.18
14. Goubin, L., Patarin, J.: DES and differential power analysis the "Duplication" method. In: Koç, Ç.K., Paar, C. (eds.) CHES 1999. LNCS, vol. 1717, pp. 158–172. Springer, Heidelberg (1999). https://doi.org/10.1007/3-540-48059-5_15
15. Ishai, Y., Prabhakaran, M., Sahai, A., Wagner, D.: Private circuits II: keeping secrets in tamperable circuits. In: Vaudenay, S. (ed.) EUROCRYPT 2006. LNCS, vol. 4004, pp. 308–327. Springer, Heidelberg (2006). https://doi.org/10.1007/11761679_19
16. Ishai, Y., Sahai, A., Wagner, D.: Private circuits: securing hardware against probing attacks. In: Boneh, D. (ed.) CRYPTO 2003. LNCS, vol. 2729, pp. 463–481. Springer, Heidelberg (2003). https://doi.org/10.1007/978-3-540-45146-4_27

17. Kocher, P., Jaffe, J., Jun, B.: Differential power analysis. In: Wiener, M. (ed.) CRYPTO 1999. LNCS, vol. 1666, pp. 388–397. Springer, Heidelberg (1999). https://doi.org/10.1007/3-540-48405-1_25

18. Miteloudi, K., Batina, L., Daemen, J., Mentens, N.: ROCKY: rotation countermeasure for the protection of keys and other sensitive data. In: Orailoglu, A., Jung, M., Reichenbach, M. (eds.) SAMOS 2021. LNCS, vol. 13227, pp. 288–299. Springer, Cham (2021). https://doi.org/10.1007/978-3-031-04580-6_19

19. Reparaz, O., et al.: CAPA: the spirit of beaver against physical attacks. In: Shacham, H., Boldyreva, A. (eds.) CRYPTO 2018. LNCS, vol. 10991, pp. 121–151. Springer, Cham (2018). https://doi.org/10.1007/978-3-319-96884-1_5

20. Schneider, T., Moradi, A., Güneysu, T.: ParTI – towards combined hardware countermeasures against side-channel and fault-injection attacks. In: Robshaw, M., Katz, J. (eds.) CRYPTO 2016. LNCS, vol. 9815, pp. 302–332. Springer, Heidelberg (2016). https://doi.org/10.1007/978-3-662-53008-5_11

21. Shahmirzadi, A.R., Rasoolzadeh, S., Moradi, A.: Impeccable circuits II. In: 57th ACM/IEEE Design Automation Conference, DAC 2020, San Francisco, 20–24 July 2020, pp. 1–6. IEEE (2020). https://doi.org/10.1109/DAC18072.2020.9218615

Probabilistic Related-Key Statistical Saturation Cryptanalysis

Muzhou Li[1,4], Nicky Mouha[3], Ling Sun[1,2,4,5], and Meiqin Wang[1,2,4(✉)]

[1] School of Cyber Science and Technology, Shandong University, Qingdao, China
muzhouli@mail.sdu.edu.cn, {lingsun,mqwang}@sdu.edu.cn
[2] Quan Cheng Shandong Laboratory, Jinan, China
[3] Strativia, Largo, MD, USA
nicky@mouha.be
[4] Key Laboratory of Cryptologic Technology and Information Security,
Ministry of Education, Shandong University, Jinan, China
[5] State Key Laboratory of Cryptology, P.O. Box 5159, Beijing 100878, China

Abstract. The related-key statistical saturation (RKSS) attack is a cryptanalysis method proposed by Li *et al.* at FSE 2019. It can be seen as the extension of previous statistical saturation attacks under the related-key setting. The attack takes advantage of a set of plaintexts with some bits fixed, while the other bits take all possible values, and considers the relation between the value distributions of a part of the ciphertext bits generated under related keys. Usually, RKSS distinguishers exploit the property that the value distribution stays invariant under the modification of the key. However, this property can only be deterministically verified if the plaintexts cover all possible values of a selection of bits. In this paper, we propose the *probabilistic RKSS cryptanalysis* which avoids iterating over all non-fixed plaintext bits by applying a statistical method on top of the original RKSS distinguisher. Compared to the RKSS attack, this newly proposed attack has a significantly lower data complexity and has the potential of attacking more rounds. As an illustration, for reduced-round Piccolo, we obtain the best key recovery attacks (considering both pre- and post-whitening keys) on both versions in terms of the number of rounds. Note that these attacks do not threaten the full-round security of Piccolo.

Keywords: Related-Key Statistical Saturation · Piccolo · Statistic

1 Introduction

Integral cryptanalysis is a cryptanalytic method for symmetric-key ciphers. First proposed by Daemen *et al.* as a dedicated attack on the Square cipher [9], the technique was later generalized by Knudsen and Wagner as the integral attack [18]. The integral distinguisher used in such an attack exploits the propagation of well-chosen sets of plaintexts through the cipher. In practice, a part of the plaintext bits is often fixed to some constant while all possible values

© The Author(s), under exclusive license to Springer Nature Switzerland AG 2024
C. Carlet et al. (Eds.): SAC 2023, LNCS 14201, pp. 213–232, 2024.
https://doi.org/10.1007/978-3-031-53368-6_11

are taken for the other bits, and the evolution of the variable bits in the cipher state is tracked. To reduce its data complexity, the statistical integral attack [33] was proposed by Wang *et al.* at FSE 2016. It avoids iterating over all non-fixed plaintext bits by applying a statistical technique on top of the original integral attack. In [13], Dobraunig *et al.* introduced a related-tweak square attack on KIASU-BC that extends the single-key attack by one round.

The statistical saturation attack [7] was proposed by Collard and Standaert. It uses the same set of plaintexts as integral distinguishers, however, it tracks the evolution of a non-uniform value distribution of the ciphertext. At FSE 2019, Li *et al.* introduced the related-key statistical saturation (RKSS) attack [19] for key-alternating ciphers [10]. It also takes advantage of a set of plaintexts with some bits fixed while the others take all possible values, however, it considers the relation between the value distributions of a part of the ciphertext bits generated under related keys. RKSS distinguishers exploit the property that a part of the ciphertexts keeps their value distribution invariant under the modification of the key. However, this property can only be deterministically verified if the plaintexts cover all possible values of a selection of bits.

In this paper, we revisit the RKSS cryptanalysis and propose a new method that can address such limitations with the help of a statistical model. This new method is referred to as *probabilistic RKSS cryptanalysis*. Compared to the original method, the data complexity here can be much smaller with only a small decrease in success probability. An intuitive comparison of these two methods is shown by their applications on Piccolo [29].

We now provide a detailed overview of the contributions of this paper.

Probabilistic RKSS Cryptanalysis. In Sect. 3, we will introduce the probabilistic RKSS cryptanalysis method, which avoids iterating over all non-fixed plaintext bits. In this way, we require less data than the original RKSS method, but the same value distribution property of the original RKSS will not strictly hold.

However, we can still distinguish between a right key guess and a wrong key guess by choosing an appropriate statistic that considers the different distributions in these two cases. First, we recall the value distribution property that the original RKSS method relies on. Let s be the number of plaintext bits that take all possible values while the other bits are fixed. For all these 2^s plaintexts, we encrypt them under related-key pairs and obtain two sets of ciphertexts. Denote t as the number of ciphertext bits whose value distribution is considered here. For any t-bit value of this part, we have the same number of occurrences in these two sets of ciphertexts. When less than 2^s plaintexts are available, the occurrences of each t-bit value may not be the same anymore, but their differences may be small if enough plaintexts are given. Hence, the statistic is constructed by summing all 2^t squared differences of the number of occurrences counted under these two related keys. With the help of Stuart-Maxwell tests for marginal homogeneity [24, 30], we can prove that such a statistic follows a χ^2-distribution with different parameters for right and wrong key guesses. The validity of this statistical model is also confirmed experimentally on a toy cipher.

With this statistical model, the data complexity of the RKSS attack can be reduced from 2^s to

$$N = 2^s - (2^s - 1) \frac{q_{\alpha_1}^{(2^t-1)}}{q_{1-\alpha_0}^{(2^t-1)}},$$

where $q_{\alpha_1}^{(2^t-1)}$ and $q_{1-\alpha_0}^{(2^t-1)}$ represent the quantiles of the central χ^2-distribution with each having a degree of freedom equal to $2^t - 1$. Meanwhile, α_0 (resp. α_1) is the probability of rejecting the right key (resp. of accepting a wrong key). This new attack has a success probability of $\Pr_s = 1 - \alpha_0$. Note that the trade-off between the success probability $\Pr_s$ and the data complexity N allows the attack to cover more rounds than the original RKSS method.

Improved Key Recovery Attacks on Round-Reduced Piccolo with both Whitenings.
Piccolo [29] is a 64-bit ultra-lightweight key-alternating block cipher designed by Shibutani *et al.* at CHES 2011. It is suitable for constrained environments such as RFID tags and sensor nodes. The cipher supports 80-bit and 128-bit keys, denoted as Piccolo-80 and Piccolo-128, respectively.

Since its proposal, many key recovery attacks have been introduced such as (conditional) linear attacks [2], (multidimensional) zero-correlation linear attacks [1,15], meet-in-the-middle attacks [16,21,22,32], and (related-key) impossible differential attacks [4,25,31]. In addition, there are some other results such as biclique attacks [17,34]. However, there is a consensus in the literature that biclique attacks are not a threat to a cipher, as they require an exhaustive search over a reduced number of rounds of the cipher.

From all these attacks, we find that the security resistance of Piccolo is different depending on whether the pre/post-whitening key layers are included or not. Specifically, when both whitenings are considered, the best-known attack on Piccolo-80 is on 8 rounds [2], not including biclique attacks. Meanwhile, the best result on Piccolo-128 with both whitenings is a biclique attack [17]. When including none or only one of these two whitening key layers, the best key recovery attack can cover 14 rounds for Piccolo-80 [21,32] and 18 rounds for Piccolo-128 [21]. This confirms that key whitening may strengthen the security of Piccolo. Thus, we are motivated to investigate its real impact on security, and try to narrow the gap between the cryptanalytic results in the above two cases.

In Sect. 4, we mount several key recovery attacks on both variants of Piccolo using the probabilistic RKSS method. To show the effectiveness of this new method, we also propose attacks using the RKSS method in Sect. 4. All these results are presented in Table 1. Compared to previous results, they are the best key recovery attacks containing both pre- and post-whitening keys on Piccolo.

From Table 1, for 16-round Piccolo-128, we can see that the probabilistic RKSS method needs only 3.44% of the number of plaintexts required in the RKSS attack with only a little decrease in its success probability from 100% to 99%. Moreover, the probabilistic RKSS method can cover one more round than the RKSS method. As for Piccolo-80, the data complexity used in the new method is only 10% of that required in the RKSS method where its success probability is 99%.

Table 1. Comparison of attacks on Piccolo containing both pre- and post-whitening key layers. Time complexities are evaluated in encryption units, while memory costs are evaluated in bits, and #k denotes the number of different keys used.

Cipher	Attacks	Rounds	Data	Time	Memory	#k	Ref.
Piccolo-128	RKSS	16	2^{49}	$2^{114.19}$	2^{38}	2	Sect. 4.2
	Prob. RKSS	16	$2^{44.14}$	$2^{114.18}$	2^{38}	2	Sect. 4.2
	Prob. RKSS	17	$2^{60.14}$	$2^{115.44}$	$2^{67.14}$	2	Sect. 4.3
Piccolo-80	Cond. Linear	8	2^{54}	2^{54}	N.A.	1	[2]
	RKSS	10	2^{41}	$2^{74.49}$	$2^{33.81}$	2	Sect. 4.1
	Prob. RKSS	10	$2^{37.68}$	$2^{74.48}$	$2^{33.81}$	2	Sect. 4.1

2   Preliminaries

Key-alternating ciphers form a significant subset of modern block ciphers, which was introduced by Daemen and Rijmen in [10]. Many block ciphers, including almost all Substitution-Permutation Networks (SPNs) and some Feistel ciphers, belong to this subset [11].

Definition 1 (*Key-Alternating Block Cipher* [10]). *Given an r-round iterative block cipher E, let k_i represent its i-th round key with $1 \leq i \leq r$. If k_i is XORed into the state at the end of the i-th round and there exists a subkey k_0 introduced by XORing with the plaintext before the first round, the block cipher E is a key-alternating block cipher.*

The related-key statistical saturation (RKSS) attack [19] is a new cryptanalytic method for key-alternating ciphers proposed by Li *et al.* at FSE 2019. This method can be regarded as an extension of statistical saturation attack [7] in the related-key setting. As pointed out in [19], this method is also applicable for tweak/tweakey-alternating ciphers, where related-tweak/tweakey are taken into consideration, since tweak/tweakey can be seen as a kind of key. For simplicity, all of these are referred to as RKSS attacks in this paper. The main idea of the RKSS attack is that we fix a part of the plaintext bits and take all possible values for the other bits, and then consider the relation between the value distributions of a part of the ciphertext bits under related-key pairs $(z, z' = z \oplus \Delta z)$, where Δz is a fixed value for all possible values of the key z. To obtain such RKSS distinguishers, Li *et al.* [19] introduced a conditional equivalent property between the KDIB distinguisher [6] and the RKSS distinguisher.

The KDIB technique [6] is another method proposed for key-alternating ciphers, which can be seen as an extension of linear cryptanalysis [23]. Linear cryptanalysis typically uses a linear trail. Denote $\theta = (\theta_0, \theta_1, \cdots, \theta_r)$ as an r-round linear trail, where θ_{i-1} is the input mask of round i ($1 \leq i \leq r$) and θ_i is the output mask. Its bias ε_θ is related to the unknown key z. For key-alternating ciphers, only the sign of ε_θ is affected by z. A linear hull (u, w) consists of all trails satisfying $u = \theta_0$ and $w = \theta_r$ [27], whose bias is evaluated by summing all biases of these trails under the same key z. Hence, the bias of a linear hull can be invariant if it is evaluated under related-key pairs (z, z') fulfilling some specific key difference Δz. This is the fact that the KDIB distinguisher exploits.

To explain the conditional equivalent property between KDIB and RKSS distinguishers, we adopt the same notation used in [19]. Denote $\mathbb{F}_2^n$ as the space of n-dimensional binary vectors over $\mathbb{F}_2 = \{0, 1\}$. Let $H : \mathbb{F}_2^n \times \mathbb{F}_2^k \to \mathbb{F}_2^n$ be the target block cipher with block size n and key size k. The n-bit input of H is split into two parts (x, y), where x is the part fixed and y is the part taking all possible values. Note that these two parts can be composed of arbitrary input bits. Similarly, the output of H is also divided into two parts $(H_1(x, y, z), H_2(x, y, z))$ and only the value distribution of $H_1(x, y, z)$ is considered. Thus, we have

$$H : \mathbb{F}_2^r \times \mathbb{F}_2^s \times \mathbb{F}_2^k \to \mathbb{F}_2^t \times \mathbb{F}_2^u, \ H(x, y, z) = (H_1(x, y, z), H_2(x, y, z)).$$

Fixing x to a constant value I and only focusing on the H_1 part of the output, we can obtain the function $T_I : \mathbb{F}_2^s \times \mathbb{F}_2^k \to \mathbb{F}_2^t$, $T_I(y, z) = H_1(I, y, z)$. In an RKSS distinguisher, we will consider the relation between the value distributions of $T_I(y, z)$ and $T_I(y, z')$ after encrypting all possible values of y.

Given the above notation, the conditional equivalent property between the KDIB and the RKSS distinguishers can be described in Theorem 1. Once the KDIB distinguisher is found, an RKSS distinguisher covering the same rounds can also be obtained using Theorem 1.

Theorem 1 *(Conditional Equivalent Property* [19]). *Let (Γ, Λ) be the linear hull of the target block cipher with $\Gamma = (\Gamma_{in}, 0)$ and $\Lambda = (\Lambda_{out}, 0)$, where $\Gamma_{in} \in \mathbb{F}_2^r$ and $\Lambda_{out} \in \mathbb{F}_2^t \setminus \{0\}$. Given a fixed Δz, if for all possible mask pairs $(\Gamma_{in}, \Lambda_{out})$, the bias is invariant under related-key pairs $(z, z' = z \oplus \Delta z)$, $T_I(y, z)$ will have the same value distribution as $T_I(y, z')$ when y takes all possible values and vice versa. In other words, for any $c \in \mathbb{F}_2^t$, we have $\#\{y \in \mathbb{F}_2^s \mid T_I(y, z) = c\} = \#\{y \in \mathbb{F}_2^s \mid T_I(y, z') = c\}$. Note that this holds for any $I \in \mathbb{F}_2^r$.*

Note that in Theorem 1, the restriction to masks of the form $(\Gamma_{in}, 0)$ and $(\Lambda_{out}, 0)$, where the last bits are fixed to zeros, is solely for the simplicity of notation. As pointed out in [19], the positions of the zero bits do not affect the applicability of this property.

From Theorem 1, we can see that the RKSS distinguisher exploits the property that the value distribution of some ciphertext bits stays invariant under the modification of the key. When mounting the RKSS key recovery attack, we have to traverse all possible values of y under a fixed value of x, and ask for ciphertexts under z and z'. Thus, we can observe whether $T_I(y, z)$ has the same value distribution with $T_I(y, z')$ after guessing the corresponding key bits. If so, the guessed key bits will be taken as the right key bits. Otherwise, they will be discarded. According to Theorem 1, for a right key guess, $T_I(y, z)$ always has the same value distribution with $T_I(y, z')$. Hence, the probability of rejecting the right key α_0 is zero. As for the probability of accepting a wrong key α_1, they proved that $\log_2(\alpha_1)$ is no more than $(2^t - 1 - t) 2^{s+1} - 2^{s(2^t-1)/2}$, which is extremely small. For instance, when Li *et al.* [19] attacked 10-round QARMA-64 [3] with $s = 56$ and $t = 4$, it was found that $\log_2(\alpha_1) \leq -2.7 \times 10^{126}$, which implies that $\alpha_1 \approx 0$.

3 Probabilistic Related-Key Statistical Saturation Attack

3.1 Introducing a Statistical Model into RKSS Cryptanalysis

In this subsection, we adopt the notation introduced in Sect. 2. Let q_j (resp. q'_j) denote the probability that $T_I(y, z) = j$ (resp. $T_I(y, z') = j$) when iterating over all possible values of $y \in \mathbb{F}_2^s$. Thus, $\sum_{j=0}^{2^t-1} q_j = 1$ and $\sum_{j=0}^{2^t-1} q'_j = 1$. Note that in the RKSS attack, q_j and q'_j can take various values for different wrong key candidates z and z', while $q_j = q'_j$ holds for any j for a right key guess. Let $\chi^2(l, \lambda)$ represent the noncentral χ^2-distribution with degree of freedom l and noncentrality parameter λ. For an RKSS distinguisher, we can obtain Lemma 1 for both wrong and right key guesses, according to Stuart-Maxwell [24,30] tests for marginal homogeneity. Due to the limit of paper length, proof of Lemma 1 is shown in the full version [20].

Lemma 1. *When 2^s is sufficiently large, for a wrong key guess, the statistic* $\gamma = \sum_{j=0}^{2^t-1} \frac{(2^s q_j - 2^s q'_j)^2}{2^s q_j + 2^s q'_j}$ *approximately follows* $\chi^2(2^t - 1, 0)$. *For the right key guess, the statistic* $\gamma = 0$.

The only way to reduce the data complexity of an RKSS attack is to reduce the number of y that are chosen. However, the same value distribution property under a right key guess will not hold if we choose some random values for y. The advantage is that we can distinguish a right key guess from a wrong one by constructing a statistic with the information of similar frequencies of each possible output under related-key pairs (z, z'), if a considerable number of distinct values of plaintexts are reachable. This new kind of RKSS attack with reduced data complexity will be referred to as a *probabilistic RKSS* attack hereafter.

Assume that we have obtained two independent randomly chosen distinct plaintext sets S and S' with the same size N. All plaintexts share the same fixed I. For each $y \in S$ (resp. $y' \in S'$), we can get a t-bit value $T_I(y, z)$ (resp. $T_I(y', z')$) that is computed under z (resp. z'). Then we respectively add one to the counter $V[j_1]$ and $V'[j_2]$, where $j_1 = T_I(y, z)$ and $j_2 = T_I(y', z')$. After traversing all these N values of y and N values of y', we can construct an efficient distinguisher by investigating the distribution of the following statistic

$$\mathcal{C} = \sum_{j=0}^{2^t-1} \frac{(V[j] - V'[j])^2}{2N \cdot 2^{-t}},$$

where $V[j] = \#\{y \in S \mid T_I(y, z) = j\}$ and $V'[j] = \#\{y' \in S' \mid T_I(y', z') = j\}$.

This statistic $\mathcal{C}$ considers different distributions determined by whether we are dealing with an actual cipher (right key guess) or a random permutation (wrong key guess). These two distributions of $\mathcal{C}$ are derived under Hypothesis 1. The validity of this hypothesis has been verified experimentally in [20].

Hypothesis 1. *For any $0 \leq i \leq 2^t - 1$, $0 \leq j \leq 2^t - 1$, we assume that $q_i q_j \approx (2^{-t})^2$, $q_i' q_j' \approx (2^{-t})^2$, and $q_i + q_j' \approx 2 \cdot 2^{-t}$ hold when 2^s is sufficiently large[1].*

Proposition 1. *Denote $\mathcal{C}_{random}$ as the statistic $\mathcal{C}$ for a wrong key guess and $\mathcal{C}_{cipher}$ as the statistic $\mathcal{C}$ for the right key guess. Under Hypothesis 1, for sufficiently large N, the statistic*

$$\frac{2^s - 1}{2^s - N} \mathcal{C}_{cipher} \sim \chi^2 \left(2^t - 1, 0\right),$$

while the statistic

$$\mathcal{C}_{random} \sim \chi^2 \left(2^t - 1, 0\right).$$

To prove this proposition, we have to recall the following lemma.

Lemma 2. *(See [12]) Let $\boldsymbol{X} = (X_1, X_2, \cdots, X_d)^T$ be a d-dimensional statistic vector that follows the multivariate normal distribution with expectation $\boldsymbol{\mu}$ and covariance matrix $\boldsymbol{\Sigma}$, where $\boldsymbol{\Sigma}$ is a symmetric matrix of rank $r \leq d$. If $\boldsymbol{\Sigma}^2 = \boldsymbol{\Sigma}$ and $\boldsymbol{\Sigma}\boldsymbol{\mu} = \boldsymbol{\mu}$, we have $\boldsymbol{X}^T \boldsymbol{X} \sim \chi^2 \left(r, \boldsymbol{\mu}^T \boldsymbol{\mu}\right)$.*

With Hypothesis 1 and Lemmas 1 and 2, we can prove Proposition 1 as follows. Due to the limit of paper length, we only show the sketch of our proof. Details are shown in the full version [20].

Proof. (Sketch) Recall that when mounting probabilistic RKSS attacks, the counters $V[T_I(y, z)]$ and $V'[T_I(y', z')]$ are generated by encrypting two independently chosen values y and y' under z and z'. Therefore, these two counters are independent of each other.

Since we choose distinct values of y (sampling without replacement), the statistic vector $(V[0], V[1], \cdots, V[2^t - 1])$ follows a multivariate hypergeometric distribution with parameters $(\boldsymbol{K}, 2^s, N)$ where $\boldsymbol{K} = (Nq_0, Nq_1, \cdots, Nq_{2^t-1})$. Similarly, the vector $(V'[0], V'[1], \cdots, V'[2^t - 1])$ also follows a multivariate hypergeometric distribution however the parameters are $(\boldsymbol{K}', 2^s, N)$ where $\boldsymbol{K}' = (Nq_0', Nq_1', \cdots, Nq_{2^t-1}')$. When N is sufficiently large, both hypergeometric distributions can be approximated into multivariate normal ones.

For any $0 \leq j \leq 2^t - 1$, define $\widetilde{X}_j = V[j] - V'[j]$. Then we have that $\widetilde{\boldsymbol{X}} = (\widetilde{X}_0, \widetilde{X}_1, \cdots, \widetilde{X}_{2^t-1})$ also follows a multivariate normal distribution. Since expectation of $\widetilde{X}_j$ is $\mathbf{E}(V[j] - V'[j]) = \mathbf{E}(V[j]) - \mathbf{E}(V'[j]) = Nq_j - Nq_j'$, the expectation of $\widetilde{\boldsymbol{X}}$ can be obtained. The covariance between $\widetilde{X}_i$ and $\widetilde{X}_j$ can be computed by $\mathbf{Cov}(\widetilde{X}_i, \widetilde{X}_j) = \mathbf{Cov}(V[i], V[j]) + \mathbf{Cov}(V'[i], V'[j])$.

Let $X_j = \widetilde{X}_j / \sqrt{2N2^{-t}\frac{2^s - N}{2^s - 1}}$. Then $\boldsymbol{X} = \widetilde{\boldsymbol{X}} / \sqrt{2N2^{-t}\frac{2^s - N}{2^s - 1}}$ also follows a multivariate normal distribution with expectation $\boldsymbol{\mu} = (\mu_0, \mu_1, \cdots, \mu_{2^t-1})$ where

$$\mu_j = \mathbf{E}(\widetilde{X}_j) / \sqrt{2N2^{-t}\frac{2^s - N}{2^s - 1}} = (Nq_j - Nq_j') / \sqrt{2N2^{-t}\frac{2^s - N}{2^s - 1}},$$

---

[1] In our experimental verification, $s = 12$ and it is enough to ensure the validity of this hypothesis, as well as other assumptions used in this paper.

and covariance matrix $\boldsymbol{\Sigma}$ where

$$\boldsymbol{\Sigma}_{i,i} = \frac{q_i(1 - q_i) + q_i'(1 - q_i')}{2 \cdot 2^{-t}}, \quad \boldsymbol{\Sigma}_{i,j} = \frac{-q_i q_j - q_i' q_j'}{2 \cdot 2^{-t}}.$$

Due to Hypothesis 1, $\boldsymbol{\Sigma}_{i,i} \approx 1 - 2^{-t}$ and $\boldsymbol{\Sigma}_{i,j} \approx -2^{-t}$. Notice that $\boldsymbol{\Sigma}$ is symmetric and its rank is $2^t - 1$. It is easy to verify that $\boldsymbol{\Sigma}^2 = \boldsymbol{\Sigma}$ and $\boldsymbol{\Sigma}\boldsymbol{\mu} = \boldsymbol{\mu}$. According to Lemma 2, we can conclude that

$$\frac{2^s - 1}{2^s - N} \sum_{j=0}^{2^t-1} \frac{(V[j] - V'[j])^2}{2N2^{-t}} \sim \chi^2(2^t - 1, \lambda) \text{ with } \lambda = \frac{2^s - 1}{2^s - N} \sum_{j=0}^{2^t-1} \frac{(Nq_j - Nq_j')^2}{2N2^{-t}}.$$

Under Hypothesis 1, γ in Lemma 1 can be approximated as

$$\gamma \approx \sum_{j=0}^{2^t-1} \frac{(2^s q_j - 2^s q_j')^2}{2 \cdot 2^s \cdot 2^{-t}}$$

and then $\lambda \approx \frac{2^s-1}{2^s-N} \frac{N}{2^s} \gamma$. Thus, for a right key guess, $\lambda = 0$ since $\gamma = 0$. In other words,

$$\frac{2^s - 1}{2^s - N} \mathcal{C}_{cipher} \sim \chi^2 \left(2^t - 1, 0\right).$$

While for a wrong key guess, $\frac{2^s}{N} \frac{2^s-N}{2^s-1} \lambda \sim \chi^2(2^t - 1, 0)$ according to Lemma 1. Thus, the distribution of $\mathcal{C}_{random}$ can be obtained with the characteristic functions of χ^2-distributions.   □

To decide whether the obtained statistic $\mathcal{C}$ is computed from the *cipher* (a *right key* guess) or the *random permutation* (a *wrong key* guess), we have to perform a statistic test. In this test, we compare $\mathcal{C}$ to a threshold value τ. If $\mathcal{C} \leq \tau$, we conclude that $\mathcal{C}$ is obtained from the cipher; otherwise, it is from a random permutation. The data complexity needed to perform the statistic test and the threshold value τ can be computed as follows, given error probabilities. Due to the limit of paper length, proof of Corollary 1 is shown in the full version [20].

Corollary 1. *Denote α_0 as the probability of rejecting the right key and α_1 as the probability of accepting a wrong key. Under the assumption of Proposition 1, the number of distinct plaintexts encrypted under a single key is*

$$N = 2^s - (2^s - 1) \frac{q_{\alpha_1}^{(2^t-1)}}{q_{1-\alpha_0}^{(2^t-1)}},$$

and the threshold value is $\tau = q_{\alpha_1}^{(2^t-1)} = \frac{2^s-N}{2^s-1} q_{1-\alpha_0}^{(2^t-1)}$, *where* $q_{\alpha_1}^{(2^t-1)}$ *and* $q_{1-\alpha_0}^{(2^t-1)}$ *are the respective quantiles of* $\chi^2(2^t - 1, 0)$.

According to Corollary 1, we can see that the data encrypted under a single key in the probabilistic RKSS attack is less than 2^s, which is the data collected under a single key of the original RKSS attack. In other words, our newly proposed method needs less data than the original one. Meanwhile, the success probability of this attack is $\Pr_s = 1 - \alpha_0$. Note that such a trade-off between $\Pr_s$ and N can make it possible to mount attacks that cover more rounds than the original RKSS method. Further comparisons between these two methods are shown in the full version [20].

3.2 Experimental Verification of the Statistical Model

To verify the theoretical model, we implement a distinguishing attack on a mini version of an SPN cipher denoted as SmallSPN (a variant of Mini-AES [28]).[2]

SmallSPN is a 20-round key-alternating cipher with a block size of 16 bits. Its round function contains four operations, $i.e.$, SB, SR, MC, and AK. Additionally, there is another AK operation before the first round. The 16-bit plaintext $P = P_0||P_1||P_2||P_3$ is arranged into a 2×2 matrix $\begin{bmatrix} P_0 & P_1 \\ P_2 & P_3 \end{bmatrix}$ and SB uses 4-bit S-box in QARMA-64 [3]. SR is the operation interchanging P_2 and P_3. The matrix used in MC is $\begin{bmatrix} 0 & 1 \\ 1 & 1 \end{bmatrix}$. Denote rk^i as the round key in the i-th round, $0 \le i \le 20$, and rk^i_j is the j-th nibble of rk^i where $0 \le j \le 3$. Each subkey rk^i will be XORed with the nibbles in AK operations, all of which are chosen uniformly at random.

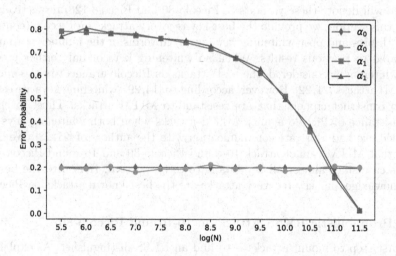

Fig. 1. Experimental results related to the statistical model using SmallSPN.

The 20-round RKSS distinguisher used here can be described as follows: when we fix P_3 and iterate over all 2^{12} possible values of $P_0||P_1||P_2$, the value

---

[2] SmallSPN has a structure that is similar to Mini-AES, but they have a different number of rounds, S-box, linear matrix, and key schedule.

distributions of C_3 obtained under K and C_3' obtained under K' will be the same. K' and K only have non-zero differences on rk_0^0, rk_1^0, rk_2^0, rk_1^1, rk_2^1, rk_3^1, rk_1^2, rk_3^2, rk_3^3, rk_1^{18}, rk_0^{19}, rk_3^{18}, rk_0^{20}, rk_1^{20}, and rk_2^{20}. Now we mount the probabilistic RKSS attack using the statistical model described in Proposition 1 where $s = 12$ and $t = 4$. Setting $\alpha_0 = 0.2$ and choosing different values for N, we can obtain α_1 and τ according to Corollary 1. In each experiment, we independently and randomly collect two plaintext sets with size N, where all plaintexts share the same fixed I, and query their ciphertexts generated with SmallSPN. After computing the statistic $\mathcal{C}$ and comparing it with τ, we can decide whether we are facing the real cipher. By launching this experiment 1000 times, we can obtain the empirical error probability $\hat{\alpha_0}$. Similarly, if we generate these ciphertexts with random permutations, we can obtain the empirical error probability $\hat{\alpha_1}$ following the same procedure. Thereafter, we can compare these error probabilities with theoretical ones α_0 and α_1, which is illustrated in Fig. 1. From Fig. 1, we can see that the test results for error probabilities are in good accordance with those for the theoretical model. Thus, our statistical model is accurately constructed.

4 Improved Key Recovery Attacks on Piccolo Considering Pre- And Post-whitening

At CHES 2011, Piccolo was proposed by Shibutani *et al.* [29] as a lightweight block cipher with a 64-bit block size. The key size can be either 80 or 128 bits, and we will denote these variants as Piccolo-80 and Piccolo-128, respectively.

In this section, we provide the best key recovery attacks on Piccolo (containing both pre- and post-whitening key layers) in terms of the number of rounds, compared to previous results. When no whitening keys or only either pre- or post-whitening is considered, the best attacks on Piccolo are meet-in-the-middle (MITM) attacks [21,22]. However, according to [14,29], whitening keys are essential to construct ciphers that are resistant to MITM attacks. Thus, to check the resistance of Piccolo against MITM attacks when both whitening keys are included, we had a private communication with the authors of [21,22]. We both agree that MITM cannot attack 10-round Piccolo-80 and 16-round Piccolo-128 in this case since almost all key bits have to be guessed. Hence, to the best of our knowledge, our key recovery attacks are the best-known attacks on Piccolo.

4.1 Probabilistic RKSS Attack on 10-Round Piccolo-80

The first step to mount attacks is to find an RKSS distinguisher. As explained in Sect. 2, Li *et al.* [19] constructed a search algorithm for KDIB distinguishers, and then RKSS distinguishers covering the same rounds can be obtained using Theorem 1. To make our paper self-contained, we briefly recall the principle of this automatic search algorithm. For more details, we refer to [19].

Their search algorithm is based on STP,[3] which is a Boolean Satisfiability Problem (SAT) [8]/Satisfiability Modulo Theories (SMT) problem [5] solver. The

---

[3] http://stp.github.io/.

application of STP as an automatic search tool for differential cryptanalysis was first suggested by Mouha and Preneel in [26]. It takes a set of equations as input and decides whether or not they have a valid solution. Therefore, when using STP to find KDIB distinguishers, we have to build some equations that describe the propagation properties of each operation. More specifically, for operations in the round function, the word-level mask propagation properties should be described; while for each operation in the key schedule, we have to describe its bit-level difference propagation property. Moreover, there are also some equations required to describe the relation between the masks and the key difference. Inserting all these equations into STP, we can obtain a KDIB distinguisher for a fixed number of rounds or conclude that no KDIB distinguishers exist.

Like other related-key attacks, the starting round of the distinguisher has an impact on the length of the distinguisher. Using this automatic search algorithm, we found an 8-round KDIB distinguisher with the pre-whitening key layer starting from the third round. Detailed distinguisher is shown in the full version [20]. The key difference of this distinguisher is $\Delta k_4[1] = \beta$ which can be any non-zero value in $\mathbb{F}_2^4$. Denote the 16-bit value X as $X = X[0]||X[1]||X[2]||X[3]$ with $X[i] \in \mathbb{F}_2^4$, and let $X[i,j]$ represents $X[i]||X[j]$. Combining the 8-round KDIB distinguisher with Theorem 1 leads to the following RKSS distinguisher.

Corollary 2. *With the notation of Fig. 2, for the 8-round Piccolo-80 including pre-whitening key layer, when we take all 2^{40} plaintexts with $P_0[0,2,3]||P_2[0,2,3]$ fixed, the value distribution of the 12-bit value $W_1[0,2,3] \oplus k_2[0,2,3]$ stays invariant under (K, K'), where K and K' only differ at $k_4[1]$.*

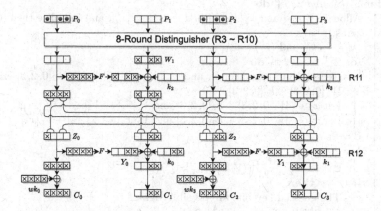

Fig. 2. Probabilistic RKSS attack on 10-round Piccolo-80 with full whitening, where ● are active nibbles and × are nibbles that we need to know in the key recovery procedure.

Using this distinguisher, a probabilistic key recovery attack on 10-round Piccolo-80 can be carried out by adding two rounds and the post-whitening key layer at the end. Algorithm 1 and Fig. 2 show the details of this attack. As usual, we collect N plaintexts P with $P_0[0,2,3]$ and $P_2[0,2,3]$ fixed. For each plaintext, we can query its corresponding ciphertext. Since wk_2 and wk_3 have been guessed, we can compute x_1 and increase $V_1[x_1]$ by one. With a similar procedure, another counter V_1' can be obtained from another N plaintexts P' where $P_0'[0,2,3] = P_0[0,2,3]$ and $P_2'[0,2,3] = P_2[0,2,3]$. With another guess of k_0^R and k_1^L, we can obtain the counters V_2 and V_2' from V_1 and V_1', respectively. Using the statistical model proposed in Sect. 3, we can get the right key after checking its validity with two new plaintext-ciphertext pairs.

Algorithm 1: Key recovery attack procedure of 10-round Piccolo-80 containing both pre- and post-whitening keys.

---

1   **for** 2^{16} wk_2 and 2^{16} wk_3 **do**

2   Allocate and initialize two arrays $V_1[x_1]$ and $V_1'[x_1']$ with $|x_1| = 28 = |x_1'|$;

3      $wk_2' = wk_2 \oplus 0x0\beta00$ and $wk_3' = wk_3$;

4   **for** N plaintexts P with $P_0[0,2,3]$ and $P_2[0,2,3]$ fixed **do**

5   Query the ciphertexts C under K;

6   Decrypt C_0, C_2 to get $Y_0[2,3]$, $Z_0[0]$, $Y_1[0,1]$ and $Z_2[2,3]$;

7   Let $x_1 \leftarrow Z_0[0]||(Y_0[2,3] \oplus C_1[2,3])||Z_2[2,3]||(Y_1[0,1] \oplus C_3[0,1])$ and $V_1[x_1] \leftarrow V_1[x_1] + 1$;

8   **for** N plaintexts P' with $P_0'[0,2,3] = P_0[0,2,3]$ and $P_2'[0,2,3] = P_2[0,2,3]$ **do**

9   Query the ciphertexts C' under K';

10   Decrypt C_0', C_2' to get $Y_0'[2,3]$, $Z_0'[0]$, $Y_1'[0,1]$ and $Z_2'[2,3]$;

11   Let $x_1' \leftarrow Z_0'[0]||(Y_0'[2,3] \oplus C_1'[2,3])||Z_2'[2,3]||(Y_1'[0,1] \oplus C_3'[0,1])$ and $V_1'[x_1'] \leftarrow V_1'[x_1'] + 1$;

12   **for** 2^8 k_0^R and 2^8 k_1^L **do**

13   Allocate $V_2[x_2]$ and $V_2'[x_2']$ with $|x_2| = 12 = |x_2'|$, and initialize them to zeros;

14          $(k_0')^R = k_0^R$ and $(k_1')^L = k_1^L$;

15   **for** 2^{28} x_1 and x_1' **do**

16   Decrypt half-round for x_1 and x_1' to get $W_1[0,2,3] \oplus k_2[0,2,3]$ and $W_1'[0,2,3] \oplus k_2'[0,2,3]$;

17   Let $x_2 \leftarrow W_1[0,2,3] \oplus k_2[0,2,3]$ and $V_2[x_2] \leftarrow V_2[x_2] + V_1[x_1]$;

18   Let $x_2' \leftarrow W_1'[0,2,3] \oplus k_2'[0,2,3]$ and $V_2'[x_2'] \leftarrow V_2'[x_2'] + V_1'[x_1']$;

19          $\mathcal{C} = 0$;

20   **for** 2^{12} x **do**

21             $\mathcal{C} \leftarrow \mathcal{C} + \sum_{x=0}^{2^{12}-1} \left((V_2[x] - V_2'[x])^2/(2N \cdot 2^{-12}) \right)$;

22   **if** $\mathcal{C} \leq \tau$ **then**

23   The guessed key bits are possibly right;

24   **for** 2^{16} k_2, 2^8 k_0^L and 2^8 k_1^R **do**

25   Use two plaintext-ciphertext pairs to check if they are right;

Suppose that one memory access to an array of size 2^{28} costs less than one encryption of 10-round Piccolo-80. Then, the time complexity of this key recovery attack is at most $T = 2^{32} N \cdot 2 \cdot (1+1) + 2^{32} \cdot 2^{16} \cdot 2^{28} \cdot 2 \cdot (1/2) \cdot (1/10) + 2 \cdot 2^{80} \alpha_1$, where N can be computed using Corollary 1 after choosing the values of α_0 and α_1. Here, we set $\alpha_0 = 0.01$ and $\alpha_1 = 2^{-7.16}$. In this way, $N \approx 2^{36.68}$, $\tau \approx 2^{11.92}$. Hence, the data complexity is $D = 2N \approx 2^{37.68}$ chosen plaintext-ciphertext pairs, while the time complexity is $T = 2^{74.48}$ 10-round encryptions. The memory requirements are $M = 2 \cdot 2^{28} \cdot 28 \approx 2^{33.81}$ bits needed for arrays.

To show the advantages of our newly proposed method, we also give the complexity of the original RKSS attack using the same distinguisher. Since we have to iterate over all possible values of $P_0[1]\|P_1\|P_2[1]\|P_3$ in the original RKSS attack, the data complexity will be $\tilde{D} = 2^{41}$ chosen plaintext-ciphertext pairs. The time complexity can be computed as before except that it is 2^{32} rather than $2^{80}\alpha_1$ and $N = 2^{40}$, which is $\tilde{T} = 2^{74.49}$ times a 10-round encryption. The memory requirement is $\tilde{M} = M$. As we can see, $D < \tilde{D}$. More precisely, $D = 10\% \times \tilde{D}$.

4.2 Probabilistic RKSS Attack on 16-Round Piccolo-128

In this subsection, we provide a probabilistic RKSS key recovery attack on 16-round Piccolo-128 containing both pre- and post-whitening layers. This attack is based on the 11-round RKSS distinguisher starting from the 14-th round described in Corollary 3.

Corollary 3. *With the notation of Fig. 3, for the 11-round Piccolo-128, when we take all 2^{48} input values of 14-th round with $X_0[0,1]\|X_2[2,3]$ fixed, the value distribution of the 16-bit value $W_3 \oplus k_3$ stays invariant under (K, K'), where K and K' only differ at $k_0[2,3] = \beta \in \mathbb{F}_2^8 \backslash \{0\}$.*

The probabilistic RKSS attack on 16-round Piccolo-128 can be mounted by adding the pre-whitening key layer before the distinguisher and five rounds, as well as the post-whitening key layer at the end. The detailed key recovery procedure is illustrated in Fig. 3 and described in Algorithm 2. One thing we should mention here is that to get the same value distribution property, we have to encrypt two independent data sets with $X_0[0,1]$ and $X_2[2,3]$ fixed under related keys. Since $wk_1[2,3] = k_0[2,3]$ has a non-zero known difference β, we can obtain the same fixed $X_2[2,3]$ by setting $P'[2,3] = P[2,3] \oplus \beta$.

Suppose that one memory access to an array of size 2^{32} costs less than one encryption of 16-round Piccolo-128. Then, the time complexity of this key recovery attack can be computed as $T = 2^{64}N \cdot 2 \cdot (1 + 4/16 + 1) + 2^{64} \cdot 2^{16} \cdot 2^{32} \cdot 2 \cdot (1/2) \cdot (1/16) + 2 \cdot 2^{128}\alpha_1$. By setting $\alpha_0 = 0.01$ and $\alpha_1 = 2^{-14.89}$, we can obtain $N \approx 2^{43.14}$ with $\tau \approx 2^{15.97}$ according to Corollary 1. Thus, the data complexity is $D \approx 2^{44.14}$ chosen plaintext-ciphertext pairs, while the time complexity is $T \approx 2^{114.18}$ 16-round encryptions. The memory requirements are $M = 2 \cdot 2^{32} \cdot 32 = 2^{38}$ bits needed for these arrays.

Compared to the RKSS key recovery attack using the same distinguisher, which needs $\tilde{D} = 2^{49}$ chosen plaintext-ciphertext pairs and $\tilde{T} \approx 2^{114.19}$ 16-round encryptions, the probabilistic RKSS method performs much better than the original one. Specifically, $D = 3.44\% \times \tilde{D}$.

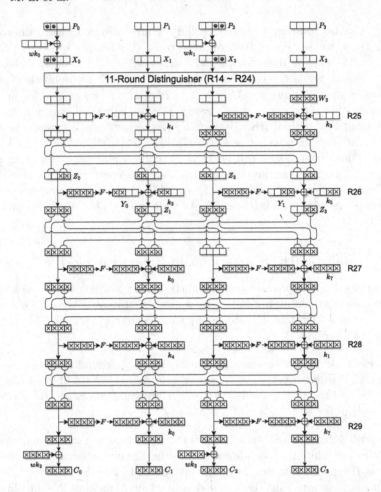

Fig. 3. Probabilistic RKSS attack on 16-round Piccolo-128 with full whitening, where • are active nibbles and × are nibbles that we need to know in the key recovery procedure.

4.3   Probabilistic RKSS Attack on 17-Round Piccolo-128

Using the same distinguisher introduced in Corollary 3, we can mount a 17-round key recovery attack on Piccolo-128 by adding an extra round before it. This key recovery attack is the best one on Piccolo-128 considering both pre- and post-whitening keys in terms of the number of rounds, compared to previous known results.

Due to Corollary 3, to guarantee that $W_3 \oplus k_3$ has the same value distribution with $W_3' \oplus k_3'$, we need to iterate over all possible values of the input of 14-th round $X = X_0 \| X_1 \| X_2 \| X_3$ with $X_0[0, 1] \| X_2[2, 3]$ fixed, which is equivalent to all possible values of $U = U_0 \| U_1 \| U_2 \| U_3$ with U_1 fixed (See Fig. 4). In other words, $s = 48$ and $t = 16$ here. Under $\alpha_0 = 0.01$ and $\alpha_1 = 2^{-14.89}$, we need

---

Algorithm 2: Key recovery attack procedure of 16-round Piccolo-128 with both pre- and post-whitening keys.

---

1 **for** 2^{16} k_4, 2^{16} k_7, 2^{16} k_0 and 2^{16} k_1 **do**
2   $\quad wk_2 = k_4^L \| k_7^R$ and $wk_3 = k_7^L \| k_4^R$;
3   $\quad wk_2' = wk_2$, $wk_3' = wk_3$, $k_4' = k_4$, $k_7' = k_7$, $k_0' = k_0 \oplus 0x00\beta$ and $k_1' = k_1$;
4   $\quad$ Allocate and initialize two arrays $V_1[x_1]$ and $V_1'[x_1']$ with $|x_1| = 32 = |x_1'|$;
5   $\quad$ **for** N plaintexts P with $P_0[0,1]$ and $P_2[2,3]$ fixed **do**
6   $\quad\quad$ Query the ciphertext C for P under K;
7   $\quad\quad$ Decrypt C to get $Z_0[2,3]$, $Z_1[0,1]$, $Z_2[0,1]$, $Z_3[2,3]$, $Y_0[0,1]$ and $Y_1[2,3]$;
8   $\quad\quad$ Let $x_1 \leftarrow Z_0[2,3]\|(Z_1[0,1]\oplus Y_0[0,1])\|Z_2[0,1]\|(Z_3[2,3]\oplus Y_1[2,3])$ and $V_1[x_1] \leftarrow V_1[x_1] + 1$;
9   $\quad$ **for** N plaintexts P' with $P_0'[0,1] = P_0[0,1]$ and $P_2'[2,3] = P_2[2,3] \oplus \beta$ **do**
10 $\quad\quad$ Decrypt C' to get $Z_0'[2,3]$, $Z_1'[0,1]$, $Z_2'[0,1]$, $Z_3'[2,3]$, $Y_0'[0,1]$ and $Y_1'[2,3]$;
11 $\quad\quad$ Let $x_1' \leftarrow Z_0'[2,3]\|(Z_1'[0,1]\oplus Y_0'[0,1])\|Z_2'[0,1]\|(Z_3'[2,3]\oplus Y_1'[2,3])$ and $V_1'[x_1'] \leftarrow V_1'[x_1'] + 1$;
12 $\quad$ **for** 2^8 k_2^L and 2^8 k_5^R **do**
13 $\quad\quad$ $(k_2')^L = k_2^L$ and $(k_5')^R = k_5^R$;
14 $\quad\quad$ Allocate and initialize two arrays $V_2[x_2]$ and $V_2'[x_2']$ with $|x_2| = 16 = |x_2'|$;
15 $\quad\quad$ **for** 2^{32} x_1 and x_1' **do**
16 $\quad\quad\quad$ Decrypt half-round for x_1 and x_1' to get $W_3 \oplus k_3$ and $W_3' \oplus k_3'$;
17 $\quad\quad\quad$ Let $x_2 \leftarrow W_3 \oplus k_3$, and $V_2[x_2] \leftarrow V_2[x_2] + V_1[x_1]$;
18 $\quad\quad\quad$ Let $x_2' \leftarrow W_3' \oplus k_3'$, and $V_2'[x_2'] \leftarrow V_2'[x_2'] + V_1'[x_1']$;
19 $\quad\quad$ $\mathcal{C} = 0$;
20 $\quad\quad$ **for** 2^{16} x **do**
21 $\quad\quad\quad$ $\mathcal{C} \leftarrow \mathcal{C} + \sum_{x=0}^{2^{16}-1} \left((V_2[x] - V_2'[x])^2/(2N \cdot 2^{-16})\right)$;
22 $\quad\quad$ **if** $\mathcal{C} \leq \tau$ **then**
23 $\quad\quad\quad$ The guessed key bits are possibly right;
24 $\quad\quad\quad$ **for** 2^8 k_2^R, 2^{16} k_3, 2^8 k_5^L and 2^{16} k_6 **do**
25 $\quad\quad\quad\quad$ Use two plaintext-ciphertext pairs to check if they are right;

$N \approx 2^{43.14}$ U with the same U_1 and the threshold value $\tau \approx 2^{15.97}$. To generate these N values of U, we traverse all possible values of P_0 and P_2, randomly choose $2^{11.14}$ values for P_3, and set $P_2 = F(P_0 \oplus wk_0)$ after guessing wk_0. U' can be obtained similarly. All key bits can then be recovered following Algorithm 3.

Suppose that one memory access to an array of size 2^{32} or of size $2^{59.14}$ costs less than one encryption of 17-round Piccolo-128. Then, the time complexity of this attack is $T = 2^{59.14} \cdot 2 + 2^{59.14} \cdot 4 + 2^{64} \cdot 2^{43.14} \cdot 4 + 2^{64} \cdot 2^{43.14} \cdot 2 \cdot (4/17+1) + 2^{64} \cdot 2^{16} \cdot 2^{32} \cdot 2 \cdot (1/2) \cdot (1/17) + 2 \cdot 2^{128}\alpha_1 \approx 2^{115.44}$ 17-round encryptions. The data complexity is $D = 2 \cdot 2^{16} N \approx 2^{60.14}$ chosen plaintext-ciphertext pairs. The dominant memory requirements are to store these plaintext-ciphertext pairs, about $M = 4 \cdot 2^{59.14} \cdot 64 = 2^{67.14}$ bits are needed for these arrays.

To show the advantage of this new method, we also try to mount an RKSS attack based on the same distinguisher. However, we have to use $\tilde{D} = 2 \cdot 2^{16} \cdot 2^{48} = 2^{65}$ chosen plaintext-ciphertext pairs in such an attack. In other words, the full

---

Algorithm 3: Key recovery attack procedure of 17-round Piccolo-128 with both pre- and post-whitening keys.

---

1 Allocate and initialize four arrays $V_P[]$, $V_P'[]$, $V_C[]$ and $V_C'[]$ with size $2^{59.14}$;
2 Take $2^{11.14}$ distinct random values of P_3 and store them in a set S;
3 Choose another $2^{11.14}$ distinct random values of P_3' and store them in a set S';
4 $a \leftarrow 0$;
5 **for** 2^{16} P_0, 2^{16} P_1, and 2^{16} P_2 **do**
6   $\quad$ **for** $2^{11.14}$ P_3 in set S **do**
7    $\quad\quad$ Query the ciphertexts C for P under K;
8    $\quad\quad$ $V_P[a] = P$, $V_C[a] = C$, and increase a by one;
9 $a \leftarrow 0$;
10 **for** 2^{16} P_0, 2^{16} P_1, and 2^{16} P_2 **do**
11 $\quad$ **for** $2^{11.14}$ P_3' in set S' **do**
12   $\quad\quad$ Query the ciphertexts C' for P' under K';
13   $\quad\quad$ $V_P'[a] = P'$, $V_C'[a] = C'$, and increase a by one;
14 **for** 2^{16} k_4, 2^{16} k_7, 2^{16} k_0, and 2^{16} k_1 **do**
15 $\quad$ $wk_0 = k_0^L \| k_1^R$, $wk_2 = k_4^L \| k_7^R$, and $wk_3 = k_7^L \| k_4^R$, $wk_0' = wk_0$, $wk_2' = wk_2$, $wk_3' = wk_3$, $k_4' = k_4$, $k_7' = k_7$, $k_0' = k_0 \oplus 0x00\beta_1\beta_2$, and $k_1' = k_1$;
16 $\quad$ Allocate and initialize two arrays $V_1[x_1]$ and $V_1'[x_1']$ with $|x_1| = 32 = |x_1'|$;
17 $\quad$ **for** 2^{16} P_0, 2^{16} P_2, and $2^{11.14}$ P_3 in set S **do**
18   $\quad\quad$ Compute $P_1 = F(P_0 \oplus wk_0)$;   // We have $2^{43.14}$ U with the same U_1
19   $\quad\quad$ Access $V_P[]$ with $P_0\|P_1\|P_2\|P_3$ and get the index a, then access $V_C[a]$ to get the corresponding ciphertexts C;
20   $\quad\quad$ Decrypt C to get $Z_0[2,3]$, $Z_1[0,1]$, $Z_2[0,1]$, $Z_3[2,3]$, $Y_0[0,1]$ and $Y_1[2,3]$;
21   $\quad\quad$ Let $x_1 \leftarrow Z_0[2,3]\|(Z_1[0,1] \oplus Y_0[0,1])\|Z_2[0,1]\|(Z_3[2,3] \oplus Y_1[2,3])$ and $V_1[x_1] \leftarrow V_1[x_1] + 1$;
22 $\quad$ **for** 2^{16} P_0, 2^{16} P_2, and $2^{11.14}$ P_3' in set S' **do**
23   $\quad\quad$ Compute $P_1 = F(P_0 \oplus wk_0)$;// We have $2^{43.14}$ U' with $U_1' = U_1$
24   $\quad\quad$ Access $V_P'[]$ with $P_0\|P_1\|P_2\|P_3'$ and get the index a, then access $V_C'[a]$ to get the corresponding ciphertexts C';
25   $\quad\quad$ Decrypt C' to get $Z_0'[2,3]$, $Z_1'[0,1]$, $Z_2'[0,1]$, $Z_3'[2,3]$, $Y_0'[0,1]$, $Y_1'[2,3]$;
26   $\quad\quad$ Let $x_1' \leftarrow Z_0'[2,3]\|(Z_1'[0,1] \oplus Y_0'[0,1])\|Z_2'[0,1]\|(Z_3'[2,3] \oplus Y_1'[2,3])$ and $V_1'[x_1'] \leftarrow V_1'[x_1'] + 1$;
27 $\quad$ **for** 2^8 k_2^L and 2^8 k_5^R **do**
28   $\quad\quad$ $(k_2')^L = k_2^L$ and $(k_5')^R = k_5^R$;
29   $\quad\quad$ Allocate and initialize two arrays $V_2[x_2]$ and $V_2'[x_2']$ with $|x_2| = 16 = |x_2'|$;
30   $\quad\quad$ **for** 2^{32} x_1 and x_1' **do**
31    $\quad\quad\quad$ Decrypt half-round for x_1 and x_1' to get $W_3 \oplus k_3$ and $W_3' \oplus k_3'$;
32    $\quad\quad\quad$ Let $x_2 \leftarrow W_3 \oplus k_3$, and $V_2[x_2] \leftarrow V_2[x_2] + V_1[x_1]$;
33    $\quad\quad\quad$ Let $x_2' \leftarrow W_3' \oplus k_3'$, and $V_2'[x_2'] \leftarrow V_2'[x_2'] + V_1'[x_1']$;
34   $\quad\quad$ $\mathcal{C} = 0$;
35   $\quad\quad$ **for** 2^{16} x **do**
36    $\quad\quad\quad$ $\mathcal{C} \leftarrow \mathcal{C} + \sum_{x=0}^{2^{16}-1} \left((V_2[x] - V_2'[x])^2 / (2N \cdot 2^{-16}) \right)$;
37   $\quad\quad$ **if** $\mathcal{C} \leq \tau$ **then**
38    $\quad\quad\quad$ The guessed key bits are possibly right;
39    $\quad\quad\quad$ **for** 2^8 k_2^R, 2^{16} k_3, 2^8 k_5^L and 2^{16} k_6 **do**
40     $\quad\quad\quad\quad$ Use two plaintext-ciphertext pairs to check if they are right;

codebook is used, and the attack would not be valid. Therefore, the probabilistic RKSS method can make it possible to cover one more round than the original RKSS method.

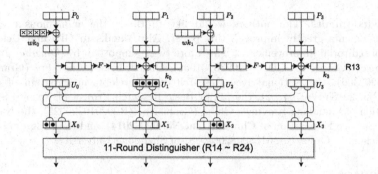

Fig. 4. One round added before the distinguisher when attacking 17-round Piccolo-128, where • are active nibbles and × are nibbles that we need to know in the key recovery procedure.

5   Conclusion and Future Work

In this paper, we revisited the RKSS cryptanalysis technique and proposed a new method called probabilistic RKSS cryptanalysis, which requires a lower data complexity and has the potential of attacking more rounds than the original RKSS method. This new method was proposed by adopting an appropriate statistic that considers different χ^2-distributions under right and wrong key guesses. The statistic is constructed as the squared Euclidean distance between the partial-value distributions of two ciphertext sets obtained from encrypting two independently chosen plaintext sets under related keys. The distributions of this statistic have been proved rigorously under several reasonable assumptions and confirmed experimentally using a toy cipher.

To show the effectiveness of this new method, we have applied it to the reduced-round Piccolo. As a result, we obtained the best key recovery attacks containing both pre- and post-whitening keys on 10-round Piccolo-80 and 17-round Piccolo-128. Note that we only use 10% of the number of plaintexts required for RKSS attacks on the 10-round Piccolo-80 and the success probability only decreases by 1%. Meanwhile, the data complexity needed in the new method on 16-round Piccolo-128 is only 3.44% of that required in the RKSS method. Moreover, we can cover one additional round on Piccolo-128 using the new method.

To make a more clear comparison between the probabilistic RKSS method and the original RKSS method, some theoretical discussions, as well as key recovery attacks on reduced-round SKINNY-128-256 and full-round LiCi-2, are given in the full version due to space constraints.

The probabilistic RKSS method has shown its advantage compared to the original RKSS by new cryptanalysis results on Piccolo, SKINNY-128-256 and LiCi-2. The applications of this new method on other primitives are an interesting topic to explore in future work.

Acknowledgments. The authors would like to thank the anonymous reviewers whose comments greatly improved this paper. Also thanks to Giovanni Uchoa de Assis for editorial improvements. This work was supported by Qingdao Innovation project (Grant No. QDBSH20230101008), Quan Cheng Laboratory (Grant No. QCLZD202306), the National Key Research and Development Program of China (Grant No. 2018YFA0704702), the Major Basic Research Project of Natural Science Foundation of Shandong Province, China (Grant No. ZR202010220025), the National Natural Science Foundation of China (Grant No. 62032014), and the Program of Qilu Young Scholars (Grant No. 61580082063088) of Shandong University.

References

1. Ahangarkolaei, M.Z., Najarkolaei, S.R.H., Ahmadi, S., Aref, M.R.: Zero correlation linear attack on reduced round Piccolo-80. In: ISCISC 2016, pp. 66–71. IEEE (2016). https://doi.org/10.1109/ISCISC.2016.7736453
2. Ashur, T., Dunkelman, O., Masalha, N.: Linear cryptanalysis reduced round of Piccolo-80. In: Dolev, S., Hendler, D., Lodha, S., Yung, M. (eds.) CSCML 2019. LNCS, vol. 11527, pp. 16–32. Springer, Cham (2019). https://doi.org/10.1007/978-3-030-20951-3_2
3. Avanzi, R.: The QARMA block cipher family. Almost MDS matrices over rings with zero divisors, nearly symmetric Even-Mansour constructions with non-involutory central rounds, and search heuristics for low-latency S-boxes. IACR Trans. Symmetric Cryptol. **2017**(1), 4–44 (2017). https://doi.org/10.13154/tosc.v2017.i1.4-44
4. Azimi, S.A., Ahmadian, Z., Mohajeri, J., Aref, M.R.: Impossible differential cryptanalysis of Piccolo lightweight block cipher. In: ISCISC 2014, pp. 89–94. IEEE (2014). https://doi.org/10.1109/ISCISC.2014.6994028
5. Barrett, C.W., Sebastiani, R., Seshia, S.A., Tinelli, C.: Satisfiability modulo theories. In: Biere, A., Heule, M., van Maaren, H., Walsh, T. (eds.) Handbook of Satisfiability, Frontiers in Artificial Intelligence and Applications, vol. 185, pp. 825–885. IOS Press (2009). https://doi.org/10.3233/978-1-58603-929-5-825
6. Bogdanov, A., Boura, C., Rijmen, V., Wang, M., Wen, L., Zhao, J.: Key difference invariant bias in block ciphers. In: Sako, K., Sarkar, P. (eds.) ASIACRYPT 2013. LNCS, vol. 8269, pp. 357–376. Springer, Heidelberg (2013). https://doi.org/10.1007/978-3-642-42033-7_19
7. Collard, B., Standaert, F.-X.: A statistical saturation attack against the block cipher PRESENT. In: Fischlin, M. (ed.) CT-RSA 2009. LNCS, vol. 5473, pp. 195–210. Springer, Heidelberg (2009). https://doi.org/10.1007/978-3-642-00862-7_13
8. Cook, S.A.: The complexity of theorem-proving procedures. In: Harrison, M.A., Banerji, R.B., Ullman, J.D. (eds.) Proceedings of the 3rd Annual ACM Symposium on Theory of Computing, Shaker Heights, Ohio, USA, 3–5 May 1971, pp. 151–158. ACM (1971). https://doi.org/10.1145/800157.805047
9. Daemen, J., Knudsen, L., Rijmen, V.: The block cipher square. In: Biham, E. (ed.) FSE 1997. LNCS, vol. 1267, pp. 149–165. Springer, Heidelberg (1997). https://doi.org/10.1007/BFb0052343

10. Daemen, J., Rijmen, V.: The Design of Rijndael: AES - The Advanced Encryption Standard. Information Security and Cryptography. Springer, Cham (2002). https://doi.org/10.1007/978-3-662-04722-4

11. Daemen, J., Rijmen, V.: Probability distributions of correlation and differentials in block ciphers. J. Math. Cryptol. **1**(3), 221–242 (2007). https://doi.org/10.1515/JMC.2007.011

12. DasGupta, A.: Asymptotic Theory of Statistics and Probability. Springer, New York (2008). https://doi.org/10.1007/978-0-387-75971-5

13. Dobraunig, C., Eichlseder, M., Mendel, F.: Square attack on 7-round Kiasu-BC. In: Manulis, M., Sadeghi, A.-R., Schneider, S. (eds.) ACNS 2016. LNCS, vol. 9696, pp. 500–517. Springer, Cham (2016). https://doi.org/10.1007/978-3-319-39555-5_27

14. Fouque, P.-A., Karpman, P.: Security amplification against meet-in-the-middle attacks using whitening. In: Stam, M. (ed.) IMACC 2013. LNCS, vol. 8308, pp. 252–269. Springer, Heidelberg (2013). https://doi.org/10.1007/978-3-642-45239-0_15

15. Fu, L., Jin, C., Li, X.: Multidimensional zero-correlation linear cryptanalysis of lightweight block cipher Piccolo-128. Secur. Commun. Netw. **9**(17), 4520–4535 (2016). https://doi.org/10.1002/sec.1644

16. Isobe, T., Shibutani, K.: Security analysis of the lightweight block ciphers XTEA, LED and Piccolo. In: Susilo, W., Mu, Y., Seberry, J. (eds.) ACISP 2012. LNCS, vol. 7372, pp. 71–86. Springer, Heidelberg (2012). https://doi.org/10.1007/978-3-642-31448-3_6

17. Jeong, K., Kang, H., Lee, C., Sung, J., Hong, S.: Biclique cryptanalysis of lightweight block ciphers PRESENT, Piccolo and LED. Cryptology ePrint Archive, Paper 2012/621 (2012). https://eprint.iacr.org/2012/621

18. Knudsen, L., Wagner, D.: Integral cryptanalysis. In: Daemen, J., Rijmen, V. (eds.) FSE 2002. LNCS, vol. 2365, pp. 112–127. Springer, Heidelberg (2002). https://doi.org/10.1007/3-540-45661-9_9

19. Li, M., Hu, K., Wang, M.: Related-tweak statistical saturation cryptanalysis and its application on QARMA. IACR Trans. Symmetric Cryptol. **2019**(1), 236–263 (2019). https://doi.org/10.13154/tosc.v2019.i1.236-263

20. Li, M., Mouha, N., Sun, L., Wang, M.: Probabilistic related-key statistical saturation cryptanalysis. IACR Cryptology ePrint Archive, p. 1245 (2023). https://eprint.iacr.org/2023/1245

21. Liu, Y., Cheng, L., Liu, Z., Li, W., Wang, Q., Gu, D.: Improved meet-in-the-middle attacks on reduced-round Piccolo. Sci. China Inf. Sci. **61**(3), 032108:1–032108:13 (2018). https://doi.org/10.1007/s11432-016-9157-y

22. Liu, Y., et al.: New analysis of reduced-version of Piccolo in the single-key scenario. KSII Trans. Internet Inf. Syst. **13**(9), 4727–4741 (2019). https://doi.org/10.3837/tiis.2019.09.022

23. Matsui, M.: Linear cryptanalysis method for DES cipher. In: Helleseth, T. (ed.) EUROCRYPT 1993. LNCS, vol. 765, pp. 386–397. Springer, Heidelberg (1994). https://doi.org/10.1007/3-540-48285-7_33

24. Maxwell, A.E.: Comparing the classification of subjects by two independent judges. Br. J. Psychiatry **116**, 651–655 (1970). https://doi.org/10.1192/bjp.116.535.651

25. Minier, M.: On the security of *Piccolo* lightweight block cipher against related-key impossible differentials. In: Paul, G., Vaudenay, S. (eds.) INDOCRYPT 2013. LNCS, vol. 8250, pp. 308–318. Springer, Cham (2013). https://doi.org/10.1007/978-3-319-03515-4_21

26. Mouha, N., Preneel, B.: Towards finding optimal differential characteristics for ARX: application to Salsa20. Cryptology ePrint Archive, Paper 2013/328 (2013). https://eprint.iacr.org/2013/328

27. Nyberg, K.: Linear approximation of block ciphers. In: De Santis, A. (ed.) EURO-CRYPT 1994. LNCS, vol. 950, pp. 439–444. Springer, Heidelberg (1995). https://doi.org/10.1007/BFb0053460

28. Phan, R.C.: Mini advanced encryption standard (Mini-AES): a testbed for crypt-analysis students. Cryptologia **26**(4), 283–306 (2002). https://doi.org/10.1080/0161-110291890948

29. Shibutani, K., Isobe, T., Hiwatari, H., Mitsuda, A., Akishita, T., Shirai, T.: *Piccolo*: an ultra-lightweight blockcipher. In: Preneel, B., Takagi, T. (eds.) CHES 2011. LNCS, vol. 6917, pp. 342–357. Springer, Heidelberg (2011). https://doi.org/10.1007/978-3-642-23951-9_23

30. Stuart, A.: A test for homogeneity of the marginal distribution of a two-way classification. Biometrika **42**, 412–416 (1955). https://doi.org/10.1093/biomet/42.3-4.412

31. Todo, Y.: Impossible differential attack against 14-round Piccolo-80 without relying on full code book. IEICE Trans. Fundam. Electron. Commun. Comput. Sci. **99-A**(1), 154–157 (2016). https://doi.org/10.1587/transfun.E99.A.154

32. Tolba, M., Abdelkhalek, A., Youssef, A.M.: Meet-in-the-middle attacks on reduced round Piccolo. In: Güneysu, T., Leander, G., Moradi, A. (eds.) LightSec 2015. LNCS, vol. 9542, pp. 3–20. Springer, Cham (2016). https://doi.org/10.1007/978-3-319-29078-2_1

33. Wang, M., Cui, T., Chen, H., Sun, L., Wen, L., Bogdanov, A.: Integrals go statistical: cryptanalysis of full skipjack variants. In: Peyrin, T. (ed.) FSE 2016. LNCS, vol. 9783, pp. 399–415. Springer, Heidelberg (2016). https://doi.org/10.1007/978-3-662-52993-5_20

34. Wang, Y., Wu, W., Yu, X.: Biclique cryptanalysis of reduced-round piccolo block cipher. In: Ryan, M.D., Smyth, B., Wang, G. (eds.) ISPEC 2012. LNCS, vol. 7232, pp. 337–352. Springer, Heidelberg (2012). https://doi.org/10.1007/978-3-642-29101-2_23

Compactly Committing Authenticated Encryption Using Encryptment and Tweakable Block Cipher

Shoichi Hirose[1]([✉]) [iD] and Kazuhiko Minematsu[2,3] [iD]

[1] University of Fukui, Fukui, Japan
`hrs_shch@u-fukui.ac.jp`
[2] NEC, Kawasaki, Japan
`k-minematsu@nec.com`
[3] Yokohama National University, Yokohama, Japan

Abstract. Message franking is a feature of end-to-end encrypted messaging introduced by Facebook that enables users to report abusive contents in a verifiable manner. Grubbs et al. (CRYPTO 2017) formalized a symmetric-key primitive usable for message franking, called compactly committing authenticated encryption with associated data (ccAEAD), and presented schemes with provable security. Dodis et al. (CRYPTO 2018) proposed a core building block for ccAEAD, called encryptment, and presented a generic construction of ccAEAD combining encryptment and conventional AEAD. We show that ccAEAD can be built on encryptment and a tweakable block cipher (TBC), leading to simpler and more efficient constructions of ccAEAD than Dodis et al.'s methods. Our construction, called EnCryptment-then-TBC (ECT), is secure under a new but feasible assumption on the ciphertext integrity of encryptment. We also formalize the notion of remotely keyed ccAEAD (RK ccAEAD) and show that our ECT works as RK ccAEAD. RK ccAEAD was first considered by Dodis et al. as a useful variant of ccAEAD when it is implemented on a platform consisting of a trusted module and an untrusted (leaking) module. However, its feasibility was left open. Our work is the first to show its feasibility with a concrete scheme.

Keywords: Authenticated encryption · Commitment · Tweakable block cipher · Remotely keyed encryption

1 Introduction

Background. End-to-end encrypted messaging systems are now widely deployed, such as Facebook Messenger [15], Signal [33], and Whatsapp Messenger [35]. Accordingly, new security issues arise in addition to those on the privacy and authenticity of messages. A significant problem is preventing malicious senders from sending harassing messages and harmful/abusive contents. To achieve this goal, Facebook introduced message franking [16]. It is a cryptographic protocol allowing users to report the receipt of abusive messages in a verifiable manner to Facebook.

C. Carlet et al. (Eds.): SAC 2023, LNCS 14201, pp. 233–252, 2024.
https://doi.org/10.1007/978-3-031-53368-6_12

At Crypto 2017, Grubbs et al. [18] initiated the formal study of message franking and presented a new variant of AEAD, called compactly committing AEAD (ccAEAD), as a symmetric-key primitive that is useful for message franking. For ccAEAD, a small part of the ciphertext works as a commitment to the message and the associated data. They also presented two generic constructions of ccAEAD. One is called CtE (Commit-then-Encrypt), which consists of commitment and AEAD. The other is called CEP (Committing Encrypt-and-PRF). It consists of a pseudorandom generator, a pseudorandom function (PRF), and a collision-resistant PRF.

At Crypto 2018, Dodis et al. [13] further studied ccAEAD and proposed a new primitive, called encryptment, as a core component of ccAEAD. They show that, given encryptment, ccAEAD can be built from an additional common cryptographic primitive. Concretely, they presented two transformations. One transformation needs a call to (randomized) AEAD in addition to encryptment, and the other needs two calls to a related-key-secure PRF. The former is a randomized scheme, and the latter is nonce-based. In addition, they considered remotely keyed ccAEAD (RK ccAEAD) in the full version [14] of [13]. Here, RK ccAEAD is an extension of ccAEAD inheriting the property of remotely keyed encryption, which was proposed by Blaze [7] and extensively studied in the late 90's [8,23,29,30]. Its goal was to enable secure encryption under a setting where one could use a resource-limited personal device storing secret keys and computing cryptographic functions. The problem was how to do bulk encryption and decryption by utilizing the power of a host and the security of the personal device. Dodis et al. [14] suggested RK ccAEAD as a useful variant of ccAEAD under such environments. However, they left open its feasibility and concrete constructions.

Our Contributions. Focusing on the work of Dodis et al. [13,14], this paper makes two contributions. First, we present a new construction of ccAEAD based on encryptment, dubbed ECT (EnCryptment-then-TBC). While Dodis et al. [13,14] used AEAD as an additional component, we show that an additional single call of a tweakable block cipher (TBC) [27,28] is sufficient. Since the integrity mechanism provided by AEAD is not needed, our proposal allows simpler and more efficient ccAEAD compared with Dodis et al.'s proposals. In more detail, when encryptment, Dodis et al.'s method needs AEAD taking two elements, B (for associated data) and L (for plaintext) as an input in addition to a secret key, while ECT simply encrypt L with tweak B by a TBC. The latter is arguably much simpler. See Fig. 1 for their illustrations. Note that the encryption output C_1 of AEAD in Dodis et al.'s method contains a random nonce and a tag in addition to the "raw" ciphertext of $|L|$ bits as otherwise decryption is not possible. Hence, ECT is more efficient in terms of bandwidth[1]. The security requirements of ECT are reduced to those of the underlying encryptment and a TBC. In particular, the ciphertext integrity of ECT requires a new but feasible

---

[1] The second method of Dodis et al. has also larger bandwidth than ours for the existence of tag. A concrete comparison is not possible as it is nonce-based.

type of ciphertext unforgeability for the encryptment. Actually, we show that HFC [13] – a hash-based efficient encryptment scheme proposed by Dodis et al. – satisfies this new ciphertext unforgeability in the random oracle model. We note that HFC originally assumed the random oracle, so we do not introduce any new assumption.

Second, we provide the first formalization of remotely keyed (RK) ccAEAD, and show that ECT is secure RK ccAEAD. This answers the aforementioned open question posed by Dodis et al. positively. Our formalization is based on that of RK authenticated encryption by Dodis and An [12]. The confidentiality of ECT as RK ccAEAD requires a new variant of confidentiality for encryptment. It is also shown that HFC satisfies the new variant of confidentiality in the random oracle model. ECT has a similar structure to the AEAD scheme named CONCRETE [6], which offers ciphertext integrity in the presence of nonce misuse and leakage. As mentioned above, remotely keyed encryption [7] is practically relevant when composing a trusted (small) module with an untrusted/leaking module. We think this similarity exhibits an interesting relationship with RK ccAEAD and leakage-resilient AEAD, where the latter has been actively studied in recent years, e.g., [4,5,11,31,32].

Related Work. Authenticated encryption is one of the central topics in symmetric cryptography. Its formal treatments were initiated by Katz and Yung [24] and by Bellare and Namprempre [3].

A variation of message franking scheme that enables a receiver to report an abusive message by revealing only the abusive parts was investigated independently by Leontiadis and Vaudenay [26] and by Chen and Tang [10]. Huguenin-Dumittan and Leontiadis formalized and instantiated a secure bidirectional channel with message franking [21]. Yamamuro et al. [36] proposed forward secure message franking and presented a scheme based on ccAEAD, a forward secure pseudorandom generator, and a forward secure MAC. Tyagi et al. [34] formalized asymmetric message franking and constructed a scheme from signatures of knowledge [20] for designated verifier signatures [22].

Hirose [19] proposed a generic construction of nonce-based ccAEAD. The proposal is similar to the second method of Dodis et al. Since it simply replaces a PRF with a TBC, it needs two additional TBC calls, while ECT needs only one TBC call. In addition, his scheme is nonce-based while ours is randomized as originally proposed. Thus, ECT is less restrictive and more efficient in computation.

Dodis and An [12] proposed and investigated a cryptographic primitive called concealment. They formalized RK authenticated encryption as an application and provided a generic construction with concealment and authenticated encryption.

Farshim et al. [17], Albertini et al. [1], Len et al. [25], Bellare and Hoang [2], and Chan and Rogaway [9] discussed so-called committing authenticated encryption. While their definitions and security goals are not identical, their primary goal was basically to decrease the risk of error or misuse by application design-

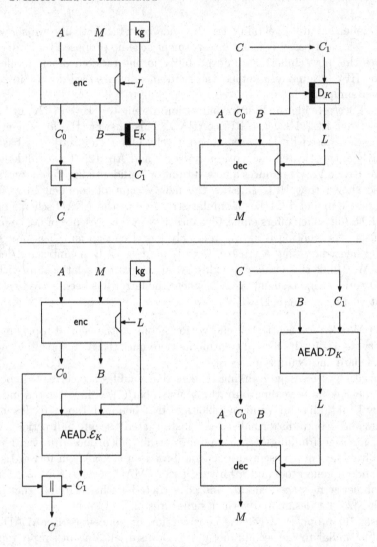

Fig. 1. Encryption and decryption algorithms of ccAEAD. (Top) our proposal, ECT, (Bottom) Dodis et al.'s method using AEAD [13]. For both cases, enc and dec are encryptment and decryptment algorithms of the encryptment scheme. The ccAEAD decryption algorithms omit the case of verification failures. In ECT, E_K and D_K denote the TBC's encryption and decryption, where the thick line is tweak input.

ers, and message franking was out of scope for the lack of opening key needed by ccAEAD.

Organization. Section 2 introduces notations and formalizes tweakable block ciphers, ccAEAD, and encryptment. Section 3 describes the generic construction of ccAEAD, called ECT, and confirms its security. Section 4 formalizes RK ccAEAD. Section 5 confirms the security of ECT as RK ccAEAD. Section 6 concludes the paper.

2 Preliminaries

Let $\Sigma := \{0,1\}$. For any integer $l \geq 0$, let Σ^l be the set of all Σ-sequences of length l. Let $\Sigma^* := \bigcup_{i \geq 0} \Sigma^i$. The length of $x \in \Sigma^*$ is denoted by $|x|$. Concatenation of $x_1, x_2 \in \Sigma^*$ is denoted by $x_1 \| x_2$. A uniform random choice of an element s from a set S is denoted by $s \leftarrow S$.

2.1 Tweakable Block Cipher

A TBC is formalized as a pair of encryption and decryption functions $\mathsf{TBC} := (\mathsf{E}, \mathsf{D})$ such that $\mathsf{E} : \Sigma^{n_k} \times \Sigma^{n_t} \times \Sigma^{n_b} \to \Sigma^{n_b}$ and $\mathsf{D} : \Sigma^{n_k} \times \Sigma^{n_t} \times \Sigma^{n_b} \to \Sigma^{n_b}$. Σ^{n_k} is a set of keys, Σ^{n_t} is a set of tweaks, and Σ^{n_b} is a set of plaintexts or ciphertexts. For every $(K, T) \in \Sigma^{n_k} \times \Sigma^{n_t}$, both $\mathsf{E}(K, T, \cdot)$ and $\mathsf{D}(K, T, \cdot)$ are permutations, and $\mathsf{D}(K, T, \mathsf{E}(K, T, \cdot))$ is the identity permutation over Σ^{n_b}.

Let $\mathcal{P}_{n_t, n_b}$ be the set of all tweakable permutations: For every $p \in \mathcal{P}_{n_t, n_b}$ and $T \in \Sigma^{n_t}$, $p(T, \cdot)$ is a permutation over Σ^{n_b}. Let $p^{-1} \in \mathcal{P}_{n_t, n_b}$ be the inverse of $p \in \mathcal{P}_{n_t, n_b}$: $p^{-1}(T, p(T, \cdot))$ is the identity permutation for every $T \in \Sigma^{n_t}$.

The security requirement of a TBC is formalized as indistinguishability from a uniform random tweakable permutation. Let $\mathbf{A}$ be an adversary with oracle access to a tweakable permutation (and its inverse) in $\mathcal{P}_{n_t, n_b}$. $\mathbf{A}$ can make adaptive queries to the oracle(s) and finally outputs 0 or 1. The advantage of $\mathbf{A}$ against TBC for a tweakable pseudorandom permutation (TPRP) is

$$\mathrm{Adv}_{\mathsf{TBC}}^{\mathrm{tprp}}(\mathbf{A}) := \left| \Pr[\mathbf{A}^{\mathsf{E}_K} = 1] - \Pr[\mathbf{A}^{\varpi} = 1] \right|,$$

where $K \leftarrow \Sigma^{n_k}$ and $\varpi \leftarrow \mathcal{P}_{n_t, n_b}$. Similarly, the advantage of $\mathbf{A}$ against TBC for a strong tweakable pseudorandom permutation (STPRP) is

$$\mathrm{Adv}_{\mathsf{TBC}}^{\mathrm{stprp}}(\mathbf{A}) := \left| \Pr[\mathbf{A}^{\mathsf{E}_K, \mathsf{D}_K} = 1] - \Pr[\mathbf{A}^{\varpi, \varpi^{-1}} = 1] \right|.$$

2.2 ccAEAD

Syntax. ccAEAD [18] is formalized as a tuple of algorithms $\mathsf{CAE} := (\mathsf{Kg}, \mathsf{Enc}, \mathsf{Dec}, \mathsf{Ver})$. It is involved with a key space $\mathcal{K} := \Sigma^n$, an associated-data space $\mathcal{A} \subseteq \Sigma^*$, a message space $\mathcal{M} \subseteq \Sigma^*$, a ciphertext space $\mathcal{C} \subseteq \Sigma^*$, an opening-key space $\mathcal{L} \subseteq \Sigma^\ell$, and a binding-tag space $\mathcal{T} := \Sigma^\tau$. The "cc" (compactly committing) property requires that $\tau = O(n)$ is small.

- The key-generation algorithm Kg returns a secret key $K \in \mathcal{K}$ chosen uniformly at random.
- The encryption algorithm Enc takes as input $(K, A, M) \in \mathcal{K} \times \mathcal{A} \times \mathcal{M}$ and returns $(C, B) \in \mathcal{C} \times \mathcal{T}$.
- The decryption algorithm Dec takes as input $(K, A, C, B) \in \mathcal{K} \times \mathcal{A} \times \mathcal{C} \times \mathcal{T}$ and returns $(M, L) \in \mathcal{M} \times \mathcal{L}$ or $\perp \notin \mathcal{M} \times \mathcal{L}$.
- The verification algorithm Ver takes as input $(A, M, L, B) \in \mathcal{A} \times \mathcal{M} \times \mathcal{L} \times \mathcal{T}$ and returns $b \in \Sigma$.

Kg and Enc are randomized algorithms, and Dec and Ver are deterministic algorithms. For every $l \in \mathbb{N}$, $\Sigma^l \subseteq \mathcal{M}$ or $\Sigma^l \cap \mathcal{M} = \emptyset$. For $(C, B) \leftarrow \mathsf{Enc}(K, A, M)$, $|C|$ depends only on $|M|$, and there exists a function clen : $\mathbb{N} \to \mathbb{N}$ such that $|C| = \mathsf{clen}(|M|)$.

CAE satisfies correctness. Namely, for any $(K, A, M) \in \mathcal{K} \times \mathcal{A} \times \mathcal{M}$, if $(C, B) \leftarrow \mathsf{Enc}(K, A, M)$, then there exists some $L \in \mathcal{L}$ such that $\mathsf{Dec}(K, A, C, B) = (M, L)$ and $\mathsf{Ver}(A, M, L, B) = 1$.

Security Requirements. The security requirements of ccAEAD are confidentiality, ciphertext integrity, and binding properties.

Confidentiality. The games MO-REAL and MO-RAND shown in Fig. 2 are introduced to formalize the confidentiality as real-or-random indistinguishability in the multi-opening setting. The advantage of an adversary $\mathbf{A}$ for confidentiality is

$$\mathrm{Adv}_{\mathsf{CAE}}^{\mathrm{mo\text{-}ror}}(\mathbf{A}) := \left| \Pr[\text{MO-REAL}_{\mathsf{CAE}}^{\mathbf{A}} = 1] - \Pr[\text{MO-RAND}_{\mathsf{CAE}}^{\mathbf{A}} = 1] \right|.$$

$\mathbf{A}$ is allowed to make queries adaptively to the oracles **Enc**, **Dec**, and **ChalEnc**. In both of the games, **Enc** and **Dec** work in the same ways. For each query (A, C, B), **Dec** returns $(M, L) \leftarrow \mathsf{Dec}(K, A, C, B)$ only if the query is a previous reply from **Enc**.

Ciphertext Integrity. The game MO-CTXT shown in Fig. 3 is introduced to formalize the ciphertext integrity as unforgeability in the multi-opening setting. The advantage of an adversary $\mathbf{A}$ for ciphertext integrity is

$$\mathrm{Adv}_{\mathsf{CAE}}^{\mathrm{mo\text{-}ctxt}}(\mathbf{A}) := \Pr[\text{MO-CTXT}_{\mathsf{CAE}}^{\mathbf{A}} = \mathsf{true}].$$

$\mathbf{A}$ is allowed to make queries adaptively to the oracles **Enc**, **Dec**, and **ChalDec**. The game outputs **true** if $\mathbf{A}$ asks a query (A, C, B) to **ChalDec** such that $\mathsf{Dec}(K, A, C, B) \neq \perp$ without obtaining it from **Enc** by a previous query.

Binding Properties. Binding properties are defined for a sender and a receiver. Receiver binding describes that a malicious receiver cannot report a non-abusive sender for sending an abusive message. The advantage of an adversary $\mathbf{A}$ for receiver binding is

$$\mathrm{Adv}_{\mathsf{CAE}}^{\mathrm{r\text{-}bind}}(\mathbf{A}) := \Pr[((A, M, L), (A', M', L'), B) \leftarrow \mathbf{A} : (A, M) \neq (A', M')$$
$$\wedge \mathsf{Ver}(A, M, L, B) = \mathsf{Ver}(A', M', L', B) = 1].$$

```
K ← Kg; 𝒴 ← ∅
b ← A^{Enc,Dec,ChalEnc}
return b

Enc(A, M)
(C, B) ← Enc(K, A, M)
𝒴 ← 𝒴 ∪ {(A, C, B)}
return (C, B)

Dec(A, C, B)
if (A, C, B) ∉ 𝒴 then
    return ⊥
end if
(M, L) ← Dec(K, A, C, B)
return (M, L)

ChalEnc(A, M)
(C, B) ← Enc(K, A, M)
return (C, B)
```

```
K ← Kg; 𝒴 ← ∅
b ← A^{Enc,Dec,ChalEnc}
return b

Enc(A, M)
(C, B) ← Enc(K, A, M)
𝒴 ← 𝒴 ∪ {(A, C, B)}
return (C, B)

Dec(A, C, B)
if (A, C, B) ∉ 𝒴 then
    return ⊥
end if
(M, L) ← Dec(K, A, C, B)
return (M, L)

ChalEnc(A, M)
(C, B) ←$ Σ^{clen(|M|)} × Σ^τ
return (C, B)
```

(a) MO-REAL$^A_{CAE}$ (b) MO-RAND$^A_{CAE}$

Fig. 2. Games for confidentiality of ccAEAD

```
K ← Kg; 𝒴 ← ∅          Enc(A, M)                      ChalDec(A, C, B)
win ← false           (C, B) ← Enc(K, A, M)          if (A, C, B) ∈ 𝒴 then
A^{Enc,Dec,ChalDec}    𝒴 ← 𝒴 ∪ {(A, C, B)}                return ⊥
return win            return (C, B)                  end if
                                                     if Dec(K, A, C, B) ≠ ⊥ then
                      Dec(A, C, B)                       win ← true
                      return Dec(K, A, C, B)         end if
                                                     return Dec(K, A, C, B)
```

Fig. 3. Game MO-CTXT$^A_{CAE}$ for ciphertext integrity of ccAEAD

The advantage of **A** for strong receiver binding is

$$\text{Adv}^{\text{sr-bind}}_{\text{CAE}}(\mathbf{A}) := \Pr[((A, M, L), (A', M', L'), B) \leftarrow \mathbf{A} : (A, M, L) \neq (A', M', L')$$
$$\wedge \text{Ver}(A, M, L, B) = \text{Ver}(A', M', L', B) = 1].$$

It holds that $\text{Adv}^{\text{r-bind}}_{\text{CAE}}(\mathbf{A}) \leq \text{Adv}^{\text{sr-bind}}_{\text{CAE}}(\mathbf{A})$ for any CAE and **A**.

Sender binding describes that a malicious sender of an abusive message cannot prevent the receiver from reporting it. The advantage of **A** for sender binding is

$$\text{Adv}^{\text{s-bind}}_{\text{CAE}}(\mathbf{A}) := \Pr[(K, A, C, B) \leftarrow \mathbf{A} : \text{Dec}(K, A, C, B) \neq \perp$$
$$(M, L) \leftarrow \text{Dec}(K, A, C, B) \wedge \text{Ver}(A, M, L, B) = 0].$$

Message Franking Using ccAEAD. A service provider is assumed to relay all communication among users. Users encrypt their communication with ccAEAD. For a ciphertext from a sender, the service provider computes a tag with a MAC function for the binding tag in the ciphertext and transfers the ciphertext to the receiver together with the tag. Suppose that an abusive message is recovered from the ciphertext. Then, the receiver reports it to the service provider with the opening key, binding tag, and the tag attached by the service provider. The receiver binding prevents malicious receivers from blaming non-abusive senders. The sender binding prevents malicious senders from denying abusive reports by honest receivers.

2.3   Encryption

Syntax. Encryption [13] is roughly one-time ccAEAD. It is formalized as a tuple of algorithms $\mathsf{EC} = (\mathsf{kg}, \mathsf{enc}, \mathsf{dec}, \mathsf{ver})$. It is involved with a key space $\mathcal{K}_{ec} := \Sigma^\ell$, an associated-data space $\mathcal{A} \subseteq \Sigma^*$, a message space $\mathcal{M} \subseteq \Sigma^*$, a ciphertext space $\mathcal{C} \subseteq \Sigma^*$, and a binding-tag space $\mathcal{T} := \Sigma^\tau$.

- The key-generation algorithm kg returns a secret key $K_{ec} \in \mathcal{K}_{ec}$ chosen uniformly at random.
- The encryption algorithm enc takes as input $(K_{ec}, A, M) \in \mathcal{K}_{ec} \times \mathcal{A} \times \mathcal{M}$ and returns $(C, B) \in \mathcal{C} \times \mathcal{T}$.
- The decryption algorithm dec takes as input $(K_{ec}, A, C, B) \in \mathcal{K}_{ec} \times \mathcal{A} \times \mathcal{C} \times \mathcal{T}$ and returns $M \in \mathcal{M}$ or $\bot \notin \mathcal{M}$.
- The verification algorithm ver takes as input $(A, M, K_{ec}, B) \in \mathcal{A} \times \mathcal{M} \times \mathcal{K}_{ec} \times \mathcal{T}$ and returns $b \in \Sigma$.

kg is a randomized algorithm, and enc, dec and ver are deterministic algorithms. For $(C, B) \leftarrow \mathsf{enc}(K_{ec}, A, M)$, it is assumed that $|C|$ depends only on $|M|$.

EC satisfies correctness: For any $(K_{ec}, A, M) \in \mathcal{K}_{ec} \times \mathcal{A} \times \mathcal{M}$, if $(C, B) \leftarrow \mathsf{enc}(K_{ec}, A, M)$, then $\mathsf{dec}(K_{ec}, A, C, B) = M$ and $\mathsf{ver}(A, M, K_{ec}, B) = 1$. A stronger notion of correctness called strong correctness is also introduced: For any $(K_{ec}, A, C, B) \in \mathcal{K}_{ec} \times \mathcal{A} \times \mathcal{C} \times \mathcal{T}$, if $M \leftarrow \mathsf{dec}(K_{ec}, A, C, B)$, then $\mathsf{enc}(K_{ec}, A, M) = (C, B)$.

Security Requirements. The security requirements of encryption are confidentiality, second-ciphertext unforgeability, and binding properties.

Confidentiality. Two games otREAL and otRAND shown in Fig. 4 are introduced to formalize the confidentiality. In both of the games, an adversary **A** asks only a single query to the oracle **enc**. The advantage of **A** for confidentiality is

$$\mathrm{Adv}_{\mathsf{EC}}^{\text{ot-ror}}(\mathbf{A}) := \left| \Pr[\text{otREAL}_{\mathsf{EC}}^{\mathbf{A}} = 1] - \Pr[\text{otRAND}_{\mathsf{EC}}^{\mathbf{A}} = 1] \right|,$$

where "ot-ror" stands for "one-time real-or-random."

Second-Ciphertext Unforgeability. An adversary **A** asks only a single query $(A, M) \in \mathcal{A} \times \mathcal{M}$ to $\mathsf{enc}_{K_{ec}}$ and gets (C, B) and K_{ec}, where $K_{ec} \leftarrow \mathsf{kg}$ and $(C, B) \leftarrow \mathsf{enc}_{K_{ec}}(A, M)$. Then, **A** outputs $(A', C') \in \mathcal{A} \times \mathcal{C}$. The advantage of **A** for second-ciphertext unforgeability is

$$\mathrm{Adv}_{\mathsf{EC}}^{\text{scu}}(\mathbf{A}) := \Pr[(A, C) \neq (A', C') \wedge \mathsf{dec}_{K_{ec}}(A', C', B) \neq \bot].$$

$$K_{ec} \leftarrow kg$$
$$b \leftarrow \mathbf{A}^{enc}$$
$$\textbf{return } b$$

$$\textbf{enc}(A, M)$$
$$(C, B) \leftarrow enc(K_{ec}, A, M)$$
$$\textbf{return } (C, B)$$

$$b \leftarrow \mathbf{A}^{enc}$$
$$\textbf{return } b$$

$$\textbf{enc}(A, M)$$
$$(C, B) \twoheadleftarrow \Sigma^{clen(|M|)} \times \Sigma^{\tau}$$
$$\textbf{return } (C, B)$$

(a) otREAL$_{EC}^{A}$ (b) otRAND$_{EC}^{A}$

Fig. 4. Games for confidentiality of encryptment

Binding Properties. The advantage of $\mathbf{A}$ for receiver binding is

$$\text{Adv}_{EC}^{\text{r-bind}}(\mathbf{A}) := \Pr[((K_{ec}, A, M), (K'_{ec}, A', M'), B) \leftarrow \mathbf{A} : (A, M) \neq (A', M')$$
$$\wedge \, \text{ver}(A, M, K_{ec}, B) = \text{ver}(A', M', K'_{ec}, B) = 1].$$

The advantage of $\mathbf{A}$ for strong receiver binding is

$$\text{Adv}_{EC}^{\text{sr-bind}}(\mathbf{A}) := \Pr[((K_{ec}, A, M), (K'_{ec}, A', M'), B) \leftarrow \mathbf{A} :$$
$$(K_{ec}, A, M) \neq (K'_{ec}, A', M') \wedge \text{ver}(A, M, K_{ec}, B) = \text{ver}(A', M', K'_{ec}, B) = 1].$$

The advantage of an adversary $\mathbf{A}$ for sender binding is

$$\text{Adv}_{EC}^{\text{s-bind}}(\mathbf{A}) := \Pr[(K_{ec}, A, C, B) \leftarrow \mathbf{A}, M \leftarrow dec(K_{ec}, A, C, B) :$$
$$M \neq \perp \wedge \text{ver}(A, M, K_{ec}, B) = 0].$$

For strongly correct encryptment, Dodis et al. [13] reduced second-ciphertext unforgeability to sender binding and receiver binding. The following proposition shows that it can be reduced only to receiver binding. On the other hand, receiver binding cannot be reduced to second-ciphertext unforgeability. Suppose that EC is secure except that it has a weak key such that receiver binding is broken using the weak key. For second-ciphertext unforgeability, the probability that the weak key is chosen is negligible for a query made by an adversary.

Proposition 1. *Let* EC *be a strongly correct encryptment scheme. Then, for any adversary* $\mathbf{A}$ *against* EC *for second-ciphertext unforgeability, there exists an adversary* $\dot{\mathbf{A}}$ *such that* $\text{Adv}_{EC}^{\text{scu}}(\mathbf{A}) \leq \text{Adv}_{EC}^{\text{r-bind}}(\dot{\mathbf{A}})$ *and the run time of* $\dot{\mathbf{A}}$ *is at most about that of* $\mathbf{A}$.

The proof is omitted due to the page limit.

3   ccAEAD Using Encryptment and TBC

3.1   Scheme

New ccAEAD construction ECT (EnCryptment-then-TBC) ECT = (KG, ENC, DEC, VER) is proposed. It uses an encryptment scheme EC = (kg, enc, dec, ver) and a TBC TBC = (E, D). For ECT, let $\mathcal{K} := \Sigma^n$ be its key space, $\mathcal{A}$ be its associated-data space, $\mathcal{M}$ be its message space, $\mathcal{C}$ be its ciphertext space, $\mathcal{L} := \Sigma^\ell$ be its opening-key space, and $\mathcal{T} := \Sigma^\tau$ be its binding-tag space. Then, for EC, $\mathcal{L}$ is its key space, $\mathcal{A}$ is its associated-data space, $\mathcal{M}$ is its message space, $\mathcal{C}$ is its ciphertext space, and $\mathcal{T}$ is its binding-tag space. For TBC, its set of keys is $\mathcal{K}$, its set of tweaks is $\mathcal{T}$, and its set of plaintexts or ciphertexts is $\mathcal{L}$.

ENC and DEC are shown in Fig. 5. Also refer to Fig. 1 for illustration. They are also depicted in Fig. 1. KG selects a secret key K for TBC from Σ^n. VER simply runs ver.

ENC(K, A, M)	DEC(K, A, C, B)
$L \leftarrow \mathsf{kg}$	$C_0 \| C_1 \leftarrow C$
$(C_0, B) \leftarrow \mathsf{enc}(L, A, M)$	$L \leftarrow \mathsf{D}_K(B, C_1)$
$C_1 \leftarrow \mathsf{E}_K(B, L)$	if $\mathsf{dec}(L, A, C_0, B) = \perp$ then
$C \leftarrow C_0 \| C_1$	$\quad$ return $\perp$
return (C, B)	else
	$\quad M \leftarrow \mathsf{dec}(L, A, C_0, B)$
	$\quad$ return (M, L)
	end if

Fig. 5. The encryption and decryption algorithms of ECT

3.2 Security

ECT replaces AEAD of the Dodis et al. scheme with TBC. This change does not impact the confidentiality or binding properties. However, it does affect the ciphertext integrity. With ECT, a candidate for the opening key can always be obtained for a ciphertext. Thus, to ensure the ciphertext integrity, it must be intractable to create a new valid ciphertext for the binding tag of the original ciphertext and the opening key candidate.

Confidentiality. The confidentiality of ECT is reduced to the confidentiality of EC and the TPRP property of TBC. The proof is omitted due to the page limit.

Theorem 1 (Confidentiality). *Let $\mathbf{A}$ be an adversary against ECT making at most q_e, q_d, and q_c queries to* **Enc**, **Dec**, *and* **ChalEnc**, *respectively. Then, there exist adversaries $\dot{\mathbf{A}}$ and $\mathbf{D}$ such that*

$$\mathrm{Adv}_{\mathsf{ECT}}^{\mathrm{mo\text{-}ror}}(\mathbf{A}) \leq q_c \cdot \mathrm{Adv}_{\mathsf{EC}}^{\mathrm{ot\text{-}ror}}(\dot{\mathbf{A}}) + 2 \cdot \mathrm{Adv}_{\mathsf{TBC}}^{\mathrm{tprp}}(\mathbf{D}) + (q_e^2 + (q_e + q_c)^2)/2^\ell.$$

The run time of $\dot{\mathbf{A}}$ and $\mathbf{D}$ is at most about that of MO-REAL$_{\mathsf{ECT}}^{\mathbf{A}}$. $\mathbf{D}$ makes at most $(q_e + q_c)$ queries to its oracle.

Ciphertext Integrity. For the ciphertext integrity of ECT, a new notion is introduced to the ciphertext unforgeability of encryption EC:

Definition 1 (Targeted Ciphertext Unforgeability). *Let* $\mathbf{A} := (\mathbf{A}_1, \mathbf{A}_2)$ *be an adversary acting in two phases. First,* $\mathbf{A}_1$ *takes no input and outputs* $(B, state)$, *where* $B \in \mathcal{T}$ *and state is some state information. Then,* $\mathbf{A}_2$ *takes* $(B, state)$ *and* K_{ec} *as input, where* $K_{ec} \leftarrow \mathsf{kg}$, *and outputs* $(A, C) \in \mathcal{A} \times \mathcal{C}$. *The advantage of* $\mathbf{A}$ *for targeted ciphertext unforgeability is*

$$\mathrm{Adv}_{\mathsf{EC}}^{\mathsf{tcu}}(\mathbf{A}) := \Pr[\mathsf{dec}(K_{ec}, A, C, B) \neq \perp].$$

It is not difficult to see that the HFC encryption scheme [13] satisfies targeted ciphertext unforgeability in the random oracle model.

The ciphertext integrity of ECT is reduced to the second-ciphertext unforgeability and the targeted ciphertext unforgeability of EC and the STPRP property of TBC:

Theorem 2 (Ciphertext Integrity). *Let* $\mathbf{A}$ *be an adversary against* ECT *making at most* q_e, q_d, *and* q_c *queries to* **Enc**, **Dec**, *and* **ChalDec**, *respectively. Then, there exist adversaries* $\dot{\mathbf{A}}$, $\ddot{\mathbf{A}}$, *and* $\mathbf{D}$ *such that*

$$\mathrm{Adv}_{\mathsf{ECT}}^{\mathsf{mo\text{-}ctxt}}(\mathbf{A}) \leq q_e \cdot \mathrm{Adv}_{\mathsf{EC}}^{\mathsf{scu}}(\dot{\mathbf{A}}) + (q_d + q_c) \cdot \mathrm{Adv}_{\mathsf{EC}}^{\mathsf{tcu}}(\ddot{\mathbf{A}}) + \mathrm{Adv}_{\mathsf{TBC}}^{\mathsf{stprp}}(\mathbf{D})$$
$$+ (q_e + q_d + q_c)^2 / 2^{\ell+1}.$$

The run time of $\dot{\mathbf{A}}$, $\ddot{\mathbf{A}}$, *and* $\mathbf{D}$ *is at most about that of* MO-CTXT$_{\mathsf{ECT}}^{\mathbf{A}}$. $\mathbf{D}$ *makes at most* $q_e + q_d + q_c$ *queries to its oracle.*

Proof. The game MO-CTXT$_{\mathsf{ECT}}^{\mathbf{A}}$ is shown in Fig. 6. Without loss of generality, it is assumed that $\mathbf{A}$ terminates right after *win* gets **true**.

The game MO-CTXT-G$_1^{\mathbf{A}}$ in Fig. 7 is different from MO-CTXT$_{\mathsf{ECT}}^{\mathbf{A}}$ in that the former records all the histories of E_K and D_K by "$P[B, C_1] \leftarrow L$" and uses them to answer to queries to **Dec** and **ChalDec**. Thus,

$$\mathrm{Adv}_{\mathsf{ECT}}^{\mathsf{mo\text{-}ctxt}}(\mathbf{A}) = \Pr[\text{MO-CTXT}_{\mathsf{ECT}}^{\mathbf{A}} = \mathbf{true}] = \Pr[\text{MO-CTXTG}_1^{\mathbf{A}} = \mathbf{true}].$$

The game MO-CTXT-G$_2^{\mathbf{A}}$ in Fig. 8 is different from MO-CTXT-G$_1^{\mathbf{A}}$ in that the former uses a random tweakable permutation ϖ instead of TBC. Let $\mathbf{D}$ be an adversary against TBC. $\mathbf{D}$ has either $(\mathsf{E}_K, \mathsf{D}_K)$ or (ϖ, ϖ^{-1}) as an oracle and simulates MO-CTXT-G$_1^{\mathbf{A}}$ or MO-CTXT-G$_2^{\mathbf{A}}$ with the use of its oracle. Thus,

$$\mathrm{Adv}_{\mathsf{TBC}}^{\mathsf{stprp}}(\mathbf{D}) = \big| \Pr[\text{MO-CTXT-G}_1^{\mathbf{A}} = \mathbf{true}] - \Pr[\text{MO-CTXT-G}_2^{\mathbf{A}} = \mathbf{true}] \big|.$$

$\mathbf{D}$ makes at most $q_e + q_d + q_c$ queries to its oracle, and its run time is at most about that of MO-CTXT$_{\mathsf{ECT}}^{\mathbf{A}}$.

In the game MO-CTXT-G$_3^{\mathbf{A}}$ shown in Fig. 8, **Dec** and **ChalDec** select L uniformly at random from Σ^{ℓ}, while they call ϖ^{-1} in MO-CTXT-G$_2^{\mathbf{A}}$. As long as no collision is found for L, the games are equivalent to each other. Thus,

$$\big| \Pr[\text{MO-CTXT-G}_2^{\mathbf{A}} = \mathbf{true}] - \Pr[\text{MO-CTXT-G}_3^{\mathbf{A}} = \mathbf{true}] \big| \leq (q_e + q_d + q_c)^2 / 2^{\ell+1}.$$

Now, $\Pr[\text{MO-CTXT-G}_3^{\mathbf{A}} = \mathbf{true}]$ is evaluated. Suppose that *win* is set **true** by a query (A^*, C^*, B^*) to **ChalDec**. Let Win$_1$, Win$_2$, and Win$_3$ be the cases that

1. $P[B^*, C_1^*] \neq \perp$ and $P[B^*, C_1^*]$ is already set by **Enc**,
2. $P[B^*, C_1^*] \neq \perp$ and $P[B^*, C_1^*]$ is already set by **Dec** or **ChalDec**, and
3. $P[B^*, C_1^*] = \perp$,

respectively, where C_1^* is the least significant ℓ bits of C^*. Then,

$$\Pr[\text{MO-CTXT-G}_3^A = \text{true}] = \Pr[\text{Win}_1] + \Pr[\text{Win}_2] + \Pr[\text{Win}_3].$$

For Win_1, suppose that **Enc** sets $P[B^*, C_1^*]$ while computing a reply $(\dot{C}, B^*)$ to a query $(\dot{A}, \dot{M})$. Then, $(\dot{A}, \dot{C}) \neq (A^*, C^*)$ since $(\dot{A}, \dot{C}, B^*) \in \mathcal{Y}$ and $(A^*, C^*, B^*) \notin \mathcal{Y}$. Thus, the following adversary $\dot{A}$ with the oracle $\text{enc}_{\dot{L}}$ against second-ciphertext unforgeability is successful. $\dot{A}$ runs MO-CTXT-G$_3^A$ except that $\dot{A}$ guesses $(\dot{A}, \dot{M})$, asks it to $\text{enc}_{\dot{L}}$ and gets $(\dot{C}, B^*)$ and $\dot{L}$. Finally, $\dot{A}$ outputs (A^*, C^*) satisfying $\text{dec}(\dot{L}, A^*, C^*, B^*) \neq \perp$. Thus, $\text{Adv}_{\text{EC}}^{\text{scu}}(\dot{A}) = \Pr[\text{Win}_1]/q_e$.

For Win_2 and Win_3, the following adversary $\ddot{A} = (\ddot{A}_1, \ddot{A}_2)$ against targeted ciphertext unforgeability is successful. First, $\ddot{A}_1$ runs MO-CTXT-G$_3^A$ and guesses (B^*, C_1^*). It interrupts the execution of MO-CTXT-G$_3^A$ right after it obtains (B^*, C_1^*) and outputs $(B^*, state^*)$. Then, $\ddot{A}_2$ takes $(B^*, state^*)$ and $\ddot{L} \leftarrow \Sigma^\ell$ as input and resumes the execution of MO-CTXT-G$_3^A$ by making use of $state^*$. Finally, $\ddot{A}_2$ outputs (A^*, C_0^*) satisfying $\text{dec}(\ddot{L}, A^*, C_0^*, B^*) \neq \perp$. Thus, $\text{Adv}_{\text{EC}}^{\text{tcu}}(\ddot{A}) = (\Pr[\text{Win}_2] + \Pr[\text{Win}_3])/(q_d + q_c)$. □

```
K ← Σⁿ; 𝒴 ← ∅                    ChalDec(A, C, B)
win ← false                       if (A, C, B) ∈ 𝒴 then
A^Enc,Dec,ChalDec                    return ⊥
return win                        end if
                                  C₀‖C₁ ← C
Enc(A, M)                         L ← D_K(B, C₁)
L ← Σˡ                            if dec(L, A, C₀, B) = ⊥ then
(C₀, B) ← enc(L, A, M)               return ⊥
C₁ ← E_K(B, L)                    else
C ← C₀‖C₁                            win ← true
𝒴 ← 𝒴 ∪ {(A, C, B)}                  M ← dec(L, A, C₀, B)
return (C, B)                        return (M, L)
                                  end if
Dec(A, C, B)
C₀‖C₁ ← C
L ← D_K(B, C₁)
return dec(L, A, C₀, B)
```

Fig. 6. Game MO-CTXT$_{\text{ECT}}^A$

Binding Properties. ECT inherits (strong) receiver binding from EC.

ECT also inherits sender binding from EC. Suppose that (K, A, C, B) satisfies $\text{DEC}(K, A, C, B) \neq \perp$ and $\text{VER}(A, M, L, B) = 0$, where $(M, L) \leftarrow \text{DEC}(K, A, C, B)$. Then, $L = D_K(B, C_1)$, $\text{dec}(L, A, C_0, B) = M$ and $M \neq \perp$, where $C = C_0\|C_1$. In addition, $\text{ver}(A, M, L, B) = 0$.

```
K ← Σⁿ; 𝒴 ← ∅                         ChalDec(A, C, B)
win ← false                           if (A, C, B) ∈ 𝒴 then
A^Enc,Dec,ChalDec                         return ⊥
return win                            end if
                                      C₀‖C₁ ← C
Enc(A, M)                             if P[B, C₁] ≠ ⊥ then
L ← Σ^ℓ                                    L ← P[B, C₁]
(C₀, B) ← enc(L, A, M)                else
C₁ ← E_K(B, L)                            L ← D_K(B, C₁)
C ← C₀‖C₁                                 P[B, C₁] ← L
𝒴 ← 𝒴 ∪ {(A, C, B)}                   end if
P[B, C₁] ← L                          if dec(L, A, C₀, B) = ⊥ then
return (C, B)                             return ⊥
                                      else
Dec(A, C, B)                              win ← true
C₀‖C₁ ← C                                 M ← dec(L, A, C₀, B)
if P[B, C₁] ≠ ⊥ then                      return (M, L)
    L ← P[B, C₁]                      end if
else
    L ← D_K(B, C₁)
    P[B, C₁] ← L
end if
return dec(L, A, C₀, B)
```

Fig. 7. MO-CTXT-G_1^A. All the entries of the table P are initialized by $\perp$.

4   Remotely Keyed ccAEAD

RK ccAEAD is a particular type of ccAEAD. Their difference is that, for RK ccAEAD, some parts of encryption and decryption are done by a trusted device keeping the secret key. A user or a host performs encryption and/or decryption by making use of the trusted device. The amount of computation for the trusted device is required to be independent of the lengths of a message, associated data, and a ciphertext due to the common case that the computational power of the trusted device is limited.

Dodis et al. [14] left it as an open problem to formalize and construct RK ccAEAD schemes. An answer will be given to the problem in this section.

4.1   Syntax

RK ccAEAD is formalized as a tuple of algorithms RKCAE = (RKKg, RKEnc, RKDec, RKVer). It is involved with a key space $\mathcal{K} := \Sigma^n$, an associated-data space $\mathcal{A} \subseteq \Sigma^*$, a message space $\mathcal{M} \subseteq \Sigma^*$, a ciphertext space $\mathcal{C} \subseteq \Sigma^*$, an opening-key space $\mathcal{L} := \Sigma^\ell$, and a binding-tag space $\mathcal{T} := \Sigma^\tau$.

In the formalization below, for simplicity, it is assumed that the trusted device is called only once during encryption and decryption:

- The key generation algorithm RKKg returns a secret key $K \in \mathcal{K}$ chosen uniformly at random.

```
ϖ ← P_{τ,ℓ}; 𝒴 ← ∅                          ChalDec(A, C, B)
win ← false                                  if (A, C, B) ∈ 𝒴 then
A^{Enc,Dec,ChalDec}                              return ⊥
return win                                   end if
                                             C_0‖C_1 ← C
Enc(A, M)                                    if P[B, C_1] ≠ ⊥ then
L ←$ Σ^ℓ                                          L ← P[B, C_1]
(C_0, B) ← enc(L, A, M)                      else
C_1 ← ϖ(B, L)                                    G_2: L ← ϖ^{-1}(B, C_1)/G_3: L ←$ Σ^ℓ
‾‾‾‾‾‾‾‾‾‾                                        ‾‾‾‾‾‾‾‾‾‾‾‾‾‾‾‾‾‾‾‾‾‾‾‾‾‾‾‾‾‾‾‾‾
C ← C_0‖C_1                                      P[B, C_1] ← L
𝒴 ← 𝒴 ∪ {(A, C, B)}                          end if
P[B, C_1] ← L                                if dec(L, A, C_0, B) = ⊥ then
return (C, B)                                    return ⊥
                                             else
Dec(A, C, B)                                     win ← true
C_0‖C_1 ← C                                      M ← dec(L, A, C_0, B)
if P[B, C_1] ≠ ⊥ then                            return (M, L)
    L ← P[B, C_1]                            end if
else
    G_2: L ← ϖ^{-1}(B, C_1)/G_3: L ←$ Σ^ℓ
    ‾‾‾‾‾‾‾‾‾‾‾‾‾‾‾‾‾‾‾‾‾‾‾‾‾‾‾‾‾‾‾‾‾
    P[B, C_1] ← L
end if
return dec(L, A, C_0, B)
```

Fig. 8. MO-CTXT-G_2^A and MO-CTXT-G_3^A

- The encryption algorithm RKEnc takes as input $(K, A, M) \in \mathcal{K} \times \mathcal{A} \times \mathcal{M}$ and returns $(C, B) \in \mathcal{C} \times \mathcal{T}$. K is given to an algorithm TE, and it is run by a trusted device. The encryption proceeds in the following three steps:

$$(Q_e, S_e) \leftarrow \mathsf{Pre\text{-}TE}(A, M); R_e \leftarrow \mathsf{TE}_K(Q_e); (C, B) \leftarrow \mathsf{Post\text{-}TE}(R_e, S_e),$$

where S_e is some state information.
- The decryption algorithm RKDec takes as input $(K, A, C, B) \in \mathcal{K} \times \mathcal{A} \times \mathcal{C} \times \mathcal{T}$ and returns $(M, L) \in \mathcal{M} \times \mathcal{L}$ or $\perp \notin \mathcal{M} \times \mathcal{L}$. K is given to an algorithm TD, and it is run by a trusted device. The decryption proceeds in the following three steps:

$$(Q_d, S_d) \leftarrow \mathsf{Pre\text{-}TD}(A, C, B); R_d \leftarrow \mathsf{TD}_K(Q_d); (M, L)/\perp \leftarrow \mathsf{Post\text{-}TD}(R_d, S_d),$$

where S_d is some state information.
- The verification algorithm RKVer takes as input $(A, M, L, B) \in \mathcal{A} \times \mathcal{M} \times \mathcal{L} \times \mathcal{T}$ and returns $b \in \Sigma$.

As well as CAE, RKCAE satisfies correctness. For every $l \in \mathbb{N}$, $\Sigma^l \subseteq \mathcal{M}$ or $\Sigma^l \cap \mathcal{M} = \emptyset$. For any message M and the corresponding ciphertext C, $|C|$ depends only on $|M|$ and let $|C| = \mathsf{clen}(|M|)$.

4.2 Security Requirement

For RK ccAEAD, an adversary is allowed to have direct access to the trusted device. Thus, the adversary can run RKEnc and RKDec by using TE_K and TD_K as oracles, respectively.

Confidentiality. Confidentiality of RK ccAEAD is defined as real-or-random indistinguishability. The games RK-REAL and RK-RAND shown in Fig. 9 are introduced. An adversary $\mathbf{A}$ is given access to oracles $\mathbf{E}$, $\mathbf{D}$, and $\mathbf{ChalEnc}$. $\mathbf{A}$ is not allowed to decrypt (A, C, B) obtained by asking (A, M) to $\mathbf{ChalEnc}$. The advantage of $\mathbf{A}$ for confidentiality is

$$\mathrm{Adv}_{\mathrm{RKCAE}}^{\mathrm{rk\text{-}ror}}(\mathbf{A}) := \left| \Pr[\mathrm{RK\text{-}REAL}_{\mathrm{RKCAE}}^{\mathbf{A}} = 1] - \Pr[\mathrm{RK\text{-}RAND}_{\mathrm{RKCAE}}^{\mathbf{A}} = 1] \right|.$$

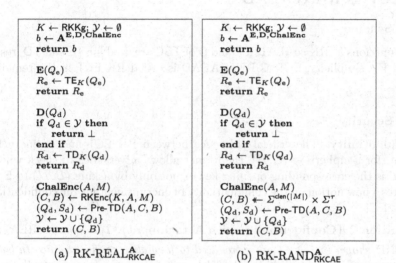

(a) RK-REAL$_{\mathrm{RKCAE}}^{\mathbf{A}}$ (b) RK-RAND$_{\mathrm{RKCAE}}^{\mathbf{A}}$

Fig. 9. Games for confidentiality of RK ccAEAD

Ciphertext Integrity. The game RK-CTXT$_{\mathrm{RKCAE}}^{\mathbf{A}}$, shown in Fig. 10, is introduced. An adversary $\mathbf{A}$ is given access to oracles $\mathbf{E}$, $\mathbf{D}$, and $\mathbf{ChalDec}$. $\mathbf{A}$ is not allowed to repeat the same queries to $\mathbf{ChalDec}$. The game outputs **true** if the number of valid ciphertexts produced by $\mathbf{A}$ is greater than the number of queries to $\mathbf{E}$ made by $\mathbf{A}$. The advantage of $\mathbf{A}$ for ciphertext integrity is

$$\mathrm{Adv}_{\mathrm{RKCAE}}^{\mathrm{rk\text{-}ctxt}}(\mathbf{A}) := \Pr[\mathrm{RK\text{-}CTXT}_{\mathrm{RKCAE}}^{\mathbf{A}} = \mathbf{true}].$$

Binding Properties. $\mathrm{Adv}_{\mathrm{RKCAE}}^{\mathrm{r\text{-}bind}}$, $\mathrm{Adv}_{\mathrm{RKCAE}}^{\mathrm{sr\text{-}bind}}$, and $\mathrm{Adv}_{\mathrm{RKCAE}}^{\mathrm{s\text{-}bind}}$ are defined as $\mathrm{Adv}_{\mathrm{CAE}}^{\mathrm{r\text{-}bind}}$, $\mathrm{Adv}_{\mathrm{CAE}}^{\mathrm{sr\text{-}bind}}$, and $\mathrm{Adv}_{\mathrm{CAE}}^{\mathrm{s\text{-}bind}}$, respectively, simply by replacing Dec with RKDec and Ver with RKVer.

```
K ← RKKg                    E(Q_e)                      ChalDec(A, C, B)
win ← false; ctr ← 0        ctr ← ctr + 1               if RKDec(K, A, C, B) ≠ ⊥ then
A^E,D,ChalDec               return TE_K(Q_e)                ctr ← ctr − 1
if ctr < 0 then                                         end if
    win ← true              D(Q_d)                      return RKDec(K, A, C, B)
end if                      return TD_K(Q_d)
return win
```

Fig. 10. Game RK-CTXT$_{\mathsf{RKCAE}}^{\mathbf{A}}$ for ciphertext integrity of RK ccAEAD

5 ECT as RK ccAEAD

5.1 Scheme

ECT functions as RK ccAEAD if E and D of TBC are used for TE and TD, respectively. For simplicity, ECT as RK ccAEAD is called RK ECT in the remaining parts.

5.2 Security

Confidentiality. The crucial difference between RK ECT and ordinary ECT is that, for a ciphertext (C, B), the former allows adversaries to check whether $L' \in \mathcal{L}$ is the corresponding opening key or not only by asking (B, L') to E_K. It requires a new notion on the confidentiality of encryption for the confidentiality of RK ECT:

Definition 2 (Confidentiality with Attachment). *Two games* $\widetilde{\mathrm{otREAL}}$ *and* $\widetilde{\mathrm{otRAND}}$ *shown in Fig. 11 are introduced to formalize confidentiality. In both of the games, an adversary* $\mathbf{A}$ *is allowed to ask only a single query to the oracle* enc, *while* $\mathbf{A}$ *is allowed to ask multiple queries adaptively to the oracle* (ϖ, ϖ^{-1}). *The advantage of* $\mathbf{A}$ *for confidentiality is*

$$\widetilde{\mathrm{Adv}}_{\mathsf{EC}}^{\text{ot-ror}}(\mathbf{A}) := \left| \Pr[\widetilde{\mathrm{otREAL}}_{\mathsf{EC}}^{\mathbf{A}} = 1] - \Pr[\widetilde{\mathrm{otRAND}}_{\mathsf{EC}}^{\mathbf{A}} = 1] \right|,$$

It is not difficult to see that the HFC encryption scheme [13] satisfies confidentiality with attachment in the random oracle model.

The confidentiality of RK ECT is reduced to the confidentiality of EC with attachment and the STPRP of TBC. The proof is omitted due to the page limit.

Theorem 3 (Confidentiality). *Let* $\mathbf{A}$ *be an adversary against RK ECT making at most* q_e, q_d, *and* q_c *queries to* $\mathbf{E}$, $\mathbf{D}$, *and* $\mathbf{ChalEnc}$, *respectively. Then, there exist adversaries* $\dot{\mathbf{A}}$ *and* $\mathbf{D}$ *such that*

$$\mathrm{Adv}_{\mathsf{ECT}}^{\text{rk-ror}}(\mathbf{A}) \leq q_c \cdot \widetilde{\mathrm{Adv}}_{\mathsf{EC}}^{\text{ot-ror}}(\dot{\mathbf{A}}) + 2 \cdot \mathrm{Adv}_{\mathsf{TBC}}^{\text{stprp}}(\mathbf{D}) + q_c(q_e + q_d + q_c)/2^{\ell-1}.$$

The run time of $\dot{\mathbf{A}}$ *and* $\mathbf{D}$ *is at most about that of* RK-REAL$_{\mathsf{ECT}}^{\mathbf{A}}$. $\dot{\mathbf{A}}$ *makes at most* $q_e + q_d + q_c$ *queries to the uniform random tweakable permutation* (ϖ, ϖ^{-1}). $\mathbf{D}$ *makes at most* $q_e + q_d + q_c$ *queries to its oracle.*

$K_{ec} \leftarrow \text{kg}; \varpi \leftarrow \mathcal{P}_{\tau,\ell}$ $b \leftarrow \mathbf{A}^{\text{enc},(\varpi,\varpi^{-1})}$ **return** b $\text{enc}(A,M)$ $(C,B) \leftarrow \text{enc}(K_{ec},A,M)$ $C' \leftarrow \varpi(B,K_{ec})$ **return** (C,B,C')	$K_{ec} \leftarrow \text{kg}; \varpi \leftarrow \mathcal{P}_{\tau,\ell}$ $b \leftarrow \mathbf{A}^{\text{enc},(\varpi,\varpi^{-1})}$ **return** b $\text{enc}(A,M)$ $(C,B) \leftarrow \Sigma^{\text{clen}(|M|)} \times \Sigma^{\tau}$ $C' \leftarrow \varpi(B,K_{ec})$ **return** (C,B,C')
(a) $\widetilde{\text{otREAL}}_{\text{EC}}^{\mathbf{A}}$	(b) $\widetilde{\text{otRAND}}_{\text{EC}}^{\mathbf{A}}$

Fig. 11. The games for confidentiality of encryption

Ciphertext Integrity. The ciphertext integrity of RK ECT is reduced to the receiver-binding and the targeted ciphertext unforgeability of EC and the STPRP property of TBC. The proof is omitted due to the page limit.

Theorem 4 (Ciphertext Integrity). *Suppose that the encryption scheme used for RK ECT satisfies strong correctness. Let* **A** *be an adversary against RK ECT making at most* q_e, q_d, *and* q_c *queries to* **E**, **D**, *and* **ChalDec***, respectively. Then, there exist adversaries* $\dot{\mathbf{A}}$, $\ddot{\mathbf{A}}$, *and* **D** *such that*

$$\text{Adv}_{\text{ECT}}^{\text{rk-ctxt}}(\mathbf{A}) \leq \text{Adv}_{\text{EC}}^{\text{r-bind}}(\dot{\mathbf{A}}) + (q_d + q_c) \cdot \text{Adv}_{\text{EC}}^{\text{tcu}}(\ddot{\mathbf{A}}) + \text{Adv}_{\text{TBC}}^{\text{stprp}}(\mathbf{D})$$
$$+ (q_e + q_d + q_c)^2/2^\ell.$$

The run time of $\dot{\mathbf{A}}$, $\ddot{\mathbf{A}}$, *and* **D** *is at most about that of* $\text{RK-CTXT}_{\text{ECT}}^{\mathbf{A}}$. **D** *makes at most* $q_e + q_d + q_c$ *queries to its oracles.*

Binding Properties. To see ECT as RK ccAEAD does not affect the binding properties. Thus, as discussed in Sect. 3.2, RK ECT inherits both (strong) receiver binding and sender binding from EC.

6 Conclusions

We have studied the problem of constructing compactly committing AEAD (ccAEAD) based on encryptment, originally proposed by Dodis et al. [13,14] in the context of end-to-end messaging. We proposed ECT, a conceptually simplified, more efficient construction than those proposed by Dodis et al. by using a TBC instead of AEAD. We also present a formalization of remotely keyed variant of ccAEAD (RK ccAEAD) and show that our ECT is indeed RK ccAEAD, which addresses the open question posed by Dodis et al. [14] positively. This indicates that ECT is useful when ccAEAD is implemented on the platform consisting of (small, slow) trusted and untrusted (but cheap and fast) modules. Future work is to explore the relationship between remotely keyed ccAEAD and leakage-resilient AEAD. It is also interesting to see if other generic constructions such as CtE and CEP in [18] can be simplified.

Acknowledgements. The authors thank Akiko Inoue for fruitful discussions. The first author was supported by JSPS KAKENHI Grant Number 21K11885.

References

1. Albertini, A., Duong, T., Gueron, S., Kölbl, S., Luykx, A., Schmieg, S.: How to abuse and fix authenticated encryption without key commitment. In: Butler, K.R.B., Thomas, K. (eds.) 31st USENIX Security Symposium, USENIX Security 2022, pp. 3291–3308. USENIX Association (2022). https://www.usenix.org/conference/usenixsecurity22/presentation/albertini

2. Bellare, M., Hoang, V.T.: Efficient schemes for committing authenticated encryption. In: Dunkelman, O., Dziembowski, S. (eds.) EUROCRYPT 2022. LNCS, vol. 13276, pp. 845–875. Springer, Heidelberg (2022). https://doi.org/10.1007/978-3-031-07085-3_29

3. Bellare, M., Namprempre, C.: Authenticated encryption: relations among notions and analysis of the generic composition paradigm. In: Okamoto, T. (ed.) ASIACRYPT 2000. LNCS, vol. 1976, pp. 531–545. Springer, Heidelberg (2000). https://doi.org/10.1007/3-540-44448-3_41

4. Bellizia, D., et al.: Mode-level vs. implementation-level physical security in symmetric cryptography. In: Micciancio, D., Ristenpart, T. (eds.) CRYPTO 2020. LNCS, vol. 12170, pp. 369–400. Springer, Cham (2020). https://doi.org/10.1007/978-3-030-56784-2_13

5. Berti, F., Guo, C, Pereira, O., Peters, T., Standaert, F-X.,: TEDT, a leakage-resistant AEAD mode for high physical security applications. IACR Trans. Cryptogr. Hardw. Embed. Syst. **2020**(1), 256–320 (2020). https://doi.org/10.13154/tches.v2020.i1.256-320

6. Berti, F., Pereira, O., Standaert, F.-X.: Reducing the cost of authenticity with leakages: a CIML2−secureAE scheme with one call to a strongly protected tweakable block cipher. In: Buchmann, J., Nitaj, A., Rachidi, T. (eds.) AFRICACRYPT 2019. LNCS, vol. 11627, pp. 229–249. Springer, Cham (2019). https://doi.org/10.1007/978-3-030-23696-0_12

7. Blaze, M.: High-bandwidth encryption with low-bandwidth smartcards. In: Gollmann, D. (ed.) FSE 1996. LNCS, vol. 1039, pp. 33–40. Springer, Heidelberg (1996). https://doi.org/10.1007/3-540-60865-6_40

8. Blaze, M., Feigenbaum, J., Naor, M.: A formal treatment of remotely keyed encryption. In: Nyberg, K. (ed.) EUROCRYPT 1998. LNCS, vol. 1403, pp. 251–265. Springer, Heidelberg (1998). https://doi.org/10.1007/BFb0054131

9. Chan, J., Rogaway, P.: On committing authenticated-encryption. In: Atluri, V., Pietro, R.D., Jensen, C.D., Meng, W. (eds.) ESORICS 2022. LNCS, vol. 13555, pp. 275–294. Springer, Heidelberg (2022). https://doi.org/10.1007/978-3-031-17146-8_14

10. Chen, L., Tang, Q.: People who live in glass houses should not throw stones: targeted opening message franking schemes. Cryptology ePrint Archive, Report 2018/994 (2018). https://eprint.iacr.org/2018/994

11. Dobraunig, C., et al.: Isap v2.0. IACR Trans. Symm. Cryptol. **2020**(S1), 390–416 (2020). https://doi.org/10.13154/tosc.v2020.iS1.390-416

12. Dodis, Y., An, J.H.: Concealment and its applications to authenticated encryption. In: Biham, E. (ed.) EUROCRYPT 2003. LNCS, vol. 2656, pp. 312–329. Springer, Heidelberg (2003). https://doi.org/10.1007/3-540-39200-9_19

13. Dodis, Y., Grubbs, P., Ristenpart, T., Woodage, J.: Fast message franking: from invisible salamanders to encryptment. In: Shacham, H., Boldyreva, A. (eds.) CRYPTO 2018. LNCS, vol. 10991, pp. 155–186. Springer, Cham (2018). https://doi.org/10.1007/978-3-319-96884-1_6

14. Dodis, Y., Grubbs, P., Ristenpart, T., Woodage, J.: Fast message franking: from invisible salamanders to encryptment. Cryptology ePrint Archive, Paper 2019/016 (2019). https://eprint.iacr.org/2019/016
15. Facebook: Facebook messenger. https://www.messenger.com. Accessed 09 Oct 2022
16. Facebook: Messenger secret conversations. Technical Whitepaper (2016). https://about.fb.com/wp-content/uploads/2016/07/messenger-secret-conversations-technical-whitepaper.pdf
17. Farshim, P., Orlandi, C., Rosie, R.: Security of symmetric primitives under incorrect usage of keys. IACR Trans. Symm. Cryptol. **2017**(1), 449–473 (2017). https://doi.org/10.13154/tosc.v2017.i1.449-473
18. Grubbs, P., Lu, J., Ristenpart, T.: Message franking via committing authenticated encryption. In: Katz, J., Shacham, H. (eds.) CRYPTO 2017. LNCS, vol. 10403, pp. 66–97. Springer, Cham (2017). https://doi.org/10.1007/978-3-319-63697-9_3
19. Hirose, S.: Compactly committing authenticated encryption using tweakable block cipher. In: Kutylowski, M., Zhang, J., Chen, C. (eds.) NSS 2020. LNCS, vol. 12570, pp. 187–206. Springer, Heidelberg (2020). https://doi.org/10.1007/978-3-030-65745-1_11
20. Huang, Q., Yang, G., Wong, D.S., Susilo, W.: Efficient strong designated verifier signature schemes without random oracle or with non-delegatability. Int. J. Inf. Secur. **10**(6), 373–385 (2011). https://doi.org/10.1007/s10207-011-0146-1
21. Huguenin-Dumittan, L., Leontiadis, I.: A message franking channel. In: Yu, Yu., Yung, M. (eds.) Inscrypt 2021. LNCS, vol. 13007, pp. 111–128. Springer, Cham (2021). https://doi.org/10.1007/978-3-030-88323-2_6
22. Jakobsson, M., Sako, K., Impagliazzo, R.: Designated verifier proofs and their applications. In: Maurer, U. (ed.) EUROCRYPT 1996. LNCS, vol. 1070, pp. 143–154. Springer, Heidelberg (1996). https://doi.org/10.1007/3-540-68339-9_13
23. Jakobsson, M., Stern, J.P., Yung, M.: Scramble all, encrypt small. In: Knudsen, L. (ed.) FSE 1999. LNCS, vol. 1636, pp. 95–111. Springer, Heidelberg (1999). https://doi.org/10.1007/3-540-48519-8_8
24. Katz, J., Yung, M.: Complete characterization of security notions for probabilistic private-key encryption. In: Proceedings of the Thirty-Second Annual ACM Symposium on Theory of Computing, pp. 245–254 (2000)
25. Len, J., Grubbs, P., Ristenpart, T.: Partitioning oracle attacks. In: Bailey, M., Greenstadt, R. (eds.) 30th USENIX Security Symposium, USENIX Security 2021, pp. 195–212. USENIX Association (2021). https://www.usenix.org/conference/usenixsecurity21/presentation/len
26. Leontiadis, I., Vaudenay, S.: Private message franking with after opening privacy. Cryptology ePrint Archive, Report 2018/938 (2018). https://eprint.iacr.org/2018/938
27. Liskov, M., Rivest, R.L., Wagner, D.: Tweakable block ciphers. In: Yung, M. (ed.) CRYPTO 2002. LNCS, vol. 2442, pp. 31–46. Springer, Heidelberg (2002). https://doi.org/10.1007/3-540-45708-9_3
28. Liskov, M.D., Rivest, R.L., Wagner, D.A.: Tweakable block ciphers. J. Cryptol. **24**(3), 588–613 (2011). https://doi.org/10.1007/s00145-010-9073-y
29. Lucks, S.: On the security of remotely keyed encryption. In: Biham, E. (ed.) FSE 1997. LNCS, vol. 1267, pp. 219–229. Springer, Heidelberg (1997). https://doi.org/10.1007/BFb0052349
30. Lucks, S.: Accelerated remotely keyed encryption. In: Knudsen, L. (ed.) FSE 1999. LNCS, vol. 1636, pp. 112–123. Springer, Heidelberg (1999). https://doi.org/10.1007/3-540-48519-8_9

31. Naito, Y., Sasaki, Y., Sugawara, T.: Secret can be public: low-memory AEAD mode for high-order masking. In: Dodis, Y., Shrimpton, T. (eds.) CRYPTO 2022. LNCS, vol. 13509, pp. 315–345. Springer, Heidelberg (2022). https://doi.org/10.1007/978-3-031-15982-4_11

32. Shen, Y., Peters, T., Standaert, F., Cassiers, G., Verhamme, C.: Triplex: an efficient and one-pass leakage-resistant mode of operation. IACR Trans. Cryptogr. Hardw. Embed. Syst. **2022**(4), 135–162 (2022). https://doi.org/10.46586/tches.v2022.i4.135-162

33. Signal Foundation: Signal. https://signal.org/. Accessed 09 Oct 2022

34. Tyagi, N., Grubbs, P., Len, J., Miers, I., Ristenpart, T.: Asymmetric message franking: content moderation for metadata-private end-to-end encryption. In: Boldyreva, A., Micciancio, D. (eds.) CRYPTO 2019. LNCS, vol. 11694, pp. 222–250. Springer, Cham (2019). https://doi.org/10.1007/978-3-030-26954-8_8

35. WhatsApp: WhatsApp Messenger. https://www.whatsapp.com. Accessed 09 Oct 2022

36. Yamamuro, H., Hara, K., Tezuka, M., Yoshida, Y., Tanaka, K.: Forward secure message franking. In: Park, J.H., Seo, S. (eds.) ICISC 2021. LNCS, vol. 13218, pp. 339–358. Springer, Heidelberg (2021). https://doi.org/10.1007/978-3-031-08896-4_18

Post-Quantum Analysis
and Implementations

Bit Security Analysis of Lattice-Based KEMs Under Plaintext-Checking Attacks

Ruiqi Mi[1,2]([⊠]) [iD], Haodong Jiang[3], and Zhenfeng Zhang[1,2]

[1] University of Chinese Academy of Sciences, Beijing 100049, China
[2] Trusted Computing and Information Assurance Laboratory, Institute of Software, Chinese Academy of Sciences, Beijing 100190, China
{ruiqi2017,zhenfeng}@iscas.ac.cn
[3] Henan Key Laboratory of Network Cryptography Technology, Zhengzhou, Henan, China

Abstract. Plaintext-checking attack (PCA) is a type of attack where an adversary recovers the secret key with the help of a plaintext-checking (PC) oracle that decides if a given ciphertext decrypts to a given plaintext. In particular, PCA exists in both the key misuse attacks for IND-CPA-secure lattice-based KEMs and generic side-channel attacks for IND-CCA-secure lattice-based KEMs. The query number of PC-oracle is a vital criterion for evaluating a PCA attack. Recently, Qin et al. [ASI-ACRYPT 2021] gave a systematic approach to finding the theoretical lower bound of PC-oracle query numbers for NIST-PQC lattice-based KEMs. Most of the prior works consider the substantial Oracle queries needed to recover the entire key. However, the adversary often has inadequate access to PC Oracles to fully recover the secret key. The concrete bit security loss with arbitrary PC Oracle access is unknown.

In this paper, we give a unified method to analyze the bit security loss with arbitrary PC Oracle access for lattice-based KEMs. First, we model the information leakage in the PC Oracle by PC-hint, and give a generic transformation from PC-hints to the perfect inner-product hint, which allows the adversary to integrate PC-hints progressively. Then, following the security analysis for LWE with the perfect inner-product hint given in Dachman-Soled et al. [CRYPTO 2020], we give a concrete relationship between the PC Oracle query number and the bit-security of the lattice-based KEM under PCA. Our proposed method is applicable to all CCA-secure NIST candidate lattice-based KEMs. Applying our methods to NIST-PQC lattice-based KEMs, we get the bit-security loss of the lattice-based KEM under PCA. Take Kyber768 (original 182-bit-security) as an example, the bit security of Kyber768 is reduced to 128 after 444 PC-oracle queries and reduced to 64 after 998 PC-oracle queries, while in Qin et al. [ASIACRYPT 2021] 1774 queries are required to recover the whole secret key. Our analysis also demonstrates the possibility of reducing the Oracle queries needed in PCA. The adversary may stop querying plaintext-checking oracle and solves the remaining part of reused secret offline with the help of lattice reduction algorithms when the cost of lattice reduction algorithms becomes acceptable.

C. Carlet et al. (Eds.): SAC 2023, LNCS 14201, pp. 255–274, 2024.
https://doi.org/10.1007/978-3-031-53368-6_13

Keywords: Lattice-based cryptography · Plaintext-checking Attacks · KEM · Learning With Errors · Kyber

1 Introduction

Current Diffie-Hellman key exchange and other widely used public key cryptography based on factoring or discrete logarithm problems will no longer be secure if large-scale quantum computers become available. According to the roadmap released by the US National Institute of Standards and Technology (NIST) and the Department of Homeland Security [13], the transition to post-quantum standards should be completed by 2030.

NIST began the call for post-quantum cryptography algorithms from all over the world in February 2016 [12]. In the third round, there are 4 finalists and 5 alternative candidates for Public Key Encryption (PKE) or Key Encapsulation Mechanism (KEM). There are 3 lattice-based KEMs among the 4 finalists. After careful analysis, NIST has selected one finalist and four alternate candidates to move on to the fourth round. Crystals-Kyber [2] is the first PKE/KEM candidate to be standardized, which is based on the lattice assumption [14].

The construction of CPA-secure PKE usually follows the design pattern given in [10]. Most of the lattice-based NIST candidate CPA-secure KEMs are designed in such a pattern (e.g. Crystals-Kyber [2], Saber [4], FrodoKEM [11], NewHope [16]), and their hardness comes from the Learning With Errors (LWE) problem [20]. All LWE-based KEMs in Rounds 2 and 3 of the NIST standardization use a Fujisaki-Okamoto (FO) transformation [6] to achieve IND-CCA security.

The ongoing standardization process raises an important question: a plaintext-checking attack may happen when the public key is reused, thus there is no security guarantee on both IND-CPA and IND-CCA KEMs. For IND-CPA secure KEM, the plaintext-checking attack runs as follows. Suppose Alice reuses her public key pk_A. The adversary $\mathcal{A}$ impersonates Bob and tries to recover each coefficient of Alice's reused secret key sk_A with the help of the plaintext-checking oracle (PC Oracle) $\mathcal{O}$. $\mathcal{A}$ crafts ciphertext ct and shared secret K and sends ct, K to $\mathcal{O}$. $\mathcal{O}$ determines if the two shared keys match or not. For each coefficient $sk_A[i]$ of sk_A, $\mathcal{A}$ determines the subset to which $sk_A[i]$ belongs based on $\mathcal{O}$'s reply. For IND-CCA secure KEMs, a plaintext-checking attack can also be launched with the help of side-channel information. According to [19], FO transformation can be bypassed by accessing physical decapsulation devices and collecting useful match or mismatch information.

Practically, the adversary $\mathcal{A}$ often has limitations in gathering sufficient perfect side-channel information and constructing a PC Oracle. In plaintext-checking attacks, users may stop misusing their public key in a short time. Thus, the adversary has restricted time to query the PC Oracle and fully recover the secret key. For example, the adversary $\mathcal{A}$ can only access a PC Oracle that is constructed from a USB key for online banking service before the users report the loss. PC Oracle constructed by reusing the KEM's public key cannot be accessed when users stop reusing the public key. Thus, an optimal plaintext-checking attack has the least number of plaintext-checking Oracle queries for successful key recovery. There are numerous works on reducing oracle queries in the plaintext-checking attack [5,9,15,17,18]. All these attacks aim to fully recover the reused secret with as few queries as possible. Qin et al. [18] gave a systematic approach to finding the theoretical lower bound of PC-oracle query numbers for all NIST-PQC lattice-based IND-CPA/IND-CCA secure KEMs. The calculation of their lower bounds is essentially the computation of a certain Shannon entropy. Thus, one cannot find a better attack with fewer queries on average for full key recovery. Their lower bounds are also confirmed by experiments.

Most of the prior works about plaintext-checking attacks to lattice-based KEMs focus on recovering the full reused secret key. However, the adversary may not have enough oracle access to construct a reliable plaintext-checking oracle for recovering the full secret. Thus, compared to recovering the full secret with substantial amounts of oracle queries, one may be interested in the following question: *How to analyze the concrete bit security loss of PKE/KEM after a limited number of oracle queries in plaintext-checking attacks?*.

Some works already analyzed the effects of information leakage on the LWE problem. For example, Dachman-Soled et al. [3] give a general framework to analyze the influence of side-channel information. They provide four types of side-channel information ("hint") and analyze the concrete security loss for each type of hint. However, the side-channel information leaked in the plaintext-checking attack ("plaintext-checking hint") has not been considered. Thus, it remains unclear how to analyze the influence of plaintext-checking attacks on the hardness of LWE information.

Let $\mathcal{S} = \{S_0, S_1, ..., S_{n-1}\}$ be the set of all possible values for one coefficient block and its corresponding probabilities $\{P_0, P_1, ..., P_{n-1}\}$. For a single coefficient block $sk_A[i]$, $P_j = Pr(sk_A[i] = S_j | sk_A[i] \leftarrow \mathcal{S})$ for $j = 0, 1, ..., n-1$. Let $H(\mathcal{S})$ the Shannon entropy for $\mathcal{S}$, Typically, we have $H(\mathcal{S}|PChint) \leq H(\mathcal{S})$. In other words, each oracle query decreases the Shannon entropy of Alice's reused secret sk_A. $\mathcal{O}$ returns a bit b depending on whether the plaintext matches or not. Intrinsically, for each coefficient of reused secret key sk_A, the querying process can be described as a function f of reused secret key sk_A, plaintext pt, ciphertext ct, in which:

$$f(sk_A, ct, pt) = b \in \{0, 1\}$$

We define such type of side-channel information as a plaintext-checking hint. Suppose the adversary $\mathcal{A}$ tries to recover the i-th coefficient of sk_A. Let v be a unit vector with $v[i] = 1$. Thus it is very natural to express $f(sk_A, ct, pt)$ as:

$$f(sk_A, ct, pt) := f(\langle sk_A, v \rangle)$$

$f(sk_A, ct, pt)$ is a general description of plaintext-checking hint. We find a solution to transform plaintext-checking hints to known hints for lattice-based KEMs.

Contributions. The main contributions of this paper include:

- We give a unified method to analyze the bit security loss even with very little PC Oracle access for all lattice-based NIST candidate KEMs. Our basic idea is to give a unified description of the information leakage in the PC-oracle (called PC-hint). PC-hint is described in the form of $f(sk_A, ct, pt)$, which is suitable for analyzing a security loss when the adversary has limited Oracle access. Then, we give a generic transformation from the least number of PC-hints to the perfect inner-product hint for lattice-based KEMs in the form of $\langle sk_A, v \rangle = l$. The least number of PC-hints needed in such a transformation is the lower bound of oracle queries needed to recover a single coefficient block as analyzed in [18]. We show that PC-hints can be transformed into a perfect inner-product hint when a coefficient block of sk_A is recovered, and the adversary can integrate PC-hints progressively. Finally, by following the security analysis for LWE with the perfect inner-product hint given in Dachman-Soled et al. [3], we establish a concrete relationship between the PC-oracle query number and the bit-security of the lattice-based KEM under PCA in Sect. 4. Our proposed method is applicable to all CPA-secure and CCA-secure NIST candidate lattice-based KEMs.
- We analyze the bit security loss under the plaintext-checking attack for all lattice-based NIST candidate KEMs with the help of the toolbox given in [3]. We present the relationship between bit security and plaintext-checking oracle query times in Table 1. The number in parentheses is the Oracle query needed when classical bit security is 100 (original classical bit-security less than 128). Note that the classical bit security of Kyber512 is 118. The classical bit security of LightSaber is 118. The classical bit security of NewHope512 is 112. The bit security of Kyber768 is reduced to 128 after 444 PC-oracle queries and further reduced to 64 after 998 PC-oracle queries, whereas 1774 queries are required to recover the entire secret key, as indicated in [18]. We provide the concrete relationship between the number of oracle queries and classical/quantum bit security in Sect. 5. Such a result reminds us that the loss of security is non-negligible even when the adversary cannot fully recover the secret key.
- Based on the analysis above, the plaintext-checking attack can be further enhanced by combining Qin's plaintext-checking attack [18] with standard lattice reduction techniques. The adversary may stop querying the plaintext-checking oracle and solve the remaining part of the reused secret offline with the help of lattice reduction algorithms when the cost of lattice reduction algorithms becomes acceptable. We present a detailed analysis of dimension, volume, and lattice basis after each PC-hint integration in Sect. 4.3. These results can be directly used as input to lattice reduction algorithms when the cost becomes acceptable.

Organizations. We start with some preliminaries in Sect. 2. Section 3 models the secret leakage in plaintext-checking attack (plaintext-checking hint). Section 4 gives a concrete mathematical expression of plaintext-checking hint (Sect. 4.2), explains how to integrate plaintext-checking hint into the lattice

Table 1. Relationship between the number of queries and classical bit security of all lattice-based NIST KEMs, $E(\#Queries)$ denotes the theoretical lower bound for the number of queries given in [18]. The number in parentheses is the Oracle queries needed when classical bit security is 100 (original classical bit-security less than 128).

Bit	Kyber512		Kyber768		Kyber1024	
Security	(E(#Queries)=1312)		(E(#Queries)=1774)		(E(#Queries)=2365)	
128(100)	(80)		444		950	
64	533		998		1459	
Bit	LightSaber		Saber		FireSaber	
Security	(E(#Queries)=1460)		(E(#Queries)=2091)		(E(#Queries)=2642)	
128(100)	(228)		612		1181	
64	631		1230		1782	
Bit	Frodo640		Frodo976		Frodo1344	
Security	(E(#Queries)=18329)		(E(#Queries)=26000)		(E(#Queries)=29353)	
128	833		8177		14006	
64	8005		15445		20234	
Bit	NewHope512			NewHope1024		
Security	(E(#Queries)=1660)			(E(#Queries)=3180)		
128(100)	(137)			1406		
64	571			2140		

(Sect. 4.3). Section 5 gives experimental results. It shows the concrete relationship between bit security and the number of oracle queries for NIST second-round KEM candidates: Kyber, Saber, Frodo and NewHope.

Independent and Concurrent Work. Very recently, Guo and Mårtensson [8] showed an improved plaintext-checking attack that recovers multiple secret coefficients in a parallel way. The comparisons are summarized below:

1 Guo and Mårtensson showed how to recover partial information of multiple secret entries in each oracle call. The adversary split the two-dimensional plane for two secret coefficients and decides from the mismatch oracle call which part the two coefficients belong to. Compared to the lower bound given in [18], the attack given in [8] reduces the number of queries needed by 0.08%, 10.6%, 10.6% for Kyber512, Kyber768, Kyber1024, and 3.4%, 5.01%, 8.1% for LightSaber, Saber, FireSaber.

2 In the discussion part, they give a rough estimation of the query sample complexity for Kyber and Saber when post-processing is allowed. They employ the lattice estimator given in [1]. They did not give concrete relationship between the number of queries and the geometry of the lattice in theory.

2 Preliminaries

A lattice is a discrete additive subgroup of $\mathbb{R}^m$, denoted as Λ. Lattice Λ is generated by a set of linearly independent *basis* $\{b_j\} \subset \mathbb{R}^m$, that is $\Lambda :=$

$\{\Sigma_j z_j \boldsymbol{b}_j : z_j \in \mathbb{Z}\}$. The i-th *successive minimum* of a lattice, $\lambda_i(\Lambda)$, is the radius of the smallest ball centered at the origin containing at least i linearly independent lattice vectors.

We denote the dimension of lattice Λ as m and the rank as n. If $n = m$, the lattice is full rank. Matrix $\boldsymbol{B}$ having all basis vectors as rows can be called a *basis*. The volume of the lattice is defined as $Vol(\Lambda) := \sqrt{det(\boldsymbol{BB}^T)}$. The dual lattice of Λ in $\mathbb{R}^n$ is defined as:

$$\Lambda^* := \{\boldsymbol{y} \in Span(\boldsymbol{B}) \mid \forall x \in \Lambda, \langle \boldsymbol{x}, \boldsymbol{y} \rangle \in \mathbb{Z}\} \tag{1}$$

Definition 1 (search-LWE problem with short secrets). *Let n, m, q be positive integers, and let χ be a distribution over $\mathbb{Z}$. The search LWE problem (with short secrets) for parameters (n, m, q, χ) is:*
  Given the pair $(\boldsymbol{A} \in \mathbb{Z}_q^{m \times n}, \boldsymbol{b} = \boldsymbol{z}\boldsymbol{A}^T + \boldsymbol{e} \in \mathbb{Z}_q^m)$ where:

1. *$\boldsymbol{A} \in \mathbb{Z}_q^{m \times n}$ is sampled uniformly at random.*
2. *$\boldsymbol{z} \leftarrow \chi^n$, and $\boldsymbol{e} \leftarrow \chi^m$ are sampled with independent and identically distributed coefficients following the distribution χ.*

Find $\boldsymbol{z}$.

The complexity of solving (search-)LWE against primal attack consists of viewing the LWE as an instance of (Distorted-)Bounded Distance Decoding problem, reducing DBDD to uSVP(via Kannan's Embedding, and finally applying lattice reduction algorithm to solve the uSVP instance. DBDD accounts for potential distortion in the distribution of the secret noise vector that is to be recovered, and the secret noise vector is found at a lower cost.

Definition 2 (γ-uSVP). *given a lattice Λ such that $\lambda_2(\Lambda) > \gamma\lambda_1(\Lambda)$, find a shortest nonzero vector in Λ.*

Definition 3 (Distorted Bounded Distance Decoding Problem, DBDD). *Let $\Lambda \subset \mathbb{R}^d$ be a lattice, $\boldsymbol{\Sigma} \in \mathbb{R}^{d \times d}$ be a symmetric matrix and $\boldsymbol{\mu} \in Span(\Lambda) \subset \mathbb{R}^d$ such that $Span(\boldsymbol{\Sigma}) \subsetneq Span(\boldsymbol{\Sigma} + \boldsymbol{\mu}^T\boldsymbol{\mu}) = Span(\Lambda)$*
  The Distorted Bounded Distance Decoding Problem $DBDD_{\Lambda,\boldsymbol{\mu},\boldsymbol{\Sigma}}$ is:
  Given $\boldsymbol{\mu}, \boldsymbol{\Sigma}$ and a basis of Λ.
  Find the unique vector $\boldsymbol{x} \in \Lambda \cap E(\boldsymbol{\mu}, \boldsymbol{\Sigma})$.
  Where $E(\boldsymbol{\mu}, \boldsymbol{\Sigma})$ denotes the ellipsoid

$$E(\boldsymbol{\mu}, \boldsymbol{\Sigma}) := \{\boldsymbol{x} \in \boldsymbol{\mu} + Span(\boldsymbol{\Sigma}) \mid (\boldsymbol{x} - \boldsymbol{\mu}) \cdot \boldsymbol{\Sigma}^{\sim} \cdot (\boldsymbol{x} - \boldsymbol{\mu})^T \le rank(\boldsymbol{\Sigma})\} \tag{2}$$

  The triple $I = (\Lambda, \boldsymbol{\mu}, \boldsymbol{\Sigma})$ will be referred to as the instance of the $DBDD_{\Lambda,\boldsymbol{\mu},\boldsymbol{\Sigma}}$ problem.

Definition 4 (Primitive Vectors). *A set of vector $\boldsymbol{y}_1, \cdots, \boldsymbol{y}_k \in \Lambda$ is said primitive with respect to Λ if $\Lambda \cap Span(\boldsymbol{y}_1, \cdots, \boldsymbol{y}_k)$ is equal to the lattice generated by $\boldsymbol{y}_1, \cdots, \boldsymbol{y}_k$. Equivalently, it is primitive if it can be extended to a basis of Λ. If $k = 1$, $\boldsymbol{y}_1$, this is equivalent to $\boldsymbol{y}_1/i \notin \Lambda$ for any integer $i \ge 2$.*

3   Side-Channel Information in Plaintext-Checking Attacks

3.1   The Meta-Structure of IND-CPA Secure KEM

Suppose there exists six *additive Abelian groups* $S_{sk}, S_A, S_B, S_t, S_U, S_V$ and four *bilinear mappings*(denoted as $\times$). The four bilinear mappings are $S_A \times S_{sk} \to S_B$, $S_U \times S_{sk} \to S_V$, $S_t \times S_A \to S_U$, $S_t \times S_B \to S_V$. The multiplication satisfies associativity in the sense that $(t \times A) \times sk = t \times (A \times sk)$ for all $t \in S_t$, $A \in S_A$, and $sk_A \in S_{sk}$. The multiplication works as **block 1** on Fig. 1.

We list the meta-structure of CPA-secure KEM in Algorithm 1, in which:

Algorithm 1. The meta-structure of IND-CPA secure KEM

1: **function** $setup(1^\lambda)$
2:    setup the algebra
3:    define public parameter pp
4:    **return** pp

1: **function** $Gen(pp; coin_A)$
2:    $A \xleftarrow{\$} S_A$
3:    $sk_A \xleftarrow{\$} S_{sk}$
4:    $d \xleftarrow{\$} s_B$
5:    randomness comes from $coin_A$
6:    $B \leftarrow A \times sk_A + d$
7:    $pk_A \leftarrow (A, B)$
8:    **return** (sk_A, pk_A)

1: **function** $Enc(pp, pk_A, pt; coin_B)$
2:    *parse* $pk_A = (A, B)$

3:    $t \xleftarrow{\$} S_t, e \xleftarrow{\$} S_U, f \xleftarrow{\$} S_V$
4:    randomness comes from $coin_B$
5:    $\bar{U} \leftarrow t \times A + e$
6:    $\bar{V} \leftarrow t \times B + f + encode(pt)$
7:    $U \leftarrow Compress(\bar{U})$
8:    $V \leftarrow Compress(\bar{V})$
9:    $K \leftarrow H(pt \| ct = (U, V))$
10:   **return** K

1: **function** $Dec(pp, sk_A, ct)$
2:    $Parse\ ct = (U, V)$
3:    $\bar{U} \leftarrow Decompress(U)$
4:    $\bar{V} \leftarrow Decompress(V)$
5:    $W \leftarrow \bar{V} - \bar{U} \times sk_A$
6:    $pt' \leftarrow decode(W)$
7:    $K' \leftarrow H(pt' \| ct = (U, V))$
8:    **return** K'

- For t, d, f, e, sk, such sparse elements are chosen to be sampled from discrete Gaussian distribution or central binomial distribution B_η whose sample is generated by $\Sigma_{i=1}^{\eta}(a_i - b_i)$, where $a_i, b_i \leftarrow \{0, 1\}$ and mutually independent. A sample is chosen according to B_η means every component is chosen randomly from B_η.
- the *encode* : $\mathcal{M} \to S_V$, *decode* : $S_V \to \mathcal{M}$ is not necessary but usually employed. The encode is an injective function. A typical code is $D - v$ lattice code. Message bits are encoded by multiplication to $L = (q - 1)/2$ and represented v times in $Y = encode(pt)$. NewHope [16] selects $v = 2$, thus $Y_i = Y_{i+256} = pt_i \cdot (q - 1)/2$. The decoding process of $Y = encode(pt)$ is finding the value b that minimizes $|Y_i - b \cdot \frac{q-1}{2}| + |Y_{i+256} - b \cdot \frac{q-1}{2}|$.
- The Compress/Decompress is usually used to decrease the communication cost. Typically, a ciphertext $\bar{V}$ is replaced by $V = Compress(\bar{V}, p) =$

$\lceil p/q \cdot \bar{V} \rfloor \bmod p$ and the decompress operates in an opposite way $\bar{V} = Compress(V, p) = \lceil q/p \cdot V \rfloor$.

Almost all NIST candidate lattice-based CPA-secure KEM are designed as Algorithm 1. We give two examples below: NewHope [16], Crystals-Kyber [2].

Example 1. Kyber defines $S_{sk} = \mathcal{R}_q^k$, $S_B = \mathcal{R}_q^k$, $S_U = \mathcal{R}_q^k$, $S_t = \mathcal{R}_q^k$, $S_V = \mathcal{R}_q$, $S_A = \mathcal{R}_q^{k \times k}$. Kyber does not use *encode/decode* algorithm. Elements in $\mathcal{R}_q$ are considered as polynomials in variable X modulo $X^n + 1$. Elements in $\mathcal{R}_q^k$ are considered as vector with components in $\mathcal{R}_q$. Elements in $\mathcal{R}_q^{k \times k}$ are considered as matrix with components in $\mathcal{R}_q$. In Kyber512-KEM, e, f, d is sampled sparsely from B_3. In Kyber768-KEM abd Kyber1024-KEM, t, d, f, e, sk are sampled from B_2. Other parameters for Kyber is $q = 3329, n = 256$. $k = 2/3/4$ for Kyber512/Kyber 768/Kyber 1024.

Example 2. NewHope-CPA-PKE defines $S_{sk} = S_A = S_B = S_t = S_U = S_V = \mathcal{R}_q$. Elements in R_q are considered as polynomials in variable X modulo $X^n + 1$. For t, d, f, e, sk, sparse elements are sampled from centered binomial distribution B_8. For NewHope512/NewHope1024, the parameters are $n = 512, n = 1024$ and $q = 12289$. The *encode/decode* algorithm are described as above.

3.2   Model of Plaintext-Checking Attack

In a plaintext-checking attack, the adversary interacts with plaintext checking oracle $\mathcal{O}$, which works as shown in Algorithm 2. $\mathcal{O}$ is a plaintext checking oracle which receives ct and pt, returning one bit showing if ct decrypts to pt. IND-CPA secure public key encryption/key encapsulation mechanisms are vulnerable to plaintext-checking attack.

The plaintext-checking oracle exists in many cases. In the client-server protocol where the ciphertext is the encryption of some symmetric key k. The adversary can construct faulty ciphertexts that may or may not decode to k and deliver them to the server. Then the adversary can see if secure messaging works and hence simulates a plaintext-checking oracle $\mathcal{O}$. IND-CCA secure KEM may also suffer a plaintext-checking attack since the adversary can create oracle $\mathcal{O}$ by a test-based template approach as given in [7].

Algorithm 2. Plaintext-Checking Attack

1: $sk'_A \leftarrow \mathcal{A}^{\mathcal{O}}(pk_A)$	1: **ORACLE** $\mathcal{O}(ct = (U, V), K)$
2: **if** $sk'_A = sk_A$ **then**	2: $\quad K' \leftarrow KEM.Dec(ct)$
3: $\quad$ **return** 1	3: $\quad$ **if** $K = K'$ **then**
4: **else**	4: $\quad\quad$ **return** 1
5: $\quad$ **return** 0	5: $\quad$ **else**
	6: $\quad\quad$ **return** 0

3.3 Secret Leakage Model in Plaintext-Checking Attack

Since many lattice-based IND-CPA secure KEMs use the same meta-structure, they may have similar plaintext-checking attack procedures. Suppose Alice reuses her public key $pk_A = (A, B)$. As described in Algorithm 2, the adversary $\mathcal{A}$ crafts different plaintext and ciphertext ct, pt to recover Alice's secret key sk_A with as fewer oracle access as possible. Each coefficient of sk_A is sampled independently from $\mathcal{S} \subset S_{sk}$.

When the adversary $\mathcal{A}$ tries to recover the i-th coefficient of sk_A, each oracle call leaks information about $\mathcal{S}$. Without loss of generality, let

$$\mathcal{S} = \{S_0, S_1, ..., S_{n-1}\}$$

be the set of all possible values of the original sparse secret distribution. Let P_j be the probability that $sk_A[i] = S_j$ where $sk_A[i]$ is generated from the distribution $\mathcal{S}$, that is, $P_j = Pr[sk_A[i] = S_j | sk_A[i] \leftarrow \mathcal{S}]$ for $j = 0, 1, ..., n-1$. Denote the new secret distribution after the oracle query as $\mathcal{S}'$ after querying plaintext checking oracle $\mathcal{O}$. When the adversary gets a returned value from the Oracle, he can narrow the range of $sk_A[i]$ from $\mathcal{S}$ to $\mathcal{S}'$ until the exact value of $sk_A[i]$ is determined.

The change of secret distribution is shown in Fig. 1. As described in Sect. 3.1, block 1 (in a dashed rectangle) represents the multiplication of Abelian groups S_A, S_B, S_t, S_U, S_V (the yellow blocks) before the adversary $\mathcal{A}$ queries the PC Oracle $\mathcal{O}$. The blue block in block 1 represents the secret distribution $\mathcal{S} \subset S_{sk}$ before the adversary queries the PC Oracle $\mathcal{O}$. The green block in block 2 represents the new secret distribution $\mathcal{S}' \subset S_{sk}$ after $\mathcal{A}$ queries the PC Oracle $\mathcal{O}$. Other Abelian groups remain unchanged.

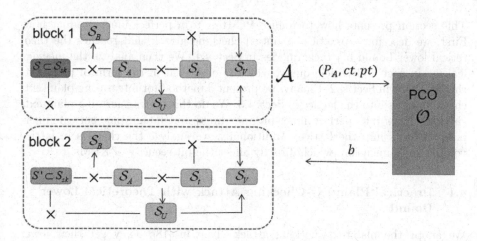

Fig. 1. Oracle query in Plaintext-Checking Attack and the change of secret distribution.

In plaintext-checking attack, the adversary $\mathcal{A}$ tries to recover the reused secret by accessing oracle $\mathcal{O}$ as few as possible. In other words, each oracle query decreases the Shannon entropy of reused secret sk_A. $\mathcal{A}$ tries to reduce the entropy of $\mathcal{S}$ as much as possible. Intrinsically, for each coefficient of Alice's reused secret key sk_A, the querying process can be described as a function f of reused secret key sk_A, secret distribution $\mathcal{S}$, ciphertext $ct \in S_U \times S_V, pt \in \mathcal{M}$. Formally, we can define the information leakage in plaintext-checking attack as:

Definition 5 (Plaintext-Checking Hint). *A plaintext-checking hint on the reused secret sk_A is the crafted plaintext pt, ciphertext ct, such that $f(sk_A, ct, pt) = b \in \{0, 1\}$.*

Let v be a unit vector with $v[i] = 1$. The expression of plaintext-checking hint $f(sk_A, ct, pt)$ can be simplified as $f(\langle sk_A, v \rangle) = b \in \{0, 1\}$ since the adversary tries to recover the i-th coefficient of sk_A.

Most of the prior works consider the Oracle access times for recovering the full reused key. Since the adversary may be prohibited from gathering sufficient side-channel information to build a plaintext-checking oracle, the adversary $\mathcal{A}$ does not have sufficient access to a plaintext-checking oracle to completely recover the reused secret. For example, PC Oracle constructed by reusing KEM's public key cannot be accessed when users stop reusing the public key. Thus one may be interested in a more precise analysis of $f(sk_A, ct, pt)$ to learn security loss after certain times of Oracle access. To investigate security loss after limited times of Oracle queries, one possible way is to express $f(sk_A, ct, pt)$ in the form that can be integrated into the lattice.

4   Reducing PC-Hint to Perfect Inner-Product Hint

This section presents how to reduce PC-Hint to a perfect inner-product hint. First, we describe a practical plaintext-checking attack that reaches the theoretical lower bound of oracle queries in Sect. 4.1. We then analyze the message leakage in each PC Oracle query, which is described in the form of plaintext-checking hint in Sect. 4.2. Finally, we present a method for integrating plaintext-checking hints into the lattice in Sect. 4.3. We do this by transforming plaintext-checking hints into perfect inner-product hints and integrating perfect inner-product hints into the lattice. Additionally, we analyze the changes in lattice volume and dimension, which directly affect the bit security of KEMs.

4.1   Practical Plaintext-Checking Attack with Theoretical Lower Bound

We adopt the plaintext-checking attack given in [18]. They get their lower bounds for all lattice-based NIST KEM candidates by building the optimal Binary Recovery Tree (BRT), and they show that the calculation of these bounds becomes essentially the computation of a certain Shannon entropy, which means that on average one cannot find a better attack with fewer queries than their results in the full key recovery.

The lower bound of oracle access for recovering a single coefficient of reused secret sk_A has been analyzed in Theorem 1 in [18]. Let $min\ E(\mathcal{S})$ represent the lower bound for the minimum average number of queries. Moreover, let $H(\mathcal{S})$ represent the Shannon entropy for $\mathcal{S}$. Then, we have $H(\mathcal{S}) \leq min\ E(\mathcal{S}) < H(\mathcal{S}) + 1$. In the following section, we give a brief explanation of their attack.

Take plaintext-checking attack to IND-CPA secure Kyber512 as an example. The adversary selects proper ciphertext $ct = (U, V)$ as inputs to $\mathcal{O}$. Then, the adversary is able to recover Alice's reused secret sk_A from the oracle response $\hat{s}$. The recovery of each coefficient is mutually independent. We give the approach to recover the first coefficient block $sk_A[0]$ of sk, other coefficient blocks can be recovered similarly.

The attacker selects plaintext $pt = (1, 0, ..., 0)$ and $ct = (U, V)$, where $\bar{U} = (\lceil \frac{q}{16} \rfloor, 0, ..., 0)$, $U = Compress(\bar{U}, 2^{d_U})$ and $V = (h, 0, ..., 0)$. $d_U = 10, d_V = 4$ is the parameter selected by Kyber512. Then the attack query the plaintext-checking oracle $\mathcal{O}$ with ct. The oracle $\mathcal{O}$ calculates $\bar{U} = Decompress(U, 2^{d_U}), \bar{V} = Decompress(V, 2^{d_V}) = (\lceil \frac{q}{16} h \rfloor, 0, ..., 0)$.

Thus, the adversary constructs a relationship between $pt'[0]$ and $sk_A[0]$ after decryption as $pt'[0] = Compress((\bar{V} - sk_A^T \cdot \bar{U})[0], 2) = \lceil \frac{2}{q} (\bar{V}[0] - (sk_A^T \cdot \bar{U})[0]) \rfloor \bmod 2$.

Since $\bar{V}[0] = \lceil \frac{q}{16} h \rfloor$ and $(sk_A^T \cdot \bar{U})[0] = sk_A^T[0]\bar{U}[0] = sk_A[0]\lceil \frac{q}{16} \rfloor$, it holds that $pt'[0] = \lceil \frac{2}{q} (\lceil \frac{q}{16} h \rfloor - sk_A^T[0][\frac{q}{16}]) \rfloor \bmod 2$, where h is a parameter chosen by the attacker. Let $h = 4$, if $sk_A[0] \in [0, 3], pt'[0] = 0$, then the oracle $\mathcal{O}$ will output 0. Otherwise, $sk_A[0] \in [-3, -1], pt'[0] = 1$, the oracle $\mathcal{O}$ will output 1.

The attacker could adaptively choose h to recover $sk_A[0]$ based on the sequence $\hat{s}$ from oracle $\mathcal{O}$. If the attacker uses well-selected h, he could recover $sk_A[0]$ with as few queries as possible. With the help of the optimal binary recovery tree, the adversary divides the range of the coefficient block in half each time and tries to recover $\mathcal{S}_i$ with the biggest probability as soon as possible. We list the selection of h in Table 2. In such a plaintext-checking attack, each query divides the possible range of $sk_A[0]$ into (nearly) half. [18] gives the selection of h and the corresponding changes of states in Sect. 4.1.

Table 2. The choice of h and the States for Kyber512

	State1	State2	State3	State4	State5	State6
h	4	3	9	12	13	7
$\mathcal{O} \to 0$	State4	$sk_A[0] = -1$	$sk_A[0] = -3$	$sk_A[0] = 0$	$sk_A[0] = 1$	$sk_A[0] = 3$
$\mathcal{O} \to 1$	State2	State3	$sk_A[0] = -2$	State5	State6	$sk_A[0] = 2$

According to Theorem [18], The lower bound for Kyber512, Kyber768, and Kyber1024, in theory, is 1216, 1632, 2176. The expectation of queries needed to recover a single coefficient in sk_A is $\frac{5}{16} \times 2 + \frac{15}{64} \times (3+2) + \frac{3}{32} \times (4+3) + \frac{1}{32} \times 3 = 2.56$. The average number of queries needed in a plaintext-checking attack for Kyber512, Kyber768, and Kyber1024, in theory, is 1312, 1774, and 2365. The gap is less than 9%. Besides, Qin et al. also did an experiment to verify their theory. The experiment result shows that the number of queries is 1311, 1777, 2368 separately.

4.2 Message Leakage in Each Query

Suppose Alice reuses her public key, the corresponding secret key is sk_A. The adversary tries to recover the first coefficient of sk_A. The analysis is similar to other coefficients.

In Sect. 3.3, we give a plaintext-checking hint $f(sk_A, ct, pt)$ to describe the change of secret distribution after each oracle query. For Kyber512, $\mathcal{A}$ sets $ct = (U, V)$. If $sk_A[0] \in [0, 3]$, set $h = 4$, $pt'[0] = \lceil \frac{2}{q}(\lceil \frac{q}{16}h \rceil - sk_A^T[0][\frac{q}{16}]) \rfloor \mod 2 = 0$, then $\mathcal{O} \to 0$. Otherwise $pt'[0] = 1$, $\mathcal{O} \to 1$. The plaintext-checking hint can be described as: $f(sk_A, ct = (U, V), pt) = \lceil \frac{2}{q}(\bar{V}[0] - (sk_A^T \cdot \bar{U})[0]) \rfloor \mod 2$.

Let v be a unit vector with $v[0] = 1$. Since the adversary tries to recover a certain coefficient in each oracle query, it is very natural to express $f(sk_A, ct, pt)$ as $f(\langle sk_A, v \rangle)$. Specifically, we have:

- $h = 4$, after the first query, plaintext-checking hint $PCHint_1$: $f(\langle sk_A, v \rangle) = \lceil \frac{2}{q}(\lceil \frac{q}{16} \cdot 4 \rceil - sk_A^T[0][\frac{q}{16}]) \rfloor \mod 2 = 0$, and $\langle sk_A, v \rangle \in [0, 3]$.
- $h = 12$, after the second query, plaintext-checking hint $PCHint_2$: $f(\langle sk_A, v \rangle) = \lceil \frac{2}{q}(\lceil \frac{q}{16} \cdot 12 \rceil - sk_A^T[0][\frac{q}{16}]) \rfloor \mod 2 = 1$, and $\langle sk_A, v \rangle \in [1, 3]$.
- $h = 13$, after the third query, plaintext-checking hint $PCHint_3$: $f(\langle sk_A, v \rangle) = \lceil \frac{2}{q}(\lceil \frac{q}{16} \cdot 13 \rceil - sk_A^T[0][\frac{q}{16}]) \rfloor \mod 2 = 1$, and $\langle sk_A, v \rangle \in [2, 3]$.
- $h = 7$, after the fourth query, plaintext-checking hint $PCHint_4$: $f(\langle sk_A, v \rangle) = \lceil \frac{2}{q}(\lceil \frac{q}{16} \cdot 7 \rceil - sk_A^T[0][\frac{q}{16}]) \rfloor \mod 2 = 0$, and $\langle sk_A, v \rangle = 3$.

Now the adversary collect four plaintext-checking hints $PCHint_1$, $PCHint_2$, $PCHint_3$, $PCHint_4$. Then the adversary can transform these hints into "perfect hint" as described in [3]: $\langle sk_A, v \rangle = sk_A[0]$.

Let $\mathcal{S} = \{S_0, S_1, ..., S_{n-1}\}$ be the set of all possible values of the original sparse secret distribution. Denote by H_i the number of plaintext-checking hints $\mathcal{A}$ needs to determine the coefficient block when it is exactly S_i, which is actually the oracle access need to determine the coefficient block as analyzed at the beginning of Sect. 4. Let $E(\#PCHint)$ be the average number we needed to transform a plaintext-checking hint into a perfect hint. According to the analysis above, we have $E(\#PCHint) = \Sigma_{i=0}^{n-1} P_i H_i$.

Intrinsically, the average number we needed to transform plaintext-checking hints into a perfect hint is the average number of oracle queries $\mathcal{A}$ needed to recover a single coefficient block. Thus the lower bound of $E(\#PCHint)$ can be derived from [18]. We list $E(\#PCHint)$ for all lattice-based NIST KEMs (both IND-CPA/IND-CCA) in Table 3.

Table 3. $E(\#PCHint)$ against lattice-based NIST KEMs

Schemes	$E(\#PCHint)$	Schemes	$E(\#PCHint)$	Schemes	$E(\#PCHint)$
Kyber512	2.77	Saber	2.73	Frodo1344	2.73
Kyber768	2.31	FireSaber	2.56	NewHope512	3.24
Kyber1024	2.31	Frodo640	3.59	NewHope1024	3.11
LightSaber	2.88	Frodo976	3.34	–	–

In the following parts, we describe how to predict security loss after collecting several PC hints and transformed these PC hints into a perfect hint.

4.3 Integrating Plaintext-Checking Hints into Lattice

The intuition behind estimating security loss (under primal attack) is to estimate the hardness of the underlying LWE problem (as defined in Definition 1) after integrating plaintext-checking hints. The adversary $\mathcal{A}$ collects plain LWE samples as shown in line 5, 6 in function Enc of Algorithm 1. Then $\mathcal{A}$ transforms the LWE problem to DBDD problem (Definition 3) and constructs a lattice basis. Then $\mathcal{A}$ integrates the plaintext-checking hints into the DBDD problem. Finally, $\mathcal{A}$ transforms the DBDD problem to uSVP problem (Definition 2). The uSVP problem can be solved by lattice reduction algorithm.

The solution of the LWE problem is (e, sk_A). It can be extended to a short vector $(e, sk_A, 1)$, which is an short vector of the lattice $\Lambda = \{(\boldsymbol{x}, \boldsymbol{y}, w) \in \mathbb{Z}^{n+m+1} | \boldsymbol{x} + \boldsymbol{y}\boldsymbol{A}^T - \boldsymbol{b}w\} = 0 \bmod q$, which is of full rank in $\mathbb{R}^d$ and has volume q^m. The row vectors of $\begin{bmatrix} q\boldsymbol{I}_m & 0 & 0 \\ \boldsymbol{A}^T & -\boldsymbol{I}_n & 0 \\ \boldsymbol{b} & 0 & 1 \end{bmatrix}$ constitute a basis of Λ. For a single coefficient block $sk_A[b]$, $P_i = Pr(sk_A[b] = \boldsymbol{S}_i | sk_A \leftarrow \mathcal{S})$ for $i = 0, 1, ..., n - 1$. We denote the average and variance of the LWE original secret distribution $\mathcal{S}$ as μ and σ^2. Such a LWE instance can be converted to a $DBDD_{\Lambda,\mu,\Sigma}$ instance with $\boldsymbol{\mu} = [\mu, ..., \mu, 1]$, $\boldsymbol{\Sigma} = \begin{bmatrix} \sigma^2 \boldsymbol{I}_{m+n} & 0 \\ 0 & 0 \end{bmatrix}$.

To integrate plaintext-checking hints into $DBDD$ problem, the adversary $\mathcal{A}$ collect several plaintext-checking hints until they can be transformed to a perfect hint $\langle sk_A, v \rangle = sk_A[0]$ as shown in Sect. 4.2. Suppose $\mathcal{A}$ recovers the first coefficient of sk_A. v can be extended to $\bar{v} := (\boldsymbol{0}; v; -l)$, where $\boldsymbol{0}$ is an all-zero vector of dimension m, $v = (1, 0, \cdots, 0)$ of dimension n, $l = sk_A[0]$. The adversary $\mathcal{A}$ can integrate $\bar{v}$ by modifying $DBDD_{\Lambda,\mu,\Sigma}$ to $DBDD_{\Lambda',\mu',\Sigma'}$.

Integrating $\bar{v}$ into $DBDD_{\Lambda,\mu,\Sigma}$ means finding an intersection between Λ and an hyperplane orthogonal to $\bar{v}$. We denote the new lattice as Λ'. Intuitively, Λ' has lower dimension than Λ, meaning that solving $DBDD_{\Lambda',\mu',\Sigma'}$ is easier than $DBDD_{\Lambda,\mu,\Sigma}$.

The new mean $\boldsymbol{\mu}'$ and new covariance $\boldsymbol{\Sigma}'$ can be derived according to the equation given in equations (12) and (13) in [3]. Specifically, we have $\boldsymbol{\Sigma}' = \boldsymbol{\Sigma} - \frac{(\bar{v}\boldsymbol{\Sigma})^T \bar{v}\boldsymbol{\Sigma}}{\bar{v}\boldsymbol{\Sigma}\bar{v}^T}$, and $\boldsymbol{\mu}' = \boldsymbol{\mu} - \frac{\langle \bar{v}, \mu \rangle}{\bar{v}\boldsymbol{\Sigma}\bar{v}^T} \bar{v}\boldsymbol{\Sigma}$. Since $\bar{v}$ is an all-zero vector with dimension

$m+n+1$ except that the $m+1$-th coefficient is 1 and the $m+n+1$-th coefficient is $-sk_A[0]$. Thus we have $\bar{v}\Sigma$ is an all-zero vector except that the $m+1$-th coefficient is σ^2.

Thus we have $\Sigma' = \Sigma - \frac{1}{\sigma^2}M$, where M is a $m+n+1$-dimension diagonal matrix with $M_{m+1,m+1} = \sigma^4, M_{m+n+1,m+n+1} = 0$ and all other diagonal elements 0. Thus Σ' is a $m+n+1$-dimension diagonal matrix with $M_{m+1,m+1} = 0, M_{m+n+1,m+n+1} = 0$ and all other diagonal elements σ^2. $\mu' = [\mu, ..., \mu, 1] - (\mu - sk_A[0])\frac{1}{\sigma^2}\bar{v}\Sigma$. Thus μ' is an all-μ vector except that $\mu'_{m+1} = sk_A[0], \mu'_{m+n+1} = 1$. The volume of Λ' is analyzed in Theorem 1.

Theorem 1. *Given the LWE sample $(A \in \mathbb{Z}_q^{m \times n}, b = sk_A^T A + e \in \mathbb{Z}_q^m)$. Suppose the adversary $\mathcal{A}$ collects $\#PCHint$ plaintext-checking hints $f_1, ..., f_{\#PCHint}$ when recovering $sk_A[i]$. The adversary $\mathcal{A}$ can transform $f_1, ..., f_{\#PCHint}$ into a perfect hint $\bar{v} := (0; v; -l)$, where 0 is an all-zero vector of dimension m, v is a unit vector with $v[i] = 1$ and dimension n, $l = sk_A[i]$. Including hint $\bar{v}$ modifies $DBDD_{\Lambda,\mu,\Sigma}$ to $DBDD_{\Lambda',\mu',\Sigma'}$ with dimension $dim(\Lambda')$ and volume $Vol(\Lambda')$:*

$$\dim(\Lambda') = \dim(\Lambda) - 1$$
$$Vol(\Lambda') = Vol(\Lambda) \cdot \sqrt{1 + sk_A[i]}^2 \cdot det(\mathbf{\Pi}_\Lambda) \tag{3}$$

When $\bar{v}$ is a primitive vector, we have

$$Vol(\Lambda') = Vol(\Lambda)\sqrt{1 + sk_A[i]^2} \tag{4}$$

Proof. When $\bar{v}$ is a primitive vector($\bar{v}$ can be extended to a basis of Λ), the volume of the lattice after integrating hint $\bar{v}$ is $Vol(\Lambda) = \|\bar{v}\| \cdot Vol(\Lambda) = Vol(\Lambda) \cdot \sqrt{1 + sk_A[i]^2}$(see Lemma 12 of [3]).

When $\bar{v}$ is not in the span of Λ, we can also apply orthogonal projection $\bar{v}' = \bar{v} \cdot \mathbf{\Pi}_\Lambda$ of $\bar{v}$ onto Λ. Replacing $\bar{v}$ by $\bar{v}'$ is still valid. The orthogonal projection matrix is $\mathbf{\Pi}_\Lambda = \mathbf{\Pi}_{\Sigma'} = \sqrt{\Sigma'}^{\sim} \cdot \Sigma' \cdot \sqrt{\Sigma'}^{\sim T}$, where $\Sigma' = \Sigma + \mu^T \cdot \mu$ is the covariance matrix after homogenization, $\sqrt{\Sigma'}^{\sim}$ is the restricted inverse of $\sqrt{\Sigma'}$(see definition 3 of [3]). Thus we have $Vol(\Lambda') = Vol(\Lambda) \cdot \sqrt{1 + sk_A[i]^2} \cdot det(\mathbf{\Pi}_\Lambda))$, where $\mathbf{\Pi}_\Lambda$ is the orthogonal projection onto Λ.

It is predicted that the $BKZ - \beta'$ can solve a $uSVP_{\Lambda'}$ after $E(\#PCHint)$ queries s.t. $\sqrt{\beta'} \le \delta_{\beta'}^{2\beta'-dim(\Lambda')-1} \cdot Vol(\Lambda')^{1/dim(\Lambda')}$, where $dim(\Lambda'), Vol(\Lambda')$ are as described in Eq. (3, 4). The expectation of $\#PCHint$ ($E(\#PCHint)$) and the transformation from plaintext-checking hints to perfect hints has been described in Sect. 4.2.

5   Experiment Results

5.1   Kyber

Figure 2 gives the concrete relationship between the number of queries and bit-security for all parameter sets of Kyber in the NIST third-round submission.

In Table 4, we present the number of queries needed for Kyber512/ Kyber768/ Kyber1024 when the bit security of the underlying LWE reaches 128, 64, 48, 32, 24, 16 under primal and dual attacks. Taking Kyber512 as an example, the adversary $\mathcal{A}$ can query PC Oracle $\mathcal{O}$ for only 867 times instead of 1312 times. The classical bit security of the LWE problem is decreased to 32. The adversary may stop querying the PC Oracle and solve the remaining part of the secret key using the lattice reduction algorithm.

For our experiment, we make use of the LWE estimator from [3]. Estimating the hardness needs the dimension of the lattice Λ and its volume only. According to Theorem 1, for Kyber512/Kyber768/ Kyber1024, every 2.77/2.31/2.31 queries reduces the dimension of the lattice by 1. After integrating short vectors into the lattice, we get the concrete dimension of the lattice Λ, which tells us the security of current LWE problem after certain times of queries. The number in parentheses is the Oracle queries needed when classical/quantum bit security is 100 (The original classical bit security of Kyber is 118).

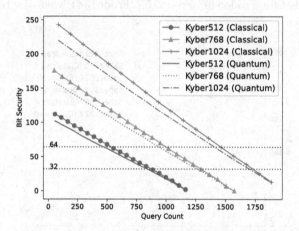

Fig. 2. Relationship between query and security under primal attack for Kyber.

Table 4. Classical&Quantum Query-Security For Kyber 512/768/1024.

Bit Security	Kyber512 (classical/quantum)		Kyber768 (classical/quantum)		Kyber1024 (classical/quantum)	
–	Primal	Dual	Primal	Dual	Primal	Dual
128(100)	(80)/(65)	(150)/(129)	444/333	562/543	950/848	1274/1205
64	533/464	657/624	998/938	1112/1096	1459/1404	1732/1673
48	699/646	761/733	1144/1098	1206/1176	1593/1550	1805/1773
32	867/831	865/838	1292/1259	1320/1302	1728/1699	1915/1893
24	953/925	922/906	1366/1343	1396/1361	1796/1775	1973/1959
16	1033/1016	981/962	1437/1423	1481/1476	1862/1849	2095/2029

5.2 Saber

Figure 3 gives the relationship between the number of queries and security for all parameter sets of Saber in NIST third round submission. We list the number of queries needed for LightSaber/Saber/FireSaber when the bit security of the underlying LWE reaches 128, 64, 48, 32, 24, 16 in Table 5 under primal/dual attack.

According to Theorem 1, for LightSaber/ Saber/ FireSaber, every 2.88/ 2.73/ 2.56 queries reduce the dimension of the lattice by 1. After integrating short vectors into the lattice, we get the concrete dimension of the lattice $\varLambda$, which tells us the security of current LWE problem after certain times of queries.

5.3 Frodo

Figure 4 gives the relationship between the number of queries and security for all parameter sets of Frodo in NIST second round submission. We list the number of queries needed for Frodo640/ Frodo976/ Frodo1344 when the bit security of

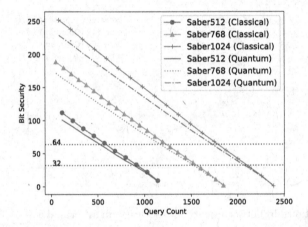

Fig. 3. Relationship between query and security under primal attack for Saber.

Table 5. Classical&Quantum Query-Security For LightSaber/Saber/FireSaber.

Bit Security	LightSaber (classical/quantum)		Saber (classical/quantum)		FireSaber (classical/quantum)	
–	Primal	Dual	Primal	Dual	Primal	Dual
128(100)	(228)/(124)	(407)/(352)	612/487	832/817	1181/1063	1395/1364
64	631/553	844/799	1230/1162	1446/1415	1782/1718	1963/1929
48	839/772	933/902	1390/1339	1550/1517	1941/1890	2067/2029
32	1075/1023	1029/1003	1554/1521	1656/1625	2100/2066	2179/2165
24	1204/1164	1096/1066	1638/1611	1714/1699	2179/2153	2257/2223
16	1340/1311	1155/1138	1717/1701	1774/1759	2258/2243	2326/2289

the underlying LWE reaches 128, 64, 48, 32, 24, 16 in Table 6 under primal/dual attack. The number in parentheses is the Oracle queries needed when classical/quantum bit security is 100 (The original quantum bit security of Frodo640 is 124).

Table 6. Classical&Quantum Query-Security For Frodo 640/976/1344

Bit Security	Frodo640 (classical/quantum)		Frodo976 (classical/quantum)		Frodo1344 (classical/quantum)	
–	Primal	Dual	Primal	Dual	Primal	Dual
128(100)	833/(2755)	2943/(4861)	8177/6734	12546/11986	14006/12761	17859/16758
64	8005/7230	10508/9961	15445/14670	19863/19384	20234/19556	23284/23009
48	9899/9296	12001/11474	17368/16754	21041/20792	21872/21370	24257/23812
32	11821/11419	13572/13230	19346/18918	22368/21994	23577/23205	25217/25124
24	12796/12509	14577/14235	20334/20014	23154/22773	24429/24145	25841/25581
16	13772/13571	15475/15162	21296/21109	23609/23527	25259/25084	26304/26174

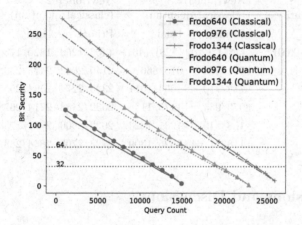

Fig. 4. Relationship between query and security under primal attack for Frodo.

5.4 NewHope

Figure 5 gives the relationship between the number of queries and security for all parameter sets of NewHope in NIST second round submission. We list the number of queries needed for NewHope512/ NewHope1024 when the bit security of the underlying LWE reaches 128, 64, 48, 32, 24, 16 in Table 7 under primal/dual attack. The number in parentheses is the Oracle queries needed when classical/quantum bit security is 100 (The original classical bit security of NewHope512 is 112).

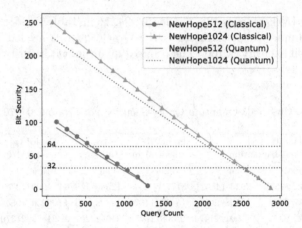

Fig. 5. Relationship between query and security under primal attack for NewHope.

Table 7. Classical&Quantum Query-Security For NewHope 512/1024

Bit Security	NewHope512 (classical/quantum)		NewHope1024 (classical/quantum)	
–	Primal	Dual	Primal	Dual
128(100)	(137)/(20)	(528)/(461)	1406/1260	1820/1756
64	571/490	915/866	2140/2062	2475/2438
48	772/710	1054/1011	2333/2274	2594/2555
32	979/934	1173/1148	2532/2488	2714/2678
24	1083/1050	1231/1224	2632/2600	2771/2738
16	1183/1164	1325/1309	2728/2709	2864/2837

6   Conclusions and Discussions

In this paper, we explicitly build the relationship between the number of Oracle queries and the security loss of the reused secrets for all NIST second-round lattice-based KEMs. Our analysis can be divided into three steps. First, we model the information leakage in the PC-oracle by PC-hint and give a generic transformation from PC-hints to the perfect inner-product hint, which allows the adversary to integrate PC-hints progressively. Then, we give a concrete relationship between the PC Oracle query number and the bit security of the lattice-based KEM under PCA. Our bit security analysis is inspired by the security analysis for LWE with the perfect inner-product hint given in [3], Our proposed method is applicable to all CCA-secure NIST candidate lattice-based KEMs.

We applied our methods to NIST-PQC lattice-based KEMs, we get the bit-security loss of the lattice-based KEM under PCA. Take Kyber768 (original 182-bit-security) as an example, the bit security of Kyber768 is reduced to 128 after 444 PC-oracle queries and reduced to 64 after 998 PC-oracle queries, while in Qin et al. [18] 1774 queries are required to recover the whole secret key. Our analysis also demonstrates the possibility of reducing the Oracle queries needed in PCA. The adversary may stop querying plaintext-checking oracle and solves the remaining part of reused secret offline with the help of lattice reduction algorithms when the cost of lattice reduction algorithms becomes acceptable.

The bit-security analysis in this paper works under perfect PC Oracle. Recently, Shen et al. [21] presents a new checking approach in the plaintext-checking attacks, which is preferable when the constructed PC Oracle is imperfect. Imperfect PC Oracle may occur due to environmental noises, or simply the measurement limitations in implementing the PC Oracle. Their basic idea is to design new detection codes that efficiently find the problematic entries in the recovered secret key and corrects problematic entries with a small number of additional traces. When the raw oracle accuracy is fixed, Their new attack requires only 41% of the EM traces needed in a majority-voting attack in our experiments. It is appealing to analyze the relationship between imperfect PC Oracle queries and bit-security of lattice-based KEMs.

Acknowledgements. We thank the anonymous reviewers for their valuable comments and suggestions to improve the quality of the paper. Ruiqi Mi is supported by the National Key R&D Program of China (Grant No. 2021YFB3100100). Haodong Jiang is supported by National Natural Science Foundation of China (Grant No. 62002385).

References

1. Albrecht, M.R., Player, R., Scott, S.: On the concrete hardness of learning with errors. J. Math. Cryptol. **9**(3), 169–203 (2015). http://www.degruyter.com/view/j/jmc.2015.9.issue-3/jmc-2015-0016/jmc-2015-0016.xml

2. Avanzi, R., et al.: CRYSTALS-Kyber: Algorithm Specifications and Supporting Documentation (2019/2020). https://pq-crystals.org/kyber/index.shtml

3. Dachman-Soled, D., Ducas, L., Gong, H., Rossi, M.: LWE with side information: attacks and concrete security estimation. In: Micciancio, D., Ristenpart, T. (eds.) CRYPTO 2020, Part II. LNCS, vol. 12171, pp. 329–358. Springer, Cham (2020). https://doi.org/10.1007/978-3-030-56880-1_12

4. D'Anvers, J.P., Karmakar, A., Roy, S.S., Vercauteren, F., et al.: SABER: Mod-LWR based KEM algorithm specification and supporting documentation. Submission to the NIST post-quantum project (2019/2020). https://www.esat.kuleuven.be/cosic/pqcrypto/saber/

5. Ding, J., Fluhrer, S., Rv, S.: Complete attack on RLWE key exchange with reused keys, without signal leakage. In: Susilo, W., Yang, G. (eds.) ACISP 2018. LNCS, vol. 10946, pp. 467–486. Springer, Cham (2018). https://doi.org/10.1007/978-3-319-93638-3_27

6. Fujisaki, E., Okamoto, T.: Secure integration of asymmetric and symmetric encryption schemes. J. Cryptol. **26**(1), 80–101 (2013). https://doi.org/10.1007/s00145-011-9114-1

7. Goodwill, G., Jun, B., Jaffe, J., Rohatgi, P.: A testing methodology for side channel resistance (2011)

8. Guo, Q., Mårtensson, E.: Do not bound to a single position: near-optimal multi-positional mismatch attacks against Kyber and Saber. IACR Cryptology ePrint Archive, p. 983 (2022). https://eprint.iacr.org/2022/983

9. Huguenin-Dumittan, L., Vaudenay, S.: Classical misuse attacks on NIST round 2 PQC. In: Conti, M., Zhou, J., Casalicchio, E., Spognardi, A. (eds.) ACNS 2020, Part I. LNCS, vol. 12146, pp. 208–227. Springer, Cham (2020). https://doi.org/10.1007/978-3-030-57808-4_11

10. Lyubashevsky, V., Peikert, C., Regev, O.: On ideal lattices and learning with errors over rings. J. ACM **60**(6), 43:1–43:5 (2013). https://doi.org/10.1145/2535925

11. Naehrig, M., Alkim, E., et al.: Frodokem learning with errors key encapsulation: algorithm specification and supporting documentation. Submission to the NIST post-quantum project (2019/2020). https://frodokem.org/

12. NIST: Call For Proposals. https://csrc.nist.gov/Projects/post-quantum-cryptography/post-quantum-cryptography-standardization/Call-for-Proposals

13. NIST: Preparing for Post-Quantum Cryptography: Informatic (2021). https://www.dhs.gov/sites/default/files/publications/post-quantum_cryptography_infographic_october_2021_508.pdf

14. NIST: Selected algorithms 2022 (2022). https://csrc.nist.gov/Projects/post-quantum-cryptography/selected-algorithms-2022

15. Okada, S., Wang, Y., Takagi, T.: Improving key mismatch attack on NewHope with fewer queries. In: Liu, J.K., Cui, H. (eds.) ACISP 2020. LNCS, vol. 12248, pp. 505–524. Springer, Cham (2020). https://doi.org/10.1007/978-3-030-55304-3_26

16. Poppelmann, T., Alkim, E., et al.: NewHope: algorithm specification and supporting documentation (2019/2020). https://newhopecrypto.org/

17. Qin, Y., Cheng, C., Ding, J.: An efficient key mismatch attack on the NIST second round candidate Kyber. IACR Cryptology ePrint Archive, p. 1343 (2019). https://eprint.iacr.org/2019/1343

18. Qin, Y., Cheng, C., Zhang, X., Pan, Y., Hu, L., Ding, J.: A systematic approach and analysis of key mismatch attacks on lattice-based NIST candidate KEMs. In: Tibouchi, M., Wang, H. (eds.) ASIACRYPT 2021, Part IV. LNCS, vol. 13093, pp. 92–121. Springer, Cham (2021). https://doi.org/10.1007/978-3-030-92068-5_4

19. Ravi, P., Roy, S.S., Chattopadhyay, A., Bhasin, S.: Generic side-channel attacks on CCA-secure lattice-based PKE and KEMs. IACR Trans. Cryptogr. Hardw. Embed. Syst. **2020**(3), 307–335 (2020). https://doi.org/10.13154/tches.v2020.i3.307-335

20. Regev, O.: On lattices, learning with errors, random linear codes, and cryptography. In: Gabow, H.N., Fagin, R. (eds.) Proceedings of the 37th Annual ACM Symposium on Theory of Computing, Baltimore, MD, USA, 22–24 May 2005, pp. 84–93. ACM (2005). https://doi.org/10.1145/1060590.1060603

21. Shen, M., Cheng, C., Zhang, X., Guo, Q., Jiang, T.: Find the bad apples: an efficient method for perfect key recovery under imperfect SCA oracles - a case study of Kyber. IACR Trans. Cryptogr. Hardw. Embed. Syst. **2023**(1), 89–112 (2023). https://doi.org/10.46586/tches.v2023.i1.89-112

Quantum Cryptanalysis of OTR and OPP: Attacks on Confidentiality, and Key-Recovery

Melanie Jauch and Varun Maram[(✉)] [ID]

Department of Computer Science, ETH Zurich, Zurich, Switzerland
mjauch@student.ethz.ch, vmaram@inf.ethz.ch

Abstract. In this paper, we analyze the security of authenticated encryption modes OTR (Minematsu, Eurocrypt 2014) and OPP (Granger *et al.*, Eurocrypt 2016) in a setting where an adversary is allowed to make encryption queries in *quantum* superposition. Starting with OTR – or more technically, AES-OTR, a third-round CAESAR candidate – we extend prior quantum attacks on the mode's unforgeability in the literature to provide the first attacks breaking confidentiality, i.e., IND-qCPA security, of AES-OTR in different settings depending on how the associated data is processed. On a technical level, one of our IND-qCPA attacks involves querying the quantum encryption oracle on a superposition of data with *unequal* length; to the best of our knowledge, such an attack has never been modelled before in the (post-)quantum cryptographic literature, and we hence believe our technique is of independent interest. Coming to OPP, we present the first *key-recovery* attack against the scheme which uses only a *single* quantum encryption query.

Keywords: AES-OTR · OPP · Authenticated Encryption · IND-qCPA Security · Key-Recovery · Simon's Algorithm · Deutsch's Algorithm

1 Introduction

With the development of large-scale quantum computers on the horizon, the security of widely-deployed cryptographic systems faces new threats. Specifically, public-key cryptosystems that rely on the hardness of factorization or computing discrete-logs would suffer from devastating attacks based on Shor's algorithm [28]. This has led to the setting of so-called *post-quantum* secure public-key cryptography gaining a lot of attention over the last few years, which includes efforts by NIST [3] to standardize such quantum-resistant algorithms.

Coming to the *symmetric-key* cryptography setting however, the impact of quantum computers has been assumed to be significantly less severe for a long time. It was widely believed that quantum attacks on symmetric primitives such as block ciphers would only improve by a quadratic speed up due to Grover's algorithm [12], and that we cannot do any better. Naturally, it was hence assumed that

C. Carlet et al. (Eds.): SAC 2023, LNCS 14201, pp. 275–296, 2024.
https://doi.org/10.1007/978-3-031-53368-6_14

it is enough to simply double the key size of the affected primitives to restore the same level of security as in the classical setting. However, the community quickly realized that it is not sufficient to just consider the quantum security of standalone primitives such as block ciphers – since they are rarely used in isolation in practice – but to also consider their associated *modes of operation*. Such modes are typically designed to provide enhanced security guarantees such as confidentiality, integrity, and authenticity of encrypted messages. In this paper, we will be focusing on modes related to authenticated encryption (AE).

Starting with the work of Kaplan et al. [18] which showed how to break the authenticity guarantees of classical AE modes such as GCM and OCB in the quantum setting in *polynomial-time* (in contrast to the generic quadratic speed up offered by Grover's algorithm), follow-up works by Bhaumik et al. [4] and Bonnetain et al. [7] improved the quantum attacks against the latter OCB modes, albeit still targeting authenticity. At a high-level, the above attacks fundamentally rely on other well-known quantum algorithms such as Simon's period finding algorithm [29] and Deutsch's algorithm [8]. Subsequently, Maram et al. [22] extended the aforementioned authenticity attacks to also break confidentiality of the OCB modes in the quantum setting; more formally, the authors targeted a quantum security notion called "IND-qCPA security" [5], which differs from the classical IND-CPA security notion in that the adversary is allowed to make quantum encryption queries. It is worth pointing out that the practicality of this model (also generically called "Q2 security" in the literature) where the attacker has quantum access to the secret-keyed encryption functionality is still currently debated in the community (e.g., see [2,4,6,16,18]); however we consider this discussion beyond the scope of our work.

Now focusing on the OCB modes, they are one of the most well-studied and widely influential classical AE modes. OCB has three versions: OCB1 [27], OCB2 [26] and OCB3 [19]. While OCB1 and OCB3 are provably secure AE schemes in the classical setting, a breakthrough result by Inoue et al. [13] showed that OCB2 is classically broken as an AE mode. More specifically, Inoue and Minematsu [14] first came up with classical attacks on the authenticity guarantees of OCB2. After their attacks became public, Poettering [25] and Iwata [15] proceeded to extend them to also break confidentiality of OCB2 in the classical setting. In this context, the aforementioned work of Maram et al. [22] can be seen as translating this strategy to the quantum setting to break (IND-qCPA) confidentiality of the three OCB modes starting with the quantum forgery attacks in [4,7,18]. However at the same time, Inoue et al. [13] observed that their classical attacks on OCB2 do not extend to other popular AE designs based on OCB such as OTR [23] and OPP [11]; this is due to some subtle differences in the structures of these modes when compared to OCB. In this paper, we analyze if one would observe something similar regarding the effects of quantum insecurity of OCB on the OTR and OPP modes.

Starting with OTR [23], it is technically a block cipher mode to realize a nonce-based authenticated encryption with associated data (AEAD) scheme. We specifically focus on an instantiation of the mode with AES as the underlying block cipher called AES-OTR [24], which also includes an additional way to process associated data when compared to the generic OTR. AES-OTR was also a third-round candidate in the CAESAR competition [1] aimed at standardizing a portfolio of authenticated encryption schemes. In the classical setting, AES-OTR was shown to offer provable security guarantees as an AE scheme [24]. Coming to the quantum setting however, works by Kaplan *et al.* [18] and Chang *et al.* [20] proposed ways to attack the authenticity guarantees of AES-OTR in the quantum superposition model using Simon's algorithm. However the confidentiality of AES-OTR in the same quantum setting has not been addressed in the literature. Hence, following the work of Maram *et al.* [22] on the quantum (IND-qCPA) confidentiality of OCB2, and given the status of AES-OTR as a third-round CAESAR candidate, this leads us to pose the question:

Is the AES-OTR mode IND-qCPA secure?

Coming to OPP [11], it is a (public) permutation-based AE mode unlike OCB and OTR. OPP essentially generalizes OCB3 by replacing the underlying block cipher by an efficiently invertible public permutation and a different form of masking. This ensures fast encryption and full parallelization, hence making OPP an ideal candidate in applications requiring high efficiency of underlying primitives. However in contrast to the OCB and OTR modes, the quantum security of OPP – related to either authenticity or confidentiality – has not been analyzed in the literature at all. This motivates us to ask the following question:

Is the OPP mode quantum secure?

1.1   Our Contributions

In this paper, we answer the above questions concerning the quantum security of both AES-OTR and OPP modes by presenting tailor-made quantum attacks. Along the way, some of our attacks involve techniques that we believe will be of independent interest to the broader (post-)quantum cryptographic community. Our concrete results are listed below:

Attacks on IND-qCPA Security of AES-OTR. In Sect. 3, we present the first IND-qCPA attacks against AES-OTR. Specifically, our quantum attacks are tailored to three different settings depending on how the associated data (AD) is processed: namely, the settings with parallel and serial processing of AD, and the setting where no AD is used at all.

For the first two settings with non-empty AD, our attacks work in the weak adversarial setting where the nonces used by the challenger to answer encryption queries in the IND-qCPA security game are generated uniformly at random (instead of the nonces being chosen by the adversary). On a high level, the attack breaking IND-qCPA security w.r.t. parallel AD processing uses Simon's algorithm as well as Deutsch's algorithm to gain *raw block cipher access*, i.e., the ability to evaluate the underlying block cipher on arbitrary inputs. With this access, it is straightforward to break IND-qCPA security. This attack strategy is similar to that used in [22] to break confidentiality of the OCB modes. However, we need to make an extra assumption for our attack to be efficient: namely that the authentication tags produced by the AES-OTR encryption oracle are not (significantly) truncated. It is worth noting that the specification of AES-OTR [24] recommends parameters with untruncated tags. But interestingly, in the process we were also able to point out a gap in the quantum cryptanalysis of OCB2's confidentiality (with non-empty AD) in [22], since the corresponding IND-qCPA attack there uses a similar assumption of untruncated tags *implicitly*. This was later confirmed by one of the authors [21].

Coming to the setting where no AD is used in AES-OTR, our attack assumes a stronger adversarial setting where the adversary is now allowed to adaptively choose the (classical) nonces for its quantum encryption queries in the IND-qCPA security game. This setting is the same as considered in [22, Section 4.4] with respect to their IND-qCPA attack against OCB2 as a "pure" AE (i.e., no AD) scheme. However, what makes our attack a non-trivial extension of the above attack on OCB2 is that for AES-OTR there is an additional formatting function applied to the nonce before it is AES-encrypted. We thus have to perform some additional steps that increase the overall complexity of our attack. The attack is described in detail in the full version of this paper [17].

Quantum Queries over *Unequal*-Length Data. Our IND-qCPA attack on AES-OTR w.r.t. serial AD processing involves a novel paradigm which, to the best of our knowledge, has never been considered in the (post-)quantum cryptanalytic literature. Note that in the IND-qCPA security definition, an adversary is allowed to make encryption queries on a quantum superposition of data. However, according to the laws of quantum physics, a superposition is defined only over states with the same number of qubits. Hence in our IND-qCPA scenario, this translates to the seemingly implicit restriction of an adversary only being able to make superposition queries over *equal*-length data.

In our work, we show how to overcome this restriction by modelling the quantum encryption oracle in the IND-qCPA security game in a way which allows an adversary to also make superposition queries over *unequal*-length data (see Sect. 3.3 for more details). Furthermore, to give evidence of the power of this new quantum cryptanalytic paradigm, we show how an adversary can immediately gain raw block cipher access in our IND-qCPA attack on AES-OTR with serial AD processing using *only* Simon's algorithm; this is in contrast to the IND-qCPA attacks against OCB in [22] and against AES-OTR with parallel AD processing discussed above which also require Deutsch's algorithm to obtain this raw access. It's also worth pointing out that using this novel paradigm, we no longer have to rely on the above extra assumption of the AES-OTR authentication tags being untruncated in the serial AD case. Finally, our paradigm can also be extended to cryptanalysis in the more realistic *post*-quantum setting, i.e., where the adversary has quantum access only to *public* cryptographic oracles (also called "Q1 security" in the literature) such as hash functions in the so-called Quantum Random Oracle Model (QROM).

A Quantum Key-Recovery Attack on OPP. We present the first quantum key-recovery attack on OPP in Sect. 4. Our attack is conducted in the weak adversarial setting similar to our IND-qCPA attacks on AES-OTR, where the nonces are chosen uniformly at random by the challenger. In contrast to AES-OTR being based on a block cipher which may only be inverted knowing the key, OPP is built upon an efficiently invertible public permutation P. We exploit this specific property to formulate our key recovery attack. On a high level, we are able to recover a value $\Omega = P(\ldots \| K)$ using only a *single* quantum encryption query via an application of Simon's algorithm, where K is the key used in OPP; hence, applying P^{-1} to Ω allows us to recover the key K.

2 Preliminaries

Notation. Denote by $\{0,1\}^*$ the set of all finite-length bit strings and $\{0,1\}^{8*}$ the set of all finite-length byte strings. We let the parameters $n, k, \tau, \kappa \geq 0$ define the block length, the size of the key, tag, and nonce respectively. For $b \in \mathbb{N}$ we let $[b] := \{1, \ldots, b\}$. Given $x, y \in \{0,1\}^*$, the concatenation of x and y is denoted as $x \| y$. We let the length of x in bits be denoted as $|x|$ and we define $|x|_b := \max\{1, \lceil X/b \rceil\}$. We use the symbols $\oplus, \ll, \gg, \lll, \ggg$ to denote bit-wise XOR, left-shift, right-shift, left-rotation and right-rotation, respectively.

Further, we define the following padding function that, for a given input X, extends it to a desired length m

$$\mathrm{pad}_m^0 : \{0,1\}^{\leq m} \to \{0,1\}^m, X \mapsto X \| 0^{m-|X|}$$

and for $0 \leq |X| < m$, we write $\underline{X} = X \| 10^{m-|X|-1}$ as the 10* padding.

By $\mathrm{msb}_l(x)$ we mean the sequence of first l left-most bits of the bit sting x and for any non-negative integer q, let $\mathrm{bin}(q, m)$ denote the standard m-bit encoding of q.

We want to highlight the difference in notation for the encryption functions used for AES-OTR in Sect. 3 and for OPP in Sect. 4. By OTR-$\mathcal{E}_{K,\cdot}(\cdot)$ we indicate the encryption algorithm of AES-OTR with an underlying block cipher (AES to be precise) encryption function E_K with key K. On the other hand we use OPP-$\mathcal{E}(K, \cdot)$ to denote the encryption algorithm of OPP with key K that uses a public permutation instead of a block cipher.

In the context of AES-OTR we use notations such as $2X, 3X$ or $7X$ for an n-bit string X. Following [24], we here interpret X as a coefficient vector of the polynomial in $\mathrm{GF}(2^n)$. So by $2X$ we essentially mean multiplying the generator of the field $\mathrm{GF}(2^n)$, which is the polynomial x, and X over $\mathrm{GF}(2^n)$. This process is referred to as *doubling*. Similarly, $2^i X$ denotes i-times doubling X and we denote $3X = X \oplus 2X$ as well as $7X = 2^2 X \oplus 2X \oplus X$. Field multiplication over $\mathrm{GF}(2^n)$ for $n = 128$ can be implemented as

$$2X = \begin{cases} X \ll 1 & \text{if } \mathrm{msb}_1 X = 0. \\ (X \ll 1) \oplus 0^{120}10000111 & \text{if } \mathrm{msb}_1 X = 1. \end{cases}$$

We omit the details here and refer to [24] for further details.

Simon's Algorithm. Simon's algorithm is a quantum algorithm that is able to solve the following problem referred to as *Simon's problem*. This algorithm is the key element of most of our quantum attacks against AES-OTR and OPP.

Definition 1. *(Simon's Problem) Given quantum access to a Boolean function* $f : \{0,1\}^n \rightarrow \{0,1\}^n$ *(called Simon's function) for which it holds:* $\exists s \in \{0,1\}^n :$ $\forall x, y \in \{0,1\}^n$

$$f(x) = f(y) \iff y \in \{x, x \oplus s\},$$

the goal is to find the period s of f.

This problem of course can be solved in a classical setting by searching for collisions in $\Theta(2^{n/2})$, when we are given classical access to the function f. However, when we are able to query the function f quantum-mechanically, and we are thus allowed to make queries of arbitrary quantum superpositions of the form $|x\rangle|0\rangle \mapsto |x\rangle|f(x)\rangle$, Simon's algorithm can solve this problem with query complexity $\mathcal{O}(n)$. On a high level, Simon's algorithm is able to recover a random vector $y \in \{0,1\}^n$ in a *single* quantum query to f that is orthogonal to the period s, i.e. $y \cdot s = 0$. This subroutine is repeated $\mathcal{O}(n)$ times such that one obtains $n - 1$ independent vectors where each is orthogonal to s with high probability. Therefore s can be recovered by solving the corresponding system of linear equations. For more details on the subroutine, we refer to [18].

Also [18] showed that Simon's algorithm recovers the hidden period s with $\mathcal{O}(n)$ quantum queries even if f has some "unwanted periods" – i.e., values $t \neq s$ such that $f(x) = f(x \oplus t)$ holds with probability $\leq 1/2$ over a random choice of x. As we will show, this condition is always satisfied in our attacks.

Deutsch's Algorithm. Deutsch's algorithm solves the following problem.

Definition 2. *Given quantum access to a Boolean function* $f : \{0,1\} \rightarrow \{0,1\}$, *the goal is to decide whether f is constant, i.e. $f(0) = f(1)$, or f is balanced, i.e. $f(0) \neq f(1)$.*

The algorithm can solve this problem with a *single* quantum query to f with success probability 1; note that any algorithm with classical access to f would need two queries for the same. To be precise, Deutsch's algorithm solves the above problem by computing the value $f(0) \oplus f(1)$ using a single quantum query to f.

IND-qCPA Security of AEAD Schemes. Below we define IND-qCPA security for nonce-based authenticated encryption with associated data (AEAD) schemes; the formal definitions for such nonce-based AEAD schemes are provided in the full version [17].

Definition 3. *(IND-qCPA with random nonces) A nonce-based AEAD scheme* $\Pi = (Enc, Dec)$ *is indistinguishable under quantum chosen-plaintext attack (IND-qCPA secure) with random nonces, if there is no efficient quantum adversary $\mathcal{A}$ that is able to win the following security game, except with probability at most $\frac{1}{2} + \epsilon$ where $\epsilon > 0$ is negligible.*

Key generation: *A random key* $K \leftarrow \mathcal{K}$ *and a random bit* $b \leftarrow \{0,1\}$ *are chosen by the challenger.*

Queries: *In any order the adversary* $\mathcal{A}$ *is allowed to make two types of queries:*

- *Encryption queries: The challenger first randomly chooses a nonce* $N \leftarrow \{0,1\}^\kappa$ *and forwards it to* $\mathcal{A}$. *The adversary now can choose a message-AD pair* (M, A), *possibly in superposition, and the challenger encrypts* (N, A, M) *with the classical nonce* N *and returns the output* (C, T) *to* $\mathcal{A}$.

- *Challenge query: The challenger picks a random nonce* $N \leftarrow \{0,1\}^\kappa$ *once more and gives it to the adversary. Afterwards,* $\mathcal{A}$ *chooses two same sized classical message-AD pairs* $(M_0, A), (M_1, A)$ *and forwards them to the challenger which in turn encrypts* (N, A, M_b) *with the previously chosen classical nonce* N. *The output* (C^*, T^*) *is again given to* $\mathcal{A}$.

Guess: *The adversary outputs a bit* b' *and wins if* $b = b'$.

Let p *be the probability that* $\mathcal{A}$ *wins the above game. Then its IND-qCPA advantage with respect to the AEAD scheme* Π *is given by* $Adv_\Pi^{IND-qCPA}(\mathcal{A}) = |p - \frac{1}{2}|$. *So* Π *is said to be IND-qCPA secure under randomly chosen nonces if* $Adv_\Pi^{IND-qCPA}(\mathcal{A})$ *of any polynomial-time quantum adversary* $\mathcal{A}$ *is negligible.*

3   Quantum Attacks on Confidentiality of OTR

The *AES-OTR* block cipher mode emerged from the *Offset Two-Round* (OTR) mode [23] as a part of the CAESAR competition [1] and is based on the AES block cipher as proposed in [24]. It is a nonce based authenticated encryption with associated data (AEAD) scheme and provides two methods for associated data processing. AES-OTR has a provable security in the classical setting under the assumption that AES is a pseudorandom function as argued in [24].

However, in this section we will show that we can exploit the way AD is processed in both cases, namely in parallel and serial, to break IND-qCPA security. In this case, we assume a setting where the adversary has quantum access to an encryption oracle and the nonces the challenger uses to answer encryption queries are picked uniformly at random. We even go one step further and break IND-qCPA security of AES-OTR considered as a pure AE scheme, i.e., with empty AD. To do so, we consider a stronger adversarial setting in which the adversary is allowed to pick the classical nonces adaptively; this attack is described in detail in the full version [17]. In the following, we will be extending upon techniques as utilized in [22].

3.1   Specifications of AES-OTR

We begin by describing the AES-OTR mode by following the specifications as proposed in [24] for the third round of the CAESAR competition. Let n, k, τ, κ as labeled in Sect. 2, where $k \in \{128, 192, 256\}$, $\tau \in \{32, 40, ..., 128\}$ and $\kappa \in \{8, 16, ..., 120\}$ are of a fixed length. Since AES-OTR uses AES as its underlying block cipher, $n = 128$ is fixed as well and we assume E_K to denote the AES encryption function with key K. Also, the lengths of both a plaintext M and associated data A are required to fulfill $|M|, |A| \in \{0,1\}^{8*}$ such that $|M|_8, |A|_8 \leq 2^{64}$. We note that [24] provides sets of recommended parameters which imply that for both instantiations of AES-OTR either with AES-128 or AES-256 a 16-byte tag should be used. This recommendation becomes relevant for our attack in Sect. 3.2. For further details on the parameters we refer to [24].

Below, we provide a simplified description of AES-OTR for both variants of processing AD, namely in parallel (on the left) and in serial (on the right). To indicate how the AD is processed, we use p for parallel and s for serial processing and write OTR-$\mathcal{E}_{K,p}(N, A, M)$ or OTR-$\mathcal{E}_{K,s}(N, A, M)$ respectively. We omit the description of the decryption algorithm, as decryption is not relevant for our attacks. We again refer to [24] for the details. To be more precise, Algorithm 4 corresponds to the encryption core and Algorithms 5 and 6 describe the authentication core of the AEAD scheme described in Algorithm 1 and 2 for parallel and serial AD processing respectively. Note that the encryption core of AES-OTR with parallel (normal box) and serial (dashed box) AD processing only differ in the way U is defined. Algorithm 3 outlines how the nonce N is formatted before being incorporated into the mask U, used to encrypt the plaintext. (This formatting plays an important role for our attack with adaptive nonces, as described in the full version [17].) Notice that for a single block message AES-OTR only encrypts it by xor-ing it with some value depending on U. We will exploit this property for our IND-qCPA attacks.

Algorithm 1. OTR-$\mathcal{E}_{K,p}(N, A, M)$
1: $(C, TE) \leftarrow$ EF-P$_{K,\tau}(N, M)$
2: if $A \neq \varepsilon$ then
3:     $TA \leftarrow$ AF-P$_K(A)$
4: else $TA \leftarrow 0^n$
5: $T \leftarrow$ msb$_\tau(TE \oplus TA)$
6: return (C, T)

Algorithm 2. OTR-$\mathcal{E}_{K,s}(N, A, M)$
1: if $A \neq \varepsilon$ then
2:     $TA \leftarrow$ AF-S$_K(A)$
3: else $TA \leftarrow 0^n$
4: $(C, TE) \leftarrow$ EF-S$_{K,\tau}(N, M, TA)$
5: $T \leftarrow$ msb$_\tau(TE)$
6: return (C, T)

Algorithm 3. Format(τ, N)
return bin$(\tau \bmod n, 7)||0^{n-8-\kappa}||1||N$

Algorithm 4. $\boxed{\text{EF-P}_{K,\tau}(N,M)}$, $\overline{\text{EF-S}_{K,\tau}(N,M,TA)}$

1: $\underline{\Sigma \leftarrow 0^n}$
2: $\boxed{U \leftarrow E_K(\text{Format}(\tau,N))}$
3: $\overline{U \leftarrow 2\big(E_K(\text{Format}(\tau,N)) \oplus TA\big)}$
4: $L \leftarrow U,\ L^\# \leftarrow 3U$
5: $M_1||...||M_m \leftarrow M$ s.t. $|M_i| = n$
6: **for** $i \in \{1,...,\lceil m/2 \rceil - 1\}$ **do**
7: $\qquad C_{2i-1} \leftarrow E_K(L \oplus M_{2i-1}) \oplus M_{2i}$
8: $\qquad C_{2i} \leftarrow E_K(L^\# \oplus C_{2i-1}) \oplus M_{2i-1}$
9: $\qquad \Sigma \leftarrow \Sigma \oplus M_{2i}$
10: $\qquad L \leftarrow L \oplus L^\#,\ L^\# \leftarrow 2L^\#$
11: **if** m is even **then**
12: $\qquad Z \leftarrow E_K(L \oplus M_{m-1})$
13: $\qquad C_m \leftarrow \text{msb}_{|M_m|}(Z) \oplus M_m$
14: $\qquad C_{m-1} \leftarrow E_K(L^\# \oplus \underline{C_m}) \oplus M_{m-1}$
15: $\qquad \Sigma \leftarrow \Sigma \oplus Z \oplus \underline{C_m}$
16: $\qquad L^* \leftarrow L^\#$
17: **else if** m is odd **then**
18: $\qquad C_m \leftarrow \text{msb}_{|M_m|}(E_K(L)) \oplus M_m$
19: $\qquad \Sigma \leftarrow \Sigma \oplus \underline{M_m}$
20: $\qquad L^* \leftarrow L$
21: **if** $|M_m| \neq n$ **then**
22: $TE \leftarrow E_K(3^2 L^* \oplus \Sigma)$
23: **else** $TE \leftarrow E_K(7L^* \oplus \Sigma)$
24: $C \leftarrow C_1||...||C_m$
25: **return** (C, TE)

Algorithm 5. AF-P$_K(A)$

1: $\Xi \leftarrow 0^n$
2: $Q \leftarrow E_K(0^n)$
3: $A_1||...||A_a \leftarrow A$, s.t. $|A_i| = n$
4: **for** $i \in \{1,...,a-1\}$ **do**
5: $\qquad \Xi \leftarrow \Xi \oplus E_K(Q \oplus A_i)$
6: $\qquad Q \leftarrow 2Q$
7: $\Xi \leftarrow \Xi \oplus \underline{A_a}$
8: **if** $|A_a| \neq n$ **then**
9: $\qquad TA \leftarrow E_K(3Q \oplus \Xi)$
10: **else** $TA \leftarrow E_K(3^2 Q \oplus \Xi)$
11: **return** TA

Algorithm 6. AF-S$_K(A)$

1: $\Xi \leftarrow 0^n$
2: $Q \leftarrow E_K(0^n)$
3: $A_1||...||A_a \leftarrow A$, s.t. $|A_i| = n$
4: **for** $i \in \{1,...,a-1\}$ **do**
5: $\qquad \Xi \leftarrow E_K(A_i \oplus \Xi)$
6: $\Xi \leftarrow \Xi \oplus \underline{A_a}$
7: **if** $|A_a| \neq n$ **then**
8: $\qquad TA \leftarrow E_K(2Q \oplus \Xi)$
9: **else**
10: $\qquad TA \leftarrow E_K(4Q \oplus \Xi)$
11: **return** TA

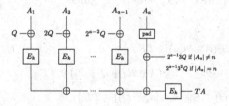

Fig. 1. Computation of the value TA of the authentication core of AES-OTR with parallel AD processing with $Q = E_K(0^n)$.

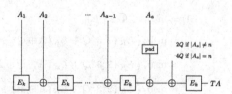

Fig. 2. Computation of the value TA of the authentication core of AES-OTR with serial AD processing with $Q = E_K(0^n)$.

In the pictorial description of how the value TA in Algorithms 5 and 6 for parallel and serial AD processing is computed, the value Q is used as part of the masking and is defined as $Q = E_K(0^n)$. Note that Q is a constant value and is independent of the nonce N. This is the key observation we use in our attacks in Sects. 3.2 and 3.3 that exploit the way AD is being processed.

It is worth mentioning that there are some prior works (specifically [18,20]) which proposed approaches to attack *unforgeability* of AES-OTR using Simon's algorithm when given quantum access to the corresponding encryption oracle. On a high level, the above works exploit the way AD is processed to compute collisions in the intermediate variable TA (see Figs. 1 and 2); we present a detailed description of their attacks in the full version [17]. We will use similar ideas for our following quantum attacks on the *confidentiality* of AES-OTR.

3.2   IND-qCPA Attack on AES-OTR with Parallel AD Processing

In this section, we show that AES-OTR is insecure in the IND-qCPA setting with random nonces when it is used as an AEAD scheme with associated data processed in parallel. In our IND-qCPA attack, we exploit the way AD is processed to find collisions for the output value TA of Algorithm 5, as well as exploit the fact that the encryption algorithm essentially performs a one-time pad encryption when given a single-block message.

As a general attack strategy, we want to create a periodic function f_1, whose period can be computed using Simon's algorithm. To construct our Simon's function f_1, we use a similar approach as described in [22, Section 4.3] for breaking IND-qCPA security of OCB2. Note that the way OCB2 authenticates AD in [22, Figure 3] is (up to multiplication with constants) essentially the same as for AES-OTR in Algorithm 5. Thus, we can follow a very similar argument.

We define $f_1 : \{0,1\}^n \to \{0,1\}^\tau$

$$f_1(A) = \text{OTR-}\mathcal{E}_{K,p}(N, A\|A\|0^n, \varepsilon).$$

As the plaintext is chosen to be empty, the ciphertext is empty as well which is the reason the quantum encryption oracle $\text{OTR-}\mathcal{E}_{K,p}(N, \cdot)$ returns a tag of length τ only.[1] Now notice that f_1 has period $s = 3Q = Q \oplus 2Q$ since

$$\begin{aligned}
f_1(A) &= \text{msb}_\tau(TA \oplus TE)\\
&= \text{msb}_\tau\Big(E_K(2^2 3^2 Q \oplus E_K(A \oplus Q) \oplus E_K(A \oplus 2Q)) \oplus TE\Big)\\
&= \text{msb}_\tau\Big(E_K(2^2 3^2 Q \oplus E_K(A \oplus Q \oplus 2Q \oplus 2Q) \oplus E_K(A \oplus 2Q \oplus Q \oplus Q)) \oplus TE\Big)\\
&= \text{msb}_\tau\Big(E_K(2^2 3^2 Q \oplus E_K(A \oplus 3Q \oplus 2Q) \oplus E_K(A \oplus 3Q \oplus Q)) \oplus TE\Big)\\
&= f_1(A \oplus s).
\end{aligned}$$

---

[1] We notice that in the context of Simon's algorithm the domain and the co-domain of Simon's function are required to be of the same dimension. Since the size of the tag τ is possibly less than n, we technically need to append an additional $n - \tau$ bits of zeros (or any other fixed bit string of size $n - \tau$). Importantly, this does not change the periodicity of f_1, as these bits are fixed. For the sake of convenience however, we refrain from appending them in each step of the analysis of f_1.

Following the arguments made in [22, Section 3.1], using a single quantum query to the encryption oracle OTR-$\mathcal{E}_{K,p}(N, \cdot)$, the function f_1 can be computed in superposition. We need this to be done in a single quantum query, as the nonce N changes with each quantum query made to the oracle. We thus can apply Simon's algorithm to f_1, which computes a vector $y \in \{0,1\}^n$ that is orthogonal to the period $s = 3Q = 3E_K(0^n)$. Notice that there do not exist any "unwanted periods" as defined in Sect. 2 with overwhelming probability, since we can apply the same reasoning as in [18, Section 5.3] using that AES is a PRP.

It is important that the period is independent of the nonce N, such that despite the nonce changing with each quantum query, Simon's algorithm still returns a random vector y orthogonal to the fixed period. This means, after recovering $O(n)$ such independent orthogonal vectors y, we can recover the value $3Q = 3E_K(0^n)$ and thus the value $E_K(0^n)$ as well with $O(n)$ quantum queries to the AES-OTR encryption oracle.

For the rest of this section, we assume that AES-OTR is instantiated using the recommended parameter sets from [24]. In particular, we assume that the size of the tag is 16-bytes, i.e., $\tau = n$. It turns out that not only is this assumption necessary for our attack to succeed efficiently but is also necessary for the IND-qCPA attack on OCB2 in [22, Section 4.3]. We discuss this assumption in detail in the full version [17].

As a next step towards breaking IND-qCPA security we want to gain raw block cipher access i.e. the ability to compute $E_K(inp)$ for any given input $inp \in \{0,1\}^n$. To realize this, we use Deutsch's algorithm like done in [22] as follows. Having recovered the value $Q = E_K(0^n)$, define two fixed single-block associated data inputs $\alpha_0 = 3^2 Q$ and $\alpha_1 = 3^2 Q \oplus inp$ for any given input $inp \in \{0,1\}^n$. We continue by considering the n functions $f^{(i)} : \{0,1\} \rightarrow \{0,1\}$,

$$f^{(i)}(b) = i\text{th bit of } \{ \text{OTR-}\mathcal{E}_{K,p}(N, \alpha_b, \varepsilon)\} \tag{3.1}$$

for a random nonce N and empty message. Here again, the output of OTR-$\mathcal{E}_{K,p}(N, \cdot)$ is only the tag of length $\tau = n$, as the message is kept empty. Following the argument in [22], we can compute $f^{(i)}(b)$ in superposition with a single quantum query to the AES-OTR encryption oracle by also truncating out the unneeded $n - 1$ bits of the output of OTR-$\mathcal{E}_{K,p}(N, \cdot)$. This gives us the ability to apply Deutsch's algorithm on $f^{(i)}$ and recover the value

$$f^{(i)}(0) \oplus f^{(i)}(1) = i\text{th bit of}\{TE \oplus E_K(\alpha_0 \oplus 3^2 Q)\}$$
$$\oplus\, i\text{th bit of}\{TE \oplus E_K(\alpha_1 \oplus 3^2 Q)\}$$
$$= i\text{th bit of}\{E_K(0^n) \oplus E_K(inp)\} \tag{3.2}$$

with a single quantum query. Thus, by applying Deutsch's algorithm to each of the n functions $f^{(i)}$, we are able to recover all n bits of $\left(E_K(0^n) \oplus E_K(inp)\right)$ and from this, since we already know $E_K(0^n)$, we can recover $E_K(inp)$. It is worth pointing out, that despite the nonce N changes with each application of Deutsch's algorithm, we are still able to recover $\left(E_K(0^n) \oplus E_K(inp)\right)$ since it is independent of N; note that the nonce-dependent value TE gets "xored-out" in Eq. (3.2).

As a result of the observations above, we can now sketch our IND-qCPA attack against AES-OTR with parallel AD processing:

1. Recover the value $3Q$ and thus the value $E_K(0^n)$ using $O(n)$ quantum queries with Simon's algorithm as discussed above.
2. Pick arbitrary but different single-block messages M_0 and M_1 and define the associated data to be empty, i.e. $A = \varepsilon$. We now give these values as an input to the challenger and record the nonce N which is used to encrypt M_b as well as the output (C^*, T) of the challenger.
3. Using Deutsch's algorithm $2n$ times (i.e., using raw block cipher access twice) as described above, we compute the value $V = E_K\Big(E_K\big(\text{Format}(\tau, N)\big)\Big)$ using a total of $2n$ quantum queries. Here, we use the nonce N the challenger used to encrypt the challenge query.
4. Output the bit $b'' = b'$ if $C^* = V \oplus M_{b'}$.

It remains to show that our attack outputs the correct bit b'':

To see this, we notice that for a single-block message M and empty AD the output of the encryption oracle is the ciphertext-tag pair (C^*, T) where

$$C^* = \text{msb}_{|M|}\big(E_K(L)\big) \oplus M$$

with $L = E_K(\text{Format}(\tau, N))$ following the description of Algorithm 4. Since the attack relies on recomputing exactly the value used to encrypt M_b in a one-time pad-like manner, the attack succeeds with high probability.

3.3 IND-qCPA Attack on AES-OTR with Serial AD Processing

The aim of this section is to break IND-qCPA security of AES-OTR used as an AEAD scheme with random nonces but now with associated data processed in serial by Algorithm 6. We again exploit the way AD is processed to compute collisions for the variable TA.

Similar to the attack above, we define a periodic function f_2 whose period can be computed using Simon's algorithm. In this case however, as a consequence of our choice of f_2, computing the period of the function already gives us raw block cipher access. This is in contrast to the IND-qCPA attack in [22, Section 4.3] and our previous attack in Sect. 3.2, where we first recover $E_K(0^n)$ and then gain raw block cipher access via Deutsch's algorithm. In this section, Simon's function is defined in a very different fashion than before, as the function can distinguish two different cases depending on an input bit b and treat them accordingly – this affects either having one or two blocks of associated data as an input to the quantum encryption oracle respectively. We therefore also need to argue why we actually have quantum access to Simon's function we define below.

This is precisely the scenario we described in Sect. 1.1 w.r.t. an adversary being able to query a superposition of (associated) data with *unequal* length to the quantum encryption oracle. We achieve this by a novel modelling of the encryption oracle in our quantum circuit for f_2, such that the circuit also queries the encryption oracle only *once* each time f_2 is queried; we emphasize the latter aspect is due to the changing nonces as described in Sect. 3.2. At this point however, we make the assumption that we have quantum access to the Simon's function f_2 and are able to compute it with a single query to the quantum encryption oracle. We later validate this assumption and further discuss the quantum accessibility as well as the issue of having to achieve this with a single quantum query near the end of this section.

We realize gaining raw block cipher access by choosing an arbitrary $B \in \{0,1\}^n$ (for which we want to know its encryption $E_K(B)$) and set Simon's function to be $f_2 : \{0,1\}^{n+1} \to \{0,1\}^\tau$,

$$
f_2(b||A) = \begin{cases} \text{OTR-}\mathcal{E}_{K,s}(N, B||A, \varepsilon) & \text{if } b = 0 \\ \text{OTR-}\mathcal{E}_{K,s}(N, A, \varepsilon) & \text{if } b = 1 \end{cases}
$$

where $b \in \{0,1\}$ is a single bit and $A \in \{0,1\}^n$ represents one block of associated data of size n. Note that here f_2 gives us a value in $\{0,1\}^\tau$, since the ciphertext is empty as a result of the plaintext being chosen as empty. More precisely, for a general set of associated data D and empty plaintext we get by Algorithm 4 and Algorithm 2 that

$$
\text{OTR-}\mathcal{E}_{K,s}(N, D, \varepsilon) = \text{msb}_\tau \left(E_K \left(3^3 2 \Big(TA_D \oplus E_K \big(\text{Format}(\tau, N) \big) \Big) \right) \right)
$$

where $TA_D = \text{AF-S}_K(D)$. This implies that the period s of f_2 only depends on the function $\text{AF-S}_K(D)$. Therefore, we define a new function $g : \{0,1\}^{n+1} \to \{0,1\}^n$,

$$
g(b||A) = \begin{cases} \text{AF-S}_K(B||A) & \text{if } b = 0 \\ \text{AF-S}_K(A) & \text{if } b = 1 \end{cases}
$$

We claim that g, and therefore f_2 as well, has period $s = 1||E_K(B)$. Indeed:

$$
\begin{aligned}
g\big(0||A \oplus 1||E_K(B)\big) = g\big(1||A \oplus E_K(B)\big) &= \text{AF-S}_K\big(A \oplus E_K(B)\big) \\
&= E_K(4Q \oplus A \oplus E_K(B)) = \text{AF-S}_K(B||A) = g(0||A) \quad (3.3)
\end{aligned}
$$

$$
\begin{aligned}
g(1||A \oplus 1||E_K(B)) = g(0||A \oplus E_K(B)) &= \text{AF-S}_K(B||A \oplus E_K(B)) \\
&= E_K\Big(4Q \oplus A \oplus E_K(B) \oplus E_K(B) \Big) = E_K(4Q \oplus A) \\
&= \text{AF-S}_K(A) = g(1||A) \quad\quad (3.4)
\end{aligned}
$$

where $Q = E_K(0^n)$, and for Eqs. 3.3 and 3.4, we used the definition of Algorithm 6.

Under the assumption that we can in fact compute f_2 in superposition using a *single* quantum query to the encryption oracle $\text{OTR-}\mathcal{E}_{K,s}(N, \cdot)$, we can apply Simon's algorithm to f_2. Hence, with a similar argument as in Sect. 3.2 we can recover the value $s = 1||E_K(B)$ and thus the value $E_K(B)$ for any $B \in \{0,1\}^n$ with $O(n)$ quantum queries. It is important to mention that the period s is again independent of the nonce. So even though the nonce, and hence f_2 changes with each quantum query, Simon's algorithm still returns a random vector orthogonal to the *fixed* period $s = 1||E_K(B)$ in each of the n iterations. We conclude that this grants us raw block cipher access without having to use Deutsch's algorithm like in the attack described in Sect. 3.2.

Unlike our IND-qCPA attack in Sect. 3.2, this attack succeeds with high probability even if the tags were truncated. This is justified because in the previous section truncation only became an issue when we applied Deutsch's algorithm. Here, we do not use Deutsch's algorithm but Simon's algorithm only. Since the function f_2 is still periodic as its periodicity is unaffected by the truncation of the tag, running Simon's algorithm does not run into any issues.

Now we can again sketch an IND-qCPA attack against AES-OTR but this time with serial AD processing:

1. Pick arbitrary but different single-block messages M_0 and M_1 and define the AD to be empty. We give these values as an input to the challenger and record the nonce N which was used to encrypt either M_0 or M_1 as well as the output (C^*, T) of the challenger.
2. Compute the value $V = E_K\left(2 \cdot E_K\big(\text{Format}(\tau, N)\big)\right)$ using $2\mathcal{O}(n)$ quantum encryption queries via two applications of Simon's algorithm (using the raw block cipher access twice as discussed above.).
3. Output the bit $b'' = b'$ if $M_{b'} = C^* \oplus V$.

To see that the above attack succeeds we note that for a single-block message M of size n and empty AD we have

$$\text{OTR-}\mathcal{E}_{K,s}(N, \varepsilon, M)\Big|_C = E_K\left(2 \cdot E_K\big(\text{Format}(\tau, N)\big)\right) \oplus M.$$

where by $|_C$ we indicate truncating out the tag T. This is essentially a one-time pad encryption with mask V. Since we are able to compute V, we also recover the correct bit b''.

On the Quantum Accessibility of Function f_2. It remains to argue that we actually have quantum access to the function f_2 with a *single* query to the encryption oracle each time we query f_2. This is done by coming up with a suitable quantum circuit that describes f_2 such that it uses only a single encryption unitary gate; this is because the nonce N changes with each quantum query made to the encryption oracle.

To achieve this, we have to modify the quantum encryption oracle queries in a slight way: we add an additional n-qubit input register which encodes the length of our message. By doing so, the encryption oracle knows how many bits of the message it should actually encrypt. Thus, we also need to define f_2 in a different manner:

$$f_2(b||A) = \begin{cases} \text{OTR-}\tilde{\mathcal{E}}_{K,s}(N, \text{bin}(2n,n)||B||A, \varepsilon) & \text{if } b = 0. \\ \text{OTR-}\tilde{\mathcal{E}}_{K,s}(N, \text{bin}(n,n)||A||0^n, \varepsilon) & \text{if } b = 1. \end{cases}$$

The circuit also uses so-called Fredkin gate (as described e.g. in [30, Section 2.2]), which is a controlled swap gate. The Fredkin gate, upon input basis state (b, I_1, I_2) with b a single bit, produces output (b, O_1, O_2) where $O_1 = \bar{b}I_1 + bI_2$, $O_2 = bI_1 + \bar{b}I_2$. So the gate essentially swaps the inputs when $b = 1$ and does nothing if $b = 0$. Note that the way f_2 is defined, both $|\text{bin}(2n, n)||B||A\rangle$ and $|\text{bin}(n, n)||A||0^n\rangle$ are $3n$ qubit states and hence can be swapped (the swap gate can only operate on inputs that are of the same length, as the swapping is done qubit wise). In this case, when the encryption oracle gets such an input, it first parses the first n qubits of the query to figure out how many blocks of the input have to be encrypted. For $b = 0$ it just takes $B||A$ as an input but if $b = 1$ then it ignores the remaining 0^n block of the query and only encrypts A. The corresponding quantum circuit therefore looks as follows (Fig. 3):

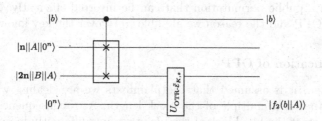

Fig. 3. The quantum circuit implementing f_2 using a single quantum query via the gate $U_{\text{OTR-}\tilde{\mathcal{E}}_{K,s}}$. We indicate the n-bit encoding of n and $2n$ with bold letters.

Note that the output of the second register is set to $|\mathbf{n}||A||0^n\rangle$ if $b = 0$ and $|\mathbf{2n}||B||A\rangle$ if $b = 1$. For the third register it is the other way round.

Comparison with the Quantum Attack on CMAC in [18]. Note that the serial AD processing component of AES-OTR (Algorithm 6) is essentially equivalent to the message authentication code CMAC [9]. And Kaplan et al. [18] show how to break the quantum unforgeability of CMAC using Simon's algorithm (technically they present a quantum attack against the closely related CBC-MAC, but it is straightforward to extend the attack to CMAC).

On a high-level, the extension of their CMAC attack to AES-OTR with serial AD processing would proceed as follows. Choose two arbitrary blocks $B_0, B_1 \in \{0,1\}^n$ and define the function $\tilde{g}(b||A) = \text{AF-S}_K(B_b||A)$ (corresponding to Simon's function $\tilde{f}_2(b||A) = \text{OTR-}\mathcal{E}_{K,s}(N, B_b||A, \varepsilon)$). It is not hard to see that $\tilde{g}$ (and $\tilde{f}_2$) has period $\tilde{s} = 1||(E_K(B_0) \oplus E_K(B_1))$. Hence we can use Simon's algorithm as in [18, Section 5.1] to recover the value $E_K(B_0) \oplus E_K(B_1)$. Also note that we no longer need to query the quantum encryption oracle on a superposition of unequal length AD, unlike our IND-qCPA attack above. However, just knowing $E_K(B_0) \oplus E_K(B_1)$ is not sufficient to obtain the raw block cipher access $E_K(\cdot)$ we would need to break IND-qCPA security, even if B_0, B_1 are under our control.

4 Quantum Key-Recovery Attack on OPP

The *Offset Public Permutation Mode* (OPP) was proposed in [10] and [11] and it essentially tries to generalize OCB3 by replacing the underlying block cipher by a public permutation and a different form of masking. In this section we will show that using a public permutation the way OPP does, actually leads to a devastating key recovery attack in the quantum setting.

Our attack uses a similar strategy as the IND-qCPA attack against OCB2 in [22, Section 4.4] with adaptively chosen nonces; but instead of choosing a new nonce adaptively to break IND-qCPA security, we are able to recover the value $\Omega := P(X\|K)$ where P is an efficiently invertible public permutation and K is the key (X can be seen as a formatting of the nonce). In contrast to OTR being based on a block cipher that may only be inverted knowing the key, we are here dealing with a public permutation that can be inverted efficiently. This is the key issue of OPP and the reason we are able to recover the key knowing Ω.

4.1 Specification of OPP

In this section, it is assumed that the plaintexts we are dealing with always have a size that is a multiple of the block length. As a consequence, it is not necessary to treat the last block of the plaintext any differently in our analysis, and furthermore we are also excluding the specifications for how OPP encrypts plaintexts that do not meet this assumption. In the same manner this also applies to the way we describe the processing of associated data.

Let n, k, τ, κ as labeled in Sect. 2 such that $\kappa \leq n - k - 1$. We begin by describing the OPP mode as proposed in [10] in a simplified manner that also maintains consistent labeling of variables in previous descriptions of modes such as OTR.

A set of functions $\Phi = \{\alpha, \beta, \gamma\}$ is given by $\alpha, \beta, \gamma : \{0,1\}^n \to \{0,1\}^n, \alpha(x) = \varphi(x), \beta(x) = \varphi(x) \oplus x$ and $\gamma(x) = \varphi^2(x) \oplus \varphi(x) \oplus x$ where for $x = x_0\|...\|x_{15}$ and $x_i \in \{0,1\}^{64}$ the function $\varphi : \{0,1\}^{1024} \to \{0,1\}^{1024}$ is defined as

$$\varphi(x_0, ..., x_{15}) = \big(x_1, ..., x_{15}, (x_0 \lll 53) \oplus (x_5 \ll 13)\big).$$

OPP uses the so called tweakable Even-Mansour construction MEM, where a tweak space $\mathcal{T}$ of the form $\mathcal{T} \subseteq \{0,1\}^{n-k} \times \mathbb{N}^3$, as outlined in [10, Lemma 4], is considered. For further details about tweaks and tweakable block ciphers we refer to [10] as this specific notion is not relevant for the subsequent attack.

The encryption function $\widetilde{E} : \{0,1\}^k \times \mathcal{T} \times \{0,1\}^n \to \{0,1\}^n$ is then defined as

$$\widetilde{E}(K, X, \bar{i}, M) = P\big(\delta(K, X, \bar{i}) \oplus M\big) \oplus \delta(K, X, \bar{i})$$

where $\delta : \{0,1\}^k \times \mathcal{T} \to \{0,1\}^n$ is called the masking function and for $\bar{i} = (i_0, i_1, i_2) \in \mathbb{N}^3$ it is set to be $\delta(K, X, \bar{i}) = \gamma^{i_2} \circ \beta^{i_1} \circ \alpha^{i_0}\big(P(X\|K)\big)$. For convenience the shorthand notation $\widetilde{E}_{K,X}^{\bar{i}}(M) = \widetilde{E}(K, X, \bar{i}, M)$ is being used in the algorithmic description of OPP.

The decryption function $\widetilde{D}$ corresponding to $\widetilde{E}$ is defined in a straightforward manner. However it should be noted that P is a public permutation such that P^{-1} can be computed efficiently, since the inverse permutation is necessary to perform decryption.

Below, we present a simplified description of the OPP mode based on the specification in [10]. We only provide a description of the encryption and authentication part of the algorithm, as the details regarding decryption are not relevant to our attack and are therefore omitted. To be precise, the authentication core of OPP is described in Algorithm 9 and the encryption core corresponds to Algorithm 8.

Algorithm 7. OPP-$\mathcal{E}(K, N, AD, M)$

1: $X \leftarrow \mathrm{pad}_{n-\kappa-k}^0(N)$
2: $C, S \leftarrow \mathrm{OPPEnc}(K, X, M)$
3: $T \leftarrow \mathrm{OPPAbs}(K, X, AD, S)$
4: **return** C, T

Algorithm 8. OPPEnc(K, X, M)

1: $M_0||...||M_{m-1} \leftarrow M, \mathrm{s.t.} \; |M_i| = n$
2: $C \leftarrow \varepsilon$
3: $S \leftarrow 0^n$
4: **for** $i \in \{0, ..., m-1\}$ **do**
5: $\quad C_i \leftarrow \widetilde{E}_{K,X}^{i,0,1}(M_i)$
6: $\quad C \leftarrow C||C_i$
7: $\quad S \leftarrow S \oplus M_i$
8: **return** $C, \widetilde{E}_{K,X}^{m-1,2,1}(S)$

Algorithm 9. OPPAbs(K, X, A, S)

1: $A_0||...||A_{a-1} \leftarrow A, \mathrm{s.t.} \; |A_i| = n$
2: $S' \leftarrow 0^n$
3: **for** $i \in \{0, ..., a-1\}$ **do**
4: $\quad S' \leftarrow S' \oplus \widetilde{E}_{K,X}^{i,0,0}(A_i)$
5: **return** $\mathrm{msb}_\tau(S' \oplus S)$

4.2 Our Quantum Key-Recovery Attack

In this attack, we adapt the techniques used in [22, Section 4.4] for breaking IND-qCPA security of OCB2 with adaptively chosen nonces. However, in this case we are able to recover the key instead. Our attack is focused solely on the encryption part, so OPP is used as a pure AE scheme, and does not make use of the way associated data is processed. This is in contrast to our previous attacks in Sects. 3.2 and 3.3 as there we could exploit the fact that AD processing was not dependent on a nonce but rather on the constant value $Q = E_k(0^n)$. In the case of OPP this is different because the nonce is used in the associated data processing, as the value $P(X||K)$ where $X = \mathrm{pad}_{n-\kappa-k}^0(N)$ is dependent on the nonce N (see Algorithm 7). Since the nonce changes with each call to the encryption oracle, OPP never processes a fixed set of AD the same way. This is the reason we can't apply Simon's algorithm (which calls the oracle multiple times) in the same manner.

Before we formulate the attack itself, we observe a crucial property of the xor of two consecutive ciphertext blocks considered as a function of its corresponding plaintext blocks. Define $\Omega = P(X\|K)$ and recall that OPP encrypts the i-th plaintext block M_i as $C_i = P(\delta(K, X, (i, 0, 1)) \oplus M_i) \oplus \delta(K, X, (i, 0, 1))$ where $\delta(K, X, (i, 0, 1)) = \varphi^{i+2}(\Omega) \oplus \varphi^{i+1}(\Omega) \oplus \varphi^i(\Omega)$. We now define functions $f_i : \{0, 1\}^n \to \{0, 1\}^n$ such that

$$f_i(M) = P\big(\delta(K, X, (i, 0, 1)) \oplus M\big) \oplus \delta(K, X, (i, 0, 1)),$$

which correspond to the i-th ciphertext block C_i considered as a function of its underlying plaintext block M. Further, by defining $s := \varphi^{i+3}(\Omega) \oplus \varphi^i(\Omega)$ we see that

$$
\begin{aligned}
&f_i(M \oplus s) \oplus f_{i+1}(M \oplus s) \\
&= P\Big(\varphi^{i+2}(\Omega) \oplus \varphi^{i+1}(\Omega) \oplus \varphi^i(\Omega) \oplus M \oplus s\Big) \\
&\quad \oplus P\Big(\varphi^{i+3}(\Omega) \oplus \varphi^{i+2}(\Omega) \oplus \varphi^{i+1}(\Omega) \oplus M \oplus s\Big) \oplus \varphi^{i+3}(\Omega) \oplus \varphi^i(\Omega) \\
&= P\Big(\varphi^{i+3}(\Omega) \oplus \varphi^{i+2}(\Omega) \oplus \varphi^{i+1}(\Omega) \oplus M\Big) \\
&\quad \oplus P\Big(\varphi^{i+2}(\Omega) \oplus \varphi^{i+1}(\Omega) \oplus \varphi^i(\Omega) \oplus M\Big) \oplus \varphi^{i+3}(\Omega) \oplus \varphi^i(\Omega) \\
&= f_{i+1}(M) \oplus f_i(M).
\end{aligned}
$$

So if we define $F_{i,i+1} : \{0, 1\}^n \to \{0, 1\}^n$ as $F_{i,i+1}(M) = f_i(M) \oplus f_{i+1}(M)$ we see from the above calculations that $F_{i,i+1}(M \oplus s) = F_{i,i+1}(M)$, i.e., $F_{i,i+1}$ is a periodic function with period $s = \varphi^{i+3}(\Omega) \oplus \varphi^i(\Omega)$.

The idea is now to apply a linear function to $2n + 1$ ciphertext blocks to capture this observation and create a periodic function that itself contains n copies of the periodic function $F_{i,i+1}$ from above. To do so consider the function $g : \{0, 1\}^{(2n+1)n+\tau} \to \{0, 1\}^{(n+1)n}$

$$g(C_0, C_1, ..., C_{2n}, t) = (C_0, C_1 \oplus C_2, ..., C_{2n-1} \oplus C_{2n}).$$

Here, the C_i's are n-bit blocks and t is a τ-bit block. It is not hard to see that g is in fact a linear function - i.e., it satisfies $g(C \oplus C') = g(C) \oplus g(C')$ for any valid inputs C and C'. Furthermore let $\tilde{f}_N : \{0, 1\}^{n^2} \to \{0, 1\}^{(n+1)n}$ such that

$$\tilde{f}_N(M_1, ..., M_n) = g \circ \text{OPP-}\mathcal{E}(K, N, \varepsilon, 0^n\|M_1\|M_1\|M_2\|...\|M_n\|M_n) \qquad (4.1)$$

for some randomly chosen nonce N and empty associated data. We can also reformulate $\tilde{f}_N$ in terms of the functions f_i and $F_{i,i+1}$ from above. To be precise, it holds

$$\tilde{f}_N(M_1, ..., M_n) = \big(f_0(0^n), F_{1,2}(M_1), ..., F_{2n-1,2n}(M_n)\big). \qquad (4.2)$$

Moreover, we have included an all-zero plaintext block at the beginning, which will be useful later on for verifying correctness of the recovered key.

The crucial property required for the success of the attack is that $\tilde{f}_N$ has n linearly independent periods $\langle s_i \rangle_{i \in [n]}$ where

$$s_i = \Big((0^n)^{i-1}\|\varphi^{2i+2}(\Omega) \oplus \varphi^{2i-1}(\Omega)\|(0^n)^{n-i}\Big).$$

This directly follows from the observation on the periodicity of $F_{i,i+1}$ and the fact that each pair of the two consecutive ciphertext blocks C_{2i-1} and C_{2i} for $i \in [n]$ encrypt the same plaintext block M_i but with different mask δ.

Following the same argument as in [22, Section 4.4], we can apply [4, Lemma 2] which assures the ability to compute a linear function of a quantum oracle's output. Therefore, we can compute $\tilde{f}_N$ with a single quantum query to the OPP-$\mathcal{E}(K, N, \cdot)$ oracle. Once more, we can apply Simon's algorithm to $\tilde{f}_N$ which, with a single quantum query, recovers a vector $y = (y_1, ..., y_n) \in \{0,1\}^{n^2}$ with $y_i \in \{0,1\}^n \ \forall i \in [n]$ that is orthogonal to each of the periods s_i. The algorithm successfully computes such a vector with overwhelming probability as there do not exist any "unwanted periods" to which y could be orthogonal to.

We justify this claim by building upon the argument presented in [4, Section 3.2], which treats the absence of "unwanted periods" in a very similar attack on a variant of OCB. We recall that OCB uses a block cipher instead of a public permutation like it is the case for OPP, so we need to adjust the reasoning to the setting of a public permutation. If we assume the existence of an unwanted period $\tilde{s}$ of $\tilde{f}_N$ with a probability greater than $\frac{1}{2}$, then at least one of the $F_{i,i+1}$ in Eq. 4.2 would also have to admit an unwanted period $\tilde{s}_{i,i+1}$ with probability greater than $\frac{1}{2n}$. We now draw upon the reasoning presented in [18, Section 3.2], which shows the non-occurrence of higher order differentials in the Even-Mansour construction. More accurately, $F_{i,i+1}$ admitting such an unwanted period is equivalent to saying that P admits a high-probability higher-order differential. But these only happen with negligible probability for a random choice of P according to [18]. This argument makes sure that the probability for unwanted periods to appear is bounded and thus Simon's algorithm computes a vector y as described above with overwhelming probability.

By orthogonality of y we get n equations of the form

$$y_i \cdot \left(\varphi^{2i+2}(\Omega) \oplus \varphi^{2i-1}(\Omega)\right) = 0. \tag{4.3}$$

Before we can proceed, we recall that for $x = x_0 || ... || x_{15}$ and $x_i \in \{0,1\}^{64}$ the function φ is defined as

$$\varphi(x_0, ..., x_{15}) = \left(x_1, ..., x_{15}, (x_0 \lll 53) \oplus (x_5 \lll 13)\right)$$

As described in [10] we see that the function φ is in fact a linear map and it therefore can be represented by a matrix M. Following this, Eq. 4.3 is equivalent to

$$y_i \cdot \left(M^{2i+2} \cdot \Omega \oplus M^{2i-1} \cdot \Omega\right) = 0 \tag{4.4}$$

Knowing M and using associativity of matrix multiplication, we are able to solve the n Equations in 4.4 and thus recover the value $\Omega = P(X||K)$. But since P is a public permutation and its inverse is assumed to be computable efficiently due P^{-1} being needed for decryption, we can just apply P^{-1} to Ω and we thus are able to acquire $X||K$. In particular, we gain possession of the key K.

Observe, that in addition when running Simon's algorithm, we recover the fixed classical value of the first ciphertext block $C_0 = \tilde{E}_{K,X}^{0,0,1}(0^n)$ when we measure the quantum register corresponding to the output of $\tilde{f}_N$ as part of our application of Simon's algorithm. It is important that we fix the value to 0^n (or any other arbitrary fixed classical value of length n also works) in order for C_0 to be a classical value.

We sketch our key-recovery attack below:

1. Given access to a quantum encryption oracle of OPP for a random nonce N, i.e., OPP-$\mathcal{E}(K, N, \varepsilon, \cdot)$, we recover with a single quantum encryption query the classical values $\Omega = P(X\|K)$ and $C_0 = \widetilde{E}_{K,X}^{0,0,1}(0^n)$ as discussed above. In particular, we recover the classical value of the key K.
2. We perform a sanity check on the key: using Ω we recompute the encryption $\widetilde{C}$ of the one-block plaintext 0^n with respect to the same key K and nonce N as used in the above encryption oracle query as

$$\widetilde{C} = P\big(\varphi^2(\Omega) \oplus \varphi(\Omega) \oplus \Omega\big) \oplus \varphi^2(\Omega) \oplus \varphi(\Omega) \oplus \Omega.$$

Check that $C_0 = \widetilde{C}$. If this turns out to be false we repeat step 1., else we are certain to have recovered the right key K.

It remains to argue why this attack is successful. We perform a sanity check in order to assure correctness of the key K. This is where the first ciphertext block is useful. Indeed, having recovered the key K as described above, we can now just recompute the encryption of 0^n, again with respect to the same key-nonce pair (K, N) as in the provided encryption oracle, as

$$\widetilde{C} = P\big(\delta(K, X, (0,0,1)) \oplus 0^n\big) \oplus \delta(K, X, (0,0,1))$$
$$= P\big(\varphi^2(\Omega) \oplus \varphi(\Omega) \oplus \Omega\big) \oplus \varphi^2(\Omega) \oplus \varphi(\Omega) \oplus \Omega$$

where $\Omega = P(X\|K)$ and $X = \mathrm{pad}_{n-\kappa-k}^0(N)$. If now $\widetilde{C} = C_0$, i.e. the encryption of the oracle and our manual computation coincide, we can be sure that we recovered the right key K. Else, we can just repeat the attack until the assertion returns to be true.

With the included sanity check, we are certain to recover the key K at some point, as step one of our attack involves an application of Simon's algorithm that already succeeds with high probability thanks to the non-existence of "unwanted periods" as argued before. Finally, we compare our quantum key-recovery attack on OPP with the corresponding attack on the generic Even-Mansour construction of [18] in the full version [17].

Acknowledgements. It is our pleasure to thank Xavier Bonnetain for helpful discussions, and the anonymous reviewers of SAC 2023 for their constructive comments and suggestions.

References

1. Caesar: Competition for authenticated encryption: Security, applicability, and robustness, 2012-2019. https://competitions.cr.yp.to/caesar.html. Accessed 23 Mar 2023
2. Alagic, G., Bai, C., Katz, J., Majenz, C.: Post-quantum security of the Even-Mansour cipher. In: Dunkelman, O., Dziembowski, S. (eds.) EUROCRYPT 2022, Part III. LNCS, vol. 13277, pp. 458–487. Springer, Cham (2022). https://doi.org/10.1007/978-3-031-07082-2_17
3. Alagic, G., et al.: Status report on the third round of the NIST post-quantum cryptography standardization process (2022)
4. Bhaumik, R., et al.: QCB: efficient quantum-secure authenticated encryption. In: Tibouchi, M., Wang, H. (eds.) ASIACRYPT 2021. LNCS, vol. 13090, pp. 668–698. Springer, Cham (2021). https://doi.org/10.1007/978-3-030-92062-3_23
5. Boneh, D., Zhandry, M.: Secure signatures and chosen ciphertext security in a quantum computing world. In: Canetti, R., Garay, J.A. (eds.) CRYPTO 2013. LNCS, vol. 8043, pp. 361–379. Springer, Heidelberg (2013). https://doi.org/10.1007/978-3-642-40084-1_21
6. Bonnetain, X., Hosoyamada, A., Naya-Plasencia, M., Sasaki, Yu., Schrottenloher, A.: Quantum attacks without superposition queries: the offline Simon's algorithm. In: Galbraith, S.D., Moriai, S. (eds.) ASIACRYPT 2019. LNCS, vol. 11921, pp. 552–583. Springer, Cham (2019). https://doi.org/10.1007/978-3-030-34578-5_20
7. Bonnetain, X., Leurent, G., Naya-Plasencia, M., Schrottenloher, A.: Quantum linearization attacks. In: Tibouchi, M., Wang, H. (eds.) ASIACRYPT 2021. LNCS, vol. 13090, pp. 422–452. Springer, Cham (2021). https://doi.org/10.1007/978-3-030-92062-3_15
8. Deutsch, D.: Quantum theory, the Church-Turing principle and the universal quantum computer. Proc. R. Soc. Lond. Ser. A **400**(1818), 97–117 (1985)
9. Dworkin, M.: Recommendation for block cipher modes of operation: the CMAC mode for authentication. Technical Report NIST Special Publication (SP) 800-38B, National Institute of Standards and Technology, Gaithersburg, MD (2005)
10. Granger, R., Jovanovic, P., Mennink, B., Neves, S.: Improved masking for tweakable blockciphers with applications to authenticated encryption. Cryptology ePrint Archive, Paper 2015/999 (2015). https://eprint.iacr.org/2015/999
11. Granger, R., Jovanovic, P., Mennink, B., Neves, S.: Improved masking for tweakable blockciphers with applications to authenticated encryption. In: Fischlin, M., Coron, J.-S. (eds.) EUROCRYPT 2016. LNCS, vol. 9665, pp. 263–293. Springer, Heidelberg (2016). https://doi.org/10.1007/978-3-662-49890-3_11
12. Grover, L.K.: A fast quantum mechanical algorithm for database search. In: Proceedings of the Twenty-Eighth Annual ACM Symposium on Theory of Computing, pp. 212–219 (1996)
13. Inoue, A., Iwata, T., Minematsu, K., Poettering, B.: Cryptanalysis of OCB2: attacks on authenticity and confidentiality. In: Boldyreva, A., Micciancio, D. (eds.) CRYPTO 2019. LNCS, vol. 11692, pp. 3–31. Springer, Cham (2019). https://doi.org/10.1007/978-3-030-26948-7_1
14. Inoue, A., Minematsu, K.: Cryptanalysis of OCB2. Cryptology ePrint Archive, Report 2018/1040 (2018). https://eprint.iacr.org/2018/1040
15. Iwata, T.: Plaintext recovery attack of OCB2. Cryptology ePrint Archive, Report 2018/1090 (2018). https://eprint.iacr.org/2018/1090

16. Jaeger, J., Song, F., Tessaro, S.: Quantum key-length extension. In: Nissim, K., Waters, B. (eds.) TCC 2021. LNCS, vol. 13042, pp. 209–239. Springer, Cham (2021). https://doi.org/10.1007/978-3-030-90459-3_8

17. Jauch, M., Maram, V.: Quantum cryptanalysis of OTR and OPP: attacks on confidentiality, and key-recovery. Cryptology ePrint Archive, Paper 2023/1157 (2023). https://eprint.iacr.org/2023/1157

18. Kaplan, M., Leurent, G., Leverrier, A., Naya-Plasencia, M.: Breaking symmetric cryptosystems using quantum period finding. In: Robshaw, M., Katz, J. (eds.) CRYPTO 2016. LNCS, vol. 9815, pp. 207–237. Springer, Heidelberg (2016). https://doi.org/10.1007/978-3-662-53008-5_8

19. Krovetz, T., Rogaway, P.: The software performance of authenticated-encryption modes. In: Joux, A. (ed.) FSE 2011. LNCS, vol. 6733, pp. 306–327. Springer, Heidelberg (2011). https://doi.org/10.1007/978-3-642-21702-9_18

20. Chang, L., Wei, Y., Wang, X., Pan, X.: Collision forgery attack on the AES-OTR algorithm under quantum computing. Symmetry (2022). https://doi.org/10.3390/sym14071434

21. Maram, V.: Private communication (2023)

22. Maram, V., Masny, D., Patranabis, S., Raghuraman, S.: On the quantum security of OCB. IACR Trans. Symmetric Cryptol. **2022**(2), 379–414 (2022)

23. Minematsu, K.: Parallelizable rate-1 authenticated encryption from pseudorandom functions. In: Nguyen, P.Q., Oswald, E. (eds.) EUROCRYPT 2014. LNCS, vol. 8441, pp. 275–292. Springer, Heidelberg (2014). https://doi.org/10.1007/978-3-642-55220-5_16

24. Minematsu, K.: AES-OTR V3.1. Third-Round Candidate Submission to CAESAR Competition (2016). https://competitions.cr.yp.to/round3/aesotrv31.pdf

25. Poettering, B.: Shorter double-authentication preventing signatures for small address spaces. Cryptology ePrint Archive, Report 2018/223 (2018). https://eprint.iacr.org/2018/223

26. Rogaway, P.: Efficient instantiations of tweakable blockciphers and refinements to modes OCB and PMAC. In: Lee, P.J. (ed.) ASIACRYPT 2004. LNCS, vol. 3329, pp. 16–31. Springer, Heidelberg (2004). https://doi.org/10.1007/978-3-540-30539-2_2

27. Rogaway, P., Bellare, M., Black, J., Krovetz, T.: OCB: a block-cipher mode of operation for efficient authenticated encryption. In: ACM CCS 2001: 8th Conference on Computer and Communications Security, pp. 196–205 (2001)

28. Shor, P.W.: Polynomial-time algorithms for prime factorization and discrete logarithms on a quantum computer. SIAM Rev. **41**(2), 303–332 (1999)

29. Simon, D.R.: On the power of quantum computation. SIAM J. Comput. **26**(5), 1474–1483 (1997)

30. Thapliyal, H., Ranganathan, N., Kotiyal, S.: Reversible logic based design and test of field coupled nanocomputing circuits. In: Anderson, N.G., Bhanja, S. (eds.) Field-Coupled Nanocomputing. LNCS, vol. 8280, pp. 133–172. Springer, Heidelberg (2014). https://doi.org/10.1007/978-3-662-43722-3_7

Fast and Efficient Hardware Implementation of HQC

Sanjay Deshpande[1]([✉]) [iD], Chuanqi Xu[1] [iD], Mamuri Nawan[2] [iD],
Kashif Nawaz[2] [iD], and Jakub Szefer[1] [iD]

[1] CASLAB, Department of Electrical Engineering, Yale University, New Haven, USA
{sanjay.deshpande,chuanqi.xu,jakub.szefer}@yale.edu
[2] Cryptography Research Centre, Technology Innovation Institute, Abu Dhabi, UAE
{mamuri,kashif.nawaz}@tii.ae

Abstract. This work presents a hardware design for constant-time implementation of the HQC (Hamming Quasi-Cyclic) code-based key encapsulation mechanism. HQC has been selected for the fourth round of NIST's Post-Quantum Cryptography standardization process and this work presents the first, hand-optimized design of HQC key generation, encapsulation, and decapsulation written in Verilog targeting implementation on FPGAs. The three modules further share a common SHAKE256 hash module to reduce area overhead. All the hardware modules are parametrizable at compile time so that designs for the different security levels can be easily generated. The design currently outperforms the other hardware designs for HQC, and many of the fourth-round Post-Quantum Cryptography standardization process, with one of the best time-area products as well. For the combined HighSpeed design targeting the lowest security level, we show that the HQC design can perform key generation in 0.09 ms, encapsulation in 0.13 ms, and decapsulation in 0.21 ms when synthesized for an Xilinx Artix 7 FPGA. Our work shows that when hardware performance is compared, HQC can be a competitive alternative candidate from the fourth round of the NIST PQC competition.

Keywords: HQC · Hamming Quasi-Cyclic · PQC · KEM · Key Encapsulation Mechanism · Post-Quantum Cryptography · FPGA · Hardware Implementation

1 Introduction

Since 2016 NIST has been conducting a standardization process with the goal to standardize cryptographic primitives that are secure against attacks aided by quantum computers. There are today five main families of post-quantum cryptographic algorithms: hash-based, code-based, lattice-based, multivariate, and isogeny-based cryptography. Very recently NIST has selected one algorithm for standardization in the key encapsulation mechanism (KEM) category, CRYSTALS-Kyber, and four fourth-round candidates that will continue in the process. One of the four fourth-round candidates is HQC. It is a code-based KEM based on structured codes.

© The Author(s), under exclusive license to Springer Nature Switzerland AG 2024
C. Carlet et al. (Eds.): SAC 2023, LNCS 14201, pp. 297–321, 2024.
https://doi.org/10.1007/978-3-031-53368-6_15

As the standardization process is coming to an end after the fourth round, the performance as well as hardware implementations of the algorithms are becoming very important factor in selection of the algorithms to be standardized. The motivation for our work is to understand how well hand-optimized HQC hardware implementation can be designed and realized on FPGAs. To date, most of the post-quantum cryptographic hardware has focused on lattice-based candidates, with code-based algorithms receiving much less attention. All existing hardware implementations for HQC are based on either high-level synthesis (HLS) [1,3] or are hardware-software co design [20]. Our design is first full hardware, hand-optimized design of HQC. While HLS can be used for rapid prototyping, in our experience it cannot yet outperform Verilog or other hand optimized designs. Indeed, as we show in this work, our design outperforms the existing HQC HLS design. Further, our design beats the existing hardware-software co-design implementation in terms of time taken to perform key generation, encapsulation, and decapsulation.

In addition, our hardware design competes very well with the hardware designs for other candidates currently in the fourth round of NIST's process: BIKE, Classic McEliece, and SIKE. The presented design has best time-area product as well as time for key generation and decapsulation compared to the hardware for these designs. We also achieve similar time-area product for encapsulation when compared to BIKE. Due to limited breakdown of data for SIKE's hardware [16] comparison to SIKE for all aspects is more difficult, but we believe our design is better since for similar area cost, their combined encapsulation and decapsulation times are two orders of magnitude larger. Detailed comparison to related work is given in Sect. 3. As this work aims to show, code-based designs such as HQC can be realized very efficiently when optimized hardware is developed. Further, our design is constant-time, eliminating timing-based attacks. We believe our work shows that HQC can be a strong contender in the fourth round of NIST's process. The list of contributions our design includes:

- We provide the first hand-optimized, fully specification-compliant FPGA implementation of HQC, that includes key generation, encapsulation, and decapsulation, as well as a joint design of all three operations, adherent to the latest (fourth-round) HQC specification.
- We provide an improved SHAKE256 module which is based on Keccak module given in [23]. With our improvement, our hash module design runs two time faster than the existing one from [23]. Also, improving the overall time-area product.
- We provide first hardware implementations and evaluation for two variants of constant-time fixed-weight vector generation, namely Constant Weight Word fixed-weight vector generation [22] and a novel Fast and Non-Biased fixed-weight vector generation algorithm, which is based on fixed-weight vector generation process given in [1].
- We also provide an implementation of a parameterized binary field polynomial multiplication unit that uses half the Block RAM when compared to the existing state-of-the-art while providing better performance.

– Our designs are constant-time providing protection against the timing side-channel attacks and providing compile-time parameters to switch between different security levels and performances.

We evaluate the resource requirements and performance numbers of our designs on a Xilinx Artix 7 FPGA as it is a defacto standard for the evaluation of NIST PQC hardware designs. For all our hardware designs, we report the resource utilization in terms of Slices, Look Up Tables (LUTs)[1], Digital-Signal Processing Units (DSPs), FlipFlops (FF) Block RAM (BRAM). We also report Time which is computed by dividing the number of clock cycles taken per operation by design with the maximum clock frequency of the design. In order to consolidate the overall performance and for comparison with other hardware designs from the literature, we use Time Area Product (T $\times$ A = Time $\times$ Slices) as a metric. Functional correctness of our modules is ensured by generating the testvectors from the reference software implementation (provided in [2]). These testvectors are then fed into our design via testbenches performing pre- and post-synthesis simulations. The hardware design generated output is then compared with the reference software implementation output.

1.1 Open-Source Design

All our hardware designs reported in this paper are fully reproducible. The source code of our hardware designs is available under an open-source license at https://github.com/caslab-code/pqc-hqc-hardware.

2 Hardware Design of HQC

HQC Key Encapsulation Mechanism (HQC-KEM) consists of three main primitives: Key Generation, Encapsulation, and Decapsulation. The algorithms for each primitive are given in Figure 3 of specification document [2]. These primitives are built upon the HQC Public Key Encryption (HQC-PKE) primitives also given in Figure 2 of the specification document [2], which in turn are composed of more basic building blocks. In this work, we implement optimized and parameterizable hardware designs for all the primitives and the building blocks from scratch. In the following subsections, we briefly discuss all the building blocks and provide comparisons with any existing designs. The main building blocks involved for each of the primitives are as follows:

– Key Generation: Fixed weight vector generator, PRNG based random vector generator, polynomial multiplication, modular addition, and SHAKE256
– Encapsulation: Encrypt, SHAKE256
– Decapsulation: Decrypt, Encrypt, SHAKE256

---

[1] We report both Slices and LUTs in our tables since slices can be often partially used based on the optimization strategy of the synthesis tool, which makes slice utilization not a complete indication of the density of the design.

2.1   Modules Common Across the Design

In this section, we give a high-level overview of hardware designs of the building blocks that are used across the HQC-KEM and HQC-PKE.

SHAKE256. HQC uses SHAKE256 for multiple purposes e.g., as a PRNG for fixed weight vector generation and random vector generation in Key Generation, as a PRNG for fixed weight vector generation in Encryption, and for hashing in encapsulation and decapsulation. We improve the SHAKE256 module described in [8] (which was originally designed based on Keccak design from [23]) to perform SHAKE256 operations. We further tailor the SHAKE256 hardware module as per the requirement for our hardware design. Following is a list of improvements we make to the design of the SHAKE256 module:

The SHAKE256 from [23] module has a fixed 32-bit data input and output ports, and has a performance parameter (parallel_slices) which represents the number of combinatorial logic units that can be run in parallel inside the round function. The SHAKE256 from [23] did not work for parallel_slices > 16. We made significant changes in the control logic to fix this issue. The design now supports up to parallel_slices = 32. The time and area results can be seen in Table 1. We note from Table 1, that the time area product improves as we increase the parallel_slices. However, we could not add the support parallel_slices beyond 32 due to the other constraints of the state size of SHAKE256 (1600 bits) and fixed data port sizes (32 bits) in the way that SHAKE256 is used in our HQC implementation.

The existing SHAKE256 module from [23] operates with a command-based interface where the number of input bits to be processed, and the number of output bits required is specified before starting the hash operation. Based on the required weight, the fixed weight vector generation process requires pseudorandom bits to be generated from the SHAKE256 module for a specified input seed. Suppose the generated pseudorandom bits fail to satisfy the conditions to achieve the necessary weight or need a second fixed-weight vector generated from the same seed. In that case, another round of pseudorandom bits is generated from SHAKE256. As per the HQC specification, the internal SHAKE256 state is maintained as starting point for generation of the next set of pseudorandom bits. The original SHAKE256 module from [23] was not optimized nor designed to support preserving of the SHAKE256 state between invocations. We modified parts of datapath and the control logic to preserve the state. Since our modification of SHAKE256 holds the current state and does not automatically return to its new input loading state, we modify the operation of the existing forced exit signal to return the SHAKE256 module to the default state.

Using the existing module from [23] directly, it was not possible to implement the constant-time solution for the fixed weight vector generation since there is no command to request for additional bytes. We modify the existing design and add an additional command that can request additional bytes. The purpose of adding this command is to support and optimize the overall time taken to generate pseudo-random bits required for the fixed weight vector generation process described in Sect. 2.1. This optimization gives a significant amount of

Table 1. SHAKE256 module area and timing information, data based on synthesis results for Artix 7 board with xc7a200t-3 FPGA chip. The formula for the time-area product, T × A, is (SLICES * Time).

Parallel Slices	Resources								
	Logic			Memory		F	Cycles	Time	T × A
	(SLICES)	(LUT)	(DSP)	(FF)	(BR)	(MHz)	(cyc.)	(us)	
1	496	1,437	0	498	0	163	2,408	14.77	7,325
2	537	1,558	0	466	0	167	1,206	7.22	3,877
4	560	1,625	0	370	0	157	604	3.85	2,156
8	675	1,958	0	280	0	158	302	1.91	1,289
16	972	2,819	0	236	0	164	150	0.91	884
Our Improvement									
32	1,654	4,797	0	191	0	166	74	0.45	744

improvement in terms of clock cycles (time), for e.g., in the case of the hqc128 parameter set, the number of clock cycles taken by the SHAKE256 module from [23] to facilitate the random bits needed for generating the second fixed weight vector is equal to 639 clock cycles. With our improvements to the module, we achieve the same in 434 clock cycles (i.e., 32% improvement in time). And this improvement is up to 65% in larger parameter sets of HQC.

In addition to the aforementioned changes, we further explored options for optimizing the maximum clock frequency by pipelining the critical path. We note that there are several such critical paths throughout the design, and pipelining each path added severe overhead in terms of clock cycles with minimal improvement in the maximum clock frequency. Consequently, the results presented in Table 1 are optimal time and area results for the given hardware architecture. We use a similar performance parameter parallel_slices as described in the original keccak/SHAKE256 design in [23]. The SHAKE256 module has a fixed 32-bit data ports, and data input and output is based on typical ready-valid protocol. The results targeting Xilinx Artix 7 xc7a200t FPGA are shown in Table 1. The clock cycle numbers provided in the Table 1 are for processing 320-bits input (sample input size chosen as per the seed size used in HQC) and generating one block of output (where each block size is 1088-bits). There are six options for the parallel_slices, which provide different time-area trade-offs. We choose parallel_slices = 32 as it provides the best time-area product. For brevity, we represent all the ports interfacing with the SHAKE256 module with ⇔ in all further block diagrams in this paper.

Polynomial Multiplication. HQC uses polynomial multiplication operation in all the primitives of HQC-KEM. The polynomial multiplication operation is multiplication of two polynomials with n components in $\mathbb{F}_2$. After profiling all the polynomial multiplication operations from the HQC specification document and the reference design [2], we note that in all the polynomial multiplication operations, one of the inputs is a sparse fixed weight vector (with weight w or w_r given in Table 5 of the specification document [2]) of width n-bits. Consequently, we design a sparse polynomial multiplication technique with an interleaved reduction $X^n - 1$ (values of n can be found in Table 5 of the specification document [2]).

The motivation behind our polynomial multiplication unit is as follows: we represent the non-sparse arbitrary polynomial as arb_poly and the sparse fixed-weight polynomial by sparse_poly. For sparse_poly, rather than storing the full polynomial we only store the indices for non-zero values. Then, the multiplication is performed by left shifting arb_poly with each index of sparse_poly and then performing reduction of the resultant vector in an interleaved fashion. Since the value of n is large in all parameter sets of HQC, we take a sequential approach for performing the left shift. We implement a sequential left shift module similar to one in [12]. The shift module described [12] uses a register based approach and is not scalable when the length of the input is as large as the n value for the HQC parameters (due to a larger resource utilization and complex routing). This issue is circumvented in our design by implementing a block RAM based sequential variable shift module with a dual port BRAM and small barrel rotation unit. The barrel rotation unit and the block RAM widths are used as performance parameter (BW - Block Width) for the shift module and in turn for the whole polynomial multiplication unit. A similar implementation of sequential variable shift module was previously described in [10], however we could not readily use their implementation because the shift module is tightly embedded with the other modules for a different application and we re-implemented our version.

The hardware design of our polynomial multiplication module (poly_mult) is given in Fig. 7b of our extended online version of this work [11]. The arb_poly input to the poly_mult module is loaded sequentially and the width is of each chunk of arb_poly is equal to BW (making total number of chunks in polynomial equal to RAMDEPTH = ceil(n/BW)). We store the least significant part of the polynomial at the lowest address of the block RAM and the most significant part at the highest address. Since the polynomial length in HQC parameters is equal to n and is not divisible by BW (n is a prime) we pad the most significant part of the polynomial with zeros. For sparse_poly, one index is loaded at a time. While performing the shift operation we also perform the reduction $(X^n - 1)$ in an interleaved fashion. As the result of multiplying two n-bit polynomials could be a $2n$-bit polynomial and reduction of $2n$-bit polynomial to $(X^n - 1)$ in $\mathbb{F}_2$ is equivalent to slicing of the $2n$-bit polynomial into two parts of n-bit polynomials and then performing a bitwise XOR. As result, when the shift operation is performed on each chunk we also compute the address value (ADDR_2N) (signifying the degree of the resultant polynomial). If we notice that this degree of the resultant polynomial is greater that n we perform XOR of this chunk to the lower chunk by decoding the address based on the value of ADDR_2N. We perform similar operation over all the indices of the sparse_poly to achieve the final multiplied resultant value.

The clock cycles taken by our poly_mult module for one polynomial multiplication can be computed using the following formula where W_{SPARSE} is weight of the sparse polynomial, n is length of the polynomial, BW is the block width, 3 cycles represents the number of pipeline stages and 2 cycles are for the start and done synchronization with interfacing modules. The clock cycles taken for shift and interleaved reduction for one index is $(3 + \text{ceil}(n/\text{BW}))$. Our poly_mult module is constant time and we achieve that by fixing the W_{SPARSE} to a specific value (w and w_r) based on the parameter set.

Table 2. Comparison of our area and timing information `poly_mult` module with the other sparse polynomial multiplication units targeting Artix 7 board with `xc7a200t` FPGA chip.

BW (bits)	Resources					F (MHz)	Cycles (cyc.)	Time (us)	T × A
	Logic			Memory					
	(SLICES)	(LUT)	(DSP)	(FF)	(BR)				
Our `poly_mult` module, Polynomial Length* = 12,323, W^*_{SPARSE} = 71									
32	134	396	0	181	1	270	27,621	0.10	14
64	202	599	0	205	2	277	13,918	0.05	10
128	486	1,438	0	456	4	238	7,102	0.03	14
General Sparse Multiplier, Polynomial Length* = 12,323, W^*_{SPARSE} = 71 [17]									
32	132	319	0	127	2	234	27,691	0.12	16
64	197	549	0	190	4	222	13,988	0.06	12
128	378	1,136	0	381	8	185	7,172	0.04	15
Sparse Multiplier, Polynomial Length* = 10,163, W^*_{SPARSE} = 71 [15]									
32	100		—	—	2	240	15,8614	0.66	66
64	157		—	—	3	220	90,880	0.41	64
128	292		—	—	5	210	51,688	0.24	70

† = Slices (no info on LUTs), + Length of the non-sparse arbitrary polynomial, * = Weight of the sparse polynomial input

$$latency_{\texttt{poly\_mult}} = W_{SPARSE} \times (3 + \texttt{ceil}(n/\texttt{BW})) + 2$$

Table 2 shows the results for our `poly_mult` module compared with the related work. We note that our sparse polynomial multiplication module performs better in terms of time while utilizing half the Block RAM resources when compared to the existing designs. Table 3 shows results for our `poly_mult` module for the parameter sizes used for HQC hardware design.

Polynomial Addition/Subtraction. HQC uses polynomial addition/ subtraction in all of its primitives. Since all addition and subtraction operations happen in $\mathbb{F}_2$, the addition and subtraction could be realized as the same operation. We design two variants of constant-time adders namely `xor_based_adder` and `location_based_adder` that could be attached with our polynomial multiplication module described in Sect. 2.1. We design our adder modules as an extension for polynomial multiplication because the addition/subtraction always appears with the polynomial multiplication as shown in Fig. 3 of the specification document [2]. The adders operate on the contents of block RAM since the polynomials are stored inside the block RAM. Both of the adder module designs do not use any additional block RAM resources, they load the polynomial multiplication output, perform the addition, and write the value back to the same block RAM inside the polynomial.

The `xor_based_adder` design performs addition in a regular $\mathbb{F}_2$ fashion by performing bit-wise `exclusive-OR` operation. The module performs addition sequentially by generating one block RAM address per clock cycle to load inputs from two block RAMs and then performs addition and writes them back to one of the specified block RAMs at the same block RAM address.

Table 3. Time and area information of our `poly_mult` module for different HQC parameter sizes with different performance parameter (BW) sizes, data based on synthesis results for Artix 7 board with `xc7a200t-3` FPGA chip.

Input Length+ (bits)	W^*_{sparse}	Resources					F (MHz)	Cycles (cyc.)	Time (us)	T × A
		Logic			Memory					
		(SLICES)	(LUT)	(DSP)	(FF)	(BR)				
Our poly_mult module (BW = 32)										
17,669 (hqc128)	66	139	412	0	189	1	287	36,698	0.13	18
35,851 (hqc192)	100	131	387	0	193	2	257	112,402	0.44	57
57,637 (hqc256)	131	134	397	0	199	2	267	236,457	0.89	119
Our poly_mult module (BW = 64)										
17,669 (hqc128)	66	209	620	0	245	2	270	18,482	0.07	14
35,851 (hqc192)	100	219	649	0	249	2	286	56,402	0.20	43
57,637 (hqc256)	131	218	644	0	223	2	283	118,426	0.42	91
Our poly_mult module (BW = 128)										
17,669 (hqc128)	66	486	1,439	0	496	4	238	9,374	0.04	19
35,851 (hqc192)	100	488	1,445	0	500	4	240	28,402	0.12	58
57,637 (hqc256)	131	489	1,448	0	474	4	245	59,476	0.24	119

+ Length of the non-sparse polynomial, * = Weight of the sparse polynomial input

Table 4. Polynomial addition modules (`xor_based_adder` and `loc_based_adder` with datapath width 128-bits) area and timing information, data based on synthesis results for Artix 7 board with `xc7a200t-3` FPGA chip.

Input Length (bits)	Resources					F (MHz)	Cycles (cyc.)	Time (us)	T × A
	Logic			Memory					
	(SLICES)	(LUT)	(DSP)	(FF)	(BR)				
xor_based_adder (BW = 128)									
17,669	74	143	0	159	0	330	142	0.43	31
35,851	73	142	0	161	0	318	284	0.89	65
57,637	73	142	0	161	0	311	455	1.46	106
loc_based_adder (BW = 128)									
17,669	86	160	0	174	0	316	69	0.22	18
35,851	88	161	0	174	0	300	103	0.34	30
57,637	92	161	0	175	0	300	134	0.45	41

The `location_based_adder` is an optimized adder designed to perform addition when one of the input is a sparse vector. This module is mainly designed to perform operations $x + h \cdot y$ from KeyGen algorithm from Fig. 3 of specification document [2] and $r_1 + h \cdot r_2$ and $s \cdot r_2 + e$ from Encrypt Algorithm from Fig. 2 of specification document [2]. In these operations the values of x, r_1, and e are sparse, fixed-weight vectors so the addition is optimized by only flipping the bits of the other input in the position of one. The `location_based_adder` module takes location of ones from the sparse vector as input and computes the address to load out the part of non-sparse polynomial from the block RAM and flips the bit on the appropriate location and writes it back to the same location. The process is repeated until all locations with ones are covered. Since there are a fixed, and known number of ones in the fixed-weight vector, there is a fixed

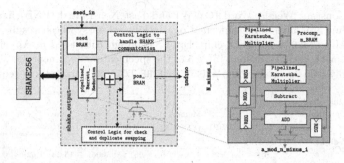

Fig. 1. Hardware design of Constant Weight Word Fixed-Weight vector generator (`fixed_weight_vector_cww`) module.

number of operations and timing does not reveal any sensitive information. Results of our polynomial addition `location_based_adder` module for one performance parameter (width = 128) are shown in Table 4.

Fixed-Weight Vector Generator. The fixed-weight vector generator function generates a uniformly random n-bit fixed-weight vector of a specified input weight (w). The algorithm for a fixed-weight generation as specified in [1] first generates $24 \times w$ random bits. These random bits are then arranged into w 24-bit integers. These 24-bit integers undergo a threshold check and are rejected if the integer value is beyond the threshold. ($949 \times 17, 669, 467 \times 35, 851, 291 \times 57, 637$ for hqc-128, hqc-192 and hqc-256 respectively). After the threshold check, these integers are reduced modulo n. After the threshold check and reduction process, if the weight is not equal to w, then more random bits are drawn from RNG, and the process is repeated until w integers are achieved. After the threshold check and reduction then, a check for duplicates is performed over all the reduced integers. In case any duplicate is found, that integer is discarded, and more random bits are requested drawn from the RNG, which again undergoes threshold check, reduction, and duplicate check. This process is repeated until a uniform fixed-weight vector is generated.

The main pitfall with the fixed-weight vector approach proposed in [1] is that it may show non-constant-time behavior in the rejection sampling process (i.e., the threshold check and duplicate detection as discussed earlier). A timing attack on existing software reference implementation of HQC [1] was performed in [13]. The authors use the information of rejection sampling routine (that is part of fixed-weight generation) being invoked during the deterministic re-encryption process in decapsulation and show that this leaks secret-dependent timing information. The timing of the rejection sampling routine depends upon the given seed. This seed is derived for the encrypt function in encapsulation and decapsulation procedures using the message. The decapsulation operation is dependent on the decoded message and this dependency allows to construct a plaintext distinguisher (described in detail in [13]) which is then used to mount the timing attack.

Although the attack has not been demonstrated on a hardware implementation of HQC yet, we implement two variants of fixed-weight generation to

Table 5. Constant Weight Word (CWW) and Fast Non-Biased (FNB) fixed-weight vector module area and timing information, data based on synthesis results for Artix 7 board with `xc7a200t-3` FPGA chip. For FNB design (discussed in Appendix 1.A), the w_r parameter is derived from Table 5 of the specification document [2]. The CWW design is fully constant-time so no `ACCEPTABLE_REJECTIONS` parameter is required.

Design	Weight (w_r)	Resources					F (MHz)	Cycles (cyc.)	Time (us)	T × A	Failure[+] Prob.
		Logic			Memory						
		(SLICES)	(LUT)	(DSP)	(FF)	(BR)					
Constant Weight Word (CWW)											
hqc128	75	67	201	4	229	1.0	201	3,062	15.23	1,020	0
hqc192	114	71	211	5	245	1.0	200	6,817	34.09	2,420	0
hqc256	149	72	216	5	248	1.0	204	11,487	56.31	4,054	0
Fast and Non-Biased Design with `ACCEPTABLE_REJECTIONS` = w_r (discussed in Appendix 1.A)											
hqc128	75	106	316	0	124	2.0	223	1,479	6.63	702	2.8×2^{-199}
hqc192	114	100	295	0	125	2.0	236	2,226	9.43	1,075	1.1×2^{-280}
hqc256	149	107	314	0	192	2.5	242	3,248	13.42	1,435	4.9×2^{-355}

[+] = Probability of our design failing to behave constant-time.

Algorithm 1. Constant Weight Word Fixed Weight Vector Generation

---

    Input: $N, w, seed$
    Output: w distinct elements in range 0 to $N - 1$
1:   $rand\_bits \leftarrow prng(input = seed, output\_size = 32 \times w)$
2:   **for** $i \leftarrow w - 1$ to 0 **do**
3:     $pos[i] = i + (rand\_bits[32 + 32 * i - 1 : 32 * i])\%(N - i)$
4:   **end for**
5:   **for** $j \leftarrow w - 1$ to 0 **do**
6:     $duplicate\_found \leftarrow 0$
7:     **for** $k \leftarrow j + 1$ to $w - 1$ **do**
8:       **if** $pos[j] == pos[k]$ **then**
9:         $duplicate\_found \leftarrow 1$
10:      **end if**
11:     **end for**
12:     **if** $duplicate\_found == 1$ **then**
13:       $pos[j] = j$
14:     **end if**
15:   **end for**
16:   **return** pos

---

prevent the attack from being possible in hardware. The two variants are Constant Weight Word Fixed-Weight Vector Generation and Fast and Non-Biased Fixed-Weight Vector Generation; discussed in Appendix 1.A due to limited space.

Constant Weight Word (CWW) Fixed Weight Vector Generation: The CWW fixed-weight vector generation variant comes as a fourth-round recommendation from the HQC authors [2]. It was introduced as a fix for the non-constant time behavior of the earlier fixed-weight algorithm (given in [1]) at the cost of small bias. The CWW was originally proposed by Sendrier in (Algorithm 5 of [22]). Shown in Algorithm 1, we rewrite the CWW fixed-weight vector generation algorithm as implemented in our hardware design. The CWW fixed-weight algorithm first generates $32 \times w$ random bits. These random bits are arranged into 32-bit integer array with indices 0 to $w - 1$. Each 32-bit integer from the array is then modulo-reduced to N - `ARRAY_INDEX`, and the reduced number is then added with the `ARRAY_INDEX`. After the reduction, a compare and swap is performed, as shown in steps 5–14 of Algorithm 1. This compare and swap step ensures no duplicate elements exist in the final fixed-weight vector.

Our hardware design uses the SHAKE256 module (described in Sect. 2.1) as the PRNG. The 32-bit interface from our `SHAKE256` module helps us avoid the 32-bit arrangement of random bits (given in steps 2–4 of Algorithm 1). We design a pipelined Barrett reduction [6] unit to perform the modular reduction (where both the input and modulo value can be changed at runtime, note that in most other design the modulo is fixed at compile time which makes the design of the reduction unit simpler). The operation is shown in step 3 of Algorithm 1. To perform the integer multiplication inside the Barrett reduction, we design karatsuba multiplication [7] unit using the Digital Signal Processing (DSP) units available on the target FPGA. If the DSP resources are unavailable on the target· FPGA, we note that our design can naturally be synthesized to use LUTs. We store the reduced values in a dual-port BRAM (`pos_BRAM` shown in Fig. 1) of depth w. Once the BRAM is filled, we perform the compare and swap step with the help of the control logic interfaced with the two ports on the BRAM. We note that the pseudorandom number generation, Barrett reduction is performed in constant-time and since the compare and swap procedure is always over a fixed number of memory locations, we achieve a fully constant time hardware implementation for the fixed-weight vector generation process. Although the CWW algorithm ensures the constant time behavior in generating fixed-weight vectors, there is a small bias between the uniform distribution and the algorithm's output. The security analysis performed in [22] for BIKE's parameters [4] shows that this bias has negligible impact on security.

The time and area results for our hardware design are given in Table 5. Because the compare and swap operation requires combinatorial logic between two ports of the dual port BRAM, this becomes the critical path for the design. The compare and scan step takes $w \times (w - 1)/2$ clock cycles. Consequently, as shown in the Table 5, as w increases, the number clock cycles also increases.

2.2 Encode and Decode Modules

The encode and decode modules are building blocks of the encrypt and decrypt modules, respectively. We describe the encode and decode modules here, before describing the bigger encrypt and decrypt modules in Sect. 2.3.

Encode Module. As specified in [2], HQC Encode uses concatenation of two codes namely Reed–Muller and Reed–Solomon codes. The hardware design of our encode module is shown in Fig. 2. The Encode function takes K-bit input and first encodes it with the Reed–Solomon code. The Reed–Solomon encoding process involves systematic encoding using a linear feedback shift register (LFSR) with a feedback connection based on the generator polynomial (shown on page 23, section 2.5.2 of [2]). The Reed–Solomon code generates a n_1-bit output (as given in [2] the value for n_1 is 368, 448, and 720 for hqc128, hqc192,

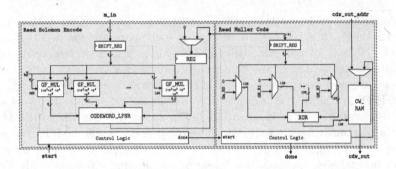

Fig. 2. Hardware design of `encode` module (formed by concatenating two encode functionalities, Reed-Solomon on the left side and Reed-Muller on the right side).

Table 6. `Encode` module area and timing information, data based on synthesis results for Artix 7 board with `xc7a200t-3` FPGA chip.

Design	Resources								
	Logic			Memory		F	Cycles	Time	T × A
	(SLICES)	(LUT)	(DSP)	(FF)	(BR)	(MHz)	(cyc.)	(us)	
hqc128	280	858	0	922	2	270.34	97	0.36	100
hqc192	358	1,011	0	1,088	2	298.32	131	0.44	157
hqc256	514	1,503	0	1,689	2	293.51	189	0.64	331
HLS design - {Reed–Solomon Encode + Reed–Muller Encode} [3]									
hqc128	—	2,019	0	603	0	—	7,244	47.18	—

and `hqc256` respectively). For the Galois field multiplication unit (for the field $\mathbb{F}_2[x]/(x^8+x^4+x^3+x^2+1)$) we design an LFSR-based optimized multiplication unit similar to the one described in [19]. The number of Galois field multiplication units we run in parallel is equal to the degree of the generator polynomial. The outputs from Galois field multipliers are fed in to a LFSR after each cycle. At the end of encoding process the module generates a n_1-bit output.

The n_1-bit output from Reed–Solomon code is then encoded by Reed–Muller code. The Reed–Muller encoding is achieved by performing vector-matrix multiplication where each byte from input is the vector and the matrix is the generator matrix (**G**) shown in Appendix 1A of our extended online version of this work [11]. In our design we store the generator matrix rows (each row is of length 128-bits) in ROM and we select the matrix rows based on each input byte. We store the output after multiplying input byte into a block RAM in chunks of 128-bits. Based on the security parameter set the code word output from Reed–Muller code has a multiplicity value (i.e., number of times a code word or in our case number of times each block RAM location is repeated). As per the specification [2], `hqc128` has multiplicity value of 3 and `hqc192` and `hqc256` have multiplicity value of 5. To optimize the storage, we only store one copy of code word, and while accessing the code word we compute the block RAM address in a way that the multiplicity is achieved. The time and area results for our `encode` module targeting Artix 7 board with `xc7a200t-3` FPGA are shown in Table 6.

Table 7. Decode module area and timing information, data based on synthesis results for Artix 7 board with xc7a200t-3 FPGA chip.

Design	Resources					F	Cycles	Time	T × A
	Logic			Memory					
	(SLICES)	(LUT)	(DSP)	(FF)	(BR)	(MHz)	(cyc.)	(ms)	
hqc128	952	2,817	0	3,779	2.5	205	4,611	0.02	19
hqc192	1,100	3,257	0	4,727	2.5	212	5,485	0.03	33
hqc256	1,243	3,679	0	5,574	2.5	206	9,199	0.04	50
HLS design - {Reed–Muller Decode + Reed–Solomon Decode} [3]									
hqc128	—	10,154	0	2,569	3	—	68,619	592.00	—

Decode Module As given in the specification [2], the ciphertext is first decoded with duplicated Reed-Muller code and then with shortened Reed-Solomon code. To decode duplicated Reed-Muller code, the transformation module expands and adds multiple code words into expanded code word, and then the Hadamard transformation is applied to the expanded code word. Finally, Find_Peak module finds the location of the highest absolute value of the Hadamard_Transformation output. Figure 6 in our extended online version of this work [11] describes detailed hardware design of Reed-Muller Decoder. expand_and_sum module collects data inputs into m x 128-bit shift register, then add and shift the last 2-bit lsb of each shift register to produce a pair of data outputs. The data pair is then processed in hadamard_transformation module which consist of 7 layers of similar blocks of radix-2 butterfly structure. With the outputs from hadamard_transformation coming in pairs, finding peak can be done in parallel inside the Find_Peak module and compare the peaks of each to be the final peak. The whole processes then repeated n_1 times to produce n_1 data output to Reed-Solomon Decoder. To decode Reed-Solomon code, we need to sequentially compute syndromes S_i, coefficients σ_i of error location polynomial $\sigma(x)$, roots of error location polynomial $(\alpha^i)^{-1}$, pre-defined helper polynomial $Z((\alpha^i)^{-1})$, errors e_i, and finally correct the output of decode of Reed-Muller code based on the errors.

Evaluation. Table 6 and Table 7 show time and area results for our decode module. Out of the existing other hardware designs [2,3,20] (i.e., HLS and hardware-software codesign), only [3] provides a breakdown of the performance for encode and decode modules. As shown in Table 7 and Table 6 our hardware design outperforms the other designs by a significant margin in all aspects. To the best of our knowledge our implementation of encode and decode is the first hand-optimized hardware implementation of concatenated encode (shortened Reed–Solomon encode + duplicated Reed–Muller encode) and decode (duplicated Reed–Muller decode and shortened Reed–Solomon decode) modules. There are other hand-optimized hardware designs in the literature for Reed–Solomon and Reed–Muller encode and decode (given in [5,14,21]), but their target was not a cryptographic application. Hence, the implementation strategy is highly focused on timing, throughput, and area performance rather than a secure implementation (e.g., constant-time). Consequently, although our design is very efficient, it will not be fair to compare our hardware implementations with them.

2.3   Encrypt and Decrypt Modules

The encrypt and decrypt modules are building blocks of the encapsulation and decapsulation modules, respectively. We describe the encrypt and decrypt modules here, before describing the bigger encapsulation and decapsulation modules later.

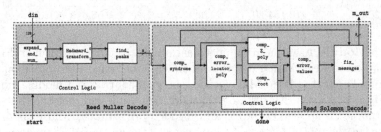

Fig. 3. Hardware design of decode module (formed by concatenating two decode functionalities, Reed-Muller on the left side and Reed-Solomon on the right side).

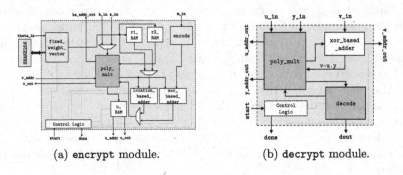

(a) encrypt module.   (b) decrypt module.

Fig. 4. Hardware design of encrypt and decrypt modules.

Encrypt Module. The encrypt module (shown in Fig. 2 of the specification document [2]) takes public key $(\mathbf{h}, \mathbf{s})$, message $\mathbf{m}$, and seed (θ) and generates a ciphertext $(\mathbf{u},\mathbf{v})$ as the output. The hardware design for the encrypt module is shown in Fig. 4a. We use our CWW fixed-weight vector module (fixed_weight_vector_cww) described in Sect. 2.1.A to generate $\mathbf{r}_1$, $\mathbf{r}_2$, and e fixed-weight vectors of weight w_r by expanding theta_in and in parallel we run encode module (described in Sect. 2.2). After the generation of $\mathbf{r}_2$ we start the polynomial multiplication of $\mathbf{h}.\mathbf{r}_2$ in parallel to the e generation. For polynomial multiplication, we use the poly_mult module with BW = 128 described in Sect. 2.1. The addition of $\mathbf{r}_1$ in $\mathbf{u}$ computation and e in $\mathbf{v}$ computation is performed by our location_based_adder and addition with $\mathbf{t}$ is performed by xor_based_adder (described in Sect. 2.1).

From the encrypt algorithm (given in Fig. 2 of the specification document [2]), we observe that both $\mathbf{h.r_2}$ and $\mathbf{s.r_2}$ multiplications can be performed in parallel, consequently, we design a `parallel_encrypt` module targeting higher performance where we use two polynomial multiplications in parallel (shown in Fig. 8a of our extended online version of this work [11]). We provide a choice of using either `encrypt` or `parallel_encrypt` module as a parameter. Table 8 shows results for both encrypt hardware implementations targeting Xilinx Artix 7 xc7a200t FPGA. We note that the major contributor to the overall time in encrypt operation is due to polynomial multiplication and using two `poly_mult` modules in parallel reduces the overall time by 40–60% across different parameter sets. The area results do not include the `SHAKE256` module as the SHAKE256 is shared among all primitives. Figure 3 shows the hardware block design on our `decode` module and Table 7 shows the time and area results for our `decode` module.

Table 8. Encrypt module area and timing information, data based on synthesis results for Artix 7 board with xc7a200t-3 FPGA chip.

Design	Resources†					F	Cycles	Time	T × A
	Logic			Memory		F	Cycles	Time	T × A
	(SLICES)	(LUT)	(DSP)	(FF)	(BR)	(MHz)	(cyc.)	(us)	
encrypt module – uses one poly_mult module with with BW = 128									
hqc128	1,230	3,642	4	1,773	10	179	28,217	0.16	194
hqc192	1,283	3,797	5	1,966	10	182	79,889	0.44	563
hqc256	1,438	4,256	5	2,542	10	192	160,489	0.84	1,202
parallel_encrypt module – two poly_mult modules with BW = 128 running in parallel									
hqc128	1,734	5,132	4	2,179	12	179	17,202	0.10	173
hqc192	1,793	5,308	5	2,376	12	196	46,857	0.24	429
hqc256	1,934	5,725	5	2,931	12	196	91,862	0.47	908

† = Given resources does not include the area for `SHAKE256` module.

Table 9. Decrypt module area and timing information, data based on synthesis results for Artix 7 board with xc7a200t-3 FPGA chip.

Design	Resources†					F	Cycles	Time	T × A
	Logic			Memory		F	Cycles	Time	T × A
	(SLICES)	(LUT)	(DSP)	(FF)	(BR)	(MHz)	(cyc.)	(us)	
hqc128	2,146	6,352	0	5,730	10.5	194	14,198	0.07	150
hqc192	2,378	7,038	0	6,787	10.5	187	34,313	0.18	428
hqc256	2,886	8,544	0	8,740	13	186	69,356	0.37	1,067

Decrypt Module. The `decrypt` module (shown in Fig. 2 of the specification document [2]) takes secret key $(\mathbf{x}, \mathbf{y})$, ciphertext $(\mathbf{u}, \mathbf{v})$, and generates the message $(\mathbf{m'})$. Figure 4b shows our hardware design for `decrypt` module. The module accepts part of the secret key $(\mathbf{y})$ as locations with ones (since it is a sparse fixed weight vector). We use our `poly_mult` module with BW = 128 described in Sect. 2.1 to compute $\mathbf{u}.\mathbf{y}$ and use `xor_based_adder` module (described in Sect. 2.1) to compute $\mathbf{v} - \mathbf{u}.\mathbf{y}$. We then use the `decode` module (described in Sect. 2.2) to decode $\mathbf{v} - \mathbf{u}.\mathbf{y}$ and retrieve the message. Table 9 shows our hardware implementation results for `decrypt` module targeting Xilinx Artix 7 xc7a200t FPGA.

2.4   Key Generation

We now begin to describe the top-level modules, starting with the key generation, followed in later sections with encapsulation and decapsulation.

The key generation (shown in Fig. 2 of the specification document [2]) takes the secret key seed and public key seed as an input and generates secret key $(\mathbf{x}, \mathbf{y})$ and public key $(\mathbf{h}, \mathbf{s})$ respectively as output. Figure 8b in our extended online version of this work [11] shows the hardware design of our `keygen` module. Our `keygen` module assumes that the public key seed and the secret key seed are generated by some other hardware module implementing a true random number generator. We use our CWW fixed-weight vector module (`fixed_weight_vector_cww`) module described in Sect. 2.1.A to generate $(\mathbf{x}, \mathbf{y})$ from the secret key seed. $\mathbf{x}$ and $\mathbf{y}$ are fixed weight vectors of weight w and length n-bits. To optimize the storage, rather than storing full n-bit sparse vector we only output locations of ones. There is also an optional provision to output the full vector as described in Sect. 2.1. The `vector_set_random` uses the `SHAKE256` module to expand the public key seed and generates $\mathbf{h}$. We then use `poly_mult` module with BW = 128 (described in Sect. 2.1) to compute $(\mathbf{h}.\mathbf{y}$ and finally use `location_based_adder` module (described in Sect. 2.1) to compute $\mathbf{s}$. We note that in the Fig. 8b (in our extended online version of this work [11]) only a block RAM for $\mathbf{x}$ storage (X_RAM) is visible because the $\mathbf{y}, \mathbf{h}, \mathbf{s}$ are stored in the block RAMs which are inside `fixed_weight_vector`, `poly_mult`, and `location_based_adder` modules respectively.

Table 10 shows the results for the `keygen` module. The area results do not include the `SHAKE256` module because it is shared among all other primitives. When we compare our `hqc128 keygen` design with existing designs from literature, we note that our design runs at least 3× faster than existing hardware designs while utilizing 80% lesser FPGA footprint. We highlight that this improvement is due to our optimized `fixed_weight_vector_cww` and `poly_mult` modules discussed in Sect. 2.1 and Sect. 2.1 respectively.

Table 10. Keygen module area and timing information, data based on synthesis results for Artix 7 board with xc7a200t-3 FPGA chip.

Design	Resources[†]					F	Cycles	Time	T × A
	Logic			Memory					
	(SLICES)	(LUT)	(DSP)	(FF)	(BR)	(MHz)	(cyc.)	(ms)	
hqc128	809	2,396	4	901	10	179	15,759	0.09	72
hqc192	791	2,342	5	926	10	189	42,106	0.22	177
hqc256	791	2,342	5	942	10	188	82,331	0.44	347
hqc128-perf HLS*[2]	3,900	12,000	0	9,000	3	150	40,000	0.27	1,053
hqc128-comp. HLS*[2]	1,500	4,700	0	2,700	3	129	630,000	4.80	7,200
hqc128-optimized. HLS*[3]	3,921	11,484	0	8,798	6	150	40,427	0.27	1,058
hqc128-pure HLS*[3]	8,359	24,746	0	21,746	7	153	40,427	0.27	2,256

[†] = Given resources does not include the area for SHAKE256 module, * = Target FGPA is Artix-7 xc7a100t-1

2.5   Encapsulation Module

The encapsulate operation (shown in Fig. 3 of the specification document [2]) takes public key (**h**, **s**) and message **m** as an input and generates shared secret (K) and ciphertext (**c** = (**u**,**v**)) and **d**. The hardware design of the encap module is shown in Fig. 9a of our extended online version of this work [11]. Our encap module assumes that **m** is generated by some other hardware module implementing a true random number generator and provided as an input to our module. Since the SHAKE256 module is extensively used in encapsulate operation we design a HASH_processor module which handles all the communication with the SHAKE256 module. HASH_processor modules reduces the multiplexing logic of inputs to the SHAKE256 module significantly.

The Hash_processor modules helps in expanding **m** to generate θ. We then use our encrypt module (described in Sect. 2.3) to encrypt **m** using θ and the public key as inputs and generates ciphertext. After the generation of r_1, r_2, and **e** inside the encrypt module (described in Sect. 2.3) we then run HASH_processor module in parallel to encrypt module to generate **d**. After the encryption of **m** we then use the HASH_processor to compute $\mathcal{K}(\mathbf{m}, \mathbf{c})$ to generate the shared secret K. Our design is constant-time since all the underlying modules are constant-time and the control logic from the encap module does not depend on any secret input. Table 11 shows the results for the encap module with our encrypt and parallel_encrypt. The area results do not include the SHAKE256 module because it is shared among all other primitives. We note that our hqc128 encap with parallel_encrypt design runs at least 4.5× faster than existing hardware designs from the literature while using 64% lesser FPGA footprint. Hence, achieving the best Time-Area product. We highlight that this improvement comes mainly from our optimized encode, and poly_mult hardware designs discussed in Sect. 2.2, and Sect. 2.1 respectively.

Table 11. Encap module area and timing information, data based on synthesis results for Artix 7 board with xc7a200t-3 FPGA chip.

Design	Resources†					F	Cycles	Time	T × A
	Logic			Memory					
	(SLICES)	(LUT)	(DSP)	(FF)	(BR)	(MHz)	(cyc.)	(ms)	
our encap module with encrypt									
hqc128	1,400	4,145	4	2,128	13	179	33,438	0.19	262
hqc192	1,445	4,278	5	2,412	15	182	90,346	0.50	716
hqc256	1,625	4,809	5	3,041	15	182	177,154	0.97	1,582
our encap module with parallel_encrypt									
hqc128	1,969	5,828	4	2,531	15	179	22,423	0.13	247
hqc192	2,174	6,434	5	2,821	17	196	57,314	0.29	636
hqc256	2,330	6,898	5	3,417	17	196	108,527	0.55	1,292
hqc128 perf HLS*[2]	5,500	16,000	0	13,000	5	151	890,00	0.59	3,245
hqc128 comp. HLS*[2]	2,100	6,400	0	4,100	5	127	1,500,000	12.00	25,200
hqc128 optimized HLS*[3]	5,575	16,487	0	13,390	10	152	89,110	0.59	3,289
hqc128 pure HLS*[3]	9,955	29,496	0	26,333	11	148	89,131	0.59	5,873

† = Given resources does not include the area for SHAKE256 module, * = Target FGPA is Artix-7 xc7a100t-1

2.6 Decapsulation Module

The decapsulate operation (shown in Fig. 3 of the specification document [2]) takes secret key $(\mathbf{x}, \mathbf{y})$, public key $(\mathbf{h}, \mathbf{s})$, ciphertext $(\mathbf{c} = (\mathbf{u}, \mathbf{v}))$, $\mathbf{d}$ as an input and generates shared secret (K). Figure 9b of our extended online version of this work [11] shows hardware design the decap module. We use our decrypt module (described in Sect. 2.3) to decrypt the input ciphertext using secret key $(\mathbf{y})$ and generate the $\mathbf{m}'$. We then use encap module to perform re-encryption of $\mathbf{m}'$ and generate $\mathbf{u}'$, $\mathbf{v}'$ and $\mathbf{d}'$. We then pause the encap module to verify the $\mathbf{u}'$, $\mathbf{v}'$ and $\mathbf{d}'$ against $\mathbf{u}$, $\mathbf{v}$ and $\mathbf{d}$. After the verification we set a signal (optional port mprime_fail) if the verification fails. Irrespective of verification result we still continue with the generation of the shared secret K to maintain the constant-time behavior. Table 12 shows the results for the decap module using encrypt and parallel _encrypt (for performing the encryption). The area results do not include the SHAKE256 module because it is shared among all the primitives. When we compare our hqc128 decap with parallel_encrypt design with the existing designs from literature, we note that our design runs at least 5.7× faster while using 40% lower FPGA footprint. Hence, achieving the best Time Area product. We highlight that this improvement comes mainly from our optimized decode, encode, and poly_mult designs discussed in Sect. 2.2, Sect. 2.2, and Sect. 2.1 respectively.

Table 12. **Decap** module area and timing information, data based on synthesis results for Artix 7 board with **xc7a200t-3** FPGA chip.

Design	Resources†					F	Cycles	Time	T × A
	Logic			Memory					
	(SLICES)	(LUT)	(DSP)	(FF)	(BR)	(MHz)	(cyc.)	(ms)	
our decap module with encrypt									
hqc128	3,035	8,984	4	6,596	20	192	48,212	0.25	758
hqc192	3,368	9,969	5	7,911	22	186	125,805	0.68	2,290
hqc256	3,693	10,931	5	9,424	22	186	248,338	1.33	4,,911
our decap module with parallel_encrypt									
hqc128	3,702	10,959	4	7,003	22	179	37,197	0.21	777
hqc192	4,025	11,915	5	8,320	24	186	92,773	0.50	2,012
hqc256	4,347	12,868	5	9,794	24	186	179,711	0.97	4,216
hqc128 perf HLS*[2]	6,200	19,000	0	15,000	9.0	152	190,000	1.20	7,440
hqc128 comp. HLS*[2]	2,700	7,700	0	5,600	10.5	130	2,100,000	16.00	43,200
hqc128 optimized HLS*[3]	6,223	18,739	0	15,243	18.0	152	193,082	1.27	7,903
hqc128 pure HLS*[3]	8,434	24,898	0	21,680	18.0	150	193,004	1.27	10,711

† = Given resources does not include the area for SHAKE256 module, * = Target FGPA is Artix-7 xc7a100t-1

3 HQC Joint Design and Related Work

In this section, we present our joint hardware design of a HQC combining our **keygen**, **encap**, and **decap** modules (described in Sect. 2.4, Sect. 2.5, and Sect. 2.6 respectively) into one overall design. Following that we compare our joint design with other HQC combined designs from the literature in Sect. 3.2. In addition to that, we also conduct a comprehensive literature survey focusing on full hardware designs of the other three fourth-round public-key encryption and key-establishment algorithms in NIST's standardization process: BIKE, Classic McEliece, and SIKE. We also include the CRYSTALS-Kyber, a public-key encryption and key-establishment algorithm selected for standardization at the end of the prior third round. Due to limited space we discuss this part in Appendix 1.A.

3.1 HQC Joint Design

In this work, we present two designs, *Balanced* and *HighSpeed*. The main difference between our *Balanced* and *HighSpeed* designs is that our *Balanced* design uses the regular **encrypt** module (shown in Fig. 4a), and our *HighSpeed* design uses the **parallel_encrypt** module (shown in Fig. 8a of our extended online version of this work [11]) for performing the encryption and re-encryption operations in encapsulation and decapsulation. The In order to build a resource-efficient yet performant joint design, we start by identifying the common sub-modules among the three **keygen**, **encap**, and **decap** by using **hqc128** parameter set as an example:

SHAKE256: The SHAKE256 module is used in all the primitives (keygen, encap, and decap) in HQC. As shown in Table 1, the SHAKE256 with parallel_slices = 32 has a high area utilization. Consequently, we share one SHAKE256 module among all the primitives.

Polynomial Multiplication: The poly_mult module is also common among all the primitives. Table 3 shows the area utilization of the poly_mult module. In our *Balanced* design, we use only one poly_mult module which takes up 60%, 35% and 16% of area resources in overall keygen, encap, and decap modules respectively. And in our *HighSpeed* design, we use two poly_mult modules for faster Encrypt and Re-encrypt operations as described in Sect. 2.5 and Sect. 2.6 this takes up 50% and 26% of overall area resources in encap, and decap modules respectively.

Encapsulation: As specified in Sect. 2.6, we use the encap module (described in Sect. 2.5) inside decap module to perform re-encryption and hash computation. This encap module takes up 46% of the overall decap resources in the *Balanced* design and 53% in the *HighSpeed* design. Consequently, sharing one encap module to perform both encapsulation and decapsulation would save a significant amount of area.

In order to save the resource overhead due to the duplication of modules, we decide to share the aforementioned modules between the three primitives in our joint design. To differentiate between different operations, we provide a 2-bit port in the interface, which helps in choosing the operation between Key Generation, Encapsulation, and Decapsulation. The results for our combined *Balanced* and *HighSpeed* implementations are shown in Table 13 in comparison with the most recent related work. Our results are generated targeting the Artix 7 (xc7a100t-csg324-3) FPGA. This is the same target FPGA family type as used in the related works [2,3,20]. Our data is from synthesis and implementation reports, while data for the other related works are from the cited papers.

3.2   Evaluation and Comparison to Existing HQC Hardware Designs

Previously, a hardware design for HQC has been generated using high-level synthesis (HLS) [2], and code targeting Artix-7 is available online.[2] The generated code can obtain the performance numbers: 0.3 ms for key generation, 0.6ms for encapsulation, and 1.2ms for decapsulation, the times correspond to the *HighSpeed* implementation of the lowest security level. Authors also provide *LightWeight* version for the lowest security level, but did not provide hardware designs for other security levels. A different HLS-based design with better results has been presented in [3]. This HLS design can achieve the performance of: 0.27 ms for key generation, 0.59 ms for encapsulation, and 1.27 ms for decapsulation with their *HighSpeed* version. Apart from the HLS designs, a recent hardware

---

[2] https://pqc-hqc.org/implementation.html.

Table 13. Comparison of our HQC hardware design with the related work.

Design	Resources					F	Encap		Decap		KeyGen	
	Logic			Memory								
	(Slices)	(LUT)	(DSP)	(FF)	(BR)	(MHz)	(Mcyc.)	(ms)	(Mcyc.)	(ms)	(Mcyc.)	(ms)
Security Level 1 — Classical 128-bit Security												
HQC – Our Work, HDL design, Artix 7 (xc7a100t)												
Balanced	4,684	13,865	8	6,897	22	164	0.03	0.20	0.05	0.29	0.02	0.10
HighSpeed	5,246	15,214	8	7,293	24	178	0.02	0.13	0.04	0.21	0.02	0.09
HQC – [20], HW/SW codesign, Artix 7 (xc7a100t)												
HW/SW	—	8,000	0	2,400	3	100	0.13	1.3	0.56	5.6	0.06	0.56
HQC – [3], HLS design, Artix 7 (xc7a100t)												
LightWeight	—	8,876	0	6,405	28.0	132	1.48	11.85	2.15	17.21	0.62	5.01
HighSpeed	—	20,169	0	16,374	25	148	0.09	0.59	0.19	1.27	0.04	0.27
HQC – [2], HLS design, Artix 7 (xc7a100t)												
LightWeight	3,100	8,900	0	6,400	14.0	132	1.50	12.00	2.10	16.00	0.63	4.80
HighSpeed	6,600	20,000	0	16,000	12.5	148	0.09	0.60	0.19	1.20	0.04	0.30

HW/SW = Hardware-Software CoDesign, FF = flip-flop, F = F_{max}, BR = BRAM

design [20] presented a hardware-software codesign approach and reports better performance numbers than that of *LightWeight* versions of both the HLS designs. Note, however, that there is area overhead of the CPU core. The HLS designs and hardware-software codesign only provide the lowest security level version. Meanwhile, both *Balanced* and *HighSpeed* variants of our design are faster for all three operations when compared to all existing designs. We also achieve the best time area product, and cover all three security levels.

4 Conclusion

This work presented two performance-targeted and constant-time hardware designs of the HQC KEM. This work presented first, hand-optimized design of HQC key generation, encapsulation, and decapsulation written in Verilog targeting FPGAs and provides compile-time parameters to switch between all security levels and performances. This work also presented a memory-optimized Polynomial Multiplication module and a SHAKE256 module, which runs two times faster when compared to the existing work. This work also presented the first hardware implementation of two variants of constant-time solutions for the fixed-weight vector generation process. Our HQC design currently outperforms the other existing hardware designs for HQC. As this work showed, code-based designs such as HQC can be realized very efficiently in optimized hardware.

Acknowledgement. We would like to thank the reviewers for the valuable feedback and Dr. Cuauhtemoc Mancillas López for constructive comments and shepherding our article. We would like to thank Dr. Victor Mateu and Dr. Carlos Aguilar Melchor for their helpful discussions. We would like to thank Dr. Shanquan Tian for his optimization recommendations for the SHAKE256 module. The work was supported in part by a research grant from Technology Innovation Institute.

Appendix 1.A Fast and Non-Biased (FNB) Fixed-Weight Vector Generation

Although the CWW design is constant in time, it does have a small bias. As an alternative, we propose a new FNB fixed-weight vector generation design which is based on fixed-weight vector generation technique given in [1]. Our FNB fixed-weight generation module can be parametrized to create design with an arbitrarily small probability of timing attack being possible. In our hardware module, have a parameter ACCEPTABLE_REJECTIONS, which can be used to specify how many indices could be rejected in either rejection sampling or in duplicated detection and still, the design will behave constant time. The parameter (ACCEPTABLE_REJECTIONS) can be set based on user's target failure probability. If the actual failures are within the failure probability set by the selected parameter value, then the timing side channel given in [13] is not possible.

We use SHAKE256 module described in Sect. 2.1 to expand 320-bit seed to a $24 \times w$-bit string. Since the SHAKE256 module has 32-bit interface, the seed is loaded in 32-bit chunks, and the seed is stored in a BRAM. The 32-bit chunk from SHAKE256 is broken into 24-bit integer by preprocess unit and stored in the ctx_RAM then threshold check and reduction are performed. For the reduction, we use Barrett reduction [6]. Unlike the variable Barrett reduction discussed in Sect. 2.1.A, this specific Barrett reduction is optimized as we always reduce the inputs to a specific fixed value (n). After the reduction, the integer values (locations) are stored in a BRAM. Once the locations BRAM is filled, the duplicate detection module is triggered. The duplicate detection module helps detect potential duplicates values in the locations BRAM by traversing through all address locations and updating the value stored in a dual-ported BRAM. While the duplicate detection module checks for duplicates, the SHAKE256 module generates the next $24 \times w$-bit string to tackle any potential duplicates and stores them in another BRAM. This way, we can hide any clock cycles taken for seed expansion. Our hardware design uses a PRNG to generate the uniformly random bits required for the fixed weight vector generation from an input seed of length 320-bits. Our hardware design includes this PRNG in the form of SHAKE256 and assumes that the seed will be initialized by some other hardware module implementing a true random number generator. Our FNB fixed-weight generation module can be parametrized to create design with an arbitrarily small probability of timing attack being possible. In our hardware module, have a parameter name is ACCEPTABLE_REJECTIONS, which can be used to specify how many indices could be rejected, and still, the design will behave constant time (at the cost of extra area for more storage and extra cycles). The extra area is needed because we generate additional (based on parameter value) uniformly random bits in advance and store them in the a BRAM. The extra clock cycles are needed because even after we found the required number of indices that are under the threshold value, we still go over all the locations to maintain constant time behavior. For the duplicate detection logic inside the duplicate detection module, the control logic is programmed to take the same cycles in both cases of duplicate being detected or not. The parameter (ACCEPTABLE_REJECTIONS) can be set based on the user's target failure probability. If the actual failures

Table 14. Comparison of the time and area of state-of-the-art hardware implementations of other (NIST PQC competition) round 4 KEM candidates.

Design	Resources					F	Encap		Decap		KeyGen	
	Logic			Memory								
	(SLICES)	(LUT)	(DSP)	(FF)	(BR)	(MHz)	(Mcyc.)	(ms)	(Mcyc.)	(ms)	(Mcyc.)	(ms)
Security Level 1 — Classical 128-bit Security												
HQC – Our Work, HDL design, Artix 7 (xc7a200t)												
BAL	4,560	13,481	8	6,897	22	164	0.03	0.20	0.05	0.29	0.02	0.10
HS	5,133	15,195	8	7,293	24	178	0.02	0.13	0.04	0.21	0.02	0.09
BIKE – [18], HDL design, Artix 7 (xc7a35t)												
LW	4,078	12,868	7	5,354	17.0	121	0.20	1.2	1.62	13.3	2.67	21.9
HS	15,187	52,967	13	7,035	49.0	96	0.01	0.1	0.19	1.9	0.26	2.7
BIKE – [17], HDL design, Artix 7 (xc7a200t)												
LW	3,777	12,319	7	3,896	9.0	121	0.05	0.4	0.84	6.89	0.46	3.8
TO	5,617	19,607	9	5,008	17.0	100	0.03	0.3	0.42	4.2	0.18	1.9
HS	7,332	25,549	13	5,462	34.0	113	0.01	0.1	0.21	1.9	0.19	1.7
Classic McEliece – [8], HDL design, Artix 7 (xc7a200t)												
LW	—	23,890	5	45,658	138.5	112	0.13	1.1	0.17	1.5	8.88	79.2
HS	—	40,018	4	61,881	177.5	113	0.03	0.3	0.10	0.9	0.97	8.6
SIKE – [16], HDL design, Artix 7 (xc7a100t)												
LW	3,415	—	57	7,202	21	145	—	25.6	—	27.2	—	15.1
HS	7,408	—	162	11,661	37	109	—	15.3	—	16.3	—	9.1
Kyber – [9], HDL design, (xc7a200t)												
HS	—	9,457	4	8,543	4.5	220	0.003	0.01	0.004	0.02	0.002	0.01
Kyber – [24], HDL design, (xc7a12t-1)												
BAL	2,126	7,412	2	4,644	3	161	0.005	0.23	0.006	0.04	0.003	0.02

LW = LightWeight, HS = HighSpeed, TO = TradeOff, BAL = Balanced, FF = flip-flop, F = F_{max}, BR = BRAM

are within the failure probability set by the selected parameter value, then the timing side channel given in [13] is not possible.

Table 5 shows the comparison of our new FNB design to the CCW design. The area results shown in Table 5 exclude SHAKE256 module as the SHAKE256 is shared among all primitives. The reported frequency in Although the CWW algorithm ensures the constant time behavior in generating fixed-weight vectors, there is a small bias between the uniform distribution and the algorithm's output. Meanwhile, for the new FNB algorithm, there is no bias. Further, FNB is faster than CWW, and the time-area product is better. These benefits come at the cost of extremely small probabilities that the design is not constant time, but only if it happens that there are more rejections than w_r. Table 5 shows that the probability of non-constant time behavior for FNB can be 2^{-200} or even smaller. To compute the failure probability (given in Table 5) for each parameter set, we take into account both threshold check failure and duplicate detection probabilities for the respective parameter sets.

Comparison to Hardware Designs for Other Round 4 Algorithms

We also provide Table 14 where we tabulate latest hardware implementations of all other post-quantum cryptographic algorithm hardware implementations from the fourth round of NIST's standardization process, plus the to-be standardized Kyber algorithm. We focus on comparison of the hardware designs for lowest level of security, Level 1, as all publications give clear time and area numbers.

References

1. Aguilar Melchor, C., et al.: HQC. Technical report, National Institute of Standards and Technology (2020). https://pqc-hqc.org/doc/hqc-specification_021-06-06.pdf
2. Aguilar Melchor, C., et al.: HQC. Technical report, National Institute of Standards and Technology (2023). http://pqc-hqc.org/doc/hqc-specification_2023-04-30.pdf
3. Aguilar-Melchor, C., et al.: Towards automating cryptographic hardware implementations: a case study of HQC. Cryptology ePrint Archive, Paper 2022/1425 (2022). https://eprint.iacr.org/2022/1425
4. Aragon, N., et al.: BIKE. Technical report, National Institute of Standards and Technology (2020). https://csrc.nist.gov/projects/post-quantum-cryptography/round-3-submissions
5. Azad, A.A., Shahed, I.: A compact and fast FPGA based implementation of encoding and decoding algorithm using Reed Solomon codes. Int. J. Future Comput. Commun. 31–35 (2014)
6. Barrett, P.: Implementing the Rivest Shamir and Adleman public key encryption algorithm on a standard digital signal processor. In: Odlyzko, A.M. (ed.) CRYPTO 1986. LNCS, vol. 263, pp. 311–323. Springer, Heidelberg (1987). https://doi.org/10.1007/3-540-47721-7_24
7. Bernstein, D.D.: Fast multiplication and its applications (2008)
8. Chen, P., et al.: Complete and improved FPGA implementation. https://doi.org/10.46586/tches.v2022.i3.71-113
9. Dang, V.B., Mohajerani, K., Gaj, K.: High-speed hardware architectures and FPGA benchmarking of CRYSTALS-Kyber, NTRU, and saber. Cryptology ePrint Archive, Paper 2021/1508 (2021). https://eprint.iacr.org/2021/1508
10. Deshpande, S., del Pozo, S.M., Mateu, V., Manzano, M., Aaraj, N., Szefer, J.: Modular inverse for integers using fast constant time GCD algorithm and its applications. In: Proceedings of the International Conference on Field Programmable Logic and Applications. FPL (2021)
11. Deshpande, S., Xu, C., Nawan, M., Nawaz, K., Szefer, J.: Fast and efficient hardware implementation of HQC. Cryptology ePrint Archive, Paper 2022/1183 (2022). https://eprint.iacr.org/2022/1183
12. Gigliotti, P.: Implementing barrel shifters using multipliers. Technical report, XAPP195, Xilinx (2004). https://www.xilinx.com/support/documentation/application_notes/xapp195.pdf
13. Guo, Q., Hlauschek, C., Johansson, T., Lahr, N., Nilsson, A., Schröder, R.L.: Don't reject this: key-recovery timing attacks due to rejection-sampling in HQC and bike. IACR Trans. Cryptogr. Hardw. Embed. Syst. **2022**(3), 223–263 (2022). https://doi.org/10.46586/tches.v2022.i3.223-263. https://tches.iacr.org/index.php/TCHES/article/view/9700
14. Hashemipour-Nazari, M., Goossens, K., Balatsoukas-Stimming, A.: Hardware implementation of iterative projection-aggregation decoding of reed-muller codes. In: 2021 IEEE International Conference on Acoustics, Speech and Signal Processing (ICASSP), ICASSP 2021, pp. 8293–8297 (2021). https://doi.org/10.1109/ICASSP39728.2021.9414655

15. Hu, J., Wang, W., Cheung, R.C., Wang, H.: Optimized polynomial multiplier over commutative rings on FPGAS: a case study on bike. In: 2019 International Conference on Field-Programmable Technology (ICFPT), pp. 231–234 (2019). https://doi.org/10.1109/ICFPT47387.2019.00035

16. Massolino, P.M.C., Longa, P., Renes, J., Batina, L.: A compact and scalable hardware/software co-design of SIKE. IACR Trans. Cryptogr. Hardw. Embed. Syst. **2020**(2), 245–271 (2020). https://doi.org/10.13154/tches.v2020.i2.245-271. https://tches.iacr.org/index.php/TCHES/article/view/8551

17. Richter-Brockmann, J., Chen, M.S., Ghosh, S., Güneysu, T.: Racing bike: improved polynomial multiplication and inversion in hardware. IACR Trans. Cryptogr. Hardw. Embed. Syst. **2022**(1), 557–588 (2021). https://doi.org/10.46586/tches.v2022.i1.557-588. https://tches.iacr.org/index.php/TCHES/article/view/9307

18. Richter-Brockmann, J., Mono, J., Guneysu, T.: Folding bike: scalable hardware implementation for reconfigurable devices. IEEE Trans. Comput. **71**(5), 1204–1215 (2022). https://doi.org/10.1109/TC.2021.3078294

19. Sandoval-Ruiz, C.: VHDL optimized model of a multiplier in finite fields. Ingenieria y Universidad **21**(2), 195–212 (2017). https://doi.org/10.11144/Javeriana.iyu21-2.vhdl. https://revistas.javeriana.edu.co/index.php/iyu/article/view/195

20. Schöffel, M., Feldmann, J., Wehn, N.: Code-based cryptography in IoT: a HW/SW co-design of HQC. CoRR abs/2301.04888 (2023). https://doi.org/10.48550/arXiv.2301.04888

21. Scholl, S., Wehn, N.: Hardware implementation of a Reed-Solomon soft decoder based on information set decoding. In: 2014 Design, Automation & Test in Europe Conference & Exhibition (DATE), pp. 1–6 (2014). https://doi.org/10.7873/DATE.2014.222

22. Sendrier, N.: Secure sampling of constant-weight words - application to bike. Cryptology ePrint Archive, Paper 2021/1631 (2021). https://eprint.iacr.org/2021/1631

23. Wang, W., Tian, S., Jungk, B., Bindel, N., Longa, P., Szefer, J.: Parameterized hardware accelerators for lattice-based cryptography and their application to the HW/SW co-design of qTESLA. IACR Trans. Cryptogr. Hardw. Embed. Syst. **2020**(3), 269–306 (2020). https://doi.org/10.13154/tches.v2020.i3.269-306. https://tches.iacr.org/index.php/TCHES/article/view/8591

24. Xing, Y., Li, S.: A compact hardware implementation of CCA-secure key exchange mechanism CRYSTALS-KYBER on FPGA. IACR Trans. Cryptogr. Hardw. Embed. Syst. **2021**(2), 328–356 (2021). https://doi.org/10.46586/tches.v2021.i2.328-356. https://tches.iacr.org/index.php/TCHES/article/view/8797

Homomorphic Encryption

On the Precision Loss in Approximate Homomorphic Encryption

Anamaria Costache[1]([✉])[ID], Benjamin R. Curtis[2][ID], Erin Hales[3][ID],
Sean Murphy[3], Tabitha Ogilvie[3], and Rachel Player[3][ID]

[1] Norwegian University of Science and Technology (NTNU), Trondheim, Norway
anamaria.costache@ntnu.no
[2] Zama, Paris, France
ben.curtis@zama.ai
[3] Royal Holloway, University of London, Egham, UK
{erin.hales.2018,tabitha.ogilvie.2019}@live.rhul.ac.uk,
{s.murphy,rachel.player}@rhul.ac.uk

Abstract. Since its introduction at Asiacrypt 2017, the CKKS approximate homomorphic encryption scheme has become one of the most widely used and implemented homomorphic encryption schemes. Due to the approximate nature of the scheme, application developers using CKKS must ensure that the evaluation output is within a tolerable error of the corresponding plaintext computation. Choosing appropriate parameters requires a good understanding of how the noise will grow through the computation. A strong understanding of the noise growth is also necessary to limit the performance impact of mitigations to the attacks on CKKS presented by Li and Micciancio (Eurocrypt [34]).

In this work, we present a comprehensive noise analysis of CKKS, that considers noise coming both from the encoding and homomorphic operations. Our main contribution is the first average-case analysis for CKKS noise, and we also introduce refinements to prior worst-case noise analyses. We develop noise heuristics both for the original CKKS scheme and the RNS variant presented at SAC 2018. We then evaluate these heuristics by comparing the predicted noise growth with experiments in the HEAAN and FullRNS-HEAAN libraries, and by comparing with a worst-case noise analysis as done in prior work. Our findings show mixed results: while our new analyses lead to heuristic estimates that more closely model the observed noise growth than prior approaches, the new heuristics sometimes slightly underestimate the observed noise growth. This evidences the need for implementation-specific noise analyses for CKKS, which recent work has shown to be effective for implementations of similar schemes.

1 Introduction

Homomorphic Encryption (HE) enables computation on ciphertexts without revealing any information about the underlying plaintexts. The first scheme was proposed by Gentry [19] and since then, many homomorphic encryption

C. Carlet et al. (Eds.): SAC 2023, LNCS 14201, pp. 325–345, 2024.
https://doi.org/10.1007/978-3-031-53368-6_16

schemes have been proposed [5,10,11,18], based on the security of the Learning with Errors (LWE) problem [39] and its variants.

One of the most popular schemes is the approximate homomorphic encryption scheme CKKS [10]. Ciphertexts in all homomorphic encryption schemes based on LWE variants contain noise, which grows with each evaluation operation, and must be carefully controlled to ensure correct decryption. The main insight of [10] is that it may be tolerable for decryption to be approximate, for example in applications where we expect small errors to occur. This enables the CKKS scheme to natively support real-valued plaintexts, making it attractive for application settings such as privacy-preserving machine learning [4,27,37]. In contrast, other similar schemes such as BGV [5] or BFV [18], are exact, and thus have a finite plaintext space that data must be encoded into. CKKS has been extensively optimised [8,9,28] and is implemented in many prominent open-source homomorphic encryption libraries [2,23,25,30,38,40].

Homomorphic encryption schemes involve many different parameters, and it can be a challenge to choose appropriate parameters that balance efficiency, security and noise growth. This is particularly true for the CKKS scheme, for two main reasons. Firstly, unlike for exact schemes, encoding and encryption noises must be considered together. Secondly, in CKKS, we have to track not only the level of ciphertexts (as in BFV and BGV), but we must also track the scaling factor Δ. Unfortunately, there is no clear guidance for choosing Δ and a trial-and-error approach is usually advised[1].

Prior noise analyses for CKKS [8–10,21,28] employ a worst-case analysis in the canonical embedding, in analogue to the line of work [13,15,20] for analysing noise growth in BGV and BFV. In particular, a worst-case bound on the noise of each ciphertext in the canonical embedding is tracked through each homomorphic operation. This leads to a bound on the noise in the output ciphertext, which can be used to set parameters for correctness. These worst-case bounds are developed assuming that the random variable falls within a certain multiple of standard deviations (e.g. six [20] or ten [21]) from its mean. We can thus expect the bounds to be loose even from the beginning of the computation (as a freshly sampled noise is likely to be closer to the mean than several standard deviations away), and that the looseness will compound as we move further through the computation. This intuition was confirmed in experiments of [15] for the BFV and BGV schemes, whose operations are similar to those of CKKS.

An alternative, average-case approach to noise analysis was proposed in [12] for the CGGI scheme [11], in which the noise is modelled as a Gaussian, and its variance is tracked through each homomorphic operation. The noise in the output ciphertext is finally bounded from the output variance, in order to pick parameters for correctness. Adopting a similar approach for CKKS appears challenging, as the noise after a homomorphic multiplication is a product of the noises in the two input ciphertexts, whereas as the output distribution of the product of two subgaussians is not necessarily subgaussian, and can have a much heavier tail [36].

---

[1] See e.g. https://ibm.github.io/fhe-toolkit-linux/html/helib/md_.opt_.i_b_m_.f_h_e-distro_.h_.elib_.c_k_k_s-security.html.

In this work, we will demonstrate how a Central Limit Theorem approach can be applied to give a heuristic average-case noise growth analysis for CKKS.

Contributions: Our first contribution is a new result relating the CKKS message and plaintext spaces. Recall that CKKS encoding maps an element from the (complex) message space into an element in the (polynomial ring) plaintext space via a scaled restriction of the inverse canonical embedding. In Theorem 1, we provide a new, tighter bound relating the size of an error in the plaintext space to the size of the induced error in the message space. Moreover, we prove that this bound is the best possible. In addition, we show that the worst case expansion factor in either the real or complex part of our message equals the worst case expansion factor of the entire embedding. This means that, perhaps surprisingly, bounding a decrypted and decoded message over only the real part, rather than the whole embedding, provides no benefit for worst-case analyses.

Our next contribution is to present the first average-case noise analysis for CKKS. In Theorem 3 we give a result showing that the product of two Normally distributed polynomials has Normally distributed coefficients under a Central Limit assumption. Using this result we are able to heuristically model all CKKS noise operations as operations on Normal random variables, thus recovering an analysis similar to [12]. We present our noise analyses for 'Textbook' CKKS as originally presented in [10] and the RNS variant presented in [9].

In order to evaluate the efficacy of our average-case noise analysis for CKKS, we compare the noise heuristics developed under this analysis with the worst-case bounds of prior work. We also present refinements to these prior worst-case noise analyses using the techniques of [26]. We parameterise all our noise bounds in terms of a failure probability, α, rather than a-priori fixing a one dimensional failure probability as in prior work [13,15,20]. We evaluate the bounds arising from all these noise analyses with experiments in HEAAN v1.0 [24] and FullRNS-HEAAN [22]. We note that neither the Textbook CKKS nor the RNS variant noise analysis is implementation-specific, and we chose the HEAAN library as it is the implementation that most closely resembles the theoretical description of both variants of the scheme.

Our experimental results are given in Table 4 for Textbook CKKS heuristics as compared with HEAAN v1.0 [24] and in Table 5 for heuristics for the RNS variant [9] as compared with FullRNS-HEAAN [22]. Our results show that our new heuristics improve upon prior noise analyses in terms of modelling more closely the observed noise. However, we also observe that our heuristics may underestimate the noise growth observed in practice. Prior work [16] for BGV has noted another example of a noise analysis that was not implementation specific that also led to underestimates of the observed noise. Our work can therefore be seen as an improved starting point for a tight noise analysis for CKKS, but an implementation-specific analysis may be more suitable for applications that cannot afford this underestimate.

Related work: Average-case noise analyses were presented for the BGV scheme in [35], by applying results from the present work. An implementation-specific average-case noise analysis for the BGV scheme was presented in [16]. An average-case noise analysis for BFV was presented in [3]. Lee *et al.* [32] use the signal-to-noise ratio to analyse CKKS noise, and proposes to track the variance of the errors, rather than an upper bound. The variances of the noise in multi-key BFV and CKKS operations were tracked in [7], but a proof that the noises are distributed as Gaussians was not presented. Our work thus provides a theoretical justification for these approaches. Our study of encoding also provides theoretical support for the heuristics in [21].

Structure: In Sect. 2 we introduce relevant background material and notation, including the Textbook CKKS scheme [10] and its RNS variant [9]. In Sect. 3 we study the precision loss coming from encoding and decoding in CKKS. In Sect. 4 we describe the three methods for noise analysis that we will apply to Textbook CKKS and its RNS variant. We then apply this to Textbook CKKS. In Sect. 5 we describe the modifications required to the noise analysis methods for the RNS setting, and provide heuristics for this setting. In Sect. 6 we report on experimental results to evaluate the noise analysis approaches that we introduced and we draw conclusions. For reasons of space, we are omitting proofs from Sects. 3 and 4 and refer the reader to the full version of the paper instead [14].

2   Preliminaries

Notation: Vectors are denoted in small bold font $\mathbf{z}$, and z_j refers to the jth element of a vector, indexing from zero. The notation $\lfloor \cdot \rceil$ is used for rounding to the nearest integer and $[\cdot]_q$ represents reduction modulo q. For $z = x + iy \in \mathbb{C}$, we denote by $\lceil z \rfloor := \lceil x \rfloor + i \lceil y \rfloor$ the rounding of both its real and imaginary components, and extend this componentwise to define the rounding $\lceil \mathbf{z} \rfloor$ of a complex vector $\mathbf{z} \in \mathbb{C}^{N/2}$. Unless otherwise stated, log will always mean $\log_2$.

In this work, we will consider several different norms. We denote the p-norm by $\|\cdot\|_p$ and the infinity norm by $\|\cdot\|_\infty$. We consider norms on a polynomial m both as a vector of its coefficients and under the canonical embedding, and denote these norms by $\|m\|$ and $\|m\|^{\text{can}}$ respectively. We use $s \leftarrow D$ to denote sampling s according to the distribution D.

We use the notation $\mathrm{N}(\mu, \sigma^2)$ to refer to a univariate Normal distribution with mean μ and variance σ^2, and $\mathrm{N}(\boldsymbol{\mu}; \Sigma)$ to refer to an N-dimensional multivariate Normal distribution with N-dimensional mean vector $\boldsymbol{\mu}$ and $N \times N$ covariance matrix Σ. For a polynomial $Z(X) \in \mathbb{R}[X]/(X^N + 1)$, we will write $Z \sim \mathrm{N}(\boldsymbol{\mu}, \rho^2 I_N)$ to indicate that each coefficient of Z is independently and identically normally distributed, i.e., $Z_i \sim \mathrm{N}(\mu_i, \rho^2)$. We denote by $\mathtt{erf}$ the (Gauss) error function, by $\mathtt{erf}^{-1}$ its inverse, and by $\mathtt{erfc}$ the complementary function.

The Textbook CKKS Scheme: The CKKS scheme as originally presented in [10] is a levelled HE scheme that we refer to as *Textbook CKKS*. For reasons of space, we omit the presentation of the scheme, and only detail that of its RNS variant.

The Textbook CKKS scheme is parameterised by L, p, q_0, N, λ, χ, S, V, and Δ. The base $p > 0$ and modulus q_0 are used to form the scale parameter and the chain of moduli (one for each level) as follows: $\Delta = 2^p$ and $Q_\ell = \Delta^\ell q_0$ for $1 \leqslant \ell \leqslant L$. The dimension N is typically chosen as a power of two, and we will only use such N in this work. The dimension N and the chain of moduli parameterise the underlying plaintext and ciphertext rings. The plaintext space is $\mathcal{R} = \mathbb{Z}[X]/(X^N+1)$. We denote by Q some fixed level in the description below, so that the ciphertext space at any given moment is $\mathcal{R}_Q = \mathbb{Z}_Q[X]/(X^N + 1)$.

The security parameter is λ. The Ring-LWE error distribution is denoted by χ and is such that each coefficient is sampled as a discrete Gaussian with standard deviation $\sigma = 3.2$ [1]. The parameter S denotes the secret key distribution, which is specified in [10] to be $HWT(h)$, i.e. the secret is ternary with Hamming weight exactly h. The parameter V denotes the ephemeral secret distribution, which is specified in [10] to be $ZO(\rho)$ with $\rho = 0.5$, i.e. the secret is ternary with coefficients having probability $\rho/2$ for each of -1 and 1, and probability $1 - \rho$ of being 0.

The CKKS scheme uses the canonical embedding to define an encoding from the message space $\mathbb{C}^{N/2}$ to the plaintext space $\mathbb{Z}[X]/(X^N + 1)$ in the following way: an isomorphism $\tau : \mathbb{R}[X]/(X^N + 1) \to \mathbb{C}^{N/2}$ can be defined via considering the canonical embedding restricted to $N/2$ of the $2N^{\text{th}}$ primitive roots and discarding conjugates. Encoding and decoding then use this map τ, as well as a precision parameter Δ, as follows: $\text{Encode}(\mathbf{z}, \Delta) = \lceil \Delta \tau^{-1}(\mathbf{z}) \rfloor$ and $\text{Decode}(m, \Delta) = \frac{1}{\Delta}\tau(m)$, where $\mathbf{z} \in \mathbb{C}^{N/2}$, $m \in \mathbb{Z}[X]/(X^N +1)$, and $\lceil \cdot \rfloor$ is taken coefficient-wise.

RNS Variants of CKKS: Variants of CKKS using RNS have been proposed [9, 28]. In this work, we focus on the RNS-CKKS scheme as described in [9]. This scheme is specified in Fig. 1.

In RNS variants of CKKS [9,28], the chain of ciphertext moduli changes compared to the original scheme. The ℓth ciphertext modulus is given by $Q_\ell = \prod_{j=0}^{\ell} q_j$ where the jth ciphertext slot is with respect to the modulus q_j. In the RNS variant [9], the key switching procedure requires the large modulus P to be formed similarly from a set of k pairwise coprime p_i as $P = \prod_{i=0}^{k} p_i$. The other parameters as specified in [9], and the encoding and decoding, are the same as for Textbook CKKS.

Precision Loss: in this work we are concerned with bounding the precision loss in CKKS, which we can define informally as the difference between evaluating a circuit in the clear and evaluating the same circuit homomorphically. A more formal description is given below.

Definition 1. *Consider a normed space* $(\mathcal{M}, || \cdot ||)$, *messages* $m_1, ..., m_n \in \mathcal{M}$, *and a circuit* $C : \mathcal{M}^n \to \mathcal{M}$. *Then we define the* **precision loss** *associated with calculating the circuit* C *homomorphically as the distance* $||\tilde{m} - m||$, *where* $\tilde{m}$ *is the output of the homomorphic evaluation of* $C(m_1, ..., m_n)$, *and* m *is the true value of the circuit.*

SecretKeyGen(λ): Sample $s \leftarrow S$ and output $\mathtt{sk} = (1, s)$.

PublicKeyGen(sk): For $\mathtt{sk} = (1, s)$, for all $0 \leq j \leq L$, a representative $a^{(j)}$ is sampled uniformly from R_{q_j}, and $b^{(j)} \leftarrow -a^{(j)}s + e \mod q_j$ is set. Output $\mathtt{pk} = (\mathtt{pk}^{(j)})_{0 \leq j \leq L} = (b^{(j)}, a^{(j)})_{0 \leq j \leq L}$.

EvaluationKeyGen(sk, w): Sample $e' \leftarrow \chi$. Output $(\mathtt{evk}^{(0)}, \ldots, \mathtt{evk}^{(k+L)})$ $=$ $((b'^{(0)}, a'^{(0)}), \ldots, (b'^{(k+L)}, a'^{(k+L)}))$, where, for $0 \leq i < k$, $a'^{(i)} \leftarrow R_{p_i}$ uniformly and $b'^{(i)} = -a'^{(i)}s + e' \mod p_i$; and for $0 \leq j \leq L$, $a'^{(k+j)} \leftarrow R_{q_j}$ uniformly and $b'^{(k+j)} = -a'^{(k+j)}s + [P]_{q_j}s^2 + e' \mod q_j$.

Encrypt(pk, m): For $m \in R$. Sample $v \leftarrow V$ and $e_0, e_1 \leftarrow \chi$. For all $0 \leq j \leq L$, and for the public key $\mathtt{pk} = (\mathtt{pk}^{(j)})_{0 \leq j \leq L} = (b^{(j)}, a^{(j)})_{0 \leq j \leq L}$, output $\mathtt{ct} = (\mathtt{ct}^{(j)})_{0 \leq j \leq L}$ where $\mathtt{ct}^{(j)} = (b^{(j)}v + e_0 + m, a^{(j)}v + e_1) \in R_{q_j}^2$.

Decrypt(sk, ct): For $\mathtt{ct} = (\mathtt{ct}^{(j)})_{0 \leq j \leq \ell}$, output $m' = \left\langle \mathtt{ct}^{(0)}, \mathtt{sk} \right\rangle \mod q_0$.

Add($\mathtt{ct}_0, \mathtt{ct}_1$): For $0 \leq j \leq \ell$, for input ciphertexts $\mathtt{ct}_1 = \{\mathtt{ct}_1^{(j)}\}$ and $\mathtt{ct}_2 = \{\mathtt{ct}_2^{(j)}\}$, output $\mathtt{ct}_{\mathrm{add}} = (\mathtt{ct}_{\mathrm{add}}^{(j)})_{0 \leq j \leq \ell}$ where $\mathtt{ct}_{\mathrm{add}}^{(j)} = \mathtt{ct}_1^{(j)} + \mathtt{ct}_2^{(j)} \mod q_j$.

Pre-Multiply($\mathtt{ct}_0, \mathtt{ct}_1$): For $0 \leq j \leq \ell$, for input ciphertexts $\mathtt{ct}_1 = \{\mathtt{ct}_1^{(j)}\} = \left\{ \left(c_0^{(j)}, c_1^{(j)} \right) \right\}$ and $\mathtt{ct}_2 = \{\mathtt{ct}_2^{(j)}\} = \left\{ \left(C_0^{(j)}, C_1^{(j)} \right) \right\}$, output $\mathtt{ct}_{\mathrm{pre\text{-}mult}} = \{\mathtt{ct}_{\mathrm{pre\text{-}mult}}^{(j)}\}_{0 \leq j \leq \ell} = \{(d_0^{(j)}, d_1^{(j)}, d_2^{(j)})\}$ where $d_0^{(j)} = c_0^{(j)}C_0^{(j)} \mod q_j$, $d_1^{(j)} = c_0^{(j)}C_1^{(j)} + c_1^{(j)}C_0^{(j)} \mod q_j$, and $d_2^{(j)} = c_1^{(j)}C_1^{(j)} \mod q_j$.

KeySwitch(ct, evk): For $0 \leq j \leq \ell$, for input ciphertext $\mathtt{ct}_{\mathrm{pre\text{-}mult}} = \{\mathtt{ct}_{\mathrm{pre\text{-}mult}}^{(j)}\}_{0 \leq j \leq \ell} = \{(d_0^{(j)}, d_1^{(j)}, d_2^{(j)})\}$, output $\mathtt{ct}_{\mathrm{ks}} = \{\mathtt{ct}_{\mathrm{ks}}^{(j)}\}_{0 \leq j \leq \ell} = \left\{ \left(c_0^{(0)}, c_1^{(0)} \right), \ldots, \left(c_0^{(\ell)}, c_1^{(\ell)} \right) \right\}$, where $\left(c_0^{(j)}, c_1^{(j)} \right) = \left([d_0^{(j)} + \hat{c}_0^{(j)}]_{q_j}, [d_1^{(j)} + \hat{c}_1^{(j)}]_{q_j} \right)$, for $\hat{c}_0^{(j)}$ and $\hat{c}_1^{(j)}$ as defined in the full version [14].

Rescale(ct): For $0 \leq j \leq \ell$, for input ciphertext $\mathtt{ct} = \{\mathtt{ct}^{(j)}\}_{0 \leq j \leq \ell} = \left(\left(c_0^{(j)}, c_1^{(j)} \right) \right)_{0 \leq j \leq \ell}$ output $\mathtt{ct}_{\mathrm{rs}} = \{\mathtt{ct}_{\mathrm{rs}}^{(j)}\}_{0 \leq j \leq \ell-1} = \{(c_0'^{(j)}, c_1'^{(j)})\}_{0 \leq j \leq \ell-1}$, where $c_0'^{(j)} = q_\ell^{-1}(c_0^{(j)} - c_0^{(\ell)}) \mod q_j$ and $c_1'^{(j)} = q_\ell^{-1}(c_1^{(j)} - c_1^{(\ell)}) \mod q_j$.

Multiply($\mathtt{ct}_0, \mathtt{ct}_1$): Output Rescale(KeySwitch(Pre-Multiply($\mathtt{ct}_0, \mathtt{ct}_1$), evk)).

Fig. 1. The RNS-CKKS Scheme

This definition is similar to Definition 10 of [33]. We will consider precision loss in three spaces: firstly, the plaintext space R with infinity norm on the vector of coefficients; secondly, the message space $\mathbb{C}^{N/2}$ with infinity norm, which is equivalent to R with infinity canonical norm; and lastly the projection to the real part $\mathbb{R}^{N/2}$ with infinity norm.

3   Encoding Analysis

In this section, we give theoretical bounds on the precision loss from encoding and decoding. Proofs of the results can be found in the full version [14]. To understand precision loss due to encoding, as well as translate noise bounds derived in the plaintext space to noise bounds in the message space, we investigate how distance measured in $\mathbb{R}[X]/(X^N + 1)$ corresponds to distance measured in $\mathbb{C}^{N/2}$, when we move between the two via τ for N a power of 2.

If we measure using the 2-norm in both spaces, these two distances correspond exactly as here τ gives a scaled isometry with $\|\tau(m)\|_2 = \sqrt{\frac{N}{2}} \|m\|_2$. However, we will use the infinity norm in both spaces to support our Worst Case in the Ring analysis (see Sect. 4). We find that, in the worst case, there is an $O(N)$ expansion in the infinity norm under the map τ and unlike the 2-norm, there is no contraction under the map τ^{-1}.

The section is organised as follows. In Sect. 3.1, we develop new theoretical results on the relationships between distances in the two spaces. In Sect. 3.2, we then apply these results in the context of CKKS encoding and decoding.

3.1 Mapping Theory

Lemma 1 ([17]). *Let $m \in \mathbb{R}^N$. Then $\|m\|_\infty \leqslant \|m\|_\infty^{\mathsf{can}}$.*

This inequality is best possible in the sense that it is achieved: let $m = \tau^{-1}(\mathbf{z})$ and let $z_k = B\zeta_k^j$ for $0 \leqslant k \leqslant \frac{N}{2} - 1$, so that $\|\mathbf{z}\|_\infty = B$. Then we find $\|m\|_\infty^{\mathsf{can}} = \|\mathbf{z}\|_\infty = B = |m_j| = \|m\|_\infty$. In particular, there is no contraction as we move from $\mathbb{C}^{N/2}, \|\cdot\|_\infty$ to $\mathbb{R}^N, \|\cdot\|_\infty$ but there is an expansion as we move the other way. The prior result on this bound is as follows.

Lemma 2 ([17,20]). *Let $m \in \mathbb{R}^N$. Then $\|m\|_\infty^{\mathsf{can}} \leqslant N \|m\|_\infty$.*

Using generic proof methods and properties of the norm, we can reduce this factor to $N/\sqrt{2}$. Before improving further, we require some definitions and a Lemma. The proof technique of the following Lemmas 3 and 4 is adapted from [6]. We introduce the notation $I(N, j)$ and $I(N)$ as follows:

$$I(N, j) := \sum_{k=0}^{N-1} \left| \sin\left(\frac{jk\pi}{N}\right) \right|, \qquad I(N) := \max_{0 \leqslant j \leqslant N-1} I(N, 2j + 1).$$

Lemma 3. *For $j \in \mathbb{Z}$, we have that $I(N, 2j + 1) = I(N, 1)$, so that $I(N) = I(N, 1)$.*

Lemma 4. $\lim_{N \to \infty} \frac{1}{N} I(N) = \frac{2}{\pi}$, *and this limit is approached from below.*

Theorem 1. *Let $m \in \mathbb{R}^N$. Then $\|m\|_\infty^{\mathsf{can}} \leqslant \sqrt{I(N)^2 + 1} \|m\|_\infty$, and this bound is the best possible for fixed N.*

Corollary 1. *Suppose for all $m \in \mathbb{R}^N$ we have $\|m\|_\infty^{\mathsf{can}} \leqslant N \cdot M(N) \|m\|_\infty$ with $M(N)$ a least upper bound. Then $M(N) \to \frac{2}{\pi}$ as $N \to \infty$.*

We now bound just the real component of the canonical embedding of m, although the following results apply equally to the imaginary component. We use the notation $\|m\|_\infty^{\mathrm{can,Re}} = \max_j |\mathrm{Re}(m(\zeta_j))|$. We find that, in the limit, the upper bound on expansion of just the real component equals the upper bound on the entire expansion.

Lemma 5. *Let $m \in \mathbb{R}^N$. Then $\|m\|_\infty^{\mathrm{can,Re}} \leqslant I(N)\,\|m\|_\infty$, and this result is best possible.*

Corollary 2. *Let $m \in \mathbb{R}^N$. If for all N we have that $\|m\|_\infty^{\mathrm{can,Re}} \leqslant kN\,\|m\|_\infty$ then $k \leqslant \frac{2}{\pi}$ and $k \to \frac{2}{\pi}$ as $N \to \infty$.*

3.2   Application to Encoding

In this section, we apply the results from Sect. 3.1 to produce bounds on the growth of polynomials under encoding and decoding. Our first result enables us to produce bounds in the plaintext space given bounds in the message space.

Lemma 6. *Suppose $m \in \mathbb{R}^N$ and $\mathbf{z} \in \mathbb{C}^{N/2}$ are such that $m = \mathrm{Encode}(\mathbf{z}, \Delta)$. Then $\|m\|_\infty \leqslant \Delta\,\|\mathbf{z}\|_\infty + \frac{1}{2}$.*

The result in Theorem 1 enables us to give bounds in the message space given bounds in the plaintext space.

Lemma 7. *Suppose $m \in \mathbb{R}^N$ has $\|m\|_\infty \leqslant B$. If $\mathbf{z} = \mathrm{Decode}(m, \Delta)$ we have that $\|\mathbf{z}\|_\infty \leqslant \frac{\sqrt{I(N)^2+1}}{\Delta}B$, and this bound is the best possible.*

Due to the fast convergence of $I(N)$ to $\frac{2N}{\pi}$, we can replace this result by its limiting value. We can therefore precisely bound the error introduced during encoding.

Corollary 3. *Suppose $\mathbf{z} \in \mathbb{C}^{N/2}$ is encoded under scale factor Δ. Then the precision lost in each slot as a result of encoding is bounded by $\frac{\sqrt{I(N)^2+1}}{2\Delta}$, and this bound tends to $\frac{N}{\pi\Delta}$ as $N \to \infty$.*

We can also give analogous results for the real and imaginary components alone.

Lemma 8. *Suppose $m \in \mathbb{R}^N$ has $\|m\|_\infty \leqslant B$. Then if $\mathbf{z} = \mathrm{Decode}(m, \Delta)$ we have that $\|Re(\mathbf{z})\|_\infty, \|Im(\mathbf{z})\|_\infty \leqslant \frac{2N}{\pi\Delta}B$, and this bound is the best possible.*

Corollary 4. *Suppose $\mathbf{z} \in \mathbb{C}^{N/2}$ is encoded under scale factor Δ. Then the precision lost on both the real and imaginary components of each slot is bounded by $\frac{N}{\pi\Delta}$.*

This shows that, perhaps surprisingly, if using a worst case analysis, it is not possible to achieve a tighter analysis of precision loss by considering only the error on the real part of the message. To benefit from restricting our attention to only the real part, we must be able to specify statistical, rather than worst case, behaviour.

4   Noise Analysis Methods

In this section, we present the three noise analysis methods considered in this work, and apply them to give noise heuristics for the Textbook CKKS scheme [10]. Proofs of the results can be found in the full version [14]. We first introduce some notation and definitions.

Noise Definitions and Notation: For a Textbook CKKS ciphertext $(\mathtt{ct}_0, \mathtt{ct}_1)$ at level ℓ encrypting a message m, we define its noise as the polynomial ϵ such that $\langle \mathtt{ct}, \mathtt{sk} \rangle = m + \epsilon \mod Q_\ell$ where this noise ϵ is small. We denote by ρ^2 the (component) variance of a noise polynomial ϵ. Some operations, such as key switching, introduce an additive noise term, whose variance we denote by η^2. We treat noise polynomials as continuous random variables for simplicity, but the distributional results are applicable to the corresponding discrete random variables for practical purposes.

Variance: We will use the following variance results. A polynomial f with coefficients distributed uniformly in $[-k/2, k/2]$, has coefficient variance $\rho_f^2 = k^2/12$. A polynomial sampled from $ZO(\rho)$ has coefficient variance ρ. A polynomial sampled from the Ring-LWE error distribution has coefficient variance σ^2.

4.1   Bounding Noise Random Variables

In this subsection, we introduce our refinement for bounding a random variable of a given variance. Given a (multivariate) random variable, we wish to identify a reasonable upper bound on the size of the components of the random variable(s). It has been common practice [13,15,20] to give an upper bound using the fact that $\mathtt{erfc}(6) \approx 2^{-55}$. Instead of deferring to such a bound in all contexts, we express our bounds on distributions in terms of a new failure probability parameter α, defined as follows.

Definition 2. *Suppose a random variable Z has real support. We will say B is a probability $1 - \alpha$ bound on Z if $\Pr(Z > B) = \alpha$. Equivalently, we will say B has failure probability α, or that B has error tolerance α.*

This refinement enables us to determine bounds on a random variable that hold with probability $(1 - \alpha)$. In Theorem 2, we give bounds both for the canonical embedding as in prior CKKS analyses (e.g. [10]), and for the plaintext ring. When applying Theorem 2 in real and complex settings respectively, we use the following functions for notational convenience:

$$H_{\mathbb{R}}(\alpha, N) := \mathtt{erf}^{-1}((1-\alpha)^{\frac{1}{N}}) \text{ and } H_{\mathbb{C}}(\alpha, N) := (-\ln(1 - (1-\alpha)^{\frac{2}{N}}))^{\frac{1}{2}}.$$

For example, a ciphertext with noise variance ρ^2 can be bounded in the canonical embedding as $\sqrt{N} \cdot \rho \cdot H_{\mathbb{C}}(\alpha, N)$ using Theorem 2 part(3).

Theorem 2. *Suppose* $Z \sim \mathrm{N}(\mathbf{0}, \rho^2 I_N)$. *Then:*

1. *A probability* $(1 - \alpha)$ *bound on the random variable* $\|Z\|_\infty$ *is given by*

$$B = \sqrt{2} \; \rho \; \mathtt{erf}^{-1}((1 - \alpha)^{\frac{1}{N}}).$$

2. *Let* τ *denote the map used in encoding and decoding and consider* $\tau(Z)$. *Then we have that* $Re(\tau(Z)), Im(\tau(Z)) \sim \mathrm{N}(\mathbf{0}, \frac{N}{2}\rho^2 I_{N/2})$, *and a probability* $(1 - \alpha)$ *bound on both* $\|Re(\tau(Z))\|_\infty$ *and* $\|Im(\tau(Z))\|_\infty$ *is given by*

$$B = \sqrt{N} \; \rho \;\; \mathtt{erf}^{-1}((1 - \alpha)^{\frac{2}{N}}).$$

3. *A probability* $(1 - \alpha)$ *bound on the random variable* $\|Z\|_\infty^{\mathsf{can}}$ *is given by*

$$B = \sqrt{N}\rho \left(- \ln(1 - (1 - \alpha)^{\frac{2}{N}})\right)^{\frac{1}{2}}.$$

4.2 Worst-Case Noise Analysis Methods

In this subsection, we introduce the two worst-case noise analysis methods considered in this work.

Worst-Case Canonical Embedding Analysis: The first noise analysis method we consider is a refinement of the standard approach for analysis of CKKS noise, as e.g. in [10]. This method tracks bounds on the noise polynomials under the canonical embedding, $\|\epsilon\|_\infty^{\mathsf{can}}$, i.e. the bounds are presented in the message space. We improve on the canonical embedding bounds in [10] by following the Iliashenko approach [26]. For a noise polynomial that consists of several summands, this approach calculates the coefficient variance of the whole sum and then maps under the canonical embedding to obtain a bound on the noise. In contrast, the prior approach relies on repeated applications of the triangle inequality to bound individual summands that are then combined into a final bound. The Iliashenko approach is expected to provide tighter bounds than the prior approach [15]. We use Theorem 2 or triangle inequalities to derive bounds in the canonical embedding. We use the fact that $\|p(X)q(X)\|_\infty^{\mathsf{can}} \leq \|p(X)\|_\infty^{\mathsf{can}} \|q(X)\|_\infty^{\mathsf{can}}$ is the worst case bound on a product of polynomials.

Worst-Case Analysis in the Ring: In this method, like the other worst-case analyses, we track how a bound $\|\epsilon\|_\infty$ on the size of the largest coefficient of the noise polynomial grows with each homomorphic operation. The difference is that we give the bound 'in the ring', i.e. the bounds are presented in the plaintext space, into which decryption takes place. We again use triangle inequalities and Theorem 2 to derive bounds in the ring. We use the fact that $\|p(X)q(X)\|_\infty \leq N \|p(X)\|_\infty \|q(X)\|_\infty$ is the worst case bound on a product. We note that this noise analysis method has has been considered for other homomorphic encryption schemes, as e.g. in [31], and this is the first work that considers it for CKKS.

4.3   Average-Case Noise Analysis Method

We present the main result of this section, Theorem 3, that considers the product of two Normally distributed polynomials. We then show how Theorem 3 enables us to develop the first average-case noise analysis for CKKS using Heuristic 1.

Theorem 3. *Suppose that* $Z \sim \mathrm{N}(\boldsymbol{\mu}; \rho^2 I_N)$ *and* $Z' \sim \mathrm{N}(\boldsymbol{\mu}'; \rho'^2 I_N)$, *then the polynomial product* ZZ' *(modulo* $X^N + 1$*) has mean vector* $\mathbf{E}(ZZ')$ *and covariance matrix* $\mathrm{Cov}(ZZ')$ *given by*

$$\mathbf{E}(ZZ') = \boldsymbol{\mu}^* \quad and \quad \mathrm{Cov}(ZZ') = \rho_*^2 I_N + S,$$

where $\boldsymbol{\mu}^*$ *is the polynomial product of* $\boldsymbol{\mu}$ *and* $\boldsymbol{\mu}'$, $\rho_*^2 = N\rho^2\rho'^2 + \rho'^2 \|\boldsymbol{\mu}\|_2^2 + \rho^2 \|\boldsymbol{\mu}'\|_2^2$ *and* S *is an off-diagonal matrix with entries*

$$S_{i,i'} = \rho'^2 \sum_{j=0}^{N-1} \xi(i-j)\xi(i'-j)\mu_{i-j}\mu_{i'-j} + \rho^2 \sum_{j=0}^{N-1} \xi(i-j)\xi(i'-j)\mu'_{i-j}\mu'_{i'-j},$$

for a modified sign function ξ *given by* $\xi(z) = \mathrm{Sign}(z)$ *for* $z \neq 0$ *and* $\xi(0) = 1$. *Furthermore, the components* $(ZZ')_i$ *of this polynomial product can be approximated as a Normal* $\mathrm{N}(\mu_i^*, \rho_*^2)$ *distribution.*

Theorem 3 gives the mean and covariance of the product $Y = ZZ'$, and shows the components Y_i of Y can be well-approximated as Normal. Our average-case analysis will model ZZ' as a multivariate Normal distribution of the established mean and covariance. This is expressed in Heuristic 1 and will be justified below.

Heuristic 1. *Suppose that* $Z \sim \mathrm{N}(\boldsymbol{\mu}; \rho^2 I_N)$ *and* $Z' \sim \mathrm{N}(\boldsymbol{\mu}'; \rho'^2 I_N)$. *Then, for* $\boldsymbol{\mu}^*$, ρ_*^2 *and* S *as specified in Theorem 3, the polynomial product* ZZ' *(modulo* $X^N + 1$*) can be approximated as a multivariate Normal distribution as*

$$ZZ' \sim \mathrm{N}\left(\boldsymbol{\mu}^*; \rho_*^2 I_N + S\right).$$

Small-S Assumption: To simplify our analysis, we make the assumption that the off-diagonal matrix S encountered in Theorem 3 is negligible. While we believe this assumption is reasonable in many circumstances of interest, we note that it would not hold e.g. if the mean vectors have large constant components.

Definition 3. *A covariance matrix of the form* $\rho_*^2 I_N + S$ *with constant component covariance* ρ_*^2 *and off-diagonal matrix* S *satisfies the* Small-S *assumption if this off-diagonal matrix* S *is negligible compared to* $\rho_*^2 I_N$.

Average-Case Noise Analysis: In an average-case noise analysis, we track the how the variance of the noise polynomial ϵ develops with each homomorphic operation, rather than tracking how a bound on the coefficients of ϵ develops. In our average-case noise analysis of CKKS, we consider how the variance of ϵ develops 'in the ring', i.e., in the plaintext space. Heuristic 1 shows that, in the ring, the polynomial product (modulo $X^N + 1$) of multivariate Normal vectors can be well-approximated as a multivariate Normal distribution. Moreover, under the Small-S assumption, we can model the input and output polynomials in an application of Heuristic 1 as Normal random variables of a specified component variance. This enables us to track the variance of the noise polynomial through each homomorphic operation using the results presented below in Corollary 5. Given the variance in an output ciphertext, we can then use Theorem 2 to derive a bound on the noise in the output ciphertext.

Corollary 5. *Suppose that $Z \sim N(\boldsymbol{\mu}; \rho^2 I_N)$ and $Z' \sim N(\boldsymbol{\mu}'; \rho'^2 I_N)$ are independent, λ is a constant vector. Approximations to the distribution of $Z + Z'$, λZ and the rounding $\lfloor Z \rceil$ are then given by:*

$$Z + Z' \sim N(\mathbf{0}, (\rho^2 + \rho'^2)I_N), \lambda Z \sim N\left(\lambda \boldsymbol{\mu} \; ; \; \rho^2 \|\lambda\|_2^2 I_N\right), \lfloor Z \rceil \sim N\left(\boldsymbol{\mu}, \; \rho^2 + \tfrac{1}{12}\right).$$

Furthermore, an approximation to the distribution of ZZ' when the Small-S assumption is valid for ZZ' and an approximation to the distribution of Z^2 when the Small-S assumption is valid for Z^2 are given by:

$$ZZ' \sim N\left(\boldsymbol{\mu}\boldsymbol{\mu}' \; ; \; (N\rho^2\rho'^2 + \rho'^2 \|\boldsymbol{\mu}\|_2^2 + \rho^2 \|\boldsymbol{\mu}'\|_2^2)I_N\right)$$
$$\text{and } Z^2 \sim N\left(\boldsymbol{\mu}^2 \; ; \; 2\rho^2(N\rho^2 + 2 \|\boldsymbol{\mu}\|_2^2)I_N\right).$$

4.4 Summary of Textbook Noise Heuristics

In this subsection, we summarise the noise heuristics obtained when analysing the Textbook CKKS scheme [10] according to the three different noise analysis methods presented in this work. Table 1 gives the worst-case analyses in the ring (WCR) and in the canonical embedding (CE) for Textbook CKKS [10]. Table 2 gives the average-case analysis in terms of the variance of the noise after each homomorphic operation, and illustrates how this variance could be converted to a bound on the noise in the output ciphertext using Theorem 2.

The full justification for the distributional results leading to the noise heuristics in Tables 1 and 2 is given in the full version [14]. This gives a variance for the noise polynomial after each operation, directly giving the average-case analysis. The variances can then be converted to a bound in either the canonical embedding or the ring after each operation to give the respective worst-case analyses, using Theorem 2.

The worst-case bounds developed in this work can be contrasted with the worst-case canonical embedding bounds given in prior work (as e.g. in [10]). These are restated for completeness in the full version [14].

5   Application of Methods to RNS-CKKS

In this section we discuss the application of the noise analysis methods described in Sect. 4 to RNS variants of CKKS [9,28]. We focus mainly on [9].

Table 1. Worst-case bounds for Textbook CKKS [10]. Here, B_1, B_2, and B denote input noise bounds in the ring or canonical embedding, as appropriate, and $\eta_{ks} = \sqrt{\frac{1}{12}\left(P^{-2}NQ_\ell^2\sigma^2 + \mathbb{1}_{P\nmid Q_\ell}(h+1)\right)}$.

Operation	WCR	CE
Fresh	$\sigma\sqrt{N+2h+2}\cdot H_\mathbb{R}(\alpha, N)$	$\sigma\sqrt{\frac{N^2}{2}+hN+N}\cdot H_\mathbb{C}(\alpha, N)$
Add	$B_1 + B_2$	$B_1 + B_2$
PreMult	$N\cdot\left(\|m_1\|_\infty B_2 + \|m_2\|_\infty B_1 + B_1B_2\right)$	$\|m_1\|_\infty^{\mathsf{can}} B_2 + \|m_2\|_\infty^{\mathsf{can}} B_1 + B_1B_2$
Key-Switch	$B + \sqrt{2}\cdot\eta_{ks}\cdot H_\mathbb{R}(\alpha, N)$	$B + \sqrt{N}\cdot\eta_{ks}\cdot H_\mathbb{C}(\alpha, N)$
Rescale	$\Delta^{-1}B + \sqrt{\frac{1}{6}(h+1)}\,H_\mathbb{R}(\alpha, N)$	$\Delta^{-1}B + \sqrt{\frac{N}{12}(h+1)}H_\mathbb{C}(\alpha, N)$

Table 2. Average-case noise analysis for Textbook CKKS [10]. Here, ρ_1, ρ_2, and ρ denote input noise variances. The final output variance can be converted to (e.g.) a canonical embedding bound using Theorem 2.

Operation	Output Variance	Final output bound (CE)
Fresh	$\rho_{\mathsf{fresh}}^2 = (\frac{N}{2}+h+1)\sigma^2$	$\sqrt{N}\cdot\rho_{\mathsf{fresh}}\cdot H_\mathbb{C}(\alpha, N)$
Add	$\rho_{\mathsf{add}}^2 = \rho_1^2 + \rho_2^2$	$\sqrt{N}\cdot\rho_{\mathsf{add}}\cdot H_\mathbb{C}(\alpha, N)$
PreMult	$\rho_{\mathsf{pre\text{-}mult}}^2 = N\rho_1^2\rho_2^2 + \rho_2^2\|m_1\|_2^2 + \rho_1^2\|m_2\|_2^2$	$\sqrt{N}\cdot\rho_{\mathsf{pre\text{-}mult}}\cdot H_\mathbb{C}(\alpha, N)$
Key-Switch	$\rho_{\mathsf{ks}}^2 = \rho^2 + \frac{1}{12}\left(P^{-2}NQ_\ell^2\sigma^2 + \mathbb{1}_{P\nmid Q_\ell}(h+1)\right)$	$\sqrt{N}\cdot\rho_{\mathsf{ks}}\cdot H_\mathbb{C}(\alpha, N)$
Rescale	$\rho_{\mathsf{rs}}^2 = \frac{\rho^2}{\Delta^2} + \frac{1}{12}(h+1)$	$\sqrt{N}\cdot\rho_{\mathsf{rs}}\cdot H_\mathbb{C}(\alpha, N)$

5.1 Differences from Textbook CKKS

The operations in RNS variants of CKKS are performed 'slotwise' with respect to the constituent moduli q_j making up the ℓth ciphertext modulus $Q_\ell = \prod_{j=0}^\ell q_j$. In [9], for all $0 \le j \le L$, a distinct $q_j = 1 \mod 2N$ is chosen to support NTT operations in each slot. It is also required that $\Delta/q_j \approx 1$ for all $1 \le j \le L$ and q_0 is sufficiently large for correctness. The need for distinct q_j that are not exactly equal to Δ incurs an approximation error not present in Textbook CKKS.

The changes in parameters in the RNS variants require modifications to the rescale and key switch operations. The other operations carry over to the RNS case in a more straightforward way. When rescaling from Q_ℓ to $Q_{\ell-1}$ in RNS variants, instead of dividing by Δ, we divide by q_ℓ. The key switching procedure presented in [9] translates the key switching approach of [10] to the RNS setting and so requires the large modulus P to be formed from a set of k pairwise coprime p_i as $P = \prod_{i=0}^k p_i$. We also note that a hybrid key switching is possible in the RNS setting, for example as done in [28].

The definition of noise in the RNS variant [9] also differs from the Textbook CKKS definition. A RNS ciphertext $\mathtt{ct}$ at level ℓ can be expressed as a vector of its RNS representatives $(\mathtt{ct}^{(j)})_{0 \le j \le \ell}$. The noise in a ciphertext is defined in [9] as ϵ such that $\langle\mathtt{ct}^{(0)}, \mathtt{sk}\rangle = m + \epsilon \mod q_0$.

5.2 Distribution of Noise Polynomials for the RNS Variant [9]

In this subsection we derive the distributions of the noise polynomials for the RNS variant [9] that differ from Textbook CKKS, namely, for the rescale and key switch operations. The analysis for the other operations is analogous to the Textbook CKKS case as presented in Sect. 4.4. Proofs for the results in this subsection are presented in the full version [14].

Lemma 9 [Key Switch – RNS]. *The* RNS-CKKS Key Switch *operation applied to a ciphertext at level ℓ introduces an additive error such that the output noise is given by $\epsilon_{ks} := \epsilon + \varepsilon_{ks}$ if the input noise is given by ϵ. The additive error ε_{ks} has a Normal distribution given by*

$$\varepsilon_{ks} \sim \mathrm{N}(\mathbf{0}, \eta_{ks}^2 I_N), \quad \text{where } \eta_{ks}^2 = \tfrac{1}{12} P^{-2} N Q^2 (\ell^2 + 1)\sigma^2 + \tfrac{1}{12}(k^2 + 1)(\|s\|_2^2 + 1).$$

For example, if the secret is sparse with fixed Hamming weight h, we have $\eta_{ks}^2 = \tfrac{1}{12} P^{-2} N Q^2 (\ell^2 + 1)\sigma^2 + \tfrac{1}{12}(k^2 + 1)(h + 1)$.

Lemma 10 [Rescale – RNS]. *Let* ct *be a ciphertext encrypting m with noise ϵ. Let* ct$_{rs}$ *encrypting m be the ciphertext with noise ϵ_{rs} resulting from the* Rescale *operation. The* Rescale *noise $\epsilon_{rs} \sim N(0; \rho_{rs}^2 I_N)$, where the component variance ρ_{rs}^2 is given by*

$$\rho_{rs}^2 = \frac{\rho^2}{q_\ell^2} + \left(\tfrac{1}{12}(\|s\|_2^2 + 1)\right).$$

For example, if the secret is sparse with fixed Hamming weight h, we have $\rho_{rs}^2 = \frac{\rho^2}{q_\ell^2} + \tfrac{1}{12}(h + 1)$.

5.3 Summary Tables of Noise Bounds

In this subsection, we present noise heuristics for the RNS variant [9] that were developed by applying the noise analyses of Sect. 4 to this variant. Table 3 summarises the worst-case canonical embedding and average-case noise heuristics for the RNS variant [9]. These heuristics can be justified in the same manner as explained in Sect. 4.4 for the Textbook CKKS case, using the distributional results presented in Sect. 5.2.

6 Experimental Results

In this section we evaluate the efficacy of the noise analyses developed in this work for Textbook CKKS and the RNS variant of [9] as compared with their implementations HEAAN [24] and FullRNS-HEAAN [22] respectively. We also compare the new heuristics with those obtained from a worst-case canonical embedding approach as in prior work (denoted as P-CE). The code used to generate our results is available at https://github.com/bencrts/CKKS_noise.

Table 3. Worst-case canonical embedding bounds (CE) and average-case noise analysis (CLT) for RNS CKKS [9]. Here, B_1 and B_2 denote input noise bounds in the canonical embedding; ρ_1, ρ_2, and ρ denote input noise variances; and $\eta_{ks}^2 = \frac{1}{12}P^{-2}NQ^2(\ell^2 + 1)\sigma^2 + \frac{1}{12}(k^2 + 1)(h + 1)$.

Operation	CE	Output variance (CLT)
Fresh	$\sigma\sqrt{\frac{N^2}{2} + hN + N} \cdot H_{\mathbb{C}}(\alpha, N)$	$\rho_{fresh}^2 = (\frac{N}{2} + h + 1)\sigma^2$
Add	$B_1 + B_2$	$\rho_{add}^2 = \rho_1^2 + \rho_2^2$
PreMult	$\|m_1\|_\infty^{can} B_2 + \|m_2\|_\infty^{can} B_1 + B_1 B_2$	$\rho_{pre\text{-}mult}^2 = N\rho_1^2\rho_2^2 + \rho_2^2 \|m_1\|_2^2 + \rho_1^2 \|m_2\|_2^2$
Key-Switch	$B + \sqrt{N}\,\eta_{ks}\,H_{\mathbb{C}}(\alpha, N)$	$\rho_{ks}^2 = \rho^2 + \eta_{ks}^2$
Rescale	$q_\ell^{-1}B + \sqrt{\frac{N}{12}(h + 1)}\,H_{\mathbb{C}}(\alpha, N)$	$\rho_{rs}^2 = \frac{\rho^2}{q_\ell^2} + \frac{1}{12}(h + 1)$

Experimental Framework: We run experiments in the HEAAN v1.0 [24] and FullRNS-HEAAN [22] libraries. We note that neither the Textbook CKKS nor the RNS variant noise analysis is implementation-specific, and we chose the HEAAN library as it is the implementation most closely resembles the theoretical description of both variants of the scheme.

The LWE parameters (ring dimension N, ciphertext modulus q, error standard deviation σ, secret distribution S) were set as follows. Following [1], we used $(\log_2(N), \log_2(q)) \in \{(13, 109), (14, 219), (15, 443)\}$ in HEAAN v1.0. We used $(\log_2(N), \log_2(q)) \in \{(12, 100), (13, 100), (14, 220), (15, 420)\}$ in FullRNS-HEAAN. We used $\sigma = 3.2$ and the default secret distribution in both libraries. We set the error tolerance as $\alpha = 0.0001$ and the scale parameter as $\Delta = 2^{40}$.

For FullRNS-HEAAN the moduli chains are parameterised by L and k. The bit-size of the top-level modulus is generated by FullRNS-HEAAN as $60 + (L-1) \cdot \log_2(\Delta)$. For $\log(N) \in \{13, 14, 15\}$, we choose L to allow for a top-level modulus which is close to the choices in HEAAN v1.0. For $\log(N) = 12$ we choose a modulus large enough to support one multiplication. We always set the default library selection of $k = L + 1$.

For both libraries we evaluate the following circuit, similarly to [15]. We generate fresh ciphertexts ct_0, ct_1 and ct_2 and evaluate the circuit $ct_2*(ct_1+ct_0)$, i.e. a homomorphic addition, followed by a (full) homomorphic multiplication. In each experiment, we iterate 1000 times and record the average, and maximum, observed noise. In Tables 4 and 5 we report the observed noises together with the noise predicted from the heuristics developed in this work: the average-case approach (CLT), and the worst-case heuristics (WCR and CE). We also compare with the noise predicted from the prior heuristics (P-CE). For the multiplication operation estimates we use worst-case message bounds, specifically Δ for WCR, $N\Delta^2$ for CLT, and $\frac{2N\Delta}{\pi}$ for CE.

In Table 4 we report the experimental results for HEAAN v1.0 [24] in two settings. We first (in the rows marked as 'Ring') report the observed noise in the plaintext space. In these experiments, in each trial, we generate a random plaintext with coefficients in $[-\Delta, \Delta]$, evaluate the specified circuit, and measure noise in the ring after each operation. We also (in the rows marked as 'Real' and 'Complex') report the observed noise in the message space. In Table 5 we report the experimental results for FullRNS-HEAAN [22] in the message space.

For the HEAAN v1.0 [24] and FullRNS-HEAAN [22] experiments in the message space, in each trial, we generate a vector of random numbers, encode them, encrypt them, and homomorphically evaluate the circuit as described above. Then, we decrypt and decode and measure the precision loss. The rows marked as 'Real' correspond to generating numbers with real part and imaginary part both uniform in $[0, 1]$, encoding and decoding with scale factor Δ, and reporting only the real error on the computation. The rows marks as 'Complex' correspond to generating numbers with real part and imaginary part both uniform in $[0, 1]$ and reporting the magnitude of the largest error.

While in exact schemes, it is trivial to observe the noise, this is not so straightforward for CKKS. Our methodology was to generate three plaintexts m_1, m_2 and m_3, and to run the circuit both in the plaintext space and in the ciphertext space. In other words, the noise reported in Tables 4 and Table 5 is the result of

$$((m_1 + m_2) \cdot m_3) - \text{Dec}((\text{Enc}(m_1) + \text{Enc}(m_2)) \cdot \text{Enc}(m_3)).$$

Results: The plaintext space experiments of Table 4 illustrate that for Textbook CKKS [10], the average case noise approach (CLT) introduced in this work, and our refinements to the prior worst case canonical embedding approach (CE), both improve on the heuristics given in prior work (P-CE), in the sense of predicting a value closer to the observed noise. For CLT compared to P-CE, the heuristic-to-practical gap reduces from around 8 bits to less than 1 bit. However, the CLT approach slightly underestimates the maximal noise, and sometimes slightly underestimates the maximum noise (as illustrated in the column **gap**). The WCR approach leads to a large heuristic-to-practical gap after multiplication, which we also observed in the Complex experiments (in the message space), so we omit it in the FullRNS-HEAAN experiments.

For the message space results in Table 4, the addition and multiplication results are similar for both the Real and Complex case. The CLT and CE approaches both underestimate the average and maximum noise by 3 to 7 bits. The WCR approach correctly bounds the noise: tightly for addition, but very loosely after multiplication.

The results in Table 5 illustrate that for the RNS variant of [9], the CLT approach and the CE approach both improve on the prior approach (P-CE), in the sense of predicting a value closer to the observed noise. For CLT compared to P-CE, the heuristic-to-practical gap typically reduces from around 6 bits to less than 1 bit. However, we again very frequently observe the CLT giving an underestimate. At $\log N = 14$, a jump is seen in the observed noise values, and in this case the prior approach P-CE gives a tight bound on the noise.

Discussion: Our results illustrate that, for the plaintext space for Textbook CKKS, and for the message space in the RNS variant of [9], both the average-case noise analysis introduced in this work and the refinement of the prior

Table 4. Average and maximum bits of noise observed in the ring and message space over 1000 trials in HEAAN compared with noise predicted by the CLT, WCR and CE noise analyses. The column **gap** denotes the difference between the predicted CLT noise value and the maximum experimental observation, with a negative value representing a heuristic underestimate.

$\log(N)$	$\log(q)$	Average	Maximum	CLT	WCR	CE	P-CE	gap
			Ring Addition noise.					
13	109	4.58	5.52	4.32	4.82	10.87	12.77	−1.20
14	219	4.63	5.39	4.35	4.85	11.40	13.27	−1.04
15	443	4.68	5.49	4.37	4.87	11.92	13.77	−1.12
			Ring Multiplication noise.					
13	109	5.18	6.19	5.67	19.32	12.61	14.32	−0.52
14	219	5.21	6.04	5.70	20.35	13.13	14.82	−0.34
15	443	5.27	6.09	5.72	21.37	13.66	15.32	−0.37
			Real Addition error.					
13	109	−25.37	−23.42	−29.70	−22.83	−29.13	−27.22	−6.28
14	219	−24.41	−22.55	−29.18	−21.80	−28.60	−26.72	−6.63
15	443	−23.35	−21.32	−28.65	−20.78	−28.08	−26.22	−7.33
			Real Multiplication error.					
13	109	−25.07	−23.00	−28.35	−8.33	−27.39	−25.68	−5.35
14	219	−24.03	−21.77	−27.83	−6.30	−26.87	−25.18	−6.06
15	443	−23.03	−20.98	−27.30	−4.28	−26.34	−24.68	−6.32
			Complex Addition error.					
13	109	−24.81	−23.12	−29.63	−22.83	−29.13	−27.22	−6.51
14	219	−23.81	−22.22	−29.10	−21.80	−28.60	−26.72	−6.88
15	443	−22.76	−21.17	−28.58	−20.78	−28.08	−26.22	−7.41
			Complex Multiplication error.					
13	109	−24.45	−22.52	−28.28	−8.33	−27.39	−25.68	−5.76
14	219	−23.47	−21.53	−27.75	−6.30	−26.87	−25.18	−6.22
15	443	−22.41	−20.61	−27.23	−4.28	−26.34	−24.68	−6.62

worst-case canonical embedding approach improve upon prior noise analyses in terms of modelling more closely the observed noise. Our work can thus represent an improved starting point for manual parameter selection compared to prior approaches.

However, some discrepancies can be seen between the observed results and the predictions from the heuristic analyses. For example, in the multiplication results in the ring in Table 4, the WCR respectively CE bounds seem to increase by 1 respectively 0.5 bits as $\log N$ increases by 1 bit, while the average observed noise shows a much slower growth. As another example, in the message space results in Table 4, the prior canonical embedding approach (P-CE) also leads

Table 5. Average and maximum bits of noise observed in the message space over 1000 trials in FullRNS-HEAAN compared with noise predicted by the CLT, CE and P-CE noise analyses. The column **gap** denotes the difference between the predicted CLT noise value and the maximum experimental observation, with a negative value representing a heuristic underestimate.

$\log(N)$	$\log(q)$	L	k	Average	Maximum	CLT	CE	P-CE	gap
				Real Addition error.					
12	100	2	3	−24.38	−24.21	−24.25	−23.63	−18.89	−0.04
13	100	2	3	−23.16	−22.93	−23.23	−22.61	−17.89	−0.30
14	220	5	6	−22.07	−21.75	−22.21	−21.59	−16.89	−0.46
15	420	10	11	−21.00	−20.74	−21.19	−20.57	−15.89	−0.45
				Real Multiplication error.					
12	100	2	3	−21.86	−21.80	−22.96	−21.62	−17.39	−1.16
13	100	2	3	−21.70	−21.41	−21.94	−20.61	−16.39	−0.53
14	220	5	6	−17.79	−17.67	−20.92	−19.59	−15.39	−3.25
15	420	10	11	−16.77	−16.73	−19.90	−18.57	−14.39	−3.17
				Complex Addition error.					
12	100	2	3	−24.03	−23.78	−24.17	−23.63	−18.89	−0.39
13	100	2	3	−22.83	−22.42	−23.16	−22.61	−17.89	−0.74
14	220	5	6	−21.84	−21.52	−22.14	−21.59	−16.89	−0.62
15	420	10	11	−20.76	−20.57	−21.12	−20.57	−15.89	-0.55
				Complex Multiplication error.					
12	100	2	3	−21.17	-21.08	−22.88	−21.62	−17.39	−1.80
13	100	2	3	−21.03	−20.95	−21.86	−20.61	−16.39	−0.91
14	220	5	6	−16.94	−16.82	−20.84	−19.59	−15.39	−4.02
15	420	10	11	−15.93	−15.90	-19.82	−18.57	−14.39	−3.92

to underestimates of the predicted noise. Moreover, in the multiplication results of Table 5, there seems to be a jump in the observed noise after $\log N = 14$, whereas the noise heuristics all grow more smoothly as $\log N$ grows. This means that, for larger $\log N$, the P-CE approach gives a correct and tight noise growth prediction, while for smaller $\log N$, the CLT and CE approaches give a closer prediction of the observed noise. This discussion suggests a fundamental issue with the modelling in all existing noise analysis approaches, including those prior to this work, suggesting that a refined theory of CKKS noise is needed.

One of the most crucial observations is that our heuristics underestimate the noise growth in many places (denoted by negative **gap** values in Tables 4 and 5). Similar underestimates have been observed in the literature before [3,16]. In more detail, the authors of [3] show that an average-case analysis of the BFV scheme that assumes independence of the coefficients of the noise leads to underestimates of the multiplication noise, and they develop a correcting function to account for this discrepancy. The authors of [16] compare experimental results of the BGV scheme as implemented in HElib to the theoretical bounds from the work of [29], and observe that the latter also underestimates the noise growth in practice. In contrast, the implementation-specific analysis of [16] is shown to very closely match the observed noise growth. Our heuristics are not specific to the implementations in HEAAN v1.0 [24] or Full-RNS HEAAN [22], and assumptions on which the heuristics rely may not hold for each implementation. For example, our experiments indicate that in HEAAN v1.0 [24] (though not in Full-RNS HEAAN [22]), the independence heuristic between coefficients of the noise polynomial fails at encryption. We believe that developing implementation-specific noise analyses for CKKS is an important direction for future work.

References

1. Albrecht, M., et al.: Homomorphic encryption security standard. HomomorphicEncryption.org, Technical report (2018)
2. Al Badawi, A., et al.: Openfhe: open-source fully homomorphic encryption library. Cryptology ePrint Archive, Paper 2022/915 (2022). https://eprint.iacr.org/2022/915
3. Biasioli, B., Marcolla, C., Calderini, M., Mono, J.: Improving and automating BFV parameters selection: an average-case approach. Cryptology ePrint Archive, Paper 2023/600 (2023). https://eprint.iacr.org/2023/600
4. Boemer, F., Costache, A., Cammarota, R., Wierzynski, C.: ngraph-he2: a high-throughput framework for neural network inference on encrypted data. In: Brenner, M., Lepoint, T., Rohloff, K. (eds.) Proceedings of the 7th ACM Workshop on Encrypted Computing & Applied Homomorphic Cryptography, WAHC@CCS 2019, London, UK, 11–15 November 2019, pp. 45–56. ACM (2019)
5. Brakerski, Z., Gentry, C., Vaikuntanathan, V.: (Leveled) fully homomorphic encryption without bootstrapping. In: Goldwasser, S. (ed.) ITCS 2012, pp. 309–325. ACM (2012)
6. Brisebarre, N., Joldeş, M., Muller, J.-M., Naneş, A.-M., Picot, J.: Error analysis of some operations involved in the cooley-tukey fast fourier transform. ACM Trans. Math. Softw. (TOMS) **46**(2), 1–27 (2020)
7. Chen, H., Dai, W., Kim, M., Song, Y.: Efficient multi-key homomorphic encryption with packed ciphertexts with application to oblivious neural network inference. In: Cavallaro, L., Kinder, J., Wang, X.F., Katz, J. (eds.) ACM CCS 2019, pp. 395–412. ACM Press (2019)
8. Cheon, J.H., Han, K., Kim, A., Kim, M., Song, Y.: Bootstrapping for approximate homomorphic encryption. In: Nielsen, J.B., Rijmen, V. (eds.) EUROCRYPT 2018. LNCS, vol. 10820, pp. 360–384. Springer, Cham (2018). https://doi.org/10.1007/978-3-319-78381-9_14
9. Cheon, J.H., Han, K., Kim, A., Kim, M., Song, Y.: A full RNS variant of approximate homomorphic encryption. In: Cid, C., Jacobson Jr, M.J. (eds.) SAC 2018, vol. 11349 of LNCS, pp. 347–368. Springer, Heidelberg (2019). https://doi.org/10.1007/978-3-030-10970-7_16
10. Cheon, J.H., Kim, A., Kim, M., Song, Y.: Homomorphic encryption for arithmetic of approximate numbers. In: Takagi, T., Peyrin, T. (eds.) ASIACRYPT 2017. LNCS, vol. 10624, pp. 409–437. Springer, Cham (2017). https://doi.org/10.1007/978-3-319-70694-8_15

11. Chillotti, I., Gama, N., Georgieva, M., Izabachène, M.: Faster fully homomorphic encryption: bootstrapping in less than 0.1 seconds. In: Cheon, J.H., Takagi, T. (eds.) ASIACRYPT 2016. LNCS, vol. 10031, pp. 3–33. Springer, Heidelberg (2016). https://doi.org/10.1007/978-3-662-53887-6_1

12. Chillotti, I., Gama, N., Georgieva, M., Izabachène, M.: TFHE: fast fully homomorphic encryption over the torus. J. Cryptology **33**(1), 34–91 (2020)

13. Costache, A., Smart, N.P.: Which ring based somewhat homomorphic encryption scheme is best? In: Sako, K. (ed.) CT-RSA 2016. LNCS, vol. 9610, pp. 325–340. Springer, Cham (2016). https://doi.org/10.1007/978-3-319-29485-8_19

14. Costache, A., Curtis, B.R., Hales, E., Murphy, S., Ogilvie, T., Player, R.: On the precision loss in approximate homomorphic encryption. Cryptology ePrint Archive, Paper 2022/162 (2022). https://eprint.iacr.org/2022/162

15. Costache, A., Laine, K., Player, R.: Evaluating the effectiveness of heuristic worst-case noise analysis in FHE. In: Chen, L., Li, N., Liang, K., Schneider, S. (eds.) ESORICS 2020. LNCS, vol. 12309, pp. 546–565. Springer, Cham (2020). https://doi.org/10.1007/978-3-030-59013-0_27

16. Costache, A., Nürnberger, L., Player, R.: Optimisations and tradeoffs for helib. In: Topics in Cryptology-CT-RSA 2023: Cryptographers' Track at the RSA Conference 2023, San Francisco, CA, USA, 24–27 April 2023, Proceedings, pp. 29–53. Springer, Heidelberg (2023). https://doi.org/10.1007/978-3-031-30872-7_2

17. Damgård, I., Pastro, V., Smart, N., Zakarias, S.: Multiparty computation from somewhat homomorphic encryption. In: Safavi-Naini, R., Canetti, R. (eds.) CRYPTO 2012. LNCS, vol. 7417, pp. 643–662. Springer, Heidelberg (2012). https://doi.org/10.1007/978-3-642-32009-5_38

18. Fan, J., Vercauteren, F.: Somewhat practical fully homomorphic encryption. Cryptology ePrint Archive, Report 2012/144 (2012). http://eprint.iacr.org/2012/144

19. Gentry, C.: Fully homomorphic encryption using ideal lattices. In: Mitzenmacher, M. (ed.) 41st ACM STOC, pp. 169–178. ACM Press (2009)

20. Gentry, C., Halevi, S., Smart, N.P.: Homomorphic evaluation of the AES circuit. In: Safavi-Naini, R., Canetti, R. (eds.) CRYPTO 2012. LNCS, vol. 7417, pp. 850–867. Springer, Heidelberg (2012). https://doi.org/10.1007/978-3-642-32009-5_49

21. Halevi, S., Shoup, V.: Design and implementation of HElib: a homomorphic encryption library. Cryptology ePrint Archive, Report 2020/1481 (2020). https://eprint.iacr.org/2020/1481

22. Fullrns-heaan. https://github.com/KyoohyungHan/FullRNS-HEAAN. Version as at October 2018

23. Heaan v2.1. https://github.com/snucrypto/HEAAN. Version as at September 2021

24. Heaan v1.0. https://github.com/snucrypto/HEAAN/releases/tag/1.0. Version as at September 2018

25. HElib. https://github.com/shaih/HElib. Version as at January 2019

26. Iliashenko, I.: Optimisations of fully homomorphic encryption. PhD thesis, KU Leuven (2019)

27. Kim, A., Song, Y., Kim, M., Lee, K., Cheon, J.H.: Logistic regression model training based on the approximate homomorphic encryption. BMC Med. Genom. **11**(4), 83 (2018)

28. Kim, A., Papadimitriou, A., Polyakov, Y.: Approximate homomorphic encryption with reduced approximation error. In: Galbraith, S.D. (ed.) CT-RSA 2022. LNCS, vol. 13161, pp. 120–144. Springer, Cham (2022). https://doi.org/10.1007/978-3-030-95312-6_6

29. Kim, A., Polyakov, Y., Zucca, V.: Revisiting homomorphic encryption schemes for finite fields. In: Tibouchi, M., Wang, H. (eds.) ASIACRYPT 2021. LNCS, vol. 13092, pp. 608–639. Springer, Cham (2021). https://doi.org/10.1007/978-3-030-92078-4_21

30. Lattigo v2.2.0. http://github.com/ldsec/lattigo. Version as at July 2021. EPFL-LDS

31. Lepoint, T., Naehrig, M.: A comparison of the homomorphic encryption schemes FV and YASHE. In: Pointcheval, D., Vergnaud, D. (eds.) AFRICACRYPT 2014. LNCS, vol. 8469, pp. 318–335. Springer, Cham (2014). https://doi.org/10.1007/978-3-319-06734-6_20

32. Lee, Y., Lee, J.W., Kim, Y.S., Kim, Y., No, J.S., Kang, H.: High-Precision Bootstrapping for Approximate Homomorphic Encryption by Error Variance Minimization. In: Dunkelman, O., Dziembowski, S. (eds.) EUROCRYPT 2022. LNCS, vol. 13275, pp. 551–580. Springer, Cham (2022). https://doi.org/10.1007/978-3-031-06944-4_19

33. Li, B., Micciancio, D., Schultz, M., Sorrell, J.: Securing approximate homomorphic encryption using differential privacy. In: Annual International Cryptology Conference, pp. 560–589. Springer, Heidelberg (2022). https://doi.org/10.1007/978-3-031-15802-5_20

34. Li, B., Micciancio, D.: On the security of homomorphic encryption on approximate numbers. In: Canteaut, A., Standaert, F.-X. (eds.) EUROCRYPT 2021. LNCS, vol. 12696, pp. 648–677. Springer, Cham (2021). https://doi.org/10.1007/978-3-030-77870-5_23

35. Murphy, S., Player, R.: A central limit framework for ring-lwe decryption. Cryptology ePrint Archive, Report 2019/452 (2019). https://eprint.iacr.org/2019/452

36. Murphy, S., Player, R.: Discretisation and product distributions in Ring-LWE. J. Math. Cryptol. 15(1), 45–59 (2021)

37. Ogilvie, T., Player, R., Rowell, J.: Improved privacy-preserving training using fixed-hessian minimisation. In: Brenner, M., Lepoint, T. (eds.) Proceedings of the 8th Workshop on Encrypted Computing and Applied Homomorphic Cryptography (WAHC 2020) (2020). https://doi.org/10.25835/0072999

38. PALISADE Lattice Cryptography Library (release 1.11.5). https://palisade-crypto.org/. Accessed Sept 2021

39. Regev, O.: On lattices, learning with errors, random linear codes, and cryptography. J. ACM (JACM) 56(6), 1–40 (2009)

40. Microsoft SEAL (release 3.6). Microsoft Research, Redmond, WA. https://github.com/Microsoft/SEAL. Version as at November 2020

Secure Function Extensions to Additively Homomorphic Cryptosystems

Mounika Pratapa$^{(\boxtimes)}$ and Aleksander Essex

Western University, London, Canada
{mpratapa,aessex}@uwo.ca

Abstract. The number-theoretic literature has long studied the question of distributions of sequences of quadratic residue symbols modulo a prime number. In this paper, we present an efficient algorithm for generating primes containing chosen sequences of quadratic residue symbols and use it as the basis of a method extending the functionality of additively homomorphic cryptosystems.

We present an algorithm for encoding a chosen Boolean function into the public key and an efficient two-party protocol for evaluating this function on an encrypted sum. We demonstrate concrete parameters for secure function evaluation on encrypted sums up to eight bits at standard key sizes in the integer factorization setting. Although the approach is limited to applications involving small sums, it is a practical way to extend the functionality of existing secure protocols built on partially homomorphic encryption schemes.

Keywords: Secure computation · Additive homomorphic encryption · Quadratic residues · Residue symbol sequences

1 Introduction

Ever since Yao's Millionaires' problem [29], distrusting parties have been computing things of mutual interest without sharing their respective inputs. Secure function evaluation (SFE) has many interesting applications in areas such as privacy-preserving machine learning [24], private information retrieval [10], similarity search in private databases such as genotype and other medical data [25], online voting [2], auctions [11] and private credit checking [18].

Despite recent advances in fully homomorphic encryption, *partially* homomorphic schemes (i.e., those offering homomorphic operations with respect to a single operation) still play an important role in secure computation. For example, Switzerland requires internet-based elections to be cryptographically verifiable[1] and the first certified implementation is based around mix nets built from additively homomorphic encryption.[2]

---

[1] Swiss Federal Chancellery Ordinance on Electronic Voting. Available: https://www.fedlex.admin.ch/eli/cc/2022/336/en.

[2] The Swiss Post E-voting System. Available: https://gitlab.com/swisspost-evoting.

C. Carlet et al. (Eds.): SAC 2023, LNCS 14201, pp. 346–366, 2024.
https://doi.org/10.1007/978-3-031-53368-6_17

In applications where partially homomorphic encryption is sufficient, such schemes can offer more clear-cut parameterizations, more mature hardness assumptions, more straightforward implementations, and faster executions relative to their fully homomorphic counterparts.

This paper presents a method for extending the functionality of additive homomorphic encryption schemes (specifically those with efficient full decryption) by working in groups containing sequences of quadratic residues and non-residues with a correspondence to a chosen Boolean function. Given an encrypted value $\mathsf{Enc}(x)$ and a Boolean function $f : \mathbb{Z}_t \to \{0,1\}$, we present an efficient method for homomorphically evaluating $\mathsf{Enc}(f(x))$ in a single public-key operation across a short (but non-trivial) interval $0 \leq x < t$.

Let $\mathsf{QR} : \mathbb{Z} \times \mathbb{Z} \to \{0,1\}$ be a function testing the quadratic residuosity of an integer $x \in \mathbb{Z}_p$, defined as

$$\mathsf{QR}(x,p) = \begin{cases} 0 & \text{if } x \text{ is a quadratic residue modulo } p. \\ 1 & \text{otherwise.} \end{cases}$$

Given $f(\cdot)$ and an integer sequence of the form $[\alpha x + \beta \mid 0 \leq x < t, \text{ and } \alpha, \beta > 0]$, our approach involves three components:

1. An efficient algorithm for finding a prime p for which

$$\mathsf{QR}(\alpha x + \beta, p) = f(x).$$

2. An additively homomorphic public-key cryptosystem embedding the required quadratic residue symbol sequence into the plaintext space, i.e., $\mathcal{M} \subset \mathbb{Z}_p$.
3. A public homomorphic operation that can blind the encryption of $\alpha x + \beta$ while preserving its quadratic residue symbol modulo p (and hence the output of the function $f(x)$).

Taken together, these components allow $f(x)$ to be securely evaluated on an encrypted sum in the range $0 \leq x < t$ for small (but non-trivial) values of t in a single public-key operation.

Previously, patterns in quadratic residues have been exploited for the evaluation of specific functions such as secure integer comparison [17], sign function evaluation [1,30], and threshold functions [16]. However, secure evaluation of *arbitrary* functions using quadratic residue patterns appears to be a novel direction. Our work extends the approach of [16] to the general case.

Contribution. We present an algorithm for generating primes with arithmetic sequences containing chosen quadratic residue symbols. These sequences extend the functionality of additively homomorphic cryptosystems and generalize the approach to secure evaluation of arbitrary functions by generating the candidate primes that facilitate the required quadratic residue symbol sequences. Using an additively homomorphic scheme with efficient full decryption (such as the schemes due to Paillier [22] and Okamoto-Uchiyama [21]), given an encrypted sum $\mathsf{Enc}(x)$, we present parameters for evaluating arbitrary functions $\mathsf{Enc}(f(x))$ for x up to $t = 256$ at the 4096-bit prime range and sums up to $t = 512$ where larger public-keys are acceptable.

2   Related Work

Finding patterns in quadratic residues and non-residues has been a subject in the number theory literature for a long time. Gauss posed the problem of finding the smallest quadratic non-residue n_p modulo a prime p [19], and papers over the past century have continued to refine this bound, most recently by Carella [8] showing $n_p \ll (\log p)(\log \log p)$.

Much of the subsequent literature has focused on distributions of consecutive runs of residues and non-residues, providing bounds on the size of a prime necessary to observe a specified run length. For some $a \geq \frac{1}{4}\sqrt{e}$, a sequence of length $p^{1/4}$ for a given p contains at least one residue and one non-residue according to Burgess [7]. Research has long explored primes with at least ℓ consecutive quadratic residues or non-residues. Studies by Brauer [5] and Davenport [14] examined arbitrary combinations of residues and non-residues, but these were restricted to very short sequences ($t < 10$).

Records for run lengths were improved with the rise of scientific computing in the 1980s. For example, Buell [6] experimentally studied the smallest primes exhibiting a consecutive sequence of ℓ residues followed by ℓ non-residues. For a residue symbol sequences of the form $\mathsf{QR}(a + x, p)$ for $0 \leq x < t$, they achieved $\ell = 9$ and thus $t = 18$ for $p = 414463$.

Since there are an equal number of residues and non-residues modulo an odd prime p, the probability that a particular integer will be a residue or non-residue would be $1/2$ across all primes if the distribution were uniform and random. Peralta [23] presented the probability of finding an arbitrary residue symbol sequence modulo p given the length of sequence t and found it deviates from random by a factor no more than $t(3 + \sqrt{p})/p$. Later research exploited the random-looking distributions of residue symbols for applications in watermarking [4] and pseudorandom bit generators [13, 26, 27], approximate pattern matching [15].

While there are several interesting applications exploiting the patterns in quadratic residues, Feige et al. [17] proposed a minimal model for secure integer comparison by exploiting the fact that, for $p = 7$, the Legendre symbols $\left(\frac{x}{p}\right) \forall x = a - b \mid a, b \in [-2, 2]$ coincide with the sign function of $x \in [-2, 2]$. Following this, improved secure function evaluation protocols were proposed [1, 30] to evaluate sign function by generating primes with the required quadratic residue symbol patterns modulo a prime number, specifically a Blum prime ($p \equiv 3 \bmod 4$). However, both these approaches [1, 30] rely on finding consecutive long runs of quadratic residues alone, thus only useful to perform secure comparison based on sign function. The work in [16] used brute force to search for consecutive sequences of ℓ residues followed by ℓ non-residues, where the quadratic residuosity function is calculated as $\mathsf{QR}(x + a, p)$. The maximum value attained in this approach is $t = 52$, for $a = 1134844$ and $p = 2269739$. Such runs were exploited to evaluate the threshold function, i.e., a Heaviside function $H(x)$, which is off until $x = c$.

Our approach. As we prove in the next section, the number of primes exhibiting a given residue symbol sequence is infinite. However, in contrast to previous work, instead of relying on the Legendre symbols of consecutive numbers modulo a prime p, we present parameters to find arithmetic sequences of the form $\alpha x + \beta$, which can be used to generate primes toward secure evaluation of an arbitrary function with an integer domain and Boolean range.

3   Cryptographic Preliminaries

Let f be a function where, $f : \mathbb{Z}_t \to \{0,1\}$ is defined over an integer input x for $0 \leq x < t$. Our objective is to securely evaluate f without revealing its inputs. To achieve this, we present relevant notations and an algorithm that can provably generate primes embedding arithmetic residue symbol sequences that implement f. Such primes are useful to extend the functionality of additively homomorphic cryptosystems.

Definition 1 (Legendre Symbol). *The Legendre symbol is a function* $L : \mathbb{Z} \times \mathbb{Z} \mapsto \{-1, 0, 1\}$ *defined as:*

$$\left(\frac{x}{p}\right) \equiv \begin{cases} 1 & \text{if } x \text{ is quadratic residue mod } p \\ -1 & \text{if } x \text{ is quadratic non-residue mod } p \\ 0 & \text{if } x \equiv 0 \bmod p. \end{cases}$$

It can be directly established that the quadratic residuosity function $\mathsf{QR} : \mathbb{Z} \times \mathbb{Z} \to \{0,1\}$, as defined in the introduction:

$$\mathsf{QR}(x, p) = \begin{cases} 0 & \text{if } x \text{ is a quadratic residue modulo } p. \\ 1 & \text{otherwise.} \end{cases}$$

is a modification of the Legendre symbol's co-domain where

$$\mathsf{QR}(x, p) = \frac{\left(\frac{x}{p}\right) + 1}{2}.$$

Since the Legendre symbol is a completely multiplicative function of its top argument, so is the quadratic residuosity function.

3.1   Linear Embeddings of Boolean Functions in Residue Sequences

We deal with the following functions:

- A function $f : \mathbb{Z}_t \to \{0,1\}$ that needs to be securely evaluated over an input x, for $0 \leq x < t$ and $t \in \mathbb{Z}^+$.
- The quadratic residuosity function $\mathsf{QR} : \mathbb{Z} \times \mathbb{Z} \to \{0,1\}$ for secure evaluation of f.

– A mapping function $h : \mathbb{Z} \to \mathbb{Z}_p$, that maps an input x into $h(x) = (\alpha x + \beta) \bmod p$. Here, $\{\alpha, \beta\} \in \mathbb{Z}^+$ and are given as input parameters to facilitate the application of QR function.

We are interested in locating primes p which contain some residue symbol sequences modulo a prime p that imitate the range of f. In other words, given and integers $\{\alpha, \beta\}$ we are looking for some p that can compute:

$$QR(h(x), p) = f(x)$$

for $0 \leq x < t$.

Approach to Secure Computation. We can homomorphically evaluate f using an additive scheme as follows. Let $\mathsf{CS} = \{\mathsf{Gen}, \mathsf{Enc}, \mathsf{Dec}\}$ be an additively homomorphic public-key cryptosystem that display the following homomorphisms:

$$\mathsf{Enc}(x_1) \cdot \mathsf{Enc}(x_2) = \mathsf{Enc}(x_1 + x_2 \bmod p)$$

and

$$\mathsf{Enc}(x_1)^{x_2} = \mathsf{Enc}(x_1 x_2 \bmod p).$$

Given an encrypted value $\mathsf{Enc}(x)$ in the range $0 \leq x < t$, and an $\alpha, \beta > 0$, one can homomorphically compute $\mathsf{Enc}(h(x))$ as follows:

$$\mathsf{Enc}(h(x)) = \mathsf{Enc}(x)^{\alpha} \cdot \mathsf{Enc}(\beta) = \mathsf{Enc}(\alpha x + \beta \bmod (p)).$$

Applying the quadratic residue function to the decryption $\mathsf{Enc}(h(x))$ yields.

$$QR(\mathsf{Dec}(\mathsf{Enc}(h(x))), p) = QR(h(x), p) = f(x).$$

This demonstrates the basic mechanics of the secure evaluation of f. Clearly, however, the decrypter could recover x from seeing $h(x)$, and thus a homomorphic blinding function will be presented later in Sect. 4.

3.2   Prime Numbers with Chosen Residue Symbol Sequences

We begin with the Legendre symbol as a standard notation and later re-frame the discussion in terms of a quadratic residuosity function QR. To proceed further, we propose two theorems.

Theorem 1. *Given a list of t distinct primes $\{a_1, \ldots, a_t\}$ and a list of Legendre symbols $\{\ell_1, \ldots, \ell_t\}$ where $\ell_x \in \{-1, 1\}$. For all $1 \leq x \leq t$, a prime p can be generated such that*

$$\left(\frac{p}{a_x}\right) = \ell_x.$$

Proof. The proof proceeds in two parts. In the first part, we prove the existence of an integer p' containing the chosen residue symbol sequence. In the second part, we prove the existence of p' implies the existence of a prime p with the same properties. Because each a_x is prime, each $0 < b_x < a_x$ is to be co-prime to a_x, Chinese Remainder Theorem guarantees the existence of a unique solution p' to the system of congruences formed by $[a_x], [b_x]$:

$$p' \equiv b_0 \bmod a_0$$
$$\vdots$$
$$p' \equiv b_t \bmod a_t.$$

Since

$$\left(\frac{b_x}{a_x}\right) = \ell_x, \text{ and} p' \equiv b_x \bmod a_x,$$

for each $1 \leq x < t$ we have

$$\left(\frac{p'}{a_x}\right) = \ell_x.$$

Now we show the existence of an integer p' implies the existence of a prime p with the same congruences. Since $p \equiv p' \bmod A_{prod}$, and therefore $p \equiv b_x \bmod a_x$, then

$$\left(\frac{p}{a_x}\right) = \ell_x.$$

Finally, since p' is relatively prime to A_{prod}, Dirichlet's theorem guarantees there are infinitely many primes of the form $k A_{prod} + p'$.   □

Theorem 2. *For all $t \in \mathbb{Z}^+$ and all functions $f : \mathbb{Z}_t \to \{0, 1\}$ there exists a prime p and two integers $0 < \alpha, \beta < p$ such that for all $0 \leq x < t$*

$$\frac{\left(\dfrac{\alpha x + \beta}{p}\right) + 1}{2} = f(x)$$

where $\left(\frac{\alpha x + \beta}{p}\right)$ denotes the Legendre symbol of $\alpha x + \beta$ modulo p.

Proof. Let α, β, t be positive integers such that $\alpha x + \beta$ is prime for all $0 \leq x < t$. The existence of such an α, β is guaranteed for all $t > 0$ by a theorem due to Green and Tao [20], which proves the primes contain arbitrarily long arithmetic sequences, and, therefore, there exists an α, β for all $t > 0$ such that $\alpha x + \beta$ is prime for all $0 \leq x < t$. Given such a linear sequence of $(\alpha x + \beta)$'s where all of them are prime valued,[3] Theorem 1 guarantees there exists a prime p such that for all $0 \leq x < t$,

$$\left(\frac{p}{\alpha x + \beta}\right) = 2f(x) - 1.$$

---

[3] Requiring all $(\alpha x + \beta)$ be prime is only done to facilitate the existence proof. In practice, Algorithm Gen (see Sect. 4.1) can generate suitable keypairs in the presence of composite $(\alpha x + \beta)$'s.

Suppose there existed a p such that $p \equiv 1 \bmod 4$. By the law of quadratic reciprocity,

$$\left(\frac{\alpha x + \beta}{p}\right) = \left(\frac{p}{\alpha x + \beta}\right) = 2f(x) - 1, \tag{1}$$

and therefore,

$$f(x) = \frac{\left(\dfrac{\alpha x + \beta}{p}\right) + 1}{2}.$$

In the alternate case where all such primes p were congruent to 3 mod 4, Theorem 1 also guarantees there exists a prime p such that

$$\left(\frac{p}{\alpha x + \beta}\right) = \begin{cases} 2f(x) - 1 & \text{if } \alpha x + b \equiv 1 \bmod 4 \\ 1 - 2f(x) & \text{if } \alpha x + b \equiv 3 \bmod 4. \end{cases}$$

For all $\alpha x + \beta \equiv 1 \bmod 4$, quadratic reciprocity again gives us

$$\left(\frac{\alpha x + \beta}{p}\right) = \left(\frac{p}{\alpha x + \beta}\right) = 2f(x) - 1.$$

Finally, for all $\alpha x + \beta \equiv 3 \bmod 4$,

$$\left(\frac{\alpha x + \beta}{p}\right) = -\left(\frac{p}{\alpha x + \beta}\right) = -(1 - 2f(x)) = 2f(x) - 1.$$

Therefore

$$f(x) = \frac{\left(\dfrac{\alpha x + \beta}{p}\right) + 1}{2} \tag{2}$$

for all $0 \le x < t$. □

4   Our Cryptosystem

Let $\mathsf{CS} = \{\mathsf{Gen}, \mathsf{Enc}, \mathsf{Dec}, \mathsf{Add}, \mathsf{Smul}, \mathsf{Eval}\}$ be an additively homomorphic public-key cryptosystem. Let $\mathcal{M}$ be the plaintext space and $m \in \mathcal{M}$ be a message. Without loss of generality and for the sake of a concrete description, we build CS based on the cryptosystem due to Okomoto and Uchiyama [21], which has a message space cardinality $|\mathcal{M}| = p$ for a large prime p. Given pre-computed sequence parameters α, β, and a Boolean function $f : \mathbb{Z}_t \to \{0,1\}$ we define CS with the following functionalities:

- $\mathsf{Gen}(1^\rho, \alpha, \beta, f)$: Outputs secret key $\mathcal{SK} = \{p, q\}$ and public key $\mathcal{PK} = \{n\}$ where $n = p^2 q$. Here p is chosen such that $\mathsf{QR}(\alpha x + \beta, p) = f(x)$ for $0 \le x < t$. To facilitate efficient generation for non-trivial values of t, p is generated using the algorithm presented in Sect. 4.1. By contrast, q is randomly chosen using standard methods. Both $|p| = |q| = \lambda$, where λ is a standard length at the ρ-bit security level in the integer factorization setting.

- Enc($\mathcal{PK}, m$): Encryption function accepting a public key $\mathcal{PK}$, plaintext m and outputting a ciphertext $c = [\![m]\!]$.
- Dec($\mathcal{SK}, c$): Decryption function accepting a private key $\mathcal{SK}$, ciphertext $c = [\![m]\!]$ and outputting plaintext m.
- Add(c_1, c_2): Homomorphic addition accepting two encrypted messages $c_1 = [\![m_1]\!]$ and $c_2 = [\![m_2]\!]$ and outputting a ciphertext $c' = [\![(m_1 + m_2) \bmod p]\!]$.
- Smul(s, c): Scalar homomorphic multiplication accepting a ciphertext $c_1 = [\![m_1]\!]$ and a scalar m_2, outputting a ciphertext $c' = [\![(m_1 m_2) \bmod p]\!]$.

The properties of CS can be further used to securely evaluate f on an encrypted plaintext. Toward that end, a sixth functionality Eval, is defined:

- Eval($\mathcal{PK}, \alpha, \beta, c$): Secure evaluation of f on an encrypted plaintext $c = [\![m]\!]$. First, a non-zero blinding parameter r_c is uniformly sampled from the message space $\mathcal{M}$. Since $\mathcal{M} = \mathbb{Z}_p$ and p is a private value, we sample uniformly from the public interval $r_c \leftarrow [1, 2^\lambda]$.[4] The function computes:

$$\mathsf{Smul}(r_c^2, \mathsf{Add}(\mathsf{Smul}([\![m]\!], \alpha), \mathsf{Enc}(\beta))) = [\![r_c^2 \cdot (\alpha m + \beta) \bmod p]\!].$$

Note that decrypting $[\![(\alpha m + \beta) \bmod p]\!]$ directly would reveal m, as α, β are public. Hence, a blinding operation is applied to randomize this value while preserving its residuosity. The result of Eval is the encryption of uniform quadratic residue in $\mathbb{Z}_p$ if $\mathsf{QR}(\alpha m + \beta) = 1$, and a uniform non-residue otherwise. The output of Eval can then be decrypted by the private key holder and the quadratic residuosity of the plaintext tested to reveal the outcome of $f(m)$.

4.1 Key Generation

To securely evaluate a function of the form $f : \mathbb{Z}_t \mapsto \{0, 1\}$, we work in an additive group modulo a prime p which contains an arithmetic sequence $S \subset \mathbb{Z}_p^*$ such that for each $s_m \in S$, $\mathsf{QR}(s_m) = f(m)$, or, in Legendre symbol form, where:

$$\left(\frac{s_m}{p}\right) = 1 - 2 \cdot f(m).$$

This section describes a method for generating a prime p containing such a sequence.[5]

Step 1: Let $S = \{s_m \mid s_m = \alpha m + \beta, 0 \leq m < t\}$ be an odd sequence for some $\alpha, \beta \in \mathbb{Z}^+$.

---

[4] If implementing CS based on an additive cryptosystem in which $|\mathcal{M}| = n$ is a public value, such as in the case of DGK [12] or Paillier [22], blinding factor r_c can be chosen from $\mathbb{Z}_n$.

[5] See our Python3 implementation of the key generation algorithm with example parameters: https://github.com/mounikapratapa/SFEPHE.

Step 2: For each $s_m \in S$, let $s_{m,0}^{(e_{m,0})}, \ldots, s_{m,\rho_m}^{(e_{m,\rho_m})}$ represent all of the prime factors of s_m for which $e_{m,j}$ is an odd power.[6] The multiplicative properties of the Legendre symbol give us

$$\left(\frac{s_m}{p}\right) = \left(\frac{s_{m,0}^{(e_{m,0})} \cdot \ldots \cdot s_{m,\rho_m}^{(e_{m,\rho_m})}}{p}\right) = \left(\frac{s_{m,0}}{p}\right) \cdot \ldots \cdot \left(\frac{s_{m,\rho_m}}{p}\right) = 1 - 2 \cdot f(m)$$

This can be rewritten in terms of applications of QR by replacing multiplications with additions when expressing the factorization of individual sequence elements:

$$QR(s_m, p) = QR(s_{m,0}, p) + \ldots + QR(s_{m,\rho_m}, p) \equiv f(m) \bmod 2. \qquad (3)$$

Expressing residues and non-residues in this form (i.e., as an addition modulo 2) instead of Legendre symbols (as a multiplication of signs) allows us to obtain a system of equations capturing the relationship between the unique prime factors of a sequence element and the function evaluated at that position.

Step 3: Let $A = \{a_0, \ldots, a_{u-1}\}$ represent the set of u unique prime factors from the combined set of all sequence factors $s_{m,j}$ across all sequence elements s_m. That is, $a_i \in A$ if there is some s_m such that $a_i \mid s_m$ and $a_i \nmid s_j$ for all other $j \neq m$. Non-unique factors will not be utilized in this calculation and are assigned a fixed, implicit target residue symbol of 1. For each sequence element $s_m \in S$ and each unique prime factor $a_j \in A$, we define a function $d(a_j, s_m)$ such that

$$d(a_j, s_m) = \begin{cases} 1 & \text{if } a_j \mid s_m \\ 0 & \text{otherwise.} \end{cases}$$

Step 4: Define a $(t \times u)$ matrix M. Let the last column represent function f evaluated at m. Form an augmented matrix representing the system of equations arising from Equation (3):

$$\begin{array}{c} \\ s_0 \\ s_1 \\ \vdots \\ s_{t-1} \end{array} \begin{pmatrix} a_0 & a_1 & \cdots & a_{u-1} & \\ d(a_0, s_0) & d(a_1, s_0) & \cdots & d(a_{u-1}, s_0) & f(0) \\ d(a_0, s_1) & d(a_1, s_1) & \cdots & d(a_{u-1}, s_1) & f(1) \\ \vdots & \vdots & \vdots & \vdots & \vdots \\ d(a_0, s_{t-1}) & d(a_1, s_{t-1}) & \cdots & d(a_{u-1}, s_{t-1}) & f(t-1) \end{pmatrix}$$

Step 5: Using Gaussian elimination, convert M into reduced row echelon form, i.e., compute $M' \leftarrow \text{RREF}(M)$. If the system of equations implied by M' is consistent and exactly determined, each $a_j \in A$ implies a

---

[6] Factors $s_{m,j}^{e_{m,j}}$ of even power will have a fixed residue symbol of 1 and are excluded from the generation algorithm (having no bearing on the outcome).

residue value $\sigma_j \in \{0,1\}$ which will satisfy the overall requirement that $\mathsf{QR}(s_m) = f(m)$ for $0 \leq m < t$. If the system is consistent and *under-determined*, select a single valid solution uniformly at random and proceed to Step 6. Otherwise repeat the same process from Step 1 with a different α, β.

Step 6: For each factor $a_j \in A$ and each residue value $\sigma_j \in \{0,1\}$ computed in the previous step, select b_j uniformly from $[1, a_j)$ such that $\mathsf{QR}(b_j, a_j) = \sigma_j$.

Step 7: For each pair a_j, b_j, apply Chinese remaindering to compute a p' satisfying the following system of congruences:

$$p' \equiv b_0 \bmod a_0$$
$$p' \equiv b_1 \bmod a_1$$
$$\vdots$$
$$p' \equiv b_{u-1} \bmod a_{u-1}.$$

Step 8: Compute:

$$p \leftarrow k\left(\prod_{j=0}^{u-1} a_j\right) + p'$$

for $k \xleftarrow{R} [k_{min}, k_{max}]$ sampled uniformly from the largest interval such that $|p| = \lambda$.

Step 9: If $p \equiv 1 \bmod 4$ and p is prime, continue to the next step, otherwise repeat Steps 6–8 until such a p is found.

Step 10: Generate a random prime q of length λ using a standard generation method suitable for the integer factorization setting.

Step 11: Output p, q.

4.2   Encryption and Decryption

We recall the Okamoto-Uchiyama cryptosystem [21], which is the basis for CS.

Key Generation: Run the key generation algorithm in Sect. 4.1 to obtain large primes p, q. Compute $n = p^2 q$. Select a uniform $g \in \{2, \ldots, n-1\}$ such that:

$$g^{p-1} \not\equiv 1 \bmod p^2.$$

Set $h \leftarrow g^n \bmod n$. Return $\mathcal{SK} \leftarrow \{p, q\}$ and $\mathcal{PK} \leftarrow \{n, g, h\}$.

Observe: $\mathbb{Z}_n^*$ is a cyclic group of order $p(p-1)(q-1)$. Let us define two subgroups: $\mathbb{G}_p \subset \mathbb{Z}_n^*$, the subgroup of order p, and $\mathbb{G}_\phi \subset \mathbb{Z}_n^*$, the subgroup of order $\phi = (p-1)(q-1)$. An isomorphism $\mathbb{Z}_n^* \cong \mathbb{G}_p \times \mathbb{G}_\phi$ exists such that $g \in \mathbb{Z}_n^*$ can be rewritten as $g_p g_\phi \bmod n$, for some $g_p \in \mathbb{G}_p$ and $g_p \in \mathbb{G}_\phi$ respectively. Thus g has order $p \cdot \phi$ whereas $h = g^n = g^{p^2 q} = g_p^{p^2 q} g_\phi^{p^2 q} = g_p^0 g_\phi^{p^2 q} \equiv g_\phi^{\hat{r}} \bmod n$ has order ϕ.

Encryption: A plaintext $0 \leq m < p$ is encrypted as follows. Uniformly sample $r \leftarrow \mathbb{Z}_n^*$. Output:

$$c \leftarrow g^m h^r \bmod n.$$

Observe: Following our notation, $c = (g_p g_\phi)^m (g_\phi^{\hat{r}})^r = g_p^m g_\phi^{m + \hat{r}r} \equiv g_p^m g_\phi^{\bar{r}} \bmod n$. In other words, m is captured in the subgroup of order p and $g_\phi^{\bar{r}}$ is indistinguishable from a uniform element in $\mathbb{G}_\phi$.

Decryption: A ciphertext c is decrypted as follows. First compute

$$\hat{c} \leftarrow c^\phi \bmod n.$$

Observe: $\hat{c} = c^\phi = (g_p^m g_\phi^{\bar{r}})^\phi = (g_p^m)^\phi (g_\phi^{\bar{r}})^\phi = g_p^{m\phi} g_\phi^0 = g_p^{m\phi} \bmod n$.

Compute the discrete logarithm of $g_p^{m\phi}$ to recover $m\phi$. An efficient algorithm exists for computing discrete logarithms in $\mathbb{G}_p \subset \mathbb{Z}_{p^2 q}^*$ given knowledge of p (which we omit for space). Finally, compute

$$(m\phi) \cdot \phi^{-1} \equiv m \bmod p$$

and return m.

4.3   Correctness of the Evaluation Function

The Eval function defined in Sect. 4 is used to homomorphically evaluate $[\![f(m)]\!]$ on encrypted plaintext $[\![m]\!]$.

Theorem 3. *Given* $c = \mathsf{Enc}(m)$, $\mathsf{QR}(\mathsf{Dec}(\mathcal{SK}, \mathsf{Eval}(\mathcal{PK}, \alpha, \beta, c)), p) = f(m)$ *in the range* $0 \leq m < t$.

Proof. Given ciphertext $c = \mathsf{Enc}(m)$, a blinding factor r_c sampled from the public interval $r_c \leftarrow [1, 2^\lambda]$, and public sequence parameters α, β, Eval computes:

$$c' = \mathsf{Eval}(\mathcal{PK}, \alpha, \beta, c) = (c^\alpha \cdot [\![\beta]\!])^{r_c^2} \bmod n$$

$$= ([\![m]\!]^\alpha \cdot [\![\beta]\!])^{r_c^2}$$

$$= [\![(\alpha m + \beta) \cdot r_c^2]\!].$$

Decrypting c' returns $(\alpha m + \beta) \cdot r_c^2 \bmod p$. Therefore applying the QR-function to the decryption result we have

$$\mathsf{QR}((\alpha m + \beta) \cdot r_c^2, p) = \mathsf{QR}(\alpha m + \beta, p) \cdot \mathsf{QR}(r_c^2, p)$$

$$= f(m) \cdot 1$$

$$= f(m).$$

$\square$

5   Semantic Security of CS

We prove that CS is semantically secure under common hardness assumptions. While CS partially depends on the semantic security of the underlying Okamoto-Uchiyama [21] cryptosystem, the key-generation algorithm has been modified from the general case by the quadratic residuosity function. Here we argue that the modified key-generation function does not affect the semantic security of the underlying cryptosystem. First, we recall some definitions.

Definition 2. *A function $f : \mathbb{N} \mapsto \mathbb{R}$ is negligible with respect to $n \in \mathbb{N}$, if for all positive polynomials p, there exists some $M \in \mathbb{Z}$ such that it holds $f(n) < \frac{1}{p(n)}$ every time $n > M$.*

Definition 3. *Given an encryption function $\mathsf{Enc}_k(m)$, message length $|m|$, random number r and a security parameter 1^n, a cryptosystem CS is semantically secure if there exists a pair of probabilistic polynomial time algorithms $\mathcal{A}$ and $\mathcal{A}'$ such that, for every such pair:*

$$Pr[\mathcal{A}(1^n, \mathsf{Enc}_k(m), r) = m] - Pr[\mathcal{A}'(1^n, |m|, r) = m] < \frac{1}{p(n)}.$$

Note that $\mathcal{A}$ has access to the ciphertext $\mathsf{Enc}_k(m)$, where as $\mathcal{A}'$ has access only to the message length $|m|$, while the rest of the information both the algorithms have access to remain equal. Intuitively, the above definition thus implies that the ciphertext $\mathsf{Enc}_k(m)$ does not reveal any additional information about the underlying plaintext message.

Now, we proceed to establish the security proof of CS involving quadratic residuosity function by proving that the semantic security of the cryptosystem CS reduces to deciding the quadratic residuosity of a plaintext message m modulo a prime p, i.e., $\mathsf{QR}(m, p)$.

Definition 4. *Given $a \in \mathbb{Z}_n^*$ and $n = p^2 q$ for unknown p, q, the p-th residue decision problem, denoted as $PRDP$, is the problem of deciding if there exists a b such that $a \equiv b^p \bmod n$.*

The semantic security of Okamoto-Uchiyama cryptosystem can be stated in terms of the $PRDP$. Particularly, for a message $m = 0$, the ciphertext $c = \mathsf{Enc}(0)$ is a p-th residue modulo n, since $c = g^0 h^r = h^r \bmod n$. Recall from Sect. 4.2 that $h = g^n = g^{p^2 q} \bmod n$ is a p-th residue.

Definition 5. *Given $\mathsf{Enc}(m)$ and an unknown p, the quadratic residuosity mod p decisional problem, denoted as $QRPDP$, is the computational problem of determining whether m is a quadratic residue modulo p, computing $\mathsf{QR}(m, p)$.*

Theorem 4. *The p-th residue decision problem is polynomially reducible to the quadratic residuosity decision problem, i.e., $PRDP \leq_p QRPDP$.*

Proof. Let $\mathcal{A}$ be an algorithm computing the quadratic residuosity of message $QR(m, p)$. For a key-size λ and a ciphertext $c = \mathsf{Enc}(m)$, we construct an algorithm $\mathcal{B}(c)$ that returns *True* if c is a p-th residue modulo in a polynomial factor of $\mathcal{A}$'s runtime with non-negligible advantage.

---

function $\mathcal{B}(c)$
  Uniformly sample $\gamma \xleftarrow{R} [1, 2^{\lambda}]$
  Compute $c' \leftarrow c \cdot \mathsf{Enc}(\gamma^2)$
  if $\mathcal{A}(c') == False$ **then**
    return *False*
  end if
  return *True*
end function

function $\mathcal{A}(c)$
  Given $c = \mathsf{Enc}(m)$
  Compute $y \leftarrow QR(m, p)$
  return y
end function

Algorithm: $\mathcal{B}$ Algorithm: $\mathcal{A}$

Consider the case when $m = 0$. $QR(0 + \gamma^2) = QR(0) \cdot QR(\gamma^2) = 1 \cdot 1 = 1$ for all γ. Therefore

$$Pr[\mathcal{B}(c) = True \,|\, m = 0] = 1.$$

For any other value of $m > 0$, the output of $\mathcal{B}(c)$ depends on the residuosity of $(m + \gamma^2)$, which in turn depends on the distribution of quadratic residues modulo p, giving us

$$Pr[\mathcal{B}(c) = True \,|\, m > 0] = \left(\frac{1}{2}\right) + \epsilon.$$

The overall probability

$$
\begin{aligned}
Pr[\mathcal{B}(c) = True \,|\, m \leftarrow [0, \lambda]] &= (Pr[\mathcal{B}(c) = True \,|\, m = 0] \cdot Pr[m = 0]) \\
&\quad + (Pr[\mathcal{B}(c) = True \,|\, m > 0] \cdot Pr[m > 0]) \\
&= \left(1 \cdot \frac{1}{2^{\lambda}}\right) + \left(\left(\frac{1}{2} + \epsilon\right) \cdot \left(1 - \frac{1}{2^{\lambda}}\right)\right) \geq \epsilon
\end{aligned}
$$

is non-negligible. This implies that as long as the semantic security of underlying encryption scheme holds, the $QR()$ function does not reveal any additional information about the underlying plaintext message.   □

Security in the Presence of Factor Base $[a_x]$. Since the input parameters α, β and the range of $f(x)$ are public, it is easy to determine the sequence and factor base $[a_x]$. The array $[b_x]$ used for CRT is chosen randomly and it remains hidden. Since the chosen $[b_x]$ and k varies with each iteration of the key-generation algorithm, this adds additional randomness to the choice of primes.

Leaking the Quadratic Residuosity of Elements in $\mathbb{Z}_p$. The public nature of α, β and the function $f(x)$ creates access to a limited oracle that provides information about quadratic residuosity $QR(x,p)$ for t elements, where t is the function size. Due to this reason, the security of our system relies on a slightly weaker assumption than factoring $n = p^2q$. The alternate hardness assumption we propose here is factoring $n = p^2q$ in the presence of the quadratic residuosity oracle $QR(x,p)$. Although the information provided by such an oracle is highly restricted relative to $\mathbb{Z}_n$, whether this information can be exploited to factorize n remains an open question and requires further cryptanalytic efforts.

6 Protocol

Protocol π is conducted between two semi-honest parties P_A and P_B. Let P_A input a vector of plaintexts $X = \{x_1, \ldots, x_a\}$ and P_B input a vector of plaintexts $Y = \{y_1, \ldots, y_b\}$ for $x_i, y_j \in \mathcal{M}$. Let $CS = \{Gen, Enc, Dec, Add, Smul, Eval\}$ be an additively homomorphic cryptosystem with the functionalities defined in Sect. 4. Let P_A be the holder of the private-key $\mathcal{SK}$.

Since our protocol is framed as an *extension* of existing protocols based on additive schemes (e.g., vector addition, weighted sums etc.). We begin by defining a sub-protocol π_{sub}, which capturing the existing protocol conducted on X and Y using the conventional functionalities $\{Enc, Add, Smul\}$. Suppose the output of π_{sub} results in P_A receiving a single ciphertext $[\![m]\!]$ where m represents the nominal outcome of π_{sub}. Protocol π extends π_{sub} with the Eval functionality to homomorphically compute $f(m)$ given $[\![m]\!]$. The full protocol π is presented in Fig. 1.

Public: Public-key $\mathcal{PK}$, sequence parameters $\{\alpha, \beta\}$, $f : \mathbb{Z}_t \mapsto \{0,1\}$, the description of a secure sub-protocol π_{sub} invoking conventional additively homomorphic functionalities $Enc, Add, Smul$.
Private Input (P_A): Plaintexts $X = \{x_1, \ldots, x_a\}$. Private key $\mathcal{SK} = \{p, q\}$.
Private Input (P_B): Plaintexts $Y = \{y_1, \ldots, y_b\}$.
Output: Given $[\![m]\!] \leftarrow \pi_{sub}(X, Y)$, P_A learns $f(m)$. P_B learns $\perp$.

- P_A, P_B : Run $\pi_{sub}(X, Y)$. P_B receives $[\![m]\!]$ as output. P_A receives $\perp$.
- P_B : Compute:
$$c' \leftarrow Eval(\mathcal{PK}, \alpha, \beta, [\![m]\!]).$$
- $P_B \rightarrow P_A$: P_B sends c' to P_A.
- P_A : Decrypt $c' \leftarrow Dec(\mathcal{SK}.c')$ to obtain $m' \leftarrow (\alpha \cdot m + \beta) \cdot r_c^2$.
- P_A : Compute $QR(m', p) = f(m)$.

Fig. 1. Secure Function Evaluation Protocol π

Theorem 5. *The secure evaluation of function $f : \mathbb{Z}_t \mapsto \{0,1\}$ by the protocol π is correct.*

Proof. From Theorem 3 we previously established that $\mathsf{QR}(\mathsf{Dec}(\mathcal{SK}, c'))$ returns $f(m)$ as

$$\mathsf{QR}(\mathsf{Dec}(\mathcal{SK}, c'), p)) = f(m).$$

6.1 Participant Privacy During the Protocol π

Participant privacy while running the protocol π in two party setting guarantees that there is no inadvertent leakage of information in the presence of semi-honest adversaries. Such adversaries follow the protocol exactly but try to learn more information than allowed based on their respective inputs and any intermediate transcripts during the protocol execution. To formalize this idea, we adopt privacy by simulation approach by creating the view of the parties without the knowledge of any keys. Security proof is established by constructing a simulator S that generates a view for adversary that is computationally indistinguishable from its real view. Privacy by simulation requires certain notations to proceed further.

- $f = (f_{P_A}, f_{P_B})$ is the two-party functionality that is computed by the protocol π.
- The view of P_A and P_B denoted as $View^\pi_{P_A}$ and $View^\pi P_B$ are defined as:

$$\mathsf{View}^\pi_{P_A}(x) = (x_{P_A}, r_{P_A}, m_{P_B}),$$

$$\mathsf{View}^\pi_{P_B}(x) = (x_{P_B}, r_{P_B}, m_{P_A}).$$

where, $x = (x_{P_A}, x_{P_B})$ represent the inputs of the participants to the protocol, $r = (r_{P_A}, r_{P_B})$ are the random values generated during the transaction and $m = (m_{P_A}, m_{P_B})$ are the messages sent by the respective parties during the protocol.
- We say that π securely computes f in the presence of a semi-honest adversary if we are able to construct the algorithms S_{P_B} to simulate P_B's view to establish P_A's privacy and S_{P_A} to simulate P_A's view to establish P_B's privacy.

P_A's **Privacy** For P_A's privacy, we need to establish that P_B's view is simulatable given P_B's input x_{P_B} and output $f_{P_B}(x_{P_A}, x_{P_B}) = \perp$. We have output by P_A denoted as $\mathsf{Output}^\pi_{P_A}$, which is a result of the execution of protocol π on the combined input from both the parties.

Theorem 6 (P_A's **privacy**). *There exists a probabilistic polynomial time algorithm S_{P_B} such that*

$$\left[S_{P_B}(x_{P_B}, \perp), f(x_{P_A}, x_{P_B})\right] \stackrel{c}{\equiv} \left[\mathsf{View}^\pi_{P_B}, \mathsf{Output}^\pi_{P_A}(x)\right].$$

where $\stackrel{c}{\equiv}$ indicates ciphertext indistinguishability.

Proof. The proof of P_A's privacy is simple because P_B only receives the ciphertext $c = \mathsf{Enc}(x)$, i.e., $m_{P_A} = c$. To simulate P_B's view the simulator just needs to sample the messages of the form $c \leftarrow \mathbb{Z}_n^*$. Due to the semantic security of the CS, it is easy to establish that a ciphertext $c = \mathsf{Enc}(x)$ is computationally indistinguishable from an element of $\mathbb{Z}_n^*$. S_{P_B} can now compute the output using public key $\mathcal{PK}$, c and P_B's input x_{P_B} and computing $f(x_{P_A}, x_{P_B})$ homomorphically, thereby simulating $View_{P_B}$. $\square$

6.2 P_B's Privacy

We rely on the similar approach to the proof of P_A's privacy. We establish that $View_{P_A}$ is simulatable given P_A's input denoted as x_{P_A}. Note that, the privacy proof relies on the hiding properties of blinding factor b. Let $QR, NR \subset \mathbb{Z}_n$ respectively denote the subsets of quadratic residues and non-residues modulo prime n. P_A decrypts ciphertext c', this results in random looking message $m' = (f(x_{P_A}, x_{P_B})\alpha + \beta) \cdot r_c^2 \bmod n$ where r_c is a uniform element modulo n and thus r_c^2 is uniform in QR.

Theorem 7 (P_B's privacy). *There exists a probabilistic polynomial time algorithm S_{P_A} such that*

$$[S_{P_A}(x_{P_A}, f(x_{P_A}, x_{P_B}))] \overset{c}{\equiv} [\mathsf{View}_{P_A}^\pi, \bot]$$

Proof. Algorithm S_{P_A} will begin by directly computing encryptions using $\mathcal{PK}$ and the P_A's input x_{P_A} and outputs $f(x_{P_A}, x_{P_B})$. S_{P_A} now computes the quadratic residuosity using $\mathsf{QR}(f(x_{P_A}, x_{P_B}))$ to check for the output, for 0 the decrypted plaintext would be of the form $m' \in NR$. S_{P_A} samples $m' \leftarrow_R NR$ for each $0 \le j < k-1$ and computes the corresponding ciphertexts $c = \mathsf{Enc}(m')$ using $\mathcal{PK}$. If $f(m) = 1$, then, plaintext would be of the form $m \in QR$. If $(f(x_{P_A}, x_{P_B})\alpha + \beta)$ is a quadratic residue (resp. non-residue), then the term $(f(x_{P_A}, x_{P_B})\alpha + \beta) \cdot r_c^2$ is indistinguishable from a random element in QR (resp. NR) as proved in [16], implying m' values are indistinguishable from a real-world plaintext $(f(x_{P_A}, x_{P_B})\alpha + \beta) \cdot r_c^2 \bmod p$. $\square$

7   Results and Discussion

7.1   Experiments

We implemented all the experiments in Python3 on a local Intel i7 quad-core processor @ 1.8 GHz with 8 GB RAM.

Finding Sequence Parameters α, β. As part of the key generation algorithm in Sect. 4.1, our goal is to find some linear sequence defined by $s_m = \alpha m + \beta$ and some prime p for which the Legendre symbol of s_m modulo p matches a given Boolean function evaluated at $f(m)$ over $0 \le m < t$.

For this to be true for all possible Boolean functions f, we require the residue symbols of each s_m to be, in essence, independently programmable. This is not possible for most sequences. For example, the factorization of elements of the sequence $3m + 2$ is: $2, 5, 2^3, 11, \ldots$. Here, no matter what prime p is chosen, the Legendre symbol of s_0 is always the same as s_2. Conversely, the factorization of $4m + 3$ is: $3, 7, 11, 3 \cdot 5, \ldots$. Here, no matter the Legendre symbol of s_0, the symbol for s_3 can be set independently by choosing a prime p for which 5 has the necessary symbol to give s_3 the required symbol to match $f(3)$.

In general, we can independently "program" each symbol of the sequence so long as each s_m contains at least one unique odd-powered prime factor. This condition is simple and sufficient, although not strictly necessary (cf. steps 3–5 of Sect. 4.1)

We took a brute-force approach to finding sequence parameters α, β for different values of t. We began with the smallest step size (α) and starting point (β), incrementing β across a heuristically chosen intervals at each function size t. For example, at $t = 512$, we searched in the range $\alpha < 6000, \beta < 100$ and recorded the parameters yielding the minimal bit-length $|p|$. These parameters are not optimal. The goal was to demonstrate practical, concrete values of α, β. Finding more efficient algorithms and computing optimal bounds on $|p|$ is left to future work.

For each candidate α/β, we generated the sequence $[\alpha x + \beta]$ for $0 \leq x < t$. We factored each sequence element, and for each prime factor $(s_m)^{e_m}$ for which e_m is odd, we added s_m to the set factors A as defined in Step 3 of Sect. 4.1. Let the product of this set be $\prod A$. Since $p > \prod A$ (see step 8 in Sect. 4.1), we set $|p| = \lceil \log_2(\prod A) \rceil$ representing the lower bound of $|p|$. For each domain cardinality t, we report the α, β leading to the smallest $|p|$ found in our search. For example, the linear sequence formed by $\alpha = 342, \beta = 787$ contains unique factors sufficient to produce sub 3000-bit primes for evaluating 8-bit Boolean functions. See Table 1 for our experimentally found sequence parameters.

Generating Prime p . Once suitable α, β are found, the steps to find p are implemented according to the key-generation algorithm described in Sect. 4.1. We ran our implementation of the key generation function Gen for various function sizes. From table 2, the most time is taken to iteratively find the right set of b_x. To speed up this step, we built a look up table containing sets of all quadratic residues and non-residues with respect to each a_x and for each iteration, the suitable b_x is randomly chosen. Additionally, the CRT step has to be computed each time we find a new set of b_x's. CRT has complexity $O((S_1 + S_2)^2)$, where S_i denotes the number of digits in the modulus, making it proportional to the number of congruences.

We also performed the comparison of our approach with its predecessor from [16]. Whereas the previous work focused on a specific function class (thresholds), our approach works across the entire class of Boolean functions, and at larger domain sizes. In fact, due to the usage of pre-determined α, β values, generating the right prime for the largest function size of 512 took less than 2 minutes, including all the steps. The search-based approach introduced in [16] takes more than 20 min to produce a sequence of size 26.

Table 1. Sample α, β

Domain cardinality t	α	β	$|p|$ (bits)
8	2	27	46
16	6	29	97
32	20	53	263
64	84	305	719
128	90	197	1218
256	342	787	2858
512	1938	31	7066

Table 2. Run times for Gen

Function size (domain cardinality t)	512	256	128	50
Gaussian Elimination	0.236	0.078	0.015	0.004
Test for consistency	0.016	0.009	0.002	0.001
Finding the right b_x	87.30	21.00	3.900	0.560
CRT	25.24	3.6	0.142	0.062

7.2 An Example Case of Secure Function Evaluation Using π

Our scheme has several potential applications that involve secure function evaluation. Specifically, we eliminate the need to display intermediate computations to either party involved in the transaction. For example: in case of similar patients query, the state of the art approaches [3,9,25,28,31] using either homomorphic encryption or other multiparty computation techniques require several communication rounds to retrieve the records of patients sharing similar genetic makeup. To reduce the communication overhead, they display the similarity score for each record directly to the querying party leading to regression based database re-identification attacks. There is a scope for such attacks in other applications such as secure machine learning inference, especially in classification problems. Our scheme can be applied to display the class labels directly while hiding intermediate scores. To test the performance of our parameters, we implemented a simple secure function evaluation on threshold functions protocol from Sect. 6. The threshold function denoted as $\tau_t(x)$ is similar to that of the one implemented in [16]. Note that we implemented the same threshold function to demonstrate the efficiency of our protocol. However, we can implement any function with a boolean co-domain using the same protocol. The range of a threshold function is $\{0, 0, 0, ..., 1, 1, 1\}$, with a maximum length of k. For a fixed threshold value t, the inputs to Gen would be $\{\alpha, \beta, f(x) = \{0\}_{x=0}^{t} \parallel \{1\}_{x=t+1}^{k}\}$. With p, q from Gen and $n = p^2 q$, compute $g \in 2, \cdots, n - 1$ such that $g^{p-1} \not\equiv 1 \bmod p^2$ and $h = g^n \bmod n$. Finally, $\mathcal{PK} = (\alpha, \beta, n, g, h)$ and $\mathcal{SK} = (p, q)$. Similar to the work in [16], the protocol uses Dice coefficient as a similarity metric to perform linkage between two datasets that consist of user names. The records are linked approximately to address any variations or errors in the strings being compared. Accordingly, the records will be considered a match if the Dice coefficient between two strings is above a threshold value. The protocol is performed between two parties P_A, P_B as shown below. The details for sub-protocols 1 and 2 can be referred from [16]. The difference with our protocol is during computing the evaluation function, which is in Step 6 of sub-protocol 2 in [16]. Particularly, Protocol 1 in [16] is modified as follows:

- **Public parameters:** $\mathcal{PK}, \alpha, \beta$ and for a threshold value t maximum set cardinality μ, where $\mu = t$
- **Private parameters:** Party P_A holds a list of strings $[a_1, \ldots, a_n]$ and private keys. Party P_B holds a list of strings $[b_1, \ldots, b_n]$
- P_A, P_B produce set intersection cardinalities between the private inputs using sub-protocol 1 from [16]
- By modifying the final step in sub-protocol 2 in [16] both parties compute threshold dice coefficient d_{ij} such that $d_{ij} = \mathsf{Eval}(\mathcal{PK}, \alpha, \beta, [\![\theta_{\ell_b}]\!]) = (([\![\theta_{\ell_b}]\!])^\alpha \cdot \beta)^{r_c^2}$
- **Output:** For all threshold dice coefficient values, if $\mathsf{QR}(\mathsf{Dec}(\mathcal{SK}, d_{ij}), p) = 1$, P_A outputs the index.

For a given threshold function, we can compute the dice-coefficient for more precise threshold values compared to [16]. Due to the ability of Gen to generate primes as per the $f(x)'$s range, we can compute any kind of functions securely unlike the approaches in [1, 16, 30] (see table 3).

Table 3. Comparison between secure function evaluation protocols that rely on the runs of quadratic residues.

Performance Indicator	Noisy Legendre Symbol [1]	Yu's Protocol [30]	Residue PHE [16]	Our Protocol
Domain cardinality (t)	623	$\Omega(log(p))$	26	512
Residue symbol sequence type	$\{1\}^t$	$\{1\}^t$	$[0]^t \,\|\, [1]^t$	$\{0,1\}^t$
Secure function evaluation type	Specific (sign functions)	Specific (sign functions)	Specific (thresholds)	General (Boolean)

8   Conclusion

This paper discusses a method to extend the functionality of additively homomorphic schemes in applications where the encrypted sum is below a threshold t

based on chosen patterns on quadratic residues modulo a prime. We developed a novel algorithm to encode such patterns into the private keys of cryptosystems in the integer factorization setting. We presented a protocol with concrete parameterizations for efficiently evaluating arbitrary Boolean functions on encrypted sums up to $t = 512$.

Future work will seek to push the domain cardinality t to higher values and will also explore the possibility of integrating of this technique in the fully homomorphic setting.

References

1. Abspoel, M., Bouman, N.J., Schoenmakers, B., de Vreede, N.: Fast secure comparison for medium-sized integers and its application in binarized neural networks. In: Matsui, M. (ed.) CT-RSA 2019. LNCS, vol. 11405, pp. 453–472. Springer, Cham (2019). https://doi.org/10.1007/978-3-030-12612-4_23
2. Adida, B.: Helios: web-based open-audit voting. In: USENIX Security Symposium, vol. 17, pp. 335–348 (2008)
3. Asharov, G., Halevi, S., Lindell, Y., Rabin, T.: Privacy-preserving search of similar patients in genomic data. In: Proceedings on Privacy Enhancing Technologies, vol. 2018, no. 4, pp. 104–124 (2018)
4. Atallah, M.J., Wagstaff Jr, S.S.: Watermarking with quadratic residues. In: Security and Watermarking of Multimedia Contents, vol. 3657, pp. 283–288. International Society for Optics and Photonics (1999)
5. Brauer, A.: Combinatorial methods in the distribution of k-th. power residues. Comb. Math. Appl. 14–37 (1969)
6. Buell, D.A., Hudson, R.H.: On runs of consecutive quadratic residues and quadratic nonresidues. BIT Numer. Math. 24(2), 243–247 (1984)
7. Burgess, D.A.: The distribution of quadratic residues and non-residues. Mathematika 4(2), 106–112 (1957)
8. Carella, N.A.: Consecutive quadratic residues and quadratic nonresidue modulo p. arXiv preprint arXiv:2011.11054 (2020)
9. Cheng, K., Hou, Y., Wang, L.: Secure similar sequence query on outsourced genomic data. In: Proceedings of the 2018 on Asia Conference on Computer and Communications Security, pp. 237–251 (2018)
10. Chor, B., Goldreich, O., Kushilevitz, E., Sudan, M.: Private information retrieval. In: Proceedings of IEEE 36th Annual Foundations of Computer Science, pp. 41–50. IEEE (1995)
11. Damgard, I., Geisler, M., Kroigaard, M.: Homomorphic encryption and secure comparison. Int. J. Appl. Cryptogr. 1(1), 22–31 (2008)
12. Damgård, I., Geisler, M., Krøigaard, M.: Efficient and secure comparison for online auctions. In: Pieprzyk, J., Ghodosi, H., Dawson, E. (eds.) ACISP 2007. LNCS, vol. 4586, pp. 416–430. Springer, Heidelberg (2007). https://doi.org/10.1007/978-3-540-73458-1_30
13. Damgård, I.B.: On the randomness of legendre and jacobi sequences. In: Goldwasser, S. (ed.) CRYPTO 1988. LNCS, vol. 403, pp. 163–172. Springer, New York (1990). https://doi.org/10.1007/0-387-34799-2_13
14. Davenport, H.: On the distribution of quadratic residues (mod p). J. Lond. Math. Soc. 1(1), 49–54 (1931)

15. Egidi, L., Manzini, G.: Better spaced seeds using quadratic residues. J. Comput. Syst. Sci. **79**(7), 1144–1155 (2013)
16. Essex, A.: Secure approximate string matching for privacy-preserving record linkage. IEEE Trans. Inf. Forensics Secur. **14**(10), 2623–2632 (2019)
17. Feige, U., Killian, J., Naor, M.: A minimal model for secure computation. In: Proceedings of the Twenty-Sixth Annual ACM Symposium on Theory of Computing, pp. 554–563 (1994)
18. Frikken, K., Atallah, M., Zhang, C.: Privacy-preserving credit checking. In: Proceedings of the 6th ACM Conference on Electronic Commerce, pp. 147–154 (2005)
19. Gauss, C.F.: Disquisitiones arithmeticae, vol. 157. Yale University Press, Yale (1966)
20. Green, B., Tao, T.: The primes contain arbitrarily long arithmetic progressions (2004)
21. Okamoto, T., Uchiyama, S.: A new public-key cryptosystem as secure as factoring. In: Nyberg, K. (ed.) EUROCRYPT 1998. LNCS, vol. 1403, pp. 308–318. Springer, Heidelberg (1998). https://doi.org/10.1007/BFb0054135
22. Paillier, P.: Public-key cryptosystems based on composite degree residuosity classes. In: International Conference on the Theory and Applications of Cryptographic Techniques, pp. 223–238. Springer, Heidelberg (1999). https://doi.org/10.1007/3-540-48910-x_16
23. Peralta, R.: On the distribution of quadratic residues and nonresidues modulo a prime number. Math. Comput. **58**(197), 433–440 (1992)
24. Riazi, M.S., Weinert, C., Tkachenko, O., Songhori, E.M., Schneider, T., Koushanfar, E.: Chameleon: a hybrid secure computation framework for machine learning applications. In: Proceedings of the 2018 on Asia Conference on Computer and Communications Security, ASIACCS '18, pp. 707–721. Association for Computing Machinery, New York (2018)
25. Salem, A., Berrang, P., Humbert, M., Backes, M.: Privacy-preserving similar patient queries for combined biomedical data. In: Proceedings on Privacy Enhancing Technologies, vol. 2019, no. 1, pp. 47–67 (2019)
26. Sárközy, A.: On finite pseudorandom binary sequences and their applications in cryptography. Tatra Mt. Math. Publ. **37**, 123–136 (2007)
27. Sárközy, A., Stewart, C.L.: On pseudorandomness in families of sequences derived from the legendre symbol. Period. Math. Hung. **54**(2), 163–173 (2007)
28. Schneider, T., Tkachenko, O.: Episode: efficient privacy-preserving similar sequence queries on outsourced genomic databases. In: Proceedings of the 2019 ACM Asia Conference on Computer and Communications Security, pp. 315–327 (2019)
29. Yao, A.C.C.: How to generate and exchange secrets. In: 27th Annual Symposium on Foundations of Computer Science (SFCS 1986), pp. 162–167. IEEE (1986)
30. Yu, C.H.: Sign modules in secure arithmetic circuits. Cryptology ePrint Archive (2011)
31. Zhu, R., Huang, Y.: Efficient privacy-preserving general edit distance and beyond. IACR Cryptol. ePrint Arch. **2017**, 683 (2017)

Public-Key Cryptography

Generalized Implicit Factorization Problem

Yansong Feng[1,2], Abderrahmane Nitaj[3(✉)], and Yanbin Pan[1,2(✉)]

[1] Key Laboratory of Mathematics Mechanization, Academy of Mathematics
and Systems Science, Chinese Academy of Sciences, Beijing, China
`panyanbin@amss.ac.cn`
[2] School of Mathematical Sciences, University of Chinese Academy of Sciences,
Beijing, China
[3] Normandie Univ, UNICAEN, CNRS, LMNO, 14000 Caen, France
`abderrahmane.nitaj@unicaen.fr`

Abstract. The Implicit Factorization Problem (IFP) was first introduced by May and Ritzenhofen at PKC'09, which concerns the factorization of two RSA moduli $N_1 = p_1 q_1$ and $N_2 = p_2 q_2$, where p_1 and p_2 share a certain consecutive number of least significant bits. Since its introduction, many different variants of IFP have been considered, such as the cases where p_1 and p_2 share most significant bits or middle bits at the same positions. In this paper, we consider a more generalized case of IFP, in which the shared consecutive bits can be located at *any* positions in each prime, not necessarily required to be located at the same positions as before. We propose a lattice-based algorithm to solve this problem under specific conditions, and also provide some experimental results to verify our analysis.

Keywords: Implicit Factorization Problem · Lattice · LLL
algorithm · Coppersmith's algorithm

1 Introduction

In 1977, Rivest, Shamir, and Adleman proposed the famous RSA encryption scheme [18], whose security is based on the hardness of factoring large integers. RSA is now a very popular scheme with many applications in industry for information security protection. Therefore, its security has been widely analyzed. Although it seems infeasible to break RSA with large modulus entirely with a classical computer now, there still exist many vulnerable RSA instances. For instance, small public key [7,8] or small secret key [4] can lead to some attacks against RSA. In addition, side-channel attacks pose a great threat to RSA [2,5,6], targeting the decryption device to obtain more information about the private key.

It is well known that additional information on the private keys or the prime factors can help attack the RSA scheme efficiently. In 1997, Coppersmith [8,14]

© The Author(s), under exclusive license to Springer Nature Switzerland AG 2024
C. Carlet et al. (Eds.): SAC 2023, LNCS 14201, pp. 369–384, 2024.
https://doi.org/10.1007/978-3-031-53368-6_18

proposed an attack that can factor the RSA modulus $N = pq$ in polynomial time if at least half of the most (or least) significant bits of p are given. In 2013, by using Coppersmith's method, Bernstein et al. [3] showed that an attacker can efficiently factor 184 distinct RSA keys generated by government-issued smart cards.

At PKC 2009, May and Ritzenhofen [15] introduced the Implicit Factorization Problem (IFP). It concerns the question of factoring two n-bit RSA moduli $N_1 = p_1q_1$ and $N_2 = p_2q_2$, given the implicit information that p_1 and p_2 share γn of their consecutive least significant bits, while q_1 and q_2 are αn-bit. Using a two-dimensional lattice, May and Ritzenhofen obtained a heuristic result that this implicit information is sufficient to factor N_1 and N_2 with a lattice-based algorithm, provided that $\gamma n > 2\alpha n + 2$.

In a follow-up work at PKC 2010, Faugère et al. [9] generalized the Implicit Factorization Problem to the case where the most significant bits (MSBs) or the middle bits of p_1 and p_2 are shared. Specifically, they established the bound of $\gamma n > 2\alpha n + 2$ for the case where the MSBs are shared, using a two-dimensional lattice. For the case where the middle bits of p_1 and p_2 are shared, Faugère et al. obtained a heuristic result that q_1 and q_2 could be found from a three-dimensional lattice if $\gamma n > 4\alpha n + 6$.

In 2011, Sarkar and Maitra [21] further expanded the Implicit Factorization Problem by revealing the relations between the Approximate Common Divisor Problem (ACDP) and the Implicit Factorization Problem, and presented the bound of $\gamma > 2\alpha - \alpha^2$ for the following three cases.

1. the primes p_1, p_2 share an amount of the least significant bits (LSBs);
2. the primes p_1, p_2 share an amount of most significant bits (MSBs);
3. the primes p_1, p_2 share both an amount of least significant bits and an amount of most significant bits.

In 2016, Lu et al. [13] presented a novel algorithm and improved the bounds to $\gamma > 2\alpha - 2\alpha^2$ for all the above three cases of the Implicit Factorization Problem. In 2015, Peng et al. [17] revisited the Implicit Factorization Problem with shared middle bits and improved the bound of Faugère et al. [9] up to $\gamma > 4\alpha - 3\alpha^2$. The bound was further enhanced by Wang et al. [22] in 2018 up to $\gamma > 4\alpha - 4\alpha\sqrt{\alpha}$.

It is worth noting that in the previous cases, the shared bits are located at the same position for the primes p_1 and p_2.

In this paper, we present a more generalized case of the Implicit Factorization Problem that allows for arbitrary consecutive shared locations, rather than requiring them to be identical in the primes, as in previous research. More precisely, we propose the Generalized Implicit Factorization Problem (GIFP), which concerns the factorization of two n-bit RSA moduli $N_1 = p_1q_1$ and $N_2 = p_2q_2$ when p_1 and p_2 share γn consecutive bits, where the shared bits are not necessarily required to be located at the same positions. See Fig. 1 for an example, where the starting positions for the shared bits in p_1 and p_2 may be different.

Fig. 1. Shared bits M for p_1 and p_2

We transform the GIFP into the Approximate Common Divisor Problem and then, employ Coppersmith's method with some optimization strategy, we propose a polynomial time algorithm to solve it when $\gamma > 4\alpha(1 - \sqrt{\alpha})$.

In Table 1, we present a comparison of our new bound on γ with the known former bounds obtained by various methods to solve the Implicit Factorization Problem.

Table 1. Asymptotic lower bound of γ in the Implicit Factorization Problem for n-bit $N_1 = p_1 q_1$ and $N_2 = p_2 q_2$ where the number of shared bits is γn, q_1 and q_2 are αn-bit.

	LSBs	MSBs	both LSBs-MSBs	Middle bits	General
May, Ritzenhofen [15]	2α	–	–	–	–
Faugère, et al. [9]	2α	-	-	4α	–
Sarkar, Maitra [21]	$2\alpha - \alpha^2$	$2\alpha - \alpha^2$	$2\alpha - \alpha^2$	-	–
Lu, et al. [13]	$2\alpha - 2\alpha^2$	$2\alpha - 2\alpha^2$	$2\alpha - 2\alpha^2$	-	-
Peng, et al. [17]	–	–	–	$4\alpha - 3\alpha^2$	-
Wang, et al. [22]	–	–	–	$4\alpha(1 - \sqrt{\alpha})$	–
This work	–	–	–	–	$4\alpha(1 - \sqrt{\alpha})$

It can be seen in Table 1 that the bounds for the Implicit Factorization Problem for sharing middle bits are inferior to those of other variants. This is because the unshared bits in the Implicit Factorization Problem for LSBs or MSBs or both LSBs and MSBs are continuous, and only one variable is necessary to represent the unshared bits while at least two variables are needed to represent the unshared bits in the Implicit Factorization Problem sharing middle bits or GIFP. In addition, our bound for GIFP is identical to the variant of IFP sharing the middle bits located in the same position. However, it is obvious that the GIFP relaxes the constraints for the positions of the shared bits.

Therefore, with the same bound for the number of shared bits as in the IFP sharing middle bits at the same position, we show that the Implicit Factorization Problem can still be solved efficiently when the positions for the sharing bits are located differently.

There are still open problems, and the most important one is: can we improve our bound $4\alpha(1 - \sqrt{\alpha})$ for GIFP to $2\alpha - 2\alpha^2$ or even better? A positive answer seems not easy since the bound for GIFP directly yields a bound for any known variant of IFP. Improving the bound for GIFP to the one better than $4\alpha \left(1 - \sqrt{\alpha}\right)$ means that we can improve the bound for the variant of IFP sharing the middle bits located in the same position, and improving the bound for GIFP to the one better than $2\alpha - 2\alpha^2$ means that we can improve the bound for any known variant of IFP.

Roadmap. Our paper is structured as follows. Section 2 presents some required background for our approaches. In Sect. 3, we present our analysis of the Generalized Implicit Factorization Problem, which constitutes our main result. Section 4 details the experimental results used to validate our analysis. Finally, we provide a brief conclusion in Sect. 5.

2   Notations and Preliminaries

Notations. Let $\mathbb{Z}$ denote the ring of integers, i.e., the set of all integers. We use lowercase bold letters (e.g., $\mathbf{v}$) for vectors and uppercase bold letters (e.g., $\mathbf{A}$) for matrices. The notation $\binom{n}{m}$ represents the number of ways to select m items out of n items, which is defined as $\frac{n!}{m!(n-m)!}$. If $m > n$, we set $\binom{n}{m} = 0$.

2.1   Lattices, SVP, and LLL

Let $m \geq 2$ be an integer. A lattice is a discrete additive subgroup of $\mathbb{R}^m$. A more explicit definition is presented as follows.

Definition 1 (Lattice). *Let* $\mathbf{v_1}, \mathbf{v_2}, \ldots, \mathbf{v_n} \in \mathbb{R}^m$ *be* n *linearly independent vectors with* $n \leq m$. *The lattice* $\mathcal{L}$ *spanned by* $\{\mathbf{v_1}, \mathbf{v_2}, \ldots, \mathbf{v_n}\}$ *is the set of all integer linear combinations of* $\{\mathbf{v_1}, \mathbf{v_2}, \ldots, \mathbf{v_n}\}$, *i.e.,*

$$\mathcal{L} = \left\{ \mathbf{v} \in \mathbb{R}^m \mid \mathbf{v} = \sum_{i=1}^{n} a_i \mathbf{v_i}, a_i \in \mathbb{Z} \right\}.$$

The integer n denotes the rank of the lattice $\mathcal{L}$, while m represents its dimension. The lattice $\mathcal{L}$ is said to be full rank if $n = m$. We use the matrix $\mathbf{B} \in \mathbb{R}^{n \times m}$, where each vector $\mathbf{v_i}$ contributes a row to $\mathbf{B}$. The determinant of $\mathcal{L}$ is defined as $\det(\mathcal{L}) = \sqrt{\det\left(\mathbf{BB}^t\right)}$, where $\mathbf{B}^t$ is the transpose of $\mathbf{B}$. If $\mathcal{L}$ is full rank, this reduces to $\det(\mathcal{L}) = |\det(\mathbf{B})|$.

The Shortest Vector Problem (SVP) is one of the famous computational problems in lattices.

Definition 2 (Shortest Vector Problem (SVP)). *Given a lattice* $\mathcal{L}$, *the Shortest Vector Problem (SVP) asks to find a non-zero lattice vector* $\mathbf{v} \in \mathcal{L}$ *of minimum Euclidean norm, i.e., find* $\mathbf{v} \in \mathcal{L} \backslash \{\mathbf{0}\}$ *such that* $\|\mathbf{v}\| \leq \|\mathbf{w}\|$ *for all non-zero* $\mathbf{w} \in \mathcal{L}$.

Although SVP is NP-hard under randomized reductions [1], there exist algorithms that can find a relatively short vector, instead of the exactly shortest vector, in polynomial time, such as the famous LLL algorithm proposed by Lenstra, Lenstra, and Lovasz [12] in 1982. The following result is useful for our analysis [14].

Theorem 1 (LLL Algorithm). *Given an n-dimensional lattice $\mathcal{L}$, we can find an LLL-reduced basis $\{\mathbf{v_1}, \mathbf{v_2}, \ldots, \mathbf{v_n}\}$ of $\mathcal{L}$ in polynomial time, which satisfies*

$$\|\mathbf{v_i}\| \leq 2^{\frac{n(n-1)}{4(n+1-i)}} \det(\mathcal{L})^{\frac{1}{n+1-i}}, \quad for \quad i = 1, \ldots, n.$$

Theorem 1 presents the upper bounds for the norm of the i-th vector in the LLL-basis using the determinant of the lattice.

2.2 Coppersmith's Method

In 1996, Coppersmith [8,14] proposed a lattice-based method for finding small solutions of univariate modular polynomial equations modulo a positive integer M, and another lattice-based method for finding the small roots of bivariate polynomial equations. The methods are based on finding short vectors in a lattice. We briefly sketch the idea below. More details can be found in [14].

Let M be a positive integer, and $f(x_1, \ldots, x_k)$ be a polynomial with integer coefficients. Suppose we want to find a small solution $(y_1, \ldots, y_k)$ of the modular equation $f(x_1, \ldots, x_k) \equiv 0 \pmod{M}$ with the bounds $y_i < X_i$ for $i = 1, \ldots, k$.

The first step is to construct a set G of k-variate polynomial equations such that, for each $g_i \in G$ with $i = 1, \ldots, k$, we have $g_i(y_1, \ldots, y_k) \equiv 0 \pmod{M}$. Then we use the coefficient vectors of $g_i(x_1 X_1, \ldots, x_k X_k)$, $i = 1, \ldots, k$, to construct a k-dimensional lattice $\mathcal{L}$. Applying the LLL algorithm to $\mathcal{L}$, we get a new set H of k polynomial equations $h_i(x_1, \ldots, x_k)$, $i = 1, \ldots, k$, with integer coefficients such that $h_i(y_1, \ldots, y_k) \equiv 0 \pmod{M}$. The following result shows that one can get $h_i(y_1, \ldots, y_k) = 0$ over the integers in some cases, where for $h(x_1, \ldots, x_k) = \sum_{i_1 \ldots i_k} a_{i_1 \ldots i_k} x_1^{i_1} \cdots x_1^{i_k}$, the Euclidean norm is defined by $\|h(x_1, \ldots, x_k)\| = \sqrt{\sum_{i_1 \ldots i_k} a_{i_1 \ldots i_k}^2}$.

Theorem 2 (Howgrave-Graham [11]). *Let $h(x_1, \ldots, x_k) \in \mathbb{Z}[x_1, \ldots, x_k]$ be a polynomial with at most ω monomials. Let M be a positive integer. If there exist k integers $(y_1, \ldots, y_k)$ satisfying the following two conditions:*

1. *$h(y_1, \ldots, y_k) \equiv 0 \pmod{M}$, and there exist k positive integers $X_1, \ldots, X_k$ such that $|y_1| \leq X_1, \ldots, |y_k| \leq X_k$,*
2. *$\|h(x_1 X_1, \ldots, x_k X_k)\| < \frac{M}{\sqrt{\omega}}$,*

then $h(y_1, \ldots, y_k) = 0$ holds over the integers.

From Theorem 1, we can obtain the vectors $\mathbf{v_1}, \mathbf{v_2}, \ldots, \mathbf{v_k}$ in the LLL reduced basis of $\mathcal{L}$. This yields k integer polynomials $h_1(x_1, \ldots, x_k)$, $\ldots$, $h_k(x_1, \ldots, x_k)$, all of which share the desired solution $(y_1, \ldots, y_k)$, that is $h_i(y_1, \ldots, y_k) \equiv 0$ (mod M) for $i = 1, \ldots, k$.

To combine Theorem 1 and Theorem 2, for $i = k$, we set

$$2^{\frac{n(n-1)}{4(n+1-i)}} \det(\mathcal{L})^{\frac{1}{n+1-i}} < \frac{M}{\sqrt{\dim(\mathcal{L})}}.$$

Ultimately, the attainment of the desired root hinges upon effectively resolving the system of integer polynomials using either the resultant method or the Gröbner basis approach. However, in order for a Gröbner basis computation to find the common root, the following heuristic assumption needs to hold.

Assumption 1. *The k polynomials $h_i(x_1, \cdots, x_k)$, $i = 1, \cdots, k$, that are derived from the reduced basis of the lattice in the Coppersmith method are algebraically independent. Equivalently, the common root of the polynomials $h_i(x_1, \cdots, x_k)$ can be found by computing the resultant or computing the Gröbner basis.*

Assumption 1 is often used in connection with Coppersmith's method in the multivariate scenario [4,13,14,21,22]. Since our attack in Sect. 3 relies on Assumption 1, it is heuristic. However, our experiments in Sect. 4 justify the validity of our attack and show that Assumption 1 perfectly holds true.

3   Generalized Implicit Factorization Problem

This section presents our analysis of the Generalized Implicit Factorization Problem (GIFP) in which p_1 and p_2 share an amount of consecutive bits at different positions.

3.1   Description of GIFP

This section proposes the Generalized Implicit Factorization Problem (GIFP), which concerns the factorization of two n-bit RSA moduli, $N_1 = p_1 q_1$ and $N_2 = p_2 q_2$, under the implicit hint that the primes p_1 and p_2 share a specific number, γn, of consecutive bits. In contrast to previous studies [9,13,15,19,20,22], where the shared bits were assumed to be located at the same positions in p_1 and p_2, the proposed GIFP considers a more general case where the shared bits can be situated at arbitrary positions.

Definition 3 (GIFP(n, α, γ)). *Given two n-bit RSA moduli $N_1 = p_1 q_1$ and $N_2 = p_2 q_2$, where q_1 and q_2 are αn-bit, assume that p_1 and p_2 share γn consecutive bits, where the shared bits may be located in different positions of p_1 and p_2. The Generalized Implicit Factorization Problem (GIFP) asks to factor N_1 and N_2.*

The introduction of GIFP expands the scope of the Implicit Factorization Problem and presents a more realistic and challenging scenario that can arise in practical applications. In real-world settings, it is more probable to encounter situations where the shared location of bits differs between primes. Therefore, it is essential to develop algorithms and analysis that can handle such cases where the shared bits are situated at different positions. By considering the Generalized Implicit Factorization Problem (GIFP), we need to avoid situations where the system that creates RSA keys lack entropy.

3.2   Algorithm for GIFP

We will show our analysis of the GIFP in this subsection. The main idea is also to relate the Approximate Common Divisor Problem (ACDP) to the Implicit Factorization Problem.

Theorem 3. *Under Assumption 1, GIFP(n, α, γ) can be solved in polynomial time when*

$$\gamma > 4\alpha \left(1 - \sqrt{\alpha}\right),$$

provided that $\alpha + \gamma \leq 1$.

Proof. Without loss of generality, we can assume that the starting and ending positions of the shared bits are known. When these positions are unknown, we can simply traverse the possible starting positions of the shared bits, which will just scale the time complexity for the case that we know the position by a factor $\mathcal{O}(n^2)$.

Hence, we suppose that p_1 shares γn-bits from the $\beta_1 n$-th bit to $(\beta_1 + \gamma)n$-th bit, and p_2 shares bits from $\beta_2 n$-th bit to $(\beta_2 + \gamma)n$-th bit, where β_1 and β_2 are known with $\beta_1 \leq \beta_2$ (see Fig. 1). Then we can write

$$p_1 = x_1 + M_0 2^{\beta_1 n} + x_2 2^{(\beta_1 + \gamma)n}, \quad p_2 = x_3 + M_0 2^{\beta_2 n} + x_4 2^{(\beta_2 + \gamma)n},$$

with $M_0 < 2^{\gamma n}$, $x_1 < 2^{\beta_1 n}$, $x_2 < 2^{(\beta - \beta_1)n}$, $x_3 < 2^{\beta_2 n}$, $x_4 < 2^{(\beta - \beta_2)n}$ where $\beta = 1 - \alpha - \gamma$. From this, we deduce

$$
\begin{aligned}
2^{(\beta_2 - \beta_1)n} p_1 &= x_1 2^{(\beta_2 - \beta_1)n} + M_0 2^{\beta_2 n} + x_2 2^{(\beta_2 + \gamma)n} \\
&= x_1 2^{(\beta_2 - \beta_1)n} + (p_2 - x_3 - x_4 2^{(\beta_2 + \gamma)n}) + x_2 2^{(\beta_2 + \gamma)n} \\
&= p_2 + (x_1 2^{(\beta_2 - \beta_1)n} - x_3) + (x_2 - x_4) 2^{(\beta_2 + \gamma)n}.
\end{aligned}
$$

Then, multiplying by q_2, we get

$$N_2 + (x_1 2^{(\beta_2 - \beta_1)n} - x_3)q_2 + (x_2 - x_4)q_2 2^{(\beta_2 + \gamma)n} = 2^{(\beta_2 - \beta_1)n} p_1 q_2.$$

Next, we define the polynomial

$$f(x, y, z) = xz + 2^{(\beta_2+\gamma)n} yz + N_2,$$

which shows that $(x_1 2^{(\beta_2-\beta_1)n} - x_3, x_2 - x_4, q_2)$ is a solutions of

$$f(x, y, z) \equiv 0 \pmod{2^{(\beta_2-\beta_1)n} p_1}.$$

Let m and t be integers to be optimized later with $0 \le t \le m$. To apply Coppersmith's method, we consider a family of polynomials $g_{i,j}(x, y, z)$ for $0 \le i \le m$ and $0 \le j \le m - i$:

$$g_{i,j}(x, y, z) = (yz)^j f(x, y, z)^i \left(2^{(\beta_2-\beta_1)n}\right)^{m-i} N_1^{\max(t-i,0)}.$$

These polynomials satisfy

$$g_{i,j}\left(x_1 2^{(\beta_2-\beta_1)n} - x_3, x_2 - x_4, q_2\right)$$

$$= (x_2 - x_4)^j q_2^j \left(2^{(\beta_2-\beta_1)n} p_1 q_2\right)^i \left(2^{(\beta_2-\beta_1)n}\right)^{m-i} N_1^{\max(t-i,0)}$$

$$= (x_2 - x_4)^j q_2^{j+i} q_1^{\max(t-i,0)} \left(2^{(\beta_2-\beta_1)n}\right)^m p_1^{\max(t-i,0)+i}$$

$$\equiv 0 \left(\mathrm{mod}\left(2^{(\beta_2-\beta_1)n}\right)^m p_1^t\right).$$

On the other hand, we have

$$\left|x_1 2^{(\beta_2-\beta_1)n} - x_3\right| \le \max\left(x_1 2^{(\beta_2-\beta_1)n}, x_3\right)$$

$$\le \max\left(2^{\beta_1 n} 2^{(\beta_2-\beta_1)n}, 2^{\beta_1 n}\right)$$

$$= 2^{\beta_2 n},$$

and

$$|x_2 - x_4| \le \max(x_2, x_4) = 2^{(\beta-\beta_1)n}.$$

Also, we have $q_2 = 2^{\alpha n}$. We then set

$$X = 2^{\beta_2 n}, \quad Y = 2^{(\beta-\beta_1)n}, \quad Z = 2^{\alpha n}.$$

To reduce the determinant of the lattice, we introduce a new variable w for p_2, and multiply the polynomials $g_{i,j}(x, y, z)$ by a power w^s for some s that will be optimized later. Similar to t, we also require $0 \le s \le m$

Note that we can replace zw in $g_{i,j}(x, y, z)w^s$ by N_2. We want to eliminate this multiple. Since $\gcd(N_2, 2N_1) = 1$, there exists an inverse of N_2, denoted as N_2^{-1}, such that $N_2 N_2^{-1} \equiv 1 \pmod{*}\left(2^{(\beta_2-\beta_1)n}\right)^m N_1^t$. We then eliminate $(zw)^{\min(s,i+j)}$ from the original polynomial by multiplying it by $N_2^{-\min(s,i+j)}$ $\pmod{*}\left(2^{(\beta_2-\beta_1)n}\right)^m N_1^t$, while ensuring that the resulting polynomial evaluation is still a multiple of $\left(2^{(\beta_2-\beta_1)n}\right)^m p_1^t$. By selecting the appropriate parameter

s, we aim to reduce the determinant of the lattice. To this end, we consider a new family of polynomials $G_{i,j}(x, y, z, w)$ for $0 \leq i \leq m$ and $0 \leq j \leq m - i$:

$$G_{i,j}(x, y, z, w) = (yz)^j w^s f(x, y, z)^i \left(2^{(\beta_2 - \beta_1)n}\right)^{m-i} N_1^{\max(t-i, 0)} N_2^{-\min(s, i+j)},$$

where $N_2^{-\min(s, i+j)}$ is computed modulo $\left(2^{(\beta_2 - \beta_1)n}\right)^m N_1^t$, and each term zw is replaced by N_2. For example, suppose $s \geq 1$, then

$$G_{0,1}(x, y, z, w) = yw^{s-1} N_2 \left(2^{(\beta_2 - \beta_1)n}\right)^m N_1^t N_2^{-1}.$$

Next, consider the lattice $\mathcal{L}$ spanned by the matrix $\mathbf{B}$ whose rows are the coefficients of the polynomials $G_{i,j}(Xx, Yy, Zz, Ww)$ where, for $0 \leq i \leq m$, $0 \leq j \leq m - i$, The rows are ordered following the rule that $G_{i,j} \prec G_{i',j'}$ if $i < i'$ or if $i = i'$ and $j < j'$. The columns are ordered following the monomials so that $x^i y^j z^{i+j-\min(s,i+j)} w^{s-\min(s,i+j)} \prec x^{i'} y^{j'} z^{i'+j'-\min(s,i'+j')} w^{s-\min(s,i'+j')}$ if $i < i'$ or if $i = i'$ and $j < j'$. Table 2 presents a matrix $\mathbf{B}$ with $m = 3$, $s = 2$, $t = 2$ where $*$ represents a nonzero term.

Table 2. The matrix of the lattice with $m = 3$, $s = 2$, $t = 2$ and $M = 2^{(\beta_2 - \beta_1)n}$.

$G_{i,j}$	w^2	yw	y^2	$y^3 z$	xw	xy	$xy^2 z$	x^2	$x^2 yz$	$x^3 z$
$G_{0,0}$	$W^2 M^3 N_1^2$	0	0	0	0	0	0	0	0	0
$G_{0,1}$	0	$YWM^3 N_1^2$	0	0	0	0	0	0	0	0
$G_{0,2}$	0	0	$Y^2 M^3 N_1^2$	0	0	0	0	0	0	0
$G_{0,3}$	0	0	0	$Y^3 Z M^3 N_1^2$	0	0	0	0	0	0
$G_{1,0}$	$*$	$*$	0	0	$XWM^2 N_1$	0	0	0	0	0
$G_{1,1}$	0	$*$	$*$	0	0	$XYM^2 N_1$	0	0	0	0
$G_{1,2}$	0	0	$*$	$*$	0	0	$XY^2 Z M^2 N_1$	0	0	0
$G_{2,0}$	$*$	$*$	$*$	0	$*$	$*$	0	$X^2 M$	0	0
$G_{2,1}$	0	$*$	$*$	$*$	0	$*$	$*$	0	$X^2 YZM$	0
$G_{3,0}$	$*$	$*$	$*$	$*$	$*$	$*$	$*$	$*$	$*$	$X^3 Z$

By construction, the square matrix B is left triangular. Hence, the dimension of the lattice is

$$\omega = \sum_{i=0}^{m} \sum_{j=0}^{m-i} 1 = \sum_{i=0}^{m} (m - i + 1) = \frac{1}{2}(m + 1)(m + 2)$$

and its determinant is

$$\det(B) = \det(\mathcal{L}) = X^{e_X} Y^{e_Y} Z^{e_Z} W^{e_W} 2^{(\beta_2 - \beta_1)n e_M} N_1^{e_N},$$

with

$$e_X = \sum_{i=0}^{m} \sum_{j=0}^{m-i} i = \frac{1}{6}m(m+1)(m+2),$$

$$e_Y = \sum_{i=0}^{m} \sum_{j=0}^{m-i} j = \frac{1}{6}m(m+1)(m+2),$$

$$e_Z = \sum_{i=0}^{m} \sum_{j=0}^{m-i} (i+j-\min(s,i+j))$$

$$= \frac{1}{3}m(m+1)(m+2) + \frac{1}{6}s(s+1)(s+2) - \frac{1}{2}s(m+1)(m+2),$$

$$e_W = \sum_{i=0}^{m} \sum_{j=0}^{m-i} (s-\min(s,i+j)) = \frac{1}{6}s(s+1)(s+2),$$

$$e_N = \sum_{i=0}^{t} \sum_{j=0}^{m-i} (t-i) = \frac{1}{6}t(t+1)(3m-t+4),$$

$$e_M = \sum_{i=0}^{m} \sum_{j=0}^{m-i} (m-i) = \frac{1}{3}m(m+1)(m+2).$$

The former results are detailed in Appendix A. To combine Theorem 1 and Theorem 2, we set

$$2^{\frac{\omega(\omega-1)}{4(\omega+1-i)}} \det(\mathcal{L})^{\frac{1}{\omega+1-i}} < \frac{\left(2^{(\beta_2-\beta_1)n}\right)^m p_1^t}{\sqrt{\omega}},$$

with $i = 2$. Then

$$\det(\mathcal{L}) < \frac{1}{2^{\frac{\omega-1}{4}}\sqrt{\omega}}\left(2^{(\beta_2-\beta_1)n}\right)^{\omega m} p_1^{t\omega},$$

and

$$X^{e_X} Y^{e_Y} Z^{e_Z} W^{e_W} 2^{(\beta_2-\beta_1)n e_M} N_1^{e_N} < \frac{1}{2^{\frac{\omega-1}{4}}\sqrt{\omega}}\left(2^{(\beta_2-\beta_1)n}\right)^{\omega m} p_1^{t\omega}. \tag{1}$$

Next, we set $s = \sigma m$ with $0 \le \sigma \le 1$, $t = \tau m$ with $0 \le \tau \le 1$, and we use $N \approx 2^n$, $p_1 \approx 2^{(1-\alpha)n}$, $X = 2^{\beta_2 n}$, $Y = 2^{(\beta-\beta_1)n}$, $Z = 2^{\alpha n}$, $W = 2^{(1-\alpha)n}$ and the most significant parts of e_X, e_Y, e_Z, e_W, e_N, e_M as

$$e_X = \frac{1}{6}m^3 + o\left(m^3\right),$$

$$e_Y = \frac{1}{6}m^3 + o\left(m^3\right),$$

$$e_Z = \frac{1}{3}m^3 + \frac{1}{6}\sigma^3 m^3 - \frac{1}{2}\sigma m^3 + o\left(m^3\right),$$

$$e_W = \frac{1}{6}\sigma^3 m^3 + o\left(m^3\right),$$

$$e_N = \frac{1}{6}\tau^2(3-\tau)m^3 + o\left(m^3\right),$$

$$e_M = \frac{1}{3}m^3 + o\left(m^3\right).$$

Similarly, we use

$$m\omega = \frac{1}{2}m^3 + o\left(m^3\right).$$

Then, after taking logarithms, dividing by nm^3, and neglecting the very small terms, i.e., $o\left(m^3\right)$, the inequality (1) implies

$$\frac{1}{6}\beta_2 + \frac{1}{6}(\beta - \beta_1) + \alpha(\frac{1}{3} + \frac{1}{6}\sigma^3 - \frac{1}{2}\sigma) + \frac{1}{6}\sigma^3(1-\alpha) + \frac{1}{3}(\beta_2 - \beta_1) + \frac{1}{6}\tau^2(3-\tau)$$
$$< \frac{1}{2}(\beta_2 - \beta_1) + \frac{1}{2}(1-\alpha)\tau.$$

Using $\beta = 1 - \alpha - \gamma$, the former inequality is equivalent to

$$\tau^2(3-\tau) - 3(1-\alpha)\tau + \sigma^3 - 3\alpha\sigma + 1 - \gamma + \alpha < 0.$$

The left side is optimized for $\tau_0 = 1 - \sqrt{\alpha}$ and $\sigma_0 = \sqrt{\alpha}$, which gives

$$3\alpha - 2\alpha\sqrt{\alpha} - 1 - 2\alpha\sqrt{\alpha} + 1 + \alpha - \gamma < 0,$$

and finally

$$\gamma > 4\alpha\left(1 - \sqrt{\alpha}\right).$$

By Assumption 1, we can get $(x_0, y_0, z_0) = (x_1 2^{(\beta_2 - \beta_1)n} - x_3, x_2 - x_4, q_2)$, so we have $q_2 = z_0$, and we calculate

$$p_2 = \frac{N_2}{q_2}.$$

Next, we have

$$2^{(\beta_2 - \beta_1)n} p_1 = p_2 + (x_1 2^{(\beta_2 - \beta_1)n} - x_3) + (x_2 - x_4)2^{(\beta_2 + \gamma)n} = p_2 + y_0 + z_0 2^{(\beta_2 + \gamma)n}.$$

Therefore, we can calculate p_1 and $q_1 = \frac{N_1}{p_1}$. This terminates the proof.   □

4   Experimental Results

We provide some experiments to verify Assumption 1 and the correctness of our analysis.

The experiments were run on a computer configured with AMD Ryzen 5 2500U with Radeon Vega Mobile Gfx (2.00 GHz). We selected the parameter $n = \log(N)$ using gradients, validated our theory starting from small-scale experiments, and continually increased the scale of our experiments. The results are presented in Table 3:

Table 3. Some experimental results for the GIFP.

n	αn	βn	$\beta_1 n$	$\beta_2 n$	γn	m	dim($\mathcal{L}$)	Time for LLL(s)	Time for Gröbner Basis(s)
200	20	40	20	30	140	6	28	1.8620	0.0033
200	20	60	20	30	140	6	28	1.8046	0.0034
500	50	100	50	75	350	6	28	3.1158	0.0043
500	50	150	50	75	300	6	28	4.23898	0.0048
1000	100	200	100	150	700	6	28	8.2277	0.0147

As can be seen from Table 3, we chose various values of n, αn, βn, $\beta_1 n$, $\beta_2 n$ and γn to investigate the behavior of our proposed algorithm. For each set of parameters, we recorded the time taken by the LLL algorithm and Gröbner basis algorithm to solve the Generalized Integer Factorization Problem (GIFP).

Our experiments confirm Assumption 1 and also the efficiency of our algorithm in handling various values of n and related parameters. As the size of the problem increases, the computation time for LLL and Gröbner basis algorithms also increases. Nevertheless, our algorithm's time complexity grows moderately compared to the problem size. Therefore, we can conclude that our algorithm is suitable for practical applications in the Generalized Integer Factorization Problem (GIFP).

Besides the Generalized Implicit Factoring Problem, we also conducted experiments on a special case, called the *least-most significant bits case* (LMSBs). This case is characterized by $\beta_1 = 0$ and $\beta_2 = \beta$. The results of these experiments are outlined below

5   Conclusion and Open Problem

In this paper, we considered the Generalized Implicit Factoring Problem (GIFP), where the shared bits are not necessarily required to be located at the same positions. We proposed a lattice-based algorithm that can efficiently factor two RSA moduli, $N_1 = p_1 q_1$ and $N_2 = p_2 q_2$, in polynomial time, when the primes share a sufficient number of bits.

Our analysis shows that if p_1 and p_2 share $\gamma n > 4\alpha \left(1 - \sqrt{\alpha}\right) n$ consecutive bits, not necessarily at the same positions, then N_1 and N_2 can be factored in

Table 4. Some experimental results for the LMSBs case.

n	αn	βn	γn	m	$\dim(\mathcal{L})$	Time for LLL(s)	Time for Gröbner Basis(s)
256	25	75	156	5	21	1.3068	0.0029
256	25	75	156	5	21	1.2325	0.0023
256	25	75	156	6	21	1.2931	0.0023
512	50	150	212	6	28	2.0612	0.0028
512	50	150	212	6	28	2.4889	0.0086
512	50	150	212	6	28	2.0193	0.0022

polynomial time. However, this bound is valid when p_i and q_i, $i = 1, 2$, are not assumed to have the same bit length, i.e., N_1 and N_2 are unbalanced moduli [16] (Table 4).

So our work raises an open question on improving the bound $4\alpha (1 - \sqrt{\alpha})$, which would lead to better bounds for specific cases such as sharing some middle bits. It is known that the unshared bits in the Most Significant Bits (MSBs) or the Least Significant Bits (LSBs) are continuous, and only one variable is required when using variables to represent the unshared bits. This makes the MSBs or LSBs case easier to solve than the generalized case and achieves a better bound of $2\alpha (1 - \alpha)$. However, the bound of the MSBs is not linear with the bound of the GIFP, which is unnatural. We hope that the gap between the bounds of the MSBs or LSBs and the GIFP case can be reduced.

Acknowledgement. The authors would like to thank the reviewers of SAC 2023 for their helpful comments and suggestions. Yansong Feng and Yanbin Pan were supported in part by National Key Research and Development Project (No. 2018YFA0704705), National Natural Science Foundation of China (No. 62032009, 12226006) and Innovation Program for Quantum Science and Technology under Grant 2021ZD0302902.

A   Details of calculations in Section 3.2

In this appendix, we present the details of calculations for the quantities e_X, e_Y, e_Z, e_W, e_N, and e_M used in Sect. 3.2. We begin by a lemma that will be easily proven by induction. This lemma is well-known and can be found in many textbooks and references on combinatorics and discrete mathematics, such as Table 174 on page 174 in [10].

Lemma 1. *The equation* $\sum_{i=0}^{n} \binom{i}{2} = \binom{n+1}{3}$ *holds for any integer n.*

Moving on, we provide the calculations for e_X as:

$$e_X = \sum_{i=0}^{m} \sum_{j=0}^{m-i} j = \sum_{i=0}^{m} \binom{m-i+1}{2} = \sum_{i=0}^{m} \binom{i+1}{2}$$

$$= \binom{m+2}{3} = \frac{1}{6} m(m+1)(m+2).$$

The calculation of e_Y is the same as e_X.
Next, we provide the calculation for e_Z:

$$
\begin{aligned}
e_Z &= \sum_{i=0}^{m}\sum_{j=0}^{m-i}(i+j-\min(s,i+j)) \\
&= \sum_{i=0}^{m}\sum_{j=0}^{m-i}\max\{i+j-s,0\} \\
&= \sum_{t=s+1}^{m}\sum_{j=0}^{t}(t-s) \quad (\text{Let } t=i+j) \\
&= \sum_{t=s+1}^{m}(t-s)(t+1) \\
&= \sum_{t=0}^{m}(t-s)(t+1) - \sum_{t=0}^{s}(t-s)(t+1) \\
&= \sum_{t=0}^{m}t(t+1) - \sum_{t=0}^{m}s(t+1) - \sum_{t=0}^{s}t(t+1) + \sum_{t=0}^{s}s(t+1) \\
&= 2\sum_{t=0}^{m}\binom{t+1}{2} - s\sum_{t=0}^{m}(t+1) - 2\sum_{t=0}^{s}\binom{t+1}{2} + s\sum_{t=0}^{s}(t+1) \\
&= 2\binom{m+2}{3} - s\binom{m+2}{2} + \frac{1}{6}\binom{s+2}{3} \\
&= \frac{1}{3}m(m+1)(m+2) + \frac{1}{6}s(s+1)(s+2) - \frac{1}{2}s(m+1)(m+2).
\end{aligned}
$$

Then, we provide the calculation for e_W:

$$
\begin{aligned}
e_W &= \sum_{i=0}^{m}\sum_{j=0}^{m-i}(s-\min(s,i+j)) \\
&= \sum_{i=0}^{s}\sum_{j=0}^{s-i}(s-i-j) \\
&= \sum_{i=0}^{s}\sum_{j=0}^{s-i}s - \sum_{i=0}^{s}\sum_{j=0}^{s-i}i - \sum_{i=0}^{s}\sum_{j=0}^{s-i}j \\
&= \frac{1}{2}s(s+1)(s+2) - \frac{1}{6}s(s+1)(s+2) - \frac{1}{6}s(s+1)(s+2) \\
&= \frac{1}{6}s(s+1)(s+2).
\end{aligned}
$$

Furthermore, we provide the calculation for e_N:

$$e_N = \sum_{i=0}^{t} \sum_{j=0}^{m-i} (t-i) = \sum_{i=0}^{t}(t-i)(m-i+1) = \sum_{i=0}^{t}(t-i)(m+2-i-1)$$

$$= (m+2)\sum_{i=0}^{t}(t-i) - \sum_{i=0}^{t}(t-i)(i+1) = (m+2)\binom{t+1}{2} - \sum_{i=0}^{t}t(i+1) + \sum_{i=0}^{t}i(i+1)$$

$$= (m+2)\binom{t+1}{2} - t\binom{t+2}{2} + \sum_{i=0}^{t}2\binom{i+1}{2} = (m+2)\binom{t+1}{2} - t\binom{t+2}{2} + 2\binom{t+2}{3}$$

$$= \frac{1}{6}t(t+1)(3m-t+4).$$

Finally, we provide the calculation for e_M:

$$e_M = \sum_{i=0}^{m}\sum_{j=0}^{m-i}(m-i) = \sum_{i=0}^{m}(m-i+1)(m-i) = \sum_{i=0}^{m}2\binom{m-i+1}{2}$$

$$= \sum_{i=0}^{m}2\binom{i+1}{2} = 2\binom{m+2}{3} = \frac{1}{3}m(m+1)(m+2).$$

References

1. Ajtai, M.: The shortest vector problem in L2 is NP-hard for randomized reductions (extended abstract). In: Symposium on the Theory of Computing (1998)
2. Bauer, A., Jaulmes, E., Lomné, V., Prouff, E., Roche, T.: Side-channel attack against RSA key generation algorithms. In: Batina, L., Robshaw, M. (eds.) CHES 2014. LNCS, vol. 8731, pp. 223–241. Springer, Heidelberg (2014). https://doi.org/10.1007/978-3-662-44709-3_13
3. Bernstein, D.J., et al.: Factoring RSA keys from certified smart cards: coppersmith in the wild. In: Sako, K., Sarkar, P. (eds.) ASIACRYPT 2013. LNCS, vol. 8270, pp. 341–360. Springer, Heidelberg (2013). https://doi.org/10.1007/978-3-642-42045-0_18
4. Boneh, D., Durfee, G.: Cryptanalysis of RSA with private key d less than $N^{0.292}$. In: Stern, J. (ed.) EUROCRYPT 1999. LNCS, vol. 1592, pp. 1–11. Springer, Heidelberg (1999). https://doi.org/10.1007/3-540-48910-X_1
5. Brumley, D., Boneh, D.: Remote timing attacks are practical. In: Proceedings of the 12th USENIX Security Symposium, Washington, D.C., USA, 4–8 August 2003. USENIX Association (2003). https://www.usenix.org/conference/12th-usenix-security-symposium/remote-timing-attacks-are-practical
6. Carmon, E., Seifert, J., Wool, A.: Photonic side channel attacks against RSA. In: 2017 IEEE International Symposium on Hardware Oriented Security and Trust, HOST 2017, McLean, VA, USA, 1–5 May 2017, pp. 74–78. IEEE Computer Society (2017). https://doi.org/10.1109/HST.2017.7951801
7. Coppersmith, D.: Finding a small root of a univariate modular equation. In: Maurer, U. (ed.) EUROCRYPT 1996. LNCS, vol. 1070, pp. 155–165. Springer, Heidelberg (1996). https://doi.org/10.1007/3-540-68339-9_14
8. Coppersmith, D.: Small solutions to polynomial equations, and low exponent RSA vulnerabilities. J. Cryptol. 10(4), 233–260 (1997). https://doi.org/10.1007/s001459900030

9. Faugère, J.-C., Marinier, R., Renault, G.: Implicit factoring with shared most significant and middle bits. In: Nguyen, P.Q., Pointcheval, D. (eds.) PKC 2010. LNCS, vol. 6056, pp. 70–87. Springer, Heidelberg (2010). https://doi.org/10.1007/978-3-642-13013-7_5

10. Graham, R.L., Knuth, D.E., Patashnik, O.: Concrete Mathematics: A Foundation for Computer Science. 2nd edn. Addison-Wesley Longman Publishing Co., Inc, USA (1994)

11. Howgrave-Graham, N.: Finding small roots of univariate modular equations revisited. In: Darnell, M. (ed.) Cryptography and Coding 1997. LNCS, vol. 1355, pp. 131–142. Springer, Heidelberg (1997). https://doi.org/10.1007/BFb0024458

12. Lenstra, A.K., Lenstra, H.W., Lovász, L.: Factoring polynomials with rational coefficients. Math. Ann. **261**, 515–534 (1982)

13. Lu, Y., Peng, L., Zhang, R., Hu, L., Lin, D.: Towards optimal bounds for implicit factorization problem. In: Dunkelman, O., Keliher, L. (eds.) SAC 2015. LNCS, vol. 9566, pp. 462–476. Springer, Cham (2016). https://doi.org/10.1007/978-3-319-31301-6_26

14. May, A.: New RSA vulnerabilities using lattice reduction methods. Ph.D. thesis, University of Paderborn (2003). http://ubdata.uni-paderborn.de/ediss/17/2003/may/disserta.pdf

15. May, A., Ritzenhofen, M.: Implicit factoring: on polynomial time factoring given only an implicit hint. In: Jarecki, S., Tsudik, G. (eds.) PKC 2009. LNCS, vol. 5443, pp. 1–14. Springer, Heidelberg (2009). https://doi.org/10.1007/978-3-642-00468-1_1

16. Nitaj, A., Ariffin, M.R.K.: Implicit factorization of unbalanced RSA moduli. IACR Cryptol. ePrint Arch. p. 548 (2014). http://eprint.iacr.org/2014/548

17. Peng, L., Hu, L., Lu, Y., Huang, Z., Xu, J.: Implicit factorization of RSA moduli revisited (Short Paper). In: Tanaka, K., Suga, Y. (eds.) IWSEC 2015. LNCS, vol. 9241, pp. 67–76. Springer, Cham (2015). https://doi.org/10.1007/978-3-319-22425-1_5

18. Rivest, R.L., Shamir, A., Adleman, L.M.: Cryptographic communications system and method (1983). US Patent 4,405,829

19. Sarkar, S., Maitra, S.: Further results on implicit factoring in polynomial time. Adv. Math. Commun. **3**(2), 205–217 (2009). https://doi.org/10.3934/amc.2009.3.205

20. Sarkar, S., Maitra, S.: Some applications of lattice based root finding techniques. Adv. Math. Commun. **4**(4), 519–531 (2010). https://doi.org/10.3934/amc.2010.4.519

21. Sarkar, S., Maitra, S.: Approximate integer common divisor problem relates to implicit factorization. IEEE Trans. Inf. Theory **57**(6), 4002–4013 (2011). https://doi.org/10.1109/TIT.2011.2137270

22. Wang, S., Qu, L., Li, C., Fu, S.: A better bound for implicit factorization problem with shared middle bits. Sci. China Inf. Sci. **61**(3), 032109:1–032109:10 (2018). https://doi.org/10.1007/s11432-017-9176-5

Differential Cryptanalysis

CLAASP: A Cryptographic Library for the Automated Analysis of Symmetric Primitives

Emanuele Bellini⬡, David Gerault⬡, Juan Grados(✉)⬡, Yun Ju Huang⬡,
Rusydi Makarim⬡, Mohamed Rachidi⬡, and Sharwan Tiwari⬡

Cryptography Research Center, Technology Innovation Institute, Abu Dhabi, UAE
{emanuele.bellini,david.gerault,juan.grados,yunju.huang,mohamed.rachidi,
sharwan.tiwari}@tii.ae

Abstract. This paper introduces CLAASP, a Cryptographic Library for the Automated Analysis of Symmetric Primitives. The library is designed to be modular, extendable, easy to use, generic, efficient and *fully* automated. It is an extensive toolbox gathering state-of-the-art techniques aimed at simplifying the manual tasks of symmetric primitive designers and analysts. CLAASP is built on top of Sagemath and is open-source under the GPLv3 license.

The central input of CLAASP is the description of a cryptographic primitive as a list of connected components in the form of a directed acyclic graph. From this representation, the library can automatically: (1) generate the Python or C code of the primitive evaluation function, (2) execute a wide range of statistical and avalanche tests on the primitive, (3) generate SAT, SMT, CP and MILP models to search, for example, differential and linear trails, (4) measure algebraic properties of the primitive, (5) test neural-based distinguishers. We demonstrate that CLAASP can reproduce many of the results that were obtained in the literature and even produce new results.

In this work, we also present a comprehensive survey and comparison of other software libraries aiming at similar goals as CLAASP.

Keywords: Cryptographic library · Automated analysis · Symmetric primitives

1 Introduction

The security targets for cryptographic primitives are well-defined, and relatively stable, after decades of cryptanalysis. In particular, a symmetric cipher should behave like a random keyed permutation, a hash function should behave like a random function, and a MAC scheme should be unforgeable. Testing a cryptographic primitive for these properties is, on the other hand, a vastly difficult task that relies on testing for known weaknesses. Such a process generally involves determining the most likely differential or linear characteristic, evaluating the resistance of the primitive to various cryptanalysis techniques such as

C. Carlet et al. (Eds.): SAC 2023, LNCS 14201, pp. 387–408, 2024.
https://doi.org/10.1007/978-3-031-53368-6_19

integral attacks, and running generic randomness tests. Fortunately, automatic techniques exist to help designers and cryptographers run such evaluations; for instance, SAT/SMT, Mixed Integer Linear Programming (MILP) or Constraint Programming (CP) are frequently used to find optimal differential and linear characteristics. These tools have, over time, become more accessible to non-experts, through libraries such as [43], that generate models (in this case, SMT) automatically from a description of the cipher. However, such tools generally focus on a single aspect, such as generating models in a given paradigm, and there is currently no single-stop toolkit that combines automated model generation, statistical testing and machine learning based analysis. We aim to fill this gap with CLAASP, a Cryptographic Library for the Automated Analysis of Symmetric Primitives. This paper introduces the first public version of CLAASP; the ambition of the project is to keep adding analysis tools in line with the state of the art, to provide cryptanalysts with a click-of-a-button solution to run all the standard analysis tools and gain an overview of the security of a given primitive.

The library's source code has been made available to the wider community and is publicly accessible at Github: https://github.com/Crypto-TII/claasp. Also, in Github: https://github.com/peacker/claasp_white_paper, you can find the scripts used to accompany this paper.

We first present existing cryptanalysis libraries in Sect. 1.1, before introducing the building blocks of CLAASP: the cipher object in Sect. 2, and the evaluators in Sect. 3. We then present the battery of tests and tools implemented in CLAASP in Sect. 4, and finish with a comparison with other cryptographic libraries in Sect. 5.

1.1 Related Works

Automated tools to support cryptanalysts have become a cornerstone for the design of new primitives. Over time, such tools were made more generic and gathered into libraries; we describe the most prominent ones in this section.

The lineartrails library [23] is dedicated to the search for linear characteristics on SPN ciphers. ARX toolkit [32,33] and YAARX [56] focus on ARX ciphers, the former testing conditions for trails to be possible, and the latter performing various analysis techniques on the components.

On the algebraic cryptanalysis side, the Automated Algebraic Cryptanalysis tool [51] tests properties of block and stream ciphers; in particular, it evaluates the randomness of a cipher through Maximum Degree Monomial tests [52].

Autoguess [27] is a tool to automate the technique guess-and-determine. This technique involves making a calculated guess of a subset of the unknown variables, which enables the deduction of the remaining unknowns using the information obtained from the guessed variables and some given relations. In order to automate this technique, SAT/SMT, MILP, and Gröbner basis solvers are used and several new modeling techniques to exploit these solver proposed. For instance, the authors of the library introduce new encodings in CP and

SAT/SMT to solve the problem of determining the minimal guess, i.e., the subset of guessed variables from which the remaining variables can be deduced. Autoguess also allows to automate the key-bridging technique. This technique is utilized in key-recovery attacks on block ciphers, wherein the attacker seeks to determine the minimum number of sub-key guesses needed to deduce all the involved sub-keys through the key schedule. The significant contribution of this work lies in integrating key-bridging techniques into tools that were previously only capable of searching for distinguishers. As a result, these enhanced tools can now be utilized as fully automatic methods for recovering keys.

CryptoSMT [53] is the first large-scale solver-based library dedicated to cryptanalysis. Based on SMT and SAT solvers, it provides an extensive toolkit, permitting the search for optimal differential and linear trails, the evaluation of the probability of a differential, the search for hash function preimages, and secret key search.

The study described in [28] presents an innovative approach to explore differentials and linear approximations. Different from methods that rely on SAT or MILP techniques, this approach transforms the search for differential and linear trails into a problem of identifying multiple long paths within a multistage graph. A practical implementation of this research, called CryptaGraph, is available in [29]. One notable feature of CryptaGraph is its automatic conversion capability, enabling C or Rust implementations of ciphers to be transformed into models for searching differentials or linear approximations using the graph-based approach mentioned earlier. An improvement of [28] can be found in [30] and its implementation was named PathFinder.

Another SMT-based library, based on ArxPy [43] is the CASCADA framework [44], which also implements techniques to search for rotational-XOR differentials, impossible-rotational-XOR, but also related-key impossible-differentials, linear approximations, and zero-correlation characteristics. The generated SMT models are expressed through the theory of bit-vectors [5], and follow the general methodology of Mouha and Preneel [39] for differential properties, Sasaki's [48] technique for impossible differentials, an SMT-based miss-in-the middle search for related-key impossible differentials of ARX ciphers [4], and a novel method proposed for zero-probability global properties. If a search can not use the previous methods, then a generic method, based on the constructions of statistical tables, such as the Differential Distribution Table (DDT), is used. Depending on the sizes of the inputs of the block cipher, these generic models could be costly, so they also proposed heuristic models by relaxing the accuracy of their properties; they called them weak models. Finally, their framework implements methods to check the properties mentioned above experimentally.

Finally, TAGADA [34] is a tool which generates Minizinc [41] models for the search for differential properties on word-based SPN ciphers, such as the AES. The search for such ciphers is typically divided into two steps, one where the word variables are abstracted as boolean values denoting the presence or absence of a difference, and one where the abstracted solutions from step 1 are instantiated to word values, when possible. The models generated by TAGADA implement the first step, including optimisations based on inferred equalities through XOR operators, in order to drastically reduce the number of incorrect solutions to be passed to step 2. Such constraints are deduced naturally from a Directed Acyclic Graph (DAG) representation of the cipher under study. The genericity of Minizinc models enables solving with a range of CP, SAT and SMT solvers, in particular, the ones participating in the MiniZinc competition, that provide an interface to MiniZinc. On the other hand, solver-specific optimisations and perks are abstracted away by the Minizinc interface, compared to models developped in the native language of a solver.

A summary of the functionalities of these libraries is presented in Table 1.

Table 1. Comparison of cryptanalysis libraries features with CLAASP. -* means that the functionality is not supported, but could easily be added from the existing code. ** means the algebraic tests works on algebraic model for cipher preimages.

		TAGADA	CASCADA	CryptoSMT	lineartrails	YAARX	Autoguess	CLAASP
Cipher types		SPN	All	All	SPN	ARX	All	All
Cipher representation		DAG	Python code	Python code	C++ code	C code	Algebraic representation	DAG
Statistical/Avalanche tests		-	-	-	-	-	-	Yes
Continuous diffusion tests		-	-	-	-	-	-	Yes
Components analysis tests		-	-	-	-	-	-	Yes
Constraint solvers	Differential trails	Truncated	Yes	Yes	-	Yes	-	Yes
	Differentials	-	Yes	Yes	-	Yes	-	Yes
	Impossible differential	-	Yes	-*	-	-	-	Yes
	Linear trails	-	Yes	Yes	Yes	-	-	Yes
	Linear hull	-	-*	-*	-	-	-	Yes
	Zero correlation approximation	-	Yes	-*	-	-	-	Yes
	Supported solvers	CP, (MiniZinc)	SMT	SMT	-	-	SAT, SMT, MILP, CP, Groebner basis	SAT, SMT, MILP, CP, Groebner basis
	Supported Scenarios	single-key related-key	single-key related-key	single-key related-key	single-key	single-key	single-key related-key single-tweak related-tweak	single-key related-key single-tweak related-tweak
Algebraic tests		-	-	-	-	-	-	Yes**
Neural-based tests		-	-	-	-	-	-	Yes
State Recovery		-	-	-	-	-	Yes	-
Key-bridging		-	-	-	-	-	Yes	-

1.2   Our Contribution

We introduce CLAASP, a Cryptographic Library for the Automated Analysis of Symmetric Primitives. CLAASP has been designed to simplify the manual tasks of symmetric cipher designers and analysts. CLAASP has been designed with the following goals:

- Be *open-source* with a GPLv3 licence.
- Be *modular*. For this reason it is built on top of Sagemath, thus inheriting Python modularity.
- Be *extendable*. The Python/Sagemath environment allows to easily integrate other powerful libraries: constraint solvers such as Cryptominisat, Cadical or Gurobi, machine learning engines such as Tensorflow, Grobner basis solvers, parallelization packages such as NumPy, etc.
- Be *usable*. Much effort has been dedicated to provide a smooth user experience for both designing and analyzing a cipher. This includes a comprehensive documentation for users and developers, and a Docker image to easily start with the library without the need of installing all the dependencies.
- Be *generic*. The wide range of pre-defined components, allows to implement a wide range of iterated symmetric ciphers, ranging from block ciphers (possibly with a tweak), cryptographic permutations, hash functions, and covering several design types such as Feistel, SPN, ARX, etc.
- Be *automated*. The concept of the library revolves around providing a cipher design as the input and getting an analysis of the cipher design as the output with respect to some desired property.
- Be *efficient*. In spite of being the most generic and fully automated tool of its kind, this library is competitive in terms of efficiency with similar tools targeting specific sectors.

The central objects of CLAASP are symmetric ciphers. They are described as directed acyclic graphs whose nodes are components (S-Boxes, linear layers, constants, Input/Output, etc.) and whose edges are input/output component connections. From this representation, the library can automatically:

1. generate the Python or C code of the evaluation function;
2. execute a wide range of statistical and avalanche tests on the primitive, including continuous diffusion tests;
3. generate a report containing the main properties of the cipher components;
4. generate SAT, SMT, CP and MILP models to search, for example, differential and linear trails;
5. measure algebraic properties of the primitive;
6. test neural-based distinguishers.

We demonstrate that CLAASP can reproduce many of the results that were obtained in the literature: in terms of différential cryptanalysis, we retrieve similar results to CASCADA for the 1 to 7 rounds of SPECK32, 64, and LEA128. Furthermore, we were able to find an optimal differential trail for Speck 128-128 reduced to 10 rounds. To the best of our knowledge, optimal trails for this specific version of Speck were only known for up to 9 rounds. This achievement was made possible by seamlessly integrating a Parallel SAT solver into CLAASP. In particular, we successfully incorporated ParKissat, the winner of the SAT competition 2022 (parallel track) [57], into the SAT module of CLAASP. In addition, we show how to use CLAASP to retrieve the known 17-rounds impossible differential on HIGHT, as well as 6-round impossible differentials on SPECK32.

Regarding linear cryptanalysis, we obtain a linear trail of Salsa with better correlation than the one reported in [17]. This discovery has the potential to enhance the correlation of the differential-linear distinguisher against Salsa reduced to 8 rounds presented in the aforementioned paper. Finally, in terms of neural cryptanalysis, CLAASP implements (and can reproduce the results of) [10], in addition to the seminal results of [26]. In addition, researchers willing to apply neural cryptanalysis to new ciphers using the techniques from [10] can do so in a straight-forward manner using the library functions.

Besides the presentation of the library, important contributions of this work are a survey and a comparison (where possible) of the main software tools trying to achieve the same goals as CLAASP.

2   Symmetric Primitives in CLAASP

In this section, we describe how a symmetric primitive is represented in CLAASP. We also present the main pre-implemented primitives that are available for testing and give some indications on how to build a custom cipher.

2.1   The Component Class

In CLAASP, a symmetric cipher is represented as a list of "connected components". The *components* of a symmetric cipher are its building blocks (S-Boxes, linear layers, etc.). Two components are *connected* when the output bits of the first component become the input bits of the second component, in a one-to-one correspondence. The library supports the following *primitive* components: the S-Box component, linear layer components (fixed and variable rotation, fixed and variable shift, bit and word permutation, multiplication by a binary or word matrix), word operations components (NOT, AND, OR, XOR, modular addition and subtraction), and the constant component. It also supports *composite* components, which are a combination of primitive components: the sigma function used in ASCON, the theta function used in Keccak, and the theta function used in Xoodoo. For example, the linear layer in ASCON can be presented by the combination of several XOR and ROTATE components, or as a composite component. Composite components can also be created at a user level.

Finally, some special components are used to represent the inputs of the cipher, and cipher intermediate and final outputs.

In CLAASP, each component requires the following minimal information: a unique component ID (e.g. "sbox_0_0"); a component type (e.g. "sbox"); the input and output bit size of the component; a list of the components that are connected to the input of the component (a list of IDs); a list of lists of bits positions specifying which output bits of the input components are connected to the component; a description containing the necessary information to finalize the definition of the component (e.g., the list of integers defining an SBox).

2.2   The Cipher Class

Ciphers as Directed Acyclic Graphs. In CLAASP, a symmetric cipher is represented as a list of connected components, forming a directed acyclic graph, and a list of basic properties, listed in Table 2.

Table 2. Parameters that are used to define a cipher in CLAASP.

Property	Description
id	unique identifier of the cipher, composed by cipher name and parameters
family_name	name of the cipher family, such as AES, ASCON, etc
type	type of the cipher (block cipher, permutation, hash or stream cipher)
inputs	inputs of the cipher, such as key and plaintext
inputs_bit_size	list of number of bits of each input parameters
output_bit_size	number of bits of the cipher output
number_of_rounds	number of rounds in the cipher
rounds	list of rounds each containing a list of components
reference_code	[optional] Python reference code (as a string) of the cipher evaluation function, used to verify the cipher correctness

CLAASP supports *iterated symmetric ciphers*, based on the composition of several round functions, which are themselves a list of connected components; each cipher must have at least one round. The round decomposition is useful and common in symmetric cipher design and cryptanalysis; in most tests, a given property is studied round by round.

CLAASP natively implements a range of well-known block ciphers (AES, TEA, DES, XTEA, LEA, Twofish, LowMC, Threefish, Midori, HIGHT, PRESENT, SKINNY, Raiden, Sparx, SIMON, SPECK), permutations (ASCON, Xoodoo, ChaCha, Spongent-π, GIFT-128, TinyJAMBU, GIMLI, Grain core, KECCAK-p, PHOTON, SPARKLE) and hash functions (SHA-1, SHA-2, MD5, BLAKE, BLAKE2). This list is meant to be expanded over time.

How to Create the Cipher Object. While native support for more primitives will be added over time, CLAASP exposes a simple interface for users to add new ones as well. This process is illustrated through a toy example of a 2-rounds cipher with 6-bit block, 6-bit key injected in every round with a XOR operation, 2 3-bit S-boxes, and a linear layer made of a left rotation of 1 bit, shown in Fig. 2, and the corresponding CLAASP implementation in Fig. 1.

The main concern of a user implementing a primitive is to correctly link the components at a bit level, and mark which component or group of components need to be reported in the output of the tests. This is because a user might be

interested not only in getting reports at every round, but, for example, after the
linear and the nonlinear layer of an SPN.

Cipher Inputs. It is important to notice that, in order to be generic, the library
has been designed to accept multiple inputs which can be labeled with different
names: for example, a key, a plaintext and a tweak, or a message and a nonce. On
the other hand, to better exploit the features of some tests, a naming convention
has been introduced for inputs such as "key" or "plaintext".

The *cipher Representation* is not unique. The *cipher representation* as a
list of connected components is *not* unique. For example, the nonlinear layer of
ASCON permutation can be represented as a circuit made of word operation
components (XOR, AND and NOT) or with a layer of parallel S-boxes.

```
from claasp.cipher import Cipher

class ToySPN(Cipher):
    def __init__(self):
        super().__init__(family_name="toyspn",
            cipher_type="block_cipher",
            cipher_inputs=["plaintext", "key"],
            cipher_inputs_bit_size=[6, 6],
            cipher_output_bit_size=6)

        sbox = [0, 5, 3, 2, 6, 1, 4, 7]
        self.add_round()
        xor = self.add_XOR_component(["plaintext", "key"
            ], [[0,1,2,3,4,5],[0,1,2,3,4,5]],6)
        sbox1 = self.add_SBOX_component([xor.id], [[0, 1,
            2]], 3, sbox)
        sbox2 = self.add_SBOX_component([xor.id], [[3, 4,
            5]], 3, sbox)
        rotate = self.add_rotate_component([sbox1.id,
            sbox2.id],[[0, 1, 2], [0, 1, 2]], 6, 1)
        self.add_round_output_component([rotate.id], [[0,
            1, 2, 3, 4, 5]], 6)

        self.add_round()
        xor = self.add_XOR_component([rotate.id, "key"
            ], [[0,1,2,3,4,5],[0,1,2,3,4,5]],6)
        sbox1 = self.add_SBOX_component([xor.id], [[0, 1,
            2]], 3, sbox)
        sbox2 = self.add_SBOX_component([xor.id], [[3, 4,
            5]], 3, sbox)
        rotate = self.add_rotate_component([sbox1.id,
            sbox2.id],[[0, 1, 2], [0, 1, 2]], 6, 1)
        self.add_cipher_output_component([rotate.id], [[0,
            1, 2, 3, 4, 5]], 6)

toyspn = ToySPN()
hex(toyspn.evaluate([0x3F,0x3F]))
```

Fig. 1. ToySPN class definition.

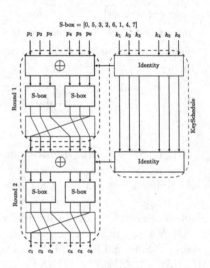

Fig. 2. ToySPN diagram.

Different *cipher representations* may affect the output of tests; for instance, a
naive differential cryptanalysis model built for an ASCON implementation using
the circuit representation is less accurate than one using a S-Box representation.
In general, the circuit model is useful when a user wishes to monitor the action
of every gate (i.e. word operation) on a single bit. On the other hand an S-Box-
based model often allows a faster evaluation function.

CLAASP implements both S-Box and circuit representations for some primitives, such as ASCON, Xoodoo, Keccak and Gimli, as well as the bit-based and
word-based such as TinyJambu representations.

3 Library: Evaluation Modules

The most basic functionality of CLAASP is to evaluate a cryptographic primitive on a given input. Basic C and Python evaluation functions provide non-optimized evaluation for single inputs, and a vectorized evaluation functions permits fast batch evaluation. For instance, using the vectorized implementation, it takes around 3 s to perform one million AES encryptions. A detailed performance review is given in the long version of this paper [8].

Base Evaluator in Python and C. In CLAASP, users can create a cipher object and call an evaluation method to evaluate a particular input. This functionality is also used internally in CLAASP by some of the modules, to run, for example, avalanche or statistical tests. The corresponding Python and C code[1] is generated automatically by scanning the list of components.

Vectorized Implementations. In Python, the NumPy library allows to vectorize function evaluations on an *array*, rather than a single input. NumPy arrays are typed and homogeneous, which, combined with NumPy's optimisations, enables significant performance gains compared to Python native lists and loops.

The cipher object provides the NumPy-based *evaluate_vectorized* function. The inputs are specified as NumPy arrays, of 8-bit unsigned integer values, arranged as one column per data point. The return value is encoded as a list containing a single NumPy array of 8-bit unsigned integer values, this time arranged as one row per data point. The choice of using bytes stems from NumPy's lack of support for integers over 64 bits.

4 Library: Test Modules

In this section, we describe all automated analysis modules that are currently supported in CLAASP. Many of the analysis tools presented here are derived from differential and linear cryptanalysis [13], the cornerstones of modern symmetric primitives evaluation. Let $S_K(X)$ be a symmetric primitive; differential cryptanalysis focuses on the probability, over all inputs, for a difference δ to propagate to γ, *i.e.*, $X, Pr[S_k(X) \oplus S_K(X \oplus \delta)] = \gamma$. Conversely, linear cryptanalysis focuses on the correlation for a linear mask Γ_0 to propagate to Γ_1, $Pr[S_k(X) \cdot \Gamma_1 = X \cdot \Gamma_0]$. In both cases, the cryptographer is interested in finding *differences* (resp. *masks*) for which this probability (resp. correlation) is high.

4.1 Component Analysis

This module allows the visualization of the "quality" of certain properties of the components used in a cipher, by means of radar charts. These properties include:

---

[1] When possible a word-oriented implementation is used, opposed to a slower bit-oriented implementation for primitives with mixed type of components.

Boolean function properties (number of terms, algebraic degree, number of variables, whether the Boolean function is APN or balanced), vectorial Boolean function properties (differential uniformity, boomerang uniformity, nonlinearity, etc.), linear layer properties (order, linear and differential branch number).

More precisely, this module allows to retrieve the list of the components used in the cipher, the number of occurrences of each component, and the corresponding properties. For example, for 2 rounds of AES-128, the user will notice that a XOR operation between 2 inputs of 128 bits each occurs 3 times. If one considers XOR output bits expressed as a Boolean function, then each of these XOR components has an algebraic degree of 1 with 2 terms, and 2 variables. The generated radar chart visualisations are provided in [8].

4.2 Statistical and Avalanche Tests

Statistical Tests. Statistical tests, such as Diehard [37], or its successor Dieharder [16], evaluate the randomness of a set of bit strings. Such tests were applied to evaluate AES candidates [7,49,50] through the NIST Statistical Test Suite (NIST STS) [6,46]. CLAASP implements both the NIST STS and Dieharder suites within the statistical test module. The statistical test process is divided into two phases, dataset generation and analysis.

Dataset Generator. The datasets used in CLAASP which covers keyed primitives are defined in [49]. Keyless primitives datasets are somehow special cases of the keyed ones. As an example, the illustration of the avalanche dataset generator is shown in Appendix B of [8]. The dataset generator, which returns a set of bit strings, is based on CLAASP's vectorized evaluation method.

Statistical Test Tools. The results of NIST STS and Dieharder are exported into a file and additionally returned as a Python dictionary for easy integration into scripts. CLAASP also features visualization of the results, as shown in Fig. 3.

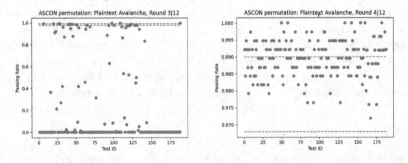

Fig. 3. CLAASP plot for the 188 NIST statistical tests pass rate of ASCON round 3 and round 4.

Performance and Experiments. To generate the plaintext avalanche test for all supported primitives (191 Gigabits), it takes 4 h. For a 100 Mbits dataset, it takes around 30 min to finish the NIST statistical tests. Figure 4 shows the number of tests that pass for each round of ASCON (left) and the percentage of the rounds needed to pass all statistical tests with respect to the 9 possible datasets for several primitives.

Avalanche Tests. This module focuses on the avalanche properties, presented in [20], of a symmetric iterated primitive. These tests evaluate the cipher with respect to three different metrics that represent what usually the literature calls *full diffusion, avalanche* and *strict avalanche* criteria. The goal of the tests is to compare how these metric evolve with respect to the computational cost of the round function; each metric is expected to satisfy a certain criterion (namely to pass a threshold) after a few rounds.

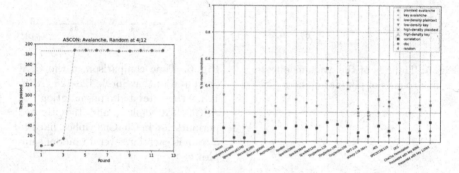

Fig. 4. Randomness graphs of ASCON generated by CLAASP. Left side is the statistical test result of avalanche dataset. Right side are all the statistical results of ASCON compared with other primitives.

Measure Avalanche Criteria. The results of the avalanche tests allow a user to: check if a criterion is satisfied at a certain round for a specific input bit difference; obtain the worst input bit differences, that are the input bit differences for which the criterion is satisfied after more rounds than the rest of the input bit differences; obtain the value of the criterion for a specific round and a specific input bit difference; obtain the average value of the criterion among all the input bit differences for a specific round. For better visualization, CLAASP can generate a heatmap graph of the output returned by the avalanche tests, as illustrated in the long version of the paper [8].

Performance. Figure 5 reports the timings of the avalanche tests for 5 rounds of some popular ciphers, using the vectorized evaluation function, up to 50,000 samples; all tests run globally in less than 5 min.

Truncated Differential Search. This module offers a range of features, including the ability to easily discover truncated differentials with only one active bit in both the input and output states. Such differentials, when paired with linear approximations, can be very useful for increasing the correlations of differential-linear distinguishers. For instance, we successfully used this module to rediscover the truncated differential outlined in [3], which has been cited and studied extensively in various papers (such as [22]). To view the script we used to rediscover this differential, you can refer to the accompanying repository for this paper.

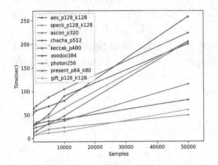

Fig. 5. Timings of the avalanche tests for five rounds of popular ciphers

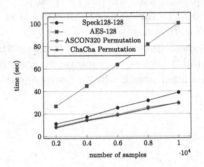

Fig. 6. Time comparison of the CAF computation for Speck 128-128, AES-128, the iterated permutation in ASCON320 cipher, and the iterated permutation in ChaCha cipher, fixed to 5 rounds each for several random samples.

4.3   Constraint Solvers for Differential and Linear Cryptanalysis

The search for strong differential or linear properties often relies on *trails, i.e.*, round by round propagation of the property under study; the final probability of the trail, under the Markov assumption that all round keys are independent, is computed as the product of the probabilities of each round. Finding such trails is a difficult combinatorial problem, traditionally handled with Matsui's algorithm [38] variations. In recent years, the use of automatic solvers, such as Mixed Integer Linear Programming (MILP), SAT, SMT, and more recently Constraint Programming (CP), have become a simpler alternative. These tools have the benefit of being extensively studied and optimized by the AI and OR communities, so that the focus shifts from implementing a search algorithm to modeling the problem properly. CLAASP can automatically generate MILP, SAT, SMT and CP models for differential and linear cryptanalysis, from a primitive's description.

Differential and Linear Models for ARX Ciphers. In order to implement the search for differential and linear trails on ARX ciphers, we utilized the techniques outlined in [19] and in [35]. Specifically, we implemented the MILP constraints described in those papers for the ARX components and were able to successfully replicate the trails reported therein. In addition to the MILP constraints described there, we also implemented SAT, CP, and SMT equivalent constraints not only for ARX ciphers but also for SPN ciphers. To accelerate the search for trails using SAT techniques, we implemented the sequential encoding method presented in [54] on CLAASP. Moreover, through modeling the cipher evaluation process (as discussed in Sect. 3) using MILP, SAT, CP, and SMT, we were able to implement the techniques outlined in [47]. Those techniques aimed to verify the validity of differential trails. In particular, by using those techniques, their authors reported some invalid trails presented in [36]. The scripts accompanying this paper demonstrate how we used CLAASP to verify differential trails.

For linear trails on ARX ciphers, we were able to rediscover trails presented in recent papers, such as those presented for two well-studied ciphers, such as Speck and ChaCha. Specifically, we rediscover the linear trails presented at [17] and the linear trails outlined in [9]. The former presents the best attacks against ChaCha reduced to 7 rounds, while the second is a recent paper attacking Speck. Again, the scripts accompanying this paper demonstrate how we used CLAASP to verify these linear trails.

New Results. Our library supports a range of SAT solvers, including parallel solvers, which we believe is a unique feature not found in other cryptanalysis libraries. By utilizing the CLAASP interface, we were able to search for differential and linear trails using parallel SAT solvers. We managed to find an optimal differential trail for 10 rounds of Speck 128-128. This accomplishment was made possible by utilizing the power of 125 AMD EPYC 7763 cores on a Ubuntu machine with 1TB of memory. To confirm the optimality of this trail, we used CLAASP in conjunction with ParKissat [57] to search for a 10-round trail of this version of Speck with a probability weight of 48. It took approximately 2.23 days to obtain as output UNSAT. The script accompanying this paper contains the details of this finding.

Regarding linear cryptanalysis, we obtain a linear trail for Salsa with better theoretical correlation than the one reported in [17]. We start from the same input bit mask described in Lemma 10 and Lemma 11 of [17]. Specifically, we found a trail with a theoretical correlation of 2^{-31} instead of 2^{-34} as described in [17]. This accomplishment was made possible by utilizing the SAT module of CLAASP. We use only 1 AMD EPYC core, and the trail was found in less than 1 min. We attempt to find a trail with a theoretical correlation of 2^{-30}, but the solver outputs UNSAT. This discovery has the potential to enhance the correlation of the differential-linear distinguisher against Salsa reduced to 8 rounds presented in the aforementioned paper. The reader can reproduce the trail by using the script accompanying this paper.

Differential and Linear Models for SPN Ciphers. SPN ciphers use Substitution Boxes (SBoxes) as their non-linear component. In addition, their linear layers can typically be expressed as a matrix multiplication. The representation of SBoxes in differential search models typically uses its *Differential Distribution Table*, or DDT. The DDT is a 2 dimensional object such that $DDT_{\delta,\gamma} = \frac{\#\{x \in \mathbb{F}_2^n : x \oplus y = \delta, SB[x] \oplus SB[y] = \gamma\}}{2^n}$. Models for linear trails use the Linear Approximation Table (LAT) built in a similar fashion instead. To represent the DDT in SAT, SMT or MILP, a constraint to forbid each invalid triplet $(\delta, \gamma, Pr[\delta \rightarrow \gamma])$ is typically introduced [55]. Techniques such as the Quine-McCluskey algorithm [42] or the heuristic *Espresso* are used to reduce the number of generated equations. In the case of Constraint Programming (CP), *table constraints* permit to directly enforce the constraint $(\delta, \gamma, Pr[\delta \rightarrow \gamma]) \in DDT$, where DDT is the set of valid tuples [25]. These techniques are implemented in CLAASP.

Differential and Linear Trails Search. CLAASP exposes functions to generate, for either paradigm among SAT, SMT, MILP or CP, a model for the search of differential or linear trails. More specifically, CLAASP implements the generation of models to find: (1) One optimal (highest objective value) trail; or (2) All trails for which the objective value is within a fixed range. The functions generating these models take, as an additional parameter, a list of variables for which the values are to be fixed, and the corresponding values. Single-key trails are found by setting the key variables to zero, while related-key trails are found by placing no restrictions.

Application to Differential Probability and Linear Hull Evaluation. Trails with identical input and output can be combined into a *differential* or a *linear hull* with higher probability than single trails. Observing differentials (or linear hulls), rather than single trails, can result in attacks on more rounds; the gap between the two cases is studied in [1]. CLAASP permits the enumeration of trails with fixed variables, so that the evaluation of the probability of a differential, by enumerating all trails better than a certain weight with a fixed input and output, is straightforward.

Application to Impossible Differential and Zero-correlation Linear Approximation Search. Impossible differentials, as well as their counterpart in the linear world, zero-correlation linear hulls, are also of interest to cryptographer. CLAASP implements a technique similar to [19] to find such properties; the main idea is to fix an input and output difference, and to look for a trail with a solver; if no trail is found, then we have an impossible differential.

As an example, we reproduce the 3 impossible differentials for 6 rounds of SPECK32/64 presented in [45] in less than 30 s using the SMT model.

4.4   Continuous Diffusion Tests

In [18], Coutinho *et. al*, describe a framework to construct continuous functions from Boolean ones. Assuming independence, these functions provide the probability or correlation between the output bits being 1 based on an input of real numbers that represent the probability of each input bit being 1. They are also able to generalize various cryptographic operations, leading to the creation of continuous versions of entire cryptographic algorithms.

Upon these continuous versions of cryptographic algorithms, they construct three metrics, namely Continuous Avalanche Factor (CAF), Continuous Neutrality Measure (CNM), and Diffusion Factor (DF). The CAF is the continuous equivalent of the avalanche factor [21], which measures the proportion of output bits that change for input Hamming distances equal to 1 on average; this proportion is expected to be 0.5 for a random permutation. In the continuous version, since there is no concept of Hamming distance, the Euclidean Distance (ED) is used to evaluate CAF. The idea behind CAF is to measure how much the output of a continuous version of an algorithm changes, on average, when the input bit's probability of being equal to 1 of a chosen random bit is slightly altered by a small real number λ. In other words, we need to evaluate, on average, the behavior of the ED between the outputs $y_0 = f(x_0)$ and $y_1 = f(x_1)$ for $x_0, x_1 \in \mathbb{B}$, when the ED of x_0 and x_1 is lesser than λ. It is expected for "good ciphers" that even with small values of λ, higher values on the ED of the propagation of these alterations, on average. For more information on the other two metrics (CNM and DF), see [18].

Within the continuous diffusion test module, CLAASP implements the continuous versions of several cryptographic operations, following Theorem 1 and Definitions 1 to 12 from [18], which can be combined to obtain the continuous version of entire primitives.

The performance of Speck 128-128, AES-128, the iterated permutations in ASCON320 and the iterated permutation in ChaCha with respect to CAF, subject to $\lambda = 0.001$, is presented in Table 3. For the iterated permutation in ChaCha, a single round is equivalent to four half-quarter rounds in the table. Figure 6 displays the timing comparison of these ciphers for various sample sizes used in computing CAF. The experiments were conducted on a Ubuntu 22.04.1 machine equipped with 256 AMD core processors and 1TB of memory.

When comparing Table 3 to Table 2 in [18], we observed slight variations in the CAF values reported in Fig. 6 compared to the values presented in [18]. This difference is due to our use of the Python Decimal package to handle small numbers, while the implementation of Table 2 in [18] employed the Relic library [2]. For instance, for five rounds of AES-128, we obtained a value of 0.777, whereas [18] reports 0.734.

Table 3. Continuous Avalanche Factor comparison for AES-128, ASCON320 permutation, ChaCha permutation, and Speck 128-128 using $\lambda = 0.001$.

Rounds	AES	ASCON	ChaCha	Speck -
1 to 4	0	0	0	0
5	0.777	0.008	0	0
6	0.971	0.761	0.019	0
7	0.999	0.962	0.257	0.002
8	–	0.998	0.694	0.067
9	–	0.999	0.939	0.318
10	–	–	0.993	0.613
11	–	–	–	0.828
12	–	–	–	0.941
13	–	–	–	0.98
14	–	–	–	0.997

4.5 Algebraic Module

The objective of this module is to study the algebraic properties and algebraic attack resistance of a specified cipher. In algebraic cryptanalysis, breaking a block or stream cipher, involves solving a set of multivariate polynomial equations over a finite field $\mathbb{F}_q$, which often has one or a few solutions in $\mathbb{F}_q$, but solving a system of multivariate random polynomials is generally a hard task.

This module generates a multivariate algebraic polynomial system corresponding to the "sbox", "linear_ layer", "mix_column", and "constant" components, together with the "XOR", "AND", "OR", "SHIFT", "ROTATE", and "NOT" operations. It provides a set of polynomials representing the components and operations involved in a particular input cipher along with connection polynomials, which represent the links between the various components. From the polynomial system, it is possible to retrieve its algebraic degree, number of polynomials, and number of variables in order to analyze its algebraic features and the difficulty of solving the system. The security of a cipher (up to a particular number of rounds) against algebraic attacks could be evaluated by solving the corresponding algebraic system up to that many rounds. The module now offers a method to test it by solving the system in a time limit using only the Gröbner basis computation [15] available on the SAGE platform.

The algebraic module is currently in its preliminary stage and will be improved in upcoming releases.

4.6 Neural Aided Cryptanalysis Module

Following Aron Gohr's seminal paper at CRYPTO'19 [26], improving the state-of-the-art differential cryptanalysis result on the SPECK32-64 cipher, neural-based approaches to cryptanalysis have gained traction in the community. In

Gohr's approach, a neural network is trained to distinguish, from an input composed of 2 ciphertexts in binary format, whether they correspond to the encryption of two unrelated plaintexts, or of two plaintexts with a given XOR difference. CLAASP implements such approaches, and other neural-based analysis tools.

Single Ciphertext Approach: Neural Network Black box Distinguisher Tests. Differential neural cryptanalysis examines pairs of plaintexts. The black box test implemented by CLAASP takes a step back, and focuses on single ciphertexts. Built from [11], this test investigates whether a neural network can find a relation between the inputs of a primitive and its output. The neural network is trained to label samples $[P, C]$ as 0 (if Y is random) or 1 if Y is the output of a given component of the primitive. This test returns the accuracy of distinguishing a ciphertext coming from an instance of the cipher with a certain key and the output of a random permutation. After a certain amount of rounds, the accuracy will converge to 0.5, meaning that the black box distinguisher is not able to distinguish the cipher output from random.

Pairs of Ciphertexts: Neural Network Differential Distinguisher Tests. This test implements the neural distinguisher described by Gohr in [26], with the simplified training pipeline described in [10], where a depth-1 neural distinguisher trained on n rounds is iteratively retrained for $n+1, \ldots n+t$ rounds, where $n+t$ is the first round where the neural distinguisher fails to learn. Specifically, the neural distinguisher is trained to label samples $[C_0 = E_K(P_0), C_1 = E_K(P_1)]$ as 0 (if $P_0 \oplus P_1$ is random) or 1 if $P_0 \oplus P_1$ is a given, fixed value δ.

Helper Function: Truncated Differential Search For Neural Distinguishers. The previous test relies on an input difference with good propagation properties. It has been observed [26] that the input difference that starts the most likely differential does not result in the best neural distinguishers. Further research [12] suggested differential-linear properties, based on highly likely truncated differentials a few rounds before the studied round, may be at play. This assumption was used as the basis to an input difference search technique [10], where a genetic algorithm explores potential input differences and ranks them based on the cumulative biases of the resulting output difference bits. This algorithm is implemented by CLAASP, and can be used to retrieve Gohr's original input difference.

These functions are illustrated in the supplementary material. The script first runs the black box test on 1 round of Speck 64, then runs the input difference search for Speck 64, and trains Gohr's neural network using the optimal difference returned by the optimizer. Note that the optimizer is not deterministic, and its parameters are adapted for a reasonably fast execution time for demonstration purposes; therefore, it may, in some rare instance, fail to find the optimal input difference $0x00400000$.

5   Benchmark Comparison with Other Libraries

In this section we compare CLAASP to similar libraries.

5.1   TAGADA

The TAGADA library focuses on the differential cryptanalysis of word-oriented ciphers with an SPN structure. For such ciphers, it is common (e.g., [14]) to divide the search into two steps. The first step aims to find truncated differential characteristics through the minimization of the non-linear operators utilized in this process. The second step enumerates the truncated differential characteristic passing to the minimum number of non-linear operators found in the previous step. It was shown [25] that the filtering of the first step may be insufficient so that too many solutions are left to explore in step 2. More advanced filtering is, therefore, beneficial and enables scaling to more rounds. This is done through additional constraints that capture linear dependencies between variables during step 1. The TAGADA library generalizes such constraints, making it very efficient for word-based ciphers. These techniques are not, at the moment, included in CLAASP, so TAGADA is expected to perform significantly better on word-based characteristics search. We are planning to include these additional constraints in the next releases of CLAASP.

On the other hand, the basic version of the first step, searching for the minimum number of active SBoxes of SPN ciphers, is implemented in CLAASP. TAGADA implements the option of running the first step search with the basic technique used in CLAASP; we attempted to run the search for 3 and 4 rounds of AES-128, but we were not able to reproduce the known results from [24,31,40] with TAGADA, which reported 2 and 7 SBoxes respectively, rather than the expected 3 and 9. On the other hand, CLAASP returned the expected solution. Note that TAGADA can only generate MiniZinc models, while CLAASP allows to directly write the model in the language supported by the solvers (including a MiniZinc interface).

5.2   CASCADA

We compared CLÁASP and CASCADA based on the time spent seeking optimal characteristics in single-key scenarios for ciphers Speck 32-64, Speck 64-128, and LEA across multiple rounds, using SMT solvers: MathSAT, Yices, and Z3. Average timings from five repetitions per round were considered. Testing was on an Ubuntu 22.04.1 machine with 256 AMD cores and 1TB RAM. With the Yices solver, CLAASP's performance mirrored CASCADA. However, it outperformed with MathSAT and Z3. See a detailed graph in the appendix of the longer version of this paper [8].

In terms of functionalities, CASCADA includes the search for impossible differentials, in particular through the method of [19]. In this method, the variables corresponding to the input and output differences of a differential are fixed to a value that the analyst wants to test, and the solver is run. If the solver finds a solution, then the differential is possible; otherwise, it is impossible. In this method, the analyst usually tests all the pairs of input and output differences of low hamming weight (typically 1). A similar technique can be used for zero-correlation linear approximations. Using this method, CLAASP can for instance retrieve the 17-rounds impossible differential on HIGHT presented in [19] in under 10 min on a single core.

6   Conclusion

The fast-paced publication of new cryptanalysis techniques, of improvement of existing ones, makes it crucial to have an efficient way to test a given property on a large number of primitives; CLAASP aims to fulfill this need. In its current form, it already offers a vast array of cipher analysis techniques, from component analysis, to automatic models building, through neural cryptanalysis. Future releases will add more primitives, as well as further analysis techniques, such as guess-and-determine or meet-in-the-middle techniques. More importantly, the CLAASP team is strongly committed to include new state-of-the-art improvements to automated techniques as it evolves, and provide a one-stop shop to evaluate, compare and experiment with modifications on existing methods. Finally, the open-source status of the library is an invitation to researchers from the community to not only use, but also improve CLAASP as they see fit.

References

1. Ankele, R., Kölbl, S.: Mind the gap - a closer look at the security of block ciphers against differential cryptanalysis. In: Cid, C., Jr., M.J.J. (eds.) SAC 2018. LNCS, vol. 11349, pp. 163–190. Springer, Cham (2018). https://doi.org/10.1007/978-3-030-10970-7_8
2. Aranha, D.F., Gouvêa, C.P.L., Markmann, T., Wahby, R.S., Liao, K.: RELIC is an efficient library for cryptography. https://github.com/relic-toolkit/relic
3. Aumasson, J.-P., Çalık, Ç., Meier, W., Özen, O., Phan, R.C.-W., Varıcı, K.: Improved cryptanalysis of skein. In: Matsui, M. (ed.) ASIACRYPT 2009. LNCS, vol. 5912, pp. 542–559. Springer, Heidelberg (2009). https://doi.org/10.1007/978-3-642-10366-7_32
4. Azimi, S.A., Ranea, A., Salmasizadeh, M., Mohajeri, J., Aref, M.R., Rijmen, V.: A bit-vector differential model for the modular addition by a constant and its applications to differential and impossible-differential cryptanalysis. Des. Codes Cryptogr. **90**(8), 1797–1855 (2022)
5. Barrett, C., Fontaine, P., Tinelli, C.: The Satisfiability Modulo Theories Library (SMT-LIB). www.SMT-LIB.org (2016)
6. Bassham, L., et al.: Special Publication (NIST SP) - 800–22 Rev 1a: A Statistical Test Suite for Random and Pseudorandom Number Generators for Cryptographic Applications (2010)
7. Bassham, L., Soto, J.: NISTIR 6483: randomness testing of the advanced encryption standard finalist candidates. NIST Internal or Interagency Reports (2000)

8. Bellini, E., et al.: CLAASP: a cryptographic library for the automated analysis of symmetric primitives. Cryptology ePrint Archive, Paper 2023/622 (2023). https://eprint.iacr.org/2023/622

9. Bellini, E., Gérault, D., Grados, J., Makarim, R.H., Peyrin, T.: Fully automated differential-linear attacks against ARX ciphers. In: Rosulek, M. (ed.) CT-RSA 2023. LNCS, vol. 13871, pp. 252–276. Springer, Cham (2023). https://doi.org/10.1007/978-3-031-30872-7_10

10. Bellini, E., Gerault, D., Hambitzer, A., Rossi, M.: A Cipher-agnostic neural training pipeline with automated finding of good input differences. Cryptology ePrint Archive, Paper 2022/1467 (2022). https://eprint.iacr.org/2022/1467

11. Bellini, E., Hambitzer, A., Protopapa, M., Rossi, M.: Limitations of the use of neural networks in black box cryptanalysis. In: Ryan, P.Y., Toma, C. (eds.) SecITC 2021. LNCS, vol. 13195, pp. 100–124. Springer, Heidelberg (2021). https://doi.org/10.1007/978-3-031-17510-7_8

12. Benamira, A., Gerault, D., Peyrin, T., Tan, Q.Q.: A deeper look at machine learning-based cryptanalysis. In: Canteaut, A., Standaert, F.-X. (eds.) EUROCRYPT 2021. LNCS, vol. 12696, pp. 805–835. Springer, Cham (2021). https://doi.org/10.1007/978-3-030-77870-5_28

13. Biham, E., Shamir, A.: Differential cryptanalysis of des-like cryptosystems. J. Cryptol. 4(1), 3–72 (1991)

14. Biryukov, A., Nikolić, I.: Automatic search for related-key differential characteristics in byte-oriented block ciphers: application to AES, Camellia, Khazad and others. In: Gilbert, H. (ed.) EUROCRYPT 2010. LNCS, vol. 6110, pp. 322–344. Springer, Heidelberg (2010). https://doi.org/10.1007/978-3-642-13190-5_17

15. Brickenstein, M., Dreyer, A.: Polybori: a framework for Gröbner-basis computations with Boolean polynomials. J. Symb. Comput. 44(9), 1326–1345 (2009)

16. Brown, R.G.: DieHarder: A Random Number Test Suite Version 3.31.1 (2021). https://webhome.phy.duke.edu/~rgb/General/dieharder.php

17. Coutinho, M., Passos, I., Vásquez, J.C.G., de Mendonça, F.L.L., de Sousa, R.T., Borges, F.: Latin dances reloaded: improved cryptanalysis against salsa and chacha, and the proposal of forró. In: Agrawal, S., Lin, D. (eds.) Advances in Cryptology - ASIACRYPT 2022, LNCS, vol. 13791, pp. 256–286. Springer (2022)

18. Coutinho, M., de Sousa Júnior, R.T., Borges, F.: Continuous diffusion analysis. IEEE Access 8, 123735–123745 (2020)

19. Cui, T., Chen, S., Fu, K., Wang, M., Jia, K.: New automatic tool for finding impossible differentials and zero-correlation linear approximations. Sci. China Inf. Sci. 64(2) (2021)

20. Daemen, J., Hoffert, S., Assche, G.V., Keer, R.V.: The design of Xoodoo and Xoofff. IACR Trans. Symmetric Cryptol. 2018(4), 1–38 (2018)

21. Daum, M.: Cryptanalysis of Hash functions of the MD4-family (2005)

22. Dey, S., Garai, H.K., Maitra, S.: Cryptanalysis of reduced round chacha - new attack & deeper analysis. IACR Trans. Symmetric Cryptol. 2023(1), 89–110 (2023)

23. Dobraunig, C., Eichlseder, M., Mendel, F.: Heuristic tool for linear cryptanalysis with applications to CAESAR candidates. In: Iwata, T., Cheon, J.H. (eds.) ASIACRYPT 2015. LNCS, vol. 9453, pp. 490–509. Springer, Heidelberg (2015). https://doi.org/10.1007/978-3-662-48800-3_20

24. Fouque, P.-A., Jean, J., Peyrin, T.: Structural evaluation of AES and chosen-key distinguisher of 9-round AES-128. In: Canetti, R., Garay, J.A. (eds.) CRYPTO 2013. LNCS, vol. 8042, pp. 183–203. Springer, Heidelberg (2013). https://doi.org/10.1007/978-3-642-40041-4_11

25. Gérault, D., Lafourcade, P., Minier, M., Solnon, C.: Computing AES related-key differential characteristics with constraint programming. Artif. Intell. **278**, 103183 (2020)

26. Gohr, A.: Improving attacks on round-reduced Speck32/64 using deep learning. In: Boldyreva, A., Micciancio, D. (eds.) CRYPTO 2019. LNCS, vol. 11693, pp. 150–179. Springer, Cham (2019). https://doi.org/10.1007/978-3-030-26951-7_6

27. Hadipour, H., Eichlseder, M.: Autoguess: a tool for finding guess-and-determine attacks and key bridges. In: Ateniese, G., Venturi, D. (eds.) ACNS 2022. LNCS, vol. 13269, pp. 230–250. Springer, Cham (2022). https://doi.org/10.1007/978-3-031-09234-3_12

28. Hall-Andersen, M., Vejre, P.S.: Generating graphs packed with paths estimation of linear approximations and differentials. IACR Trans. Symmetric Cryptol. **2018**(3), 265–289 (2018)

29. Hall-Andersen, M., Vejre, P.S.: Cryptagraph. https://github.com/psve/cryptagraph (2019)

30. Indrøy, J.P., Raddum, H.: Trail search with CRHS equations. IACR Cryptol. ePrint Arch, p. 1329 (2021)

31. Khoo, K., Lee, E., Peyrin, T., Sim, S.M.: Human-readable proof of the related-key security of AES-128. IACR Trans. Symmetric Cryptol. **2017**(2), 59–83 (2017)

32. Leurent, G.: Analysis of differential attacks in ARX constructions. In: Wang, X., Sako, K. (eds.) ASIACRYPT 2012. LNCS, vol. 7658, pp. 226–243. Springer, Heidelberg (2012). https://doi.org/10.1007/978-3-642-34961-4_15

33. Leurent, G.: Construction of differential characteristics in ARX designs application to skein. In: Canetti, R., Garay, J.A. (eds.) CRYPTO 2013. LNCS, vol. 8042, pp. 241–258. Springer, Heidelberg (2013). https://doi.org/10.1007/978-3-642-40041-4_14

34. Libralesso, L., Delobel, F., Lafourcade, P., Solnon, C.: Automatic Generation of Declarative Models For Differential Cryptanalysis. In: Michel, L.D. (ed.) 27th International Conference on Principles and Practice of Constraint Programming, CP 2021, Montpellier, France (Virtual Conference), October 25–29, 2021. LIPIcs, vol. 210, pp. 40:1–40:18. Schloss Dagstuhl - Leibniz-Zentrum für Informatik (2021)

35. Lipmaa, H., Moriai, S.: Efficient algorithms for computing differential properties of addition. In: Matsui, M. (ed.) FSE 2001. LNCS, vol. 2355, pp. 336–350. Springer, Heidelberg (2002). https://doi.org/10.1007/3-540-45473-X_28

36. Liu, Y., Witte, G.D., Ranea, A., Ashur, T.: Rotational-XOR cryptanalysis of reduced-round SPECK. IACR Trans. Symmetric Cryptol. **2017**(3), 24–36 (2017)

37. Marsaglia, G.: The Marsaglia Random Number CDROM including the Diehard Battery of Tests of Randomness (1995). https://web.archive.org/web/20160125103112. http://stat.fsu.edu/pub/diehard/

38. Matsui, M.: Linear cryptanalysis method for DES Cipher. In: Helleseth, T. (ed.) EUROCRYPT 1993. LNCS, vol. 765, pp. 386–397. Springer, Heidelberg (1994). https://doi.org/10.1007/3-540-48285-7_33

39. Mouha, N., Preneel, B.: A Proof that the ARX Cipher Salsa20 is secure against differential cryptanalysis. IACR Cryptol. ePrint Arch, p. 328 (2013)

40. Mouha, N., Wang, Q., Gu, D., Preneel, B.: Differential and linear cryptanalysis using mixed-integer linear programming. In: Wu, C.-K., Yung, M., Lin, D. (eds.) Inscrypt 2011. LNCS, vol. 7537, pp. 57–76. Springer, Heidelberg (2012). https://doi.org/10.1007/978-3-642-34704-7_5

41. Nethercote, N., Stuckey, P.J., Becket, R., Brand, S., Duck, G.J., Tack, G.: MiniZinc: towards a standard CP modelling language. In: Bessière, C. (ed.) CP 2007. LNCS,

vol. 4741, pp. 529–543. Springer, Heidelberg (2007). https://doi.org/10.1007/978-3-540-74970-7_38

42. Quine, W.V.: A way to simplify truth functions. Amer. Math. Monthly **62**, 627–631 (1955)

43. Ranea, A., Liu, Y., Ashur, T.: An easy-to-use tool for rotational-XOR cryptanalysis of ARX block ciphers. IACR Cryptol. ePrint Arch, p. 727 (2020)

44. Ranea, A., Rijmen, V.: Characteristic automated search of cryptographic algorithms for distinguishing attacks (CASCADA). IET Inf. Secur. **16**(6), 470–481 (2022)

45. Ren, J., Chen, S.: Cryptanalysis of reduced-round speck. IEEE Access **7**, 63045–63056 (2019)

46. Rukhin, A., et al.: Special Publication (NIST SP) - 800–22: A Statistical Test Suite for Random and Pseudorandom Number Generators for Cryptographic Applications (2001)

47. Sadeghi, S., Rijmen, V., Bagheri, N.: Proposing an MILP-based method for the experimental verification of difference-based trails: application to SPECK. SIMECK. Des. Codes Cryptogr. **89**(9), 2113–2155 (2021)

48. Sasaki, Yu., Todo, Y.: New impossible differential search tool from design and cryptanalysis aspects. In: Coron, J.-S., Nielsen, J.B. (eds.) EUROCRYPT 2017. LNCS, vol. 10212, pp. 185–215. Springer, Cham (2017). https://doi.org/10.1007/978-3-319-56617-7_7

49. Soto, J.: NISTIR 6390: Randomness testing of the advanced encryption standard candidate algorithms. NIST Internal or Interagency Reports (1999)

50. Soto, J.: Statistical testing of random number generators. In: Proceedings of the 22nd National Information Systems Security Conference, vol. 10, p. 12. NIST Gaithersburg, MD (1999). https://csrc.nist.gov/CSRC/media/Publications/conference-paper/1999/10/21/proceedings-of-the-22nd-nissc-1999/documents/papers/p24.pdf

51. Stankovski, P.: Automated algebraic cryptanalysis, pp. 11. ECRYPT II (2010). tools for Cryptanalysis 2010; Conference date: 22–06-2010 Through 23–06-2010

52. Stankovski, P.: Greedy distinguishers and nonrandomness detectors. In: Gong, G., Gupta, K.C. (eds.) INDOCRYPT 2010. LNCS, vol. 6498, pp. 210–226. Springer, Heidelberg (2010). https://doi.org/10.1007/978-3-642-17401-8_16

53. Stefan Kölbl: CryptoSMT: an easy to use tool for cryptanalysis of symmetric primitives. https://github.com/kste/cryptosmt

54. Sun, L., Wang, W., Wang, M.: Accelerating the search of differential and linear characteristics with the SAT method. IACR Trans. Symmetric Cryptol. **2021**(1), 269–315 (2021)

55. Sun, S., Hu, L., Wang, P., Qiao, K., Ma, X., Song, L.: Automatic security evaluation and (related-key) differential characteristic search: application to SIMON, PRESENT, LBlock, DES(L) and other bit-oriented block ciphers. In: Sarkar, P., Iwata, T. (eds.) ASIACRYPT 2014. LNCS, vol. 8873, pp. 158–178. Springer, Heidelberg (2014). https://doi.org/10.1007/978-3-662-45611-8_9

56. Vesselinux, Laboratory of Algorithmics, C., of Luxembourg University, S.L.: Vesselinux/yaarx: Yet another toolkit for analysis of ARX cryptographic algorithms. https://github.com/vesselinux/yaarx

57. Zhang, X., Chen, Z., Cai, S.: Parkissat: Random shuffle based and pre-processing extended parallel solvers with clause sharing. SAT COMPETITION, 51 (2022)

Parallel SAT Framework to Find Clustering of Differential Characteristics and Its Applications

Kosei Sakamoto[1(✉)], Ryoma Ito[2], and Takanori Isobe[3]

[1] Mitsubishi Electric Corporation, Kamakura, Japan
Sakamoto.Kosei@dc.MitsubishiElectric.co.jp
[2] NICT, Koganei, Japan
itorym@nict.go.jp
[3] University of Hyogo, Kobe, Japan
takanori.isobe@ai.u-hyogo.ac.jp

Abstract. The most crucial but time-consuming task for differential cryptanalysis is to find a differential with a high probability. To tackle this task, we propose a new SAT-based automatic search framework to efficiently figure out a differential with the highest probability under a specified condition. As the previous SAT methods (e.g., the Sun et al.'s method proposed at ToSC 2021(1)) focused on accelerating the search of an optimal single differential characteristic, these are not optimized for evaluating a clustering effect to obtain a tighter differential probability of differentials. In contrast, our framework takes advantage of a method to solve incremental SAT problems in parallel using a multi-threading technique, and consequently, it offers the following advantages compared with the previous methods: (1) speedy identification of a differential with the highest probability under the specified conditions; (2) efficient construction of the truncated differential with the highest probability from the obtained multiple differentials; and (3) applicability to a wide class of the symmetric-key primitives. To demonstrate the effectiveness of our framework, we apply it to the block cipher PRINCE and the tweakable block cipher QARMA. We successfully figure out the tight differential bounds for all variants of PRINCE and QARMA within the practical time, thereby identifying the longest distinguisher for all the variants, which improves existing ones by one to four more rounds. Besides, we uncover notable differences between PRINCE and QARMA in the behavior of differential, especially for the clustering effect. We believe that our findings shed light on new structural properties of these important primitives.

Keywords: Differential · SAT-based automatic search · Incremental SAT problem · Low-latency primitives

Due to the page limitation, we leave the part of (1) descriptions of several basic algorithms and SAT models, (2) a detailed explanation of our investigation about the impact of multi-threading techniques, (3) key-recovery attacks, and (4) discussion of good parameters in our algorithms to the full version of this paper (https://eprint.iacr.org/2023/1227).

© The Author(s), under exclusive license to Springer Nature Switzerland AG 2024
C. Carlet et al. (Eds.): SAC 2023, LNCS 14201, pp. 409–428, 2024.
https://doi.org/10.1007/978-3-031-53368-6_20

1   Introduction

Background. The most crucial but time-consuming part of differential cryptanlysis [7] is to determine a pair of plaintext differences and the corresponding ciphertext differences and construct a differential distinguisher with high probability. To this end, cryptographers frequently use a *differential characteristic*, which is a sequence of the internal differences in each round. However, from the attackers' viewpoint, they are interested in not the internal differences but only a pair of the input and output differences, which is called a *differential* in literature. A differential is more useful than a differential characteristic for the attackers, as a differential has a higher probability than that of a differential characteristic.

Several studies investigated the relationship between a differential characteristic and a differential, revealing that a gap between their probabilities can be significant [2,8,18]. Most of these studies focused on a differential constructed by only a differential characteristic with the highest probability, which is called the *optimal* differential characteristic. This seems reasonable, as the probability of the optimal differential characteristic dominates the probability of a differential in numerous designs. However, Kölbl and Roy [19] demonstrated an interesting case in Simeck32 [29] where a differential with a higher probability can be constructed by the non-optimal differential characteristic. Although this appears to be a special case, it can be valid for any design. From these aspects, finding a differential with a higher probability still remains a challenging task.

Finding such a differential is not only useful from the attackers' aspect but also crucial from the designers' aspect. In particular, the ultra-low-latency designs must be carefully designed against differential cryptanalysis, because they are usually based on a substitution-permutation network with a small number of rounds, and the growth of the differential probability is not sufficient at the beginning of the rounds. In fact, the designers of MANTIS [6] and SPEEDY [21] invested significant efforts into guaranteeing the resistance against differential cryptanalysis in their works. Nevertheless, they were broken by differential cryptanalysis [10,15]. Furthermore, the best attack to the first low-latency design PRINCE [9] is also (multiple) differential cryptanalysis on 10 (out of 12) rounds proposed by Canteaut et al. [12]. Hence, it is evidently important to investigate a differential in detail, especially for low-latency designs.

Limitations of SAT-Based Automatic Search Tools. The existing SAT-based automatic search tools, proposed by Sun et al. [26,27], focused on accelerating the search for an optimal differential characteristic by incorporating the Matsui's bounding conditions [24]. These tools are valid for evaluating a single differential characteristic, but the Matsui's bounding conditions are not suitable for the purpose of evaluating the clustering effect of multiple differential characteristics; thus, the existing tools are not suitable for efficiently finding a differential with a higher probability. Certainly, it can be applied to evaluate the clustering effect of multiple differential characteristics by removing the Matsui's bounding conditions and adding some new conditions. However, such a straightforward adjustment can be inefficient because Sun et al. assumed only an environment with a single-thread execution even though their SAT solver accepts an execution on multiple threads. Considering that the evaluation for the clustering effect of multiple differential characteristics having different input and output differences requires a much more computational cost than that for finding the optimal differential characteristic, the tool for finding a differential with the highest possible probability should be optimized for execution on multiple threads. Moreover, it is also of great importance to investigate the impact of the relation on the efficiency between the number of threads to be assigned to solve a single SAT problem and the degree of the parallelization for the evaluation of the clustering effect, as we have to evaluate the clustering effect for each found differential characteristic having different input and output differences with a high probability. Therefore, without these considerations, it is hard to efficiently investigate the clustering effect of numerous differential characteristics having different input and output differences in detail. This investigation leads to understanding the behavior of the probability about differentials more deeply; thus, optimizing these SAT-based tools to evaluate for the clustering effect of differential characteristics is crucial.

Our Contributions. In this study, we propose a new generic SAT-based automatic search framework that aims to figure out a differential with a higher probability under the specified condition, in contrast to existing approaches. The main concept of the framework involves investigating the clustering effect of all differential characteristics having different input and output differences with a specified range of weight and identifying the good differential. Our framework fully leverages a method to solve *incremental SAT problems*, which can efficiently solve a SAT problem with small modifications multiple times, in parallel using a multithreading technique. As an incremental SAT problem can be efficiently solved by the *bounded variable elimination method* [16], it is known that we can efficiently evaluate the clustering effect by converting the evaluation of the clustering effect into an incremental SAT problem. In our method, we also take advantage of an incremental SAT problem to efficiently find all differential characteristics having different input and output differences that are seeds to construct differentials, as well as the evaluation of the clustering effect. By carefully investigating the most suitable parameters, such as the number of threads to be assigned to solve a single incremental SAT problem and the degree of the parallelization for the evaluation of the clustering effect, to solve multiple incremental SAT problems efficiently, our framework enables us to thoroughly evaluate the clustering effect of such all differential characteristics not only with the highest probability but also with any probability. Hence, we evaluate the probability of differentials more comprehensively than any other previous methods.

Identifying Good Differentials on PRINCE and QARMA. To demonstrate the effectiveness of our framework, we apply it to PRINCE [9] and QARMA [3], which are the reflection ciphers for low-latency applications. As a result, we significantly improve previous differential bounds for all variants of these ciphers as shown in

Table 1. Comparison of our results with existing ones regarding distinguishers.

Cipher	Total # Rounds	Attacked # Rounds	Setting[†]	Type[‡]	Time/Data	Reference
PRINCE PRINCEv2	12	4	SK	ID	–	[14]
		6	SK	D	2^{62}	[2]
		6	SK	I	2^{62}	[11]
		6	SK	D	$2^{56.42}$	[12]
		7	SK	D	$2^{55.771}$	Section 4.1
QARMA64	16	6	SK	ID	–	[28]
		7	SK	D	$2^{58.921}$	Section 4.2
		4.5	RT	ID	–	[23]
		7	RT	ID	–	[30]
		8	RT	SS	2^{57}	[22]
		9	RT	ZC/I	2^{44}	[1]
		10	RT	D	$2^{60.831}$	Section 4.2
QARMA128	24	6	SK	ID	–	[28]
		10	SK	D	$2^{121.549}$	Section 4.2
		6.5	RT	ID	–	[23]
		8	RT	TDIB	$2^{124.1}$	[22]
		12	RT	D	$2^{120.024}$	Section 4.2

[†] SK: Single-Key, RT: Related-Tweak
[‡] D: Differential, I: Integral, ID: Impossible Differential, SS: Statistical Saturation, ZC: Zero-Correlation, TDIB: Tweak Difference Invariant Bias

Table 1, and our differential distinguishers are the longest ones among existing ones. It is important to note that while the previous attacks may have been adjusted for key recovery, identifying the longest distinguisher is very important to deeply comprehend the structural properties of these primitives as pseudo random permutations. These results demonstrate that the proposed framework is effective for evaluating the tight differential bounds.

Difference in Behavior of Clustering Effect Between PRINCE and QARMA. We look into the difference between PRINCE and QARMA in the behavior of a differential. Our experiments observe that the gaps in the probability between a differential characteristic and a differential can be large in QARMA under the SK setting compared to that in PRINCE. Specifically, QARMA under the single-key (SK) setting has a large impact on the clustering effect, and the case reported by Kölbl and Roy [19] can occur in QARMA under the SK setting. A detailed investigation of such gaps reveals that they are influenced by different design strategies for the linear layers (i.e., matrices). After conducting the additional experiments using four types of matrices with different properties, we find that the target cipher has a good resistance to a clustering effect when each output bit of the round function depends on as many input bits of the round function as possible. We conclude that a cipher using a matrix with the same property as that used in QARMA has a large impact on a clustering effect, and a clustering effect in non-optimal weights can strongly affect the probability of a differential.

Our framework can be applied to any symmetric-key primitive. Also, it is very important to analyze the tight differential bound in the field of symmetric-key cryptanalysis. Therefore, we believe that our work is a significant contribution in terms of the tight security analysis for a wide class of symmetric-key primitives.

2 Preliminaries

2.1 Definitions of Differential Characteristic and Differential

We frequently use terms *differential characteristic* and *differential* throughout this paper. To avoid mixing these terms, we specify their definitions and how to calculate their probabilities. Further, we provide the definition of *weight* that is also frequently used in this paper. Notably, we explain a differential characteristic and differential over an r-round iterated block cipher $E(\cdot) = f_r(\cdot) \circ \cdots \circ f_1(\cdot)$.

Definition 1 (*Differential characteristic*). *A differential characteristic is a sequence of differences over E defined as follows:*

$$C = (c_0 \xrightarrow{f_1} c_1 \xrightarrow{f_2} \cdots \xrightarrow{f_r} c_r) := (c_0, c_1, \cdots, c_r),$$

where $(c_0, c_1, \cdots, c_r)$ denotes the differences in the output of each round, i.e., c_0 and c_r denote the differences in a plaintext and ciphertext, respectively.

The probability of a differential characteristic is estimated by the product of the corresponding differential probabilities for each round on the Markov cipher assumption [20] as follows:

$$\Pr(C) = \prod_{i=1}^{r} \Pr(c_{i-1} \xrightarrow{f_i} c_i).$$

Definition 2 (*Differential*). *A differential is a pair of the input and output differences (c_0, c_r).*

The probability of a differential is estimated by a sum of probabilities for all differential characteristics sharing the same input and output differences (c_0, c_r) as follows:

$$\Pr(c_0 \xrightarrow{E} c_r) = \sum_{c_1, c_2, \cdots c_{r-1}} \Pr(c_0 \xrightarrow{f_1} c_1 \xrightarrow{f_2} \cdots \xrightarrow{f_r} c_r).$$

We finally provide the definition of *weight* which corresponds to the probability of a differential characteristic.

Definition 3 (*Weight*). *A weight w is a negated value of the binary logarithm of the probability P_r defined as follows:*

$$w = -\log_2 P_r$$

2.2   SAT-Based Automatic Search for Differential Characteristics

SAT. When a formula consists of only AND ($\wedge$), OR ($\vee$), and NOT ($\overline{\cdot}$) operations based on Boolean variables, we refer to it as a *Boolean formula*. In a SAT problem, a SAT solver checks whether there is an assignment of Boolean variables that can validate a Boolean formula or not. If such an assignment exists, a SAT solver returns *satisfiable* or "SAT". Generally, a SAT problem is an NP-complete [13]. However, owing to numerous efforts for SAT problems, nowadays, there are numerous excellent SAT solvers that can solve a SAT problem very efficiently, such as CaDiCaL, Kissat, and CryptoMiniSat5.

A Boolean formula can be converted into a *Conjunctive Normal Form* (CNF), which is expressed by the conjunction ($\wedge$) of the disjunction ($\vee$) on (possibly negated) Boolean variables, such as $\bigwedge_{a=0}^{i}(\bigvee_{b=0}^{j_a} c_{i,j})$, where $c_{i,j}$ is a Boolean variable. We call each disjunction $\bigvee_{b=0}^{j_a} c_{i,j}$ in a Boolean formula a *clause*.

SAT-Based Automatic Tools. SAT-based automatic tools are known as a valid approach to find optimal differential/linear characteristics and are more powerful than MILP-based ones as shown in [27]. To implement its approach with the SAT method, the differential/linear propagation over all operations in a primitive must be converted into a CNF, and then we check if there exists a differential/linear characteristic along with a specified weight as a SAT problem. We can know the optimal differential/linear characteristics by solving some SAT problems by changing the number of specified weights.

SAT Models for Basic Operations. Our framework is based on a pure-SAT model proposed by Sun et al. [26,27]. Due to the page limitation, we do not give the detailed modeling method (for more information, please refer to Sun et al.'s work). Herein, we specify some basic notations that are used in this study to construct a whole SAT model as follows:

$\mathcal{M}_{SAT}$: A whole SAT model that we solve.

$\mathcal{M}_{cla.operations}$: Clauses to express the propagation of differences in a certain operation. These clauses also contain variables to express a weight corresponding to the propagation of differences in a probabilistic operation.

$\mathcal{M}_{var}$: Variables to construct clauses.

In this study, we use $\mathcal{M}_{cla.xor}$, $\mathcal{M}_{cla.matrix}$, and $\mathcal{M}_{cla.sbox}$ as clauses to express the propagation of differences in PRINCE and QARMA. In addition, we also use $\mathcal{M}_{cla.input}$ and $\mathcal{M}_{cla.sec(B)}$ to evaluate a minimum weight. These clauses play a role as follows:

$\mathcal{M}_{cla.input}$: Clauses to avoid a trivial differential propagation, such as all input differences being zero at the same time.

$\mathcal{M}_{cla.sec(B)}$: Clauses to count the total weight of a primitive. More specifically, the constraint of $\sum_{i=0}^{j} p_i \leq B$ can be added, where p_i is a Boolean variable to express a weight and j is the total number of p_i. There are several methods to realize such a constraint in a Boolean formula [4,25]. Among these, we employ *Sequential Encoding Method* [25] that was used in numerous works.

Finding Differential Characteristics with Minimum Weight. With the clauses and variables introduced in this section, we construct a whole SAT model as follows:

$$\mathcal{M}_{SAT} \leftarrow (\mathcal{M}_{cla.matrix}, \, \mathcal{M}_{cla.sbox}, \, \mathcal{M}_{cla.sec}, \, \mathcal{M}_{cla.input}).$$

Now, we are ready to find a differential characteristic with the minimum weight by feeding $\mathcal{M}_{SAT}$ and $\mathcal{M}_{var}$ to a SAT solver. If a SAT solver returns "UNSAT", there is no differential characteristic with a weight of $\leq B$. In that case, we increment B and repeat it until a SAT solver returns "SAT". This means that we obtain a differential characteristic with the minimum weight of B.

Modeling for a Clustering Effect. To take a clustering effect into account, we must solve a SAT problem multiple times with the same input and output differences, while the identical internal differential propagation is deleted from the solution space of the initial SAT problem. To realize this procedure, we introduce the following clauses:

$\mathcal{M}_{cla.clust}$: Clauses to fix the input and output differences to find multiple differential characteristics with the same input and output differences.

$\mathcal{M}_{cla.\overline{clust}}$: Clauses to remove the internal differential propagation from a SAT model. These will be repeatably added to a SAT model whenever another internal differential propagation is found.

When evaluating a clustering effect, we attempt to find a differential characteristic with the weight of B, not the weight of $\leq B$ so as to calculate the exact probability of a differential due to the same reason mentioned in [26]. $\sum_{j=0}^{r \cdot i - 1} p_j = B$ can be obtained by applying both $\sum_{j=0}^{r \cdot i - 1} p_j \leq B$ and $\sum_{j=0}^{r \cdot i - 1} p_j \geq B$. The first constraint is already given above, and the second one can be easily obtained from $\sum_{j=0}^{r \cdot i - 1} p_j \leq B$ with a small change. More information is provided in the previous study [26]. Hereafter, $\mathcal{M}_{cla.\overline{sec}(B)}$ denotes the clauses to express $\sum_{j=0}^{r \cdot i - 1} p_j \geq B$. The detailed comprehensive algorithm for finding differential characteristics and evaluating the clustering effect will be given in the following section.

3   A New SAT Framework to Find the Best Differential

In this section, we propose a new generic SAT-based automatic search framework to find a differential with a higher probability under a specified condition (we refer to it as a *good* differential in this paper). Specifically, our framework can efficiently investigate the clustering effect of all differential characteristics having different (c_0, c_r) with a specified range of probability and identify a good differential. Our framework leverages a method to solve *incremental SAT problems* in parallel using a multi-threading technique, leading to an efficient search for all differentials under the specified condition. Specifically, the unique features of our framework are listed as follows:

Speedy identification of a good differential. Most of the existing studies on solver-aided search methods have focused on searching for the optimal differential characteristics as efficiently as possible. In contrast, our framework aims to identify a good differential among numerous differential characteristics having different (c_0, c_r) by evaluating the clustering effect of them within the practical time. This can be realized by taking a method to solve incremental SAT problems in parallel using a multi-threading technique into consideration. Thereby, our framework enables us to find good differentials under the specified range of the weight that the corresponding differential characteristic has.

Efficient construction of a good truncated differential. Our framework also enables us to find a good truncated differential. This can be realized by combining all the obtained differentials under the specified truncated differential. The truncated differential attack is more powerful than the ordinary differential attack; thus, our framework leads to a better differential attack on many symmetric-key primitives.

Applicability to a wide class of the symmetric-key primitives. Our framework leverages the existing SAT-based automatic search method proposed by Sun et al. [27] and maintains its availability of applications; thus, our framework can be applied to a wide class of the symmetric-key primitives. Therefore, compared with existing solver-aided tools, our framework can be the best tool to construct the (truncated) differential distinguisher for a wide class of symmetric-key primitives.

3.1 Our Approach

Conventionally, when we attempt to obtain a good differential, we adopt a strategy of searching it based on the optimal differential characteristic. This strategy seems reasonable in many cases; therefore, most of the existing studies followed this strategy and improved the differential attacks based on the differentials obtained by this strategy. However, this strategy might overlook the better one because the non-optimal differential characteristic sometimes constructs the better differentials than that by the optimal differential characteristic, as the case on Simeck32 reported by Kölbl and Roy [19].

To investigate differentials in more detail, we need to evaluate a clustering effect of numerous differential characteristics having different (c_0, c_r). Since this requires a huge computational cost, it is a time-consuming task even with the state-of-the-art approach, such as a pure SAT-based automatic search method proposed by Sun et al. [27]. To tackle this task, we focus on a method to efficiently solve an incremental SAT problem and consider a new strategy to speedily obtain all differential characteristics having different (c_0, c_r) with a specified range of weight to evaluate the clustering effect of them. The essential idea of our search strategy is very simple; we first enumerate all single differential characteristics having different (c_0, c_r) with a relatively high probability and then investigate the clustering effect of every obtained differential characteristic. Figure 1 illustrates the overview of our approach in comparison with the conventional one.

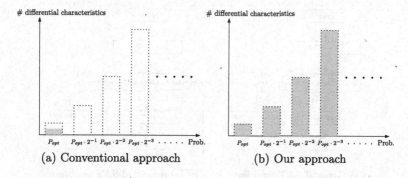

Fig. 1. Approaches to identifying a good differential. "# differential characteristics" denotes the total number of differential characteristics having different (c_0, c_r) with the corresponding probability in horizontal axis. P_{opt} denotes the probability of an optimal differential characteristic. The gray area depicts evaluated differentials.

3.2   Incremental SAT Problem

An *incremental SAT problem* is a kind of SAT problem, that solves a general SAT problem multiple times with a small modification, which the *bounded variable elimination method* [16] can efficiently realize. Several SAT solvers support the function to efficiently solve the incremental SAT problem, such as *Crypto-MiniSAT* which is the most popular SAT solver in the field of symmetric-key cryptography. Figure 2 illustrates flowcharts of solving the general and an incremental SAT problem.

Some Insights About Solving an Incremental SAT Problem. According to the Erlacher et al.'s work [17], assigning multiple threads to solve a single general SAT problem has a positive impact on reducing the runtime, but does not obtain the same degree of gain as the degree of the parallelization. From this fact, our work starts at investigating whether the same phenomenon happens in the case of an incremental SAT problem. As a result, we find that it happens in the case of an incremental SAT problem as well. Moreover, we also find that assigning multiple threads to solve a single incremental SAT problem does not improve the efficiency of the evaluation at all (see Sect. 3.4). This means that solving multiple incremental SAT problems in parallel on each single thread is more efficient than solving a single incremental SAT problem on multiple threads. We leverage this insight into our framework.

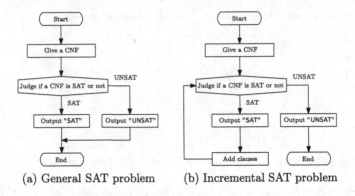

(a) General SAT problem   (b) Incremental SAT problem

Fig. 2. Flowcharts of solving the general and an incremental SAT problem.

Good Solver for an Incremental SAT Problem. There are numerous excellent SAT solvers tending to solve a general SAT problem, while not so many of them support solving an incremental SAT problem. Since our framework requires to efficiently solve not a general SAT problem but an incremental SAT problem, we must employ a SAT solver suitable for solving an incremental SAT problem. To the best of our knowledge, `CryptoMiniSat5`[1] is the most efficient SAT solver to solve an incremental SAT problem[2]. Hence, we use `CryptoMiniSat5` throughout all of our evaluations.

3.3 Finding a Good Differential

We present a new method to find a good differential under a specified condition. Our method requires several basic algorithms to find differential characteristics, such as the ones presented in [27]. Due to the page limitation, We leave a detailed explanation of them in the full version of this paper.[3]

The idea of our method is to investigate a clustering effect about all differential characteristics having different (c_0, c_r) with not only the minimum weight, but also a specified range of weight, and then identify a good differential. Before giving a detailed algorithm of our method, we explain the procedure of this method step by step as follows:

Step 1: Identify the weight W_{min} of the r-round optimal differential characteristic by $\text{SAT}_{\text{diff.min}}()$.

Step 2: Obtain all differential characteristics having different (c_0, c_r) with the weight from W_{min} to $W_{min} + \alpha$ by $\text{SAT}_{\text{diff.all}}()$.

---

[1] https://www.msoos.org/cryptominisat5/.

[2] `CryptoMiniSat5` is the winner of the incremental library track at SAT competition 2020.

[3] https://eprint.iacr.org/2023/1227.

Algorithm 1: Finding the best differential.

---

input : W_{min}, r, T_w, T_c
output: D, N

1 **begin**
2     $D \leftarrow (D_0, D_1, \ldots, D_{T_w-1})$
3     $N \leftarrow (N_0, N_1, \ldots, N_{T_w-1})$
4   **for** $i = W_{min}$ **to** $W_{min} + T_w - 1$ **do**
5        $D_{i-W_{min}} \leftarrow \text{SAT}_{\text{diff.all}}(i, r, 1, 1)$
6        $N_{i-W_{min}} \leftarrow \emptyset$
7        $j \leftarrow 0$
8   **for** *all pairs in* $D_{i-W_{min}}$ **do**
9   **add** $\text{SAT}_{\text{diff.clust}}(i, i + T_c - 1, r, D_{i-W_{in}}^{(j)})$ **to** $N_{i-W_{in}}$
10           $j \leftarrow j + 1$
11   /* j denotes the index of $D_{i-W_{in}}$, i.e., $MAX(j) = |D_{i-W_{in}}|$ */

12   **return** (D, N)

Step 3: Evaluate the clustering effect of all differential characteristics obtained in Step 2, and then find a good differential.

As can be seen in the above steps, this method can investigate the probability of differentials in more detail than any other existing tools. We give the detailed algorithm of this method in Algorithm 1.

As inputs to Algorithm 1, we provide the minimum weight W_{min}, the number of target rounds r, and two thresholds T_w and T_c. We can obtain W_{min} by $\text{SAT}_{\text{diff.min}}()$ and decide T_w as the range of weights taken into account in the whole evaluation. For example, suppose that we obtain $W_{min} = 60$ by $\text{SAT}_{\text{diff.min}}()$ and set $T_w = 3$, Algorithm 1 searches a good differential in all differential characteristics having different (c_0, c_r) with the weight of $60, 61$, and 62. We can also decide T_c as the range of weight taken into account in a clustering effect for each differential characteristic. After executing Algorithm 1, we obtain lists of D and N which store all differentials (c_0, c_r) and the number of the differential characteristics for each weight in each differential, respectively. Then, we can calculate the probability for each differential with D and N.

The computational cost of Algorithm 1 highly depends on T_w and T_c, because these two thresholds highly influence the number of times to solve an incremental SAT problem in the whole procedure of Algorithm 1. Therefore, T_w and T_c must be set depending on the computational environment. It should be noted that the clustering effect for each differential will be evaluated in parallel because of some observations discussed in Sect. 3.4.

3.4   Optimizing the Efficiency by a Multi-threading Technique

To optimize the efficiency of our algorithms, we investigate the feature of an incremental SAT problem, e.g., the most efficient way to solve multiple incremental SAT problems. We show several experimental results on the 5- and 9-round PRINCE and the 6-round QARMA64 in the single-key setting. Based on our results, we conclude that assigning a single incremental SAT problem to each thread is more advantageous than assigning many threads to a single incremental SAT problem. Due to the page limitation, we leave the detailed explanations of our investigation to the full version of this paper (see Footnote 3).

3.5   A More Efficient Algorithm to Find a Good Differential

Algorithm 1 can find a good differential under the specified condition, while a computational cost becomes vast along with increasing T_w and T_c. The downside of Algorithm 1 is that it never returns any result when all differentials cannot be found out, and this situation happens often along with a weight far from W_{min}.

To address this problem, we propose Algorithm 2, which can evaluate a clustering effect whenever a differential characteristic having different (c_0, c_r) is found. In Algorithm 2, it is not always possible to identify a good differential under a specified condition, as we discard some differentials (c_0, c_r) in the middle of the procedure. However, we place emphasis on evaluating a clustering effect as efficiently as possible. To reduce the entire computational cost, we screen the differential (c_0, c_r) depending on its differential probability by a certain threshold whenever evaluating a clustering effect. If it does not satisfy a certain threshold, the evaluation of a clustering effect for this differential (c_0, c_r) halts, and this differential is discarded. In Algorithm 2, we assume to execute it in parallel on an environment with multiple threads based on the fact in Sect. 3.4. We explain the overview of the procedure step by step as follows:

Step 1: Find the same number of differential characteristics having different (c_0, c_r) with the weight W_{min} as the degree of parallelization.

Step 2: Evaluate the clustering effect for each obtained differential characteristic in parallel. During this evaluation, we store or update the information of a differential (c_0, c_r) with the highest probability (specifically, the differential and its probability), and this information is used to specify the threshold. If the probability of a differential (c_0, c_r) in the middle of evaluating the clustering effect does not surpass a certain threshold, this evaluation halts, and such a differential is discarded. Otherwise, the evaluation proceeds and the highest probability is updated if the probability of the resulting differential exceeds the previous highest one.

Step 3: Repeat Step 1–2 until all differential characteristics having different (c_0, c_r) with the weight W_{min} are found. If it is infeasible to find all differential characteristics having different (c_0, c_r), we stop the evaluation and obtain the highest probability of a differential in this evaluation so far.

Step 4: Increase W_{min} and repeat Step 1–3 until W_{min} reaches a specified weight.

Algorithm 2: Finding the (almost) good differential for a multi-thread programming technique

---

input : $W_{min}, r, T_w, T_c, T_s, T_t, N_{thr}$
output: $(c_{opt.in}, c_{opt.out}), P_{opt}$

1 **begin**
2     $P_{opt} \leftarrow 0,\ P_{thr} \leftarrow (P_{thr}^0, P_{thr}^1, \ldots, P_{thr}^{N_{thr}-1})$
3     $D \leftarrow (D_0, D_1, \ldots, D_{N_{thr}-1})$
4   **for** $i = W_{min}$ **to** $W_{min} + T_w - 1$ **do**
5         $(\mathcal{M}_{SAT}, \mathcal{M}_{var}) \leftarrow \text{SET}_{\text{model}}(i, r)$
6   **add** *auxiliary Boolean variables of* $\mathcal{M}_{cla.\overline{sec}(i)}$ **to** $\mathcal{M}_{var}$
7   **add** $\mathcal{M}_{cla.\overline{sec}(i)}$ **to** $\mathcal{M}_{SAT}$
8         $count \leftarrow 0$
9   /* incremental SAT problem   */
10   **while** $\text{SAT}_{\text{diff.char}}(\mathcal{M}_{SAT}, \mathcal{M}_{var}) = (\text{``SAT''}, C_r)$ **do**
11             $D_{count \bmod N_{thr}} \leftarrow (c_0, c_r)$
12             $count \leftarrow count + 1$
13   **if** $count \bmod N_{thr} = 0$ **then**
14   **for** *each thread* **do**
15                     $P_{thr}^{thread} \leftarrow \text{Thread}(i, r, T_c, T_s, T_t, P_{opt}, D_{thread})$
16   **if** $MAX(P_{thr}) > P_{opt}$ **then**
17                     $(D_{opt}, P_{opt}) \leftarrow MAX(D, P_{thr})$
18   **add** $\bigvee_{k=0}^{n-1}(v_{0,k} \oplus c_{0,k}) \vee (v_{r,k} \oplus c_{r,k})$ **to** $\mathcal{M}_{SAT}$
19   **if** $count \bmod N_{thr} \neq 0$ **then**
20   **for** *each thread* **do**
21                 $P_{thr}^{thread} \leftarrow \text{Thread}(i, r, T_c, T_s, T_t, P_{opt}, D_{thread})$
22   **if** $MAX(P_{thr}) > P_{opt}$ **then**
23                 $(D_{opt}, P_{opt}) \leftarrow MAX(D, P_{thr})$

24   **return** (D_{opt}, P_{opt})

25 **Function** $\text{Thread}(W, r, T_c, T_s, T_t, P_{opt}, D)$ // A multi-threading technique
26 **begin**
27     $N \leftarrow (N_0, N_1, \ldots, N_{T_c-1})$
28     $N \leftarrow \text{SAT}_{\text{diff.clust}}(W, W + T_t - 1, r, D)$
29     $P_{tmp} \leftarrow \sum_{i=W}^{W+T_t-1}(N_{i-W} \cdot 2^{-i})$
30   **if** $T_s \cdot P_{tmp} > P_{opt}$ **then**
31         $N \leftarrow \text{SAT}_{\text{diff.clust}}(W + T_t, W + T_c - 1, r, D)$
32         $P_{tmp} \leftarrow P_{tmp} + \sum_{i=W+T_t}^{W+T_c-1}(N_{i-W} \cdot 2^{-i})$
33   **return** P_{tmp}

As inputs to Algorithm 2, we provide the same parameters in Algorithm 1 and the additional two thresholds T_s and T_t which are the bounding condition used to narrow down the search space. We specify T_t and T_s as a range of the

Table 2. Differential probabilities of (almost) good differentials of PRINCE. W_{min} denotes the same parameter as in Algorithms 1 and 2. #differentials denotes the number of different differentials with a particular weight. The minimum weight of a differential characteristic for each round is written in bold. The highest differential probability for each round is written in red. The probabilities in a white and gray cell are obtained by Algorithms 1 and 2, respectively. For all results, we set $T_w = 1$ and $T_c = 10$.

PRINCE

Rounds	4 (1+2+1)					5 (1+2+2/2+2+1)				
W_{min}	**32**	33	34	35	36	**39**	40	41	42	43
Prob.	$2^{-30.808}$	$2^{-31.861}$	$2^{-32.587}$	$2^{-33.333}$	$2^{-32.979}$	$2^{-38.810}$	$2^{-39.385}$	$2^{-40.017}$	$2^{-40.607}$	$2^{-40.837}$
# differentials	477452	3792944	4929816	5537848	5547896	576	12512	113840	598592	2231756
Time	6h06m57s	48h48m43s	47h34m17s	47h35m06s	48h01m15s	1m21s	26m09s	4h08m26s	23h14m24s	48h03m32s

Rounds	6 (2+2+2)					7 (2+2+3/3+2+2)				
W_{min}	**44**	45	46	47	48	**56**	57	58	59	60
Prob.	$2^{-43.907}$	$2^{-44.907}$	$2^{-45.195}$	$2^{-46.111}$	$2^{-46.374}$	$2^{-53.771}$	$2^{-55.887}$	$2^{-56.810}$	$2^{-57.37}$	$2^{-57.990}$
# differentials	64	512	1984	6592	25968	5632	100976	835456	205272	212280
Time	51s	4m21s	17m57s	1h07m16s	4h46m53s	5h07m16s	90h40m16s	48h00m00s	73h03m01s	71h43m12s

Rounds	8 (3+2+3)					9 (3+2+4/4+2+3)				
W_{min}	**66**	67	68	69	70	**74**	75	76	77	78
Prob.	$2^{-64.389}$	$2^{-65.384}$	$2^{-66.303}$	$2^{-66.970}$	$2^{-67.075}$	$2^{-73.888}$	$2^{-74.881}$	$2^{-74.970}$	$2^{-75.970}$	$2^{-76.166}$
# differentials	256	3584	46736	18352	24056	64	544	3400	26592	13968
Time	1h55m50s	24h34m09s	290h41m48s	47h32m37s	48h4m28s	34m49s	5h11m49s	32h10m51s	235h42m42s	48h04m53s

evaluated weight in the clustering effect before screening and a specific threshold of screening, respectively. Besides, we specify the degree of parallelization in Step 2 by N_{thr}. After executing Algorithm 2, we obtain a good differential D_{opt} with its probability P_{opt}.

4   Applications to PRINCE and QARMA

We apply our framework to PRINCE and QARMA in some rounds. To make our results clear, we show the results on each W_{min} with $T_w = 1$, i.e., we consistently set $T_w = 1$ for each W_{min}. Furthermore, we set $T_c = 10$ unless noted otherwise.

4.1   Good Differentials for PRINCE

Table 2 shows the results of PRINCE, which are evaluated on Apple M1 MAX with 64 GB of main memory. In the case where the number of all differential characteristics having different (c_0, c_r) is not so many, and the number of rounds is small, we can apply Algorithm 1, i.e., we can find a good differential with $T_c = 10$. In other cases, the cost of the evaluation of a clustering effect becomes so high that we apply Algorithm 2. For the results by Algorithm 1, the evaluation of a clustering effect is parallelized on multiple threads to make the most of our computational environment, as described in Sect. 3.3 and 3.4. For the results by Algorithm 2, we pick up the best one among results on several combinations of T_t and T_s.

Table 2 shows that the distinguishing attack can be applied up to seven rounds of PRINCE/PRINCEv2 that improves the previous best attack by one round [2,12]. It must be mentioned that the previous best distinguishing attack by differential cryptanalysis is adjusted for the key recovery that restricts the space of the input and output differences.

4.2 Good Differentials for QARMA

Table 3 shows the results of QARMA64 and QARMA128, both of which are evaluated on Linux machine with Intel Xeon Gold 6258R CPU (2.70 GHz) and 256 GB of main memory. As with the case of PRINCE, we apply Algorithm 1 when the number of all differential characteristics having different (c_0, c_r) is not so many, and the number of rounds is small. Otherwise, we apply Algorithm 2. Particularly, the computational cost becomes excessive in the evaluation of QARMA128, because the state length is 128 bits. Hence, we apply only Algorithm 2 in most cases of the evaluation of QARMA128. For the results by Algorithm 1, the evaluation of a clustering effect is parallelized on multiple threads to make the most of our computational environment, as well as the evaluation of PRINCE. For the results by Algorithm 2, we pick up the best one among results on several combinations of T_t and T_s.

As shown in Table 3, the distinguishing attack in the SK setting can be applied up to 7 and 10 rounds of QARMA64 and QARMA128, both of which improve the previous best attack [28] by 1 and 4 rounds, respectively. Further, the distinguishing attack in the RT setting can be applied up to 10 and 12 rounds of QARMA64 and QARMA128, both of which improve the previous best attacks [1,22] by 1 and 4 rounds, respectively. As with the case of PRINCE, we note that the previous best distinguishing attack may be adjusted for the key recovery. Besides, it must be mentioned that the same case reported by Kölbl and Roy [19] often happens in both QARMA64 and QARMA128, i.e., there are some better differentials corresponding to a differential characteristic with not the highest probability than that by the optimal differential characteristic.

[†] These experiments were stopped before all differentials were obtained because the program took too long to run.

4.3 Discussion: Comparison with PRINCE and QARMA

We observe that the gaps in the probability between a differential characteristic and a differential can be large in QARMA64 and QARMA128 under the SK setting compared to that in PRINCE. When looking at each construction in detail, for the non-linear layer, the 4-bit S-boxes used in PRINCE and QARMA have the same property in terms of security, such as a full diffusion property and guaranteeing the maximum differential probability and the absolute linear bias of 2^{-2}. In contrast, their linear layers are designed with a different strategy. The linear layer of PRINCE is designed to ensure 16 active S-boxes in consecutive four rounds, while that of QARMA is designed based on an almost MDS matrix suitable for hardware implementation. We summarize the difference in their matrices from the macro and micro perspectives as follows. Hereafter, we

Table 3. Differential probabilities of (almost) good differentials of QARMA. W_{min} denotes the same parameter as in Algorithms 1 and 2. #differentials denotes the number of different differentials with a particular weight. All notations and parameters are consistent with Table 2.

QARMA64 under the SK setting

Rounds	6 (2+2+2)			7 (2+2+3/3+2+2)			8 (3+2+3)		
W_{min}	**52**	53	54	**64**	65	66	**72**	73	74
Prob.	$2^{-45.741}$	$2^{-46.019}$	$2^{-46.112}$	$2^{-60.278}$	$2^{-60.111}$	$2^{-58.921}$	$2^{-64.845}$	$2^{-64.503}$	$2^{-64.693}$
# differentials	1024	18048	315360	512	16896	313280	400	21904	333776
Time	35m15s	19h47m31s	109h51m44s	48m19s	39h48m41s	186h21m10s	15h47m58s	53h01m41s	508h11m56s

QARMA64 under the RT setting

Rounds	6 (2+2+2)			7 (2+2+3/3+2+2)			8 (3+2+3)		
W_{min}	**14**	15	16	**28**	29	30	**36**	37	38
Prob.	$2^{-14.000}$	$2^{-14.913}$	$2^{-15.193}$	$2^{-27.541}$	$2^{-28.000}$	$2^{-28.286}$	$2^{-35.000}$	$2^{-36.679}$	$2^{-36.679}$
# differentials	17	202	2571	84	3030	48840	20	840	18509
Time	36s	1m44s	13m33s	5m35s	1h15m24s	15h28m20s	11m16s	30m22s	10h18m25s

Rounds	9 (3+2+4/4+2+3)			10 (4+2+4)			11 (4+2+5/5+2+4)		
W_{min}	**52**	53	54	**62**	63	64	**77**	78	79
Prob.	$2^{-51.415}$	$2^{-51.415}$	$2^{-52.246}$	$2^{-60.831}$	$2^{-60.831}$	$2^{-60.831}$	$2^{-77.000}$	$2^{-77.415}$	$2^{-77.509}$
# differentials	8	688	11290	273	4822	49585	64	7616	18424
Time	6h32m25s	10h27m32s	49h31m02s	96h12m59s	114h45m17s	303h33m25s	596h07m26s†	1317h17m08s†	1317h16m57s†

QARMA128 under the SK setting

Rounds	6 (2+2+2)			7 (2+2+3/3+2+2)			8 (2+2+4/4+2+2)		
W_{min}	**60**	61	62	**76**	77	78	**87**	88	89
Prob.	$2^{-54.494}$	$2^{-54.521}$	$2^{-54.581}$	$2^{-71.990}$	$2^{-72.321}$	$2^{-72.614}$	$2^{-84.850}$	$2^{-85.093}$	$2^{-85.539}$
# differentials	1312	98984	391352	516	32880	31960	16	708	14300
Time	15h27m17s	499h19m12s	1316h25m40s†	40h57m50s	530h05m58s	430h44m47s	57h59m37s	92h7m23s	693h25m04s

Rounds	9 (3+2+4/4+2+3)			10 (3+2+5/5+2+3)		
W_{min}	**106**	107	108	**125**	126	127
Prob.	$2^{-104.285}$	$2^{-103.616}$	$2^{-106.255}$	$2^{-121.549}$	$2^{-121.667}$	$2^{-122.304}$
# differentials	240	561	1172	12	54	31
Time	249h25m14s†	1004h00m44s†	1004h00m32s†	794h25m35s†	794h25m23s†	794h25m13s†

QARMA128 under the RT setting

Rounds	7 (2+2+3/3+2+2)			8 (3+2+3)			9 (3+2+4/4+2+3)		
W_{min}	**28**	29	30	**42**	43	44	**64**	65	66
Prob.	$2^{-28.000}$	$2^{-27.415}$	$2^{-28.000}$	$2^{-42.000}$	$2^{-42.415}$	$2^{-42.187}$	$2^{-63.679}$	$2^{-64.415}$	$2^{-64.679}$
# differentials	32	2144	64368	64	5248	203200	1815	6870	26105
Time	38m43s	4h51m52s	48h32m23s	21h17m20s	52h32m19s	470h54m17s	1154h39m26s†	1154h39m16s†	1154h39m05s†

Rounds	10 (4+2+4)			11 (4+2+5/5+2+4)			12 (5+2+5)		
W_{min}	**80**	81	82	**100**	101	102	**125**	126	127
Prob.	$2^{-78.005}$	$2^{-79.005}$	$2^{-78.408}$	$2^{-96.460}$	$2^{-97.929}$	$2^{-96.521}$	$2^{-120.324}$	$2^{-123.499}$	$2^{-124.084}$
# differentials	2	72	51	9	6	2	3	3	2
Time	978h51m03s†	1316h34m33s†	1316h33m53s†	794h24m09s†	794h23m59s†	1036h39m39s†	794h16m56s†	1036h44m17s†	1036h44m02s†

mainly take a comparison between PRINCE and QARMA64 as an example for a better understanding.

Macro perspective. When looking at the matrices of PRINCE and QARMA64 as a single 64×64 matrix, the matrix of PRINCE consists of two 16×16 matrices $\widehat{M}^{(0)}$ and $\widehat{M}^{(1)}$ while that of QARMA64 consists of only one 16×16 matrix M. Hence, the (forward and backward) round function of PRINCE can be seen as constructed on two super S-boxes, while that of QARMA64 can be seen as constructed on the one super S-box.

Micro perspective. When focusing on output nibbles, each output nibble in the matrix of PRINCE comes from four input nibbles, while that of QARMA64

Table 4. Probability of differential characteristic and differential.

PRINCE (6 (2+2+2) rounds) $T_w = 1$, $T_c = 10$				
Matrix	Original	M_{e1}	M_{e2}	M_{e3}
W_{min}	**44**	**40**	**44**	**42**
Prob.	$2^{-43.907}$	$2^{-38.526}$	$2^{-38.616}$	$2^{-37.458}$
Gap (Prob./$2^{-W_{min}}$)	$2^{0.093}$	$2^{1.474}$	$2^{5.384}$	$2^{4.542}$
# differentials	64	256	8	272

Table 5. Distribution of differential characteristics.

PRINCE (6 (2+2+2) rounds) $T_w = 1$, $T_c = 10$											
Matrix \ Weight		W_{min}	$W_{min}+1$	$W_{min}+2$	$W_{min}+3$	$W_{min}+4$	$W_{min}+5$	$W_{min}+6$	$W_{min}+7$	$W_{min}+8$	$W_{min}+9$
# DC[†]	Original	1	0	0	0	1	0	0	0	1	0
	M_{e1}	2	0	0	0	11	0	0	0	23	0
	M_{e2}	1	2	7	16	55	116	452	848	2152	3498
	M_{e3}	1	0	5	2	56	38	358	210	1719	1102

comes from three input nibbles. Thus, each output bit of the round function of PRINCE depends on 16 input bits of the round function, while that of QARMA64 depends on 12 input bits of the round function.

To further investigate the impact of a matrix on a gap in the probability, we conduct three experiments with a change of the matrix in PRINCE focusing on the above perspectives. Hence, we change the matrix in PRINCE to:

$$M_{e1} = diag(\widehat{M}^{(0)}, \widehat{M}^{(0)}, \widehat{M}^{(0)}, \widehat{M}^{(0)});$$
$$M_{e2} = diag(circ(0, \rho^1, \rho^2, \rho^1), circ(0, 1, \rho^2, 1), circ(0, 1, \rho^2, 1), circ(0, \rho^1, \rho^2, \rho^1));$$
$$M_{e3} = diag(circ(0, \rho^1, \rho^2, \rho^1), circ(0, \rho^1, \rho^2, \rho^1), circ(0, \rho^1, \rho^2, \rho^1), circ(0, \rho^1, \rho^2, \rho^1)).$$

Notably, $circ(0, 1, \rho^2, 1)$ in M_{e2} has the same diffusion property as $circ(0, \rho^1, \rho^2, \rho^1)$ given in [3]. With M_{e1}, the round function can be viewed as constructed on the one super S-box, but each output bit of the round function still depends on 16 input bits of the round function. With M_{e2}, the round function can be viewed as constructed on two super S-boxes like the original PRINCE, but each output bit of the round function depends on 12 input bits of the round function. With M_{e3}, the matrix in PRINCE changes to the same matrix as QARMA64 into PRINCE, that is, the round function can be viewed as constructed on the one super S-box and each output bit of the round function depends on 12 input bits of the round function.

† DC: Differential Characteristic

Tables 4 and 5 show the gap in the probability of the differential characteristic and differential on the six rounds of each variant of PRINCE and their distribution of the differential characteristics, respectively. From a macro perspective, the number of super S-boxes based on a primitive does not seem to have an impact on the gap as far as comparing the cases of the original matrix with M_{e1}

and M_{e2} with M_{e3}. Meanwhile, the number of the input bits influencing each output bit seems to have a large impact on the gap as far as comparing the cases of the original matrix with M_{e2} and M_{e1} with M_{e3}. These observations can fit into MIDORI64 [5] and SKINNY64 [6], both of which have the matrix with each output nibble depending on less than four input nibbles. Ankele and Kölbl showed that the probability of the optimal differential characteristic in MIDORI64 and SKINNY is dramatically increased by considering a clustering effect [2]. When each output bit depends on 16 input bits, the number of the differential characteristics for each weight is curbed very few. Therefore, we predict that a cipher can have good resistance to a clustering effect when each output bit of the round function depends on more input bits of the round function.

In the RT setting, this gap of QARMA becomes small compared to that in the SK setting, i.e., the permutation-based tweak update function like that used in QARMA brings resistance to a clustering effect. That is mainly because the transition of the differential propagation is uniquely fixed in the tweak update function, and it contributes to making clustering difficult in the whole cipher. Therefore, we expect that a tweakable block cipher with a linear tweak (tweakey) update function can have good resistance to the clustering effect.

Finally, the case reported by Kölbl and Roy [19] can occur in any cipher, as a clustering effect in non-optimal weights can strongly affect the probability of a differential, especially for a cipher like QARMA.

5   Conclusion

We provide a new generic SAT-based automatic search framework to find a good differential under the specified conditions. Our framework introduces a method to solve incremental SAT problems in parallel using a multi-threading technique, and consequently, it allows us to evaluate differentials more comprehensively than any other previous methods.

Our framework can be applied to a wide class of symmetric-key primitives. In this study, to demonstrate the effectiveness of our framework, we apply it to PRINCE and QARMA from the aspect of distinguishing attacks. Our results are summarized as follows:

- We specify the conditions for finding a good differential to build a distinguisher and conduct experiments using our framework. As a result, we improve previous differential bounds for all variants of the target ciphers.
- We investigate the gap in the probability between a differential characteristic and a differential for PRINCE and QARMA and find that different design strategies for the linear layers have a significant impact on this gap.

For future direction, it would be interesting to expand the incremental SAT problem to more efficiently find the optimal differential/linear characteristics and other kinds of distinguishers. Further, it would be useful for future designs to more comprehensively investigate the impact of the design construction on the gap in the probability between a differential characteristic and a differential.

Acknowledgments. Takanori Isobe is supported by JST, PRESTO Grant Number JPMJPR2031. These research results were also obtained from the commissioned research (No. 05801) by National Institute of Information and Communications Technology (NICT), Japan.

References

1. Ankele, R., Dobraunig, C., Guo, J., Lambooij, E., Leander, G., Todo, Y.: Zero-correlation attacks on tweakable block ciphers with linear tweakey expansion. IACR Trans. Symmetric Cryptol. **2019**(1), 192–235 (2019)
2. Ankele, R., Kölbl, S.: Mind the gap - a closer look at the security of block ciphers against differential cryptanalysis. In: Cid, C., Jacobson, M., Jr. (eds.) SAC 2018. LNCS, vol. 11349, pp. 163–190. Springer, Cham (2018). https://doi.org/10.1007/978-3-030-10970-7_8
3. Avanzi, R.: The QARMA block cipher family. Almost MDS matrices over rings with zero divisors, nearly symmetric even-mansour constructions with non-involutory central rounds, and search heuristics for low-latency s-boxes. IACR Trans. Symmetric Cryptol. **2017**(1), 4–44 (2017)
4. Bailleux, O., Boufkhad, Y.: Efficient CNF encoding of Boolean cardinality constraints. In: Rossi, F. (ed.) CP 2003. LNCS, vol. 2833, pp. 108–122. Springer, Cham (2003). https://doi.org/10.1007/978-3-540-45193-8_8
5. Banik, S., et al.: Midori: a block cipher for low energy. In: Iwata, T., Cheon, J. (eds.) ASIACRYPT 2015. LNSC, vol. 9453, pp. 411–436. Springer, Cham (2015). https://doi.org/10.1007/978-3-662-48800-3_17
6. Beierle, C., et al.: The SKINNY family of block ciphers and its low-latency variant MANTIS. In: Robshaw, M., Katz, J. (eds.) CRYPTO 2016. LNSC, vol. 9815, pp. 123–153. Springer, Cham (2016). https://doi.org/10.1007/978-3-662-53008-5_5
7. Biham, E., Shamir, A.: Differential cryptanalysis of des-like cryptosystems. In: Menezes, A.J., Vanstone, S.A. (eds.) CRYPTO 1990. LNCS, vol. 537, pp. 2–21. Springer, Cham (1990). https://doi.org/10.1007/3-540-38424-3_1
8. Biryukov, A., Roy, A., Velichkov, V.: Differential analysis of block ciphers SIMON and SPECK. In: Cid, C., Rechberger, C. (eds.) FSE 2014. LNSC, vol. 8540, pp. 546–570. Springer, Heidelberg (2014). https://doi.org/10.1007/978-3-662-46706-0_28
9. Borghoff, J., et al.: PRINCE - a low-latency block cipher for pervasive computing applications - extended abstract. In: Wang, X., Sako, K. (eds.) ASIACRYPT 2012. LNSC, vol. 7658, pp. 208–225. Springer, Heidelberg (2012). https://doi.org/10.1007/978-3-642-34961-4_14
10. Boura, C., David, N., Boissier, R.H., Naya-Plasencia, M.: Better steady than speedy: full break of SPEEDY-7-192. IACR Cryptology ePrint Archive, p. 1351 (2022)
11. Bozilov, D., et al.: PRINCEv2 - more security for (almost) no overhead. In: Dunkelman, O., Jacobson, M.J., Jr., O'Flynn, C. (eds.) SAC 2020. LNSC, vol. 12804, pp. 483–511. Springer, Cham (2020). https://doi.org/10.1007/978-3-030-81652-0_19
12. Canteaut, A., Fuhr, T., Gilbert, H., Naya-Plasencia, M., Reinhard, J.: Multiple differential cryptanalysis of round-reduced PRINCE. In: Cid, C., Rechberger, C. (eds.) FSE 2014. LNSC, vol. 8540, pp. 591–610. Springer, Heidelberg (2014). https://doi.org/10.1007/978-3-662-46706-0_30
13. Cook, S.A.: The complexity of theorem-proving procedures. In: STOC, pp. 151–158. ACM (1971)

14. Ding, Y., Zhao, J., Li, L., Yu, H.: Impossible differential analysis on round-reduced PRINCE. J. Inf. Sci. Eng. **33**(4), 1041–1053 (2017)
15. Dobraunig, C., Eichlseder, M., Kales, D., Mendel, F.: Practical key-recovery attack on MANTIS5. IACR Trans. Symmetric Cryptol. **2016**(2), 248–260 (2016)
16. Eén, N., Biere, A.: Effective preprocessing in SAT through variable and clause elimination. In: Bacchus, F., Walsh, T. (eds.) SAT 2005. LNTCS, vol. 3569, pp. 61–75. Springer, Heidelberg (2005). https://doi.org/10.1007/11499107_5
17. Erlacher, J., Mendel, F., Eichlseder, M.: Bounds for the security of ascon against differential and linear cryptanalysis. IACR Trans. Symmetric Cryptol. **2022**(1), 64–87 (2022)
18. Kölbl, S., Leander, G., Tiessen, T.: Observations on the SIMON block cipher family. In: Gennaro, R., Robshaw, M. (eds.) CRYPTO 2015. LNSC, vol. 9215, pp. 161–185. Springer, Heidelberg (2015). https://doi.org/10.1007/978-3-662-47989-6_8
19. Kölbl, S., Roy, A.: A brief comparison of SIMON and SIMECK. In: Bogdanov, A. (ed.) LightSec 2016. LNSC, vol. 10098, pp. 69–88. Springer, Cham (2016). https://doi.org/10.1007/978-3-319-55714-4_6
20. Lai, X., Massey, J.L., Murphy, S.: Markov ciphers and differential cryptanalysis. In: Davies, D.W. (ed.) EUROCRYPT 1991. LNCS, vol. 547, pp. 17–38. Springer, Heidelberg (1991). https://doi.org/10.1007/3-540-46416-6_2
21. Leander, G., Moos, T., Moradi, A., Rasoolzadeh, S.: The SPEEDY family of block ciphers engineering an ultra low-latency cipher from gate level for secure processor architectures. IACR Trans. Cryptogr. Hardw. Embed. Syst. **2021**(4), 510–545 (2021)
22. Li, M., Hu, K., Wang, M.: Related-tweak statistical saturation cryptanalysis and its application on QARMA. IACR Trans. Symmetric Cryptol. **2019**(1), 236–263 (2019)
23. Liu, Y., Zang, T., Gu, D., Zhao, F., Li, W., Liu, Z.: Improved cryptanalysis of reduced-version QARMA-64/128. IEEE Access **8**, 8361–8370 (2020)
24. Matsui, M.: On correlation between the order of S-boxes and the strength of DES. In: De Santis, A. (ed.) EUROCRYPT 1994. LNCS, vol. 950, pp. 366–375. Springer, Heidelberg (1994). https://doi.org/10.1007/BFb0053451
25. Sinz, C.: Towards an optimal CNF encoding of Boolean cardinality constraints. In: van Beek, P. (ed.) CP 2005. LNPSE, vol. 3709, pp. 827–831. Springer, Heidelberg (2005). https://doi.org/10.1007/11564751_73
26. Sun, L., Wang, W., Wang, M.: More accurate differential properties of LED64 and Midori64. IACR Trans. Symmetric Cryptol. **2018**(3), 93–123 (2018)
27. Sun, L., Wang, W., Wang, M.: Accelerating the search of differential and linear characteristics with the SAT method. IACR Trans. Symmetric Cryptol. **2021**(1), 269–315 (2021)
28. Yang, D., Qi, W., Chen, H.: Impossible differential attack on QARMA family of block ciphers. IACR Cryptology ePrint Archive, p. 334 (2018)
29. Yang, G., Zhu, B., Suder, V., Aagaard, M.D., Gong, G.: The Simeck family of lightweight block ciphers. In: Güneysu, T., Handschuh, H. (eds.) CHES 2015. LNSC, vol. 9293, pp. 307–329. Springer, Heidelberg (2015). https://doi.org/10.1007/978-3-662-48324-4_16
30. Zong, R., Dong, X.: MILP-aided related-tweak/key impossible differential attack and its applications to QARMA, Joltik-BC. IEEE Access **7**, 153683–153693 (2019)

Deep Learning-Based Rotational-XOR Distinguishers for AND-RX Block Ciphers: Evaluations on Simeck and Simon

Amirhossein Ebrahimi[1]([✉]) [iD], David Gerault[2] [iD], and Paolo Palmieri[1] [iD]

[1] School of Computer Science and IT, University College Cork, Cork, Ireland
{a.ebrahimimodhaddam,p.palmieri}@cs.ucc.ie
[2] Cryptography Research Centre, Technology Innovation Institute, Abu Dhabi, UAE
david.gerault@tii.ael

Abstract. The use of deep learning techniques in cryptanalysis has garnered considerable interest following Gohr's seminal work in 2019. Subsequent studies have focused on training more effective distinguishers
and interpreting these models, primarily for differential attacks. In this
paper, we shift our attention to deep learning-based distinguishers for
rotational XOR (RX) cryptanalysis on AND-RX ciphers, an area that
has received comparatively less attention. Our contributions include a
detailed analysis of the state-of-the-art deep learning techniques for RX
cryptanalysis and their applicability to AND-RX ciphers like Simeck and
Simon. Our research proposes a novel approach to identify DL-based RX
distinguishers, by adapting the evolutionary algorithm presented in the
work of Bellini et al. to determine optimal values for translation (δ)
and rotation offset (γ) parameters for RX pairs. We successfully identify distinguishers using deep learning techniques for different versions
of Simon and Simeck, finding distinguishers for the classical related-key
scenario, as opposed to the weak-key model used in related work. Additionally, our work contributes to the understanding of the diffusion layer's
impact in AND-RX block ciphers against RX cryptanalysis by focusing
on determining the optimal rotation parameters using our evolutionary
algorithm, thereby providing valuable insights for designing secure block
ciphers and enhancing their resistance to RX cryptanalysis.

Keywords: AND-RX ciphers · Deep Learning · Cryptanalysis ·
Rotational-XOR cryptanalysis

1 Introduction

Cryptography plays a crucial role in ensuring the security and privacy of information in modern communication systems. Block ciphers, in particular, are widely

This publication has emanated from research supported in part by a Grant from Science
Foundation Ireland under Grant number 18/CRT/6222.

used to provide encryption for data transmission, ensuring that the content remains confidential and secure from unauthorized access. However, the effectiveness of block ciphers is always being tested, and researchers are continually exploring new ways to improve their resilience against attacks like differential [7], linear [19], algebraic attacks [3], etc. Among several cryptanalysis techniques, Rotational-XOR (RX) cryptanalysis has emerged as a powerful method to evaluate the security of block ciphers, particularly ARX and AND-RX ciphers such as Speck, Simon, and Simeck [1].

In recent years, artificial intelligence (AI) and deep learning have shown great potential in a variety of applications, including cryptanalysis. Their ability to analyze complex patterns and relationships in large datasets has motivated researchers to explore new techniques for breaking cryptographic algorithms [6, 10, 20]. This paper aims to investigate the application of deep learning in the RX cryptanalysis of AND-RX block ciphers, with a focus on Simon and Simeck, and proposes an approach to see the impact of diffusion layers in these ciphers.

The conventional cryptographic analysis techniques utilized in RX cryptanalysis commonly depend on weak-key models, wherein statistical methods are utilized to detect distinguishers and possible vulnerabilities. Nevertheless, these methods are constrained, as achieving a good distinction with a limited weak-key model may not be feasible. In this context, deep learning has been proposed as an alternative technique, offering the possibility of improved results in cryptanalysis tasks. Our proposed method has enabled us to acquire distinguishers for full-key classes concerning Simeck and Simon ciphers.

In addition to assessing the security of ciphers, finding the best parameters for diffusion layers is a crucial aspect of cipher design. The diffusion layer plays a significant role in ensuring that minimal alterations in plaintext or key inputs lead to substantial changes in the ciphertext output, making it challenging for adversaries to decipher the original data. In this paper, we propose a new approach that involves using a modified version of the optimizer in [5] to determine the best RX differential inputs and the optimal shift parameter for finding the longest round distinguisher with the aid of deep learning classifiers. Furthermore, we use this optimizer to identify the best set of rotations in the diffusion layer that works against deep learning optimizers, specifically for Simeck-like ciphers. Our approach ensures that deep learning distinguishers cannot find the optimal distinguishers, thereby enhancing the overall security of the ciphers. Therefore, our method demonstrates the potential for improving the security of ciphers while also enhancing the efficiency of the design process by utilizing deep learning classifiers in combination with an optimizer. Our findings contribute to the ongoing efforts to enhance the security of AND-RX block ciphers and highlight the potential of AI applications in Rotational-XOR cryptanalysis.

Our Deep Learning (DL)-based distinguishers demonstrate superior performance on the Simeck cipher compared to the Simon cipher. In order to juxtapose our achieved Deep Learning (DL)-based distinguishers with other related-key DL-based distinguishers for the Simeck cipher, the results are presented in Table 1. It's important to note that our distinguisher was trained exclusively on a single pair, whereas the existing literature offers distinguishers trained on eight pairs for the Simeck cipher. Consequently, we implemented the technique introduced in [11] to compute an amalgamated score for eight pairs. Furthermore, a comparison between our DL-based RX distinguishers and past RX distinguishers of the Simeck cipher can be found in Table 2.

Our work introduces a superior related-key DL distinguisher for Simeck 64/128 cipher and marginally behind for Simeck 32/64, according to Table 1. Furthermore, our research introduces a novel distinguisher that is specifically designed for RX cryptanalysis and trained on the entire key space. This distinguisher can be further scrutinized to assess how the accuracy of these distinguishers is affected by different keys.

Table 1. Comparison of related-key DL-based distinguishers for Simeck. RX: Rotational-Xor cryptanalysis, RD: Related-key Differential cryptanalysis. The Combined Accuracy Score [11] for m pairs is $\frac{1}{1+\prod_{i=1}^{m}\frac{1-p_i}{p_i}}$

Simeck 32/64	Round	Combined Accuracy Score	Pairs	Attack Type	Ref.
	13	0.9950	8	RD	[17]
	14	0.6679	8	RD	[17]
	15	0.5573	8	RD	[17]
	15	**0.5134**	**1**	**RX**	**This Work**
	15	**0.5475**	**8**	**RX**	**This Work**
Simeck 64/128	18	0.9066	8	RD	[17]
	19	0.7558	8	RD	[17]
	20	0.6229	8	RD	[17]
	20	**0.5212**	**1**	**RX**	**This Work**
	20	**0.6338**	**8**	**RX**	**This Work**

Table 2. Comparison of the RX distinguishers for different versions of Simeck

Cipher	Rounds	Data Complexity	Size of Weak Key Class	DL-based	Ref
Simeck32/64	**15**	**2^{20}**	**Full**	**Yes**	**This Work**
	15	2^{18}	2^{44}	No	[18]
	19	2^{24}	2^{30}	No	[18]
	20	2^{26}	2^{30}	No	[18]
Simeck48/96	**17**	**2^{20}**	**Full**	**Yes**	**This Work**
	16	2^{18}	2^{68}	No	[18]
	18	2^{22}	2^{66}	No	[18]
	19	2^{24}	2^{62}	No	[18]
	27	2^{44}	2^{46}	No	[18]
Simeck64/128	**20**	**2^{20}**	**Full**	**Yes**	**This Work**
	25	2^{34}	2^{80}	No	[18]
	34	2^{56}	2^{58}	No	[18]

1.1   Related Works

Simon [4] and Simeck [22] are lightweight block ciphers that have gained popularity due to their simplicity and efficiency. However, several attacks have been proposed against these ciphers, including related-key and weak-key attacks.

Liu et al. [16] propose an automatic search algorithm to find optimal differential trails in Simon and Simeck ciphers. The authors use Matsui's branch-and-bound algorithm to traverse input differences from low Hamming weight and break unnecessary branches. They also derive a more accurate upper bound on the differential probability of the Simon-like round function, which helps to improve the efficiency of the search algorithm. With this algorithm, they find the provably optimal differential trails for all versions of Simon and Simeck ciphers. In [21] a detailed analysis of Simon-like block ciphers and their related-key differential trails is presented. The authors identify that not only the Hamming weight but also the positions of active bits in the input difference affect the probability of differential trails. The authors proceed to reconstruct the Mixed Integer Linear Programming (MILP) model for Simon-like block ciphers, eliminating quadratic constraints, and introducing an accurate objective function that reduces its degree to one through the inclusion of auxiliary variants. Additionally, they investigate and identify the optimal differential trails for Simon and Simeck, utilizing this model, and they obtain related-key differential trails. Their core findings encompass the discovery of optimal related-key differential trails for various versions of Simon and Simeck (Simon32/64, Simon48/96, Simon64/128, Simeck32/64, Simeck48/96, and Simeck64/128), along with the identification of impossible differentials for several iterations of Simon and Simeck.

Rotational cryptanalysis is a technique that explores the propagation of rotational pairs, which consist of pairs $(x, x \lll \gamma)$ where γ is the rotational offset. The success of this attack can be compromised when non-rotation-invariant constants are injected into the rotational pairs. Rotational-XOR (RX) cryptanalysis, a generalized attack method, accounts for these constants by incorporating their effect into the analysis of the propagation probability. RX-cryptanalysis considers an RX-pair of the form $(x, (x \lll \gamma) \oplus \delta)$ where δ is known as the translation.

Ashur and Liu [1] introduced the concept of an RX-difference, and demonstrated how RX-differences behave around modular addition. They presented a formula for computing the transition probability of RX-differences, which was verified experimentally using Speck32/64. Additionally, they provided guidance on the optimal choice of parameters and discussed two types of constants: round constants and constants that result from a fixed key.

Khovratovich et al. [13] provided theoretical and practical support for the security of modular addition, rotation, and XOR-based (ARX) systems. They used rotational cryptanalysis to illustrate the best-known attack on reduced versions of the Threefish block cipher.

Lu et al. [18] extended RX-cryptanalysis to AND-RX ciphers that can be described using bitwise AND, XOR, and cyclic rotation operations. The authors formulated an equation for predicting the likelihood of RX-differences progressing through AND-RX rounds and established an SMT (Satisfiability Modulo

Theories) model to investigate RX-characteristics in Simon and Simeck. They discovered RX-characteristics in Simeck across diverse block sizes, specifically for expansive groups of weak keys within the related-key model, and conducted an analysis of how the key schedule and the rotation quantities of the round function affect the propagation of RX-characteristics in Simon-like ciphers.

AI and ML methods have been utilized in various data security applications such as cryptographic algorithms, cryptanalysis, steganography, and others. At CRYPTO'19, Gohr introduced a novel cryptanalysis approach that harnessed the power of machine learning algorithms [10]. By employing deep neural networks, he successfully constructed a neural-based distinguisher, outperforming existing cryptanalysis on a version of the widely examined NSA block cipher Speck. This distinguisher could be incorporated into a broader key recovery attack scheme. He could perform an attack on 11 rounds of Speck with the help of the AI-based distinguishers. Subsequently, numerous other scholarly works have been published on the application and examination of AI and deep learning-based distinguishers for cryptanalysis, following Gohr's initial contribution.

Jaewoo So presents a novel approach to cryptanalysis in [20] wherein a generic model is established using deep learning (DL) to discover the key of block ciphers through analyzing known plaintext-ciphertext pairs. The author illustrates the effectiveness of the DL-based cryptanalysis model through successful attacks on lightweight block ciphers, including simplified DES, Simon, and Speck. The experimental outcomes suggest that DL-based cryptanalysis is capable of accurately retrieving key bits when the keyspace is limited to 64 ASCII characters. Baksi et. al in [2] describe two innovative approaches that utilize machine learning to identify distinguishers in symmetric key primitives. The authors demonstrate that their techniques can significantly reduce the complexity of differential cryptanalysis for round-reduced ciphers, resulting in an approximate cube root reduction in the claimed complexity. Through experiments on various non-Markov ciphers, the authors demonstrate the efficacy of their methods. The researchers also evaluate the selection of machine learning models and illustrate that even a shallow three-layer neural network can perform effectively for their purposes. This study serves as a proof of concept for how machine learning may be utilized as a comprehensive tool in symmetric key cryptanalysis.

Another research direction in AI-assisted cryptanalysis involves the interpretation of neural network distinguishers. Benamira et al. [6] provided a comprehensive analysis of a neural distinguisher proposed by Gohr. They analyzed classified sets of data to identify patterns and gain a better understanding of Gohr's results. Their findings revealed that the neural distinguisher primarily depends on differential distribution in ciphertext pairs, as well as differential distribution in the penultimate and antepenultimate rounds. The researchers subsequently developed a distinguisher for the Speck cipher, independent of any neural network use, which matched the accuracy and efficiency levels of Gohr's neural-based distinguisher. Furthermore, the researchers developed a machine learning-based distinguisher that utilized standard machine learning tools to approximate the Differential Distribution Table (DDT) of the cipher, similar to

Gohr's neural distinguisher. This allowed for full interpretability of the distinguisher and contributed towards the interpretability of deep neural networks.

In [5], researchers presented a novel tool for neural cryptanalysis that comprises two components. Firstly, an evolutionary algorithm is proposed for the search of single-key and related-key input differences that are effective with neural distinguishers, thereby enabling the search for larger ciphers while eliminating the dependence on machine learning and prioritizing cryptanalytic methods. Secondly, DBitNet, a neural distinguisher architecture independent of the cipher structure, is introduced and demonstrated to outperform current state-of-the-art architectures. Using their tool, the researchers improved upon the state-of-the-art neural distinguishers for various ciphers and provided new neural distinguishers for others. The paper also provides a comparative review of the current state-of-the-art in neural cryptanalysis.

1.2   Our Contribution

In this paper, we present several contributions to the rotational-XOR cryptanalysis of AND-RX block ciphers such as Simon and Simeck. Our research advances the understanding of these ciphers and their resistance to attacks by incorporating deep learning techniques. Our main contributions are as follows:

1. We propose the first study of neural-assisted RX cryptanalysis. We modified the evolutionary algorithm presented in the work of Bellini et al. [5] to determine the optimal values for the translation parameter, denoted as δ, and the rotation offset parameter, represented as γ, for RX pairs, and by doing so we were able to find new RX distinguishers for Simon and Simeck ciphers
2. Our research successfully identifies RX distinguishers using deep learning techniques for different versions of Simon and Simeck in the related-key scenario, as opposed to the traditional weak-key model.
3. Our work contributes to finding the best parameters for diffusion layer for Simeck-like ciphers. The practical implications of these findings offer insights for designing secure AND-RX block ciphers and improving their resistance to RX cryptanalysis.

1.3   Outline

The current paper's structure is outlined as follows. The background concepts relevant to AND-RX ciphers, RX cryptanalysis, and deep learning-based cryptanalysis are discussed in Sect. 2. The methodology employed, which includes a modified evolutionary algorithm, is presented in Sect. 3. In Sect. 4, we report new distinguishes that have been discovered for Simon and Simeck. Section 5 proposes a technique for identifying the optimal permutation parameters for the diffusion layer of AND-RX block ciphers against DL-based attacks. Finally, Sect. 6 provides a concluding remark for the paper.

2 Preliminaries

In this section, we provide an overview of the key concepts and terms related to AND-RX ciphers, Rotational-XOR (RX) cryptanalysis, and deep learning techniques for cryptanalysis. Understanding these foundational concepts is essential for comprehending the methods and results presented in this paper.

2.1 AND-RX Ciphers

Simon and Simeck are block ciphers intended for use in environments with limited resources, such as IoT devices. They utilize the AND-RX design paradigm, which employs only three basic operations: bitwise XOR ($\oplus$), bitwise AND ($\wedge$), and left circular shift ($\lll i$) by i bits. The general round function, R, of AND-RX ciphers can be defined by the following equation:

$$R(x, y) = (y \oplus f(x) \oplus k, x),$$

where $f(x) = ((x \lll a) \wedge (x \lll b)) \oplus x \lll c$ and k is the subkey for corresponding round.

In 2013, the NSA designed a family of lightweight block ciphers called Simon [4]. Each cipher in the family employs a word size of n bits, represented as Simon$2n$ where $n \in \{16, 24, 32, 48\}$. Simon$2n$ with a key size of $m \in 2, 3, 4$ words (mn bits) is denoted as Simon$2n/mn$. For example, Simon32/64 operates on 32-bit plaintext blocks and utilizes a 64-bit key. In this paper, we focus on Simon$2n/4n$. The $f(x)$ function for Simon$2n$ encryption is $f(x) = ((x \lll 1) \wedge (x \lll 8)) \oplus x \lll 2$.

Simon's key schedule produces r key words $k_0, \ldots, k_{r-1}$ from a given key, where r is the number of rounds. This process also involves using a sequence of 1-bit round constants to remove slide properties and circular shift symmetries.

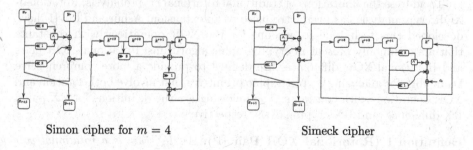

Simon cipher for $m = 4$ Simeck cipher

Fig. 1. The Simon and Simeck ciphers

In this paper, we assess another lightweight block cipher known as Simeck [22]. It is represented by Simeck$2n/mn$, where the word size n must be either 16, 24, or 32, and $2n$ is the block size, while mn represents the key size.

The round function R used in Simeck is identical to the one used in the Simon cipher, as shown by the equation. However, Simeck's function f is distinct from Simon's and is defined as

$$f(x) = (x \wedge (x \lll 5)) \oplus (x \lll 1).$$

In Simeck cipher, the round key k_i is generated from a given master key K by first dividing the master key K into four words and using them as the initial states (t_2, t_1, t_0, k_0) of a feedback shift register. To produce round keys and update the registers, the round function f is utilized as well as a 1-bit round constant c_r. The number of rounds r for Simeck32/64, Simeck48/96, and Simeck64/128 are 32, 36, and 44, respectively. Figure 1 demonstrate the round function and key schedule of Simon and Simeck ciphers.

2.2   Rotational-XOR (RX) Cryptanalysis

Rotational cryptanalysis is a technique used to analyze the security of symmetric algorithms. Khovratovich and Nikolić introduced and formalized this approach for ARX structures in their work cited as [13], and subsequently applied it to scrutinize other ciphers like Skein [14]. In this technique, the attacker focuses on rotational pairs of plaintext and ciphertext, where the input values are related through a fixed rotation. The attacker then looks for statistical biases or patterns in the ciphertexts of these pairs that can be exploited to recover the secret key.

However, rotational cryptanalysis can be less effective in the presence of constants, as these fixed values can disrupt the rotational properties of the pairs. This is because the rotation operation alone does not account for the XOR operations that involve these constants, which can be present in many cryptographic algorithms. When constants are involved, the rotational relations between the input and output values might be obscured, making it harder to analyze the cipher using traditional rotational cryptanalysis techniques.

To address the limitations of traditional rotational cryptanalysis, Rotational-XOR cryptanalysis has been introduced as an extension. Ashur and Liu [1] have developed this technique to account for the XOR operations with constants that are commonly present in cryptographic algorithms. Rotational-XOR pairs and Rotational-XOR differences are defined to provide a more comprehensive framework for analyzing cryptographic primitives that involve both rotation and XOR operations with constants. The following are the definitions for RX pairs, RX difference, and RX cryptanalysis, respectively

Definition 1 (Rotational XOR Pair [1]). *An RX-pair is a rotational pair with rotational offset γ under translations δ_1 and δ_2, defined as the pair $x_0 \oplus \delta_1, (x_0 \lll \gamma) \oplus \delta_2$. However, for the sake of simplicity, a slightly different notation is used, where an RX-pair is represented by x_0 and $x_1 = (x_0 \lll \gamma) \oplus \delta$, or alternatively as $x_0, (x_0 \lll \gamma) \oplus \delta$, where $\delta = \delta_1 \oplus \delta_2$.*

Definition 2 (Rotational XOR Difference [1]). *An RX-difference of x_0 and x_1, denoted by $\Delta_\gamma(x_0, x_1)$, is formed by the rotational XOR of x_0 with a constant*

δ such that $x_1 = (x_0 \lll \gamma) \oplus \delta$, where $0 < \gamma < n$ and $\delta \in F_n^2$ is a constant. In another word

$$\Delta_\gamma(x_0, x_1) = x_1 \oplus (x_0 \lll \gamma)$$

Definition 3 (Rotational XOR Cryptanalysis [1]). *Rotational XOR Cryptanalysis is a cryptanalytic technique that extends traditional rotational cryptanalysis to handle XOR operations with non-rotational-invariant constants between input and output pairs of a cryptographic primitive. This method aims to estimate the transition probability with respect to non-linear operations in block ciphers (like modular addition or $\wedge$ operation) of two input RX-differences to an output RX-difference. The technique introduces the concept of a (δ, γ)-Rotational-XOR-difference (or RX-difference), which represents a rotational pair with rotation γ under translation δ, i.e., $(x, (x \lll \gamma) \oplus \delta)$. The method seeks to analyze the propagation of RX-differences through the cryptographic primitive.*

The transmission of RX-differences through linear operations is known to be deterministic; however, this is not the case for nonlinear operations. Prior research conducted by Ashur et al. [1] and Lu et al. [18] delved into the investigation of the transmission of RX-differences through modular addition and AND ($\wedge$) operations, respectively.

2.3   Deep Learning and Its Application on Symmetric Cryptography

Deep learning has proven to be a game-changer in various challenging tasks, including image recognition, natural language processing, and speech recognition, to name a few. Although machine learning techniques have been applied to cryptography, much of the practical work has focused on side-channel analysis [12,20,23]. However, in 2019, Gohr explores the application of deep learning techniques for cryptanalysis [10], specifically for attacking the Speck [4] cipher. This approach aims to differentiate between real and random pairs of ciphertexts resulting from the encryption of plaintext pairs with fixed and arbitrary input differences, respectively. While pure differential distinguishers have traditionally been used for this purpose, his research has shown that deep learning (DL) can outperform their traditional counterparts. Gohr's study focused on Speck-32/64 and compared the accuracy of a pure differential distinguisher with a DL-based distinguisher for 5 to 8 rounds. The results demonstrated that the DL-based distinguisher achieved higher accuracy than the pure differential distinguisher, highlighting the potential of DL-based approaches in differential cryptanalysis.

Algorithm 1 is the algorithm employed by Gohr in training a deep learning (DL)-based distinguisher for differential attack. The algorithm considers a pair of plaintexts P_0 and P_1 with a predetermined input difference Δ, i.e., $P_0 \oplus P_1 = \Delta$. Additionally, $C_0 = E_k(P_0)$ and $C_1 = E_k(P_1)$, where E_k signifies encryption of plaintext P with key k. Furthermore, in the context of Feistel structured block ciphers, the left and right halves of a data block are typically referred to as L and R, respectively.

Algorithm 1. DL-based Differential Distinguisher for r rounds of Speck32/64

1: **Input:** r (number of rounds), AI machine, (C_0, C_1)
2: **Output:** Trained AI machine, differential distinguisher status
3: Generate 10^7 plaintext pairs (P_0, P_1) with $\Delta = (L_0 \oplus L_1, R_0 \oplus R_1) = $ (0x0040, 0x0000)
4: Randomly allocate 10^7 labels $Y \in_r \{0, 1\}$ to the pairs
5: **for** each pair (P_0, P_1) with label Y **do**
6:     **if** $Y = 0$ **then**
7:         $P_1 \leftarrow P_1 \in_r \{0, 1\}^{32}$
8:     Encrypt the pairs with r rounds of Speck32/64 to get ciphertext pairs (C_0, C_1)
9:     Store (C_0, C_1) with corresponding labels in a dataset
10: Train DL-distinguisher using the dataset and their corresponding labels
11: Repeat steps 3-11 for another 10^6 pairs for testing
12: Measure the accuracy of the DL-based distinguisher
13: **if** accuracy > 50% **then**
14:     The machine is a DL-based differential distinguisher

In deep learning (DL)-based distinguishers, determining the optimal input difference can significantly improve their performance. Gohr [10] presented a novel algorithm for identifying appropriate input differences for neural network distinguishers, without requiring prior human knowledge. This algorithm employs few-shot learning, where a neural network learns features from a large dataset and a simpler machine learning algorithm is trained on a smaller set of samples.

In [5], Bellini et al. presented an alternative approach that does not rely on neural networks for finding the best input difference for DL-based distinguishers. In order to find the best input difference they had a bias score hypothesis which states that the optimal input difference for neural distinguishers cryptographically is the input difference that maximizes the bias of output difference bits. Computing the bias score for block ciphers is infeasible due to the requirement of enumerating all keys and plaintexts. However, we can use an approximation derived from a limited number of samples t:

Definition 4 (Approximate Bias Score [5]). *Let $E : \mathbb{F}_2^n \times \mathbb{F}_2^k \to \mathbb{F}_2^n$ be a block cipher, and let $\Delta \in \mathbb{F}_2^n$ be an input difference. The Approximate Bias Score for Δ, denoted by $\tilde{b}^t(\Delta)$, is defined as the sum of the biases of each bit position j in the output difference, computed over t samples. Formally, we have:*

$$\tilde{b}^t(\Delta) = \left| \sum_{j=0}^{n-1} 2 \cdot \frac{\sum_{i=0}^{t}(E_{K_i}(X_i) \oplus E_{K_i}(X_i \oplus \Delta))_j}{t} - 1 \right|$$

The authors' hypothesis is confirmed, and they propose an evolutionary-based search algorithm that leverages the approximate bias score to explore a larger set of candidate input differences. The algorithm starts with a population of randomly generated input differences, and an approximate bias score is computed for each of them. The top 32 input differences with the highest score are retained for further evaluation. The algorithm then proceeds with 50 iterations, during which new individuals are derived and evaluated. To ensure the starting round's influence on the bias score is accounted for, the number of rounds is incremented if the maximum bias score obtained surpasses a threshold limit. At the end of the algorithm, the authors obtain a list of 32 input differences for each round. The final step involves computing a weighted cumulative bias score for all the obtained input differences from round 1 to round R. The authors' search algorithm based on the biased score demonstrates improved performance in identifying input differences compared to other methods and can be useful for cryptographic applications. Algorithm 2 can show their method. The algorithm has several key parameters, including the initial population size for each generation (P), the mutation probability (p_m), the approximate bias score sample size (t), and the relevance threshold (T). The specific values of these parameters can be adjusted as needed to optimize the algorithm's performance. Also $curr\_population_i$ indicates the ith bit of the current population we have.

Algorithm 2. Evolutionary optimizer [5]

1: $init\_population \leftarrow [\text{RandomInt}(0, 2^n - 1) \text{ for } 1024 \text{ times}]$
2: Sort $init\_population$ by $\tilde{b}_t(\cdot)$ in descending order
3: $curr\_population \leftarrow$ first P elements of $init\_population$
4: **for** $iter \leftarrow 0$ to 50 **do**
5: $\quad cand \leftarrow [\ ]$
6: $\quad$ **for** $i \leftarrow 0$ to $P - 1$ **do**
7: $\quad\quad$ **for** $j \leftarrow i + 1$ to $P - 1$ **do**
8: $\quad\quad\quad$ **if** $\text{RandomFloat}(0, 1) < p_m$ **then**
9: $\quad\quad\quad\quad m \leftarrow 1$
10: $\quad\quad\quad$ **else**
11: $\quad\quad\quad\quad m \leftarrow 0$
12: $\quad\quad\quad$ Add $curr\_population_i \oplus curr\_population_j \oplus (m \lll \text{RandomInt}(0, n - 1))$ to $cand$
13: $\quad$ Sort $cand$ by $\tilde{b}_t(\cdot)$ in descending order
14: $\quad$ $curr\_population \leftarrow$ first P elements of $cand$
$\quad$ **return** $cand$

---

3   Identification of Optimal RX Distinguishers in Cryptanalysis with Evolutionary Algorithm

In this section, we present a modified evolutionary algorithm that builds upon the algorithm of [5]. Our algorithm facilitates the discovery of novel RX differential pairs that can be leveraged to train deep-learning-based RX distinguishers. Initially, we discuss the artificial intelligence (AI) tools and deep learning model utilized in our study. Subsequently, we explore the relation between the rotational bias score and the accuracy of deep learning-based RX distinguishers. Drawing upon this insight, we introduce our evolutionary algorithm designed to identify the optimal RX input for training a deep learning-based distinguisher.

3.1   AI Tools and Model Development

In this study, we employ the Keras [9] library to develop our deep learning model, which is inspired by the architecture proposed by Aron Gohr in his groundbreaking CRYPTO'19 paper [10]. Gohr's model focuses on using a neural network to differentiate between pairs of Speck32/64 ciphertexts corresponding to fixed differences (non-random) and random message pairs (random). His neural distinguisher is a residual network comprising four main components, achieving remarkable accuracy for varying rounds of Speck32/64 and enabling practical key recovery attacks.

The input to Gohr's neural distinguisher consists of a 64-bit ciphertext pair from Speck32/64, which is reshaped and permuted into a 16-bit wide tensor with four channels. This input reshaping takes into account the unique 16-bit word structure of Speck32/64. The second component of the architecture involves a one-dimensional convolution, denoted as Conv1D with kernel size 1 and 32 filters, that slices through the four-channel bits.

Following the convolutional layer, batch normalization and ReLU activation function are applied as per conventional deep learning practices. The third component consists of residual blocks, with each block containing two convolutional layers, represented as Conv1D with kernel size 3 and 32 filters. The number of residual blocks in the network determines the depth of the neural distinguisher.

Lastly, a densely connected prediction head with ReLU activations is employed, along with an output layer featuring a single neuron with sigmoid activation. L2 regularization with a value of 10^{-5} is used throughout the network to penalize large weights and reduce the likelihood of overfitting. Also, the Adam optimization method [15] is used for this architecture.

The present research employs Gohr's neural distinguisher architecture to train RX differential distinguishers for analyzing AND-RX ciphers such as Simon and Simeck. The rationale behind this choice is that Simon and Simeck, specifically the 32-bit version, share the same 16-bit structure as Speck32/64, which is extensively investigated in Gohr's previous research. The aim of this approach is to harness the potential of deep learning to discover new RX distinguishers and enhance our comprehension of the security of these ciphers.

We also employed a sequential training approach in which we increased the number of rounds in each iteration. Previous research has shown that this approach can improve model performance [5], as it utilizes knowledge learned in previous rounds. We trained our model using a dataset of 10^7 training samples and 10^6 validation samples, with a batch size of 1000. Our model had a depth of 1 and we used 5 epochs for training.

3.2   Training DL-Based RX Distinguishers

This section outlines the training process for our RX distinguishers, which is based on deep learning. Furthermore, it elaborates on the potential of DL-based RX distinguishers in gaining insights from pairs of ciphertext.

Training Phase. The training process involves data preparation, model configuration, and evaluation of the trained model on AND-RX ciphers such as Simon and Simeck. The first step in training the RX distinguishers is data preparation. We generate a dataset consisting of pairs RX of ciphertexts, labeled as either non-random (for fixed (δ, γ)) or random (random message pairs). Since RX cryptanalysis is a related-key cryptanalysis, in addition to a translation δ that exists for the RX plaintext pairs, there may also be a translation for the keys used to encrypt each plaintext within the pair, which can be shown by δ_{key}. According to the research presented in [18], the propagation of the RX differential in AND-RX ciphers primarily depends on the Hamming weight of the difference and their rotations.

In this part, we chose to focus on an input difference zero for the initial training of the deep learning-based RX distinguisher for lightweight ciphers Simon32/64 and Simeck32/64. Specifically, we set both the input difference and key RX difference to $0x0000$ and $0x00000000$, respectively, using hexadecimal representation to represent the n-bit ($n \times m$-bit) binary representation of plaintexts (keys). By doing so, we aimed to first train the RX distinguisher as a starting point and subsequently analyze its behavior and performance in the context of Simon32/64 and Simeck32/64 ciphers, and then investigate possible improvements.

For that, we fixed $\delta = 0$ for both plaintexts and keys and iterated through all possible γs to determine the γ that would produce the best distinguisher for the longest number of rounds r for both Simon and Simeck. Our results indicated that for the case of Simeck32/64, $\gamma \in \{1, 15\}$ and for the case of Simon32/64, $\gamma \in \{4, 12\}$ produced the best distinguishers for 14 and 10 rounds, respectively. The detailed training method for r rounds is presented in Algorithm 3.

Algorithm 3. DL-based RX Distinguisher for r rounds of a Cryptographic Primitive

---

1: **Input:** r (number of rounds), AI machine, (C_0, C_1)
2: **Output:** Trained AI machine, RX distinguisher status
3: Choose a rotational offset γ and constants δ_1, δ_2, with $\delta_\gamma = \delta_1 \oplus \delta_2$
4: Generate 10^7 plaintext pairs (P_0, P_1) with RX-difference $\delta_\gamma(P_0, P_1) = (L_1 \oplus (L_0 \lll \gamma), R_1 \oplus (R_0 \lll \gamma))$
5: Randomly allocate 10^7 labels $Y \in_r \{0, 1\}$ to the pairs
6: **for** each pair (P_0, P_1) with label Y **do**
7:     **if** $Y = 0$ **then**
8:         $P_1 \in_r \{0, 1\}^{32}$
9:     Encrypt the pairs with r rounds of the cryptographic primitive to get ciphertext pairs (C_0, C_1)
10:     Store (C_0, C_1) with corresponding labels in a dataset
11: Train DL-RX-distinguisher using the dataset and their corresponding labels
12: Repeat steps 3-11 for another 10^6 pairs for testing
13: Measure the accuracy of the DL-based RX distinguisher
14: **if** accuracy $\geq 50\%$ **then**
15:     The machine is a DL-based RX distinguisher

Machine Interpretation. In this part, we present an interpretation of the deep learning-based RX distinguishers trained on AND-RX ciphers, specially on Simeck32/64. Our objective is to investigate the factors affecting the accuracy of the distinguisher and its ability to analyze RX cryptanalysis.

In prior studies on deep learning-based differential distinguishers, it has been shown that the bias of the output differential plays a crucial role in determining the accuracy and the number of rounds for which a distinguisher can be trained. To investigate the possible impact of bias on our RX distinguishers, we first define the Approximate Bias Score for RX attack, inspired by the definition presented in [5].

Definition 5 (Approximate RX Bias Score). *Let* $E : \mathbb{F}_2^n \times \mathbb{F}_2^k \to \mathbb{F}_2^n$ *be a block cipher, and let* $\delta \in \mathbb{F}_2^n$ *be an input RX-difference with a given rotational offset* γ. *The Approximate RX Bias Score for* δ, *denoted by* $\tilde{b}^t(\delta, \gamma)$, *is defined as the sum of the biases of each bit position* j *in the output RX-difference, computed over* t *samples. Formally, we have:*

$$\tilde{b}^t(\delta, \gamma) = \left| \sum_{j=0}^{n-1} 2 \cdot \frac{\sum_{i=0}^{t}((E_{K_i}(X_i)) \oplus E_{(K_i \lll \gamma) \oplus \delta}((X_i \lll \gamma) \oplus \delta)))_j}{t} - 1 \right|$$

In our study, we investigated the relationship between bias score, accuracy of the RX distinguisher, and number of rounds for the trained distinguisher.

To do this, we trained distinguishers for a range of γ values while keeping δ fixed at 0. For each distinguisher, we then calculated its bias score and accuracy across various rounds. This process was repeated for multiple iterations to ensure the robustness of our results. The Pearson correlation coefficient and The resulting scatter plot (Fig. 2) maps bias scores (x-axis) against distinguisher accuracy (y-axis), with each dot representing a different γ value for Simeck32/64. Different colors are used to denote the number of rounds for each distinguisher: red for 11 rounds, green for 12 rounds, and blue for 13 rounds.

Upon examining the plot, we observed a general trend: higher bias scores often corresponded to higher accuracy (or more rounds). There was one notable exception: $\gamma = 11$ produced the highest bias, but no distinguisher could be trained above 12 rounds with this γ value.

In order to gain a deeper understanding of these patterns, we conducted a weighted correlation analysis. This analysis validated the presence of a positive connection between the bias score and accuracy. During our experiment, we utilized formula (1) for our analysis, and the resulting score was approximately 0.65. This score indicates that there is indeed a positive correlation between the bias and the accuracy of the trained machine. In the formula, ρ represents the Pearson correlation coefficient, and a represents the accuracy of the DL-based distinguisher. We further scrutinized outliers, such as the aforementioned $\gamma = 11$ case, and hypothesize that these may be due to variations in the cipher structure or other unidentified factors that warrant further investigation.

$$\text{correlation\_coefficient} = \rho\left(\tilde{b}^t, a \times e^{2r}\right) \tag{1}$$

These results underpin our claim that the output RX difference bias score is a key determinant of the accuracy of a deep learning-based RX distinguisher. They also prompted us to introduce an adapted evolutionary algorithm aimed at identifying optimal (δ, γ) pairs for RX plaintext.

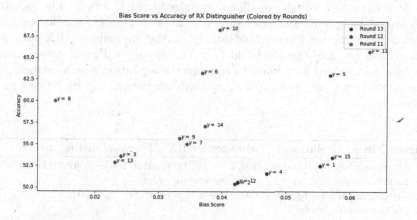

Fig. 2. Scatter plot of Bias Score vs Accuracy of RX Distinguisher (Colored by Rounds)

3.3 Evolutionary Optimization of Deep Learning RX Differential Distinguishers

Now, we propose an evolutionary optimization algorithm for finding the best RX input differences. The goal is to adapt the evolutionary-based search algorithm, leveraging the approximate RX bias score, to explore a more extensive set of candidate RX pairs. The modified algorithm will account for the rotational offset γ and the XOR translation δ.

The main modification of this algorithm involves introducing a novel search strategy for the optimal shift parameter, γ, while also evaluating the impact of input difference. Notably, to the best of our knowledge, this approach is the first to simultaneously search for both the optimal δ and γ parameters, instead of solely searching for the best δ for a fixed γ value, which is commonly set to $\gamma = 1$ in the literature. To enable this search strategy, we have developed a methodology for generating a binary representation for the shift parameter based on the block size, with the final bits appended to each member of the population. For example, for the Simeck32/64, γ and γ_{key} represented by two 4-bit words. So, we increase the number of bits in the search by an additional 8, where the final 8 bits represent the value of γ.

The new algorithm starts with a population of randomly generated input differences and corresponding rotational offsets. For each of them, an approximate RX bias score is computed. The top 32 input differences with the highest score are retained for further evaluation. The algorithm proceeds with 50 iterations, during which new individuals are derived and evaluated. If the highest bias score returned is greater than a threshold, the number of rounds is incremented by one. At the end of the algorithm, a list of 32 input differences for each round is obtained. The final step involves computing a weighted cumulative RX bias score for all the obtained input differences from round 1 to round R.

Algorithm 4 shows the modified optimizer for RX attack. The algorithm has several key parameters, including the initial population size for each generation (P), the mutation probability (p_m), the approximate RX bias score sample size (t), and the threshold (T). The specific values of these parameters can be adjusted as needed to enhance the algorithm's performance. Also, $curr\_population_{i,\delta}$ and $curr\_population_{i,\gamma}$ indicate the value of ith bit of δ and γ, respectively.

Algorithm 4. Evolutionary optimizer for RX differential distinguishers

---

1:   $init\_population \leftarrow [\text{RandomInt}(0, 2^n - 1) \| \text{RandomInt}(1, n - 1) \text{ for 1024 times}]$
2:   Sort $init\_population$ by $\tilde{b}^t_{(\delta,\gamma)}(\cdot)$ in descending order
3:   $curr\_population \leftarrow$ first P elements of $init\_population$
4: **for** $iter \leftarrow 0$ to 50 **do**
5:     $cand \leftarrow [\ \ ]$
6:     **for** $i \leftarrow 0$ to $P - 1$ **do**
7:         **for** $j \leftarrow i + 1$ to $P - 1$ **do**
8:             $m_\gamma \leftarrow 1$
9:             **if** $\text{RandomFloat}(0, 1) < p_m$ **then**
10:                 $m_\delta \leftarrow 1$
11:             **else**
12:                 $m_\delta \leftarrow 0$
13:             Add $(((curr\_population_{i,\delta} \lll \text{RandomInt}(0, n-1)) \oplus curr\_population_{j,\delta} \oplus m_\delta) \| (curr\_population_{i,\gamma} \oplus m_\gamma)$ to $cand$
14:     Sort $cand$ by $\tilde{b}_t(\cdot)$ in descending order
15:     $curr\_population \leftarrow$ first P elements of $cand$
    return $cand$

The modified algorithm presented in Algorithm 4 is specifically designed for optimizing RX differential distinguishers for cryptographic primitives such as Simon32/64 and Simeck32/64. By incorporating the rotational offset γ and the XOR translation δ, the search space for potential input differences is expanded, increasing the likelihood of discovering more effective RX input pairs for deep learning-based RX distinguishers. One significant improvement afforded by this method is the capability to identify effective RX distinguishers for full-key classes, which represents a marked advancement over prior research that only succeeded in identifying such distinguishers for classes that were not full-key.

4 Results and Discussion

In this section, we present the results of applying our evolutionary optimization method to different versions of Simon and Simeck block ciphers. Our goal is to determine the most effective RX input differences (δ) and rotational offsets (γ) for each cipher version, allowing us to train deep learning-based RX distinguishers.

In this study, we utilized an Intel(R) Core(TM) i7-6700HQ CPU @ 2.60 GHz to run the evolutionary algorithm and employed Colab [8] for training the distinguishers. The experiments for the highest weight version of Simon and Simeck lasted approximately 3 h each.

We used an evolutionary optimization approach, applying Algorithm 4 to the various versions of Simon and Simeck. The optimization was run 10 times, with each trial randomly initializing the values of δ and γ. The evolutionary algorithm subsequently updated these values to achieve higher distinguisher accuracy.

Each trial was trained on a dataset of 10^6 cipher text pairs, which were generated using different random keys. The key space was varied over the course of the trials to ensure thorough testing.

In the following subsections, we discuss our findings for each cipher version, highlighting the specific δ and γ values that led to the most effective RX distinguishers.

4.1 Simeck Cipher

For the Simeck cipher family, our evolutionary optimization method was successful in identifying effective RX distinguishers for 15, 17, 20 rounds of Simeck32/64, Simeck48/96, and Simeck/128, respectively. The results for each version of the Simeck cipher are detailed in Table 3, which includes the optimal RX input differences (δ), rotational offsets (γ), the number of rounds, and the corresponding distinguisher accuracy.

Our proposed method for training deep learning-based RX distinguishers demonstrates notable advantages despite not necessarily achieving the best possible distinguisher performance for the Simeck cipher family. Although there exist distinguishers with higher round coverage, As shown in Table 2, such as 20 rounds for Simeck32/64, 27 rounds for Simeck48/96, and 34 rounds for Simeck64/128, these distinguishers operate under significantly smaller weak key classes, specifically of size 2^{30}, 2^{46}, and 2^{58}, respectively, while our distinguishers cover the entire key space.

In our investigation, it was found that the Simeck cipher is more susceptible to RX cryptanalysis compared to Simon. While searching for vulnerabilities in Simon, we did not find any effective deep learning-based distinguishers with $\gamma \neq 0$ that perform better than conventional DL-differential distinguishers. However, this is not the case for Simeck, as shown by the results presented in Table 1, where DL-RX distinguishers can almost match the performance compared to related key distinguishers reported in the literature for the same round.

Table 3. Summary of the optimal RX input differences (δ), key differences (δ_{key}), rotational offsets (γ), the number of rounds, and distinguisher accuracy for different versions of Simeck block ciphers.

Cipher Version	δ	δ_{key}	γ	Number of Rounds	Accuracy
Simeck32/64	$(0, 0x0002)$	0002	1	15	51.34
				14	57.08
				13	70.57
Simeck48/96	$(0, 0x000002)$	0002	1	17	52.06
				16	57.67
				15	69.85
Simeck64/128	$(0, 0x00000002)$	0002	1	20	52.12
				19	57.01
				18	70.15

4.2 Simon Cipher

The results of applying our proposed method to the Simon cipher family, specifically Simon32/64, Simon64/128, and Simon128/256 is shown in Table 4. We obtained deep learning-based RX distinguishers for 11 rounds for Simon32/64, 13 rounds for Simon64/128, and 16 rounds for Simon128/256, respectively. It should be noted that these results exhibit worse performance in terms of round coverage when compared to existing distinguishers from the literature that also cover the full key space.

Additionally, we introduce RX distinguishers with rotational offsets γ other than 1, which, to the best of our knowledge, has not been previously explored. This highlights the potential of our proposed method to uncover new insights in the realm of RX cryptanalysis and contribute to the development of more secure cryptographic primitives.

In our study, we observed that the performance of the proposed method was worse for the Simon cipher family compared to the Simeck cipher family, even though both ciphers share the AND-RX design paradigm. One possible explanation could be the different structures of the diffusion layer in the round functions of Simon and Simeck ciphers. The different choices of shift parameters in these functions could result in different resistance to RX cryptanalysis. The rotation offsets in the $f(x)$ functions might interact differently with the proposed distinguishers, making it harder for the evolutionary search algorithm to find strong RX distinguishers for Simon compared to Simeck.

Table 4. Summary of the optimal RX input differences (δ), key differences (δ_k), rotational offsets (γ), the number of rounds, and distinguisher accuracy for different versions of Simon block ciphers.

Cipher Version	δ	δ_k	γ	Number of Rounds	Accuracy
Simon32/64	$(0x0, 0x0002)$	0002	3	11	54.45
				10	74.11
				9	98.48
Simon64/128	$(0x0, 0x0)$	0000	30	13	51.51
				12	73.15
				11	98.5
Simon128/256	$(0x0, 0x0)$	0000	60	16	50.62
				15	72.26
				14	96.87

5 Impact of the Diffusion Layer and Optimal Rotation Parameters

In the design of AND-RX ciphers, the choice of round constants and shift parameters are crucial in improving the security against RX cryptanalysis. While Lu et al. investigated the impact of round constants on RX cryptanalysis [18], the present study aims to extend this line of inquiry by examining the influence of shift parameters in AND-RX ciphers. Our primary focus is on identifying the ideal rotation parameters, (a, b, c) for $f(x)$ function of AND-RX ciphers that can be defined as below:

$$f(x) = ((x \lll a) \land (x \lll b)) \oplus x \lll c$$

In this section, our exploration of optimal parameters is centered on AND-RX ciphers with non-linear key schedules. The rationale behind this choice is based on our observation that Simon outperforms Simeck in resisting RX cryptanalysis. Consequently, our aim is to ascertain whether it is feasible to devise a variant of the Simeck-like cipher that could rival Simon in its defense against deep learning-based RX and differential attacks, or find other parameters that can enhance the security of Simeck-like ciphers.

In our pursuit of the optimal rotation parameters, we employed our previously discussed evolutionary algorithm (see Algorithm 4). This involved an iterative process where we tested various combinations of a, b, and c parameters for Simeck32/64. For each combination, we identified the highest bias score and the maximum number of rounds for which our algorithm could determine an appropriate input for the DL distinguisher. Notably, as our algorithm effectively searches for the best inputs with any γ values, even $\gamma = 0$, the optimal shift parameters identified also enhance resistance against both differential and RX differential attacks.

Among the shift sets found during our comprehensive exploration, (4, 6, 3) stood out due to its superior cumulative bias score, indicating enhanced resistance to these types of attacks. We could not find any distinguisher for more than 13 round for a Simeck-like cipher with these parameters as their shift parameter based on our optimizer. Notably, for other optimal parameter sets, we were successful in training DL-based distinguishers for up to 14 rounds. These findings, including the six shift parameter sets that performed optimally in our experiments, are detailed in Table 5.

Table 5. Optimal rotation sets for AND-RX ciphers with non-linear key schedule and $n = 32$ determined by the evolutionary algorithm

Rotation Set	Highest Cumulative Bias	Highest Round Distinguisher
(4, 6, 3)	14.32	13
(4, 5, 7)	17.28	14
(6, 7, 4)	17.99	14
(3, 7, 2)	18.25	14
(3, 5, 6)	18.67	14
(3, 6, 1)	18.95	14

Our findings provide useful considerations for the design of block ciphers. The optimal rotation parameters we identified demonstrate how specific configuration choices can influence a cipher's behavior against RX and related-key differential attacks. It should be noted, however, that the parameters we found optimal for security may not directly apply to practical cipher design, as designers also have to consider other factors such as hardware efficiency. Therefore, our insights should be considered along with other factors like hardware efficiency during the selection of shift parameters in the development of AND-RX ciphers. This balanced approach could yield designs that optimize both security and efficiency, aligning with the core goals of ARX/AND-RX cipher designers.

6   Conclusion

This paper has investigated the application of deep learning techniques to the RX cryptanalysis of AND-RX block ciphers, with a particular focus on the Simon and Simeck families. We have uncovered distinguishers in the related-key model, which is opposed to the conventional weak-key models found for these ciphers.

Our deep learning models have shown a promising ability to identify effective RX distinguishers for various rounds of the Simeck cipher. Specifically, a combined accuracy score of 0.5475 was achieved for 15 rounds of Simeck32/64 and 0.6429 for 18 rounds of Simeck64/128. Moreover, optimal RX input differences, key differences, and rotational offsets for different versions of Simeck and Simon block ciphers were identified.

In addition, this study presented a novel approach to optimizing diffusion layers in AND-RX block ciphers. As a result, several optimal rotation sets for Simeck-like ciphers were identified.

References

1. Ashur, T., Liu, Y.: Rotational cryptanalysis in the presence of constants. IACR Trans. Symmetric Cryptol. **2016**, 57–70 (2016)
2. Baksi, A.: Machine learning-assisted differential distinguishers for lightweight ciphers. In: Baksi, A. (ed.) Classical and Physical Security of Symmetric Key Cryptographic Algorithms. CADM, pp. 141–162. Springer, Singapore (2022). https://doi.org/10.1007/978-981-16-6522-6_6
3. Bard, G.: Algebraic Cryptanalysis. Springer, New York (2009). https://doi.org/10.1007/978-0-387-88757-9
4. Beaulieu, R., Shors, D., Smith, J., Treatman-Clark, S., Weeks, B., Wingers, L.: The SIMON and SPECK families of lightweight block ciphers. Cryptology ePrint Archive (2013)
5. Bellini, E., Gerault, D., Hambitzer, A., Rossi, M.: A cipher-agnostic neural training pipeline with automated finding of good input differences. Cryptology ePrint Archive (2022)
6. Benamira, A., Gerault, D., Peyrin, T., Tan, Q.Q.: A deeper look at machine learning-based cryptanalysis. In: Canteaut, A., Standaert, F.X. (eds.) EUROCRYPT 2021. LNSC, vol. 12696, pp. 805–835. Springer, Cham (2021). https://doi.org/10.1007/978-3-030-77870-5_28
7. Biham, E., Shamir, A.: Differential cryptanalysis of DES-like cryptosystems. J. Cryptol. **4**, 3–72 (1991). https://doi.org/10.1007/BF00630563
8. Bisong, E.: Google colaboratory, pp. 59–64. Apress, Berkeley (2019). https://doi.org/10.1007/978-1-4842-4470-8_7
9. Chollet, F.: Keras (2015). https://github.com/fchollet/keras
10. Gohr, A.: Improving attacks on round-reduced speck32/64 using deep learning. In: Boldyreva, A., Micciancio, D. (eds.) CRYPTO 2019. LNSC, vol. 11693, pp. 150–179. Springer, Cham (2019). https://doi.org/10.1007/978-3-030-26951-7_6
11. Gohr, A., Leander, G., Neumann, P.: An assessment of differential-neural distinguishers. Cryptology ePrint Archive (2022)
12. Hu, F., Wang, H., Wang, J.: Multi-leak deep-learning side-channel analysis. IEEE Access **10**, 22610–22621 (2022)
13. Khovratovich, D., Nikolić, I.: Rotational cryptanalysis of ARX. In: Hong, S., Iwata, T. (eds.) FSE 2010. LNSC, vol. 6147, pp. 333–346. Springer, Heidelberg (2010). https://doi.org/10.1007/978-3-642-13858-4_19
14. Khovratovich, D., Nikolić, I., Rechberger, C.: Rotational rebound attacks on reduced Skein. J. Cryptol. **27**, 452–479 (2014). https://doi.org/10.1007/s00145-013-9150-0
15. Kingma, D.P., Ba, J.: Adam: a method for stochastic optimization. arXiv preprint arXiv:1412.6980 (2014)
16. Liu, Z., Li, Y., Wang, M.: Optimal differential trails in SIMON-like ciphers. IACR Trans. Symmetric Cryptol. 358–379 (2017)
17. Lu, J., Liu, G., Sun, B., Li, C., Liu, L.: Improved (related-key) differential-based neural distinguishers for SIMON and SIMECK block ciphers. Cryptology ePrint Archive (2022)

18. Lu, J., Liu, Y., Ashur, T., Sun, B., Li, C.: Improved rotational-XOR cryptanalysis of Simon-like block ciphers. IET Inf. Secur. **16**(4), 282–300 (2022)
19. Matsui, M.: Linear cryptanalysis method for DES cipher. In: Helleseth, T. (ed.) EUROCRYPT 1993. LNCS, vol. 765, pp. 386–397. Springer, Heidelberg (1994). https://doi.org/10.1007/3-540-48285-7_33
20. So, J.: Deep learning-based cryptanalysis of lightweight block ciphers. Secur. Commun. Netw. **2020**, 1–11 (2020)
21. Wang, X., Wu, B., Hou, L., Lin, D.: Automatic search for related-key differential trails in SIMON-like block ciphers based on MILP. In: Chen, L., Manulis, M., Schneider, S. (eds.) ISC 2018. LNSC, vol. 11060, pp. 116–131. Springer, Cham (2018). https://doi.org/10.1007/978-3-319-99136-8_7
22. Yang, G., Zhu, B., Suder, V., Aagaard, M.D., Gong, G.: The Simeck family of lightweight block ciphers. In: Güneysu, T., Handschuh, H. (eds.) CHES 2015. LNSC, vol. 9293, pp. 307–329. Springer, Heidelberg (2015). https://doi.org/10.1007/978-3-662-48324-4_16
23. Zhang, L., Xing, X., Fan, J., Wang, Z., Wang, S.: Multilabel deep learning-based side-channel attack. IEEE Trans. Comput. Aided Des. Integr. Circ. Syst. **40**(6), 1207–1216 (2020)

Author Index

C. Carlet et al. (Eds.): SAC 2023, LNCS 14201, pp. 451–452, 2024.
https://doi.org/10.1007/978-3-031-53368-6

Printed in the United States
by Baker & Taylor Publisher Services